The Transportation Revolution

1815–1860

THE ECONOMIC HISTORY OF THE UNITED STATES

Edited by Henry David, Harold U. Faulkner, Louis M. Hacker,
Curtis P. Nettels, and Fred A. Shannon

Curtis P. Nettels: THE EMERGENCE OF A NATIONAL ECONOMY, 1775-1815

Paul W. Gates: THE FARMER'S AGE: *Agriculture, 1815-1860*

George Rogers Taylor: THE TRANSPORTATION REVOLUTION, 1815-1860

Fred A. Shannon: THE FARMER'S LAST FRONTIER:
Agriculture, 1860-1897

Edward C. Kirkland: INDUSTRY COMES OF AGE:
Business, Labor, and Public Policy, 1860-1897

Harold U. Faulkner: THE DECLINE OF LAISSEZ FAIRE, 1897-1917

George Soule: PROSPERITY DECADE:
From War to Depression, 1917-1929

Broadus Mitchell: DEPRESSION DECADE: *From New Era Through New Deal*

THE TRANSPORTATION REVOLUTION

1815–1860

By GEORGE ROGERS TAYLOR

VOLUME IV
The Economic History of
the United States

M. E. SHARPE, INC.
Armonk, New York   London, England

Cover photo courtesy of Westchester County Historical Society.

This book was originally published as volume IV of The Economic History of the United States series by Holt, Rinehart and Winston in 1951. It is here reprinted by arrangement with Holt, Rinehart and Winston, Inc.

This paperback edition first published in 1977 by M. E. Sharpe, Inc., 80 Business Park Drive, Armonk, N.Y. 10504

Library of Congress Cataloging-in-Publication Data

Taylor, George Rogers, 1895-
    The transportation revolution 1815-1860 / George Rogers Taylor.
        p.   cm.—(The Economic history of the United States ; 4)
    Reprint. Originally published: New York : Rinehart, 1951.
    ISBN 0-87332-101-4 :
    1. Transportation—United States—History—19th century. 2. United States—Economic conditions—To 1865. I. Title. II. Series.
HE204.T39   1989   89-10686
388'.0973'09034—dc20   CIP

Printed in the United States of America

ED 10 9 8 7 6 5 4 3 2 1

Foreword

WHEN this series of nine volumes on the economic history of the United States was first conceived, the nation's economy had reached a critical stage in its development. Although the shock of the depression of 1929 had been partially absorbed, the sense of bewilderment which it produced had not yet vanished, and the suffering and the bitterness of its first years were being transformed into less substantial, though still anguished, memories. Reform measures, either in operation or proposed, were being actively debated, but with less sense of urgency than earlier.

To the Editors of this series a fresh consideration of America's economic history was justified by more than the experiences of the recent past or the obscurity of the future. Rich contributions to the literature of American history had been made through cooperative series dealing with the political, social, and cultural aspects of American life. Numerous single-volume surveys of the country's economic development have been written. But, as late as the end of the fourth decade of the twentieth century, the world's foremost economic power had not yet produced an integrated, full-length, and authoritative treatment of its own economic history.

Scholarly concern with American economic history has been constantly growing during the past half century, and chairs of economic history have been established in leading universities. A more profound understanding of the role of economic forces in the nation's history has not only been developed by historians and economists, but has also won some measure of popular acceptance. The earlier thin trickle of monographs has broadened in recent years into a flood of publications. At present, such specialized studies, the many collections of documentary materials, and the mountains of government reports on different facets of American economic life, are staggering in their richness and scope.

This series has been planned to utilize these available sources in the preparation of a full-scale, balanced, cooperative, and readable survey of the growth of American economy and of its transformation from one of primitive character to world pre-eminence in industry, trade, and finance. Clearly, in nine volumes all aspects of the nation's economic life cannot be treated fully. But such a series can point the way to new fields of study and treat authoritatively, if not definitively, the main lines of economic development. Further, the series is intended to fill a present need of those professionally concerned with American economic history, to supplement the economic materials now available in general school and college histories of the United States, and finally to provide the lay reader with the fruits of American scholarship. If these objectives are attained, then the efforts which have gone into the creation of this economic history of the United States will have been amply repaid.

Contributors to the series have been chosen who have already established their competence in the particular periods they are to survey here; and they are, of course, solely responsible for the points of view or points of departure they employ. It is not intended that the series represent a school of thought or any one philosophical or theoretical position.

The major theme of Volume IV in *The Economic History of the United States* is stated in its title. It must not be thought, however, that *The Transportation Revolution: 1815–1860* is concerned exclusively with the construction and financing of roads, canals, steamboats, and railroads. Professor Taylor's focus extends far beyond these limits to embrace all the significant aspects of the nation's economic life during a period marked by changes of revolutionary magnitude. In this volume he displays not only an acute sensitivity to the importance of the interplay of the various economic factors with which he deals, but also a fresh approach to developments in the field of transportation itself. Because he looks at these in terms of their impact upon the costs and speed of the movement of goods and persons, he successfully directs attention to the transformation in the character of the whole economy between 1815 and the eve of the Civil War. By 1860, Professor Taylor points out, a national economy replaced what had been a colonially oriented economy thirty-five years earlier. The crucial place occupied by the pre-Civil War years in the industrial history of the United States is properly emphasized in *The Transportation Revolution*, for it deals fully with both the domestic and factory systems of manufacturing. Changes in the labor force in the emergence of an American movement are treated in detail, as also are the growth of urban centers.

Professor Taylor departs from the traditional treatments of this period in minimizing its tariff history. At the same time, he provides an unusually illuminating account of the United States in the international economy. His analysis of such a technically difficult problem as the balance of international indebtedness is particularly effective and clear. He is, moreover, no less concerned with internal business fluctuations and the relationship of government to the economy than he is with the economic relations of the United States to the rest of the world. His treatment of the extensive economic functions of government, particularly at the state level, in a period which has been traditionally viewed as exemplifying laissez-faire characteristics is particularly rewarding. Worthy of note, too, is the masterly survey of the primary and secondary literature which Professor Taylor has prepared for *The Transportation Revolution*.

The Editors.

Preface

Attention in this volume is focused on changes in the means of transportation and their effect on the economy of the United States. If this emphasis has at times somewhat limited attention to other aspects of the American economy during the period, I can only plead that transportation developments were so revolutionary and were so fundamental to the economic growth of the country that, in my judgment, they seemed to require the central position they have been given. The agricultural history for the years covered by this study will be dealt with in Volume III of this series. I have striven, therefore, though at times without complete success, to avoid encroaching on material falling more properly in this companion volume.

Although much original research has gone into this book, I have benefited at almost every turn from the fruits of others' labors. My chief debt, therefore, is to those workers who have tilled this field before me. In addition, I alone can be blamed if I have not benefited from excellent editorial advice: that of the Editors of this series; of my colleagues, Lester V. Chandler, Edwin C. Rozwenc, and Colston E. Warne; and of Paul W. Gates, Bray Hammond, Louis Hunter, and Edward C. Kirkland. Finally, for many hours of research assistance and typing I am under deep obligation to Mary Alice Fitzpatrick, Delphine Ormiston, and Gladys Westcott.

Amherst, Massachusetts
March, 1951

George Rogers Taylor

Contents

Illustrations

xiv

Charts, Figures, Maps, and Tables

CHAPTER I

Merchant Capitalism, 1815

POPULATION AND RESOURCES

FROM the "cutting edge" of the frontier, which already reached far into the Ohio River Valley, to the outskirts of its seaboard cities the United States was in 1815 chiefly an agricultural country. Commerce, largely sea- and river-borne, was organized and directed by the merchant capitalists residing in a few cities along the Atlantic coast. This American economy of the early nineteenth century might best be described as extractive-commercial in character. It is true that the beginnings of industrial growth were already discernible. But in this land of continental expanses only revolutionary developments in the techniques of transportation and communication would make possible that almost explosive rush of industrial expansion which characterized the later decades of the century.

About 8,400,000 people lived in the United States in 1815. Their homes were, for the most part, in the states along the Atlantic coast. Out of every 100 persons, about 37 lived in the South Atlantic states and about 48 in the Middle Atlantic and New England states. Approximately 15 out of every 100 lived farther westward.[1] Negro slaves comprised more than 1,600,000 of the total; the remainder was largely of western European descent, with by far the greatest numbers having English, Scotch-Irish, or German forebears. Most Americans of 1815 were born in the United States, for immigration had been relatively slight since the Revolution. The Napoleonic Wars, as well as the British government's opposition to emigration, had tended to check transatlantic migration.

In view of the tremendous expanse of the United States—nearly

[1] *Sixteenth Census of the United States: Population,* I, 14.

3

1,800,000 square miles after the annexation of Florida in 1819—its population was very small. But though relatively few in numbers, Americans were not long to remain so. The population of 8,400,000 in 1815 was over twice that of 1790 but only about one fourth of the total reached by 1860. The rate of increase for each decade between 1810 and 1860 varied from a low of 32.7 per cent in the years 1830–1840 to a high of 35.9 for 1840–1850.[2] Territorial expansion and immigration were favorable factors. But the rapid increase in population came chiefly as the result of natural increase. Large families were the rule, and children were welcomed as an economic asset. Probably the life expectancy of the American population was gradually increasing but conclusive data are not available.[3]

But beyond matters of mere numbers, were there as yet any significant national characteristics which contemporary observers believed they saw in the people of this new country? Even before the American Revolution the observant immigrant J. Hector St. John de Crèvecœur wrote of a peculiar quality or spirit, a kind of independence and resourcefulness which he found typical of Americans.[4] In 1815, the opening year for the period covered by this volume, Hezekiah Niles, a leading "printer" of his day, commented shrewdly on the American character. He emphasized the "almost *universal ambition to get forward*" noting that "in England it is 'once a journeyman weaver always a journeyman weaver.'" In the United States, he pointed out, "one half of our wealthy men, over 45 years of age, were once common day laborers or journeymen, or otherwise very humble in their circumstances when they began the world." Niles continues:

> Europeans, especially Englishmen, settling in the United States, who lived decently at home, have a universal complaint to make about the "impertinence of servants," meaning chiefly *women* and girls hired to do house-work. . . . These girls will not call the lady of the house *mistress* or drop a *curtsey* when honored with a command; and, if they do not like the usage they receive, will be off in an instant, and leave you to manage as well as you can. They think that the employer is quite as much indebted to them as they are to the employer. . . . Those girls who behave as they ought, soon get married and raise up families for themselves. This is what they *calculate* upon, and it is this calculation that makes them "saucy."[5]

[2] *Ibid.*, p. 16.
[3] Louis I. Dublin and Alfred J. Lotka, *Length of Life* (New York: The Ronald Press Company, 1936), pp. 44, 53–54.
[4] J. Hector St. John de Crèvecœur, *Letters from an American Farmer* (New York: Fox, Duffield and Company, 1904), pp. 48–91.
[5] *Niles' Weekly Register*, IX (December 2, 1815), 238–239.

The United States of 1815 possessed vast but largely untapped natural resources. Wherever arable lands lay close to the ocean or along easily navigable rivers flowing into it, they yielded a rich agricultural output which constituted by far the most important product of the country. From roughly the same area came such products of the forest as lumber and masts, and tar, pitch, and turpentine. Vast areas of fertile lands and primeval forests stretched to the westward awaiting the development of transportation before they could be economically utilized. Already the intense exploitation of earlier years had greatly reduced the annual yield of furs and peltries from the forests of the eastern part of the country, but the rapid spread of hunters and trappers into the territory west of the Mississippi, begun before the War of 1812, now brought another decade or two of rapid development of a resource doomed to decline with advancing settlement.

The long Atlantic coast line, with its hundreds of harbors suitable for the small sailing craft of the period, provided the chief highway for travel and transportation by methods surprisingly little changed from the days of the Phoenicians. And the unexcelled fishing grounds off the coast of New England and Newfoundland, utilized by European fishermen even before the shores were settled, continued to provide a rich harvest of cod and mackerel for successive generations of American fishermen. From one end of the country to the other the larger rivers were used for the movement of goods to market and the smaller streams to turn the water wheels for gristmills, sawmills, and bloomeries. But techniques were still lacking to make possible utilization of the tremendous power potentialities of the larger rivers such as the Connecticut, the Susquehanna, and the Potomac.

The nineteenth century is sometimes described as the age of coal, iron, and steel, and the United States is regarded as one of the leading nations of that epoch. But such developments were far from evident in 1815. The bituminous coal of Virginia was only just beginning to find an appreciable market in Philadelphia and New York, in competition with imports from England, and the anthracite beds of Pennsylvania still rested almost untouched. Iron production was relatively less important in 1815 than it had been just before the American Revolution. The bog iron deposits of eastern Massachusetts and New Jersey had been largely exhausted in the eighteenth century. Still some small-scale mining of iron ore was to be found in nearly every state. The chief productive areas in 1815 were in New York in the vicinity of Lake Champlain, in the Salisbury district of Connecticut, in Morris County, New Jersey, and especially in the state of Pennsylvania. Many small furnaces and forges operated in this last-named state, chiefly in the central valleys but also as far west as the vicinity of Pittsburgh. Practically all of the mines were small surface operations, and charcoal was used as the fuel for operating the furnaces and forges. Large mining developments were still unknown even in Pennsylvania and the ore beds of the Birmingham and Superior districts were untouched and were to remain so for decades. The lead from Missouri and the Galena district of Wisconsin and Illinois was being brought to market despite difficulties of transportation, as was salt from the New York State and Virginia deposits. Few other products were being mined. Neither the copper of the Upper Peninsula nor the rich deposits of the Far West were yet known.

THE CITIES

The United States was still a predominantly rural country in 1815. According to the census returns, the proportion of the total population living in cities of 2,500 or more increased from 5.1 in 1790 to 7.3 per cent in 1810, then declined to 7.2 per cent in 1820, and rose in subsequent decades to 19.8 in 1860. In only one decade since the first national census in 1790, that between 1810 and 1820, has the proportion of people living in places of 2,500 or more failed to rise. Just why the long trend toward urbanization was halted in this single decade is not entirely clear, but chief responsibility for this reversal of trend appears to have been due to a small decline in the percentage of urban population in New York State. As in colonial times, the cities were especially important in the northern states. By 1820 the proportion of the population living in cities was twice as great in the North as in the South.[6]

In both 1810 and 1820 about 5 per cent of the total population lived in cities of 8,000 or more. The thirteen places having at least this population in 1820 are listed in the accompanying table. In them lived about 70 per cent of the total urban population, i.e., persons living in places of 2,500 or more. In fact, more than half of the total urban population was concentrated in the six largest cities: New York, Philadelphia, Baltimore, Boston, New Orleans, and Charleston. All of these cities were great seaports and in them centered most of the commerce of the period.

[6] *Sixteenth Census of the United States: Population*, I, 18, 20–21.

The two outstanding giants were New York and Philadelphia, for together they contained more than a third of all the city dwellers in the country. The metropolis at the mouth of the Hudson had achieved first rank in 1810 and had appreciably increased its lead by 1820. No Atlantic harbor was finer than New York's, or more strategically located for the coastwise trade. And for foreign commerce only Boston of the major cities was closer to Europe. By 1815 the foreign trade of New York was already twice that of either of its immediate rivals, Boston and Philadelphia, and its great period of growth had only just begun.

POPULATION OF CITIES HAVING 8,000 OR MORE INHABITANTS,
1810 AND 1820

(*In thousands.*)

Cities in Order of Size in 1820	1810	1820
1. New York	96.4	123.7
2. Philadelphia	91.9	112.8
3. Baltimore	35.6	62.7
4. Boston	33.3	43.3
5. New Orleans	17.2	27.2
6. Charleston	24.7	24.8
7. Washington	8.2	13.2
8. Salem	12.6	12.7
9. Albany	9.4	12.6
10. Richmond	9.7	12.1
11. Providence	10.1	11.8
12. Cincinnati	2.5	9.6
13. Norfolk	9.2	8.5

Sources: J. D. B. De Bow, *Statistical View of the United States: A Compendium of the Seventh Census* (Washington: Beverley Tucker, 1854), p. 192, except for Norfolk, 1810, for which see *Sixteenth Census of the United States: Population*, I, 33.

But New York seems to have had more than natural advantages. Its citizens evidenced an aggressive energy in the years immediately following 1815 which ensured its growing lead over all rivals. As R. G. Albion has pointed out, four measures were taken by New Yorkers which contributed to this success: (1) establishment of an attractive auction system for disposing of imports; (2) organization of regular transatlantic packet service; (3) development of the coastwise trade, especially the bringing of southern cotton to New York for export; and (4) the building of the Erie Canal.[7]

From the middle to the end of the eighteenth century, Philadelphia was the first city of the country, but it took second place there-

[7] Robert Greenhalgh Albion, "New York Port and Its Disappointed Rivals, 1815–1860," *Journal of Economic and Business History*, III (1930–1931), 602–629.

after. The commerce of this Pennsylvania city, which had been built to a considerable extent upon the export of breadstuffs to southern Europe and the West Indies, suffered after 1818 from the declining importance of these markets. Like Baltimore, Philadelphia was strategically located for trade with the West, but in 1815 this commerce was as yet not of very large volume. Already a leading center for handicraft industry, it was presently to become a great industrial city and the leading entrepôt for the coal trade. But all this lay in the future. In 1815 and in the years immediately following, Philadelphians managed to retain financial leadership, but, though keeping a substantial foreign trade, Philadelphia merchants definitely surrendered primacy in this respect to their rivals to the north.

No major port grew more rapidly than Baltimore from 1810 to 1820. Already the third city of the country by 1800, its population had risen to 35,600 by 1810 and to 62,700 by 1820. Especially in the years immediately preceding and following the War of 1812, the Maryland port was able to subordinate a half-dozen rivals in the Chesapeake region and to dominate the tremendous grain and tobacco trade of Virginia, Maryland, and, by way of the Susquehanna, most of central Pennsylvania. While Philadelphians were conservative and slow to move, Baltimore merchants built swift "clipper" schooners, pressed into the coastwise and foreign markets to the south, and more aggressively than the merchants of any other city developed the overland trade with the Ohio Valley.

Boston, which had been the first city of the country in the early eighteenth century, had first lost that leadership to Philadelphia and then to New York, but it was still a port to be reckoned with. Always forced to create business, to search far and wide for cargoes because the back country, though productive of excellent sailors and traders, furnished few export staples, the merchants of this Massachusetts city continued a formidable factor in the foreign trade. Though pressed by rivals to the south, they made New England more than ever tributary to Boston and concentrated the commerce of that region more and more at its wharves as smaller ports like Salem, Newburyport, and Plymouth failed to recover from the hardships imposed by the embargo and the war. Boston was not a manufacturing city but, in 1815 and in the years immediately following, Boston merchants financed factories in other New England communities and benefited greatly from the commerce in raw and finished goods which resulted.

New Orleans and Charleston, the fifth- and sixth-ranking cities in 1820, present contrasting pictures. Charleston, once a leading port, had already become of secondary importance in the foreign trade. The population remained almost stationary at a little under 25,000 between 1810 and 1820. New Orleans, on the other hand, stood in 1815 at the beginning of its greatest period of growth. The sugar and cotton of the lower South and the food products of the Ohio Valley had already begun to find a market through the Crescent City. Even without the help of the steamboat, the commerce of this city was sure to grow. With steam transportation, New Orleans became in the late twenties securely established as the second exporting city in the country and for a few years during the late thirties and early forties its exports actually exceeded in value those from New York.

The remaining cities having a population of 8,000 or more in 1820 were much smaller than the first six. Even the largest were only a little more than half the size of Charleston. Salem, Albany, Providence, Richmond, and Norfolk were all Atlantic tidewater ports overshadowed by larger cities and showing little or no growth during the second decade of the nineteenth century. Boston, while busily swallowing the commerce of Salem, united with New York to curtail the growth of Providence. Albany became definitely subservient to New York, and Baltimore kept Richmond and Norfolk in a secondary position. Despite being burned by the British in the summer of 1814, the national capital emerged from the war, as it has after every war period since that time, with a greatly increased population.

Cincinnati is the only city in the list which was not a seaport on tidewater. A few seagoing ships built at Marietta and farther up the river made Cincinnati a port of call on their way to sea, but this was, of course, of relatively slight importance. Its growth of nearly 300 per cent within one decade was an augury of what could be expected to happen to other inland cities once steamboats, canals, and railroads had opened up the routes of inland commerce.

In nearly every part of the country there were, of course, smaller cities or towns which served as important local distributing centers. Mostly they were river towns like Springfield and Hartford in New England; Pittsburgh, Frankfort, Nashville, and St. Louis in the West; Trenton and Harrisburg in the East; and Raleigh and Atlanta farther south. Or they were minor seaports engaged chiefly in local and coastwise trade like Portland, Newport, New Haven, Wilmington, what was then Newbern, and Savannah.

MERCHANTS AND THE ORGANIZATION OF COMMERCE

The chief business of the cities was commerce, and their leading citizens were merchants. Wharves, warehouses, and stores characterized their physical appearance, and everything was tied together and directed from their nerve centers, the counting rooms. The streets of every large city led down past the warehouses to the piers. From the farms by river or road came products for export, but this was the *back country;* in 1815 every city seemed to face the sea, the direction from which came not only the needed products of every land but the news of distant nations and markets.

Nothing better illustrates this seaward orientation of life in early nineteenth-century America than the newspapers which were printed in every important seaport. Whether issued in Boston, Philadelphia, or New Orleans, the news columns of these early papers were primarily concerned with foreign affairs: political events in European countries, the shipping news of distant ports, and the state of foreign markets. Even their advertising was redolent of the sea. Whole columns were given over to offerings of ships, schooners, and brigs for freight or charter, each preceded by a small printed picture of a sailing vessel. In addition, advertisements offered for sale the staples of the port, the products of nearly every foreign land, and all the necessary supplies of a shipping community from ship bread and shooks for molasses barrels to anchor chains and marine insurance.

As in earlier decades, the leading citizens of the cities and the men who organized and directed the commerce of the country were the *merchants,* as they were then called, or the *sedentary merchants* or *merchant capitalists,* as they were called by later historians. These merchants typically owned their own ships and were engaged on their own account in the coastwise and foreign trade. Their activities comprehended almost every aspect of business. They bought and sold goods at wholesale and retail. They owned and sometimes built their own ships, which they operated as ocean carriers for their own convenience and as common carriers for others. In addition to trading on their own capital they often acted as commission agents or factors for others, assumed marine insurance risks, and performed numerous banking functions. In many cases, they also had manufacturing interests, perhaps a distillery or a ropewalk in New England or a flour mill or a tannery in Pennsylvania or Maryland.

By 1815 merchant capitalism had already passed its prime in

America and the specialization had already begun which would presently lead to the splitting up of the many functions of the merchants; i.e., exporters would ship abroad by common carriers rather than in their own vessels, banking and insurance functions would be more and more taken over by corporations organized for those purposes, and manufacturing would be carried on by industrialists who, concentrating on fabricating or processing, would leave the problems of transporting, financing, and marketing to others. But as yet the merchant held the center of the stage. In New York City the richest man in America, John Jacob Astor, with his extensive interests in the fur trade and foreign commerce, was a prototype of the sedentary merchant. In Baltimore Alexander Brown, despite the restrictions on commerce during hostilities, had brought his great mercantile house successfully through the war and was ready to extend his trading activities still wider with branch houses in Philadelphia and New York. In Philadelphia Stephen Girard, perhaps the greatest merchant of the early national period, gave increased attention to his specialized banking and investment activities after the War of 1812.

Besides the true sedentary merchants who traded on their own account there were in every city an increasing number whose activities were much less comprehensive. Thus some received goods from producers or from other traders to sell on commission. If they sold partly on their own account and partly for others, a most common practice, they were called *commission merchants*. Or if they sold no goods of their own but merely dealt in goods for others, they were called *factors* or *brokers*. Thus factors in the southern states bought cotton for their principals in northern and European cities and arranged to advance the long credits upon which the planters were typically so dependent.[8]

A development which came into prominence following the Treaty of Amiens (1802) and tended to curtail the activities of American merchants, who had previously imported British manufactures, was the auction. Though auction sales had long been customary in American cities, they had chiefly been used to dispose of damaged goods or distress merchandise. When American markets became flooded with British textiles following the war, British manufacturers gen-

---

[8] See, for example, Norman Sydney Buck, *The Development of the Organisation of Anglo-American Trade, 1800–1850* (New Haven: Yale University Press, 1925), *passim;* Kenneth Wiggins Porter, *The Jacksons and the Lees* (Vol. III of *Harvard Studies in Business History*, 2 vols., Cambridge: Harvard University Press, 1937), especially the introductions, both the one by the author and the one by N. S. B. Gras.

erally adopted the practice of sending their goods to agents in New York, who disposed of them at once through sales at auction. Buyers found that they could get their merchandise more cheaply in this way than by purchasing from the New York merchants. The British manufacturers benefited from commissions saved and from quick turnover. Moreover, in 1817 New York passed legislation which reduced the taxes on sales at auction and imposed improved procedures requiring that goods offered for sale must actually be disposed of to the highest bidders.[9]

In addition to the sedentary merchants and traders of all kinds and degrees, such as wholesalers, retailers, brokers, factors, agents, and auctioneers, were the other urban dwellers, practically all of whom performed services for the merchants. There were, of course, the professional men of whom the lawyers and preachers were perhaps somewhat more honored and respected than the general run of physicians, teachers, and port officials. Masters and mates of the larger ships and important packets were also among the more distinguished persons who served the cause of commerce. More numerous were the clerks and merchants' apprentices who formed a considerable body of the workers in every community. Ambitious boys were apprenticed to merchants to learn the trade. If able and fortunate they moved from errand boy to copyist to bookkeeper or specialist outdoor clerk and even to chief clerk. Those who showed special ability or had the always advantageous close family relationship to a member of the firm might become trusted representatives in a distant city, supercargoes, or even partners in the firm.[10]

As for the other city inhabitants, they were of the humbler sort concerning whom too little is known. Some, of course, were artisans and mechanics who, with their assistants, made the hats, shoes, and clothing for others to wear or more directly served the needs of commerce by making such needed objects as pipes, barrels, and kegs for the shipment of goods, constructing sails and rigging for the ships, or baking ship bread to feed hungry crews at sea. The roustabouts, the draymen, and the longshoremen loaded and unloaded the vessels and carted the boxes, bales, and barrels to and from the warehouses

[9] Buck, *The Development of the Organisation of Anglo-American Trade, 1800–1850*, pp. 135–150; Fred Mitchell Jones, *Middlemen in the Domestic Trade of the United States, 1800–1860* (University of Illinois *Studies in the Social Sciences*, Vol. XXI, No. 3, Urbana: University of Illinois, 1937), pp. 33–43; Ray Bert Westerfield, "Early History of American Auctions—A Chapter in Commercial History," *Transactions of the Connecticut Academy of Arts and Sciences*, XXIII (May, 1920), 159–210.

[10] See, for example, Robert Greenhalgh Albion, *The Rise of New York Port (1815–1860)* (New York: Charles Scribner's Sons, 1939), Chaps. 11–13.

and stores. Finally, the sailors themselves, hailing from many lands and often a transient and somewhat exotic element, added to the color and life of every seaport.

Even in the smaller trading towns, many of which had a population of only from 2,000 to 3,000, the merchants played the central role. Thus in Hartford and Middletown, Connecticut, towns of less than 5,000 in 1820 but commercial centers for the lower Connecticut River Valley, merchants operating much like Astor and Brown, though on a smaller scale, dominated the economic life of the area. Owning in whole or in part their own trading vessels, the leading merchants of these towns sent the lumber and provisions of the Connecticut Valley to the West Indies and brought back sugar, molasses, and tropical products which they then sold at wholesale and retail. Accustomed to assuming responsibility for every aspect of getting goods to market, storing, transporting, financing, insuring, and selling, these men were quite naturally those who, with the rapid development of specialization after 1815, were most aggressive in organizing banking, turnpike, insurance, and manufacturing companies.[11]

The products of commerce finally reached consumers, about 93 per cent of whom lived on farms or in small towns, through retail stores, public markets, or traveling peddlers. Except in the larger cities retail stores were quite unspecialized, carrying small but miscellaneous stocks made up chiefly of imported manufactured goods and tropical products such as sugar, spices, and molasses. The storekeeper was almost inevitably a dealer in the staples of the surrounding country; in exchange for his store goods he accepted the promise of cotton or tobacco in the South, and in the West or North he took in trade everything from wheat, bacon, and ashes to ginseng root and feathers. The retail stores in the interior secured their supplies from the seaboard merchants, typically on long credit. When they could, the retailers themselves traveled to New York or Baltimore or Philadelphia, visited the warehouses of the merchants, purchased their supplies for the coming year, and by sailing vessel and wagon personally supervised their transportation back to their stores in the country villages.

Following old-country tradition, every city of any size had its public market and market days when goods of all kinds were bought and sold at a public square. But roads were poor and distances long

[11] Margaret E. Martin, "Merchants and Trade of the Connecticut River Valley, 1750–1820," *Smith College Studies in History*, XXIV, Nos. 1–4 (October, 1938–July, 1939), *passim*.

in the America of 1815. Few farmers were near enough even to a
place of 2,000 to permit many visits during the year. So the peddler
with his horse and wagon or his store boat on river or stream brought
to the farmer small and easily transported articles of all kinds. Mostly
he sold notions, everything from pins and needles to yard goods and
queen's ware. But some were more specialized. Thus the van of the
Yankee tinware peddler was known from Vermont to Louisiana, and
the salesman of Connecticut clocks traveling with horse and wagon
sought customers even in the Deep South.[12]

[12] Jones, *Middlemen in the Domestic Trade of the United States, 1800–1860,*
Chaps. 5 and 6; Lewis E. Atherton, "Itinerant Merchandising in the Ante-Bellum
South," *Bulletin of the Business Historical Society,* XIX, No. 2 (April, 1945), 35–59.

(*Above*) The Conestoga Wagon. (*Left, J. L. Ringwalt, Development of Transportation Systems in the United States, p. 288. Right, R. H. Gabriel, Pageant of America, IV, 6*)

(*Left*) New York City, 1831, Broadway at St. Paul's Church, showing early traffic congestion. (*Right*) Louisville, Kentucky about 1850, a typical main street of a small city. (*Both pictures Old Print Shop*)

(*Left*) Covered bridge, Columbus, Georgia. (*Old Print Shop*) (*Right*) The Niagara Railway Suspension Bridge. (*J. L. Ringwalt, Development of Transportation Systems in the United States, p. 288*)

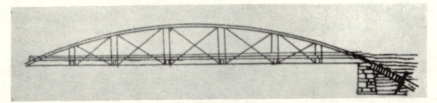

Iron truss bridge. Patented by Squire Whipple in 1841. (*J. L. Ringwalt, Development of Transportation Systems in the United States, p. 96*)

Stephen Girard, 1750–1831. (*Culver Service*)

John Jacob Astor, 1763–1848. (*Culver Service*)

John A. Roebling, 1806–1869. (*Culver Service*)

(*Right*) A good country road. (*Below*) Axles had to be high when mud was deep in country roads. (*Both pictures Culver Service*)

CHAPTER II

Roads and Bridges

THE COMMON ROADS

AS a part of the transportation system of the country, the humble rural road has seldom been given its due.[1] In 1815 a great network of these roads covered the settled portion of the country. Unbelievably poor by mid-twentieth century standards, they were hardly more than broad paths through the forest. In wet places they presented a line of ruts with frequent mud holes, and, where dry, a powdered surface of deep dust. The largest stones and stumps were removed only so far as was absolutely necessary to permit passage.[2] An early act of the Ohio legislature provided that stumps left in the road should not be more than a foot high.[3] In the most swampy places where mud rendered passage impossible, logs were laid side by side across the road to form what were known as corduroy roads. Across the rivers a few wooden bridges had been built, but for the most part fords or ferries were the only recourse.

These country roads led from the farms to the nearby village, that is, to the mill, the cotton gin, or the country store. Typically the village was located on water which was navigable at least for small boats during part of the year. If the village was not on navigable water, then the road would extend on to such a point; but the village

[1] For an exception see Jeremiah W. Jenks, "Road Legislation for the American States," *Publications of the American Economic Association,* 1st series, IV, No. 3 (May, 1889), 145–227.

[2] See Baynard Rush Hall (Robert Carlton, Esq., pseudonym), *The New Purchase; or, Early Years in the Far West* (New Albany, Ind.: J. R. Nunemacher, 1855, 2 vols. in one), pp. 46–47, 71.

[3] Laws of Ohio, 1804, cited by William F. Gephart, *Transportation and Industrial Development in the Middle West (Studies in History, Economics and Public Law,* Vol. XXXIV, No. 1, New York: Columbia University Press, 1909), p. 132.

could not be far away, for the prices paid for the bulky produce of the farms—the corn, wheat, or ashes of the North and the cotton, rice, or tobacco of the South—could not absorb the cost of extended transportation by land routes.

The fact that the years from about 1800 to 1830 have been called the "turnpike era" has diverted attention from these country roads, roads which were really much more important the country over than were the turnpikes, which were chiefly designed for travel between the larger towns or to the westward across the mountains. In view of their importance, why were these country roads permitted to continue in such extremely poor condition? In the first place, the sprawling rural communities had neither the capital nor the labor to expend on improving this tremendous network. Clearing the land, erecting dwellings, building rude schoolhouses and courthouses— these activities were more important to the farmers than fancy roads.

Second, following the ancient Anglo-Saxon tradition, road building was a community responsibility. The task was done by citizens who "worked off" their highway taxes. They assembled often in carnival mood and typically at a time of year when farm work was slack rather than when roads could best be made. With hoes, rakes, and shovels, and with plows pulled by oxen or mules they made their road under the direction of a fellow farmer who most often was an elected official of the town or county. Although skilled in felling trees and grubbing out stumps, this official was usually quite ignorant of even the rudiments of highway engineering. So, even where considerable time was spent on local roads and bridges, the results were not impressive.[4]

Finally, and probably most important, farmers did not deem it worth their while to go to great labor and expense to construct good roads. Hauling to market was indeed necessary and bad roads were an inconvenience. But it was slack-season work to be done by the farmers or their hands when farm work was least pressing. In the North, winter meant frozen roads which snow, under favorable conditions, converted into finer, smoother highways than man could build. With sleds and pungs, farmers carried their produce to mill and market with surprising ease. In the South, conditions were more difficult, especially if rains prevailed in the hauling season, but some-

[4] W. M. Gillespie, A Manual of the Principles and Practice of Road-Making (New York: A. S. Barnes and Company, 1852), pp. 341–347; Charles L. Dearing, American Highway Policy (Washington: The Brookings Institution, 1941), pp. 41–45; J. L. Ringwalt, Development of Transportation Systems in the United States (Philadelphia: J. L. Ringwalt, 1888), pp. 26–27.

how by use of mud boats and with the help of mules and oxen and slaves, the cotton could be got through the mud to the river bank. And if bad roads delayed the journey, no great loss resulted, for draft animals and slaves might as well be kept busy in the off season.[5]

To a considerable extent the local country roads had been linked together to provide longer routes of travel, so that by 1816 a continuous highway of sorts extended from Maine to Georgia. As population thinned out westward from the coast, the network of country roads disappeared, leaving only a few through roads or trails which crossed the divide to the headwaters of the tributaries of the Ohio River or connected with streams flowing into the St. Lawrence, the Great Lakes, or the Gulf of Mexico. For the most part these through routes, whether between coastal cities or leading to the West, were no better and frequently were worse than other roads. Except for brief stretches where turnpikes had been constructed, or in uncommon instances where state governments had sponsored the building of public roads, the through routes were, indeed, but a succession of country roads with necessary connecting links which were typically most ill cared for of all. The communities through which they passed were often unable or unwilling to give much attention to such through roads. The farmers had difficulty enough to provide passable roads to the local market without spending effort on main roads which were chiefly useful to travelers and stagecoach operators from distant cities.

THE MOVEMENT FOR IMPROVED ROADS

Even before the War of 1812 considerable progress had been made in the Middle Atlantic and New England states toward linking together the chief commercial centers by means of turnpikes, a term used to designate a road upon which tolls were charged. These roads were typically built by private stock companies, which were chartered by the state governments, and were erected over the most important routes of travel. The best ones, like the early Lancaster Turnpike in Pennsylvania or the Cumberland Road, were built on a solid stone foundation with a gravel dressing. Others consisted of merely a layer of loose gravel with drainage ditches on each side. Usually some attempt was made to reduce the steeper grades by cuts or fills. The poorest were little more than country roads kept in barely passable condition by the turnpike company. The excellence of the Lan-

[5] Ulrich B. Phillips, "Transportation in the Ante-Bellum South: An Economic Analysis," Quarterly Journal of Economics, XIX (May, 1905), 444.

caster Turnpike, which was completed between Philadelphia and Lancaster, Pennsylvania, in 1794, and its financial success stimulated considerable building of toll roads so that by 1815 eastern Pennsylvania, New York, New Jersey, and southern New England were served by fairly good roads between the chief commercial centers.

Intensified and almost unanimous enthusiasm for improved routes of land transportation followed the War of 1812. In part this was an outgrowth of the war experience. The extreme difficulty of moving troops on the Canadian frontier as well as on the southern boundary, due to the almost complete absence of highways, demonstrated that through roads in those areas were essential for effective national defense. Moreover, the British blockade of the Atlantic coast had compelled an unprecedented amount of land carriage and had emphasized the unsatisfactory character of the highways. Wagons carrying butter had made the long trip from New York to Charleston, South Carolina, and merchandise had been shipped in similar fashion from Boston to Philadelphia.[6] A wagon loaded with cotton cards and drawn by four horses had actually been sent from Worcester, Massachusetts, to Charleston, South Carolina. This trip took seventy-five days! [7] But the agitation for better roads also arose from the generally improved commercial conditions following the war. Farmers needed to get their war-accumulated surpluses to the seaports, merchants and manufacturers to sell their products in the interior. Especially were roads necessary to make contact with the rapidly expanding West, roads which must be built for long distances across unsettled portions of the Appalachians where no local governments existed.

The stage seemed to be set for the financing by the national government of a comprehensive scheme of internal improvements including both roads and canals. Albert Gallatin's statesmanlike plan of 1808 was still available to Congress and, although no general action had been taken to forward this proposal, the federal government had already, despite constitutional objections, sponsored a number of road-building projects. For postal as well as military purposes, federal roads had been built through the lower South in order to connect Georgia and Tennessee with Natchez. Although little more than broad paths through the forest, these roads did permit land communication through this as yet largely unsettled part of the coun-

[6] Niles' Weekly Register, Vol. IV (March 13, 1813), 32 and VI (March 26, 1814), 67.

[7] Charleston Courier, Charleston, South Carolina, March 3, 1813.

try. But the chief federal road-building project was, of course, the Cumberland Road from Cumberland, Maryland, to Wheeling, Virginia, on the Ohio. This well-constructed highway to the West, later known as the National Road, was well under way in 1815.

It also should be noted that when Ohio was made a state in 1803, Congress provided that 5 per cent of the net proceeds from the sale of public lands within the state should be set aside for the construction of roads. Of this amount two fifths were to be spent by Congress in building roads to and through the state and three fifths were to be disbursed by the Ohio legislature for laying out and constructing state roads. Down to 1830 considerable sums for the building of roads in Ohio were available from this source, but unfortunately a substantial part of these funds appears to have been diverted for political purposes.[8]

In his annual message to Congress in December, 1815, President James Madison urged "the great importance of establishing throughout our country the roads and canals which can best be executed under national authority." [9] John C. Calhoun sponsored and Henry Clay supported a bill in the House of Representatives providing for a national system of internal improvements on a scale similar to that proposed by Gallatin in 1808. As finally passed by Congress on March 1, 1817, this measure, known as the Bonus Bill, provided that funds arising from the chartering of the second Bank of the United States should be earmarked for this purpose. Madison vetoed the bill on constitutional grounds.[10] Two other presidential vetoes punctuated the long struggle. In 1822 elaborate plans were drawn up for a national system of internal improvements following the main lines of an elaborate scheme worked out by Calhoun in 1819. But again the proposal had to be dropped, for on May 4, 1822, President James Monroe vetoed a bill providing for the erection of toll gates and the collection of tolls on the Cumberland, or National Road, stating at great length his belief that federally sponsored internal improvements were and always had been unconstitutional.[11]

[8] Gephart, *Transportation and Industrial Development in the Middle West*, pp. 131–134.

[9] James D. Richardson, ed., *Messages and Papers of the Presidents, 1789–1907* (The Miscellaneous Documents of the House of Representatives, 43 Cong., 2 Sess., 1893–1894, 40 vols., Washington: Government Printing Office, 1895), I, 567.

[10] *Ibid.*, I, 584; Charles M. Wiltse, *John C. Calhoun, Nationalist, 1782–1828* (2 vols., Indianapolis: The Bobbs-Merrill Company, 1944–1949), I, 137.

[11] Richardson, *Messages and Papers of the Presidents*, II, 142–183; Jeremiah Simeon Young, *A Political and Constitutional Study of the Cumberland Road* (Chicago: The University of Chicago Press, 1904), pp. 66–77.

Finally, President Andrew Jackson, in his veto of the use of federal funds to help finance the Maysville Road (1830) and also in his annual message of December 6, 1830, opposed federal grants for internal improvements at that time. It must be emphasized, however, that Jackson took no arbitrary stand on the constitutionality of federal projects for building roads or canals but pointed out that the Maysville Road lay within a single state and was not a part of a great national system for which constitutional justification for federal aid might reasonably be argued. Actually, he went beyond constitutional questions, condemning grants for local improvements because of the serious abuses that might be expected from them and opposing large national projects because he believed it more important at that time to retire the national debt than to appropriate money for national roads and bridges, desirable though they might be. In part, also, Jackson's opposition to the Maysville project may have stemmed from the fact that it involved federal aid to a private corporation. At other times Jackson gave his approval to substantial appropriations of federal funds for building roads and canals.[12] His Maysville Road veto, therefore, hardly warrants the strict constructionist emphasis so commonly given it.

Congress debated year after year, even decade after decade, the subject of federal aid to internal improvements. Speeches taking the form of constitutional exegesis encumber the record with long and incredibly arid passages. With tireless persistency the members debated such questions as whether the power "To establish Post Offices and Post Roads" permitted the federal government merely to plan and designate post roads or whether it also authorized Congress to build, operate, and repair them. That the leaders of the time were genuinely troubled over the strict as against the broad interpretation of the Constitution and the degree to which it was desirable to centralize power in the national government cannot be doubted. But from the vantage point of the twentieth century the prolonged constitutional debates seem forced and unreal, little more than forensic shadowboxing. Despite a great parade of constitutional scruples, successive chief executives and congresses actually approved grants to aid in building specific roads, canals, and railroads. The average annual appropriation of the federal government for internal improvements increased with each administration from Jefferson

[12] Richardson, *Messages and Papers of the Presidents*, II, 483–493; 508–517. See also Marquis James, *The Life of Jackson* (New York: Garden City Publishing Company, 1940), pp. 525–527; *Congressional Globe*, 30 Cong., 1 Sess., XIX, App., 106.

through Jackson. John Quincy Adams has been known as the great champion of internal improvements, but appropriations for this purpose, which averaged $702,000 annually while he was president, increased to $1,323,000 under Andrew Jackson.[13]

The real obstacle which defeated a national system of internal improvements is to be found in the bitter state and sectional jealousies which were wracking the new nation. New England was almost solidly opposed to federally financed internal improvements. Her own roads were relatively good, and she looked with genuine alarm upon measures which would further augment the heavy migration of people from her hills to the Ohio Valley or promote the commerce of New York, Philadelphia, or Baltimore to the disadvantage of Boston. At first New York and Pennsylvania were powerful advocates of a federal system of internal improvements, for across their territory lay promising routes to the West. In fact these two states together marshaled nearly half the votes which made possible passage of the Internal Improvements, or so-called Bonus, Bill of 1817.[14] But this marked the high tide of such support from these states; each was soon financing its own system and consequently opposed to the development of competitive routes to the West at federal expense.

It is true that the South was well supplied with navigable rivers, yet no part of the country had poorer roads or stood more greatly in need of federal capital to provide internal improvements than the South. But little support for such projects came from this section. Even in 1817 Calhoun could not command a majority of southern votes in favor of his internal improvements measure. Later, as sectional issues became more clearly defined, the people of the South grew even more strongly opposed to federal grants for roads and canals. Southerners believed such expenditures would benefit other sections more than the South. But even more important to them was the fact that disbursements on internal improvements increased the need for revenue and thus gave justification for a tariff system which they bitterly opposed. Finally, the argument for federal internal improvements rested on a broad interpretation of the Constitution, a construction which became increasingly distasteful in the South as the defense of slavery gradually overshadowed all other issues.

The one section of the country which gave the most continuous

[13] John G. Van Deusen, *Economic Bases of Disunion in South Carolina* (No. 305 of *Columbia University Studies in History, Economics and Public Law*, New York: Columbia University Press, 1928), p. 128; *Senate Document* No. 450, 26 Cong., 1 Sess., pp. 3–6; *Congressional Globe*, 30 Cong., 1 Sess., XIX, App., 106.

[14] For an analysis of the vote on this bill see Wiltse *John C. Calhoun*, I, 403.

support for a national system of internal improvements was the West. Capital was scarce and the need pressing for improved routes to the East. But even in this section voters were not unanimous in their approval. The dominance of other issues as well as the existence of local jealousies always sufficed to produce some opposition.

THE RAGE FOR TURNPIKES

Greatest of all the turnpikes was the National Road. Here was a truly national project, conceived on Roman lines, and—despite sectional jealousies, a mixture of presidential vetoes and blessings, and constitutional complications which were never resolved—finally built by the federal government through the heart of the country. The road started at Cumberland, Maryland, the terminus of the Frederick Pike, which came from Baltimore. Thus, beginning not far from a central point on the Atlantic coast line, it was continued steadily westward. By 1818 Wheeling had been reached, by 1833 Columbus, Ohio, and finally, about the middle of the century, Vandalia, Illinois. Plans for its further extension were then abandoned. Begun in the early days of the turnpike enthusiasm, its construction was continued through the canal-building boom and for two decades into the railroad era. Then for more than half a century it suffered neglect until, with the coming of the automobile, it became a part of National Highway No. 40. Its sturdily constructed stone bridges, though built for oxcarts and stagecoaches, safely supported the motor-driven traffic of the gasoline age. And its remaining taverns, which had in the dull days of the latter nineteenth century become commercial hotels, country stores, or private residences, came to life again as taverns, inns, and "tourist homes." [15]

The most active period of turnpike construction in New England had come in the decade ending in 1806. But additional roads were built thereafter, so that by about 1825 southern New England was crisscrossed with many main roads, and New Hampshire and Vermont had completed or authorized turnpike construction over the chief routes of travel.[16] New York and Pennsylvania had the greatest mileage of turnpike roads. In New York, soon after the close of

[15] Philip D. Jordan, *The National Road* (Indianapolis: The Bobbs-Merrill Company, 1948), *passim*.
[16] Frederic J. Wood, *The Turnpikes of New England and Evolution of the Same through England, Virginia, and Maryland* (Boston: Marshall Jones Company, 1919), *passim*, referred to hereafter as Wood, *Turnpikes of New England*; Philip Elbert Taylor, "The Turnpike Era in New England" (manuscript thesis in Yale University Library), pp. 208, 345–349.

the War of 1812, a series of connected turnpikes was completed which extended from the Massachusetts border through Albany to a point on Lake Erie near Buffalo, and numerous additional roads fanned out from Albany and other Hudson River points. By 1821, 6,000 miles of new turnpike construction had been authorized, about 4,000 of which were completed. Road building reached its height in the next few years but declined after 1825. Pennsylvania turnpikes, which even before the war were extensive in the eastern part of the state, were after 1815 built rapidly to the westward. By 1821 about 1,800 miles of turnpike had been built. Construction continued, and the total mileage for the state reached a high point in 1832 with approximately 2,400 miles of toll road. In New Jersey, turnpikes were constructed largely in the northern and central part of the state. About 550 miles of toll roads had been completed by 1829.[17]

Although much was said in the South in the period 1815–1830 concerning the desirability of improved roads, turnpike building lagged in that region. Maryland went farthest toward erecting a highway system. Even before the War of 1812, turnpike companies had begun the construction of roads radiating from Baltimore, and after the war these were extended and a connection was made with the Cumberland Road. By 1830 the state had about 300 miles of toll road.[18] In Virginia, the Turnpike Act of 1817 permitted the state to invest in turnpike companies up to two fifths of their capital if the remainder was secured from private sources. But not until the forties were two important turnpikes completed to the West, the Staunton and Parkersburg Road and the Northwestern Turnpike, which ran from Winchester to the mouth of the Little Kanawha.[19]

South Carolina experienced a flurry of road building during the twenties. A road of sorts was finally completed across the pine barrens from Charleston to Columbia, and from Columbia northward to the North Carolina boundary. Causeways were erected across

[17] Joseph Austin Durrenberger, *Turnpikes: A Study of the Toll Road Movement in the Middle Atlantic States and Maryland* (Valdosta, Ga.: Southern Stationery and Printing Company, 1931), pp. 55–56, 61–62, referred to hereafter as Durrenberger, *Turnpikes;* Report of the Senate Committee on Roads, Bridges, and Inland Navigation of March 23, 1822, in *Hazard's Register of Pennsylvania,* II (November 27, 1828), 290; Wheaton J. Lane, *From Indian Trail to Iron Horse: Travel and Transportation in New Jersey, 1620–1860* (Princeton: Princeton University Press, 1939), p. 151, referred to hereafter as Lane, *From Indian Trail to Iron Horse.*

[18] Durrenberger, *Turnpikes,* p. 70.

[19] Isaac Figley Boughter, *Internal Improvements in Northwestern Virginia: A Study of State Policy Prior to the Civil War* (*University of Pittsburgh Bulletin,* Vol. XXVIII, No. 4, December, 1931), pp. 4–5. Referred to hereafter as Boughter, *Internal Improvements in Northwestern Virginia.*

swampy sections of the coastal plain and several short turnpikes were completed. All this was done directly by the state at a total cost for the period 1823–1828 of nearly $120,000, of which about one tenth came from tolls.[20] But state appropriations came to an end in 1829, and the turnpike era was over in South Carolina. In 1838 the South Carolina legislature agreed under certain conditions to subscribe to two fifths of the stock of turnpike companies. But by this time, chief attention was focused on railways, few if any new turnpikes were constructed, and the old ones fell into disrepair.[21]

In the lower South, very few through roads were built. The course of events in Georgia is fairly representative. The main roads were admittedly in a "shameful condition," and many plans were urged for their improvement. In the early twenties the legislature agreed to purchase stock in private turnpike companies, but no successful promoters came forward. In fact, the total accomplishments of the legislature in the matter of road building appear to have been some extended surveys which came to nothing and a small amount of road work by gangs of state-owned slaves in 1830–1833.[22]

Although the turnpike fever raged in the Old Northwest during the twenties and thirties, few roads were completed except in Ohio. There a great number of turnpike companies were formed and toll roads were established on the main routes of commerce. The companies were not effectively supervised by the state and the roads generally were not well constructed or managed.[23]

FINANCING THE TURNPIKES

The corporate form of organization appears to have been used for the turnpikes practically without exception. With capital for building any particular turnpike available only from local sources, the corporate form, which through sale of shares facilitated wide community participation, proved most acceptable. Often the state charter limited the number of shares for any company, and the

[20] Report of the Superintendent of Public Works for the Year 1828, in David Kohn and Bess Glenn, eds., *Internal Improvement in South Carolina, 1817–1828* (Washington: Privately printed, 1938), p. 577.

[21] Ulrich Bonnell Phillips, *A History of Transportation in the Eastern Cotton Belt to 1860* (New York: Columbia University Press, 1939), pp. 83–100. Referred to hereafter as Phillips, *Transportation in Eastern Cotton Belt.*

[22] *Ibid.,* pp. 102–116. For Alabama, see William Elejius Martin, *Internal Improvements in Alabama* (Johns Hopkins University *Studies in Historical and Political Science,* Vol. XX, No. 4, Baltimore: The Johns Hopkins Press, 1902), pp. 29–32.

[23] Gephart, *Transportation and Industrial Development in the Middle West,* pp. 129–147.

directors levied successive assessments on subscribers as long as additional capital was needed to complete the road. Each of the 995 shares in the Newburyport Turnpike Company in Massachusetts had repeated assessments made against it until the total investment represented by each share finally came to $420.[24]

With enthusiasm for turnpikes running high, state legislatures were generous in granting corporation charters. From 1815 to 1830 probably more charters were granted for this type of business than for any other, and by the twenties the common stocks issued by turnpike companies rivaled and possibly surpassed those which had been issued by state banks.[25]

The amount of private capital invested in turnpike companies was of considerable magnitude. In New England alone about $6,500,-000 was so invested by 1840. Though companies involving an investment of several hundred thousand dollars were not uncommon, most were capitalized for less than $100,000. Shares were sold to all in the community who wished to invest small savings—professional men, farmers, merchants, and manufacturers. But large blocks of stocks were often held by a few wealthy persons in the community. Merchant capitalists who were also active in banking and promoting local manufacturing companies were often leaders in organizing and financing the turnpike companies.[26]

In New England and the Middle Atlantic states, except for Pennsylvania, turnpikes were financed almost exclusively from private investments. Of approximately $6,000,000 which had been invested in turnpike companies in Pennsylvania by 1822, about two thirds had come from individuals and about one third from the state treasury.[27] Elsewhere in the country the large sums invested in toll roads came in large part from state funds. This seems to have followed largely from the fact that population was less dense and that less private capital was available. The outlays by the states took two different forms. In South Carolina before 1830 and in Indiana, most turnpikes

[24] Taylor, "The Turnpike Era in New England," pp. 162–163.

[25] Ibid., pp. 111–112, 135–152; Durrenberger, Turnpikes, pp. 76–82; Edward Chase Kirkland, Men, Cities and Transportation: A Study in New England History, 1820–1900 (2 vols., Cambridge: Harvard University Press, 1948), I, 41–44, referred to hereafter as Kirkland, Men, Cities and Transportation; George Heberton Evans, Jr., Business Incorporations in the United States, 1800–1943 (New York: National Bureau of Economic Research, 1948), pp. 14–20.

[26] Durrenberger, Turnpikes, pp. 96–109; Taylor, "The Turnpike Era in New England," pp. 100–102, 165–169, 211; Martin, Merchants and Trade of the Connecticut River Valley, 1750–1820, pp. 201–202.

[27] Hazard's Register of Pennsylvania, II (November 22, 1828), 292; Tenth Census of the United States: Valuation, Taxation, and Public Indebtedness, VII, 526.

were completely financed and owned outright by the state. More common, however, was state investment in the stock of privately owned companies. This was the procedure followed in Pennsylvania and, to a larger extent, in such states as Virginia and Ohio. In fact, a considerable number of southern and western states agreed to match out of state funds and, on a fairly generous basis, private investments in the stock of turnpike companies. The total amount of the investment by states in turnpikes is unknown, but it was surely a fairly substantial sum. Expenditures for bridges, turnpikes, and plank roads in Virginia totaled nearly $5,000,000 by 1861. As of 1838 the state debt of Kentucky attributable to toll-road construction was nearly $2,500,000 and that for Indiana was over $1,000,000.

Very little is known as to the contributions of capital to turnpike building by local governmental units. Such help is said to have amounted to $2,000,000 in Ohio and was of at least occasional importance in eastern states. In Pennsylvania, counties invested heavily in turnpike stock and by the terms of its Pennsylvania charter the second Bank of the United States was required to appropriate over $200,000 for stock subscriptions and outright grants to turnpike companies. Even the federal government lent a helping hand by granting public lands to Ohio for the benefit of the Columbus and Sandusky Turnpike Company.[28]

END OF THE TURNPIKE BOOM

Where well built and kept in good repair, the turnpikes provided fine hard-surfaced roads which were a great improvement over the usual public roads. To travelers, whether by carriage or stage coach, they were an unquestioned blessing. For immigrants pressing westward they literally smoothed the way, greatly reducing the hardships of that difficult trek. For local transportation with the heavy, clumsy wagons of the day they offered real advantages, though even low tolls discouraged traffic when freight was large in bulk or weight but small in value. But for long freight hauls the value of turnpikes

---

[28] *Tenth Census of the United States: Valuation, Taxation, and Public Indebtedness,* VII, 555, 526; Lewis Collins, *History of Kentucky* (2 vols., Louisville: John P. Morton and Company, n.d.), I, 540; Gephart, *Transportation and Industrial Development in the Middle West,* pp. 142–143; Federal Coordinator of Transportation, *Public Aids to Transportation* (Washington: Government Printing Office, 1938), II, 7; Matthias Nordberg Orfield, *Federal Land Grants to the States with Special Reference to Minnesota* (University of Minnesota *Studies in the Social Sciences,* No. 2, Minneapolis: *Bulletin* of the University of Minnesota, 1915), p. 92; Louis Hartz, *Economic Policy and Democratic Thought: Pennsylvania, 1776–1860* (Cambridge: Harvard University Press, 1948), pp. 46–47, 87 fn.

was sharply limited. Even where tolls were very low or nonexistent, transportation by heavy wagons with four- to eight-horse teams proved profitable only to a very limited extent.[29] As a result, though a boon to travelers, turnpikes generally did not cheapen and stimulate land transportation sufficiently to provide satisfactory earnings from tolls.

This failure of the turnpikes to provide the means of cheap transportation over considerable distances sealed their doom. Wherever tried, they proved with rare exceptions financially disappointing. This had been the history of turnpikes in western Europe; it proved no less true in every part of the United States. Far from yielding a fair return on the capital invested, many turnpike companies were unable to collect sufficient revenue to cover the cost of maintaining the roads and collecting the tolls. Very few indeed returned any part of the original capital to the investors. Even in New England, where they were relatively most successful, only 5 or 6 out of 230 turnpikes paid barely satisfactory returns to investors.[30] The most successful Massachusetts road, the Salem Turnpike, averaged dividends of 3.1 per cent over sixty years. Most prosperous in Connecticut was the short Derby Turnpike from New Haven to Derby, which over approximately one hundred years averaged dividends of 5.1 per cent. In the Middle Atlantic states a few of the best located pikes paid from 1 to 8 per cent in their most prosperous years.[31] Ohio owned nearly half the stock in 26 turnpike companies in 1838. For the year ending November 15, 1848, only 9 of these companies paid dividends on their stock. By far the best of these was the Colerain, Oxford, and Brookville Turnpike Company, which brought the state about 9 per cent on its investment.[32] Turnpike stock in which the state of Kentucky had invested more than $2,500,000 was worth only 25 or 30 cents on the dollar by 1851.[33]

Even those turnpikes which were so favorably located as to develop a large volume of traffic both from travelers and from transportation of goods found profitable operation extremely difficult. The cost of keeping the roads in repair under heavy traffic conditions

<hr />

[29] Taylor, "The Turnpike Era in New England," pp. 260–265.

[30] Ibid., p. 266.

[31] Wood, Turnpikes of New England, p. 35; Taylor, "The Turnpike Era in New England," p. 279; Durrenberger, Turnpikes, pp. 112–115; Oliver W. Holmes, "The Turnpike Era," Conquering the Wilderness (Vol. V of Alexander C. Flick, ed., History of the State of New York, 10 vols., New York: Columbia University Press, 1934), p. 269.

[32] Tenth Census of the United States: Valuation, Taxation, and Public Indebtedness, VII, 614.

[33] Ibid., p. 609.

proved a constant drain. Collection of tolls entailed burdensome operating expenses, and ensuring honest and efficient performance by tollhouse keepers was so difficult that the right to operate tollgates was often sold for a fixed sum. Finally, the traveling public showed considerable reluctance to part with money for tolls. Shunpikes— roads around the tollgates—appeared widely despite the best efforts of the turnpike companies, and teamsters waited until after sundown in order to pass free when no collector remained on duty. Perhaps most damaging of all, wherever public roads offered fair passage, as they often did especially during the more favorable seasons of the year, the teamsters demonstrated great interest in choosing more roundabout routes if tolls could be avoided.

The decline of the turnpikes can be ascribed only in small part to the competition of canals and railroads. Many turnpike companies had failed even before this competition appeared, and those which lasted after about 1830 had for the most part already demonstrated their financial unprofitability. Turnpikes were being abandoned in Massachusetts as early as 1819, and by 1835 more than half of those built were either partially or completely abandoned.[34] In 1817 some toll roads were being abandoned in New York. Joseph Durrenberger reports that about 4,000 miles of turnpike road were being operated in New York State in 1822; fourteen years later, more than half of this mileage had been given up by the turnpike companies.[35] Few turnpikes were built in New Jersey after 1828, and important companies had failed as early as 1822 and 1823.[36]

BRIDGES AND PLANK ROADS

The growth of turnpikes gave a great impetus to bridge building. Wood, abundant in most places, formed the superstructure, with stone for piers and abutments. Most common, especially in the East, was the covered bridge with roof shingled and sides clapboarded to protect the timbers from the harmful effects of the weather. The science of bridge building advanced rapidly, especially after 1830, when the special needs of the railroads had to be met. Inventions by such men as William Howe of Springfield, Massachusetts, and Squire Whipple of Utica, New York, greatly improved the truss bridge. Cast and wrought iron came into common use, and, with the development of the wire cable by John A. Roebling, the suspension

[34] Taylor, "The Turnpike Era in New England," pp. 357–358.
[35] Durrenberger, *Turnpikes*, pp. 156, 158.
[36] Lane, *From Indian Trail to Iron Horse*, pp. 151–152, 161.

bridge became increasingly popular. In fact, the strides which marked bridge building between 1816 and 1860 epitomize the transportation revolution of those years. At the beginning of the period, carpenters and masons turned bridge builders constructed, by rule of thumb, the substantial stone and wooden bridges which adequately served the horse-drawn traffic on the new Cumberland Road. In 1855 Roebling completed the Niagara Railway Suspension Bridge, one of the great engineering feats of the age. Having a span of 821 feet, this huge modern structure carried railroad trains on its upper deck and highway traffic on its lower.

Like the turnpikes the highway bridges of this period were typically built by private corporations chartered for the purpose and supported by tolls. Similarly, capital for their construction came largely from local interests, though often supplemented by public credit. But unlike the turnpikes, a considerable number of the bridge companies proved profitable ventures and, though public ownership became increasingly common, many privately owned toll bridges persisted through the nineteenth and into the twentieth century.[37]

The canal and the railroad provided what the turnpike could not—economical long-distance transportation. But for shorter distances not on trunk lines, for routes to secondary market areas, or for feeder lines to the railroad or canal centers, no satisfactory answer had been found, and farmers and merchants continued to depend upon the miserable rural roads of the time. Only against this background can the enthusiasm for plank roads following 1844 be understood.

From Russia the idea of the plank road was introduced into upper Canada in 1834, where it was adopted with considerable enthusiasm. Like the older turnpikes, plank roads were built by private corporations which collected tolls for their use. But they differed from their predecessors in construction and also in purpose. They were typically built not for long but rather for short or intermediate distance transportation. They were constructed on the same principle as the wooden sidewalks, which around 1900 were common in every Ameri-

---

[37] Wilbur J. Watson, *Bridge Architecture* (Cleveland: J. H. Jansen, 1927), pp. 115, 147, 170–174; Wilbur J. Watson and Sara Ruth Watson, *Bridges in History and Legend* (Cleveland: J. H. Jansen, 1937), pp. 182–191, 200–204, 209–212; Adelbert M. Jakeman, *Old Covered Bridges* (Brattleboro, Vt.: Stephen Daye Press, 1935), *passim;* Caroline E. MacGill, *History of Transportation in the United States before 1860* (Balthasar Henry Meyer, ed., Washington: Carnegie Institution of Washington, 1917), pp. 37–50, referred to hereafter as MacGill, *History of Transportation;* D. B. Steinman, *The Builders of the Bridge: The Story of John Roebling and His Son* (New York: Harcourt, Brace and Company, 1945), pp. 157–193.

can community. Heavy planks, usually about three inches thick and eight feet long, were laid across stringers, which were placed parallel with the direction of the road and set solidly into the roadbed. The result was a smooth surface over which heavy loads could be easily and quickly hauled to market. A Canadian editor declared that a horse driven six miles over one of these roads "seemed more in a gay frolick than at labour." [38]

Enthusiasm for these roads was also stimulated by their apparently low cost. Wherever the country was wooded, small sawmills could be set up, thus providing cheap materials and obviating transportation costs. Often such roads were built on top of abandoned turnpikes or on common roads, thus saving much expense for grading and draining. Actually the original cost does appear to have been low relative to that for turnpikes. Plank roads were built for as little as $1,000 per mile and averaged perhaps from $1,500 to $1,800.[39] Some of the early well-constructed turnpikes cost much more, the Lancaster Turnpike $7,500 a mile and the Cumberland Road $13,000 a mile. But much depended on the terrain, the quality of the road built, and other factors. Many New England turnpikes cost less than $1,000 a mile.[40] Pennsylvania turnpikes built before 1822 cost from $600 to more than $11,000 per mile, but for stone construction the cost was seldom below $3,000 or $4,000 a mile. In 1853, William Kingsford, a strong proponent of the plank road, estimated the average cost of a macadam road in New York at $3,500 a mile. Over a period of eight years, during the last year of which he figured the plank road would have to be relaid, Kingsford believed that the total cost of a macadam road would be 50 per cent greater than a single-track plank road. But his estimate on the average life of the plank road was possibly double that justified by experience.[41]

Appearing first in New York State in 1844, the mania for plank roads spread rapidly to every part of the country. Strongest in the Middle Atlantic and North Central states, by 1857 the movement had resulted in the building of some 7,000 miles of plank road in

[38] Quoted from the *Patriot* by G. P. de T. Glazebrook, *A History of Transportation in Canada* (Toronto: The Ryerson Press, 1938), p. 120.

[39] Durrenberger, *Turnpikes*, p. 149; Wood, *Turnpikes of New England*, p. 40; MacGill, *History of Transportation*, p. 300; William Kingsford, *History, Structure, and Statistics of Plank Roads, in the United States and Canada* (Philadelphia: A. Hart, 1851), pp. 6, 9, 29, referred to hereafter as Kingsford, *History of Plank Roads;* Gillespie, *A Manual of the Principles and Practice of Road-Making*, pp. 244–247.

[40] Taylor, "The Turnpike Era in New England," pp. 348–349; *Hazard's Register of Pennsylvania*, II (November 22, 1828), 298–299.

[41] Kingsford, *History of Plank Roads*, p. 10.

New York, Pennsylvania, New Jersey, and Maryland at a total cost of $10,000,000.[42] Plank roads in Ohio were valued at over $300,000 in 1853.[43] In Illinois, Michigan, and Wisconsin, many companies were organized to build these roads and considerable mileage was actually constructed.[44] Even west of the Mississippi, plank roads enjoyed a brief period of popularity in the fifties.[45] Although the contagion spread to every part of the Union, the mileage actually built was not great in New England and the South. Construction of plank roads was carried farthest in central New York State. Here the roads were typically short, radiating out from the larger cities into rich farming country and tapping subsidiary market areas. Thus the plank roads acted as feeder lines for railroads and canals.

But the movement was short-lived; only a few companies struggled on after the panic of 1857. The plank roads could no more be supported by receipts from tolls than the earlier turnpikes for, despite low original cost, the expense of upkeep and replacement proved prohibitive. Although enthusiasts believed that planked highways would last from seven to ten years, in actual practice hard wear and especially the rot caused by constant contact with the moist earth made their useful life much shorter. Repairs were costly and, unlike the turnpike, which often provided a road of sorts even though abused and neglected, the plank road became a positive menace once the surface was weakened by use or decay.[46] The failure of the plank-road movement left most short-haul land transportation literally stuck in the mud, there to remain until the later age of the rigid-surfaced road and the internal-combustion engine.

[42] Durrenberger, *Turnpikes*, p. 145.
[43] Gephart, *Transportation and Industrial Development in the Middle West*, p. 145.
[44] MacGill, *History of Transportation*, pp. 300, 303–304.
[45] Richard C. Overton, *Burlington West: A Colonization History of the Burlington Railroad* (Cambridge: Harvard University Press, 1941), pp. 49–50, referred to hereafter as Overton, *Burlington West;* S. G. Reed, *A History of the Texas Railroads* (Houston: The St. Clair Publishing Company, 1941), p. 124; Ben Hur Wilson, "Planked from Burlington," *The Palimpsest*, XVI (October, 1935), 309–323; Oscar Osburn Winther, *The Old Oregon Country* (Indiana University Publications, Social Science Series, No. 7, Bloomington: Indiana University, 1950), pp. 123–124.
[46] Bessie Louise Pierce, *A History of Chicago* (2 vols., New York: Alfred A. Knopf, Inc., 1937–1940), II, 36–37; Wilson, "Planked from Burlington," pp. 327–328; Holmes, "The Turnpike Era," pp. 272–273.

The Canal Era

THE ERIE CANAL AND THE BEGINNING OF THE BOOM

WHEN, at the close of the War of 1812, the nation turned enthusi-astically to developing more effective means of internal transporta-tion, attention was directed to canals as well as to turnpikes. Though ambitious schemes for extensive artificial waterways, including canals across the Appalachian barrier, had long been urged, actual build-ing had advanced so slowly that by 1816 only about 100 miles of canal had been constructed in the United States. Only three canals in operation at this time were more than 2 miles long. The longest (27.25 miles) was the Middlesex, which by tapping the Merri-mack River brought the products of New Hampshire to Boston Har-bor. The Santee and Cooper Canal in South Carolina gave Charles-ton access to the commerce of the Santee River. Finally, the Dismal Swamp Canal provided for passage of small boats between Norfolk and Albemarle Sound.

No great boom in canal construction such as that which followed the completion of the Bridgewater Canal in Great Britain in 1765 had yet taken place in the United States. The chief reasons are not far to seek. Canals required heavy expenditures of capital, much greater than could be easily raised, and canal engineering was an almost un-known science in America. Moreover, the canals already built had proved such unsuccessful financial ventures as to offer little en-couragement to investors. Both the Santee and the Middlesex canal companies had subjected stockholders to many heavy assessments during the long process of construction and by 1816 neither had be-come a really profitable investment nor proved the boon to transpor-tation which promoters had promised.[1]

[1] Christopher Roberts, *The Middlesex Canal 1793–1860* (Vol. LXI of *Harvard*

The building of the Erie Canal was an act of faith, the demonstration of a spirit of enterprise by an organized government that has few parallels in world history. When the bill providing for this great public work was passed by the New York legislature in 1817, the population of the state was not much more than a million persons, most of whom lived in the lower Hudson River Valley. Much of the territory between Albany and Buffalo, through which the 364-mile canal must be built, was an unsettled wilderness. The longest canal as yet built in the United States extended not quite 28 miles. Not only was the Erie to be by far the longest in the world but engineering problems greater than any previously solved in canal construction had to be surmounted in the building of its locks and aqueducts. Finally to be overcome were the doubts of the skeptical and the faint-hearted, of those who saw nothing but financial ruin for the state and a heyday for political plunderers in the building of what was termed "Clinton's Big Ditch."

Though presenting major engineering difficulties, the route of the New York canal from Albany through the valley of the Mohawk River to Buffalo on Lake Erie offered by far the most attractive artificial water route from the Atlantic to the West. At its highest point near Buffalo it rose only 650 feet above the Hudson River at Albany, ample water supplies were available, and the terrain was much less forbidding than that to be found farther to the south. Little wonder, then, that Americans had dreamed of such a project in the Mohawk Valley even before independence had been achieved, that Gallatin had included it among his recommendations, and that, prior to the War of 1812, the New York legislature had taken preliminary steps looking toward constructing such a waterway.

After the war, the plan was vigorously pushed with the powerful support of De Witt Clinton, who, more than any other, was responsible for its success. Construction of the canal was authorized by the state legislature in April, 1817, and was actually begun on the following fourth of July. At the same time provision was made for building the Champlain Canal. When completed, it connected the Hudson a few miles north of Albany with the head of navigation on Lake Champlain. The federal government having denied financial aid, the state took on the whole responsibility of raising the necessary funds and directing the building. Special commissioners with wide

Economic Studies, Cambridge: Harvard University Press, 1938), pp. 181–183; Phillips, Transportation in Eastern Cotton Belt, pp. 38–43.

powers were appointed to superintend the construction and operation of the canal.

The epic story of the building of the Erie Canal has been told
many times. The lack of professional engineers was met by appoint-
ing untrained but able persons, chiefly lawyers, to plan and superintend the construction. With energy and versatility not untypical
of the Americans of that day, Benjamin Wright and James Geddes,
and the men associated with them, constructed the Erie so well as
to earn the praise of European experts.[2] The work was pushed with
such vigor that by the end of 1819 the middle section of the canal
was open for a distance of 75 miles. In the autumn of 1823 the Champlain Canal was completed, and in October two years later the Erie
was formally opened with the pageantry, illuminations, oratory,
firing of cannon, and drinking of toasts deemed suitable to the occasion and the spirit of the times.

Even before completion, the Erie Canal gave unmistakable evidence of phenomenal success. After 1819, as successive sections of
the canal were completed, traffic crowded its waters and the revenue
from tolls rose so rapidly as to contribute materially to financing its
completion. In 1825 tolls on the Erie and Champlain canals totaled
over half a million dollars; the following year, three quarters of a
million. Already there was talk of overcrowding and the need for
enlargement. Traffic continued to increase, and in 1835, only ten
years after the canal's completion, the state of New York ordered
the whole work enlarged, the width at the water surface to be increased from 40 to 70 feet and the depth from 4 to 7 feet. This tremendous task of enlargement went forward slowly, not being completed until 1862. But in the meantime, traffic grew and revenues
from tolls increased despite financial panics and railroad competition. In fact, the tonnage carried on the Erie grew even after the
Civil War until it reached its highest point in 1880.[3]

The success of the Erie Canal provided the spark which set off
a nation-wide craze for canal building. With the need for improved
transportation so great and the financial and economic benefits to
be secured from artificial waterways now apparently assured, a veritable canal-building fury gripped the country from Maine to Vir-

[2] John A. Krout, "New York's Early Engineers," *New York State Historical Society,
Quarterly Journal*, XXVI (July, 1945), 269–277.

[3] Noble E. Whitford, *History of the Canal System of the State of New York, Supple-
ment to the Annual Report of the State Engineer and Surveyor of the State of New
York, 1905* (2 vols., Albany: 1906); Alvin F. Harlow, *Old Towpaths* (New York: D.
Appleton and Company, 1926), Chaps. 6 and 7.

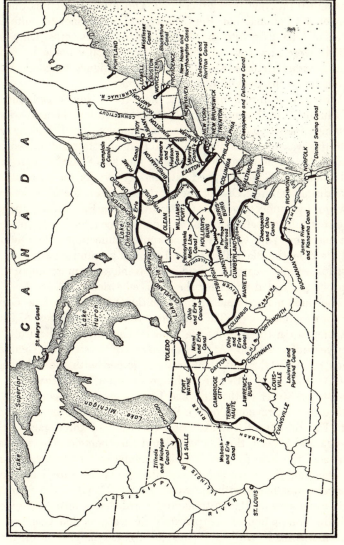

Principal Canals Built by 1860

ginia and from New Jersey to Illinois. Old projects such as that to connect the Potomac and the Ohio rivers, or schemes to unite the waters of Lake Erie with the Ohio River by routes across Ohio and Indiana were now revived. Surveys were actually made by order of the Massachusetts legislature for a canal designed to extend from Boston across the Berkshires to the Hudson.

With optimism running so high, the state of New York found itself caught up in the enthusiasm of its own creating. Though wisely avoiding dissipation of its resources on extensions until the Erie was built, this was no sooner accomplished than the state authorized the construction of one branch canal after another. Some of these carried a heavy traffic and proved valuable feeders for the Erie; others were dismal failures. One of the most successful, the 38 mile long Oswego, by connecting Lake Ontario with the Erie Canal, opened up direct inland water communication between the shores of that lake and New York City. A second route connecting Lake Ontario and the Erie, the Black River Canal, proved a sound investment. At least for a time it carried considerable traffic and, more important, it furnished needed water for the enlarged Erie.

The three major branches built southward from the Erie Canal did not turn out so well. The Chenango to Binghamton cost $2,316,-000, more than three times the total revenue produced during its forty years of operation.[4] At the western end of the state, the Genesee, which reached Olean in 1856 and was joined with the Allegheny River in 1862, was a disastrous failure. Costing more than half as much to construct as the Erie and Champlain canals combined, it yielded in total revenues only a little more than one seventh of its cost. The third southern extension consisted of three canals, the Cayuga and Seneca, the Chemung, and the Junction. These canals connected the Erie by way of Lake Cayuga and Lake Seneca and the Chemung River to a point two miles across the state line, where a junction was made with the North Branch Canal of the Pennsylvania canal system. Heavy traffic did not develop until 1858 when, with the completion of the privately owned Junction Canal, connection was made with the Pennsylvania system. Thereafter, for a few years, business improved as large shipments of Pennsylvania coal were sent to Erie Canal markets.[5]

[4] Harlow, *Old Towpaths*, p. 150.

[5] Material in this section based chiefly on Whitford, *History of the Canal System of the State of New York, passim;* Henry V. Poor, *History of the Railroads and Canals of the United States of America* (New York: 1860), pp. 353–376; Harlow, *Old Towpaths,* Chap. 15.

CANALS TO TIDEWATER: NEW ENGLAND

On the wave of enthusiasm for canal building which arose out of the success of the Erie, three types of major canals were built: (1) those designed to improve transportation between the upcountry and tidewater in states bordering on the Atlantic from Maine to Virginia; (2) those, like the Erie, designed to link the Atlantic states with the Ohio River Valley; and (3) those in the West which were planned to connect the Ohio-Mississippi system with the Great Lakes. In New York, Pennsylvania, and Ohio the main line canals were supplemented by an extensive system of branches or feeders.

Of the major tidewater canals, three were constructed in New England: the Cumberland and Oxford Canal in Maine from Sebago Pond to tidewater near Portland; the Blackstone from Worcester, Massachusetts, to Narragansett Bay in Rhode Island; and the New Haven and Northampton from New Haven, Connecticut, to Northampton, Massachusetts.

Chartered in 1820, the Cumberland and Oxford Canal was completed in 1827. Though only twenty miles long, it was supplemented by lake and river navigation and proved for many years an important outlet to tidewater for inland products. More successful than the canals of southern New England, it did not succumb to railroad competition until the 1870's.[6] Like many of the canals dug during the great building boom, the Blackstone had long been urged as a needed transportation improvement. The area around Worcester, Massachusetts, though comprising good farming land, failed to develop rapidly because produce had to bear the heavy expense of overland haul to the Boston market. Begun in 1824 and completed in 1828, the Blackstone Canal afforded a new outlet to tidewater for this previously isolated region. For a few years it proved a considerable boon to the area through which it passed, though much difficulty arose from irregular service. Frequent delays resulted from too much or too little water both in the canal itself and in that portion of the route dependent upon slack-water navigation of the Blackstone River. Sabotage by mill owners who coveted the water diverted by the canal and failure of the company to keep the canal in good

[6] Tenth Census of the United States: Transportation, IV, 756, 761; MacGill, History of Transportation, p. 143; Inland Waterways Commission, Preliminary Report, 1908, Senate Document No. 325, 60 Cong., 1 Sess., p. 205; Henry S. Tanner, A Description of the Railroads and Canals of the United States Comprehending Notices of All the Works of Internal Improvement throughout the Several States (New York: T. R. Tanner and J. Disturnell, 1840), p. 29.

operating condition added to the difficulties. Eventually these obstacles would doubtless have been overcome but time did not wait. A railroad from Boston to Worcester was completed in 1835 and from Providence to Worcester in 1847. Traffic fell off rapidly after 1835 and the last tolls were collected in 1848.[7]

The longest, most costly, and least successful of New England canals was the New Haven and Northampton. Built at a cost of well over a million dollars, this waterway, first chartered in 1822, was, after many difficulties, opened for traffic through to Northampton in 1835. Designed to capture for New Haven the trade of the rich valley extending northward into Vermont and New Hampshire by tapping the Connecticut River at Northampton, this ill-starred venture was poorly constructed, constantly short of capital, repeatedly damaged by floods, and always short of water in dry seasons. Seldom developing enough traffic to cover current operating expenses, it was abandoned in 1847.[8]

CANALS TO TIDEWATER: MIDDLE ATLANTIC STATES [9]

In the Middle Atlantic states, canals had long been urged from points in eastern Pennsylvania to the Delaware River and from that river across New York or New Jersey to tidewater. Following the success of the Erie, a number of major waterway systems were built in this area. Three extended from high ground in eastern Pennsylvania to the Delaware and there connected with three canals built across New York or New Jersey. Only the most northern, the Delaware and Hudson, was built and operated by a single company. A

[7] William Lincoln, *History of Worcester, Massachusetts, from Its Earliest Settlement to September, 1836* (Worcester: Charles Hersey, 1862), pp. 282–283, 309–310; *Tenth Census of the United States: Transportation*, IV, 757; Kirkland, *Men, Cities and Transportation*, I, 81–84.

[8] No satisfactory history of this canal has yet been written. Much information is available in old New Haven and Northampton newspapers. See Thelma M. Kistler, "The Rise of Railroads in the Connecticut River Valley," *Smith College Studies in History*, XXIII, Nos. 1–4 (October, 1937–July, 1938), 24–28; *Tenth Census of the United States: Transportation*, IV, 757–761; Kirkland, *Men, Cities and Transportation*, I, 70–81. For the best contemporary account, see *An Account of the Farmington Canal Company; and of the Hampshire and Hamden Canal Company; and of the New Haven and Northampton Company Till the Suspension of Its Canals in 1847* (New Haven: Thomas J. Stafford, 1850).

[9] This section is largely based on *Tenth Census of the United States: Transportation*, IV, 731–762; Chester Lloyd Jones, *The Economic History of the Anthracite-Tidewater Canals* (No. 22 of University of Pennsylvania *Publications in Political Economy and Public Law*, Philadelphia: The John C. Winston Company, 1908), *passim*; Lane, *From Indian Trail to Iron Horse*, pp. 221–277; MacGill, *History of Transportation*, pp. 203–234; Poor, *History of the Railroads and Canals of the United States of America*, pp. 411–413, 536–557, 602–606.

fourth waterway, the Delaware Division Canal, paralleled the Delaware River on the Pennsylvania side from Easton to Bristol. Known as "the anthracite canals" because their principal traffic arose from carrying this new fuel to Philadelphia and New York markets, they were as a whole relatively prosperous and, except for the Delaware Division Canal, under private management.

The Delaware and Hudson Canal was built from Honesdale in northeastern Pennsylvania to the Delaware River. Then, leaving the Delaware close to the northwestern corner of New Jersey, it crossed New York State in a northeasterly direction to Rondout on the Hudson. Completed in 1828, this canal tapped the anthracite region of northeastern Pennsylvania and before long did a tremendous business making this increasingly popular fuel available to New York and New England cities. Originally small—only from 25 to 30 tons could be carried by a single barge—it was enlarged by 1843 to accommodate boats carrying 40 tons, and by 1853 had been several times enlarged so as to take boats up to 140 tons. This successful canal company paid dividends of 8 per cent or better during the forties. By 1855 net profits were reported which slightly exceeded 18 per cent on the capital. Many prosperous years followed, for the peak of traffic was not reached until 1872.[10]

South of the Delaware and Hudson Canal a waterway system consisting of two privately owned canals, the Lehigh and the Morris, was completed, designed to give a second outlet for Pennsylvania anthracite. The Lehigh Canal, running from White Haven through Mauch Chunk to Easton on the Delaware, tapped a rich anthracite country. Improvement of navigation on the Lehigh River had long been urged, and as early as 1791 the state of Pennsylvania appropriated £1,000 for this purpose. Little progress was made until, in 1818, Josiah White and his associates, who had secured control of Lehigh anthracite beds, took vigorous and unique measures to get their coal to market. Difficulties of navigation on the Lehigh River were overcome in some places by wing dams—solid piers built into the river to force the water into a narrow channel—and in others by artificial freshets, a system by which a sudden flow of water was secured by opening up sluice gates in dams built across the river.

[10] *Tenth Census of the United States: Transportation*, IV, 734; *Annual Report of the Delaware and Hudson Canal Company for the Year 1855* (New York: 1856), p. 3; *Annual Report of the Delaware and Hudson Canal Company for the Year 1853* (New York: 1854), p. 3; *A Century of Progress, History of the Delaware and Hudson Company, 1823–1923* (Albany: The Delaware and Hudson Company, 1925), Chaps. 2, 3, 5, and 6.

From the mouth of the Lehigh the coal-carrying arks were floated down the Delaware to the Philadelphia market. There the boats were broken up for lumber, as the system of artificial freshets did not permit upstream navigation. This disadvantage, combined with rapidly increasing business, led to the construction of the Lehigh Canal. It was completed in 1829. Though depending in considerable part on slack-water navigation, this waterway was large, accommodating boats of 100 tons, and well constructed. Almost at once the Lehigh carried a tremendous tonnage. In its peak year, 1860, two thousand canal boats plied its waters and carried more than a million and one third tons of traffic.

At Easton, the Lehigh connected with two other canals. One, the Delaware Division Canal, led south paralleling the Delaware River to Bristol, from which point boats could proceed by the river to Philadelphia. This waterway was built by the state and operated by it until sold to a private corporation in 1858. Completed in 1830, it suffered from an inadequate water supply and was not open for navigation over its full length until nearly two years later. Through mistaken efforts at economy, the canal was built on a smaller scale than the Lehigh, with the result that the larger Lehigh canal boats could not go beyond Easton and cargoes had to be broken there. Nevertheless, the Delaware Division Canal did a large business. In its most prosperous years in the early fifties, it was the best paying of the Pennsylvania state works, yielding from 14 to 22 per cent on construction costs.

The Morris Canal also connected with the Lehigh at Easton and wound for 102 miles through the northern part of New Jersey before reaching Newark Bay. Though costing about $3,000,000, this waterway was only four feet deep and its locks would not take boats carrying more than twenty-five tons. This shortsighted planning, which excluded the larger Lehigh boats from its waters, hurt the profitability of the Morris in its early years. Moreover, the directors became primarily interested in speculation and wildcat banking, and the canal suffered in consequence. Amidst notorious scandals the company failed in 1841, but a new company took over, enlarged the canal, and, despite railroad competition, operated it with some success until after the Civil War.

Below the Morris Canal in New Jersey and connecting Bordentown on the Delaware with tidewater at New Brunswick was the Delaware and Raritan Canal. Completed in 1834, though not actually connected with the Delaware River at Bordentown until 1838, this waterway afforded a large and well-constructed route from Philadelphia to New York. Cursed by railroad ownership and irresponsible management, it nevertheless became one of the most important transportation routes in the country in the period before the Civil War. For a few years the Delaware and Raritan actually carried a greater tonnage than did the Erie.

Although considerable traffic on the Delaware and Raritan Canal originated on the Lehigh Canal, much also came north from Philadelphia, where not infrequently it had arrived by way of the Union Canal and the Schuylkill River. An early scheme to improve the navigation of the Schuylkill and to build a canal connecting the Susquehanna and Schuylkill rivers was finally accomplished during this period. The Schuylkill Navigation, a system of slack water and canals, was opened from Philadelphia to Port Carbon in 1825, and the Union Canal, uniting Reading on the Schuylkill with a point south of Harrisburg on the Susquehanna, was completed two years later. Because of topographical difficulties and shortage of water, the Union was built on such small dimensions that canal boats could carry a maximum of only twenty-five tons. Although the canal did a fair business, it was greatly handicapped because its locks would not accommodate the larger boats from the Schuylkill to the East and the Pennsylvania state canals to the West. Faced with railroad competition after 1835, the canal struggled on until, in 1850, the task of enlargement was begun. The expense proved excessive because of the great difficulty of securing sufficient water. Although traffic doubled after the enlargement, the added cost, combined with increasing railroad competition, led to declining profits after 1857.

The Susquehanna and Tidewater Canal contributed to the decline of the Union Canal. Heavily sponsored by Baltimore interests, this canal was designed to make navigable the lower Susquehanna River and thus draw away from Philadelphia the rich trade of central Pennsylvania. The Susquehanna and Tidewater, reaching from Havre de Grace forty-five miles up the river to Wrightsville, was opened to traffic in 1840, being one of the latest of the major canals to be constructed. Its cost was great, about $80,000 a mile, but its locks were large and a heavy traffic rapidly developed. The Susquehanna and Tidewater benefited not only Baltimore but also Philadelphia, for the Chesapeake and Delaware Canal had already been completed. The route of this canal between Delaware and Chesapeake bays had been surveyed as early as 1764. Repeatedly urged as a desirable project, this canal was financed on the wave of Erie enthusiasm and completed for full use in 1830. Annual tonnage on the canal increased steadily, exceeding the half-million mark in the latter 1850's.

Strictly speaking, the last three canals mentioned above—the Union, the Susquehanna and Tidewater, and the Chesapeake and Delaware—do not belong to the anthracite group, but all were important in the coal trade. The first two were links in the great system of public works in Pennsylvania, and the last, though lying outside the state, supplemented this system by providing an inland short cut for shipping between two great bays.

CANALS TO TIDEWATER: VIRGINIA

South of the canals described above, two major tidewater canals were built after 1815—the James River and Kanawha, and the Chesapeake and Ohio. Although never more than routes to tidewater, both were planned to cross the Appalachian divide and connect with the Ohio River. In addition, the Dismal Swamp Canal was enlarged and rebuilt.[11]

Improvement of navigation on the James River above Richmond, Virginia, was begun before 1800 and continued sporadically until the Civil War. Despite many difficulties, by 1840 the canal was completed over the 146 miles from Richmond to Lynchburg. Five years earlier the company had been reorganized under the name of the James River and Kanawha Company. As the name implies, it was hoped to extend the waterway across the divide to the Kanawha River, thus providing a through route to the Ohio. Actually the canal, in part slack-water navigation, was completed only a few miles beyond Buchanan. But it extended nearly 200 miles through a relatively rich country and did a very substantial business, though not on a money-making basis.[12]

George Washington had been much interested in a canal which, beginning at Georgetown on the Potomac, would follow that river to Cumberland, Maryland, and extend from there to the Ohio River. He was the first president of the Potomac Company, which erected canals around the Potomac Rapids north of Washington. But little came of the ambitious scheme of extension to the westward until the

[11] Clifford Reginald Hinshaw, Jr., "North Carolina Canals before 1860," *North Carolina Historical Review*, XXV, No. 1 (January, 1948), 24–26.
[12] Wayland Fuller Dunaway, *History of the James River and Kanawha Company* (*Studies in History, Economics and Public Law*, Vol. CIV, No. 2, New York: Columbia University Press, 1922), *passim*; MacGill, *History of Transportation*, pp. 269–273.

1820's, when Erie fever inflamed men's imaginations and loosed the strings of their pocketbooks. Immediate extension to the Ohio River seemed financially impossible, but a new organization, optimistically named the Chesapeake and Ohio Canal Company, was formed, and in 1828 work was begun on the 184-mile stretch to Cumberland. The project went forward slowly. The company was constantly short of necessary funds despite generous stock subscriptions from Virginia, Maryland, and the federal government, for the necessary outlay proved much greater than had been estimated. The actual cost of building the canal exceeded that of the Erie and Champlain canals combined, and not until 1850 was the waterway opened to Cumberland. It was built on generous lines, measuring from fifty to eighty feet wide at the water surface, and was from six to eight feet deep. Despite competition from the Baltimore and Ohio Railroad, whose tracks paralleled it over most of its route, the canal carried considerable traffic, mostly coal from around Cumberland. Though continued in use into the twentieth century, this waterway was never a paying venture, and the plan of extending it beyond Cumberland to the Ohio River was never realized.[13]

THE PENNSYLVANIA STATE CANALS

As the Erie neared completion, the merchants of Philadelphia, fearful that their trade with the West would be largely lost to New York, started a systematic agitation for a rival waterway which should extend from Philadelphia to Pittsburgh on the Ohio. Strong opposition appeared from wagoners and innkeepers on the turnpikes, who fought to protect their vested interests. A few, generally regarded as impractical visionaries, contended that railroads should be built instead of canals. Citizens in the northern half of Pennsylvania objected to the expenditure of such large funds for the benefit of Philadelphia and the southern part of the state. Finally, some, wiser than their contemporaries, pointed out that the route across Pennsylvania was so rugged and difficult that it could not successfully compete with the Erie on the basis of either speed or cost.

But the canal craze swept all opposition aside, and in 1826 Pennsylvania began her canal-building orgy. Philadelphia was already connected with the Susquehanna by the Union Canal. But, as this

[13] Walter S. Sanderlin, *The Great National Project: A History of the Chesapeake and Ohio Canal* (Johns Hopkins University *Studies in Historical and Political Science*, Vol. LXIV, No. 1, Baltimore: The Johns Hopkins Press, 1946), *passim.*

was too small, the state supplemented it by building a railroad (completed 1834) from Philadelphia to Columbia on the Susquehanna. Westward from Columbia the Main Line Canal was built, first following the Susquehanna and then the Juniata River until it reached the backbone of the Allegheny Mountains near Hollidaysburg. Here the famous Portage Railroad was built. On a series of inclined planes, cable cars designed to carry canal boats, which were built in sections for that purpose, were hauled up one side of the ridge and eased down the other. To the westward the canal followed the Conemaugh and Allegheny rivers to Pittsburgh. This so-called "Main Line" cost over $10,000,000 to build and was 395 miles long. At its highest point on the Portage Railroad near Hollidaysburg, the Pennsylvania route rose 2,200 feet above sea level, as compared to a maximum altitude on the Erie of 650 feet. Moreover, this second canal to the west had 174 locks as against the Erie's 84.

Opened over its entire length to Pittsburgh in 1834, the Main Line soon did a very considerable business, though it never became a strong competitor of the Erie. The inclined-plane railroad proved a traffic bottleneck from the beginning, the excessive lockage delayed traffic, and the necessity of shifting cargo at Columbia for shipment to Philadelphia by rail or small canal boats on the Union Canal was time consuming and costly. However, this last disadvantage was somewhat overcome when, after the completion of the Susquehanna and Tidewater Canal in 1840, large barges could descend to Chesapeake Bay and move from there directly to Philadelphia or Baltimore.

Once having begun canal building with state funds, Pennsylvania proceeded to spend money lavishly on a whole system of artificial waterways. Writing in 1831, Mathew Carey declared:

. . . every person who has at heart the honor of Pennsylvania must feel proud, that she rises to a height which has never been equalled in any part of the world; as no nation, ancient or modern, has ever expended so much money, on such vast useful improvements *in the same space of time*.[14]

Instead of first completing her Main Line route to the west and then building numerous branches as was done in New York, Pennsylvania, because of sectional political pressures, constructed a whole system of canals simultaneously with the Main Line. The total canal mileage built by 1834, the date of the completion of the Main Line, was nearly twice that necessary to complete the through route to Pittsburgh. Yet many sections of the state were still unsatisfied, and canal

---

[14] Mathew Carey, *Brief View of the System of Internal Improvement of the State of Pennsylvania* (Philadelphia: Lydia R. Bailey, 1831), p. 28.

building on a considerable scale continued with some interruptions to 1842. By that date about 772 miles of canal had been constructed, and 162 miles were in various stages of completion. But the state was in serious financial difficulties, the bubble of confidence had been pricked, and very little further building took place.

Despite rapidly increasing railroad competition, a few of the more advantageously located canals carried considerable traffic as late as the Civil War period and even for a decade or two thereafter. But with few exceptions, the Pennsylvania state works were losing financial ventures, and during the fifties the state sold most of them to the railroads or other private corporations. In her effort to meet the challenge of New York, Pennsylvania had spent on new canal construction more than any other state. In 1860 Henry V. Poor computed the total outlay on public works at $65,800,000.[15] Many factors contributed to her defeat. Of all the states, Pennsylvania was topographically the least suited to canal building. This meant excessively high original cost, expensive operation, and relatively slow movement of traffic. Also, Pennsylvania started late, with the result that she built chiefly during the thirties, when costs were highest and when the panics of 1837 and 1839 made capital for completing her system difficult to secure. Finally, almost from the beginning, the state canals encountered strong railroad competition. Unfortunately, these handicaps were not offset by careful planning or sound administration. The legislature provided for administration by a canal board of such limited powers and divided responsibilities that it seemed almost designed to promote inefficiency, logrolling, and dishonesty of officials.[16]

THE WESTERN CANALS

In Ohio the desirability of a canal connecting Lake Erie and the Ohio River had long been recognized. Word of the success of the Erie Canal preceded the flood of immigrants who streamed into the Middle West over its waters, and by 1822 the Ohio legislature was seriously considering the construction of artificial waterways for that state. Early in 1825, eight months before the formal opening of the

[15] Poor, *History of the Railroads and Canals of the United States of America*, p. 558.

[16] Avard Longley Bishop, "The State Works of Pennsylvania," *Transactions of the Connecticut Academy of Arts and Sciences* (New Haven: The Tuttle, Morehouse and Taylor Press, 1908), XIII (1907–1908), 149–288; Avard Longley Bishop, "Corrupt Practices Connected with the Building and Operation of the State Works of Pennsylvania," *Yale Review*, XV (February, 1907), 391–411; and Hartz, *Economic Policy and Democratic Thought: Pennsylvania, 1776–1860*, pp. 148–160.

Erie Canal, the Ohio legislature authorized the canal-building program which was eventually to unite the waters of Lake Erie and the Ohio River by two great state-owned canals and lead to the construction of one of the greatest systems of internal waterways in the country.

First completed (1833) was the Ohio and Erie Canal. This 308-mile waterway was built from Cleveland in the north to Portsmouth on the Ohio River at a cost of nearly eight million dollars. The other trans-Ohio canal, the Miami and Erie, built in the western part of the state from Cincinnati to Toledo, was completed from Cincinnati to Dayton in 1832 and to Toledo on Lake Erie in 1845. Both canals were well planned and constructed and built on a scale sufficiently generous to permit the passage of canal boats carrying as much as eighty tons.

Like New York and Pennsylvania, the state of Ohio was not content with main line canals, but proceeded to build branches and extensions with a lavish hand. Some of these, like the Muskingum, which extended along that river from Dresden Junction on the Ohio and Erie Canal to the Ohio River, proved to be well-considered improvements. Others, like the 25-mile Walhonding Canal, appear to have had no other justification than political logrolling. Even private companies sprang up in the thirties to make additions to the growing network of Ohio waterways. One of the most important of these, the Ohio and Pennsylvania, extended from the Ohio River near Pittsburgh across northeastern Ohio to make a junction with the Ohio and Erie Canal, thus forming a connection between the Ohio canals and the main line of the Pennsylvania state system.

As a whole, the Ohio canals did a tremendous business and were a great boon to those parts of the state through which they passed. No great volume of through traffic developed on the two lines across the state, but local traffic and shipments of goods locally produced and destined for out-of-state markets were heavy. Traffic reached its peak in about 1851. Thereafter, the Ohio waterways suffered a rapid decline. Floods were a constantly recurring problem: at best they merely disorganized and delayed the movement of traffic; at worst they caused tremendous damage to costly installations. No doubt ways would have been devised to overcome excessive damage from floods, but railroad competition presented an insuperable obstacle. In no state were railroads built during the fifties more rapidly than in Ohio, and by the middle of that decade the canals were obsolescent. Most of them were rapidly abandoned, but a few, notably the Miami,

Travel by canalboat was a leisurely affair. (*Brown Brothers*)

A barge on the Dismal Swamp Canal. (*Harper's Magazine, XIII* [1856], *444*)

On the larger canals, broad towpaths were provided. (*Culver Service*)

(*Above*) Lockport on the Erie Canal in the late thirties. (*Culver Service*) (*Center*) DeWitt Clinton, 1769–1828, Governor of New York and leading sponsor of the Erie Canal. (*Culver Service*) (*Below*) A Mississippi flatboat. Goods could be transported by this method from the upper Ohio to New Orleans in about one month. (*Bettmann Archive*)

lingered on for some time as useful supplements to the railroad system.[17]

In 1816 Indiana had incorporated the Ohio Canal Company to construct on the Indiana side of the river a short canal around the falls of the Ohio at Louisville. Though this project was abandoned, a two and one-half mile canal was completed late in 1830 on the Kentucky side by a company chartered by the Kentucky legislature. Greatly facilitating river traffic, this canal, known as the Louisville and Portland, proved tremendously profitable.[18]

No state became more disastrously involved in the general enthusiasm for canal building than Indiana. In 1827 the state legislature received a grant of land from the federal government to aid in building a canal to connect the Ohio River and Lake Erie by way of the Wabash and Maumee rivers. Construction on the canal, which was called the Wabash and Erie, was begun in 1832 and proceeded slowly and with chronic lack of funds. But in 1836 times were good, improved transportation was greatly needed, and enthusiasm for canals at fever pitch. The legislature in that year voted the Mammoth Internal Improvement Bill, which provided for an ambitious system of state canals as well as for turnpike and railroad building.

Work was begun simultaneously in many parts of the state with what proved afterward to be a maximum of incompetence, political logrolling, and large-scale peculation. By 1839 depression had descended on the country and the state of Indiana was virtually bankrupt. Her debt in 1841 was reported at over $13,000,000, of which over $9,000,000 was attributable to internal improvements. The elaborate canal system was now abandoned except for the Whitewater and the Wabash and Erie canals. The former was turned over to a private corporation which in 1846 completed this 76-mile waterway from the Ohio River near the Indiana-Ohio border to Cambridge, Indiana, on the National Road. The latter, the Wabash and Erie Canal, was continued at great effort and expense. The state of Ohio opened the necessary connecting link in that state in 1843. Work continued slowly in Indiana; by 1849 traffic was opened from Toledo

[17] Gephart, *Transportation and Industrial Development in the Middle West*, Chap 7; MacGill, *History of Transportation*, pp. 282–294; C. P. McClelland and C. C. Huntington, *History of the Ohio Canals: Their Construction, Cost, Use and Partial Abandonment* (Columbus: Ohio State Archeological and Historical Society, 1905), *passim*, referred to hereafter as McClelland and Huntington, *History of Ohio Canals.*

[18] Archer Butler Hulbert, *Waterways of Westward Expansion: The Ohio River and Its Tributaries* (Vol. IX of *Historic Highways of America*, Cleveland: The Arthur H. Clark Company, 16 vols., 1903), pp. 203–204; Harlow, *Old Towpaths*, pp. 289–290.

as far south as Terre Haute, and by 1853 the canal was declared open to Evansville on the Ohio River. The completed canal was more than 450 miles in length, the longest in the United States. But on the lower section, traffic was light, flood damage great, and funds were lacking for repairs. All operations ceased on this section about 1860. Above Terre Haute considerable traffic had developed when the canal was first opened, with tolls reaching their peak in 1852. Though kept open until 1872 from Terre Haute to Toledo, this remaining section of the Indiana canal system gradually died from neglect and railroad competition. The Wabash and Erie Canal helped to open up and develop northern Indiana; nevertheless, as a financial venture, at least, it must be regarded as one of the greatest canal failures. Total expenditures on this canal exceeded $8,000,000; total revenues were about $5,500,000, of which more than half came from the sale of lands received from the federal government.[19]

The Illinois and Michigan Canal, connecting Lake Michigan at Chicago with the Illinois River and thus with the Mississippi River, was begun by Illinois in 1836, and after great expense, which contributed to the ruin of the state bank in 1842 and for a time seriously undermined the credit of the state, was completed in 1848. Traffic grew rapidly during the fifties, with the canal contributing materially to the phenomenal rise of Chicago. Repeatedly enlarged and extended, this canal, unlike so many of the others, has continued in active use.[20]

FINANCING THE CANALS

Whereas the capital needed for the largest turnpike companies might be measured in a few hundred thousand dollars, that for a canal of any appreciable size was seldom less than a million and might be five or ten times that sum. Even for the turnpikes, at least outside New England, needed capital was secured with difficulty from private sources and, as already noted, state help was often sought and secured. The very large sums necessary for canal construction were typically not available from private savers. Large

---

[19] See *Hunt's Merchants' Magazine*, XLII (1860), 54; Elbert Jay Benton, *The Wabash Trade Route in the Development of the Old Northwest* (Johns Hopkins University *Studies in Historical and Political Science*, Vol. XXI, Nos. 1–2, Baltimore: The Johns Hopkins Press, 1903), pp. 9–112; John Bell Rae, "Federal Land Grants in Aid of Canals," *Journal of Economic History*, IV, No. 2 (November, 1944), 173.

[20] See James William Putnam, *The Illinois and Michigan Canal* (Vol. X of *Chicago Historical Society's Collection*, Chicago: The University of Chicago Press, 1918); Pierce, *A History of Chicago*, Vol. I, Chap. 4; F. Cyril James, *The Growth of Chicago Banks* (2 vols., New York: Harper & Brothers, 1938), Vol. I, see especially Chap. 4.

pools of venture capital did not yet exist in the United States, and although savings were growing, they lay chiefly in the hands of small savers who were primarily interested in security. As a result, the canals were financed, to an extent even greater than is generally recognized, either directly or indirectly through public aid. Primarily this took the form of direct ownership and operation by state governments, but even where managed by private corporations most canals received a great deal of help from the state. Emphasized by G. S. Callender long ago, the point is too often overlooked that the great contribution of New York to the canal era was not confined to engineering accomplishments; she showed that large sums could easily be raised for public works by utilizing public credit through the sale of state bonds.[21]

Congress denied help to the state of New York in building the Erie, but it later made substantial contributions toward the construction of other canals. By 1860 the federal government had granted approximately 4,000,000 acres of the public domain to canal projects in Ohio, Michigan, Indiana, Illinois, and Wisconsin. In addition, it had subscribed over $3,000,000 to the stock of canal companies, the chief beneficiary being the Chesapeake and Ohio.[22]

But it was the states which made the major capital contributions, and to a large extent they themselves built and operated these waterways. As has been shown, New York, Pennsylvania, Ohio, and Indiana adopted plans for extensive artificial waterway systems. The state governments were generally in a very favorable position to raise the unprecedented amounts necessary to build these ambitious public works. At the beginning of the canal-building era their debts were small, revenues from investment appreciable, and, for most, taxes very low indeed.[23] Their reputation for meeting their obligations inspired the confidence of investors both in America and abroad, and the large revenues received by New York from Erie tolls seemed to assure the soundness of similar ventures. Prosperity and generally rising prices aided during the early thirties, and the act of 1836, distributing the federal surplus to the states, provided vital support

[21] G. S. Callender, "The Early Transportation and Banking Enterprises of the States in Relation to the Growth of Corporations," *Quarterly Journal of Economics,* XVII (November, 1902), 151–152. See also Bishop, "The State Works of Pennsylvania," p. 188.

[22] Inland Waterways Commission, *Preliminary Report,* 1908, pp. 178–180. See also Rae, "Federal Land Grants in Aid of Canals," pp. 167–177; Sanderlin, *The Great National Project,* p. 81.

[23] B. U. Ratchford, *American State Debts* (Durham, N.C.: Duke University Press, 1941), pp. 77–79.

just as the strain of large state financing was beginning to be felt. Moreover, Indiana and Ohio were encouraged by large federal land grants, and Pennsylvania received in 1836 the promise of $2,500,000 in connection with the granting of a state charter to the second Bank of the United States.[24] But by the early forties the period of expansion was over and almost every state was in financial difficulties. Whereas the amount of state bonds issued in 1820–1824 had been only $13,-000,000, it rose to $108,000,000 in 1835–1837. Over $60,000,000 of this debt was incurred for canal-building purposes.[25] Indiana and Pennsylvania were virtually bankrupt, Ohio's credit was badly strained, and even New York was forced, for a time, to suspend all canal-building activities.

Even privately operated canals leaned heavily upon the credit of the state governments. This was most pronounced for those of Virginia and Maryland. The Dismal Swamp Canal Company raised $486,000 by the sale of shares of stock. Of this, $200,000 came from the federal government, $190,000 from the state of Virginia, and only $96,000 from individuals. Most of the investment by the state and all by the federal government was made between 1817 and 1837.[26] The James River and Kanawha Canal Company received help from banks, from municipalities, and, chiefly, from the state.[27] In 1861 Virginia had over $10,000,000 of her state debt reported as attributable to funds supplied to finance the James River and Kanawha Canal.[28] Funds supplied by the federal government and the states, chiefly Maryland, provided more than four fifths of the capital for the construction of the Chesapeake and Ohio Canal. Toward the construction of the Chesapeake and Delaware Canal the United States subscribed $450,000; Pennsylvania, $100,000; Maryland, $50,-000; and Delaware, $25,000.[29]

The privately owned canals of Ohio were heavily subsidized by the state.[30] Even in New England the three major canals built during this period received substantial public assistance. In Maine, the

[24] Bishop, "The State Works of Pennsylvania," p. 215.
[25] *Tenth Census of the United States: Valuation, Taxation, and Public Indebtedness,* VII, 523, 526.
[26] Inland Waterways Commission, *Preliminary Report,* 1908, pp. 291–292.
[27] Dunaway, *History of the James River and Kanawha Company,* pp. 97–119.
[28] *Tenth Census of the United States: Valuation, Taxation, and Public Indebtedness,* VII, 555.
[29] Inland Waterways Commission, *Preliminary Report,* 1908, pp. 276, 283–285; *The American Almanac, 1830* (Boston: Gray and Bower, 1830), p. 277.
[30] Charles N. Morris, "Internal Improvements in Ohio, 1825–1850," *Papers of the American Historical Association,* III, No. 2 (1889), 124–128; McClelland and Huntington, *History of Ohio Canals,* p. 44.

Cumberland and Oxford Canal was given the right to raise $50,000 by a lottery, and a newly organized bank was chartered with the authority to invest in canal stock.[31] Rhode Island gave banking privileges to the Blackstone Canal.[32] The New Haven and Northampton Canal depended for substantial contributions upon grants by the city of New Haven and required investments by two banks in that city. By 1840, Pennsylvania had invested over $600,000 in the stock of canal and navigation companies.[33]

Least dependent on public help were the anthracite tidewater canals of the Middle Atlantic states. Excluding valuable monopoly rights granted by charter, the Lehigh, the Schuylkill, and the Raritan canals appear to have been built with little or no public assistance. The last two had strong financial backing. Stephen Girard invested heavily in the Schuylkill Navigation. Southern slaveowners and merchants, chief of whom was John Potter of Charleston, raised between a third and a half of the capital for the Delaware and Raritan Canal. John Jacob Astor later became a heavy investor. In 1849 more than half of the stock of $3,000,000 of the joint companies (the Raritan Canal and the Camden and Amboy Railroad) was owned by the following six families: Astor, McKnight, Neilson, Potter, Stevens, and Stockton.[34] The Delaware and Raritan actually gave New Jersey a bonus of $100,000 for its charter rights and paid transit duties to the state on all traffic handled, thus reversing the usual financial relationship between privately owned canal companies and state legislatures.[35] But the other privately owned tidewater canals in the Middle Atlantic states received appreciable governmental aid. To the Susquehanna and Tidewater Canal the state of Maryland lent its credit to the amount of $1,000,000.[36] Both the Delaware and Hudson and the Morris enjoyed valuable banking privileges, and the former issued a loan of $500,000 backed by the credit of the state of New York.[37] To encourage the building of the Union Canal,

[31] MacGill, *History of Transportation*, pp. 143, 560; Frederick A. Cleveland and Fred Wilbur Powell, *Railroad Promotion and Capitalization in the United States* (New York: Longmans, Green and Co., 1909), p. 168.

[32] MacGill, *History of Transportation*, p. 560; Harlow, *Old Towpaths*, p. 159.

[33] *An Account of the Farmington Canal Company; of the Hampshire and Hamden Canal Company; and of the New Haven and Northampton Company Till the Suspension of Its Canals in 1847*, pp. 9, 14; Hartz, *Economic Policy and Democratic Thought*, p. 85.

[34] Jones, *The Economic History of the Anthracite-Tidewater Canals*, pp. 127–128; Lane, *From Indian Trail to Iron Horse*, p. 272; Robert T. Thompson, *Colonel James Neilson* (New Brunswick, N.J.: Rutgers University Press, 1940), pp. 195–196, 323–326.

[35] Lane, *From Indian Trail to Iron Horse*, pp. 258–261.

[36] Poor, *History of the Railroads and Canals of the United States of America*, p. 552.

[37] Lane, *From Indian Trail to Iron Horse*, p. 227; Jones, *The Economic History of the Anthracite-Tidewater Canals*, p. 75.

Pennsylvania not only purchased stock but also granted valuable lottery privileges and guaranteed a return of 6 per cent to subscribers of stock in that company.[38]

By 1840 the people of the United States had constructed canals totaling 3,326 miles, a distance greater than that across the continent from New York to Seattle. All but approximately 100 miles had been built since 1816, mostly between 1824 and 1840. The total canal mileage, 1,277 in 1830, increased by over 2,000 miles in the decade following.[39] Between 1816 and 1840, about $125,000,000 was spent on canal building, and at least three states had so strained their credit as to be brought to the verge of bankruptcy.

No canals of major size were begun between 1840 and 1860, although much of the work of constructing the Miami and Erie and the Chesapeake and Ohio was done during the forties, and work on the James River and Kanawha continued through the fifties. One short artificial waterway, known as Saint Marys Falls Canal, constructed in 1853–1855 to connect Lake Superior and Lake Huron, was destined—as the Sault Ste. Marie—to carry more traffic than any other in the world. But the great period of new construction in the nineteenth century was definitely over. In the decade of the forties less than 400 miles of canal were added, and by 1850 abandonments exceeded new construction. Even before 1850, about 123 miles of canal had gone out of use, and from 1850 to the Civil War, 225 additional miles became inoperative.[40]

The immediate causes for the collapse of the canal-building boom are easily identified. Just as the financial success of the Erie had led to boundless enthusiasm, so the financial crises of 1837 and 1839 brought exaggerated timidity. The cost of constructing most canals greatly exceeded the engineers' estimates, and the revenues from tolls fell far short of popular expectation. When it was realized that, instead of freeing the states from the necessity of taxation and providing numerous boons such as covering the cost of popular education, as was promised by the enthusiasts,[41] canals were costing huge

[38] Bishop, "The State Works of Pennsylvania," p. 163; Henrietta M. Larson, "S. & M. Allen—Lottery, Exchange, and Stock Brokerage," *Journal of Economic and Business History*, III (1930–1931), 432.

[39] *Hunt's Merchants' Magazine*, XXV (September, 1851), 381–382.

[40] Inland Waterways Commission, *Preliminary Report*, 1908, pp. 205–209.

[41] See, for example, Carey, *Brief View of the System of Internal Improvement of the State of Pennsylvania*, pp. 29–30; Charles Cist, *Cincinnati in 1841* (Cincinnati: The author, 1841), p. 159.

sums and producing so little revenue that public credit was threatened, and that taxes, far from being wiped out, had actually to be increased, construction slowed down and promoters of new projects found little encouragement either from voters or from domestic or foreign investors. But more than the collapse of inflated hopes lay behind the decline of canal building. Even the appearance of the railroad does not tell the whole story. Though railroad building had been delayed for a decade or two, the rate of canal construction would nevertheless have slowed down if for no other reason than that most of the natural routes for long-distance artificial waterways had been developed.

It should be emphasized that important sums were spent on canal enlargement and improvement during the forties and fifties. Some of the early canals had been poorly constructed; many were too small to permit economical handlings of heavy traffic. As a result, where traffic conditions appeared to justify the expenditure, substantial additional sums were spent on old canals. The Erie was enlarged and almost completely rebuilt at a cost of $44,500,000, a sum about six times the original investment.[42] Other canals like the Union, the Morris, and the Delaware and Hudson were enlarged and improved. Between 1816 and the Civil War something over $200,000,000 was invested in canal construction, of which about $75,000,000, or more than one third, was spent after 1840.[43]

The chief factors affecting the financial success or failure of the canals are well worth examination. The fixed investment in artificial waterways was practically always heavy, although this varied greatly and depended upon such considerations as the character of the country through which the canal was built, its size, and the number of locks. Excellent stone turnpikes could be constructed at from $5,000 to $10,000 a mile, whereas most canals required an investment of from about $20,000 to $30,000 a mile. Some needed much more than this. Two of the most expensive were the Chesapeake and Ohio, which cost $60,000 a mile, and the Susquehanna and Tidewater, which required an outlay of about $80,000 a mile.[44] On the other hand, construction costs for railroads seem to have averaged higher than those for canals. Of the short lines built across New York State and later combined to form the New York Central, three cost less than $30,000 a mile and five cost more than that sum. The solidly

[42] Inland Waterways Commission, *Preliminary Report,* 1908, p. 211.

[43] Estimated on the basis of data from many sources, the chief one being Inland Waterways Commission, *Preliminary Report,* 1908, pp. 193–311.

[44] *Tenth Census of the United States: Transportation,* IV, 738–739, 746, 761–762; Harlow, *Old Towpaths,* p. 171.

built Boston and Lowell cost $71,000 a mile, and the Baltimore and Ohio, $54,000. On the other hand, the Georgia Railroad was relatively inexpensive, costing only $17,000 a mile.[45]

Maintenance and repair expenses were extremely high for most canals. In addition to the ever-present problem of keeping the banks tight and the channel of necessary depth, floods were a possible source of serious damage to all canals, and for some they brought almost annual catastrophe. Ohio and Pennsylvania canals were repeatedly damaged by floods. The Whitewater, appreciable portions of which had to be rebuilt because of serious damage in 1846, suffered a similar disaster the following year. A single freshet in 1852 cost the Chesapeake and Ohio Canal Company $100,000 in repairs.[46]

The size of the canal, the density of traffic, and the operational efficiency were all important considerations for profitable canal operation. Actual costs of shipping goods were greatly reduced where boats of eighty tons' capacity or even more could be handled, as on the Lehigh and the Susquehanna and Tidewater; they were seriously increased when the maximum was about twenty-five tons, as on the Morris and the Union canals before they were enlarged. Only where demand was sufficiently great so as to utilize the canal fairly close to its capacity could the canal company hope to cover its normally heavy fixed charges. Thus canals which, like the New Haven and Northampton or the Genesee, never developed appreciable business could not possibly earn dividends on the investment.

Even where the demand was great, the volume of traffic which could be handled might be insufficient to permit profitable operation. An important element in the capacity of a canal was the rapidity of movement through it. Speed was greatly reduced where locks were frequent. Portage railroads and inclined planes were even more serious bottlenecks. Thus traffic on the Main Line of the Pennsylvania canal was so restricted by the Portage Railroad and the large number of locks that its operation at full capacity was annually much less than that of the Erie Canal, even though its season was often several weeks longer because of the milder climate.

The capacity of the canals as well as the demand for their services often suffered greatly from the irregularities in their service caused by droughts and floods. The poorly constructed, narrow, and shallow ditch known as the New Haven and Northampton Canal was frequently as short of water as of capital, and at other times floods made it unusable for months at a time. The Chesapeake and Ohio was

---

[45] Ringwalt, *Development of Transportation Systems in the United States*, p. 127.
[46] Harlow, *Old Towpaths*, p. 259; Sanderlin, *The Great National Project*, p. 208.

repeatedly cursed by too little or too much water. The freshet of 1852 cut off all revenues for from three to four months and hurt the canal's reputation as a reliable carrier. And stoppages of five weeks in 1853 and of two months in 1854 due to drought had a similarly unfavorable result.[47]

Finally, some of the canals, both those publicly and those privately owned, suffered from poor business management. The inefficiency and cupidity of state officials contributed to the failure of the publicly owned Pennsylvania and Indiana canals. Speculation in stocks and the financial irresponsibility of its directors brought the privately owned Morris Canal to bankruptcy.

The student of the canal era will do well not to dismiss the canals as obvious "failures." In the first place, it must be remembered that most of the canals were built during the thirties when costs were excessively high. At best these agencies with high fixed costs, were especially handicapped in the period of low prices during the forties. In similar fashion, many railroads went through bankruptcy in later financial crises. In the second place, the general decline and even disappearance of most canals during the last part of the nineteenth century led some to forget that many canals were relatively prosperous as late as 1860 and a few, in fact, did not reach their traffic peak until after the Civil War. At least this was true of such important artificial waterways as the Erie, the Illinois and Michigan, and a number of the coal-carrying canals. Third, it must not be forgotten that agencies of transportation have very often failed to pay their way in the sense of earning a fair return on the capital sunk in them. Turnpikes and railroads, as well as canals, which have failed to pay dividends have often been regarded by the communities they served as worth-while investments. An early writer expressed this attitude very well when, in discussing the Blackstone Canal, he said: "The canal has been more useful to the public, than to the owners. . . ."[48] Finally, it was the misfortune of most canals to become obsolescent even before they were opened for traffic. The advantages of the railroads were so great that even the strongest canals could not long retain a profitable share of the business. As a result such great works as the Erie, the Main Line of the Pennsylvania, and the Chesapeake and Ohio canals, which without the railroads might have become celebrated as among the most useful monuments of the age, have been generally regarded as failures and, except for the Erie, almost forgotten.

[47] Sanderlin, *The Great National Project*, pp. 207–210.
[48] Lincoln, *History of Worcester*, p. 283.

CHAPTER IV

Steamboats on
River, Lake, and Bay

RIVER NAVIGATION, 1815

WITH its continental expanse and vast inland distances the United States was from the beginning peculiarly dependent upon river transportation. Sale crops were of little value unless they could be taken to market without great expense. As but few products could bear the cost of land carriage over appreciable distances, the rivers proved the only economical routes of commerce for early inland settlements. It was said in 1818 that two thirds of the market crops of South Carolina were raised within five miles of a river and the other third not more than ten miles from navigable water.[1] Though possibly somewhat exaggerated, this picture of dependence upon river transportation applied equally well to the rest of the country and properly emphasizes the dependence upon waterways.

On ocean bays and the lower reaches of broad rivers, the small seagoing sailing ships of the time might tack their way under favorable conditions. Such vessels sailed up the Mississippi above New Orleans as far as Natchez and were at home on the lower James, Potomac, Delaware, Hudson, Connecticut, and a few other Atlantic rivers. Elsewhere swift currents, shallow water, narrow, winding channels, or high banks and forests which broke the wind rendered such navigation impracticable. As a consequence, the great bulk of the products of the country was floated down the streams and rivers on crude rafts and flatboats. Too clumsy for upriver navigation, they were usually broken up for lumber at the end of their journey. Trans-

[1] *Niles' Weekly Register*, XV (October 24, 1818), 135.

portation up the rivers proved extremely time consuming and costly. Narrow keelboats provided a limited service but their capacity was small and the labor of propelling them often so great that only small quantities of the most needed items would bear the cost of upriver shipment.

Nowhere were these difficulties greater than in the West, where river journeys of a thousand or even two thousand miles were not unusual. Flatboats from western Pennsylvania floated down to New Orleans in a month or six weeks. A few keelboats and barges made the return trip upriver. From New Orleans to Pittsburgh the 1,950-mile journey consumed four months or more and required a crew of strong men prepared to utilize every known method in overcoming the difficulties of upriver navigation. On wide expanses of water they used sails and when the river bottom was solid, they poled. At times they rowed. Where other means failed they often used the cordelle. This was a heavy rope which, attached to a tree or other object on the bank, permitted the boat to be warped forward. Where the bank provided good footing, the cordelle might be used as a towline by the boatsmen. Finally, they might resort to "bushwhacking," pulling the boat up the river by grasping bushes or branches of trees overhanging the bank.[2]

That the solution of this problem lay in the application of steam power to water transportation had been clearly recognized toward the end of the eighteenth century. Such American inventors as William Henry, James Rumsey, and John Fitch showed great ingenuity in applying steam power to river craft. Though they succeeded in demonstrating that river boats could be propelled by steam, their efforts brought only commercial failure, for steam engines had not yet been developed to a point sufficiently powerful and rugged to attract capital for significant commercial ventures. But the technique of steam-engine construction advanced rapidly and, shortly before the War of 1812, the commercial feasibility of the steamboat was demonstrated by Robert Fulton in 1807 on the Hudson and, two years later, by John Stevens on the Delaware. With the return of peace in 1815 the stage was set for a great expansion in the use of steamboats. Already Americans were building their own steam engines, steamboats had ceased to be a curiosity on the Hudson and Delaware, and in the West the *New Orleans* had in the winter of 1811–1812 steamed successfully from Pittsburgh to New Orleans.

[2] Cf. Leland D. Baldwin, *The Keelboat Age on Western Waters* (Pittsburgh: The University of Pittsburgh Press, 1941), pp. 62–67.

EASTERN STEAMBOATS

The years from 1815 to 1860 mark the golden age of the river steamboat. By 1830 it dominated American river transportation and for two decades thereafter was the most important agency of internal transportation in the country. For the most part turnpikes and canals proved feeders rather than effective competitors and not until the fifties did railroads become a serious threat. New York provided the chief center of eastern steamboat development. Its harbor, the Hudson River, and Long Island Sound offered unusually favorable conditions for steam navigation, and in New York City and on the nearby Jersey shore the country's leading engine works developed. At first, growth was slow, for Robert R. Livingston and Robert Fulton, who had successfully introduced the *Clermont* on the Hudson in 1807, secured from the state legislature exclusive rights to navigate the waters of New York with vessels driven by steam or fire. By the end of the War of 1812 they had added several boats on the Hudson, begun ferry service in New York Harbor, and established steamboat service from New York to New Brunswick on the Raritan. With the end of the British blockade in 1815, they inaugurated steamboat navigation on Long Island Sound by sending the *Fulton* to New Haven.

The steamboats were such a marked improvement over the slower and less dependable sailing craft that the demand for their services expanded rapidly and the profits of the Fulton-Livingston monopoly grew so high as to attract vigorous competition from other pioneers in steamboat development. John Stevens of Hoboken, a leading inventor and promoter of the period, challenged the monopoly on the Hudson with the first completely American-built steamship, the *Phoenix*, but pressure from the Fulton-Livingston interests led him to transfer this vessel to the Delaware, where it operated very profitably between Philadelphia and Trenton. Later, Stevens placed a second steamboat, the *Juliana*, in service as a ferry between New York and Hoboken, but in 1813 removed it to the Connecticut River in order to escape legal measures by the monopoly.[3]

The most important traffic route in the East, that between New York and Philadelphia, involved three stages: a sheltered water passage from Manhattan to a point in northern New Jersey usually

---

[3] Albion, *The Rise of New York Port*, pp. 145–147; Lane, *From Indian Trail to Iron Horse*, pp. 179–185; Archibald Douglas Turnbull, *John Stevens, an American Record* (New York: The Century Company, 1928), especially Chaps. 11–15.

on or near the Raritan River, turnpike transportation across the waist of New Jersey to Trenton or some other convenient port on the Delaware, and, finally, steam navigation down the river to Philadelphia. In their attempt to control the section of this route between New York and New Jersey, the New York monopolists finally came to grief. Aaron Ogden, for a time as politically important in New Jersey as Livingston was in New York, at first fought the New York monopoly and secured retaliatory legislation from the New Jersey legislature. But later (1815) a compromise was effected and Ogden paid the Fulton-Livingston group for the privilege of operating a steamboat from New York to Elizabeth-Town Point, now Elizabethport, on the Jersey shore. Ogden enjoyed his privileges unhindered for a brief period until he was challenged by as formidable a pair of opponents as any monopoly would wish to face. Thomas Gibbons, a southern planter of some wealth, a duelist and a stubborn and ruthless fighter, had settled in New Jersey, where he entered the steamboat business as a partner of Ogden. A sordid quarrel developed, the partnership was dissolved, and in 1818 Gibbons entered a steamship in competition with Ogden on the New York-Elizabethport run. For his captain he secured the 24-year-old Cornelius Vanderbilt, whose eight years of sailing his own ferries in New York Harbor had brought him a well-earned reputation as a bold and resourceful operator.

While Vanderbilt successfully operated the steamboat, defying the law by a hundred bold stratagems, Gibbons doggedly and vengefully fought the Livingston interests in the courts. Unsuccessful at first, he later secured the services of Daniel Webster to argue the case before the Supreme Court of the United States. There in 1824 the famous decision in the case of Gibbons v. Ogden was rendered against the monopoly. Chief Justice John Marshall stated the majority opinion, upholding the plenary power of Congress to regulate interstate commerce, making inoperative the Livingston monopoly insofar as it affected interstate movement of vessels in the coasting trade. The following year the New York legislature repealed all monopoly privileges on the internal waters of the state.[4]

The removal of legal restrictions, combined with rapid technical improvements in hull and engine construction, now led to a tremendous expansion of steam navigation on eastern rivers, harbors,

[4] Lane, *From Indian Trail to Iron Horse*, pp. 185–194; Wheaton J. Lane, *Commodore Vanderbilt: An Epic of the Steam Age* (New York: Alfred A. Knopf, Inc., 1942), pp. 27–44; 9 Wheaton 1; "The New Jersey Monopolies," *North American Review*, CIV (1867), 431–435.

and bays. Though used to some extent for freight, the eastern steamboat was primarily a passenger vessel. It reached its most notable
development on the Hudson. In 1851, the editor of the *Scientific
American*, obviously having in mind the eastern rather than the
Mississippi type of steamboat, wrote: "The form of the American
steamboat is beautiful and clean for speed: they have fine clear
runs, and bows like razors. . . . They are long and narrow, some
being in length twelve times more than in breadth of beam." [5] Though
clearly descended from the sailing ships of the time, they differed
from them in appearance as much as they did from the marine steamship. Sails, used at first for auxiliary power, largely disappeared
during the twenties. The superstructure was greatly enlarged; above
it arched the longitudinal trusses or "hog-frame" necessary to give
strength to the long hull; amidship and open to the weather oscillated
the characteristic diamond-shaped walking beams and on each side
of the vessel, reaching as high as or even higher than the superstructure, rose the arched housings of the giant paddle wheels. In the
East, low-pressure engines were almost universally used and, though
at first placed in the hold, soon were moved abovedeck in order to
decrease the damage from explosions. Engines, transmission, gearing,
and boilers became more dependable and efficient through the efforts
of a host of inventors and practical builders, probably the most notable of whom was the marine engineer and naval architect, Robert
L. Stevens, son of John Stevens.

Tremendous quantities of wood were burned to fire steamboat
engines during the twenties and thirties but, early difficulties in securing satisfactory combustion of anthracite having been overcome, this
fuel came into general use in the forties because of the growing
scarcity and rising price of wood. The competitive struggle for passengers led to an increasing emphasis on luxury in steamboat construction as well as on speed. Berths and staterooms, salons, dining
halls and bars with elegant and even garish decorations became common on the longer and more important runs, and the steamboats, with
their gilt decorations and elaborate fixtures, became known as "floating palaces." Even the engine rooms of some of the more elaborately
furnished were lined with mirrors. Racing was common between
rival lines and before the end of the period the faster boats not infrequently achieved better than twenty miles an hour.[6]

[5] Robert Macfarlane, *History of Propellers and Steam Navigation with Biographical
Sketches of the Early Inventors* (New York: G. P. Putnam & Co., 1851), p. 128.

[6] Dionysius Lardner, *Railway Economy: A Treatise on the New Art of Transport*
(New York: Harper & Brothers, 1850), pp. 313–323; Robert H. Thurston, *A History*

Though New York continued the leading steamboat center of the East, steam navigation was rapidly introduced on bays and rivers from Maine to Florida. On the Delaware and Chesapeake bays and their great tidal rivers, steam early secured a mastery. Even on the lower reaches of the less placid rivers of New England the steamboat made a bid for passenger travel and, until the advent of the railroads, moved increasing quantities of freight. On the Connecticut River below Hartford regular steamboat operation began in 1818, with several vessels giving service to New York by 1825. On the Connecticut north of Hartford, river improvements, especially the six-mile Enfield Canal, combined with the use of small steamboats of the western type, made possible steam navigation of a sort. Though passenger service was established between Hartford and Springfield, (Dickens describes his journey over this route on his visit to America in 1842), steamboats on the upper river were used chiefly to tow barges on stretches of the river between locks.[7]

STEAMERS ON THE LAKES

Wherever sailing ships operated under favorable conditions, steam navigation developed relatively slowly. So, though steamers appeared on the Great Lakes only a few years after their successful introduction on American rivers, their victory over other craft came, as it did on the ocean, more slowly than on the rivers. Steam navigation was inaugurated on Lake Ontario in 1816 by the Canadian-owned *Frontenac* and two years later on Lake Erie with the launching of the *Walk-in-the-Water*, the first steamer built by the Erie Steamboat Company of Buffalo. Steamboats remained small and few on Lake Ontario until after the opening of the Welland Canal in 1829. Thereafter, as the canal was gradually enlarged and improved, steamers passed easily in to Lake Erie, and Lake Ontario

of the Growth of the Steam-Engine (New York: D. Appleton and Company, 1907), pp. 270–279; Carl D. Lane, American Paddle Steamboats (New York: Coward-McCann, Inc., 1943), pp. 10–12; Albion, The Rise of New York Port, pp. 157–160; Macfarlane, History of Propellers and Steam Navigation, pp. 125–130; John H. Morrison, History of American Steam Navigation (New York: W. F. Sametz and Company, Inc., 1903), Chaps. 2, 3, and 5; Ringwalt, Development of Transportation Systems in the United States, p. 137.

[7] Alexander Crosby Brown, The Old Bay Line (Richmond: The Dietz Press, 1940), pp. 9 ff.; Tenth Census of the United States: Transportation, IV, 667–669, 675–679; Henry W. Erving, The Connecticut River Banking Company, 1825 (Hartford: Henry W. Erving, 1925), passim; Morrison, History of American Steam Navigation, pp. 184–189; Charles Dickens, American Notes for General Circulation (New York: Charles Scribner's Sons, 1910), pp. 84–86; Kirkland, Men, Cities and Transportation, I, 72–75.

participated in the great development of steam navigation on the lakes.

Shallow, turbulent Lake Erie early became the leading center for lake steamships. As on eastern rivers, the lake steamer was primarily a passenger vessel and, with the opening of the Erie Canal, Lake Erie steamers carried a growing horde of immigrants to Detroit and beyond. At first the railroads greatly stimulated steamship travel on the Lakes, but by the end of the fifties they began to take more and more passengers away from the lake steamers. As the West developed, steam took over from the sailing vessels the cream of the passenger business on Lakes Huron and Michigan. Steam navigation on Lake Superior was inaugurated in the spring of 1845 by the small propeller-driven *Independence,* which had been hauled overland from the Sault during the previous winter. With the opening of the Saint Marys Falls Canal in 1855, five lake steamers appeared on Lake Superior.

By 1860 the number of steam-driven ships on the Lakes totaled 369 with a tonnage of 137,771 while sailing vessels numbered 1,207 with a tonnage of 255,449.[8] The number of lake steamships as compared with those on American rivers was never large before 1860. But the size of the lake steamships increased greatly from decade to decade. The *Walk-in-the-Water,* about 330 tons, was a large vessel in its day. By the prewar decade, many lake steamships exceeded 1,000 tons and a few giants, like the 2,200-ton *City of Buffalo,* rivaled in size as well as in elegance their sisters on the Atlantic. In fact, the lake steamers with their deep hulls, relatively low superstructure, and marine lines more closely resembled ocean than river craft. But it should not be supposed that lake steamers were merely modeled after ocean steamships, for in part, at least, the reverse was true. Thus, one of the first successful commercial experiments with screw propulsion was made on Lake Ontario in 1841, and by the late fifties, when the finest ocean liners were still driven by paddle wheels, more than half the steam vessels on the Lakes were so called "propellers." [9]

[8] Computed from *Report of the Secretary of the Treasury,* June 25, 1864, *Senate Executive Document* No. 55, 38 Cong., 1 Sess., p. 144.

[9] Morrison, *History of American Steam Navigation,* pp. 366–385; Lane, *American Paddle Steamboats,* pp. 15–17; Harlan Hatcher, *The Great Lakes* (New York: Oxford University Press, 1944), pp. 227–232, and *Lake Erie* (Indianapolis: The Bobbs-Merrill Company, 1945), pp. 123–133; *Tenth Census of the United States: Transportation,* IV, 669–670; James Cooke Mills, *Our Inland Seas, Their Shipping & Commerce for Three Centuries* (Chicago: A. C. McClurg & Co., 1910), pp. 89–202; Ralph G. Plumb, *History of the Navigation of the Great Lakes* (Washington: Government Printing Office, 1911).

WESTERN STEAMBOATS [10]

Steamboats played a significant, but hardly an indispensable, role on eastern rivers and the lakes. In the great valley of the Mississippi, steam-driven vessels proved the most important factor in the great industrial development of that region from 1815 to the eve of the Civil War. No section of the country was so completely dependent upon steam for effective transportation, and in no other part of the world were so many steamboats built and operated.[11] The original experiment with the *Clermont* on the Hudson was made with navigation of the western waters in mind, and in 1811 the Fulton-Livingston group successfully sent the Pittsburgh-built steamboat *New Orleans*, 371 tons, from Pittsburgh to New Orleans. The *New Orleans* operated effectively on the lower Mississippi but did not attempt to return to the Ohio. The possibility of using steamboats in the upriver trade was demonstrated in 1815, when the *Enterprise*, built at Brownsville on the Monongahela fifty miles above Pittsburgh, successfully returned to its home port after a trip to New Orleans. By 1817 the feasibility of using steamboats for such journeys was clearly established.

The Fulton-Livingston group obtained monopoly privileges from the Territory of Orleans (after 1812 the state of Louisiana) similar to those secured from New York. Legislatures of other western states refused to grant such privileges and protested this action by Louisiana, which they feared would greatly curtail steamboat development. But neither patent rights nor monopoly grants kept Westerners from building and operating steamboats where they chose. For a few years Livingston interests fought to defend their legal rights but after 1817 they gave up the struggle. With legal difficulties at an end and the feasibility of steamboat navigation on the Ohio and Mississippi clearly established, the great period of the western steamboat began.[12]

Seventeen steamboats with a total tonnage of 3,290 operated on western rivers in 1817. Three years later, in 1820, the number had

[10] For this section and the following ones of this chapter, chief reliance has been placed on Louis C. Hunter's *Steamboats on the Western Rivers* (Cambridge: Harvard University Press, 1949).

[11] *Tenth Census of the United States: Transportation*, IV, 662–666; Annual Report on *Commerce and Navigation*, 1860, pp. 650–653.

[12] Gephart, *Transportation and Industrial Development in the Middle West*, pp. 73–76; Charles Henry Ambler, *A History of Transportation in the Ohio Valley* (Glendale, Cal.: The Arthur H. Clark Company, 1932), pp. 126–128; William J. Petersen, *Steamboating on the Upper Mississippi* (Iowa City: State Historical Society, 1937), pp. 43–45, 70, 72–73.

risen to 69 and the tonnage to 13,890. After a slight decline during the depressed period of the early twenties, the growth became truly phenomenal. By 1855 the total number was 727 and the tonnage exceeded 170,000. These figures actually minimize the increase of steam transportation services for, when account is taken of increased speed of the boats and greater carrying capacity by measured ton, the facilities for steamboat transportation on western rivers increased a hundredfold from 1820 to 1860. The most rapid steamboat development came first on the lower Ohio and the main stem of the Mississippi below Cairo. But soon the steamboat became a common sight on the chief tributaries of the Ohio, and before the period was over, the smaller steamboats ventured up the many lesser streams to the remote reaches of the Mississippi Valley. On rivers like the Wabash, Monongahela, and Cumberland, the number at times was comparable with that on any eastern river, not excluding the Hudson.

On the western branches of the Mississippi and on the upper Mississippi, steamboats served first to assist in the fur trade, to move troops and supplies to government posts, and to facilitate colonization. Later, as the country developed, they provided the means by which the growing production of this newly settled country, the timber, lead, and grain, might be carried to market. The forties and fifties witnessed a tremendous growth in steam navigation on the upper Mississippi and on the branches such as the Red, Illinois, and Missouri rivers. Though steam navigation was introduced on the Missouri before 1820, it did not develop rapidly until the late forties. By 1860, boats steamed 2,200 miles up the river's winding course to Fort Benton in Montana.[13]

The great advantage of the steamboats over the flatboats and keelboats lay, of course, in their greater speed and their economy, especially for upriver navigation. By the fifties many were more than 300 feet long and carried 300 or 400 deck passengers besides those in the cabins.[14] Yet, it should not be supposed that the older river craft were immediately put out of business by the introduction of steam power. Quite the contrary, for the steamboat to a very considerable extent stimulated and facilitated flatboat operation. With steamboat transportation available, rivermen no longer had to walk back across country or laboriously to pole their keelboats upriver

[13] Petersen, *Steamboating on the Upper Mississippi, passim;* Mildred L. Hartsough, *From Canoe to Steel Barge on the Upper Mississippi* (Minneapolis: The University of Minnesota Press, 1934), pp. 58–108; *Tenth Census of the United States: Transportation,* IV, 679.

[14] Lardner, *Railway Economy,* p. 324.

STEAMBOATS ON RIVER, LAKE, AND BAY

to Nashville, Lafayette, Marietta, or Pittsburgh. Farmers on small streams inaccessible to steamboats still had to make at least the first part of their journey to market by flatboat; many found it advantageous to continue on to New Orleans. This worked out very well, for the bulk of the downriver products greatly exceeded that of the finer goods which were brought upriver for western consumption. By 1830 the steamboat was clearly the predominant means of transportation on western rivers, but the number of flatboats continued to increase, reaching a peak in 1846–1847. The total number of flatboat arrivals at New Orleans in 1814 was 598. This figure had risen to 2,792 by 1846–1847, but then fell off rapidly, arrivals at New Orleans numbering only 541 in 1856–1857.

On the rivers of California and Oregon, steam navigation developed rapidly during the fifties. Soon after the discovery of gold, steamboats were rushed from the East to the Sacramento River. Some came in parts packed in the holds of sailing vessels; a few river steamboats actually made the sea trip all the way round Cape Horn. At least 16 steamers were operating on California rivers by the end of 1850 and the number had risen to 43 by 1860. To the northward development was almost as rapid. By 1852 at least a half dozen steamboats were operating on the Willamette and Yamhill rivers, and before the decade was over steamboats were a common sight on the Columbia River and the navigable waters of Washington Territory.[15]

Steam navigation of western rivers presented serious and unusual hazards. The level of water in the rivers was subject to exceedingly wide and sudden fluctuations. At Cincinnati the spread between high and low water might vary forty feet or more within a few weeks. Steamboats, often tied up for lack of water in summer months, had to combat the roaring floods of fall and spring. Ice which closed the river to navigation in winter became a floating menace when the spring moved northward, freeing tremendous flows in successive tributaries. Extended periods of low water made ledges and rock and sand bars a dreaded threat; to these must be added the greatest menace of all, the snags. Great trees thrown into the water by constantly crumbling banks became caught in the river bed where, year in and year out, they caused more damage to steamboats than any other single cause. Of steamboats lost in western rivers, 1811–1851, more than 40 per cent were destroyed by snags or similar obstructions.

[15] *Tenth Census of the United States: Transportation*, IV, 680–683; Jerry Mac-Mullen, *Paddle-Wheel Days in California* (Palo Alto, Cal.: Stanford University Press, 1945), pp. 17–23; Ringwalt, *Development of Transportation Systems in the United States*, pp. 138–139; Winther, *The Old Oregon Country*, pp. 160–170.

And of all western steamboats built before 1849, nearly 30 per cent were lost in accidents of one kind or another.

Under these conditions the shipbuilders on the Monongahela and the Ohio gradually developed a new type of steamboat. In order to permit navigation during periods of low water, hulls were made broad and shallow, engines were placed on deck, and huge wooden superstructures were erected on the scowlike hulls. Despite the greater danger from boiler explosions, high-pressure engines came to be universally preferred in the West, not only because they were compact and weighed less than the eastern low-pressure type, but also because they permitted the boilers to use the muddy river water, were easier to operate, were relatively cheap, and gave reserve power for emergencies. As the period advanced, stern-wheel propulsion came to be preferred because weight was saved and low-water navigation made more effective. Though both coal and wood, sometimes in combination, were used as fuel, by the fifties the chief dependence was upon coal.

Most writers have tended to attribute the unique architecture of the western steamboat and its high-pressure engine to revolutionary innovations by Henry Miller Shreve, one of the early shipbuilders of western Pennsylvania, who later became distinguished for his activities in snag removal while superintendent of western river improvements. The studies of Louis C. Hunter demonstate that Shreve's contribution has been considerably exaggerated. The peculiar construction of the flat-bottomed, western steamboat appears to have been not a sudden discovery but a gradual development in which many builders had a hand. Similarly the western steamboat engine was the product of development extending over a score of years in the course of which many mechanics made significant contribution. The names of Oliver Evans, Daniel French, and Stephen H. Long are certainly among those which must in this connection be placed beside that of Henry Shreve.[16]

The western steamboat looked like a cheaply constructed, ornate, white wooden castle floating on a raft. Though viewed as a monstrosity by deep-sea sailors, it was not without stately grandeur; above all, it admirably suited Western conditions. Its light wooden construction made it relatively inexpensive. This low cost of construction was especially important because on western rivers the average

[16] Louis C. Hunter, "The Invention of the Western Steamboat," *Journal of Economic History*, III, No. 2 (November, 1943), 201–220. Cf. Gephart, *Transportation and Industrial Development in the Middle West*, pp. 72–73; Petersen, *Steamboating on the Upper Mississippi*, pp. 71–73.

life of a steamboat was under five years. The distinctive model and
the lightness of the western steamboats were such that they could
navigate incredibly shallow water. In 1838 at least twenty steamboats on the Ohio could operate in thirty inches of water, and one
built in 1841, the *Orphan Boy* (169 tons), is reported to have drawn
but twenty-two inches of water carrying forty tons of freight and
eighty passengers. Little wonder western rivermen boasted that for
successful navigation their steamboats needed only a heavy dew.[17]

GOVERNMENTAL AID AND REGULATION

Both federal and state governments aided steamboat navigation
on inland waters, but such help was indirect and on a much smaller
scale than that received by turnpikes, canals, and railroads. Almost
no direct assistance was given either in the form of grants of money
or land or by the purchase of stock or bonds in steamboat companies. Possibly the only exception was the investment of $100,000
in a steamboat company by the state of Georgia.[18]

Public assistance to steamboats was largely confined to attempts
to improve the conditions of navigation on internal waters by deep-
ening rivers, providing slack-water navigation, and removing obstructions. For the most part these activities were carried out by the
states either directly or by chartering private companies for the
purpose. The private companies were ordinarily permitted to charge
tolls in return for building systems of slack-water navigation or constructing canals around river obstructions. Thus, the Connecticut
River Banking Company opened the upper Connecticut to steamboat navigation by building a canal above Hartford at the Enfield
Falls; the Monongahela Navigation Company built an elaborate
slack-water navigation on that important waterway; and the Louisville and Portland Canal Company, by permitting steamboats to
avoid the falls of the Ohio at Louisville, removed the chief obstruc-
tion to steamboat navigation on the Ohio River. These companies
often received substantial governmental aid. Thus by 1822 the state

---

[17] Ambler, *A History of Transportation in the Ohio Valley*, pp. 161–184; Thomas
Senior Berry, *Western Prices before 1861* (Vol. LXXIV of *Harvard Economic Studies*,
Cambridge: Harvard University Press, 1943), pp. 32–35; Lardner, *Railway Economy*,
pp. 323–324; William F. Switzler, *Report on the Internal Commerce of the United
States*, Part II of *Commerce and Navigation*, Special Report on the Commerce of the
Mississippi, Ohio, and Other Rivers, and of the Bridges Which Cross Them, 1888,
Treasury Department *Document* No. 1,039b, Bureau of Statistics, Serial No. 50,829,
pp. 187–189, 192–195; Morrison, *History of American Steam Navigation*, pp. 191–
264.

[18] Phillips, *Transportation in Eastern Cotton Belt*, p. 77.

of Pennsylvania had invested $130,000 in the stock of private navigation companies, and the United States government a few years later invested $235,000 in the stock of the Louisville and Portland Canal.[19] A number of western and southern states spent considerable sums of money directly on river improvements, much of which was wasted on ineffective and partially completed projects.[20]

Between 1815 and 1860 the federal government made a number of relatively small land grants for river improvements and many appropriations of money for the same purpose. The latter totaled nearly $6,000,000. Much of this money was spent on western rivers in removing snags, boulders, and sunken boats and in increasing the depth at bars, but as early as 1834, $70,000 was appropriated toward improving the Hudson River. Though appreciably aided by this service, steamboat navigation was by no means freed from the hazards of snags and other obstructions in the prewar period.[21]

Steamboats alone among the various agencies of internal transportation came under federal regulation before the Civil War. Undoubtedly this resulted from the effect on the popular mind of steamboat accidents, especially those caused by boiler explosions. With the earliest explosions, insistent demands arose that the federal government take action to require such standards of building and operating steamboat engines as would reasonably protect passengers. Investors in steamboats opposed such legislation, holding that the self-interest of the owners, who obviously did not wish their boats to be blown up, was the best protection to the traveling public.

But as sensational explosions continued year after year, public pressure forced action. At first a number of states imposed regulations, but these measures were weak and largely ineffective because of the interstate nature of most steamboat operation. Finally, in 1838, Congress passed the first federal legislation regulating steamboats. This law, which applied only to steam vessels carrying pas-

[19] Erving, *The Connecticut River Banking Company, 1825, passim; Tenth Census of the United States: Transportation,* IV, 744–745; *Preliminary Report of the Inland Waterways Commission,* 1908, Senate Document No. 325, 60 Cong., 1 Sess., p. 180; Gephart, *Transportation and Industrial Development in the Middle West,* pp. 107–110; *Hazard's Register of Pennsylvania,* II (November 22, 1828), 298–299.

[20] Alexander Trotter, *Observations on the Financial Position and Credit of Such of the States of the American Union as Have Contracted Public Debts* (London: Longmans, Rees, Orme, Brown and Green, 1839), pp. 245–248; Mary Verhoeff, *The Kentucky River Navigation* (No. 28 of *Filson Club Publications,* Louisville: John P. Morton and Company, 1917), pp. 23, 31; MacGill, *History of Transportation,* p. 258; Martin, *Internal Improvements in Alabama,* p. 44.

[21] *Preliminary Report of the Inland Waterways Commission,* 1908, p. 180; *Transportation by Water in the United States* (Washington: Government Printing Office, 1909), Pt. 1, p. 46; Hunter, *Steamboats on the Western Rivers,* Chap. 4.

sengers, was so limited in its requirements and established so ineffective an inspection service that explosions were unchecked and
the public soon demanded a stronger measure. In 1852, following a
period marked by an unusual number of disastrous explosions, Congress enacted the Steamboat Act of 1852, a comprehensive measure
which not only established standards for the construction, equipment, and operation of steamboat boilers but also prescribed measures for the prevention of fire and collisions. The law also provided
for the establishment of effective administrative machinery and the
hiring of competent inspectors.[22]

BUSINESS ASPECTS OF STEAMBOATING

The rivers provided public highways upon which steamboats
could operate without the expense of building and maintaining a
right of way. As a result the business could be entered with fairly
small capital. On the Ohio-Mississippi system a steamship of medium
tonnage cost only about $20,000; the very largest and best could be
secured for from $40,000 to $60,000. The large and fast Hudson River
steamboats, specializing in the passenger business, cost appreciably
more, but the capital necessary to go into the business was still not
so great as to exclude ventures by wealthy individuals or groups of
more moderate means.

In the East and on the Great Lakes, the corporation gradually
became an important type of ownership, with great lines sometimes
securing a dominant position over important routes. By the late
forties railroad companies occasionally became owners and operators
of strategic steamboat lines. But as late as 1850, single owners, part-
nerships, and corporations were important in that order on the Hudson River and on Long Island Sound.[23] Though tramp steamboats
operated on most Atlantic rivers and on the lakes, packets running
on regular schedules and as part of great steamboat lines early
achieved a dominant position.

Fluctuations in depth of the water made regular packet sailings much more difficult on western rivers. The tramp steamboat that
could go freely to those sections of the river where the water was
high and cargoes abundant often had a great advantage over packets tied down to a scheduled run. Moreover, the importance of freight

[22] Morrison, *History of American Steam Navigation*, pp. 591 ff.
[23] Robert G. Albion, "Early Nineteenth-Century Shipowning—A Chapter in Business Enterprise," *Journal of Economic History*, I, No. 1 (May, 1941), 4, 10–11.

carriage often made it more desirable for western steamboat captains to await full cargoes than to accommodate passengers by scheduled sailings. As a result, the tramp steamboat remained on the Ohio-Mississippi system, though during the forties and fifties single packets or even lines combining several packets achieved appreciable success on important runs such as those between Pittsburgh and Cincinnati, Cincinnati and Louisville, and St. Paul and La Crosse.[24]

As a result of this situation on western rivers, the typical form of ownership differed radically from that common in the East. Each steamboat tended to be a separate venture, owned either by a single man or by a small group organized as an association of part owners. Thus, between 1830 and 1860 more than half of the Ohio and Mississippi steamboats were owned by from two to four men. The financial success of the venture depended upon the skill of the captain both in navigating his craft and in finding ports where well-paying cargoes were available. Even when lines of packets sailing on schedule were formed in a particular trade, individual ownership of the steamboat was usually retained, the owners merely forming loose agreements to operate as part of a line for a single season. Western steamboats were financed very largely by local capital. Though coming at first largely from mercantile interests, appreciable contributions were made by manufacturers, farmers, and those already engaged in turnpike and canal transportation. As time went on, much capital came from the profits of those who operated steamboats or those who insured, built, repaired, or furnished supplies for them.[25]

Wherever inland waters were suitable for steam navigation, the steamboat quickly demonstrated its competitive superiority over earlier means of transportation for travelers and on many routes for freight as well. For speed and for the comfort of passengers neither canals nor turnpikes could compete, and even on the basis of cost, the steamboat had an advantage over most routes. It is true that on the great bays and tidal rivers of the East and on the Great Lakes, sailing craft continued to carry most of the bulky freight, and that on the rivers, flatboats survived in downstream traffic to perform a similar function. Especially on the larger rivers where heavy hauling was to be done and wherever a canal and river connection was made,

[24] Frederick Merk, *Economic History of Wisconsin during the Civil War Decade* (Vol. I of *Publications of the State Historical Society of Wisconsin*, Madison: The Society, 1916), pp. 348–353.

[25] Berry, *Western Prices before 1861*, pp. 35–38; Hartsough, *From Canoe to Steel Barge on the Upper Mississippi*, pp. 160–168.

the flatboats and canalboats were taken over by the steamboats with the growing practice of using the steamboats for towing purposes. Thus much of the freight on the Hudson was moved by steam tow-boats. Steam vessels were specially constructed for that purpose as early as 1825 on the Hudson and 1836 on the Ohio. On the latter river the business of moving coal barges grew tremendously, particularly in the fifties, when an efficient technique was developed by which stern-wheeled towboats pushed canalboats or barges through the water ahead of them.[26] By the fifties steam was everywhere making rapid progress against other water craft, and on the main western rivers had very nearly routed all competition.

But the railroad was another matter. Here steam navigation suffered from serious physical and commercial disadvantages similar to those already mentioned for canals. Rail travel was generally faster, more regular and dependable, and more flexible than that by steamboat. The average rate of speed even of the faster steamboats before the Civil War was seldom greater than fifteen miles an hour except on some of the luxury lines in the East, whereas by the fifties railroad passenger trains often maintained schedules faster by 50 to 100 per cent. But even more important, especially in the West, was the directness of rail as against river routes. It is true that on the Lakes and in the East this advantage was not so great; in fact, rail and water distances between Albany and New York City and between Cleveland and Detroit were nearly the same. On some routes, as that between Washington and Norfolk, steam lines were, and still are, more direct than rail. But the meandering western rivers greatly handicapped water transportation. Thus, the distance by river from Pittsburgh to Cincinnati was 470 miles, by rail 316; to St. Louis, 1,164 miles, by rail 612. From Cincinnati to Nashville, steamboats traveled 644 miles down the Ohio and up the Cumberland; by rail the mileage (301) was more than halved.

While railroads operated the year round, the lakes and rivers of the North were closed by ice from two to five months during the winter season and in the West frequently for long periods during the rest of the year by low water. Travelers and shippers alike, becoming habituated to using the rails in the closed season, often found small differences in cost insufficient to tempt them back to the rivers when they again became navigable. Finally, river position was pre-

[26] Morrison, *History of American Steam Navigation,* pp. 539–541; Ambler, *A History of Transportation in the Ohio Valley,* pp. 203–207; Berry, *Western Prices before 1861,* pp. 38–39.

determined, whereas rails might be laid over the most convenient routes for commerce, and spurs, sidings, and loading platforms often brought rail shipments directly from the producer to the industrial consumer without breaking bulk or reloading.

Rails also early developed major commercial advantages for travelers and shippers. Passengers could buy through tickets on the trains with the assurance of regularly scheduled connections when changes from one railroad to another were necessary. Irregularity of sailings and the lack of interline agreements made such arrangements unusual for river trips. Freight shipments by water were at an even greater disadvantage in this respect. Whereas merchants could bill their rail shipments through to destination even though a number of lines were involved, those who shipped by steamboat usually had to bill goods to forwarding agents wherever goods had to be shifted en route from one steamboat to another or from steamboat to railroad line. For some time the steamboats retained two advantages: lower rates and greater comfort for passengers, but even these were threatened in the fifties as rail rates over many routes came closer to, though they did not generally equal, those by water, and as improved coaches and smoother road beds greatly reduced the discomforts of rail travel.

In general, the fifties marked the peak of the steamboat's development. At first railroads often stimulated water transportation. Thus, completion of rail lines from New York to Buffalo and across southern Michigan greatly added to the demand for steamboats on Lakes Erie and Michigan. Steamboats on Long Island Sound increased their business when they were able to connect with railroads leading to Boston from Providence, Fall River, and Stonington. But when through rail routes were completed, the steamboats found their erstwhile helper their deadly enemy. First to succumb to rail competition frequently were steamboats on lesser streams where traffic had been relatively light and conditions of navigation difficult. When in 1844 Springfield was connected by rail with Hartford, steamboat navigation on the middle Connecticut fell off precipitously. A similar decline was noted on the tributaries of the Ohio wherever railroads were constructed roughly parallel to river routes. On many of the great tidal rivers of the East and on the Great Lakes, freight traffic continued to grow and passenger travel continued large though its heyday was over. On the Ohio the steamboats suffered one competitive shock after another as railroads from Pittsburgh and Wheeling were opened to Cincinnati and Louisville by 1854 and to St.

Louis in 1857. Before the decade was over, passenger traffic on the Ohio had been seriously reduced and steamboats forced to slash freight rates drastically in order to keep what they could of the freight business. Only on the upper Mississippi and its western tributaries was the star of the steamboat still rising as the railroads brought hordes of settlers and for a brief period stimulated river trade.

CHAPTER V

Railroads

ACCEPTANCE OF THE RAILROADS

IMPROVED roads, canals, and steamboats made their contribution, but they were not entirely effective in loosening the bonds which fettered the agrarian, merchant-capitalist economy of the early nineteenth century. The United States encompassed vast distances, difficult mountain barriers, virgin forests, and great unsettled plains. Only a method of transportation by land—cheap, fast, and flexible—could meet the pressing needs of agriculture and industry. The steam railroad, surely one of the most revolutionary inventions of all time, provided the solution.

Although developed largely in England, where its commercial feasibility was demonstrated by 1829, the railroad had its most dramatic growth in the United States. By 1840, all Europe had 1,818 miles of railroad; the United States, about 3,000. Why should the United States have so quickly established this railroad leadership? Though western Europe led in engineering and in the metal-working techniques and was best able to finance railroad building, the United States possessed strategic advantages. Not only did it have the urgent need for improved land transportation stressed above, but it was also relatively free from such Old World obstacles as restrictive political boundaries and customs barriers. The cheapness of land in this new country greatly facilitated railroad building, whereas high land values added tremendously to the cost of construction in western Europe. It has been estimated that up to 1868 English railroads paid out for land more than the total sum expended on all American railroads built up to that date.[1] Finally, at least on a relative basis,

[1] Henry M. Flint, *The Railroads of the United States: Their History and Statistics* (Philadelphia: John E. Potter and Company, 1868), p. 26.

American railroads were less hampered by entrenched monopolies, vested interests, and long-established customs and prejudices than were those abroad.

Of course, some opposition appeared, for no nation is too young to have vested interests, timid individuals, and conservative communities fearful of innovation. Tavern keepers, bridge and turnpike companies, wagoners, and stagecoach lines, though frequently slow to realize the threat of railroad competition, once aroused, often fought bitterly. The legislatures of at least three states sought by restrictive laws to protect their huge investment in canals. For a time, New York required railroads paralleling the Erie to pay tolls equal to those assessed on the canal and forbade the carrying of freight by such railroads except during the winter, when canal traffic was suspended. Similarly, both Pennsylvania and Ohio levied special taxes on certain traffic carried by railroads which competed directly with canals.[2] Also a certain amount of inertia and prejudice had to be overcome: a Boston editor declared a railroad from Boston to Albany "impracticable" and "as useless as a railroad to the moon," and an Ohio school board held the steam railroad "a device of Satan to lead immortal souls down to Hell." [3]

But it must be emphasized that these obstacles were exceptional. For the most part, Americans welcomed the railroad with noisy enthusiasm. People who had never seen a track, to say nothing of a steam locomotive, invested their savings and gave support to promoters who, even before many of the major technical problems of railroad building had been solved, planned ambitious lines crossing unsettled territory, spanning rivers, and tunneling mountains. The spirit was that of a young and pioneering people who were trying new things in an undeveloped country, a spirit greatly stimulated, as will be emphasized later, by the fierce competition of rival commercial centers.

THE FIRST RAILROADS

In 1825, the year which saw the completion of the Erie Canal, the Stockton and Darlington, the world's first railroad constructed

[2] Frank Walker Stevens, *The Beginnings of the New York Central Railroad: A History* (New York: G. P. Putnam's Sons, 1926), pp. 266–276; Cleveland and Powell, *Railroad Promotion and Capitalization in the United States*, pp. 73–75; MacGill, *History of Transportation*, pp. 353–356; Gephart, *Transportation and Industrial Development in the Middle West*, pp. 160–161.

[3] For these and other examples, see Cleveland and Powell, *Railroad Promotion and Capitalization in the United States*, pp. 75–77; Thurman W. Van Metre, *Early Opposition to the Steam Railroad* (no date or place of publication given), *passim*.

for general transportation purposes, began operations in England. Though the canal received major attention in the United States, significant reverberations of the railroad success were not lacking. Before the year was over, Governor Levi Lincoln of Massachusetts had, though with evident misgivings, recommended to the general court that consideration be given to a railroad from Boston to Albany; William Strickland, sent to England by the Pennsylvania Society for the Promotion of Internal Improvements in the Commonwealth, had reported that railroads would be preferable to canals in important respects; and John Stevens, an early American enthusiast for the steam railroad, had built and exhibited in operation on a small circular track a toy-sized steam engine. Of course, even earlier than this, Americans had been interested in the railroad. The Philadelphia inventor, Oliver Evans, had long been an advocate of steam railroads. In 1816, through the columns of the *National Intelligencer*, he directed the attention of Congress to the advantages of steam for use on railways or smooth roads.[4] Stevens had urged that New York State construct a double-track railroad instead of the Erie Canal. In 1815 he had actually secured a charter from the state of New Jersey authorizing construction of a railroad between Trenton and New Brunswick, but, lacking financial support, he abandoned the project.

These and other early proposals came to nought, but in the years following 1825, significant experiments rapidly took shape. First, a number of tramways were built and placed in effective operation. These were single-purpose roads operated in connection with mines and quarries. Light tracks were provided on which small cars were moved ordinarily by horses or mules. They may be distinguished from railroads, as the term has come to be used, in that they were not designed to serve as agencies of public transportation. Tracks had long been used in this way in connection with mining operations in Europe, and even in America limited experiments had been made with this device as early as 1807.[5]

The so-called Granite Railroad, located at Quincy, Massachusetts, and completed in 1826, though strictly speaking a tramway, is sometimes referred to as the first American railroad. The cars on

[4] *Niles' Weekly Register,* X (May 25, 1816), 213–214.
[5] J. H. Clapham, *The Economic Development of France and Germany 1815–1914* (Cambridge, England: The University Press, 3d ed., 1928), p. 140; J. H. Clapham, *An Economic History of Modern Britain: The Early Railway Age, 1820–1850* (Cambridge, England: The University Press, 1926), pp. 85 ff.; Cleveland and Powell, *Railroad Promotion and Capitalization in the United States,* pp. 59–60.

this road were loaded with granite at the quarry and moved by gravity and horsepower about two miles to a dock on Boston Harbor. Two much longer tramways soon played an important role in the mining of anthracite in northeastern Pennsylvania. One nine miles long was completed in 1827 at Mauch Chunk, and another sixteen miles in length was placed in operation two years later by the Delaware and Hudson Canal Company to connect coal lands at Carbondale with their canal at Honesdale. Each of these two roads made interesting experiments in motive power. On the Mauch Chunk, cars were hauled up a gradual incline by horses and mules, which then rode to the bottom of the grade in one of the cars. The first locomotive to operate in America on a commercial line was tried out on the tramway of the Delaware and Hudson Canal Company. Imported from England, this locomotive, the famous *Stourbridge Lion*, ran well enough but could not be used because it proved too heavy for the track, which had been built for relatively light, horse-drawn cars.[6]

But overshadowing these tramway developments were the plans going rapidly forward for building the first American railroads. Three important commercial cities, Baltimore, Charleston, and Boston, each struggling to enlarge its market to the West and each without important inland waterway connections, pioneered in railroad development. Baltimore's advantage in the western trade arising from the National Road was seriously endangered as New York gained from the Erie Canal, and Philadelphia threatened to secure a similar competitive advantage as soon as the great state works of Pennsylvania came into operation. The business interests of Baltimore met the challenge by building the first important railroad in America. Designed to extend westward to the Ohio, the Baltimore and Ohio Railroad was chartered in 1828 and in May, two years later, 13 miles of track were placed in operation.

Citizens of Charleston, South Carolina, sought to gain a larger share of the inland trade by building a railroad to Hamburg on the Savannah River. They hoped to secure the commerce from a rich cotton-growing region which would otherwise be channeled through Savannah at the mouth of the river. This railroad, the second in the country, was opened for regular passenger service over part of its

[6] Cleveland and Powell, *Railroad Promotion and Capitalization in the United States*, pp. 60–61; Charles Francis Adams, Jr., "The Canal and Railroad Enterprise of Boston," in *The Memorial History of Boston* (Boston: James R. Osgood and Company, 1881), IV, 116–121; Jules I. Bogen, *The Anthracite Railroads* (New York: The Ronald Press Company, 1927), pp. 10–11; Jones, *The Economic History of the Anthracite-Tidewater Canals*, pp. 15–16, 79–80.

route early in 1831 and was completed in 1833. At that time it extended 136 miles and was the longest railroad in the world under single management. Bostonians, alarmed by the growing strength of New York, began agitating for a railroad from Boston to Albany, even before the Erie Canal was completed, but progress was slow. After the Erie was opened, much time was spent in unsuccessful attempts to persuade the Massachusetts State Legislature to authorize a state railroad.[7] Finally, in 1830–1831, three Boston companies were chartered to build railroads, one reaching north to Lowell, a second west to Worcester, and a third south to Providence. All were in operation by 1835. Many other short lines were completed in southern New England during the thirties, but through connections from Boston to the Hudson River were not effected until 1841.

Although Maryland and South Carolina were the real pioneers in railroad building, Pennsylvania soon became an outstanding leader. At first many short feeder lines were built leading from coal mines to nearby canals and rivers. Soon longer roads were built directly from large centers, especially Philadelphia, to, and in some cases through, the larger coal fields. Thus the important coal railroad, the Philadelphia and Reading, was in full operation between these two cities by 1839. In addition, before the end of the thirties important links for through rail lines had been built in the Keystone State. Completed in 1834, the state-owned Philadelphia and Columbia connected Philadelphia with the great system of state canals. In the same year, the completion of the Philadelphia and Trenton to the north provided a connection with the Camden and Amboy in New Jersey and thus afforded a through route between Philadelphia and New York Harbor. To the south, a main line to Baltimore was opened in 1838 when the Philadelphia, Wilmington, and Baltimore was placed in operation.

It will be seen from the accompanying table that New York was a poor second among the states in the amount of railroad mileage built by 1840. Many short lines were constructed in New York, chiefly as the result of a struggle by such cities as New York, Albany-Schenectady-Troy, Buffalo, Rochester, and Utica to dominate and develop nearby market areas.[8] Building was somewhat retarded by the great success of the state canal system, by the burdensome legislative restraints imposed on the railroads by the canal interests, and, finally, by

[7] For early railroad agitation in Massachusetts see Edward C. Kirkland, "The 'Railroad Scheme' of Massachusetts," *Journal of Economic History*, V, No. 2 (November, 1945), 145–171.

[8] MacGill, *History of Transportation*, p. 353.

Steamboat racing on the Mississippi River. These steamboats may be compared with the eastern type shown below. (*Culver Service*)

The explosion of the *Reindeer* on the Hudson River. Accidents such as this led to federal regulation in 1838. (*Culver Service*)

(*Below left*) Cornelius Vanderbilt, 1794–1877, steamboat and railroad promoter. (*Center*) Henry M. Shreve, 1785–1851, steamboat builder and operator. (*Right*) Robert Fulton, 1765–1815. He demonstrated the commercial practicability of the steamboat. (*Three pictures Culver Service*)

(*Above*) A western stern-wheeler. These became increasingly popular because of their effectiveness in low water. (*Brown Brothers*) (*Below*) A dock scene on the lower Mississippi. River steamboats carried the bulky cotton bales to New Orleans. (*Bettmann Archive*)

(*Left*) Erastus Corning, 1794–1872, railroad magnate. (*Culver Service*) (*Right*) An early freight car on the Baltimore & Ohio. (*R. H. Gabriel, Pageant of America, IV, 34*)

(*Above*) An early freight train on the Baltimore & Ohio. (*Bettmann Archive*) (*Below*) Early passenger train. The early passenger cars were almost indistinguishable from stagecoaches. (*Culver Service*)

(*Top*) A passenger train of the early forties. (*Bottom*) American passenger coach, 1844. (*Both pictures R. H. Gabriel, Pageant of America, IV, 129, 143*) (*Below*) First American-built locomotive. Built by John Stevens, 1825. (*Insert*) John Stevens, 1749–1838, engineer and inventor. (*Both pictures Culver Service*)

the general belief that a railroad paralleling the Hudson from New York to Troy could not successfully meet water competition.

RAILROAD AND CANAL MILEAGE BY DECADES, 1830–1860

State	1830		1840		1850		1860
	Canals	Rail-roads	Canals	Rail-roads	Canals	Rail-roads	Rail-roads
New York	546	...	640	453	803	1,409	2,682
Pennsylvania	230	70	954	576	954	900	2,598
Ohio	245	...	744	39	792	590	2,946
Virginia	...	...	216	341	216	341	1,731
Tennessee	...	...	...	...	...	48	1,253
Kentucky	2	...	2	32	2	80	534
North Carolina ..	...	...	13	247	13	249	937
Massachusetts ...	74	3	89	270	89	1,042	1,264
Georgia	16	...	28	212	28	666	1,420
Indiana	...	...	150	20	214	226	2,163
South Carolina ..	52	...	52	136	52	270	973
Alabama	...	...	52	51	52	112	743
Maine	21	...	21	10	29	257	472
Illinois	...	...	...	26	100	118	2,799
Maryland	10	...	136	273	136	315	386
Missouri	...	...	...	...	...	4	817
Mississippi	...	...	...	50	...	60	862
New Jersey	20	...	142	192	142	332	560
Louisiana	...	...	14	62	14	89	335
Connecticut	34	...	36	94	36	436	601
Vermont	...	...	1	...	1	366	554
New Hampshire .	...	...	11	15	...	471	661
Michigan	...	...	...	114	...	349	779
Rhode Island	11	...	11	47	11	61	108
Arkansas	...	...	...	...	...	...	38
Delaware	14	...	14	16	14	16	127
Florida	...	...	...	52	...	52	402
Iowa	...	...	...	...	...	...	655
Wisconsin	...	...	...	...	...	20	905
Texas	...	...	...	...	...	...	307
California	...	...	...	...	...	...	23
Total	1,277	73	3,326	3,328	3,698	8,879	30,636

Sources: Hunt's Merchants' Magazine, XXV (September, 1851), 381–382 for the years 1830, 1840, and 1850; and Henry V. Poor, *Manual of the Railroads of the United States for 1868–69* (New York: H. V. and H. W. Poor, 1868), pp. 20–21 for the year 1860.

By 1840, although little more than a bare beginning had been made west of the Appalachians, 3,328 miles of railroads had been built in the United States, and all of the larger Atlantic states, except Maine, had appreciable mileage. Within little more than a decade the railroad had grown from an infant to a giant. During the thirties, more than three miles of railroad were built for every two miles of canal, so that by 1840 the total mileage constructed in the United States was very nearly equal for these two systems of transportation.[9] The accompanying table, based on contemporary compilations, gives a fair over-all picture but is not always reliable in detail, chiefly because of failure to distinguish carefully between roads completed and those under construction. For example, the 13 miles of the Baltimore and Ohio in operation in 1830 are not recorded for Maryland and tramways are apparently included in the Pennsylvania total for that year.

It must be emphasized that even these earliest railroads were new and largely independent agents of transportation, sturdy rivals of the older canals. The early railroads must not be regarded chiefly as feeder lines to waterways.[10] True, the tramways in the Pennsylvania coal fields augmented canal traffic and some of the north and south roads connecting with the Erie Canal served originally as branch lines for that canal. But far from acting primarily as feeders for canals, most of the early railroads provided alternative traffic routes. Thus the Boston and Lowell Railroad promptly sounded the death knell of the Middlesex Canal. The Boston and Worcester was a competitor of the Blackstone Canal and, when completed, the Providence and Worcester Railroad put this canal out of business. No stockholder of the Schuylkill Navigation could possibly have mistaken the Reading Railroad for a feeder line rather than a dangerous rival. The Baltimore and Ohio took business away from the Chesapeake and Ohio Canal, and the Charleston and Hamburg Railroad was designed to, and did to some extent, divert traffic from the lower Savannah River.

TECHNICAL ADVANCE

Both tracks and steam engines had reached a point of development in the late 1820's at which, although many difficulties remained, they could be successfully combined to form the first steam railroads. Experiments in the use of wooden beams and also of granite blocks as rails proved unsuccessful, and most early American railroads

[9] Based on statistics appearing in *Hunt's Merchants' Magazine*, XXV (September, 1851), 380–382. Data given in Poor, *Manual of Railroads, 1868*, are not quite as favorable to the railroads. For a convenient summary of these statistics see MacGill, *History of Transportation*, p. 573.

[10] Cf. Eliot Jones, *Principles of Railway Transportation* (New York: The Macmillan Company, 1924), p. 53; William Z. Ripley, *Railroads, Rates and Regulations* (New York: Longmans, Green and Co., 1912), p. 8; Kent T. Healy, "American Transportation before the War between the States," in Harold F. Williamson, ed., *The Growth of the American Economy* (New York: Prentice-Hall, Inc., 1944), p. 182.

adopted wooden rails often twenty to twenty-five feet long capped with an iron strap or bar. Though fairly suitable for the light horse-drawn cars on the tramways, these rails were never very satisfactory for the heavier locomotives and cars of the steam railroad. Consequently nearly every railroad management found itself under the repeated necessity of using heavier strap iron and firmer installations. The tendency of these iron straps to work loose and curl up under the weight of passing trains—of forming so-called "snake-heads" which might break through the floor of a passing coach—presented one of the serious hazards of early railroading. Robert L. Stevens, president and engineer of the Camden and Amboy Railroad, met this problem by designing the T rail. He ordered rails of this type made in England and installed them in 1831 as original equipment on his New Jersey railroad.[11] Because wood was cheap and abundant in America and iron relatively costly, the strap-iron type of construction continued to be used as late as the Civil War for roads equipped with comparatively light rolling stock. But as traffic increased and locomotives and cars grew steadily heavier, the T rail became standard equipment on the better American roads. In 1847 the state of New York required the installation of the T rail, but at least some of the strap iron then torn up was sold, to be reused on western roads then under construction.[12]

The roadbed also had to be improved to meet the needs of the steam railroad. Almost every conceivable expedient was used. A number of railroads, including the Boston and Lowell, the Mohawk and Hudson, and the Baltimore and Ohio, experimented with anchoring the rails to heavy granite blocks. Although regarded as indestructible, this construction proved especially susceptible to damage from frost heaves and was so lacking in resiliency as to prove seriously destructive to the rolling stock. In order to avoid grading the roadbed, a number of early roads were built on piles, but this method, though used with some success by the Charleston and Hamburg Railroad, was generally less satisfactory than granite blocks. The Erie is said to have spent about a million dollars in piling which was abandoned before it was placed in use. Gradually wooden sleepers firmly imbedded in gravel were found to provide the best support for the rails. Sometimes the two rails were laid on parallel logs or

[11] Lardner, *Railway Economy*, pp. 56–61, 335–336; Lane, *From Indian Trail to Iron Horse*, pp. 286–287; J. Elfreth Watkins, *The Camden and Amboy Railroad* (Washington: Gedney and Roberts, 1892), p. 29; Ringwalt, *Development of Transportation Systems in the United States*, pp. 83–86, 104.
[12] Overton, *Burlington West*, pp. 21–22.

beams, but the system of crossties, proving much superior, became accepted practice during the forties.[13]

The English adopted a gauge of 4 feet 8½ inches for their railroads, and the early lines in the United States which used British locomotives were necessarily built with that width. This peculiar gauge was that long customary for English wagons, and consequently the earlier tram lines had been built of proper gauge to fit them. But almost from the beginning, Americans began constructing their own railroad engines and experimenting with varying track widths. The resulting confusion of track widths added to the cost of rail shipment and long delayed the development of a unified railroad system. In New England the so-called "standard gauge," 4 feet 8½ inches, was generally adopted, and in the South the 5-foot gauge was common. Although most of the short lines in New York were of the standard gauge, the Erie Railroad deliberately chose 6 feet in order to prevent diversion of traffic over other lines, thus defeating itself, for in the long run this unusual construction proved a handicap, and the road was forced at great expense to change over to the standard gauge. Elsewhere there was great diversity, with Pennsylvania and Ohio leading in the so-called "war of gauges," for each had railroads representing seven different track widths. Progress toward a uniform system of track widths was slow before 1865. The publicly owned railways of Pennsylvania had been built with the standard gauge, and legislation adopted in 1852 required all lines in the state to conform to that system. But at the beginning of the Civil War there were still at least eleven different gauges in the North, and the 5-foot gauge was by no means universal in the South. Between Philadelphia and Charleston there were at least eight changes in width of track.[14]

The first American railroads were constructed before the problem of the most effective motive power had been solved. At first horses or mules were used, often with stationary engines and cables to lift the cars over the steepest inclines. Even sails and treadmills operated by horses were tried. But during the thirties the steam locomotives rapidly established their superiority, though early railroad engines were small, feeble in power, and so unreliable that horses had to be kept in reserve for emergencies and were often used exclusively dur-

[13] Lardner, *Railway Economy*, pp. 59–60; Ringwalt, *Development of Transportation Systems in the United States*, pp. 85–87; John W. Starr, Jr., *One Hundred Years of American Railroading* (New York: Dodd, Mead & Company, 1928), pp. 18–20.
[14] MacGill, *History of Transportation*, pp. 313–314, 565; Carl Russell Fish, "The Northern Railroads, April, 1861," *American Historical Review*, XXII, No. 4 (July, 1917), 785–786; Ringwalt, *Development of Transportation Systems in the United States*, p. 136.

ing the winter months. At first British locomotives were imported, but they were generally too heavy for the light rails and trestles of American roads and did not hold to the track well on the sharp curves characteristic of early American construction. But improvements came with great rapidity, many being made in the American locomotive shops which now sprang up rapidly, especially in the Middle Atlantic states. In addition to many improvements in the power plant itself, such as greatly increased steam pressures, many devices were adopted that perfected the operation of the engine upon the track. John B. Jervis, engineer for the Delaware and Hudson Company, used the swivel or bogie truck, which greatly helped in holding the locomotive to the track on sharp curves. It consisted of a set of forward wheels whose frame was connected by a kingbolt at the center of a crosspiece on the engine. This permitted the forward or guiding wheels to turn freely with the curvature of the track. Another major improvement, the equalizing beam, was invented (1839) by Joseph Harrison of Philadelphia. This device, by utilizing the principle of the lever, permitted an equalization of pressure on the drive wheels, despite unevenness in the track or the changing position of the engine. Other typical American developments were the cowcatcher, the sand box, and the enclosed cab.[15]

Because of the precedent of the turnpikes and canals it was anticipated that the first railroads might be public highways upon which shippers would pay toll for use of the rails and provide not only their own vehicles but also their own motive power.[16] But even though turnouts were provided at intervals, the plan of having traffic move more or less at will proved impracticable and, even with horse-drawn cars, sometimes disastrous. This led to the early belief that only double-track lines were feasible. But the whole matter was rather quickly solved by the rapid introduction of the steam locomotive. It soon became clear that the railroad company itself, unlike turnpikes and canal companies, must provide the necessary motive power and vehicles for passengers and freight.

Like the first automobiles, which slavishly followed the design of the horse-drawn carriage even to the inclusion of bolt holes for the whip socket, the early railroad passenger cars scrupulously copied the stagecoaches, including the elevated seat for the coachman. But both passenger and freight cars rapidly took on a more practical form

[15] Ringwalt, *Development of Transportation Systems in the United States*, pp. 94–99; Thurston, *A History of the Growth of the Steam-Engine*, p. 219.
[16] Ringwalt, *Development of Transportation Systems in the United States*, pp. 91–92.

and, though much smaller than those in use later, soon approximated their modern appearance. The hazards from flying sparks were somewhat reduced by the invention of the "spark arrester" and by the gradual substitution of coal for wood as fuel. The danger of accidents was decreased by fences on the right of way, heavier rails, improved wheels, and, finally, the telegraphic dispatching of trains. But until after 1860 brakes continued to be manually operated, link and pin couplings were used, and adequate springs were lacking. Luxurious railroad travel was a development of the future. Still a beginning was being made, for in 1836 the Cumberland Valley Railroad introduced a crude sleeping car, the forerunner of the Pullman, and the Camden and Amboy Railroad in 1840 anticipated the chair car by equipping two deluxe coaches with that great American institution, the rocking chair.[17]

RAPID SPREAD OF THE RAILWAY NET

Despite the generally depressed condition of business during the early forties, railroad construction continued at a rapid pace. Total mileage, which stood at 3,328 in 1840, reached 8,879 in another ten years. Nearly three fifths of this new mileage was added in New England and New York, where the railroad map rapidly assumed modern outlines. By the early fifties, New England, excluding Maine, was crosshatched with railroads. No similar area was so well supplied with rail transportation, and for a brief season Boston enjoyed the distinction of being the greatest railroad center in the United States. Lines radiating from that city connected it with Portland, Maine, Montreal, Albany, and New York.

The period was also one of tremendous building activity in New York, which, with new construction of 956 miles, led all the states. By 1851 two lines spanned the state connecting New York City with Lake Erie. The series of short lines from Buffalo to Albany, which had been completed in 1842, was now extended from Albany to New York to form the ultimate New York Central route. In the same year the Erie was completed through the southern counties of the state to give a second railroad to the West. This, the longest road in the country under single ownership, accounted for about half the total increase in mileage for the state during the forties. Elsewhere progress was less rapid. Little building occurred in the South except in

[17] Slason Thompson, *A Short History of American Railways* (New York: D. Appleton and Company, 1925), p. 141; Lane, *From Indian Trail to Iron Horse*, pp. 291–292.

Georgia, where about 450 miles were added, so that by 1851 Savannah was connected with Chattanooga, Tennessee. Although the great period of railroad building in the West was still to come, a substantial beginning was made by the completion of a line across Ohio from Cincinnati to Sandusky. Two lines were begun in southern Michigan which, when completed in the next decade, formed important links in direct rail routes between New York and Chicago.

New railroad mileage, especially in New England and New York, grew rapidly during the forties. But in the generally prosperous fifties, and especially to 1857, a tremendous further acceleration took place. Mileage soared from 8,879 in 1850 to 30,626 in 1860, to register an increase about four times that achieved during the previous ten-year period. The most striking advance now came in the West, where Ohio, Illinois, and Indiana experienced a railroad boom such that by 1860 Ohio and Illinois were the leading states in railroad mileage and Indiana was not far behind. In the South rapid main-line extensions were made, though the network of lines was less dense than that north of the Ohio River. In the Middle Atlantic states growth was more moderate, although Pennsylvania, which had lagged, now constructed nearly 1,700 miles. Finally, gains were least in New England, where the major lines had already been built.

The fifties were also notable as marking the beginning of the strong tendency toward the combination of short lines into larger systems, a movement which has long persisted. A few relatively long roads like the Erie, the Baltimore and Ohio, and the Illinois Central had been constructed by a single company. But for the most part, the railroads of the country were local affairs built as short lines under independent management. Thus seven different companies owned segments of the line from Albany to Buffalo. These were combined in 1853 to form the nucleus of what is now the New York Central. The Pennsylvania also became a unified system from Philadelphia to Pittsburgh. During the decade, twenty railroad combinations took place in Ohio through lease, sale, or consolidation.[18]

Though many short lines were combined during the fifties, hardly more than a beginning was made. No New York to Chicago system under unified management existed before 1860. Not until 1868 did the Boston and Albany Railroad bring the route between those two cities into a single system. The four independent companies owning parts of the original shore line from Boston to New York were not merged under one management until 1893, when the New York, New

[18] Gephart, *Transportation and Industrial Development in the Middle West*, p. 178.

Haven and Hartford finally acquired the Boston and Providence.[19]

By 1860 the railroad net east of the Mississippi approximated its present pattern, although, of course, many details were still to be added, and blank spaces, especially in the extreme North and South remained to be filled in. A few lines were pushing westward beyond the Mississippi, and one, the Hannibal and St. Joseph, had already tapped the Missouri at the latter city. Chicago, with eleven major railroads, had assumed her place as the greatest railroad center in the world. All of the major market cities of the North had been tied together by rail lines. Four rail routes permitted through shipment across the Appalachian barrier to the Old Northwest, where connections were available leading to Chicago and St. Louis. Farther south both Charleston and Savannah were connected by way of Chattanooga with Memphis on the Mississippi. On the other hand, the usual railroad map of 1860 gives too strong an impression of a really integrated railroad system. It must be remembered that there were still many independent lines (more than 300 in 1860), a variety of gauges hindered the exchange of rolling stock, and finally, many connecting links were still lacking. Only at Bowling Green, Kentucky, did northern railroads make actual physical connection with those of the South.

The suggestion of a transcontinental railroad had been made at least as early as 1820, and as railroad-building technique improved and the West Coast was added to the national territory, more and more people became convinced of the feasibility and desirability of such a project. By the last decade of this study the issue became an important one in Congress, where a southern route was favored by the South and a more northern one by the North. A deadlock ensued, not to be broken until after the southern states had seceded from the Union.

THE STATE CHARTERS

The early craze in the United States for railroad building, as well as for turnpikes and canals, cannot be understood if it is thought of only in terms of eager investors seeking large direct returns from such investments, although indeed this eagerness was sometimes a factor. It is the peculiarity of any great improvement in transporta-

[19] Alvin F. Harlow, *Steelways of New England* (New York: Creative Age Press, 1946), p. 194. For detailed statistics on railroad construction by states and by individual companies see: "Report on the Physical Characteristics of the Railroads . . . ," *Tenth Census of the United States: Transportation*, IV, 299–651.

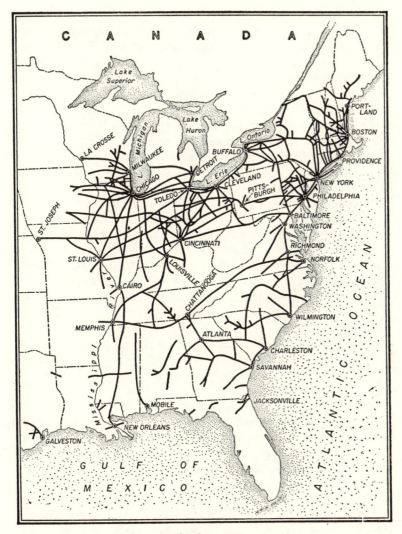

Railroads in 1860

This map provides a general view of the railroad net in 1860 but is not always reliable in details. It follows, for the most part, plate 139B in Charles O. Paullin, *Atlas of the Historical Geography of the United States* (Washington: Carnegie Institution of Washington, 1932), which is perhaps the best for this date. A really satisfactory railroad map for 1860 would require research for each individual railroad, the adoption of a uniform definition for railroads which were *completed,* or *in operation,* and a clear indication of the gauge of each piece of track.

tion that it may bring tremendous indirect benefits, that the multiplier effect of a relatively small investment in a railroad may have the result of greatly increasing the productivity of a whole area. The incidence of these gains varies depending upon circumstances, but in general farmers, manufacturers, and mine owners receive higher prices, consumers get more for their money, real-estate values mount, favorably located middlemen and bankers augment their profits, and government revenues rise. The community gains, the advantages resulting to those who were not actually investors, often greatly exceeded those which accrued to stockholders. This accounts in considerable part, at least, for the enthusiastic support which was given to state railroad ventures and to grants of public aid for railroad building, whether by federal, state, or local governments.

Had ample private capital been forthcoming, public grants might not have been thought advisable or necessary. But the private capital needed to build 30,000 miles of railroad was simply not forthcoming between 1830 and 1860. The help of governmental agencies, national, state, and local, plus substantial private investments, was needed to do the job. So much attention has been given to the lavish grants of land to railroads by the federal government after 1850 that the major role of state and local aid has been obscured. The state governments contributed to the rapid growth of the railroad net (1) by putting liberal provisions in railroad charters, (2) by actually building railroads, and (3) by supplying needed money and credit for private construction.

Because of the huge amount of capital needed and the risks involved, most American railroads were organized as corporations. Charters had, therefore, to be secured from the state legislatures. Though considerable popular suspicion of the corporate form as being a monopolistic device prevailed, especially in rural districts, this prejudice was generally subordinated to the rage for internal improvements and the necessity for chartering bridge, turnpike, and canal companies. It is true that when railroads were first built, the state legislatures tended to impose restrictions similar to those placed upon turnpikes and canals. Following English precedent, legislatures often reserved the right to purchase the road from the owners under specified conditions and to limit fares or dividends. Neither of these restrictions proved important. Limitations on railroad charges were usually so generously drawn as to impose no burden or, as in Ohio, were simply ignored. An exception was the provision in the charter of the Camden and Amboy Railroad, limiting freight rates to eight cents a ton-mile. The company exceeded this level and, in at least one case, was ordered to refund overcharges.[20] Dividend limitations were rendered generally ineffective by the issuance of stock dividends. In Massachusetts, where such dividends were prohibited, large corporate surpluses were built up and ultraconservative policies were adopted in order to avoid contributions to the state treasury.

Most of the charters granted sweeping privileges of eminent domain and, especially as the period advanced, freedom from restraints as to the form and amount of securities issued. Beyond this, special privileges of many kinds were often added. Despite the public suspicion of monopoly, a number of states (e.g., Massachusetts, New Jersey, South Carolina, Georgia, Kentucky, and Louisiana) granted monopoly privileges in certain railroad charters. Most notorious of these was that given by the New Jersey legislature to the Camden and Amboy Railroad by which this line obtained exclusive rail transportation rights between New York and Philadelphia.[21] Many charters exempted railroads from taxation in whole or in part. Exemption from property taxes in perpetuity was granted by Virginia to the Richmond, Fredericksburg and Potomac Railroad Company. More common was the imposition of a time limit on such exemption, as in the case of the Vermont Central, whose charter gave complete freedom from state taxation for ten years. Sometimes taxes were not to be imposed unless earnings exceeded a specified percentage on investment. Even where railroad charters specifically authorized taxation, the desire to encourage was so great that often no taxes were imposed. In Ohio the general property of railroads was not taxed until 1852, and then not effectively until the Civil War period. All this resulted in a very appreciable subsidy to the railroads.[22]

As in the case of canals, the railroads were sometimes given lottery or banking privileges. The former permitted the collection of capital from even the smallest savers, and the latter the creation of the money necessary to pay laborers, contractors, and suppliers. The great day of the lottery was over, but as late as 1833 two railroads, one in North Carolina and one in Missouri, were permitted to raise

[20] Lane, *From Indian Trail to Iron Horse*, pp. 297–299; Gephart, *Transportation and Industrial Development in the Middle West*, p. 122.

[21] Cleveland and Powell, *Railroad Promotion and Capitalization in the United States*, pp. 164–167; Lane, *From Indian Trail to Iron Horse*, p. 285; MacGill, *History of Transportation*, pp. 229–230.

[22] Cleveland and Powell, *Railroad Promotion and Capitalization in the United States*, pp. 176–178; Gephart, *Transportation and Industrial Development in the Middle West*, pp. 195–196; Federal Coordinator of Transportation, *Public Aids to Transportation* (Washington: Government Printing Office, 1938), II, 61–62.

funds by this means.[23] Many railroad banks were chartered during the thirties, especially in the West and South, although at least one was established in the East, the Quinebaug, chartered by Connecticut to aid the Boston, Norwich, and New London Railroad. Though some of the railroad banks, notably those in Georgia, provided substantial help in financing railroad construction, others did little more than foster wildcat banking. Finally, states sometimes required banks to purchase railroad stock as one of the prerequisites for receiving a charter.[24]

RAILROADS BUILT BY THE STATES

At the beginning of the railroad era, a few states built and owned their own railroads. Early agitation for railroads in Massachusetts was coupled with the proposal that the state should supply the capital. Though strongly supported by Boston interests, this was defeated in 1830 not primarily because of opposition to the principle of state ownership, but because those communities not on the line of the proposed railroad withheld their approval.[25] As New York and Ohio spent tremendous sums on state canals, it is not surprising that their legislatures were reluctant to embark on the building of railroads which might provide serious competition to state-owned public works already completed or projected. On the other hand, Pennsylvania built two short railroads, the Portage Railroad and the Philadelphia and Columbia, as necessary supplements to her great system of canals. When the canal system was abandoned, both lines were sold to the Pennsylvania Railroad.

In the South, Georgia and Virginia successfully built railroads when private capital was not forthcoming. In Georgia, the building of the Western and Atlantic was authorized in 1836 and completed from Atlanta to Chattanooga in 1851. Owned and operated by the state, this railroad was managed with moderate success during the ante-bellum period. Concerning this road Ulrich B. Phillips says: "Had private capital been depended upon, not only would the building of the road have been long delayed, but the whole railway development of Georgia would have been stunted and largely deprived of its success, and the general economic progress of that and

---

[23] Cleveland and Powell, *Railroad Promotion and Capitalization in the United States*, p. 167.

[24] Federal Coordinator of Transportation, *Public Aids to Transportation*, II, 64; Cleveland and Powell, *Railroad Promotion and Capitalization in the United States*, pp. 167–176; MacGill, *History of Transportation*, pp. 559–563.

[25] Kirkland, "The 'Railroad Scheme' of Massachusetts," pp. 151–160.

neighboring states would have been slackened." [26] In Virginia, private capital was lacking to construct a railroad across the Blue Ridge which would provide a connection to the West. Seventeen miles of very difficult mountain construction were completed by the state in the decade before the Civil War and then leased to the Virginia Central Railroad. An extension to the Ohio River, begun in 1855, was not yet completed when the war broke out.[27]

In the Northwest, three state governments pioneered in the building of railroads, but all disposed of their projects to private companies when hard times came in the early forties. After private ventures had failed, Michigan in 1837 began an ambitious program of state railroad construction in which it was planned to span the state with three lines. By 1846, the two most southern, the Michigan Central and the Michigan Southern, were in operation though not completed. Before work had gone very far the northern line was converted into a wagon road. In financial difficulties, the state disposed of all railroad properties.[28] In 1834 and 1836, Indiana made an appropriation for a railroad from Madison to Lafayette as part of her gigantic scheme for internal improvements. More than $1,600,000 had been spent on this road by 1843, when the state, its credit ruined, turned the road over to the Madison and Indianapolis Railroad Company. Completed between the two cities named in 1847, this was the first railroad in the state of Indiana. The earliest railroad construction in Illinois also came in connection with an ambitious plan for internal improvements. As a result of appropriations made in 1837 and 1838, a number of lines were begun, but financial difficulties following the crises of 1837 and 1839 forced the state to dispose of these properties to private companies.[29]

Troy, New York, with a population of less than 20,000, pioneered in the field of municipal ownership. Determined to best her commercial rival, Albany, this Hudson River city raised approximately

[26] Phillips, *Transportation in Eastern Cotton Belt*, p. 334. See also by the same author "An American State-Owned Railroad," *Yale Review*, XV (November, 1906), 259–282.

[27] Cleveland and Powell, *Railroad Promotion and Capitalization in the United States*, p. 108; Hannah Emily Keith, "An Historical Sketch of Internal Improvements in Michigan 1836–1846," *Publications of the Michigan Political Science Association*, Vol. IV, No. 1 (July, 1900), *passim.*

[28] Henry Greenleaf Pearson, *An American Railroad Builder: John Murray Forbes* (Boston: Houghton Mifflin Company, 1911), *passim;* MacGill, *History of Transportation*, pp. 503–504.

[29] MacGill, *History of Transportation*, pp. 506–510; Paul Wallace Gates, *The Illinois Central Rail-road and Its Colonization Work* (Vol. XLII of *Harvard Economic Studies*, Cambridge: Harvard University Press, 1934), pp. 22–26.

$600,000 through bond issues and, with the help of a $100,000 loan from the state, completed the twenty-mile-long Schenectady and Troy Railroad in 1842.[30]

STATE AND LOCAL AID

But much more important than special charter privileges or direct ownership was the tremendous financial aid given to private railroad companies by states and local governments. A census report concludes that in 1838, state debts totaling nearly $43,000,000 were attributable to railroads.[31] A student of American state debts finds that in the fifteen years before the Civil War, a group of states, including those whose credit was relatively good "borrowed more than $90,000,000, mainly to finance railroad construction." [32] As for local and municipal contributions, William Z. Ripley believes they totaled more than those of the states, and that by 1870 they equaled at least one fifth of the construction costs of the railroads then in existence. In the southern states up to 1860 more than 55 per cent of railroad capital came from state and local authorities and a very appreciable part of the help from private sources took the form of goods and services.[33]

The character of the state and local subventions is best shown by citing a few actual cases. Even in New England, where private capital was most abundant, Massachusetts gave substantial public assistance. By the time of its completion in 1841, the Western Railroad of this state had received $4,600,000 from the legislature, $600,000 of this being an investment in the stock of the company and the remainder a secured loan. Of the total capital funds used to complete this railroad, the state provided 70 per cent. Later, in 1854, the Massachusetts legislature, in order to secure a second line westward across the state, granted $2,000,000. This route, which involved building the Hoosac Tunnel, cost the state many more millions before its completion in 1875. The Western Railroad of Massachusetts was linked with Albany in 1842 by the Albany and West Stockbridge Railroad Company. In order to make possible the building of this line the city

---

[30] Stevens, *The Beginnings of the New York Central Railroad*, pp. 238–248; David Maldwyn Ellis, *Landlords and Farmers in the Hudson-Mohawk Region, 1790–1850* (Ithaca: Cornell University Press, 1946), p. 177.

[31] *Tenth Census of the United States: Valuation, Taxation and Public Indebtedness*, VII, 526.

[32] Ratchford, *American State Debts*, p. 134.

[33] Ripley, *Railroads, Rates and Regulations*, pp. 38–39; Milton S. Heath, "Public Railroad Construction and the Development of Private Enterprise in the South before 1861," *Tasks of Economic History*, Supplement X (1950), 43, 52.

of Albany issued $1,000,000 of municipal bonds, which were exchanged for stock of the Albany and West Stockbridge.[34]

The state of New York, which issued bonds totaling $3,000,000 to subsidize the Erie Railroad,[35] had advanced a little more than $9,000,000 to ten railroad companies by 1846. An amendment to the constitution of the state of New York in that year forbade further grants. But gifts to railroad projects by towns and cities increased greatly so that by 1879 they totaled nearly $30,000,000.[36] In Pennsylvania, city and county investment in railroads between 1840 and 1853 amounted to about $14,000,000.[37] In Maryland, the city of Baltimore provided much of the early capital for the Baltimore and Ohio Railroad, and throughout the South most railroad construction was heavily financed by state or local governments, or both.[38] Virginia was one of the more generous, having early agreed to take three fifths of the stock of railroads as soon as the other two fifths had been subscribed. By the opening of the Civil War, this state had furnished the railroads with more than $21,000,000, and additional contributions had been made by many localities.[39] By the same date, the part of the North Carolina state debt arising from subventions to railroads exceeded $9,000,000.[40]

No section of the country surpassed the West in enthusiasm for railroads. Believing that they were the key to prosperity, states and localities made lavish contributions. It is true that the state governments in what was formerly the Northwest Territory had so weakened their credit by banking excesses and grandiose schemes for internal improvements that their aid, with the exception of their early

[34] Kistler, "The Rise of Railroads in the Connecticut River Valley," pp. 153–155, 250; MacGill, *History of Transportation*, pp. 328–331; *Tenth Census of the United States: Valuation, Taxation and Public Indebtedness*, VII, 533; Edward C. Kirkland, "The Hoosac Tunnel Route: The Great Bore," *New England Quarterly*, XX (March, 1947), 96.

[35] MacGill, *History of Transportation*, p. 371.

[36] Frank L. McVey, "State Aid to New York Railways," *Social Economist*, VII (August, 1894), 104–106.

[37] Sharpless *et al. v.* Mayor of Philadelphia, 21 Pa. St. Rep. 147, 158 (1853), cited by J. Alton Burdine, "Governmental Regulation of Industry in Pennsylvania, 1776–1860" (unpublished thesis, Harvard University, 1939), p. 123.

[38] Cleveland and Powell, *Railroad Promotion and Capitalization in the United States*, pp. 205–206, 212–226.

[39] *Ibid.*, pp. 205, 213–214. See also Carter Goodrich, "The Virginia System of Mixed Enterprise: A Study of State Planning of Internal Improvements," *Political Science Quarterly*, LXIV (September, 1949), *passim*.

[40] Ratchford, *American State Debts*, p. 126; for the detailed story for this state, see Cecil Kenneth Brown, *A State Movement in Railroad Development* (Chapel Hill: The University of North Carolina Press, 1928). For the South in general, see R. S. Cotterill, "Southern Railroads, 1850–1860," *Mississippi Valley Historical Review*, X, No. 4 (March, 1924), 396–405.

ventures in state railroad construction, was relatively small. Still, it may be noted that Ohio invested over $700,000 in railroad stocks between 1837 and 1840.[41] The new states farther west had no such cramping restraint on their largesse, and Missouri and Minnesota made tremendous grants. To 1857, Missouri authorized loans of nearly $25,000,000 to seven railroad companies, and Minnesota marked her first year of statehood, 1858, by amending her constitution so that she could lend $5,000,000 to four railroads.[42] By 1860, Texas had lent nearly $2,000,000 and given about five million acres of state lands to encourage railroad building in her boundaries.[43]

As in the East and South, counties, cities, and towns also poured money into railroad treasuries. This was especially true in states whose constitutions forbade or limited state grants to private companies, as in Iowa, Wisconsin, and, after 1848, Illinois. To encourage railroad building, local governments in Iowa built up an indebtedness exceeding $7,000,000 by 1856.[44] The city of Milwaukee, Wisconsin, though having a population of only 45,246 in 1860, had lent $1,614,-000 to railroad companies two years earlier.[45] Capital contributions by localities sometimes took the form of outright donations often supplemented by gifts of land for railway stations and yards and of materials, such as stone and timber.[46] Not infrequently individuals living along the route of the new railroad made direct gifts of land and material.[47]

FEDERAL SUBSIDIES

Preceding the period of land grants, federal aid to railroads took two forms. First, many early railroad surveys were made by federal engineers at government expense under a law passed in 1824 and repealed in 1838.[48] Both the Baltimore and Ohio and the Charleston

[41] Cleveland and Powell, *Railroad Promotion and Capitalization in the United States*, p. 217.

[42] *Tenth Census of the United States: Valuation, Taxation, and Public Indebtedness*, VII, 632–635.

[43] Reed, *A History of the Texas Railroads*, p. 124; Robert Edgar Riegel, *The Story of the Western Railroads* (New York: The Macmillan Company, 1926), pp. 57–59.

[44] Cleveland and Powell, *Railroad Promotion and Capitalization in the United States*, p. 205.

[45] Laurence Marcellus Larson, *A Financial and Administrative History of Milwaukee* (University of Wisconsin, *Bulletin* No. 242, *Economics and Political Science Series*, IV, No. 2, Madison: 1908), pp. 74–75.

[46] Cleveland and Powell, *Railroad Promotion and Capitalization in the United States*, pp. 200, 210.

[47] See, for example, Samuel Melanchthon Derrick, *Centennial History of South Carolina Railroad* (Columbia: The State Company, 1930), pp. 35–38.

[48] 4 *U.S. Statutes at Large*, p. 22; 5 *U.S. Statutes at Large*, p. 260.

and Hamburg benefited from such surveys. The records indicate that at least sixty-one railroad surveys were made by government engineers at a total cost estimated at $75,000. As trained engineers were still very scarce in this country, the government rendered a uniquely valuable service by making its experts available for such surveys.[49]

More important in monetary terms was the provision made by Congress, 1830–1843, for reduction of the tariff duties on iron used in railroad construction. This resulted in a saving to the railroads of almost $6,000,000. Whether this be regarded as a public "grant" or "donation" to the railroads, or as the remittance of a burdensome tax, there can be no question of the marked help it gave to the railroads. However, this heavy charge on railroad construction was revived after March 3, 1843, at the behest of the manufacturers in order to subsidize the domestic manufacture of railroad iron.[50]

During the three decades of railroad history before 1860, Congress was, from time to time, under considerable pressure to grant funds and lands to aid in railroad construction. But no loans were voted and until 1850 no significant federal land grants were made for railroad construction. While the debates in Congress, as in the earlier controversies over aid to internal improvements, continued to be largely in terms of constitutional interpretation, the votes taken reflected sectional jealousies and economic interests. The Northeast and South were generally, though by no means unanimously, opposed. The new states in the West, seriously lacking local capital for railroad construction but having (except for Texas) large tracts of unsettled federal domain within their borders, strongly urged that such lands be used to accelerate railroad building. At first, and as long as such proposals were for small projects directly affecting only one or two states, the opposition in Congress from eastern and southern states proved sufficient to block favorable action. Finally, in 1850, southern and western states combined to urge grants for a north and south railroad, extending from northern Illinois to Mobile, Alabama. Representatives from western and Gulf states could not, by themselves, muster enough votes, but with considerable eastern support, the bill became a law. New York and Boston capitalists saw a

[49] Lewis Henry Haney, *A Congressional History of Railways in the United States to 1850* (University of Wisconsin, *Bulletin* No. 211, *Economics and Political Science Series*, III, Madison: 1903), pp. 275–288; Federal Coordinator of Transportation, *Public Aids to Transportation* (4 vols., Washington: Government Printing Office, 1938–1940), II, 4–5.

[50] See Haney, *A Congressional History of Railways in the United States to 1850*, pp. 298–317; *Public Aids to Transportation*, II, 5.

real advantage in the building of such a line. Railroads in which they had heavy investments were pushing into Chicago and would be given valuable connections. Moreover, the large investments which many of them had made in Illinois land, as well as in Illinois state bonds would, they believed, appreciate in value.[51]

The act, as passed September 20, 1850, provided that the states of Illinois, Mississippi, and Alabama should receive federal lands lying within their boundaries for the construction of a railroad to extend from La Salle on the Illinois and Michigan Canal to Cairo in Illinois, across Kentucky and Tennessee, and through Mississippi and Alabama to Mobile. Branches were to be built in Illinois to East Dubuque (then called Dunleith) and Chicago. Illinois, Alabama, and Mississippi passed these lands on to the railroads. The grant consisted of a two-hundred-foot right of way and alternate even sections of land on each side of the road for a depth of six miles. If lands so granted had already been taken up, the railroad could take other lands within fifteen miles of the road. It was provided that the railroads constructed under this grant should transport the property or troops of the United States "free from any toll or other charge" and that Congress should fix the rates at which the mails should be carried.[52] Substantially, this pattern was followed in other grants made previous to the Civil War.

This subsidy totaled 3,736,005 acres and made capital available for the rapid building of the railroads. In 1857, one year after the Illinois Central had been completed, its total cost for construction and equipment was $23,436,668. The money came largely from mortgages secured by railroad properties, chiefly federal lands. Less than one sixth was contributed by stockholders.[53]

Though the grant of 1850 was regarded at the time as a special case, inevitably it set a precedent, and Congress was flooded with bills designed to appropriate tremendous sections of the public domain to aid railroad construction. Most failed of passage; nevertheless, important bills passed in 1852, 1853, 1856, and 1857 granted land to ten states, benefiting approximately forty-five railroads. These grants totaled around eighteen million acres. Large in an absolute sense, they were relatively small as compared with the tremendous acreage subsequently given directly by Congress to the transcontinental railroads.[54]

[51] Gates, *The Illinois Central Rail-road and Its Colonization Work*, pp. 34–41.
[52] *Public Aids to Transportation*, II, 11.
[53] *Ibid.*, 12.
[54] Computed from Thomas Donaldson, *The Public Domain*, 1883, *House Miscellaneous Document No. 45*, Pt. 4, 47 Cong., 2 Sess., pp. 274–277.

PRIVATE CAPITAL

Although public agencies provided a substantial share of railroad capital during the period covered by this study, the role of the private investors was also important. As with the turnpike companies, many of the early railroads secured most of their private capital from merchants, small manufacturers, farmers, and professional men living along the proposed route of the new railroad. These investors bought stock in the hope that land values would rise and general business prosperity result from improved transportation, not for the most part because they sought safe or profitable investment for their small savings. This was especially true of many of the early short lines built in the East, which at the time did not seem to promise clear advantage to any of the few large cities in the country. Thus, the Auburn and Rochester Railroad Company, chartered in 1836, appears to have been financed almost exclusively by small investors living in the towns, villages, and farms along its route.[55] In Massachusetts, farmers contributed substantially to the building of the Greenfield and Northampton Railroad. Capital for the New London, Willimantic and Palmer Railroad came largely from New London businessmen who had made fortunes in whaling. Aid from city capitalists sometimes was contingent upon local stock purchases. Citizens of the little town of Amherst, Massachusetts, invested heavily in the Amherst and Belchertown Railroad on the promise of aid from New London interests.[56] Private capital for southern railroads, especially the smaller and more remote lines, came largely from small local investors whose interest was nonspeculative and indirect.[57]

In the West also the earliest roads were often but short affairs. Unable to attract eastern capital, they depended upon the limited accumulations of local residents, including those of small farmers and artisans.[58] Even when eastern promoters came in and built longer lines, great pressure was exerted to get help from persons living along the projected railroad, including those who had little or no liquid capital. Farmers, hopeful of the benefits to be derived from cheapened transportation, were persuaded to accept railroad stock in exchange for mortgages on their farms. These mortgages, sold in

[55] Stevens, *The Beginnings of the New York Central Railroad*, p. 184.
[56] Kistler, "The Rise of Railroads in the Connecticut Valley," pp. 74–79, 124–126; Charles G. Woodward, *The New London, Willimantic & Palmer Railroad Company* (Hartford, Conn.: The Case, Lockwood, and Brainard Company, 1942), pp. 3 ff.
[57] Phillips, *Transportation in Eastern Cotton Belt*, p. 387.
[58] Pierce, *A History of Chicago*, I, 116–118. See especially p. 118, fn. 224.

eastern markets by the railroads, provided money for construction expenses. From 1850 through 1857 Wisconsin farmers mortgaged their property for between $4,500,000 and $5,000,000 in order to supply capital for railroad building.[59]

But most of the available capital funds in private hands was to be found in the eastern seaport cities. Here again the lure of the indirect benefits to be gained provided the chief attraction for capital. Moreover, interest in such investment was greatly heightened by the bitter rivalry of the chief ports for what each regarded as its fair share of the commerce of the interior. The leading business and professional men of each city were bound together in a community of interest, in city-states not unlike those of ancient Greece in which the desire for the benefits of commercial growth and prosperity, reinforced by civic pride and local patriotism, led to long and bitter warfare. These intercity struggles, already a factor in the rapid expansion of canals, now became greatly intensified, for railroads could be built where, because of physiographic conditions, canals could not. So it became the object of each city to build railroads which would gather up the trade of the back country and funnel it to its own wharves and warehouses.

Thus there developed a sort of metropolitan mercantilism in which railroads, rather than merchant fleets, were the chief weapons of warfare. City-states could hardly be expected to provide the needed capital for their rivals; so to a very large extent each community had to build its railroads from its own resources. The Baltimore and Ohio Railroad was a Baltimore project toward which leading Baltimore merchants made the chief contributions of private capital. Their purpose was, as indicated in a call to one of their meetings, to secure "the best means of restoring to the city of Baltimore that portion of the western trade which has recently been diverted from it. . . ."[60] The Charleston and Hamburg Railroad was promoted by the Chamber of Commerce of Charleston, financed by its leading merchants, and designed to take the business of the back country away from Savannah.[61] Likewise, Boston capital provided the main support of the early New England railroads, but only for those which led to Boston. Lines which benefited New London or New Haven had to seek capital in those cities. New York competition was so feared that

[59] Merk, *Economic History of Wisconsin during the Civil War Decade*, pp. 241–243; see also Robert E. Riegel, "Trans-Mississippi Railroads during the Fifties," *Mississippi Valley Historical Review*, X, No. 2 (September, 1923), 156–157.

[60] Edward Hungerford, *The Story of the Baltimore & Ohio Railroad, 1827–1927* (2 vols., New York: G. P. Putnam's Sons, 1928), I, 19.

[61] Derrick, *Centennial History of South Carolina Railroad*, pp. 15–23.

when badly needed funds for the Western Railroad were offered by New York capitalists, they were refused.[62] Rivalries of interior cities were no less bitter, and they, too, put their resources into improved transportation developments in order to gain a competitive advantage.[63]

Owners of manufacturing establishments and coal lands frequently promoted and financed railroads which would enhance the value of their holdings. Cotton textile manufacturers took most of the stock in the Boston and Lowell Railroad, and Boston and Springfield capitalists interested in the growing textile center at Chicopee Falls, Massachusetts, backed the Western and the Northampton and Springfield railroads.[64] The Delaware, Lackawanna and Western Railroad was promoted and financed in considerable part by the Scrantons, who sought markets for the products of their iron foundry.[65] Most of the anthracite railroads were financed, in part at least, by holders of coal lands who thus sought to increase the value of their property. Stephen Girard, who had invested in Lehigh coal property, sank $200,000 in the ill-fated Pottsville and Danville Railroad, which was designed to provide an outlet for the coal of that area.[66]

Of course, some capital for railroad building was available also from those who were interested primarily in the return on their investment, in speculation, or in control. Philadelphia, Boston, New York, and London were the chief sources of such funds. One of the first railroads, the little Mohawk and Hudson, was financed chiefly by wealthy New Yorkers who listed it on the New York Stock Exchange in 1830.[67] The New York money market provided at least some of the funds for building the early New Jersey railroads as well as the anthracite roads of Pennsylvania. New England and New York capital, helped to build the New Jersey Railroad. Both Philadelphia and New York banking houses were interested in the Philadelphia and Reading. The second Bank of the United States

[62] Kistler, "The Rise of Railroads in the Connecticut Valley," pp. 84–105.

[63] See, for example, Ambler, A History of Transportation in the Ohio Valley, pp. 211–238; Cleveland and Powell, Railroad Promotion and Capitalization in the United States, pp. 128–132; R. S. Cotterill, "The Beginnings of Railroads in the Southwest," Mississippi Valley Historical Review, VIII, No. 4 (March, 1922), 318–326.

[64] Adams, "The Canal and Railroad Enterprise of Boston," p. 126; Kistler, "The Rise of Railroads in the Connecticut River Valley," pp. 93–103.

[65] Bogen, The Anthracite Railroads, pp. 80–81.

[66] Ibid., p. 14.

[67] Stevens, The Beginnings of the New York Central Railroad, pp. 24–25, 108–109; Margaret G. Myers, Origins and Development (Vol. I of The New York Money Market, 4 vols., New York: Columbia University Press, 1931), pp. 32–33; referred to hereafter as Myers, The New York Money Market, Vol. I.

ned in 1841 nearly one fourth of the stock of this railroad.[68]

But until the end of the second decade of railroad construction only a small part of railroad capital came from the financial districts of the eastern cities.[69] At that time, State Street in Boston and Wall Street in New York began to play a more important role, especially in connection with the construction of western lines. Thus when the state of Michigan disposed of its two partially completed railroads in 1846, Boston interests financed the Michigan Central and New Yorkers the Michigan Southern.[70] Similarly the Illinois Central was managed by eastern promoters and was financed in part by funds raised in the eastern states and abroad.[71] The financial districts of Boston and New York absorbed some railroad paper themselves, often for purposes of control, but chiefly they were intermediaries selling to investors in the East and abroad railroad securities or the western farm mortgages and municipal bonds which railroad companies had received as donations or in exchange for their stock. But the New York Stock Exchange does not appear to have played an important role in providing capital for early railroad construction. Only a small proportion of railroad stocks were even listed before 1860, and among these, leading roads such as the Pennsylvania and the Baltimore and Ohio, do not appear.[72]

American railroad securities found at least a limited sale in London before 1850, and the bonds of American states marketed abroad helped to provide capital for railroad financing. During the early fifties, British investments in American railroad securities, especially bonds, increased rapidly so that by 1853, of the total American railroad bonds outstanding, 26 per cent were foreign-owned. Railroad stocks, valued at something less than twice the figure for bonds, were only 3 per cent foreign-owned.[73] But stockownership abroad was highly concentrated in a few lines, and before the decade was over such roads as the Philadelphia and Reading and the Illinois Central were controlled by British interests.[74]

[68] Lane, *From Indian Trail to Iron Horse*, pp. 306–313; Bogen, *The Anthracite Railroads*, pp. 23–27.
[69] Cf. Winthrop M. Daniels, *American Railroads: Four Phases of Their History* (Princeton: Princeton University Press, 1932), p. 7.
[70] Pearson, *An American Railroad Builder: John Murray Forbes*, pp. 25–30, 42–43.
[71] Gates, *The Illinois Central Rail-road and Its Colonization Work*, pp. 66–83.
[72] John T. Flynn, *Security Speculation: Its Economic Effects* (New York: Harcourt, Brace and Company, 1934), pp. 90–96; Daniels, *American Railroads: Four Phases of Their History*, pp. 7–8; Myers, *The New York Money Market*, I, 34–37.
[73] Myers, *The New York Money Market*, I, 34–37; Daniels, *American Railroads: Four Phases of Their History*, pp. 7–8.
[74] Bogen, *The Anthracite Railroads*, pp. 25, 43; Gates, *The Illinois Central Railroad and Its Colonization Work*, p. 76.

In the 1850's, railroad finance began to assume the form which characterized it during the following decades. Railroad bond issues became increasingly important and were marketed chiefly through eastern financial institutions. Stocks, though still disposed of to local interests seeking the advantages of improved transportation, were issued in increasing amounts to construction companies and tended to gravitate into the hands of railroad magnates and promoters who used them for purposes of speculation and control.

Though, as always, many railroads continued to be honestly built and conservatively managed, the evils and abuses usually associated with the sixties and seventies, and often ascribed to the moral collapse following the war, became abundantly manifest in the decade preceding that contest. Said Governor Alexander W. Randall of Wisconsin in 1861: "In the history of the financial speculations of this country, so bold, open, unblushing frauds, taking in a large body of men, were never perpetrated." [75] Watered or worthless stock was peddled by clever salesmen to farmers and small investors; capital was raised for railroads whose funds disappeared before much more than a gesture toward construction had been made. Railroad presidents like Erastus Corning of the New York Central and Charles Paine of the Vermont Central pioneered in the practice, not unknown to later railroad history, by which railroad officials siphoned money into their own pockets from the railroad treasury by making favorable contracts with themselves to sell lands or supplies to the railroad. During the fifties, railroad securities became a favorite of the more daring speculators on the New York Stock Exchange, where older masters like Jacob Little gave practical lessons in the manipulation of pools, bear raids, and even the special uses of convertible bonds to eager students of these subjects like Daniel Drew, James Fisk, and Cornelius Vanderbilt. Finally, in New Jersey, Robert F. Stockton efficiently set the pattern, followed in many a state in subsequent decades, for railroad dominance of state politics. By various devices —the granting of free passes, railroad ownership of newspapers, railroad subsidies to newspapers and periodicals in the form of advertisements—successive legislatures and governors were made to do the bidding of the railroad, and New Jersey became known as the "Camden and Amboy State." [76]

But these developments should not be permitted to obscure the heart of the story. Insofar as private capital contributed to the build-

[75] Quoted by Merk, *Economic History of Wisconsin during the Civil War Decade,* p. 245.

[76] "The New Jersey Monopolies," *North American Review,* CIV (1867), 435–476.

ing of American railroads before 1860, it came from a multitude of private savers, both large and small. The primary interest of most investors lay in the indirect benefits to be gained, though as the period advanced, purchase for investment or speculation by financiers in the eastern cities and abroad began to be important.

THE TRIUMPH OF THE RAILROADS

By 1860 steam had revolutionized transportation on the ocean, on inland lakes and rivers, and, most important of all, on the land. The railroad was essentially a simple device consisting of a smooth fixed track upon which vehicles were moved by steam power. Before it could become an efficient agent of transportation many technical problems of track building, steam-engine construction, and practical railroad operation had to be solved. These came so rapidly that most of the major difficulties had been overcome by 1860. Of course, many improvements continued to be made: steel rails, the safety coupler, the automatic air brake, larger cars of steel construction, and heavier, faster, and more efficient locomotives. Important as were these improvements of the future, it is nonetheless true that by 1860 the railroad as a major instrument of transportation had come of age. Already it had built great cities, hastened the settlement of the West, made farming practicable on the prairies, and greatly stimulated the flow of internal commerce.

The railroad had definitely triumphed over competing forms of transportation. Already turnpike and plank-road companies had largely disappeared and many canals had been abandoned. It is true that some canals, like the Erie and the Delaware and Raritan were still greatly expanding their business, that natural waterways such as the Mississippi and the Hudson had not yet reached the peak of their usefulness. Nevertheless, railroads had already been built parallel to these water routes and had demonstrated their ability successfully to challenge such competition.

Wherever traffic was dense or distances were great the railroad could transport goods so much more cheaply than could be done by turnpikes that its superiority was easily established. The railroad won an easy victory over the smaller and weaker canals for the same reason. But some of the larger canals could easily meet or even better the lowest rates which the railroad could offer. Nevertheless, the railroads proved to have decisive advantage which assured their ultimate victory. In part, this superiority arose from greater dependability and flexibility. Closed by ice during at least a portion of the year and frequently subject to serious interruptions of traffic from either too little or too much water, the canal could not rival the railroad in either regularity or dependability of service. Nor could the water route often compete effectively in building short lines or sidings directly to the loading platforms or warehouses of shippers or receivers. Moreover, the railroads secured a strong competitive advantage, for shipment by rail over long distances was greatly facilitated and cheapened: first, through the consolidation of many short lines into great transportation systems; and, second, through cooperative arrangements among railroad lines providing through bills of lading and joint rates for interline shipments. Such cooperative arrangements were seldom available to shippers using joint rail and water routes.[77]

Finally, the railways triumphed because where soundly managed, well located, and built to meet present rather than future traffic needs, they often provided not only the expected advantages to the whole region through which they passed but paid a fair return to those who had put their savings into the venture. It is true that the market value of railroad stocks showed wide fluctuations with the swings of the business cycle,[78] and that many railroad stocks, especially those of the more speculative western roads, proved a poor or even a worthless investment. On the other hand, securities of many eastern roads sold above par over long periods and paid satisfactory returns to investors. Even some early western railroads earned high dividends.[79]

Turnpikes, canals, steamboats, railroads—these were the technical devices by which Americans in the forty-five years preceding the Civil War solved the problem of moving goods and persons quickly and cheaply in the interior of their vast country. The equally drastic changes which marked the development of ocean transportation provide the focus for the next chapter.

[77] Cf. Leland H. Jenks, "Railroads as an Economic Force in American Development," *Journal of Economic History*, IV, No. 1 (May, 1944), 12–13; David Maldwyn Ellis, "Rivalry between the New York Central and the Erie Canal," *New York History*, XXIX, No. 3 (July, 1948), 274–275.

[78] See Arthur H. Cole and Edwin Frickey, "The Course of Stock Prices, 1825–66," *Review of Economic Statistics*, X, No. 3 (August, 1928), 117–139.

[79] MacGill, *History of Transportation*, pp. 582–584; Gates, *The Illinois Central Rail-road and Its Colonization Work*, p. 86.

CHAPTER VI

The Merchant Marine

THE RISE OF THE PACKET LINES [1]

BRITISH merchant vessels of the Napoleonic period were but little changed from those of the time of Elizabeth, which laid the foundation for four centuries of British maritime supremacy. Nor had the American merchant marine altered greatly from early colonial times. But from 1815 to 1860 the merchant shipping of the world underwent truly revolutionary changes—changes in the organization of maritime trade and also in the structure, size, speed, and means of propulsion of ocean-going ships. This was the golden age of the United States merchant marine. Ocean shipping flourished as one of the major industries, and in many of the new developments of the period the United States was the outstanding leader.

From the functional standpoint, there were in 1815 two types of vessels engaged in the foreign trade of the United States: transients and regular traders. The transients, or tramps, were still most typical of American shipping. They followed no fixed routes, kept to no time schedules, and confined their cargoes to no particular commodities. Under the direction of a merchant-captain or a supercargo they sailed the seven seas in search of goods to carry or favorable markets in which to buy or sell. A transient sailing from an American port might not return for more than two years and might visit a dozen ports. Thus Robert Greenhalgh Albion tells of the brig *Forrester* from Salem,

---

[1] This chapter is based in considerable part on Robert Greenhalgh Albion, *Square-Riggers on Schedule* (Princeton: Princeton University Press, 1938); Albion, *The Rise of New York Port;* and John G. B. Hutchins, *The American Maritime Industries and Public Policy, 1789–1914* (Vol. LXXI of *Harvard Economic Studies*, Cambridge: Harvard University Press, 1941), hereafter referred to as Hutchins, *American Maritime Industries.*

which was absent from its home port nearly three years (1826–1828) and visited in turn New Orleans, New York, Cuba, Genoa, Marseilles, New York, New Orleans, Hamburg, and St. Ubes (later Setubal in Portugal).[2] The merchant-captain of the transient was ready for any kind of business. Often he carried goods which he had bought on his own risk or for the account of others who had made him their agent. When he could, he freighted goods as a public carrier. Not infrequently he found it profitable to sell his ship in Capetown, Canton, or Lisbon and to return home as a passenger on some other vessel.

The other type of vessel consisted of the regular traders. Their distinctive feature was that they customarily traded between a fixed number of predetermined ports. Usually owned by the more important merchants, they were likely to be relatively large vessels, often brigs or ships of between three hundred and four hundred tons. At the beginning of the period the goods shipped were largely the property of the shipowners, but increasingly the regular traders did more and more business as common carriers. The regular traders operated chiefly on the important sea routes. Thus they were especially active on the routes from New York to Liverpool, London, Le Havre, and New Orleans. As their routes were direct and their destinations reasonably certain, they were much preferred over transients for passengers and mail.

Although the regular traders operated on established routes, news of rising markets or profitable freight sometimes tempted them to unaccustomed ports. In any case their sailing dates depended on the state of business. Only when a satisfactory cargo had been assembled and placed on board and when markets were deemed favorable did the vessel set sail. In the meantime, passengers composed themselves as best they could, and shippers, dependent on the common carrier service of the regular trader, prayed that their goods would neither be injured by the delay nor fail to reach the market before prices fell.

The first important innovation to be made in ocean transportation after the War of 1812 was the introduction of the transatlantic packet lines. These lines operated two or more vessels on definite routes and differed from the regular traders in that they sailed on set schedules which did not change from month to month and on which shippers could depend. Earlier experiments at establishing such regular schedules for groups of merchant vessels on the Atlantic had not been successful, although it may be noted that the mail brigs of the British government were the forerunners of the packets. Since

[2] Albion, *Square-Riggers on Schedule*, p. 15.

early in the eighteenth century, these brigs had been operated by the British authorities for carrying mail. They sailed at scheduled times and carried a few passengers, but their routes were often indirect and they did not do a freight business. Their functions were so much better performed by the new packet lines that the British mail brigs could not compete successfully with them. Also, as Albion points out, steamboats on the Hudson River and Long Island Sound had set a precedent of regular "line" service.[3]

During the first week of January, 1818, the ship *James Monroe* sailed from New York bound for Liverpool and the ship *Courier* cleared from Liverpool headed for the port of New York. The vessels themselves were not unusual. Both were square-riggers, the first of 381 tons burden and the second of 424, and both had been regular traders. But their sailing is of great significance because it marked the beginning of regular monthly sailing on fixed dates of a group of merchant vessels between two distant ports. Along with two other ships, they formed the Black Ball Line and a ship sailed each month from each port on a specified day and hour.[4]

For four years the five New York merchants who inaugurated this first of the packet lines had no imitators. Then with rising general prosperity in 1822 the idea took hold with a rush. Two New York–Liverpool lines were established, and the Black Ball increased its sailings to twice a month from each port. Soon packet lines from New York were also in operation to Le Havre and London. By 1824 the packet-line principle had taken firm root. Each month there were four packet sailings for Liverpool, two to Le Havre and one to London, besides many in the coastwise trade. Business grew, and new and larger ships were added by the lines. In 1836 the Dramatic Line was established on the Liverpool run with exceptionally fine ships. By 1845 fifty-two transatlantic packets were sailing regularly from New York, giving that port three regular sailings a week.

Transatlantic packets from other ports were generally not so successful. Short-lived experiments were made at Boston, Baltimore, and the cotton ports, but specialization on seasonal products in the South, lack of west-bound cargoes in New England, and everywhere the aggressive competition of the established New York lines were too much for them in the end. Only at Philadelphia did a line in operation by 1822 give continuous and moderately successful overseas packet service. At least two foreign-owned packet lines were

[3] Albion, *Square-Riggers on Schedule*, pp. 17–19.
[4] Carl C. Cutler, *Greyhounds of the Sea; The Story of the American Clipper Ship* (New York: G. P. Putnam's Sons, 1930), pp. 56–59.

operated for a few years, but they offered no serious competition.

Many packet lines appeared in the coastwise trade. Between the chief commercial centers from Maine to Virginia numerous lines sprang up. Often the vessels employed were relatively small, schooners and even sloops being used. Data for 1827 indicate that a little over one half of the coasting trade of Philadelphia was carried by regularly sailing packets.[5] Between New York and the cotton ports a packet service in large square-riggers flourished comparable to that on the Atlantic shuttle. Packet lines had been established to Charleston, New Orleans, and Savannah by 1824 and to Mobile and Apalachicola, Florida, somewhat later. But the lines to the first-named cities were most important, with New Orleans taking a dominant position as cotton culture moved westward. Both in size and speed the New Orleans packets rivaled those on the transatlantic route. Indeed, in 1835 the largest packet in service was the 747-ton *Shakespeare* on the New Orleans run.

On the whole, these coastwise packets tended to be somewhat less regular in their sailings than those in the transatlantic service. Cotton dominated this trade, and shipments were so light in the spring and summer that packets sometimes deserted their schedules in order to participate in the transatlantic trade during the summer peak. Least affected by such defections was New Orleans, for in addition to being the largest cotton shipping port, she offered other valuable cargoes, such as Mexican specie, flour, lead, tobacco, sugar, skins, and a considerable list of food items known to the trade as "up-country provisions."

The success of the packets lay primarily in their regularity. Very soon they had the cream of the transatlantic business, the carrying of mails, most of the cabin passengers, and the best-paying freight, especially specie, textiles, and fine goods of all kinds. In addition, of course, they carried much bulky freight, such as cotton, flour, and tobacco. The regular receipt of news by packets meant much to merchants and editors. And passengers gained in that they no longer had to make roundabout trips on transients or suffer annoying delays while regular traders waited to complete their cargoes. Finally, importers and exporters alike had for the first time the advantage of regularly sailing common carriers. Many of the great merchants still depended in large part upon their own vessels, but others, especially the auctioneers, dry goods merchants, and the representatives of manufacturers, made profitable use of the line service.[6]

[5] *Hazard's Register of Pennsylvania*, I (February 2, 1828), 71–72.
[6] Albion, *The Rise of New York Port*, p. 43.

A second change in the merchant marine was technical—ships became larger, their design sharper, and their sail greatly increased. But conditions changed very little between the War of 1812 and about 1830. Most American vessels, as did also the British,[7] remained relatively small, for such craft best met the needs of the highly dispersed trade of the period. They could enter and easily maneuver in the several hundred ports on the Atlantic and the Gulf. And they were suitable for trips to the many small ports of foreign countries, for nowhere had a few major seaports yet been able to monopolize the great bulk of ocean commerce. These vessels could enter a small harbor and quickly find sufficient cargo to permit prompt sailing, whereas a larger one might wait for some time or have to sail with partly filled cargo space. Many vessels were owned and operated by small merchants who had a limited capital to invest in either ship or cargo. Even when larger capital was available, the highly speculative character of trade made it advantageous for the merchants to spread their risks by owning two or three small vessels rather than a single, large one.[8]

Trade along the Atlantic coast, especially to nearby ports, was carried on to a large extent in sloops. These were small craft often under 25 tons and rarely more than 100. They had but one mast and, at least after the beginning of the period, were rigged fore and aft. Except for short trips, such as those on Long Island Sound or the Hudson, during most of this period they did not compete effectively with the schooners, which tended to monopolize much of the ocean-going coastwise trade. The schooners were rigged much like the sloops, but they had two masts instead of one and normally ranged in size from 75 to 175 tons. Most numerous of all American vessels down to the Civil War, they carried much of the coastal commerce and were important also in the Boston and New York trade with the West Indies and South America.[9]

But it was the square-rigged vessels, the two-masted brigs, and the three-masted ships which were predominant on the longer sea voyages. The brigs were usually vessels of from 150 to 250 tons and, at the beginning of the period, were more common in the American

[7] Abbott Payson Usher, "The Growth of English Shipping, 1572–1922," *Quarterly Journal of Economics*, XLII (May, 1928), 475.

[8] Hutchins, *American Maritime Industries*, pp. 208–214.

[9] William E. Verplanck and Moses W. Collyer, *The Sloops on the Hudson* (New York: G. P. Putnam's Sons, 1908), see especially pp. 25–64.

registry than ships. Later, with the strong tendency toward increased size, they were soon overtaken by the ships. But brigs continued important in the trade from New York and Boston to New Orleans and South America. The full-rigged ships were the pride of the American merchant marine. As transients, regular traders, or packets, they not only operated on the Atlantic shuttle to Liverpool, London, and Le Havre and on the long coastwise route from Boston and New York to New Orleans, but also carried the American flag to St. Petersburg, Smyrna, Calcutta, Canton, and a hundred other distant ports. The smaller vessels underwent little change from the Peace of Ghent to the opening of the Civil War, but these full-rigged ships were greatly altered in size and design.

These ships (the term is here confined to square-riggers having at least three masts) of the American Merchant Marine may have averaged at the beginning of this period above 300 tons; some were less than 200 tons, and a few, 500 or more. At first, except for the few packet liners, no tendency toward larger ships appeared. Thus John G. B. Hutchins shows that for four important shipbuilding centers, Boston, Kennebunk, Hanover, and Portsmouth, the average tonnage of ships built in 1815 as compared with 1825 declined for the later year for all except Portsmouth, where there was a small increase.[10] But after about 1825 important forces were at work to cause ships to increase rapidly in size. Growing concentration of trade in major ports, the rise of the packet, and the increasing importance of ships as common carriers, the appearance of trade in bulky products, especially cotton, and the demand for speed and better passenger accommodations in Atlantic travel—these were among the factors leading to the growing demand for larger ships.

The common cargo carriers of the 1850's were about three times the size of those built in the 1820's. Cargo ships of 1,000 gross tons were regarded as very large in the early forties, but by the fifties such ships were typical and 1,500 tons not unusual. The average size of full-rigged ships built at Portsmouth was 361 tons in 1825–1829, 572 tons in 1835–1839, 833 tons in 1845–1849, and 1,087 tons in 1855–1859.[11] The *Ocean Monarch*, a square-rigged merchantman of 2,145 tons, was launched at New York in 1856 and, largest of all, the clipper *Great Republic* was christened at East Boston three years earlier.[12] The packets, too, increased greatly in burden. The twenty-four ships

---

[10] Hutchins, *American Maritime Industries*, p. 212.
[11] *Ibid.*, pp. 289–290.
[12] Albion, *The Rise of New York Port*, pp. 307, 363.

on the three original Atlantic packet lines averaged 351 tons. The largest packet in 1830 was of 647 tons burden. By 1853 the *Calhoun,* with a burden of 1,749 tons, had been placed in service on the Dramatic Line.[13]

Changes in design came more slowly. The typical ship in the twenties was bluff-bowed (convex at the bow), wide of beam (a typical ratio of length to breadth was about 4 to 1), and deep and roughly V-shaped in the hull. In the early thirties changes began to appear. Hulls became flatter, more U-shaped. This alteration is said to have been originally effected to make passage easier over the bars at the mouth of the Mississippi. At any rate, this feature, combined with a tendency toward sharper bows, a ratio of greater length to width, and increased sail area, gave faster, more streamlined ships. The East Indiamen built in Massachusetts and New Hampshire in the thirties, though snub-nosed and deep in the hull, had greater length relative to width than the earlier ships and carried a greatly increased spread of canvas. Though usually less than 500 tons, they were soundly economical, fast, of large carrying capacity for their size, and so easy to handle that they required a relatively small crew.[14]

The packets on the major Atlantic runs typify the tendencies described above. The earliest of these vessels had a length-to-beam ratio as low as 3.5 to 1; by the fifties they were much more streamlined, with increased length-to-beam ratios. The limits in both size and length-to-beam ratio were reached in the *Amazon* (1854), whose tonnage was 1,771 and whose ratio was 5.1 to 1.[15] The effect of these changes was a considerable increase in speed. Thus the average time for the packets on the westward route from Liverpool to New York during 1818–1822 was 39.0 days; thirty years later, during 1848–1852, it was 33.3 days.[16] Economy was a major result of these developments. Improved maneuverability meant smaller crews, and increased speed brought savings not only in sailors' wages and provisions, but often in lowered overhead costs. Nor were these savings offset, as in the clipper, by decreased freight-carrying capacity, for the sturdy merchantmen of the forties and fifties had ample waists and capacious holds.

The tendencies toward streamlining and greater spread of sail were given extreme expression in the clipper ships, whose sensational

---

[13] *Ibid.,* pp. 79, 274, 280.

[14] Samuel Eliot Morison, *The Maritime History of Massachusetts, 1783–1860* (Boston: Houghton Mifflin Company, 1921), pp. 254–256.

[15] Albion, *Square-Riggers on Schedule,* p. 86.

[16] *Ibid.,* p. 197.

(*Left*) Edward K. Collins, 1802–1878, shipowner. He challenged British maritime supremacy on the Atlantic. (*Right*) Captain Robert F. Stockton, 1795–1866, naval officer, politician, and canal and railroad magnate. (*Both pictures Culver Service*) (*Below top*) Harbor at Portland, Maine. Ice was an important outward freight. (*Bottom*) Harbor at Detroit, Michigan. Lake steamers were more like ocean steamships than western steamboats. (*Both pictures Old Print Shop*)

The clipper ship, *Tornado*. In 1852 she sailed from San Francisco to New York in 100 days. (*Old Print Shop*)

(*Above*) Lake steamer, *Illinois*. Steam vessels on the lakes were used chiefly for passengers. (*Bettmann Archive*) (*Below*) The ocean-going steamship *Atlantic*, Collins Line. (*D. B. Tyler, Steam Conquers the Atlantic, p. 202*)

(*Right*) A country post office. A communications center and an informal institution for adult education. (*Old Print Shop*) (*Below*) New York Post Office, 1845.

(*Bettmann Archive*)

(*Left*) Elias Howe, 1819–1867, inventor of the sewing machine. (*Right*) A telegraph linesman. During the fifties telegraph wires reached nearly every part of the country. (*Below*) Municipal fire-alarm telegraph apparatus, Boston, 1852. (*Three pictures Culver Service*)

rise, stately beauty, and unsurpassed speed have led writers to call the years from 1843 to 1860 "the clipper ship era." Gracefully narrow of beam, with concave sides and bow, the clipper cut the water like a knife as she was driven forward by clouds of sail, which rose nearly two hundred feet above the clean lines of her deck. Over every important sea route of the world the American clippers set records for speed which have never been equaled by sailing ships of their size. Eighteen clippers made single passages from Boston or New York around Cape Horn to San Francisco in less than 100 days, and in 1854 the *Flying Cloud*, perhaps the most famous of all the clippers, set a record on this course of 89 days and 8 hours. Ordinary merchantmen usually required from 150 to 200 days to make this 16,000 mile trip to San Francisco. Another clipper, the *Lightning*, while on her maiden voyage to Liverpool, covered 436 miles in 24 hours, the fastest day's run ever recorded for a sailing vessel. Never before had human beings been carried so fast over so long a course either by land or by sea. Nor were they to be again until several decades later, when the finest steamships began to equal this record.

The few relatively small clipper ships built before 1848 found profitable employment in the China trade. Then came the high tide, 1848–1854, when rising prosperity brought a greatly increased business for shipping in general, and the gold rush to California, with its imperative demand for speed and fabulously high rates for passengers and freight, made the need for clippers seem boundless. No wonder clippers could not be built fast enough to meet the demand when their merchant owners were reaping tremendous profits in the California trade; sometimes the gain was so great on the initial voyage that it equaled the original cost of the ship.

Wherever distances were long and premium freight rates were paid for speed, the clipper took the cream of the business. Thus when the British relaxed their navigation laws in 1849 and permitted American ships to compete with the British in carrying tea from China to England, American clippers commanded high rates to hurry each new crop to British markets. So also the gold rush to Australia, which began in 1851, gave profitable employment to these swift vessels.

But by 1855, the prosperous period was over. Some made money down to 1860; many were a losing venture. With the Civil War, the clipper ship era came to a close. The Americans of 1850–1854, like their descendants of 1928–1929, had mistaken a short-run boom for a new era. While the rush was on to California, clippers were built as rapidly as the shipyards could turn them out, approximately 270 being completed in the decade 1843–1853. And then the bubble burst and there were too many clippers. The truth of the matter is that the clipper was a large and expensive ship of relatively small carrying capacity; her narrow wedgelike hull, though perfect for speed, carried relatively small cargo for each registered ton. Only on long voyages where premium rates were paid for speed could she compete with the slower, round-bellied merchantmen. On the cotton run to New Orleans or on the Atlantic shuttle, clippers did not prove a paying venture. However, clipper ships might well have survived the overbuilding of the early fifties to operate profitably for many decades on the longer runs to California and the Orient were it not that a truly new era, that of effective ocean steamship transportation, had begun in the very decade in which the sailing ships reached their greatest perfection. Snub-nosed merchantman and graceful clipper alike were doomed by the modern miracle of steam.[17]

It is not surprising that the beauty and speed of the American clipper ship moved the people of the coastal cities to unbounded enthusiasm. Nor is it strange that historical writers, bemused by the romantic appeal of these fast and beautiful ships, have often given them far more attention than their importance justified.

BEGINNINGS OF THE OCEAN STEAMSHIP

More than fifty years passed after Fitch built his first steamboat in 1787 before steam was successfully adapted to ocean transportation. By 1838 river steamboats had been successfully operating for more than twenty-five years, and on land the steam railroad had clearly demonstrated its supremacy, although serious technical difficulties remained to be overcome. Yet not until 1838 was steamship service established on the Atlantic.

The slow development in the application of steam to ocean transportation was due to the necessity of overcoming substantial technical and economic obstacles much greater than those met on rivers and sheltered waters. Mechanically, steam engines were still crude and tremendously heavy. The weight and rigidity of the machinery meant that the wooden hulls of steamships must be built extraordinarily strong in order to withstand the wrenching and tossing caused by storms at sea. The walking beam which had been found most satis-

[17] Albion, *The Rise of New York Port*, pp. 354–373; Arthur H. Clark, *The Clipper Ship Era* (New York: G. P. Putnam's Sons, 1910), pp. 289–308; Raymond A. Rydell, "The California Clipper," *Pacific Historical Review*, XVIII, No. 1 (February, 1949), 70–83; and Cutler, *Greyhounds of the Sea, passim.*

factory for eastern river steamboats was not easily adapted to steam-ships. The opening in the deck of the vessel through which this beam operated might, in a storm, permit dangerous quantities of water to enter the hold; it also interfered with the proper placing of the masts. Also, the walking beam made the center of gravity incon-veniently high, and exposed working parts of the engine to the weather. So the side-lever engine was developed and widely used. But the walking beam was not entirely abandoned. In the fifties, Vanderbilt used it successfully on fast Atlantic steamships.[18]

Steamboats on inland waters or short coastal routes had fuel close at hand as well as fresh water for boilers. Although some experiments were made with carrying the large quantities of water necessary, most steamships used sea water. By using copper boilers, corrosion could be kept within bounds, but a considerable loss in efficiency re-sulted from the necessity of frequently blowing from the boilers the concentrated brine and refilling with cold sea water. When in the fifties higher-temperature and higher-pressure engines were used, scale in the boilers caused by the use of sea water became a serious matter.[19]

Fuel presented a difficult economic problem. The clumsy and inefficient side-lever engines of the early paddle-wheelers required much space and burned such large amounts of coal that cargo-carrying capacity was sharply limited. Thus the *British Queen*, a 275-foot vessel which made her first crossing in 1839, was designed to carry 750 tons of coal and 500 tons of cargo.[20] So, in order to carry sufficient coal and to have any appreciable space left for paying cargo, steamships had to be much larger than the largest sailing ves-sels at the close of the War of 1812. All of these factors, as well as competition from increasingly efficient sailing ships, lessened the financial attractiveness of investment in steamships. Down to the Civil War most Atlantic steamship companies, even those benefiting from government subsidy, did not prove to be very profitable ventures.

Ships equipped with steam engines had successfully crossed the ocean before 1838. Most famous was the crossing of the *Savannah*, which in 1819 went from Savannah, Georgia, to Liverpool in twenty-seven days and achieved the distinction of being the first ship equipped with a steam engine to cross the Atlantic Ocean. As a harbinger of things to come, the trip of the *Savannah* is of some im-

[18] W. Mack Angas, *Rivalry on the Atlantic* (New York: Lee Furman, Inc., 1939), p. 23; Lane, *Commodore Vanderbilt: An Epic of the Steam Age*, p. 156.
[19] Angas, *Rivalry on the Atlantic*, pp. 22–25.
[20] *Ibid.*, p. 26.

portance. Actually, steam power was used for only about eighty hours on the whole trip, fuel ran short, and the paddle wheels, which were collapsible, permitting them to be stored on deck when not in use, did not prove very effective. After visiting Liverpool, Stockholm, and St. Petersburg, where unsuccessful attempts were made to sell the ship, it was brought back to Savannah. As the original backers were no longer able to bear the expenses of operation, the ship was sold at auction, its engine removed, and the *Savannah* entered the coastal trade as a sailing ship.

A few other ships using steam for auxiliary power crossed the ocean in the years before 1838. One steamship, the Canadian-owned *Royal William*, crossed the North Atlantic in 1833. David Budlong Tyler reports twelve steamships as going from Europe to the West Indies or South America before 1838, but apparently only one of these, a small steamer, the *Curaçao*, owned by the Dutch Navy, made more than one round trip; nine of the steamships were British government vessels which were sent to the West Indies for use there either by the navy or for carrying mail.[21]

More impressive was the gradual progress which was being made by steamships in this same period on shorter sea voyages. England took the leadership and rapidly developed their use in the coastwise, Channel, and Irish Sea trade. By 1824 regular steamship trips were being made between Liverpool and Dublin. This journey across the Irish Sea, which might consume seven days by sailing vessel, was accomplished by the steamboats in fourteen hours. Within a few years, steamboats very largely eliminated sailboat competition in the trade between England and Ireland.[22]

Great strides were being made in America during these years in the development of the river steamboat, but progress was slow in the coastwise trade.[23] True, on such sheltered waters as Long Island Sound, steam soon established its supremacy, at least for the passenger trade. The *Fulton* maintained regular service between New York and New Haven in 1815, and the important New York to Providence route was taken over by steam when the *Connecticut* was put on this route in 1822. The running time of this vessel on her first trip between these two points was twenty-nine hours. Some notion of the improvements which were being made in steamboat engines may be gained from noting that when a new steamboat, the

[21] David Budlong Tyler, *Steam Conquers the Atlantic* (New York: D. Appleton-Century Company, 1939), pp. 18–28 and App. VI.

[22] *Ibid.*, p. 29; Hutchins, *American Maritime Industries*, pp. 333–336.

[23] Hutchins, *American Maritime Industries*, pp. 327–333.

Lexington, was put on this same route in 1835 she took only twelve hours for her first run.

But on longer and less protected coastal routes, steamships did not prove immediately practicable. An auspicious beginning was made by the *Robert Fulton*, a well-constructed steamship of 702 tons, which in 1820 began running between New York and New Orleans with stops at Charleston and Havana. This ship was operated for several years with some success, but her carrying capacity was small and her sailings were irregular. She could not compete effectively with the packets which afforded frequent, regular sailings and which could be much more economically operated. So she was withdrawn from the service and, like the *Savannah*, suffered the indignity of having her engines removed and of being converted into a sailing vessel.[24]

An ambitious attempt was made between 1834 and 1838 to establish a line of steam packets between New York and Charleston. The ships were operated on a regular schedule, one leaving each port each week. They gave as frequent and regular sailings as the sailing packets and cut the latter's travel time by one half when the weather was favorable. Moreover, they were not forced to stop at some intermediate port for repairs or protection from the elements. For a time they made serious inroads in the passenger and mail business of the sailing packets. But after a series of disasters, the worst of which was the sinking of the *Home* off Cape Hatteras in 1837 with the loss of upwards of a hundred lives, public confidence was lost and the line was soon abandoned.[25]

In the decade 1838–1848, promoters struggled to establish the steamship on the Atlantic. Although a transatlantic steamship operated in every year of the decade, technical problems and management difficulties were still so troublesome that not until toward the end of the period did steamship lines begin gradually to establish their superiority over the packets in the competition for the best-paying carrying trade.

The year 1838 opened auspiciously. British capital had finally become interested in backing steamships on the Atlantic and rival companies hurried their plans in order to win the honor of the first crossing. The race was won by the British and American Steam Navigation Company, whose small steamer *Sirius* arrived at New York

---

[24] Albion, *Square-Riggers on Schedule*, pp. 253–254; Morrison, *History of American Steam Navigation*, pp. 434–466.

[25] Albion, *Square-Riggers on Schedule*, pp. 254–255.

early on April 23, 1838. Later on the same day the *Great Western* arrived. She was owned by a group connected with the Great Western Railway, was a veritable giant for her time (1,340 tons burden), and made the trip from Bristol to New York in fifteen days. Before the year was over there had been eleven steamer sailings from New York, five by the *Great Western* and six by four other vessels. In the next year, sailings increased slightly, and the British and American Navigation Company replaced the small *Sirius* with the 1862-ton *British Queen.*[26]

But things did not go well on the New York route. Ships were withdrawn because they did not pay, mechanical difficulties gave constant trouble, and sailings were irregular. In 1841 the *President,* a sister ship of the *British Queen,* disappeared at sea with the loss of 136 lives. In the following year the *Great Western* was the only steamer left on the Atlantic route between New York and England. Although the number of steamships clearing from New York increased presently, not until 1848 were steamships again offering a serious threat to the packets on the route from New York to British ports.[27]

The only other American city to establish steamship connections with Europe during this period was Boston. There in 1840 Samuel Cunard established his line from Liverpool with the help of a British subsidy. Despite early difficulties which necessitated an increase in government aid, the Cunard line proved the most successful of the early transatlantic steamship companies. Its regular sailings, well-built ships, and superior management gave Boston better steamship service until the late forties than was enjoyed by New York.

Coastwise steamship operation over appreciable distances did not rapidly recover from the earlier reverses. Not until near the close of the period did successful operation begin on the route from New York to Charleston and to New Orleans.

STEAMSHIP LINES 1848–1860

Between 1848 and 1860 the number of steamships in the Atlantic trade grew tremendously. The total registered tonnage of steamships in the United States was 5,631 in 1847 and 97,296 in 1860.[28] In part this growth was due to the great increase in foreign trade, but it

26 *Ibid.,* pp. 258–259.
27 *Ibid.,* p. 259.
28 *Annual Report of the Commissioner of Navigation,* 1894, p. 268.

must also be noted that major technical improvements had been achieved and that better ships and abler management now made possible frequent sailings on prearranged schedules. Finally, international rivalry backed by subsidies greatly stimulated steamship development.

Steam packet lines operating between New York and European ports were rapidly established following 1847. Cunard began his New York–Liverpool steam packet service on January 1 of the next year. Later in 1848 the Ocean Steam Navigation Company of New York began operating two large steamers on a regular schedule to Bremen by way of Southampton. At about the same time two steam packet lines, one with an American subsidy and the other with a French one, began operating between France and the United States. Finally, in 1850, the Collins Line challenged Cunard on the Liverpool run with four fine new ships.

This was competition which the sailing packets could not meet. The first-class passenger traffic, the mails, and the best-paying freight were secured by the steamships, whose service was now as regular as that of the sailing packets and whose speed in crossing the Atlantic was often twice as great. So the sailing packets were forced to turn to the immigrant business and the transporting of bulky freight.

Similarly, steamship lines now succeeded in the coastwise routes. The steamship *Southerner* began operating between New York and Charleston in 1846. Regular steam packet service from New York was soon established on this route and on that from New York to New Orleans. Congress had adopted a policy of mail subsidies in 1845, and soon subsidized steam lines were in operation from New York to the Isthmus of Panama, on the Pacific from Oregon to the Isthmus, and from Charleston to Cuba. By the early fifties, steamships had taken the best-paying freight and passenger business from the sailing packets on all of the major sea lanes except the very longest. To the Far East and around Cape Horn to California the necessity of refueling made steam uneconomical, so that the sailing vessels maintained their superiority until after 1860.[29]

Improvements continued to be made in the ocean steamship. Although the fastest ships in the forties could average eleven knots an hour or a little better, by the end of the next decade a speed of thirteen knots was achieved for Atlantic crossings. Vessels grew in size as time went on, although actually the largest Atlantic steam-

[29] Morrison, *History of American Steam Navigation*, Chaps. 5, 7, and pp. 434–484, 505–506.

ship of the forties (the *Great Britain*, 3,270 tons) was not a great deal under the largest for the fifties (the *Adriatic*, 3,670 tons)—that is, of course, if we do not count the *Great Eastern*, which was of 22,500 tons' burden and strictly *sui generis*.[30] Advances were also made in the construction of marine steam engines, especially in the use of the expansive force of steam, though the heat of the condensed steam was still largely wasted. The side-lever single-cylinder engine with jet condenser remained the rule, but successful experiments were being made with the direct-acting compound engine with surface condenser. Coal was used more effectively, and Collins demonstrated that the use of American anthracite was feasible on fast mail ships.

But the most striking technical changes and those most significant for the future came from the hesitant introduction during this period of iron hulls and screw propulsion. Iron hulls were found to be much stronger and safer for the larger ships which were now being built. Not only could they better accommodate the heavy machinery, but they were generally more rugged and less likely to go to pieces or break their backs when grounded. Iron ships were more durable and had appreciably greater cargo-carrying ability both because of their greater buoyancy and because of their larger internal capacity. Though especially adapted to use with steam, they proved also advantageous for sailing vessels.[31]

The screw was not yet perfected as to pitch or number of blades; the engines had to be considerably altered in order to give the speed necessary for screw propulsion; and the practical application of the twin screw was a later development. But screw-propelled vessels already had certain advantages. They were economical of coal and, by eliminating the paddle wheels, they reduced the drag on the ship when it was under sail, took up less space in the ship, and did away with any interference with the handling of the sails. On the other hand, the propeller-driven ships suffered from considerable vibration (one of the reasons why iron hulls were superior) and, even more important, they were not yet quite as fast as the best paddle-wheel steamships. This latter reason kept Collins and Cunard from adopting the screw on their New York to Liverpool ships, where speed was a major consideration.[32]

[30] Tyler, *Steam Conquers the Atlantic*, p. 311, App., IV. Tonnage is in "old measurement."

[31] Joseph Nimmo, Jr., "Foreign Commerce and Decadence of American Shipping," *Report*, 1870, *House Executive Document* No. 111, 41 Cong., 2 Sess., pp. 17–18.

[32] Tyler, *Steam Conquers the Atlantic*, pp. 184–189; Thurston, *A History of the*

The first large ship to combine the two new principles—the iron hull and the screw—was the *Great Britain,* which crossed from Liverpool to New York in 1845. The experiment was not wholly successful. But with subsequent experiments British companies turned more and more to iron construction and, more slowly, to the use of the screw, so that by 1860 the superiority of both had gained wide recognition. But Americans for the most part clung to wooden ships and paddle wheels, for iron hulls were not yet made economically in this country, and screw propulsion was not satisfactory for large wooden ships. In the United States the iron steam tonnage actually built in the fifties averaged annually only 1,515 gross tons, and not a single major iron vessel had been produced before 1860. In part this tardy growth was due to the slow development of heavy industry and the relatively high cost of domestic iron on the Atlantic seaboard. But it was also a result of the rather contemptuous attitude which American shipbuilders, who had been so successful with wood, took toward iron construction. In consequence, the building of iron ships in this country tended to fall into the hands of boilermakers and machinists rather than into those of experienced shipbuilders.[33] On all Atlantic steamships, sails remained for many years an important source of supplementary power. The first liners carrying no canvas were placed on the Atlantic in 1899 by the White Star Line.

Although steamships had, during the fifties, been able to take over the best-paying part of the ocean trade, they had, of course, by no means driven the sailing ships from the seas nor would they completely do so before the day of the airplane. At least as late as 1860 the ocean freight of the world continued to be carried very largely by sailing craft. The chief advantage of the sailing vessels lay in the fact that they offered economical transportation. Before 1860 a steamship ordinarily cost three or four times as much as a sailing packet of comparable size, and its operating expenses were high because of necessary outlays for maintenance and repairs and because of the large consumption of coal. Moreover, the cargo capacity of the steamers continued to be restricted by the space taken up by the engine (especially large on the paddle-wheelers) and by the cargo space required to store fuel. Even with the help of subsidies, most Atlantic steamship companies found survival exceedingly difficult.

The success of the subsidized Cunard line between Liverpool and

Growth of the Steam-Engine, pp. 285 ff. and 379 ff.; Francis B. Stevens, *The First Steam Screw Propeller Boats to Navigate the Waters of Any Country* (New York: The Engineering Press, n.d.), *passim.*

[33] Hutchins, *American Maritime Industries,* pp. 441–450.

Boston in the early forties enhanced the British prestige and encouraged other countries to attempt similar subsidy lines. These ventures did not meet with much success. A Belgian company enjoying state aid sent the *British Queen* from Antwerp to New York in 1842. After three trips this ship was withdrawn. A French line which began operation in 1847 with government aid was miserably managed and lasted less than a year. In the early fifties a transatlantic line with sailings from Montreal and Portland, Maine, met with difficulties despite a Canadian subsidy.

The United States also entered the contest. The first line to receive a subsidy, the Ocean Steam Navigation Company, began operations between New York and Bremen in 1847. Its two steamships proved to be slow, and considerable alterations to their machinery were found necessary. The line appears to have done only a fair business and ceased operation when the subsidy was withdrawn ten years later. A second subsidized line operated to Le Havre. Its career was not spectacular, but under conservative management it survived for a time the withdrawal of the subsidy in 1858.

Much more sensational is the history of the well-known Collins Line, which, by operating between New York and Liverpool, offered a direct challenge to Cunard. In fact, both Congress, in awarding an annual subsidy of $385,000, and Edward K. Collins, in securing this subsidy for the United States Mail Steamship Company, seem to have been chiefly concerned to defeat Cunard and re-establish the prestige of the American merchant marine. Collins was himself a leading New York merchant and had strong financial backing. No money was spared in building four of the fastest and most luxurious ocean steamships which the New York shipyards could produce. When the first of these ships, the *Atlantic*, sailed from New York on April 27, 1850, there was great excitement. For the time being, Collins won. His ships were about a day faster than the Cunarders; the *Baltic* of the Collins Line made the westward run in 1851 in nine days and eighteen hours. The unprecedented speed, the excellent food, and the lavish appointments attracted passengers away from the Cunard Line. Also, by high-pressure lobbying, Collins got his annual subsidy raised from $385,000 to $858,000 in 1852.

This was success. But difficulties lay ahead. Collins was steadily losing money on each of his four liners, while Cunard, with a smaller subsidy, continued to operate at a profit. The speed and luxury afforded by the American line proved costly. The ships' engines were so pressed to secure speed that it is reported that secret repairs had constantly to be rushed to completion when the ships were in port. And presently ill-fortune overtook the line. The *Arctic* sank off Cape Race in 1854 as a result of a collision. In this disaster 318 lives were lost. Then in 1856 the *Pacific* disappeared at sea, never to be heard from again. The line never recovered from these losses and sailings ceased in 1858. Congress reduced its subsidy in 1857 and withdrew it completely the following year. Thus the Cunarders, although losing the first heat, won the race. Careful business management and emphasis on safety proved a better investment than luxury and excessive speed.[34]

Steam navigation of the Atlantic now passed largely into European hands. With the withdrawal of the subsidy, the American line to Bremen came to an end, although the subsidy line to Le Havre managed to survive the withdrawal of Congressional aid. Vanderbilt, operating without subsidy, sent fast steamships to Bremen and Le Havre, with stops at an English port. He cut passenger rates and gave Cunard some real competition, but his schedules were somewhat irregular and he ordinarily withdrew his ships in the winter time.[35] Just before the Civil War, two famous German lines, the Hamburg-American and the North German Lloyd, began their long careers in promoting steamship travel on the Atlantic.

The British-owned Inman Line, whose history is worthy of brief attention, continued to expand its transatlantic business. Though denied a British subsidy, this company, headed by an able Liverpool merchant, William Inman, had begun steam service between Liverpool and Philadelphia in 1850. In 1857 he shifted to New York and successfully took over the sailing dates surrendered by the Collins Line. Inman had had his share of difficulties. In 1854 one of his ships was wrecked on Cape Race, and another, the *City of Glasgow*, disappeared at sea with 460 persons aboard. But he survived this double misfortune and demonstrated the fact that a transatlantic steamship line could operate without government subventions. His success is probably correctly attributed to sound and progressive management. Inman pioneered in the use of the iron screwship when Collins and Cunard, too, were holding to wooden hulls and paddle wheels. Also, he made good profits by providing decent steerage quarters for im-

[34] Jesse E. Saugstad, *Shipping and Shipbuilding Subsidies*, United States Department of Commerce, *Trade Promotion Series* No. 129, 1932, pp. 48–57.
[35] Lane, *Commodore Vanderbilt*, pp. 147–153.

migrants, while Collins and Cunard regarded this business as beneath their dignity and the sailing packets were transporting these passengers under appalling sanitary conditions.

THE GROWTH OF THE MERCHANT MARINE

During the nineteenth century the merchant marine of the United States experienced its greatest period of sustained growth from 1815 to 1860. The magnitude as well as the details of this development are reflected in the statistics appearing in Appendix A, Table 1. The registered tonnage of the United States (i.e., that engaged in foreign commerce) increased from an annual average of 636,490 tons in 1821–1830 to more than 2,300,000 tons in the years just before the Civil War. This nearly fourfold gain is one of the most striking facts of American maritime history. Another way of measuring this development is in terms of annual American tonnage entered and cleared from ports in the United States. The data for these totals are much more reliable before 1829 than those for tonnage registered in the foreign trade. The official figures for registered tonnage are typically much inflated before 1829. They were corrected and sharply deflated in 1818 and 1829; beginning in 1829 they were corrected annually.[36] The annual tonnage of American vessels entered and cleared from American ports increased between five and six times from 1821–1830 to the closing years of the period. The former figures (those for registered tonnage) reflect the growth in the total tonnage of shipping registered for foreign trade under the American flag; the latter (those for tonnage entered and cleared) show the increased activity in the carrying trade of American-owned vessels. The fact that the tonnage entered and cleared increased more rapidly than total registered tonnage is, insofar as it is not due to an overstatement of registered tonnage in the earlier years, largely a reflection of the growing speed of the ships and more frequent sailings, although it may also show to some extent a relative decline in the number of roundabout and far distant voyages.

The course of the development of the American merchant marine during this period is reflected in Chart 1, which depicts the relative annual increase in registered tonnage, United States tonnage entered and cleared from American ports, and the combined value of American foreign exports and imports. Two warnings are necessary in order

[36] See Hans Keiler, *American Shipping: Its History and Economic Conditions* (Jena: Fischer, 1913), pp. 51, 54.

that the chart will not be misinterpreted. First, the data for years preceding 1821 are very unsatisfactory official estimates but the best available. Most confidence for these six years can be placed in the records for tonnage entered and cleared, which are based on fairly reliable records for tonnage cleared. Figures for registered tonnage are not very trustworthy until after 1829. Second, total commerce figures are for values only and therefore reflect *volume* changes im-

CHART 1

Relative Growth of Foreign Commerce and the Merchant Marine, 1815–1860
Base: 1821–1830

(Computed from data appearing in Tables 1 and 4 of Appendix A)

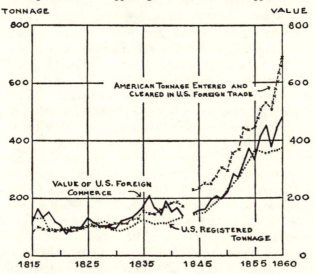

perfectly. The broad picture is one of gradually accelerating growth for both commerce and merchant marine. The expanding tendency of the merchant marine was present even in the first fifteen years of the period, although the rate of growth was relatively slow. Each subsequent decade brought a greater percentage gain.

Throughout this period American ships carried a high proportion of American commerce. It will be seen from Table 1 in Appendix A that the percentage of the value of American foreign trade carried by American vessels was never below 88 per cent in the twenties nor below 82 per cent in the thirties. Subsequent years show an irregular decline, but the percentage was still above 66 in 1860. The same table presents a similar series showing the percentage which was

American of the total tonnage cleared and entered in American ports. The percentages are again highest for the decade of the twenties, but subsequent movements follow no clear pattern. The lowest point for the whole period (60 per cent) was registered in 1850; the highest percentage reached in any year after 1831 was 71 per cent, which was recorded in three years, 1832, 1839, and 1860.

The availability of these statistical data for a period when such unbroken series are none too common has occasionally led some writers to use them uncritically.[37] A few difficulties may be noted. The percentages shown in Columns III and IV of Table 1 in Appendix A are subject to appreciable fluctuation merely as a result of the shifting of vessels between the foreign and coastwise trade. Thus the low percentage in 1850 (60 per cent) for American tonnage entered and cleared from American ports is probably largely a reflection of the demand for vessels in the coastwise trade to California. The data for tonnages of vessels entered and cleared are subject to the defect that vessels in ballast count as much as those with full cargoes. Although the series showing the percentage of value exports carried under the American flag does not present this difficulty, it may show considerable fluctuations due merely to a shift by American ships from valuable cargoes to more bulky ones.

As a consequence of these and other difficulties, no attempt has been made to read any significance into the year to year fluctuations of these figures. It does seem safe to conclude, however, that the consistently lower percentages after the 1820's reflect a comparative advantage for the foreign merchant marine which was greatest in the twenties and somewhat less in subsequent years. Nevertheless, these somewhat lower percentages should not obscure the fact that such percentages did remain fairly high throughout the period and, more important, that in absolute terms the tonnage grew rapidly and was at its crest just before the Civil War.

The tremendous growth of world shipping in this period was merely part of the complex development which has been called the industrial revolution. The increase in manufacturing and its geographical concentration, especially in England, made necessary a mighty merchant fleet to bring raw materials and to take away the finished product. Likewise the improvements in internal commerce, the steamboats, the canals, and the railroads created feeder lines which provided growing cargoes for ocean ships. At the same time

[37] See, for example, William W. Bates, *American Marine: The Shipping Question in History and Politics* (Boston: Houghton Mifflin Company, 1893), Chap. 8.

the increased size and efficiency of the merchant marine itself stimulated the development of manufacturing and encouraged improvements in internal transportation.

A fundamental cause for the growth of the American merchant marine before the Civil War was, of course, the relatively great profitability of investing capital and labor in this industry. Technically speaking, the United States merchant marine enjoyed a comparative advantage; the industry was sufficiently attractive to hold its own with other fields of investment, and costs were so low as to permit successful competition with the shipping of foreign countries. The advantage rested on numerous factors: a skilled and, in many ways, superior labor force, vigorous entrepreneurship, the integration of the merchant and carrier function, and, probably most important of all, the relative excellence and cheapness of American-built sailing vessels.

In the early decades of this period the crews of American sailing vessels were among the finest in the world. Largely farm boys recruited from the areas bordering the north Atlantic coast, they were generally rugged, sober, and filled with a typical American determination to get ahead. Many came from the rocky farms of coastal New England, where agriculture, fishing, trading, and the merchant marine were alternative forms of employment for a rapidly increasing population, and the profits and wages in agriculture were often least attractive. Promotion in the merchant marine was rapid for those who showed ability. Many a Cape Cod or Rhode Island lad went to sea before he was fifteen and, if unusually able, often became a ship's captain at the age of twenty-five or younger. In the foreign trade, most crews included some foreign sailors. The Secretary of the Navy estimated their number to be one fourth of the total in 1828.[38] But at that time they were largely English-speaking and readily assimilated.

As time went on, although many Americans continued to enter the merchant marine, conditions became relatively less attractive as wages ashore increased relative to those at sea. So, especially after the thirties, more and more foreigners were used, chiefly English, German, and Scandinavians. They also were able and rugged sailors, but with the increase in the size of this foreign group the gap widened between officers and men and promotions from the regular crew became less common. Finally, with the tremendous expansion of

[38] Secretary of the Navy *Report*, May 26, 1828, *Senate Document* No. 207, 20 Cong., 1 Sess., p. 6.

shipping in the decade of the fifties, crews for American ships were recruited wherever they could be found and the use of crimping and the press gang, long a common practice in manning British ships, became a frequent one in the larger American ports.

As important as the quality of the crews was the high standard of seamanship, reliability, and sobriety set by American sea captains. For many years the merchant marine attracted as ships' officers men of unusual ability. Owing in appreciable part to the reputation of American captains for efficiency and reliability, American flag vessels were often able to secure premium rates from shippers. These masters were hard drivers. They pushed ships and men to get the greatest amount of work out of both. Whereas in the forties British vessels of 1,000 tons carried a crew of forty men and ten boys, American ships of the same size had only twenty to thirty men for a full crew. So although wage rates were appreciably higher on American vessels, operating expenses were often less than for the British.[39]

Vigorous and aggressive entrepreneurship also played a part. The New England Yankees, who with their small sloops won a reputation for sharp and aggressive trading on every little bay and inlet from Maine to Florida, carried the same tactics on a larger scale to the ports of the world. American shipowners pioneered in the trade with the northwest coast and South America, challenged the British in the Far East, and successfully sought cargoes in remote parts of the Mediterranean. Likewise, Americans instituted the sailing packet service on the Atlantic and by efficient management, skillful use of advertising, and the provision of specialized services secured the most lucrative part of the Atlantic carrying trade.

Important in the first part of this period was the integration of the merchant and the carrying function. As long as the merchants owned their own ships and ventured with merchandise largely owned by themselves, the United States merchant marine grew *pari passu* with the rise of its foreign commerce and the success of its merchants. The itinerant sea merchant of 1815–1830 typically owned his own ship just as the peddler on land owned his horses and wagon. Later, as common carriers became more usual, functions were separated, but interests continued to overlap, and leading exporting houses often had large investments in the ships which brought cotton and tobacco

[39] Hutchins, *American Maritime Industries*, pp. 221, 306; Albion, *Square-Riggers on Schedule*, Chap. 6; Clark, *The Clipper Ship Era*, Chap. 8.

to New York and transported it across the Atlantic to Liverpool. Although perhaps of minor importance, these linkages did give some advantage to American-owned shipping.

Finally, the American merchant marine gained a great advantage from the combined excellence and low cost of the sailing vessels themselves. The success of Americans in improving the design and performance of sailing vessels has already been described. It may merely be added here that their rigging was typically so designed as to require fewer hands than most foreign vessels, and that they were so well constructed that their average life exceeded that of most foreign-built vessels.

But perhaps the greatest advantage of all arose from the lower original cost of the American-built vessels. Domestic shipyards furnished American merchants with excellent vessels at a cost appreciably below that available to their chief competitors. Thus John G. B. Hutchins finds that until about 1830 prices for ordinary merchant ships in the United States were 40 to 60 per cent of those in England and France, and that prices for some "home-built trading schooners" were only 25 per cent of similar vessels abroad.[40] With this substantial differential it is not surprising that American merchants could undercut the carrying rates quoted by foreign ship-owners and still make very attractive profits. The advantage from cheap ships depended not only upon the ability of American ship-yards to construct ships at low cost but also upon foreign legislation under which the chief competitors protected their own high-cost shipbuilding industry by prohibiting or making difficult the purchase of American vessels. Later in the period, conditions in both respects became less advantageous. After about 1835 American shipbuilders experienced gradually rising costs. Moreover, in 1849 Great Britain repealed that part of her navigation acts which prevented American-built vessels from being freely registered under her flag. So, by the end of this period, the American gain from cheap wooden ships had largely disappeared. Moreover, iron ships were rapidly introduced after 1850, and in the building of these vessels Americans were at a marked cost disadvantage. By 1857 the stage was set for the great decline that followed—a decline the evidences of which would doubtless have been more clearly foreseen in the early fifties had it not been for the remarkable technical leadership of American builders of wooden vessels and the great demand for shipping resulting from

[40] Hutchins, *American Maritime Industries*, pp. 77, 78, 221.

the discovery of gold in California and Australia and the outbreak of the Crimean War.[41]

The United States had from the beginning followed the almost world-wide practice of protecting its merchant marine by imposing discriminatory duties. Such duties were placed both on goods imported in foreign ships and on foreign tonnage entering United States ports. During the European wars, which had continued almost from the beginning of the national existence, foreign countries often did not enforce their discriminatory measures against the United States, or, even if they did, profits were often so great that they were not a serious handicap. All this was changed with the return of peace in 1815, and it was greatly feared that the merchant marine, which had grown so tremendously before we entered the War of 1812, would now be lost. So, believing that the old mercantile system was not advantageous to us, that in a fair field with no favors American ships could compete on advantageous terms with any in the world, the United States, as soon as the War of 1812 was over, adopted an aggressive policy of promoting free navigation.

Congress struck its first blow against the discriminatory system by passing the Reciprocity Act of March 3, 1815. This act empowered the President to establish complete reciprocity in the direct trade; foreign ships could enter American ports under the same terms as were granted United States ships in the ports of the foreign country. Four months after the adoption of this act a treaty in harmony with it was signed with Great Britain. This treaty did away with all discriminatory duties in the direct trade between the two countries insofar as such trade was in the products of the countries concerned.[42]

A period of active negotiation followed in which the State Department, backed by Congress, sought to extend the reciprocity principle chiefly by imposing drastic restrictions on the shipping of those nations which discriminated against the United States.[43] The two most important laws passed were the Navigation Act of 1817 and the Reciprocity Act of 1828. The first prohibited imports in foreign

[41] *Ibid.*, pp. 276–288, 296; Charles H. Cramp, *Commercial Supremacy and Other Papers* (Philadelphia: Moyer and Lesher, 1894), pp. 45–46.

[42] Vernon G. Setser, *The Commercial Reciprocity Policy of the United States, 1774–1829* (Philadelphia: University of Pennsylvania Press, 1937), pp. 184–188.

[43] John G. B. Hutchins, "One Hundred and Fifty Years of American Navigation Policy," *Quarterly Journal of Economics*, LIII (February, 1939), 242–243.

ships which did not come from the country to which the ship belonged, but this restriction was removed if a similar prohibition was not enforced by the foreign country concerned. This legislation also completely closed American coastwise trade to foreign shipping. Although in this form the provision was new, the situation was but little changed, for discriminatory duties had effectively excluded foreign tonnage from the coastwise carrying trade since 1787. The act of 1828 extended to the indirect trade the reciprocal features of earlier legislation. The reciprocity policy of the United States was so successful that by 1830 American ships traded directly with the chief ports of the world without appreciable hindrance from discriminatory regulations. Following 1830 the system was further extended to take in practically all nations and to cover the indirect as well as the direct trade. The repeal of the British navigation laws in 1849 signalized the end of the old mercantilism.

The policy during this period of promoting free navigation was essentially sound. It encouraged the growth of an activity in which the United States had a comparative advantage and furthered worldwide exchange and specialization. Even from the most strictly national point of view, this policy can hardly be justly criticized. Unfortunately, however, the subsequent decline of the merchant marine led to much false or at least careless generalization concerning the maritime history of this period. Earnest writers and speakers, much concerned with the decadence of American shipping after the Civil War and the threatened disappearance of the American flag at sea, have sought to demonstrate that the abandonment of discriminatory duties was the great cause of this decline.[44]

Toward the close of this period, Congress, recognizing the backwardness of the country in ocean steam navigation and fearing the increasing dominance of Great Britain, made a somewhat belated and, in the end, unsuccessful attempt to promote the development of American steamship lines by means of government subsidies. Under an act of March 3, 1845, and subsequent legislation, about $14,500,000 was expended by 1858 in public subsidies to steamship lines.[45] With this encouragement, lines were established to Le Havre, Bremen, and Liverpool from New York, and to Panama from both New York and the West Coast. So, temporarily at least, government

[44] Bates, *American Marine*, Chaps. 7 and 8; Winthrop L. Marvin, *The American Merchant Marine: Its History and Romance from 1620 to 1902* (New York: Charles Scribner's Sons, 1910), Chap. 9.

[45] Royal Meeker, "History of Shipping Subsidies," *Publications of the American Economic Association*, VI, No. 3 (August, 1905), 156.

subventions were a factor in the growth of the United States carrying trade, for none of the transatlantic steam lines could have operated without government help. Although lines to Panama might have developed without subsidies, the service would probably have been poorer and the lines established somewhat later.

When adopted, the subsidy plan had very wide support, chiefly, it appears, because it was a countermove to the virtual British monopoly in this field. Pride in the great accomplishments of the merchant marine and determination that England should not surpass America in any respect seem to have been the leading motives. Other considerations were belief that the British monopoly would lead to high ocean rates, that market information would be delayed for American merchants if mails were carried in British ships, and that steamships could be used as fighting vessels in time of war. Practically no attention was given to an economic analysis of the situation.

As a matter of fact, the whole experiment was poorly planned and miserably administered. Even with the then existing comparative disadvantage in steamship building, a fairly sound case could have been made on the infant industry argument for subsidizing carefully planned and integrated steam lines on routes where traffic could be expected to develop. England had successfully followed this policy in her subsidization of lines to the Mediterranean and India, and on the Atlantic. American-subsidized lines to Panama, especially on the Pacific, met these conditions and were fairly successful. But despite the cost disadvantage and the technical inferiority under which the American lines operated, and the head start which the British enjoyed on the Liverpool–New York route, the United States chose to challenge Britain on the Atlantic. The result was failure. Costs proved much greater than had been anticipated and freight and passenger rates fell as cutthroat competition developed. The two subsidy lines to the Continent required more help than was expected and failed to furnish first-rate service. That to Liverpool lost money steadily despite a great increase in the subsidy.

The failure need not have been as great, and possibly something might have been salvaged from the experiment, had both private management and government administration been better. Neither the Le Havre nor the Bremen line developed outstanding management. Collins, head of the New York–Liverpool line and formerly a successful operator of packet lines, appeared to lose his business judgment when, with the United States Treasury behind him, he set out to challenge the Cunard monopoly. He built luxury liners which did, in-

deed, take the blue ribbon for speed in Atlantic crossings, but the original cost of these ships was excessive, their operating expenses were
extremely high (in part because of their constant need of repairs),
and their rate of depreciation was so great as to make them quite
uneconomical. His last ship, the *Adriatic,* cost an unprecedented
amount (over one million dollars) and was so poorly planned and
designed as to be obsolescent at launching. Under excellent management, the Vanderbilt Line from New York and the Inman Line from
Liverpool operated profitably without subsidies.[46]

Part of the difficulty lay with the government. The cost of construction was increased by requirements designed to make the ships
convertible into warships. But, even more serious, no careful or skilled
attention was devoted to making certain that public funds were most
advantageously employed. Money was lent and subsidies were paid
without proper protection of the public interest. Subsidy contracts
ran over a considerable period of years, and government officials did
not require the prompt fulfillment of contract obligations.[47] The lack
of success of the subsidy lines, their great cost, and finally, the growing political antagonism, especially of southern congressmen, led to
the repeal of the subsidy act and the withdrawal of all subsidy aid
after 1858.

[46] Hutchins, *American Maritime Industries,* p. 358; Marguerite M. McKee, "The
Ship Subsidy Question in United States Politics," *Smith College Studies in History,* VIII,
No. 1 (October, 1922), 22–24; Lane, *Commodore Vanderbilt,* pp. 155–156.
[47] Hutchins, *American Maritime Industries,* pp. 362–368.

CHAPTER VII

Changing Costs and Speed of Transportation and Communication

FUNDAMENTAL as is the story of the rise of the new agencies of transportation to an understanding of American economic development, it must be emphasized that the foregoing account, which stresses construction, technical improvement, and financing, is but one important aspect of the transportation revolution. The impact of these developments on commerce and industry still remains to be examined. First, however, attention must be directed to the core of the revolutionary change itself, the cheapening and facilitating of the movement of goods and persons.

FREIGHT RATES BY LAND

At the close of the War of 1812, heavy wagons drawn along common roads or turnpikes by four- and six-horse teams provided the only means of moving bulky goods over appreciable distances by land. It is hard to realize how prohibitively expensive was such transportation. The following excerpt from a United States Senate Committee Report written in 1816 gives concrete illustration of the obstacles to the development of inland industry. "A coal mine," says the report, "may exist in the United States not more than ten miles from valuable ores of iron and other materials, and both of them be useless until a canal is established between them, as the price of land carriage is too great to be borne by either." [1] The same report points out that a ton of goods could be brought 3,000 miles from Europe to America for about nine dollars, but that for the same sum it could be

[1] *American State Papers: Miscellaneous*, II (1834), 287.

moved only 30 miles overland in this country.[2] Little wonder that under such conditions foreign trade flourished while domestic commerce developed only very slowly.

Any summary of the cost of land transportation presents unusual difficulties because charges depended on many factors, including the condition of the road, the season of the year, the presence or absence of back haul, the level of wages and prices, and competitive conditions; nevertheless a fairly clear picture emerges. Between 1800 and 1819 the ton-mile rate for wagon transportation appears to have varied from about 30 to 70 cents. Writing in 1814, Robert Fulton declared the "usual" cost of wagoning to be 32 cents, and in 1816 a Senate committee reckoned wagonage at 30 cents a ton-mile.[3] At freight rates of 30 cents or more a ton-mile none but the most valuable commodities could be carried very far, and farmers, unable to market their bulky produce at a distance, lacked the ability to purchase lighter manufactured products even though such items could be transported without prohibitive price increase. In 1816 wheat and corn were selling at relatively high prices in Philadelphia, averaging about $1.94 and $1.13, respectively, a bushel.[4] With costs for teaming at 30 cents a ton-mile, the mere charge for carting wheat to Philadelphia equaled its whole selling price if it were drawn 218 miles; for corn this was true for a distance of 135 miles. The month before the Erie Canal was authorized—March, 1817—a committee of the New York State Legislature found that the cost of transportation from Buffalo to New York City was three times the market value of wheat in New York City, six times that of corn, and twelve times that of oats.[5] It is not surprising that under these conditions the industrial revolution lagged in America.

Between 1819 and 1822 rates for hauling goods by wagon fell drastically. Before 1819 westward from Philadelphia and Baltimore they had ranged from 30 cents a ton-mile to more than double that figure. During 1822 they were quoted as low as 12 cents. Thereafter

[2] *Ibid.*

[3] Berry, *Western Prices before 1861,* pp. 72–75; George Rogers Taylor, "Agrarian Discontent in the Mississippi Valley Preceding the War of 1812" (unpublished thesis, University of Chicago, 1929), p. 87; MacGill, *History of Transportation,* pp. 80–93; *Niles' Weekly Register,* VI (May 14, 1814), 169; *American State Papers: Miscellaneous,* II (1834), 287.

[4] Arthur Harrison Cole, *Wholesale Commodity Prices in the United States, 1700–1861, Statistical Supplement* (Cambridge: Harvard University Press, 1938), pp. 174–175.

[5] Israel D. Andrews, "Communication from the Secretary of the Treasury," 1852, *Senate Executive Document* No. 112, 32 Cong., 1 Sess., p. 278. Hereafter referred to as the *Andrews Report.*

charges ranged down to 7 and as high as 20 cents a ton-mile, although charges between about 12 and 17 cents were most common.[6] This sharp reduction finds its chief explanation in the general price deflation of 1819–1821, one of the most drastic in American history. The spread of the turnpikes during this period may possibly have helped to reduce the rates. Some have held that these new toll roads lowered costs by as much as 50 per cent. But it is well to remember that toll charges had to be included in the expense of turnpike transportation and that many of these toll roads fell into serious disrepair soon after completion.[7]

Actual charges for wagon carriage show wide variation even within given sections of the country. Thus, for three turnpikes leading out of Boston the situation was as follows: rates northward to Concord, New Hampshire, were 20 cents a ton-mile in 1822, westward to Worcester 17.5 cents in 1833, and southward to Fall River 7.5 cents in 1828.[8] A Pennsylvania estimate of 1824 gives the cost of turnpike transportation in that state as a little more than 13 cents a ton-mile. At the time when railroads were first introduced, 20 cents a ton-mile appears to have been regarded as the average wagon charge. By the fifties, 15 cents was considered the usual rate on "ordinary highways."[9]

On even the earliest railroads rates were appreciably lower than those charged for wagon transportation. When the railroad from Boston to Worcester began operation in 1833, its charge between the two terminals was 6.25 cents a ton-mile as compared to 17.5 cents on the turnpike.[10] As railroads improved and iron rails linked the chief commercial centers of the country, land transportation became so cheap

[6] Berry, *Western Prices before 1861*, pp. 74–77, 81–83; Hunter, *Steamboats on the Western Rivers*, p. 658.

[7] MacGill, *History of Transportation*, p. 89; Arthur Twining Hadley, *Railroad Transportation* (New York: G. P. Putnam's Sons, 1903), p. 26; Frederick Jackson Turner, *Rise of the New West, 1819–1829* (Vol. XIV of Albert Bushnell Hart, ed., *The American Nation: A History*, 27 vols., New York: Harper & Brothers, 1906), p. 100; Durrenberger, *Turnpikes*, p. 127.

[8] Roberts, *The Middlesex Canal, 1793–1860*, p. 149; Taylor, "The Turnpike Era in New England," p. 319; *Report of the Board of Commissioners of Internal Improvements in Relation to the Examination of Sundry Routes for a Railway from Boston to Providence* (Boston: 1828), p. 49; *Report of the Board of Commissioners for the Survey of One or More Routes for a Railway from Boston to Albany* (Boston, 1828), pp. 49–52.

[9] George L. Vose, *Handbook of Railroad Construction: For the Use of American Engineers* (Boston: James Monroe and Company, 1857), p. 3; Logan G. McPherson, *Railroad Freight Rates in Relation to the Industry and Commerce of the United States* (New York: Henry Holt and Company, 1909), pp. 148–149; MacGill, *History of Transportation*, p. 223, fn.; *Hunt's Merchants' Magazine*, V (September, 1841), 284; *Andrews Report*, p. 380; Ringwalt, *Development of Transportation Systems in the United States*, p. 28.

[10] Taylor, "The Turnpike Era in New England," p. 319.

as to permit long-distance shipment of bulky products. Rail freight rates varied from one part of the country to another and present difficulties of comparison because special-class and commodity rates were soon adopted by each railroad. In Virginia in 1860 the Richmond and Petersburg Railroad, primarily a coal-carrying line, charged 9 cents a ton-mile for wheat and 2.5 cents for coal. But the produce-carrying Orange and Alexandria charged 5 cents a ton-mile for wheat, 3 cents for coal, and, in order to stimulate wheat production, only 2 cents on plaster and manure. Also, rates fluctuated with the business cycle and according to competitive conditions. Nevertheless, a strong trend downward to the Civil War is clearly indicated. For railroads in New York State, the average ton-mile charge was 9.04 cents for first-class freight and 5.79 for second-class in 1848. In 1851, the general average was 4.05 cents and by 1860 it was 2.2 cents. For bulky products moved over long distances rates went even lower. Just before the Civil War the charge on all-rail shipments of wheat from Chicago to New York was 34.8 cents a bushel, or about 1.2 cents a ton-mile.[11] When these rates at the end of the period are compared with those for 1815–1820 it will be seen that for shipments by land of bulky products over appreciable distances freight charges had been reduced by approximately 95 per cent. Less than half of this decline merely reflects a decline in the general level of prices; the remainder represents a real reduction in the cost of land transport. The magnitude of this change was so great as to permit a major revolution in domestic commerce.

FREIGHT RATES BY RIVER AND CANAL

During the period covered by this study, steamboats facilitated and cheapened the carriage of freight, especially upstream, and canals created new routes over which low water rates replaced the high cost of land carriage. The effect of the steamboat in reducing shipment costs was greatest on the chief navigable rivers. Even for down-river trade, flatboat shipments were not as inexpensive as might be expected, for on most large rivers the clumsy wooden craft could not make the return trip and had to be sold at a substantial loss at their

[11] Berry, *Western Prices before 1861*, pp. 71 ff.; W. M. Grosvenor, "The Railroads and the Farms," *Atlantic Monthly*, XXXII, No. 193 (November, 1873), 597; *Report on the Internal Commerce of the United States*, 1891, *House Executive Document* No. 6, Pt. 2, 52 Cong., 1 Sess., p. xxxiii; Ringwalt, *Development of Transportation Systems in the United States*, p. 132; Charles W. Turner, "Railroad Service to Virginia Farmers, 1828–1860," *Agricultural History*, XXII, No. 4 (October, 1948), 244–245.

destination. Mississippi flats costing about $75 were sold for what they would bring as lumber at New Orleans, and on the Susquehanna, flatboats carrying 40 to 50 tons, and costing $65, were sold for about $15 on their arrival at downriver markets.[12] On the Mississippi-Ohio system, freight costs declined almost as sensationally as the decline shown above for land routes. Though paucity of data for the early years and the violence of seasonal fluctuations throughout somewhat obscure the picture, careful studies now indicate that just before the Civil War downstream rates averaged 25 to 30 per cent, and upstream charges 5 to 10 per cent of their respective levels in 1815–1819. At times during the fifties the rate a hundred pounds from Cincinnati to New Orleans occasionally fell to 20 cents or even lower. A charge of 20 cents was approximately equivalent to the extremely low rate of .27 cents a ton-mile. Most of the decline came in the early twenties, thus by the third decade of the century freeing the land-locked central valley from high freights on its bulky exports and, more than any other single factor, promoting the rapid development of the trans-Appalachian frontier.[13] For other rivers similar rate studies do not appear to have been made, but conclusions drawn from fragmentary data available for rates on the Hudson indicate that freight charges on that river fell from about 6.2 cents a ton-mile in 1814 to .7 cents in 1854, a decline of nearly 90 per cent.[14]

A very substantial reduction in charges also appeared for coastwise shipments and on the Great Lakes, although it is uncertain to what extent the steamboat was responsible. As late as 1860 sailing vessels were still giving a good account of themselves in both areas despite strongly increasing steam competition. On major commodities shipped coastwise from New Orleans to Atlantic ports, freight rates declined from 60 to 75 per cent during the period [15] and shipments for long distances on the Lakes were carried for as low as .5 cents a ton-mile in 1854.[16]

The canals made their contribution by permitting relatively cheap water transportation to be substituted for high-cost movement by

[12] Baldwin, The Keelboat Age on Western Waters, p. 54; Hazard's Register of Pennsylvania, III (1829), 17–18.

[13] Berry, Western Prices before 1861, pp. 42–70, 557–561; Hunter, Steamboats on the Western Rivers, pp. 374–377, 658–659; Frank Haigh Dixon, A Traffic History of the Mississippi River System (National Waterways Commission, Document No. 11, Washington: Government Printing Office, 1917), pp. 26–28.

[14] Cf. Letter from Robert Fulton to Gouverneur Morris, quoted in Niles' Weekly Register, VI (May 14, 1814), 169, and a report of the State Engineer of New York in Hunt's Merchants' Magazine, XXXI (July, 1854), 123.

[15] Based on a careful sampling by the author of newspaper quotations.

[16] Hunt's Merchants' Magazine, XXXI (July, 1854), 123.

land. Little is known as to the rates of carriage on the least prosperous of the canals, but their very failure, except where they were subjected to severe railroad competition, suggests that they may not
have greatly lowered transportation costs. At any rate we do know
that such moderately successful artificial waterways as the Pennsylvania Main Line and the Blackstone charged rates substantially below those for wagon carriage. Thus rates a ton-mile on the Pennsylvania Canal were 2.70 cents in 1853 [17] and on the Blackstone, about
twenty years earlier, 4.5 cents.[18]

The most successful artificial waterways greatly stimulated trade
by their ability to offer extremely low-cost transportation. In 1853,
ton-mile rates on the Ohio Canal were 1.00 cents; on the Illinois,
1.40 cents. During the fifties, rates on the Chesapeake and Ohio
Canal varied from 2 cents a ton-mile for valuable commodities
shipped relatively short distances to .25 cents a ton-mile for coal.
Before the construction of the Erie Canal the expense of transportation from Buffalo to New York City was $100 a ton, but rates fell
sharply with the completion of the canal. From 1830 to 1850 they
averaged only $8.81 a ton, and in 1852 ranged from $3.00 to $7.00,
depending on the character of the shipments. Freights westward
were higher, averaging $16.12 a ton from 1830 to 1850. Converting
these data to rates a ton-mile and adding annual rates for the Erie
Canal available in the fifties give the following picture of declining
average charges over the Erie Canal route:

Date	Route	Cents a Ton-Mile
1817	Buffalo to New York	19.12
1830–1850	Buffalo to New York	1.68
1830–1850	New York to Buffalo	3.35
1853	Both directions between Albany and Buffalo	.57–1.34
1854	between Albany and Buffalo	1.1
1857	Buffalo to Albany	.799
1858	Buffalo to Albany	.797
1859	Buffalo to Albany	.672
1860	Buffalo to Albany	.994

The Erie Canal ton-mile average for 1857–1860 was .8155 cents, a
reduction of more than 95 per cent from rates a ton-mile charged
in 1817 from Buffalo to New York.[19] Ton-mile charges for the canal

[17] Ibid.
[18] Taylor, "The Turnpike Era in New England," p. 294.
[19] Hunt's Merchants' Magazine, XXIII (1850), 387, and XXXI (1854), 123;

trip from Albany to Buffalo fell from 5.51 cents in 1830 to .66 cents in 1860, and from Buffalo to Albany from 2.50 to 1.07 cents in the same period.[20] The average cost of transporting a barrel of flour from Buffalo to Albany fell from 71 cents in 1841 to 34 cents in 1858.[21] Table 2 in Appendix A summarizes the striking decline in transportation rates during the four and one half decades covered by this volume and indicates comparative charges by the different transport agencies.

SPEED OF FREIGHT SHIPMENTS

The time necessary for moving heavy freight in the turnpike and canal era seems extremely slow by later standards. Teams drawing loaded wagons did well to average twenty miles a day or 2 miles an hour. This was also about average time for heavily laden canalboats, though if traffic were dense or locks frequent, even this rate might not be achieved. From 1853 through 1858 the average rate of speed for through flour shipments on the Erie Canal was about 1.8 miles an hour.

Steamboats and steam railroads greatly speeded up freight movement. By the end of the period the fastest packets on the Ohio and Mississippi were able to average up- and downstream about 15 miles an hour, but the usual rate for western steamboats was probably under 10 miles an hour. The speediest Hudson steamboats made 20 miles an hour or a little better. But freight moved by steam on the Hudson was largely towed in barges or canalboats, and moved much more slowly. Steam tugboats greatly facilitated the movement of sailing vessels in harbors and rivers. They often saved sailing vessels two or three days' delay in entering or leaving New York Harbor. And with unfavorable winds, vessels often required weeks to ascend the river to New Orleans. As early as 1815, steamboats were used to reduce greatly the time for this passage.

Massachusetts railroads included in their official reports of 1860 the average speed of freight train movement. Minor roads, probably reporting for combination freight and passenger trains carrying very little freight, reported average speeds as high as 20 or even 30 miles

Andrews Report, p. 278; Joseph Nimmo, Jr., *Report on the Internal Commerce of the United States, House Document* No. 32, Pt. 3, 45 Cong., 3 Sess. (1879), p. 110, referred to hereafter as the *Nimmo Report*, 1879.

[20] Computed from Albion, *The Rise of New York Port*, p. 411, App. XVIII. Albion's table provides annual averages 1830–1860.

[21] *Hunt's Merchants' Magazine*, XLII (January, 1860), 118.

an hour. But the more important lines claimed a rate of only 10 to 12 miles an hour. A New York State report for 1858 gives the average rate of speed of freight trains, including stops, as 10.69 miles an hour, and the average speed while in motion as 13.95 miles an hour. For the country as a whole, the speed of railroad freight shipments over appreciable distances certainly did not by 1860 exceed that on New York lines, and in all probability was less.[22]

So by 1860 steamboats and steam railroads were moving freight approximately five times as fast as was usual by wagon and canal-boat. Though figures for the average rates of speed are helpful in showing the changes which took place, it is well to point out that they do not present the whole story. In the first place, average speeds are typically available only for single railroad lines and so may take no account of transfer delays en route for shipments over appreciable distances. In addition to the ordinary delays incident to switching and transfer, nonuniformity of track gauges often made necessary the actual transfer of goods from one freight car to another. In the second place, average rates of speed do not take account of the relatively direct, shorter-distance routes which were often available for rail as compared with water shipment. Thus the river distance from Cincinnati to Pittsburgh was 470 miles, by railroad 311 miles. In the late fifties water shipments averaged about 3 days and 6 hours between these two cities, but only 1 day and 12 hours by rail.[23]

In 1817 goods could be shipped most expeditiously from Cincinnati to New York City by keelboat to Pittsburgh, wagon to Philadelphia, and wagon, or wagon and river, to New York. Such shipments necessarily consumed more than 50 days. By the early fifties, freight sent from Cincinnati could reach the same destination in 28 days by steamboat and packet to New York via New Orleans; in 18 days by the Ohio Canal, Lake Erie, the Erie Canal, and the Hudson River; or in only 6 to 8 days by railroad.[24]

In order further to facilitate shipments, express companies sprang up in nearly every part of the country during the forties and fifties. They were service organizations designed to secure the rapid and safe delivery of money, important papers, and especially valuable

[22] Durrenberger, *Turnpikes*, p. 118; *Returns of the Railroad Corporations in Massachusetts, 1860*, Massachusetts *Public Document* No. 46 (Boston: 1861), unnumbered folding table; Harlow, *Old Towpaths*, pp. 124, 142; Morrison, *History of American Steam Navigation*, pp. 560–571; Hunter, *Steamboats on the Western Rivers*, pp. 23–24; *Niles' Weekly Register*, IX (November 4, 1815), 171; Albion, *The Rise of New York Port*, pp. 147, 158; *Hunt's Merchants' Magazine*, XL (1859), 501, XLII (1860), 118.

[23] Hunter, *Steamboats on the Western Rivers*, p. 490.

[24] See Table 3 in Appendix A.

or perishable freight. First appearing in the East in the latter part of the thirties, these companies spread rapidly with, and even ahead of, the railroads. By the fifties they were active everywhere east of the Rockies, had established service to Europe and Canada, and were doing a tremendous business carrying gold dust by stagecoach in California. In 1860 the celebrated *Pony Express* made its first trip nearly 2,000 miles across mountains and deserts from San Francisco to St. Joseph.

At first, agents traveling with carpetbags easily handled all of the traffic, but the volume and character of the business expanded rapidly. Soon special express cars became common on railroad trains. Stagecoach lines were organized to do an express business, and for local delivery the horse-drawn express wagons, still a familiar sight on American streets in the first quarter of the nineteenth century, began to appear on city streets. Even bulky products were accepted for express shipment, and by the middle fifties fast freights were operated by express companies between Chicago and New York. Business was extended to include money-order, collecting, and letter-of-credit services. Agents would even accept a Negro slave, attach a waybill to his clothing, transport him in the express car, and deliver him to his proper destination.

A tremendous number of express companies sprang up as soon as the business was shown to be profitable. Though a large number of small, local firms continued in existence, five, through consolidation and expansion, controlled most of the long-distance express business by 1860. These were the American, Wells Fargo, Adams, United States, and National companies. Anything like satisfactory information on the total amount of business done by these companies does not exist, but some indication of their importance may be derived from the following statement made by Henry Wells in 1864:

. . . the annual expenses of the Adams, American, and United companies, incurred in the transportation of freight and the salaries of agents and messengers, amount to not less than *ten millions of dollars;* that the single carpet-sack of 1839 has now grown into more than thirty cars forwarded daily from the East by the American Express Co. alone, while the Adams and United States Co's each require at least an equal amount of transportation; that the American Express conveys freight over 9,000 miles a day in a *direct* line, while its messengers travel daily more than 30,000 miles, and wherever on this extensive route there is a village with a post-office, this company has an agency at that point.[25]

[25] Henry Wells, *Sketch of the Rise, Progress, and Present Condition of the Express System* (Albany: Van Benthuysen's Printing House, 1864). See also Alvin F. Harlow,

TRANSPORTATION OF PERSONS

The accompanying table presents a picture of the striking changes which took place between 1816 and 1860 in the cost and speed of passenger travel in the United States. Commenting on the data shown for travel between Philadelphia and Quebec in 1816, a contributor to *Niles' Weekly Register* declared that it showed "expedition in travelling . . . [which] . . . cannot be equalled in any other country on the globe." [26]

TRAVEL FROM PHILADELPHIA TO QUEBEC IN 1816 AND 1860

(*By railroad in 1860*)

Mode of Travel, 1816	Expense		Hours		Miles	
	1816	1860	1816	1860	1816	1860
From:						
Philadelphia to New York by steamboats and stage	$10	$3.00	13	4:00	96	90
New York to Albany, by steamboat	7	3.00	24	9:05	160	150
Albany to Whitehall, by stages (fare $5, expense $3)	8		12		70	
Whitehall to St. Johns by steamboat	9	7.71	26	10:45	150	246
St. Johns to Montreal . .	3		4		37	
Montreal to Quebec, by steamboat	10	4.98	24	7:25	186	168
	$47	$18.69	103	31:15	699	654

Sources: Niles' Weekly Register, X (August 3, 1816), p. 381; Dinsmore's Railroad and Steam Navigation Guide, July, 1859, and September, 1860.

In 1860 the whole journey could be made by railroad over seven different lines. Railroads had shortened the distance by only about 45 miles but had reduced the actual traveling time almost 70 per cent. The cost had apparently fallen more than 50 per cent, but this comparison is complicated by the fact that the data for 1816 apparently include at least some expenses in addition to the passenger fare. The most striking comparison is that for total elapsed time for the whole journey. For 1816 the contributor to *Niles' Weekly Register* reported that the whole trip would require about 5½ successive days

Old Waybills: The Romance of the Express Companies (New York: D. Appleton-Century Company, 1934), *passim;* Pierce, *A History of Chicago*, II, 62–64; A. L. Stimson, *History of the Express Companies* (New York: 1858).
[26] *Niles' Weekly Register*, X (August 3, 1816), 381.

because it was necessary to "tarry 6 hours in New York, 9 hours in Albany, 19 at Whitehall, and 6 in Montreal." [27] By 1860 it was possible to leave Philadelphia on Monday at 2 p.m. and arrive at Quebec on Wednesday at 3:55 p.m., for a total elapsed time of 2 days, 1 hour, and 55 minutes.[28]

Stagecoaches were the symbol of rapid transportation in 1815. Though coastwise voyages were less expensive and certainly more comfortable, travelers in a hurry took the stages, whose speed was being considerably increased as a result of the rapid spread of turnpikes. In 1800 the journey by stage from Boston to New York involved overnight stops at Worcester, Hartford, and Stamford, and consumed 74 hours. By 1825 the road had been both shortened and improved so that only one overnight stop was made and the whole journey was completed in 41 hours. And in 1833, by eliminating the overnight stop, the time was reduced to 33¼ hours.[29]

On good roads, stagecoaches appear to have averaged from about 6 to 8 miles an hour, though, apparently, faster time was sometimes obtained on important routes where competition was keen. Thus, between New York and Philadelphia stagecoaches were reported in 1819 to be traveling 11½ miles an hour. On a New York plank road, stages averaged 9 miles an hour including stops. Charges for coach travel, 1815–1819, appear to have varied from 5 to 9 cents a mile, with 7 cents about the average rate. Stagecoach fares on the fine Boston-Worcester Turnpike were 5.0 cents a mile in the early thirties. By 1850 they were reported to average about 6.5 cents a mile.[30]

By canal, travel was a leisurely business and relatively cheap. The rate of movement varied from 1½ to 2 miles an hour for the Erie "line" boats, which catered to immigrants, to about 5 miles an hour for the fastest canal packets. Regular packets averaged about 3 to 4 miles an hour on the Erie and on the Main Line Canal of Pennsylvania. Between Richmond and Lynchburg on the James River and Kanawha Canal, packet boats made the good time of about 4½ miles an hour. Sometimes they moved even faster than those on the Erie when the captain or passengers were willing to pay the fine for

[27] *Ibid.*

[28] *Dinsmore's Railroad and Steam Navigation Guide,* July, 1859, and September, 1860.

[29] Taylor, "The Turnpike Era in New England," pp. 241–243.

[30] *Niles' Weekly Register,* XVI (May 1, 1819), 176; MacGill, *History of Transportation,* pp. 75, 302; *Niles' Weekly Register,* X (August 3, 1816), 381; Blake McKelvey, *Rochester: The Water-Power City, 1812–1854* (Cambridge: Harvard University Press, 1945), p. 94; Taylor, "The Turnpike Era in New England," p. 319; Ringwalt, *Development of Transportation Systems in the United States,* p. 107; Lardner, *Railway Economy,* p. 345.

exceeding the legal speed limit of 4 miles an hour. Fares varied from 1.5 to 2.0 cents a mile on the slower boats to 3.0 to 4.0 cents a mile on the speedier ones. The cost of meals was often included in the charge for transportation.[31]

The steamboat greatly speeded up travel by water. This was especially marked for upriver journeys on the Mississippi-Ohio system. Keelboats needed about 3 months to go from New Orleans to the Ohio above Louisville, and the fare was $100 to $125. The steamboat time in the fifties was 8 days or even less. Though at first passenger fares were high—the *New Orleans* charged $25 from New Orleans to Natchez in 1811—they were rapidly reduced until, during the last two decades before the Civil War, the cost of passenger travel on western rivers was the cheapest in the world.

For speed, dependability, and comfort, the eastern steamboat was greatly preferred by travelers and commuters over stagecoaches and sailing packets. The superiority of steam was immediately evident for such short runs as ferry service in New York Harbor. Here passage by steamboat was assured in a matter of minutes, whereas by sailing packet, if winds were unfavorable or failed completely, passage might actually consume hours. For longer journeys also most of the passenger traffic was soon absorbed by the steamboats. The tedious and uncomfortable stage trip from New York to Boston took about 2½ days in 1815. Steamboats operating from New York to Connecticut and Rhode Island ports greatly reduced the time and discomfort of this journey. On the Hudson, sailing packets transported passengers from New York to Albany, about 150 miles, in from 2 days to 2 weeks. The fare by sloop in 1800 was $2.00 a passenger without meals. By the thirties, steamboats completed this trip in less than 10 hours; by the fifties, under 8. In the beginning, Hudson steamboat fares were high. Until the end of the Livingston monopoly the passenger rate from New York to Albany was $7.00. Subsequently $5.00 was a common charge, often greatly reduced during sporadic periods of rate warfare. By 1850 passenger rates had fallen to fifty cents without stateroom.[32]

---

[31] Harlow, *Old Towpaths*, pp. 124, 142, 343, 360–364; McKelvey, *Rochester: The Water-Power City, 1812–1854*, p. 94; Pierce, *A History of Chicago*, II, 38–39; Dunaway, *History of the James River and Kanawha Company*, pp. 171–172; Clyde H. Freed, *The Story of Railroad Passenger Fares* (Washington: Clyde H. Freed, 1942), p. 6.

[32] MacGill, *History of Transportation*, pp. 76–77; Ambler, *A History of Transportation in the Ohio Valley*, p. 124; Berry, *Western Prices before 1861*, pp. 57–58; Albion, *The Rise of New York Port*, pp. 153–154; Lardner, *Railway Economy*, p. 319; Freed, *The Story of Railroad Passenger Fares*, pp. 17–21; John Maude, *Visit to the Falls of Niagara in 1800* (London: Longmans, Rees, Orme, Brown and Green, 1826). p. 19.

Almost from the beginning, railroads provided the fastest known method of passenger transportation. Early speeds of 10 to 15 miles an hour were about doubled, so that by 1860 a speed of 20 miles was not uncommon for the better roads, some averaging 25 to 30 miles an hour. Passenger fares, though still appreciably higher than those by water, were fairly low during the late forties and the fifties. In 1848 rates a mile averaged 3 cents or less in New England, 2.5 to 3.5 cents in New York, less than 4.5 in the West, and 4 to 5 cents in the South. By the middle fifties they appear to have been slightly lower.[33]

Railroads often cut rates to meet competition on competitive portions of their routes. Thus the Providence and Stonington Railroad, in order to meet water competition, sold tickets from Providence to New York for $1.00, but from way points charged $3.00. In 1854 rates as low as 1 cent a mile were charged by the Hudson River Railroad, which had steamboat competition. Unlike British practice, most railroads in the United States adopted a one-class system, but a few had two or even three classes and charged accordingly. Moreover, by the fifties some of the lines to the West were operating immigrant trains. The fares were very low, about 1 cent a mile, and the accommodations sometimes little more than a box car with wooden benches.[34]

COST AND SPEED OF OCEAN TRANSPORTATION

The manner in which the packets and steamships greatly facilitated sea commerce by their regular and dependable sailings has been commented upon in Chapter VI. Something has also been said of larger and faster ships, but in the preceding pages the chief emphasis has been on the changes in technique and business organization. It remains, therefore, to point out their effect, first, in greatly decreasing the time consumed for ocean voyages and, second, in reducing the cost of shipping goods by sea.

The time taken to transport goods by sea underwent a truly revolutionary reduction during the period of this study. The speed of sail-

[33] MacGill, *History of Transportation*, pp. 574–582; *Returns of the Railroad Corporations of Massachusetts, 1860*, unnumbered folding table; Turner, "Railroad Service to Virginia Farmers, 1828–1860," pp. 240–242; John Bach McMaster, *A History of the People of the United States from the Revolution to the Civil War* (8 vols., New York: D. Appleton and Company, 1883–1913), VIII, 96.

[34] Rowland Gibson Hazard, "Speech on the Act to Equalize Charges for Carrying Freight," (1851) in Caroline Hazard, ed., *Economics and Politics* (Boston: Houghton Mifflin Company, 1889), p. 66; Edgar W. Martin, *The Standard of Living in 1860* (Chicago: The University of Chicago Press, 1942), pp. 253–254.

ing ships was in 1815 much the same as it had been for over a hundred years. On the westward trip across the stormy Atlantic, vessels were fortunate to make the passage from Liverpool to New York in 40 to 50 days. In 1816 ninety-seven vessels averaged 49.4 days on this westbound route.[35] Eastbound, with the help of the prevailing westerlies and the Gulf Stream, the time was less, probably under two thirds that required westbound.[36] To more distant points, voyages took proportionately longer. Thus, to sail from China to the Atlantic ports of the United States usually required from 125 to 160 days, although much slower voyages were not uncommon.[37]

With the introduction of the first packet line in 1818 came an emphasis on increased sailing speed which grew as the period advanced. From 1818 to 1832 packets westbound from Liverpool to New York averaged 37.9 days. Nor was the effect felt by the packets alone, for as early as 1826 the average of all ships on the Liverpool–New York run had been reduced from 49.4 days in 1816 to about 42 days. By 1848–1857 the average packet time had fallen to 34.6 days. Similar reductions were achieved on other sea lanes by the packets. For example, the average duration of westbound passages from Le Havre to New York was 36.7 days in 1848–1857, as compared with 40 days in 1818–1832.[38]

These packet figures are impressive because they are averages for very considerable periods. Of course, sailing ships were greatly dependent upon the weather, and individual trips—or even averages for one year only—might reflect merely the condition of the weather. This is brought out in R. G. Albion's detailed study of the records of individual ships. Even the fastest packet would have very slow voyages when winds were unfavorable. From 1818 to 1848 packets westbound to New York from Liverpool, London, and Le Havre showed great variation in time, with the slowest trip taking 83 days and the fastest but 16.[39] A speedy packet on the Dramatic Line, experiencing strong, unfavorable winds, took 54 days to reach New York from Liverpool in 1848. Lack of wind could be just as troublesome. The packet *Erie*, proceeding from Le Havre to New York in 1837, was at sea 82 days, 40 of which she spent completely becalmed.[40]

In the final fifteen years of the period, the clipper ships, of course, still further decreased the sailing time. While regular sailing ships

[35] Albion, *The Rise of New York Port*, p. 51.
[36] Albion, *Square-Riggers on Schedule*, p. 322.
[37] Cutler, *Greyhounds of the Sea*, pp. 80–81.
[38] Albion, *Square-Riggers on Schedule*, pp. 192, 317.
[39] *Ibid.*, p. 192.   [40] *Ibid.*, p. 196.

ordinarily took 150 to 200 days to sail from Atlantic ports to California, clippers frequently made it within 110 days.[41] Before 1830 the average speed of a sailing ship was not ordinarily over five knots. General averages for the clippers are not available, but at least on their faster runs their speed was two or three times as great. Thus, the *Red Jacket* did 14.7 knots an hour for six consecutive days on the Atlantic and the *Lightning* averaged 11 knots on a speedy trip from Australia to England.[42]

Even before the clipper era the real revolution in speed was begun by the steamships. The three steamships operating between England and New York in 1839 averaged 17 days on the westward trip and a little over 15.4 days on the eastward journey, with the result that the packet time was reduced by about 50 per cent for westbound, though the reduction was considerably less for eastbound passages.[43] As the steamships improved, their time was further reduced, so that by 1860 record trips were made in less than 10 days, and Atlantic crossings by steamship requiring more than 13 or 14 days were considered unusually slow.

With the great improvements in speed and in regularity of sailing it might be supposed that freight and passenger rates on the Atlantic would have advanced. This was decidedly not the case. The increased speed and the larger size of the ships actually permitted a reduction of shipping costs, as did also improved business organization. As a result, both passenger and freight rates were greatly reduced.

As to passenger rates, information is fragmentary, and the situation is complicated by the changing character of the accommodations and the varying classes of service offered, but the downward tendency is clear enough. At the beginning of the packet service, rates were $186, food and wines included. As wine accounted for about $20 and very good Madeira was available at less than $3 a gallon, one can understand how the passengers withstood the tedium of passages which took 40 to 60 days. During the thirties the packets came to an agreement not to include wine in the price of passage. Eliminating this fee, we find packets charging $166 during the first few years, about $120 in the thirties, and as low as $75 in the forties.[44] Thereafter they carried very few first-class passengers.

[41] Albion, *The Rise of New York Port*, pp. 358–359.
[42] Morison, *The Maritime History of Massachusetts 1783–1860*, p. 343.
[43] Frank C. Bowen, *A Century of Atlantic Travel, 1830–1930* (Boston: Little, Brown & Company, 1930), p. 35.
[44] Albion, *Square-Riggers on Schedule*, pp. 233–235.

Steamship fares also declined, although fast ships could secure a premium. In 1838 both the *Great Western* and the *Sirius* had first-class rates of $140 with wine included. The much speedier Cunarders about a decade later were charging $190. In 1851 Cunard and Collins reduced their fares from about $165 to $140 as a result of competition from slower steamships which were charging less than $100. By 1852 the Inman Line to Philadelphia had reduced rates to $90 for first-class passage.[45] But for the faster ships reductions came more slowly. By 1855 Collins and Cunard were charging $130 for first-class passage, but in that year Vanderbilt on his line to Le Havre cut the rate to $110. Competition was very keen in 1857, when Vanderbilt reduced fares to Bremen to $80 and to Southampton to between $100 and $130.[46]

Reductions were greater and the picture is clearer for freight rates, at least from United States ports to Europe. Freight charges did, of course, fluctuate considerably with the season of the year and the number of ships seeking cargoes. Nevertheless, a strong downward tendency is clearly evident. J. Smith Homans provides tables showing rates on cotton a pound from New York to Liverpool and to Le Havre for most of this period. Rates to Liverpool declined from a half a penny a pound in 1823 to three sixteenths of a penny in 1855 and to Le Havre from one and one-quarter cents in 1824 to one quarter of a cent in 1855. As individual quotations may be subject to erratic variations, averages are shown in the following table:

AVERAGE FREIGHT RATES A POUND ON COTTON FROM NEW YORK TO
LIVERPOOL AND LE HAVRE, 1823–1855

Years	Liverpool (*pence a pound*)	Le Havre (*cents a pound*)
1823–1825	.5	1.25
1826–1830	.41	.95
1831–1835	.4	.88
1836–1840	.39	.9
1841–1845	.3	.83
1846–1850	.23	.7
1851–1855	.16	.38

Sources: Computed from J. Smith Homans and J. Smith Homans, Jr., *A Cyclopedia of Commerce and Commercial Navigation* (New York: Harper & Brothers, 1859), I, 451. For Le Havre, the data begin in 1824. Homans' quotations are for October 1. Where a spread of prices is indicated, the high has been used.

[45] *Ibid.*, p. 235; Bowen, *A Century of Atlantic Travel, 1830–1930*, pp. 53, 73; Tyler, *Steam Conquers the Atlantic*, p. 197.
[46] Lane, *Commodore Vanderbilt*, pp. 147–152.

Thus it will be seen that freight rates on cotton to these two ports declined about two thirds from 1823–1825 to 1851–1855.

A similar, though less drastic decline, took place in freight rates on cotton from New Orleans to the same two European ports. In

FREIGHT RATES A POUND ON COTTON FROM NEW ORLEANS TO
LIVERPOOL AND LE HAVRE, 1822–1856

Average for year	Liverpool (*pence a pound*)	Le Havre (*cents a pound*)
1822	1.09	2.31
1826	.86	1.91
1831	.76	1.60
1836	.65	1.44
1841	.50	1.03
1846	.53	1.10
1851	.47	1.00
1856	.47	1.00

Sources: Average of monthly quotations which were taken for a day as near the middle of the month as possible. Data for 1822 from the *New York Shipping and Commercial List*, New York City, and for the other years from the *New Orleans Price Current*, New Orleans. For 1822, quotations were available for eight months only. Price spreads were treated as in the foregoing table.

the decade before the War of 1812, freight rates from New Orleans to Europe were ordinarily 4 to 5 cents a pound on cotton.[47] Apparently they dropped soon after the war, for scattered quotations for 1817 through 1819 range from 2 to 4 cents a pound for cotton to France.[48] By 1822 average rates were about half what they had been before the war. The persistent downward trend in subsequent years is evident from the accompanying table. By 1856 freight rates both to Liverpool and Le Havre were less than half their average in the early twenties. Less complete data for other commodities and to other destinations indicate a general trend in freight rates similar to that which took place for cotton. Albion reports that rates for fine freight on sailing vessels was $10 a ton in the twenties and thirties.[49] Steamboat tariffs appear to have been appreciably higher. Early in 1852 it was reported that the Bremen Line had received $7.50 to $12.50 a ton for eastbound freight and $25.00 to $35.00 for westbound. But competition became very severe in this year and rates from Europe fell from £7 10s to £4 a ton.[50]

[47] Files of the *Louisiana Gazette,* New Orleans.
[48] *New York Shipping and Commercial List,* New York, December 3, 1817, and January 1, June 28, 1818; *Orleans Gazette,* New Orleans, March 11, 1819; and *Louisiana Gazette,* New Orleans, April 19 through August 23, 1819; *Niles' Weekly Register,* X (March 2, 1816), 2.
[49] Albion, *Square-Riggers on Schedule,* pp. 47. 110.
[50] *Senate Report* No. 267, 32 Cong., 1 Sess., II, 45; William Shaw Lindsay, *History*

IMPROVED COMMUNICATIONS

Accompanying the revolution in transportation came equally drastic improvements in communication. The postal service gained directly from the improved means of transportation, and the invention and development of the magnetic telegraph opened up a whole new field of rapid communication.

As a division of the Treasury Department until 1825 the Post Office was looked upon primarily as a source of revenue. Nevertheless, a strong feeling also existed that the benefits of the post should be rapidly extended to meet the needs of newly settled areas. In line with this latter policy the number of post offices was rapidly increased. Numbering only 3,000 in 1815, they had grown to 8,401 in 1830 and more than 28,000 in 1860. As late as 1825 more than half of the mail was carried by horseback riders, but stagecoaches rapidly became the chief transporters of the nation's mail and so remained possibly as late as 1850. Coastwise packets were used, but they were seldom as fast as land conveyances. Steamboat lines had been declared post routes in 1813, and railroads in 1838, but neither was always superior to the older methods. On eastern rivers steamboat lines became important mail carriers, but not so on the Ohio and Mississippi, where the irregularity of steamboat sailings defeated all attempts to set up extensive river mail routes. At first railways were neither as fast nor as certain for the delivery of mails as post riders or stagecoaches, but in the last two decades of our period improved technical operation of railroads and the rapid spread of the rail net doomed the older methods of transporting the mails in the more settled parts of the country.

Though the government showed commendable energy in extending post roads and establishing post offices in new communities, this effort seems to have exhausted its initiative, for in other respects improvements in the service came but slowly and only after long public agitation. Postal rates, though raised for revenue purposes during the War of 1812, were in 1816 restored to substantially the level of 1799. These rates were on a zonal basis and not low. Thus a letter written on one sheet of paper cost 6 cents within 30 miles. A sliding scale was provided for three intermediate zones, over 400 miles the charge being 25 cents. The postal rate was doubled if two sheets of paper

---

of *Merchant Shipping and Ancient Commerce* (London: S. Low, Marston, Searle, and Rivington, 1883), IV, 214. Both references are cited by Tyler, *Steam Conquers the Atlantic*, p. 199.

were used. Not until 1845 were these rates considerably reduced and the zone system simplified. Finally, in 1851, the rate was lowered to 3 cents for letters going under 300 miles. Government postage stamps were authorized in 1847 and prepayment of postage was finally required in 1855. Free city delivery was not inaugurated until 1863, but from early in the century private mailmen, who charged a cent or two for each letter delivered, had distributed mail in the larger cities.[51]

The slowness of the government in reducing rates and improving the service largely resulted from the reluctance of Congress to make larger appropriations. Deficits, frequent after 1838, were in considerable part due to the heavy burden placed on the department by the franking privileges, which were extended to minor government officials, deputy postmasters, and even to certain prominent citizens, and in part to the special treatment of newspapers. In that day as in this, newspapers did not bear their proportionate share of the costs of postal service, attempts to raise the rate were attacked by publishers as threats to the freedom of the press, and congressmen showed no great eagerness to antagonize the publishers.

Actually there was some justification for subsidizing the newspapers as an agency of public education, although no very good reason existed why it should have been done at the expense of letter writers. Certainly newspapers flourished and Americans became the greatest readers of newspapers in the world. By 1829 one newspaper a week was published for every fourth inhabitant of Pennsylvania; in the British Isles, in part at least because of restrictive taxes, the ratio was one newspaper a week for every 36 inhabitants. As new cities arose on the American frontier, each supported at least one newspaper often before it had schools, churches, or even a bank. About 850 newspapers and periodicals were published in 1828; this figure had increased to over 4,000 on the eve of the Civil War.[52]

Especially in the larger commercial centers the newspapers gave increasing attention to providing information as to prices, shipping, and market conditions. Thus, after 1815 they largely took the place

[51] Daniel C. Roper, *The United States Post Office* (New York: Funk & Wagnalls Company, 1917), pp. 49–95; Wesley Everett Rich, *The History of the United States Post Office to the Year 1829* (Vol. XXVII of *Harvard Economic Studies*, Cambridge: Harvard University Press, 1924), *passim; American State Papers: Post Office*, pp. 253, 258.

[52] Harold A. Innis, "The Newspaper in Economic Development," *The Tasks of Economic History* (December, 1942), p. 9; *Eighth Census of the United States: Mortality and Miscellaneous Statistics*, pp. 319–320; Frank Luther Mott, *American Journalism* (New York: The Macmillan Company, 1947), pp. 201–203, 298–302.

of long letters describing the state of the market and of printed prices current, both of which services the larger mercantile houses had furnished to their correspondents. Advertising, often highly valued by readers for its news value, formed an important feature of the newspapers and contributed substantially to their income. Newspapers typically devoted most of the front page and often a large part of the other pages to advertising matter, which was unattractively presented, usually in small type, with few illustrations, and in single columns. Specialized business and commercial journals also appeared which, in addition to providing solid articles on economic and business subjects, printed detailed financial and commercial statistics. Some of these, like *Niles' Weekly Register, Hazard's Register, Hunt's Merchants' Magazine,* and *De Bow's Review,* had a great reputation in their time and are today valuable sources of economic information for the period.

In an age of revolutionary developments in transportation and communication, perhaps the most drastic change resulted from the magnetic telegraph. Except for some slight use of the semaphoric telegraph and dependence upon homing pigeons over short distances for emergency messages, communication had from the beginning of history been tied to transportation. Messages could travel no faster than the messengers. This limitation disappeared when the invention of the magnetic telegraph made possible almost instantaneous communication over hundreds or even thousands of miles.

Many contributed to the scientific developments which finally led to the magnetic telegraph. In the United States its introduction was due largely to the genius and persistence of Samuel F. B. Morse. Trained as a painter rather than a scientist, he became convinced that electrical impulses could be used for communication purposes. Scientific and technical difficulties were overcome with the help of a young scientist, Alfred Vail, whom Morse took in as a partner. Only a small sum was necessary to permit a practical experiment with the new invention, but private capitalists refused to risk their money on so visionary a scheme. Morse finally persuaded Congress to appropriate $30,000 for the purpose, and with this money a line was completed in the spring of 1844 from Washington to Baltimore. This experimental installation definitely established the feasibility of this new method of communication.

No new device, not even the railroad, experienced a more rapid growth than the telegraph. The government dropped out of the picture as aggressive promoters took over. By the close of 1846 most of the technical obstacles had been overcome, a continuous line, except for the crossing of the Hudson, had been completed from Boston to Washington and from New York to Buffalo, and tremendous further expansion was planned. Four years later, January 1, 1852, more than 23,000 miles of line had been built; by 1860 this had reached 50,000; and in 1861 telegraph wires for the first time spanned the continent.

The telegraph was such a complete innovation that at first its possibilities were but dimly realized. So little use was found for the original line between Baltimore and Washington that chess games by telegraph were promoted between experts in the two cities. When other lines were first completed in the East they seldom had an immediate rush of business. Thus, the Magnetic Company, opened between New York and Philadelphia in early 1846, developed customers slowly, with lottery men, brokers, and the press among the first to experiment with the new service. By the fall of 1846 this company had made connections through to Washington via Baltimore, yet it was taking in only about $600 a week. But with the great extension of the lines, the original hesitancy to use the telegraph disappeared. The whole method of gathering news was rapidly revolutionized, and business, financial, and transportation interests soon began to make increasing use of the new device. Thus, steamboat owners and shippers on the Ohio-Mississippi system benefited from early information on the changes in the conditions of navigation. Later the telegraph greatly increased the speed and safety of railroad operation in this country, but for some not very obvious reason only limited use was made of it for this purpose before the Civil War. Rates charged for sending messages appear to have varied greatly from one line to another. However, by the early fifties a usual charge for a message of 10 words or less sent 100 miles was 25 cents, and the charge for a message of 20 words sent 500 miles was 1 dollar.[53]

Finally it may be noted that the first transatlantic cable was laid in 1858. It remained in operation only a few weeks before parting, but its feasibility and usefulness had been demonstrated. Capital was difficult to raise and the Civil War intervened; hence it was not relaid until after the war.[54]

[53] Robert Luther Thompson, *Wiring a Continent* (Princeton: Princeton University Press, 1947), *passim;* Alvin F. Harlow, *Old Wires and New Waves: The History of the Telegraph, Telephone, and Wireless* (New York: D. Appleton–Century Company, 1936), Chaps. 3–13.
[54] Henry M. Field, *History of the Atlantic Telegraph* (New York: Charles Scribner & Co., 1866), *passim.*

CHAPTER VIII

Domestic Trade

TURNPIKE vs. WATER AND RAIL TRANSPORTATION

EACH new method of transportation had to establish itself in a bitter competitive battle against previously existing devices, and each new traffic route had to meet competition from established ones. This competitive struggle provides one of the chief characteristics of the period, and it profoundly affected the rate and nature of American industrial development.

Turnpikes were chiefly built over routes where water transportation was not easily available, so that for the most part they served to supplement rather than to compete with water routes. Thus in New England they led inland in a generally east and west direction and avoided to a considerable extent paralleling the coast or the Connecticut River; in New York they radiated out from Hudson River towns, and in the Middle Atlantic states generally they ran at right angles to water routes or led westward over the mountains.

For travelers, stagecoaches were faster, although more expensive and much less comfortable for long journeys, than sailing packets. But where coastwise journeys were very roundabout, stagecoaches secured considerable patronage. Travelers between Boston and New York who wished to avoid the tedious voyage around Cape Cod brought a brisk business to the stages between Boston and Providence. But from Providence to New York such persons usually preferred the sailing packets and later the steamships. Similarly, those going from New York to Philadelphia increasingly avoided the time-consuming sea journey by taking coaches over the much more direct turnpike routes across New Jersey.

The steamboats on their advent quickly absorbed most of the

153

parallel turnpike traffic which had survived previous river competition. Their competition actually hurt only a few stage lines and stimulated many others, which began running so-called "accommodation" stages timed to meet the steamboats at such ports as Hartford, Connecticut; Albany and Newburgh, New York; and Richmond, Virginia. But for the transportation of goods, turnpikes could compete successfully with carriage by sea or river only under very special conditions. The large number of heavy wagons on the Boston–Providence Turnpike indicates that, for valuable freight shipments between New York and Boston, merchants often used this turnpike in order to avoid the long sea journey around Cape Cod.[1] Appreciable quantities of valuable freight also moved by wagon over the mountains from Baltimore and Philadelphia to Ohio River points, thus saving not only the tedious coastwise trip to New Orleans, but also, before steamboat carriage became important, the expensive three or four months' passage from New Orleans to the upper Ohio River.

Lead from the Galena district in southwestern Wisconsin was sent down the Mississippi and thence by sea to a market on the Atlantic coast. Not only was this route exceedingly roundabout, but steam navigation on the river between Galena and St. Louis was expensive and undependable. Unusually low water in the summer of 1839 greatly curtailed the river trade, and the successful experiment was made of shipping lead across southern Wisconsin in wagons drawn by six or eight yoke of oxen. At Milwaukee the lead was sent on to an eastern market by lake, and the wagons returned loaded with merchandise for the mining district. Once established, the trade on this overland route remained substantial during the forties despite the competition of the river route.[2]

Most turnpikes, especially those in New England and the South, were not faced with important canal competition, but where such competition did appear, results varied. At least in the case of the Middlesex Canal, the waterway won the freight business away from the teamsters only after an extended struggle. Not until the late 1820's and after repeatedly lowering its rates did this canal succeed in overcoming important turnpike competition not only in carrying raw materials and manufactured goods for the textile mills of Lowell, Massachusetts, but also for transporting such bulky county produce as

[1] Taylor, "The Turnpike Era in New England," pp. 236–240, 254–256; Lane, *From Indian Trail to Iron Horse*, pp. 159–160; Kistler, "The Rise of Railroads in the Connecticut River Valley," p. 24.
[2] Orin Grant Libby, "Significance of the Lead and Shot Trade in Early Wisconsin History," *Collection of the State Historical Society of Wisconsin*, XIII (1895), 313–325.

ashes and grain from tributary farming areas as far as 160 miles northward in New Hampshire.[3] This struggle merits attention because it
reveals the fundamental shortcomings of canals and emphasizes those
factors in land transportation which later proved so advantageous for
the railroads.

The one clear advantage of the canal was its lower ton-mile rates,
but the superintendent of the Middlesex Canal in a report submitted
in 1822 pointed out the following considerations which, unless rate
differences were sufficiently great, led shippers to prefer wagon
transportation:

1) Practically all goods had to be carried from the farms to the
canal by wagon. The teamsters having a monopoly of this business
charged very high rates. The same carriers greatly reduced their
ton-mile rates when they carried goods all the way to Boston.

2) Through shipment by team permitted avoidance of truckage
charges between the canal and the warehouse in Boston.

3) The country trader who personally accompanied his shipments, supervised the sale of his produce in Boston, and actually
purchased his return load did not have "to wait in town after making
his purchases nor at home for his goods" if he used turnpike transportation.

4) The trader who conducted his operations from his store in
the country and shipped by turnpike dealt with a single teamster
who made a round trip for him and who was held responsible for delays or damage to goods. If the merchant used the canal he dealt at
a distance and often through intermediaries with canal agents, Boston
teamsters, and merchants. This was inconvenient and frequently gave
rise to difficulties in fixing responsibility for delays or damage to
shipments.

5) The time of arrival of goods sent by canal was unpredictable,
and country traders were often put to the expense of sending teams
to secure freight at the nearest canal port only to find that their
shipments had not arrived.[4]

Of course these difficulties arose in part from the lack of fast
communications and from the imperfect commercial organization
of the time. But they illustrate the superior flexibility and convenience
of road over canal shipment.

The canals of the Middle Atlantic states promptly took away
from the turnpikes most of their long-distance freight. Thus, team-

[3] Roberts, *The Middlesex Canal, 1793–1860*, pp. 148–154, 166–170.
[4] *Ibid.*, pp. 149–151.

sters could not compete with the Morris Canal across New Jersey nor with the Erie and the Main Line of the Pennsylvania for shipments to the West. Nevertheless, they continued to do a large local business and, until the railroads came, to operate over their old routes in the winter when ice closed the canals. In middlewestern states the periods of canal and turnpike building coincided, and to a considerable extent roads were built to facilitate movement of goods to and from canals or rivers.

In the transportation of passengers, the turnpikes suffered little from canal competition. Most American canals did little or no passenger business. The Pennsylvania Main Line and the Erie were exceptional in that they carried many passengers, especially during early canal days, but this was largely new business which would not have existed but for the canals. In fact, the more successful canals like the Erie actually stimulated turnpike traffic. Impatient of the slowness of canalboats, many persons chose to travel by coach on New York turnpikes which paralleled the waterway. Turnpikes which led to the canal often became canal feeder lines, and their traffic increased with the growing population and wealth of the region.[5]

When the railroads appeared, they quickly captured the passenger business and thus took over the chief remaining turnpike traffic. Even less could the wagon lines compete effectively for freight with parallel railroad lines, though for a few years, until rail freight rates were considerably reduced, wagon routes offered occasional competition where rail lines were unusually roundabout and charges high. But for freight shipment of fifteen miles or less, railroads were at a disadvantage as compared to the more flexible wagon. In most areas the railroads actually added to the business of the teamsters, for the increased demand for short haul movements more than made up for the long-distance traffic lost to the railroads.[6]

COMPETING WATER ROUTES

The phenomenal growth of overland commerce between the Atlantic states and the West during the decades preceding 1860 should

[5] Durrenberger, *Turnpikes*, p. 142; Holmes, "The Turnpike Era," V, 270, 290–393; Lane, *From Indian Trail to Iron Horse*, pp. 161, 263; Leland D. Baldwin, *Pittsburgh: The Story of a City* (Pittsburgh: The University of Pittsburgh Press, 1937), p. 188; McKelvey, *Rochester: The Water-Power City, 1812–1854*, p. 94; Oliver W. Holmes, "The Stage-Coach Business in the Hudson Valley," New York State Historical Association, *Quarterly Journal*, XII, No. 3 (July, 1931), 246.

[6] See Kistler, "The Rise of Railroads in the Connecticut River Valley," pp. 185–189; Kirkland, *Men, Cities and Transportation*, p. 202.

not be permitted to deflect attention from what was in 1816 and remained in 1860 the most important trade route in the country, that along the Atlantic coast. This coastwise shipping lane was challenged by the development of an extensive inland waterway system paralleling the coast. Roughly following Gallatin's great plan, canals connecting bays and sounds made possible, by the 1830's, continuous shipment on this sheltered passage from New London, Connecticut, to Wilmington, North Carolina.

But long-distance shipments by this inland passage did not seriously rival those by sea. Naval stores from North Carolina and flour and tobacco from the Chesapeake region continued for the most part to move to New York and New England markets by coastwise vessels, the manufactured products of the northern states and Europe furnishing valuable return cargoes. Nevertheless, the canals were utilized for some long-distance shipments. Thus, barges laden with coal from Richmond, Virginia, arrived in New York Harbor via the James River, the Chesapeake Bay, the Chesapeake and Delaware Canal, the Delaware Bay and River, and the Delaware and Raritan Canal, and limited amounts of merchandise moved all the way back to the Chesapeake ports by this route. Even from far up the Susquehanna, barges descended to the Chesapeake and followed this inside route to New York, a journey of about seven hundred miles.

But it was over the shorter distances and primarily between Philadelphia and New York that the canal system so successfully challenged the sea route that only the bulkiest products were left for coastal vessels. Of course, a little later the railroads in turn took the most valuable freight away from the canals, and the inland and sea routes were left to divide the less valuable business between them. In the late twenties, anthracite rapidly became the great export staple of Pennsylvania. Most of the Lackawanna coal from northeastern Pennsylvania moved directly to New York over the Delaware and Hudson Canal and that from the nearby Lehigh fields reached the same market over the Morris Canal. From this latter source large quantities of anthracite also went down the Delaware Division Canal and reached New York either by way of the Delaware and Raritan Canal or by sloop around Cape May. Anthracite from the great Schuylkill area arrived at tidewater on the Delaware River via the Schuylkill Navigation or the Reading Railroad and, although much was sent on to New York by sea, the Delaware and Raritan Canal, by adjusting its tolls to meet coastwise competition, managed to capture an appreciable part of this business.[7]

[7] *Hunt's Merchants' Magazine*, VIII (1843), 546–549; Lane, *From Indian Trail to*

The prosperity of the western states depended upon their ability to exchange the products of their farms for needed manufactures and other outside products like salt, sugar, and coffee. At the beginning of this period the high cost of transportation erected a wall around the states west of the Alleghenies which seriously blocked the economic development of that area. In a sense, this barrier was overcome by the spirit of a pioneering people who, defying or ignoring difficulties, crowded into the broad western valley. Three great developments in the technique of transportation—steamboats, canals, and steam railroads—helped to raze this wall and to justify frontier optimism. The part played by steamboats and canals is here briefly summarized; the role of the railroad is examined in the following section.

At the beginning of this period the transportation to and from the Ohio River Valley moved counterclockwise in an irregular circle more than three thousand miles in circumference. Upcountry produce such as wheat, flour, butter, pork, and pork products from western Pennsylvania, Ohio, and Indiana; tobacco and hemp from Kentucky; cotton from Tennessee and lead from Missouri, Illinois, and Wisconsin—these moved southward by flatboat to New Orleans on the river arc of the circle. Transportation on this section was far from satisfactory. It was time consuming and expensive not only because the flatboats had to be sold for little or nothing at New Orleans,[8] but also because the men who manned them had, at least before steamboat days, to return home as best they could, usually by foot over the Natchez Trace, which followed the old Indian trail from Natchez through the Chickasaw country to Nashville. Also, trade moved almost exclusively in one direction. Upriver shipments were almost prohibitively expensive even for the most light and valuable merchandise.

From New Orleans, some upriver products were exported to Europe and the West Indies, but in large part they flowed around the second and longest arc of the circle, i.e., by coastwise vessels to Atlantic ports, chiefly New York, Boston, and Philadelphia. Though much the longest of the three parts of this circular route, it presented the fewest problems. Costs of ocean transportation, even on this long sea route, were, despite the danger of gulf hurricanes and the peril of storms off Cape Hatteras, remarkably low. Also, trade could move as easily in one direction as the other.

Iron Horse, pp. 257–276; Albion, *The Rise of New York Port*, pp. 134–142; MacGill, *History of Transportation*, pp. 233–234.
    [8] Baldwin, *The Keelboat Age on Western Waters*, p. 54.

In order to overcome the delays and costs of breaking cargo at New Orleans, in the first decade of the century a considerable number of seagoing vessels had been built on the Ohio River, loaded with produce for eastern or foreign markets, floated down the river to New Orleans, and then sailed to their destination. Despite many discouragements, attempts of this kind were still being made in the years immediately following the War of 1812. Thus, the fifty-ton schooner *Maria*, built at Marietta and carrying a cargo of pork, flour, and lard, arrived at Baltimore, Maryland, in July, 1816, in forty-six days.[9] But the hazards of river navigation by seagoing vessels and the rapid development of the river steamboat soon gave the *coup de grâce* to this unique development.

Finally, the circle was closed by the routes across the Appalachian Highlands from Philadelphia and Baltimore over which the West received, in return for its downriver exports, textiles, hats, shoes, hardware, china, books, tea, and so on. This overland stretch of about three hundred miles proved the least satisfactory arc of the whole route, for transportation by wagon over this short distance cost more than shipment by sea and river all the way from Pittsburgh to Philadelphia.[10] Moreover, as on the river route, freight moved chiefly in one direction, for the cost of turnpike carriage eastward across the mountains effectively discouraged return loads made up of the bulky produce of the frontier.

Developments during the four and one half decades of this study greatly affected the flow of commerce on each of the three arcs of the circle described above. The introduction of fast, regularly sailing packets added materially to the speed and dependability of shipment on the coastwise sector. On the river, steamboats greatly reduced the time and cost of shipment and made upriver traffic little more expensive than downstream. And on the bottleneck arc across the Appalachians, canals and then railroads performed a similar miracle.

By making possible upriver trade and greatly reducing transport costs both up and down the river, the steamboat gave the first great impetus to western growth. An increasing flood of western products came down the rivers, while northward from New Orleans there began to move a growing stream of eastern and European merchandise —salt, sugar, coffee, and a hundred other needed items—which frontiersmen could now afford to purchase.

Chiefly because of this technological change in river transporta-

[9] *Niles' Weekly Register*, X (May 11, 1816), 184, and X (May 20, 1816), 346.
[10] Berry, *Western Prices before 1861*, p. 81.

tion the terms of trade shifted sharply to the advantage of the westerners. This is strikingly shown in the behavior of prices of western
exports as compared with imports. Because of the deflation of 1819–
1820 the level of prices in all American markets was much lower in
1826–1830 than in 1816–1820, but the prices of western export
staples declined less in the Ohio River Valley than at New Orleans and Atlantic ports, and the prices of imports into the West
fell more drastically in the Ohio Valley than at seaport cities. Thus
during 1816–1820 a barrel of flour averaged $2.16 higher in New
Orleans than in Cincinnati. By 1826–1830 New Orleans prices were
only $1.75 higher, a 19 per cent decline. For other major exports
this differential was even greater. The difference between mess pork
prices a barrel was $7.57 in the first five-year period, while only $2.41
in the second, a 68 per cent decline.[11]

As would be expected from the fact that upriver freight rates
declined much more than did those for downriver shipments, the
price difference on imports shrank even more sharply between these
two five-year periods. Coffee which cost 16 cents more a pound in
Cincinnati than in New Orleans in the first period cost only 2.6 cents
more in the second, a decline of about 84 per cent! On sugar the difference for a hundred pounds fell from $10.33 to $2.64, or 74 per
cent.[12] Some notion of what these changes meant in terms of purchasing power to the inhabitants of the Ohio Valley may be easily illustrated. In 1816–1820 an Ohio farmer could exchange a barrel of
flour in Cincinnati for 27 pounds of sugar; in 1826–1830 it would bring
39 pounds. Or taking a more favorable ratio, a barrel of pork which
would have exchanged in the earlier period for 30 pounds of coffee
would buy about 52 pounds of coffee in 1826–1830.[13] These comparisons are, of course, in terms of wholesale prices, but there is no reason
to believe the picture would be appreciably altered were retail quotations available.

No sooner had trade adjusted itself to changes wrought by the
river steamboat, than canals, penetrating the barriers on the short
Appalachian route, further stimulated western commerce and influenced the direction of its flow. It will be remembered that the Erie
Canal was opened for through traffic in 1825, the Pennsylvania Main
Line in 1834, the two canals across Ohio respectively in 1833 and
1845, and the Illinois and Michigan Canal in 1848. The first effect of

[11] *Ibid.,* p. 106.
[12] *Ibid.,* p. 113.
[13] Computed from tables in Cole, *Wholesale Commodity Prices in the United States,*
Statistical Supplement.

these new waterways was greatly to stimulate traffic from the land-locked areas through which they passed, although before long the commerce of the whole Great Lakes area and the Ohio Valley began to feel their influence. The valuable manufactured products of the East moved in growing volume directly westward across New York and Pennsylvania. The merchants of Marietta, Cincinnati, Louisville, and even of Frankfort and Nashville secured an increasing portion of their merchandise over both northern Ohio routes and via the Pennsylvania canal system. By 1846 more than half of its manufactured imports reached the Ohio basin by this latter route. The value of goods shipped to the West by way of the Erie Canal was nearly $10,000,000 in 1836; by 1853 it was more than $94,000,000. Chicago became an important receiving and distributing point for New York merchandise and, with the opening of the Illinois and Michigan Canal in 1848, St. Louis, which had been an important distributing center for goods imported via New Orleans, began to get increasing shipments by way of the Illinois and Michigan Canal.[14]

For the first time the bulky products of the West began to flow directly eastward. By connecting with the Great Lakes, the canal system of New York had tapped the finest inland waterway in the world. The immigrants who crowded the Erie canalboats and settled first in Ohio, Indiana, and Michigan, and later in the more western lake states, soon sent back over the route they had traveled an increasing flow of flour, wheat, and other frontier products. By 1835 flour and wheat, equal to 268,000 barrels of flour, were shipped from the West to tidewater via the Erie; by 1840 shipments exceeded 1,000,000 barrels. By 1860 they totaled 4,344,000 barrels. As early as 1838 receipts at Buffalo exceeded those at the Mississippi River port. After 1848 Buffalo received wheat and flour even from faraway St. Louis via the Illinois River, the Illinois and Michigan Canal, and the Lakes.[15]

In the Ohio Basin, produce, which from the first settlement of the West had gone down the river to market, now began to reverse its flow. Produce was carried to Lake Erie by either the Miami or the Ohio Canal and thence via the Erie Canal to the New York markets. Grain and flour from Pennsylvania, Kentucky, and southern Ohio

[14] Switzler, *Report on the Internal Commerce of the United States,* p. 211; Emory R. Johnson and others, *History of Domestic and Foreign Commerce of the United States* (2 vols., Washington: Carnegie Institution of Washington, 1915), I, 232–235; Putnam, *The Illinois and Michigan Canal,* pp. 102–105.

[15] *Monthly Summary of Commerce and Finance* (January, 1900), p. 1969; *Eighth Census: Agriculture,* pp. cxlviii and clvi; Putnam, *The Illinois and Michigan Canal,* pp. 102–105.

and even some Kentucky tobacco moved to eastern markets by way of the Ohio Canal. As early as 1842 the value of farm products shipped from Cleveland at the head of the canal was about equal to the value of such products shipped from New Orleans. But most of these exports were the products of Ohio farmlands situated near the canals. Neither of the two canals across Ohio ever developed a large through traffic, despite the fact that low rates were instituted in order to encourage long-distance traffic. Apparently through traffic was discouraged by the large number of locks and the slow rate of movement possible. Nevertheless, in 1846 James L. Barton asserted that flour was being shipped from St. Louis via river to Cincinnati and thence by canal and lake to New York City. Though the freight cost via Cincinnati was $1.53 a barrel compared to $1.40 via New Orleans, he claimed the northern route was to be preferred because of the danger of souring and other damage to the flour on the southern route.[16]

The alternative direct route eastward—up the Ohio and over the Pennsylvania Main Line Canal—also provided an outlet for a number of western products. About 20,000 hogsheads of tobacco annually passed eastward over the Main Line Canal, and by 1850–1852 total shipments of pork and pork products by this route were almost as large as those sent down the river. But the total volume of through traffic eastward via this Pennsylvania canal, though considerable, fell well below that on the Erie. In 1844 it amounted to less than 75,000 tons, while that on the Erie for the same year totaled over 350,000 tons.[17]

A third direct water route to the East—through British North America by way of the Welland Canal, Lake Ontario, and the St. Lawrence River—constituted another outlet for the bulky products of the West. In fact, in the late fifties a number of ships carried western products directly from Chicago to Liverpool over this route, but for the most part cargoes were transshipped at Quebec. Much money was spent on digging canals and in improving navigation on the St. Lawrence River. Hopes ran high that a good deal of American trade

[16] *Lake Commerce*, Letter to the Hon. Robert M'Cleland (Buffalo: Jewett, Thomas and Co., 2d ed., 1846), p. 18.
[17] Ernest L. Bogart, "Early Canal Traffic and Railroad Competition in Ohio," *Journal of Political Economy*, XXI, No. 1 (January, 1913), 58–65; Johnson and others, *History of Domestic and Foreign Commerce of the United States*, I, 230–237; Berry, *Western Prices before 1861*, pp. 83–90; Switzler, *Report on the Internal Commerce of the United States*, pp. 210–211; Louis Bernard Schmidt, "The Internal Grain Trade of the United States, 1850–1860," *Iowa Journal of History and Politics*, XVIII, No. 1 (January, 1920), 94–124.

would be attracted to this northern route, but it was never able to compete effectively with the Erie Canal–Hudson River outlet. Although the cost of shipment from Chicago to Quebec was less than that to New York via the Erie Canal, the ocean freights from Quebec to Liverpool were much higher (nearly double in 1856) than from New York to the great English market. The port of Quebec was closed during the winter, lacked the excellent port facilities of its rival to the south, and held out scant promise for inbound cargoes.[18]

Despite the tremendous volume of commerce developed by the canal routes, the Mississippi trade showed no slackening in its growth. The rise in the value of receipts at New Orleans from the interior is shown in the accompanying table. For 1860 the value was the greatest in river history up to that time, and from 1820 to 1860 the total value of commerce at New Orleans from upriver had about doubled in each successive decade.

VALUE OF RECEIPTS AT NEW ORLEANS FROM THE INTERIOR FOR SELECTED YEARS, 1816–1860

(*In thousands of dollars*)

Year	Value
1816	9,749
1820	12,637
1830	22,066
1840	49,764
1850	96,898
1860	185,211

Source: William F. Switzler, *Report on the Internal Commerce of the United States*, Part II of Commerce and Navigation, *Special Report on the Commerce of the Mississippi, Ohio, and Other Rivers, and of the Bridges Which Cross Them* (Washington: Government Printing Office, 1888), pp. 199, 209.

But it should not be concluded that river traffic was unaffected by the competition of canals, beginning in the thirties, and of the railroads in the fifties. The whole West was growing so rapidly that for the time being there was more than enough business for all channels of trade. The tremendous tonnages reaching Buffalo from the Lake region consisted largely of new production made possible by the Erie Canal. At the same time that produce was being diverted eastward from the Ohio Valley, states tributary to the upper Mississippi— Illinois, Missouri, Iowa, Wisconsin, and Minnesota—were rapidly increasing their shipments down the river. Moreover, the lower Mississippi Valley was one of the most rapidly developing sections of

[18] Samuel McKee, Jr., "Canada's Bid for the Traffic of the Middle West: A Quarter-Century of the History of the St. Lawrence Waterway, 1849–1874," *Report of the Annual Meeting of the Canadian Historical Association* (May, 1940), pp. 26–35.

the country, with the result that receipts of cotton and sugar at New Orleans tremendously increased.

Although the rate of growth of commerce on the Mississippi did not slacken, major changes in its nature were taking place. New Orleans became much less important as a distributing center for the manufactured products of the East. The value of eastern products reaching the interior in 1851 was about twice as great by the Hudson and canal as by coastwise shipment and the Mississippi. At the same time the upriver shipments of such products as West Indian coffee and Louisiana sugar and molasses grew greatly as western population increased and the canals of Illinois, Indiana, and Ohio opened up new markets for southern, Caribbean, and South American products.

Significant changes also took place in the character of the downriver trade. Though the total value of river commerce continued to increase, the major part of this growth was due to increased receipts of southern staples, chiefly cotton, sugar, and molasses. In 1819–1820 western products had constituted 58 per cent of the total value of receipts at New Orleans. By 1849–1850 they were about 41 per cent of the total. It is significant that even before 1852, when through railroad connections were made with the Ohio River at Cincinnati, shipments to New Orleans of most of the major Ohio Valley products had already begun to decline in volume. Thus tobacco receipts at New Orleans reached their peak in 1843, wheat and flour and corn in 1847, butter in 1848, and pork in 1849.[19] Though upcountry produce arriving in New Orleans increased during the fifties, it was largely consumed in local delta markets or exported to the West Indies. Coastwise shipments of western products to the East showed a marked decline. Hence by 1860 the canals and railroads had almost completely substituted direct trade across the Appalachians for the old indirect route via New Orleans and the sea.[20]

RAILWAYS vs. WATERWAYS

Before 1840 the amount of traffic carried by American railways was negligible as compared with that moving on all inland waterways. By 1860 the total volume carried by the two methods was

[19] Berry, *Western Prices before 1861*, pp. 580–581; Switzler, *Report on the Internal Commerce of the United States*, pp. 209–215; Dixon, *A Traffic History of the Mississippi River System*, pp. 16, 24–26.

[20] Berry, *Western Prices before 1861*, pp. 90–91, 107; Dixon, *A Traffic History of the Mississippi River System*, p. 34.

probably about equal, and the value of goods transported by railroad greatly exceeded that carried on the internal waterways. As the railroads were opened over new routes, they almost without exception immediately took away from competing waterways most of the passenger and light freight business. Except for the Erie Canal, which long provided cheap water passage for impecunious immigrants, passenger traffic on canals collapsed as soon as rival railroads were completed. The decline was just as sharp for other water routes, though a few long coastwise passages or shorter overnight sailings, as those between Albany, Hartford, or New London and New York, long retained a part of the passenger business because of their convenience.

Before through rail lines were completed from New York City to Lake Erie at the beginning of the fifties, the Erie Canal had developed a tremendous business in transporting westward the manufactured goods of the East. This trade reached its peak in 1853, but as a result of railroad competition was more than cut in half by 1860.[21] Even in the carriage of the heavier and bulkier commodities the railroad proved an unexpectedly successful competitor. Confronted by railroads, such weak canals as the Middlesex and the Blackstone had collapsed before 1850. The Pennsylvania Main Line Canal, with its excessive lockage and its portage railroad, ceased to operate as an important through route soon after the Pennsylvania Railroad reached Pittsburgh in 1852. Most of the western canals rapidly lost the cream of their traffic to the railroads during the fifties.

River traffic was also adversely affected. Most of the trade on the upper Connecticut simply disappeared soon after rails paralleled the river. After 1852 the volume of goods shipped down the Ohio River to New Orleans declined because of railroad competition, but, so far as Ohio River traffic was concerned, this loss was more than compensated for by increased upriver shipments to the railheads at Pittsburgh and Wheeling, a growing traffic with St. Louis and the upper Mississippi River area, and greatly increased coal shipments.[22]

Railroads, which, beginning in 1853, were rapidly completed across Illinois and Wisconsin to the Mississippi River, had no trouble in getting all the business they could handle. The number of bushels

[21] S. P. Chase, "Foreign and Domestic Commerce of the United States," *Senate Document* No. 55, 38 Cong., 1 Sess. (1864), p. 181. This document is hereinafter referred to as the *Chase Report on Foreign and Domestic Commerce, 1864.*

[22] Cf. Berry, *Western Prices before 1861*, pp. 39, 90–93; Johnson and others, *History of Domestic and Foreign Commerce of the United States,* I, 244–247; Hunter, *Steamboats on the Western Rivers*, pp. 484–488.

of wheat arriving at Chicago jumped from 937,000 in 1852 to 8,-768,000 in 1856, and corn from 2,999,000 bushels in the former year to 11,888,000 in the latter. But commerce on the upper Mississippi also continued to increase during this decade. At St. Louis, the great distributing center for the whole upper Mississippi area, goods were transferred from the steamboats of the lower Mississippi built to operate in four to six feet of water to steamboats of the Missouri and upper Mississippi which might navigate in thirty inches or even less. At this great center, steamboat arrivals grew from 1,721 in 1840 to 2,879 in 1850, and to 3,454 in 1860.

In the long run, the river could not retain much traffic in competition with the railroads. The difficulties of navigation on the upper Mississippi and the long journey via New Orleans on which goods were especially likely to damage and spoilage proved much more costly than that directly eastward by rail or rail and water. But during the fifties settlement was advancing so rapidly in Illinois, Wisconsin, Minnesota, and Iowa that both the rivers and the railroads were taxed to carry the growing traffic. So both increased in absolute tonnage carried, but from about 1847 and especially after 1852 the rivers transported a decreasing proportion of the total trade of the upper Mississippi area.[23]

Even some of the cotton trade of New Orleans was surrendered to railroads. The Western and Atlantic Railroad, pushing westward from Augusta, made connections with Chattanooga in 1849, Nashville in 1854, and Memphis in 1857. As a result, thousands of bales of cotton, which would have gone down the Tennessee and Cumberland rivers and the Mississippi to the Crescent City, instead swelled the exports of Charleston and Savannah. Nevertheless, the whole West was developing so rapidly and cotton and sugar production in the delta region immediately tributary to New Orleans was advancing so tremendously that the river trade continued its rapid growth down to the war. Exports of cotton from New Orleans and the total volume of river trade both reached their peak for the ante-bellum period in 1860.[24]

In tonnage terms, most of the domestic commerce still moved by

[23] John B. Appleton, "The Declining Significance of the Mississippi as a Commercial Highway in the Middle of the Nineteenth Century," *The Bulletin of the Geographical Society of Philadelphia,* XXVIII (October, 1930), 267–284; Isaac Lippincott, *Internal Trade of the United States, 1700–1860* (*Washington University Studies,* Vol. IV, Pt. 2, No. 1, Second Study, October, 1916), p. 136.

[24] Johnson and others, *History of Domestic and Foreign Commerce in the United States,* I, 240–246; Dixon, *A Traffic History of the Mississippi River System,* pp. 32–36; Van Deusen, *Economic Bases of Disunion in South Carolina,* pp. 238 ff.

water in 1860. The direct trade between the West and the north Atlantic seaboard expanded so rapidly during the fifties that the railroads, the lakes, and the Erie Canal were all needed to deliver western products to the East. The tonnage carried by the Erie Canal grew tremendously despite railroad competition and did not actually reach its peak until 1880. The Great Lakes served as a gigantic extension of the Erie Canal, and during the fifties railroads, pushing westward from Chicago and Milwaukee, acted as feeders to the Great Lakes trade so that its volume, swollen by the corn of Iowa and the wheat of Illinois, Wisconsin, and Minnesota, grew from year to year in almost geometric ratio. By the end of the decade western flour (and wheat equivalent) transported to tidewater via the Erie Canal exceeded 4,000,000 barrels; of this probably about two thirds came from ports on Lake Michigan.[25]

The railroads also rapidly increased their eastward shipments. The tonnage of through freight carried eastward by the Pennsylvania, Erie, New York Central, and Baltimore and Ohio railroads was not yet quite equal to that transported by the Erie Canal. But it was much more valuable, for the rails transported practically all of the merchandise and livestock, most of the packing house products, and about two thirds of the flour. As a result, the heavier and bulkier products, such as grain and lumber, made up an increasingly large percentage of lake and canal traffic. This tendency is well illustrated by shipments from Chicago, a point from which commodities could be shipped eastward with equal facility by water or rail. Data available for 1859 show that heavy and bulky products, like corn, wheat, and lead, moved predominantly by water, whereas such items as hides, livestock, and general merchandise were carried chiefly by rail. Flour held an intermediate position, with 365,000 barrels being shipped eastward by lake and 307,000 by rail. But in terms of tons of western produce moved eastward to tidewater, the Erie Canal was still the predominant agency in 1860. In that year the tonnage reaching tidewater from the western states and Canada via the Erie Canal totaled 1,896,975. Through freight moving eastward by the New York Central, Erie, and Pennsylvania railroads appears to have been about half the canal tonnage.[26]

[25] Johnson and others, *History of Domestic and Foreign Commerce in the United States*, I, 231–232; Internal Waterways Commission, *Preliminary Report*, 1908, p. 233; *Eighth Census of the United States: Agriculture*, p. cl.

[26] Johnson and others, *History of Domestic and Foreign Commerce in the United States*, I, 238; Pierce, *A History of Chicago*, II, 494; and Schmidt, "The Internal Grain Trade of the United States," pp. 94–124; *Chase Report on Foreign and Domestic Com-*

Railroads had little effect on the coastal trade between New England and the southern Atlantic states. Manufactured goods, lumber, and ice moved to southern markets, and cotton, tobacco, and naval stores were received in exchange. But trade with the West was appreciably altered. Textiles and other merchandise destined for the Ohio Valley had formerly been sent by coastwise vessel to Philadelphia and Baltimore and thence overland to market. With the completion of the Western Railroad to Albany in 1841 these products began to move directly westward by rail and canal and later all the way by rail. Also, with the opening of the Erie Canal much flour had moved by sloop from Albany directly to New England coastal markets. The Western Railroad gradually secured this business so that little was left of this coastwise trade by 1860.[27]

The coastwise trade between the South Atlantic and the Middle states was also largely unaffected by the coming of the railroads. Rail lines extended north from Washington, D.C., along the coast to Boston and beyond. But south from the capital city the only coastal railroad connecting with the east and west roads of the Carolinas and Georgia was the stem extending 325 miles from near Washington to Wilmington, North Carolina. Unfortunately this route was comprised of several independent railroad companies, and as late as the Civil War had three gaps, places where rolling stock could not pass from the rails of one road to those of another. One of these barriers occurred between Washington and Acquia Creek on the Potomac River in Virginia. The other two were short breaks at Petersburg, Virginia, and Weldon, North Carolina. Passengers were transported across these breaks in the line without great difficulty, and as a result the railroads were able to compete fairly effectively with the coastwise packets for the passenger business. But the cost of reshipping freight was prohibitive. Not until well after the Civil War did the railroads begin to offer important competition for seaboard shipments south of Washington.[28]

Hope had run high that the line extending northward from Mobile and connecting with the Illinois Central at Cairo would promote intersectional rail traffic. In 1860 the lack of direct physical connection between these two rail routes still made necessary a twenty-mile

---

merce, 1864, pp. 138, 140–141; Hunt's Merchants' Magazine, XLIII (December, 1860), 701.

[27] Albion, The Rise of New York Port, pp. 128–129.

[28] Howard Douglas Dozier, "Trade and Transportation along the South Atlantic Seaboard before the Civil War," South Atlantic Quarterly, XVIII, No. 3 (July, 1919), 232–234.

shipment by ferry between Columbus, Kentucky, and Cairo, Illinois, and little through business had developed. The rail route connecting Cincinnati and New Orleans was opened in 1859 too late to permit much traffic to develop before war closed such intercourse. The overland movement of cotton to northern markets was inconsequential until the very end of the period. For the years 1852–1858 such shipments had averaged less than 10,000 bales a year. But in 1859 and 1860 they rose rapidly, so that in the final year they totaled nearly 109,000 bales, or one eighth of the total shipped northward in that year for domestic consumption. The railroad system of the South gave great assistance in moving staples to southern seaport markets, but not until the very end of the period were southern rail lines beginning to be sufficiently integrated with those of the North as to encourage long-distance rail shipments between the North and the South.[29]

THE PATTERN OF TRADE

The rapid settlement of the West, the great increase in population, and the phenomenal improvements in transportation which have been emphasized made possible the territorial specialization upon which rested the striking growth of American domestic commerce during the period of this study. The direction and magnitude of this commerce was largely determined by the growth of New York City as the great center for foreign importations, and the development of manufacturing in the Atlantic states lying north of Chesapeake Bay. The fundamental pattern of this trade was very similar to that which existed between Great Britain and this country in the colonial and early national period. The South, which in colonial days had sent its great staples directly to England and received manufactured products in return, after 1815 found a growing market for its raw materials— cotton, tobacco, and sugar—in the manufacturing East. The West, an exporter of grain and meat, carried on a similar direct trade with the manufacturing states, but it also provided the South with food products, receiving in exchange drafts on the East which were used to pay for manufactured imports. In similar manner before the Revolution, fish from New England and grain from the Middle Atlantic states had been exported to the West Indies to help permit payment for British imports. But this earlier trade had involved only the fringe of states along the Atlantic, whereas the domestic commerce rapidly

[29] Pierce, *A History of Chicago*, II, 45–46; *Nimmo Report*, 1879, pp. 122, 128.

developing during the nineteenth century presently involved a whole continent.

Though the essential pattern of American domestic trade was determined by this exchange between the agricultural West and South and the increasingly industrialized East, there were many special or subsidiary traffic movements of great importance. A few of these merit at least brief mention. As firewood grew scarce in the vicinity of the larger towns, a brisk trade in coal developed which, from a small start at the beginning of the century, grew to major importance as Virginia and Pennsylvania coal was moved northward by coastwise sloop, by canalboat, and even by rail to provide warmth for homes and fuel for factories and gas plants. Until 1827 most of this coal moved northward from the Richmond, Virginia, bituminous fields, but in the following year Pennsylvania anthracite went into the lead. Although coal shipments from Richmond continued to the end of our period, they were increasingly overshadowed by the Pennsylvania trade. By the fifties coal had become the most important cargo for canalboats on all of the tidewater canals south of the Erie, for Atlantic coastwise sloops, and for Ohio River flats.[30] Even the railroads were entering largely into this business. Thus, in 1856 no less than 42 per cent of the total tonnage of the Pennsylvania Railroad consisted of coal.[31]

Resourceful Yankees developed a number of bulky products to fill the holds of coasters which brought coal, cotton, and flour to Boston and other New England ports. To fish and lumber, which had long been export staples, they added ice, which provided a back haul for many a returning Philadelphia coal schooner or for farther-ranging vessels to southern or even foreign ports. Other bulky items, like lime and granite blocks from Maine, and plaster of Paris, which had been imported from over the border at Passamaquoddy, moved southward in large quantities to coastal markets.[32]

Equaling and at times exceeding coal as an important item of domestic trade was lumber, a commodity of greatest importance to

[30] Kathleen Bruce, *Virginia Iron Manufacture in the Slave Era* (New York: The Century Company, 1931), pp. 96–97; *Annual Report of the Delaware and Hudson Canal Company*, 1860, p. 10; *Hunt's Merchants' Magazine*, XLIII (December, 1860), 752–753. For elaborate statistical tables on coal production and trade see Howard N. Eavenson, *The First Century and a Quarter of the American Coal Industry* (Baltimore: Waverly Press, 1942), pp. 425 ff.

[31] Richmond E. Myers, "The Story of Transportation on the Susquehanna River," *New York History*, XXIX, No. 2 (April, 1948), 163; H. Haupt, *The Coal Business on the Pennsylvania Railroad* (Philadelphia: T. K. and P. G. Collins, Printers, 1857), p. 9.

[32] Johnson and others, *History of Domestic and Foreign Commerce of the United States*, I, 340–343; Richard O. Cummings, *The American Ice Harvests* (Berkeley: University of California Press, 1949), *passim*.

an age which depended upon wood not only for building houses, barns, factories, and stores, but for transportation equipment such as wagons, canalboats, ships, and railroad cars; and for furniture, farm implements, and containers, including barrels, hogsheads, and pipes. South from Maine and New Hampshire, north from South Atlantic and Gulf ports, eastward via the Great Lakes and the Erie, and down the Susquehanna River, hundreds of millions of feet of lumber moved annually to eastern markets. As early as 1827 the lumber shipped on the Susquehanna was estimated at 40,000,000 feet. The receipts of boards and scantling at Albany, New York, in 1860 amounted to 301,-000,000 feet valued at more than $5,000,000.[33] As the loggers moved into the forests of Michigan and Wisconsin, lumber vied with grain as the leading item of trade on the Lakes. By 1857 vessels engaged in the lumber trade on the Lakes were valued at $1,500,000, and Chicago became the greatest lumber port in the world. Down the upper Mississippi River, also, tremendous quantities of lumber moved southward from the pine forests of Wisconsin and Minnesota to the prairie farms.[34] In both the East and the West other building materials like stone, lime, bricks, sand, and gravel, usually destined for nearby markets, provided heavy cargoes for thousands of canal and river boats.

Finally, there was the trade with the Far West. Though at first a mere trickle over the Santa Fe Trail, it quickly became of considerable importance following the discovery of gold in California. This historic route, the Santa Fe Trail, connected Franklin, and later Independence, Missouri, with the Mexican frontier trading town of Santa Fe, nearly 800 miles to the southwest. Traders first essayed this difficult journey on a large scale with wagon trains in 1824. Despite Indian attacks and difficulties from suspicious Mexican customs officials, the trade continued, except for the years of strained relations with Mexico 1844–1848, until the appearance of railroad competition after the Civil War. Westward the slowly moving wagons carried chiefly cotton goods and hardware; returning, they brought specie, Mexican blankets, beaver skins, and buffalo robes. The total value of the merchandise sent westward over this route was small, averaging about $130,000 annually before 1844. After 1848, following the annexation of Texas and the cession of Mexican territory, this

[33] *Hunt's Merchants' Magazine*, XLIV (March, 1861), 356; *Niles' Weekly Register*, XXXII (June 30, 1827), 290.

[34] Pierce, *A History of Chicago*, I, 67, 103–105; Merk, *Economic History of Wisconsin during the Civil War Decade*, pp. 79–86; Agnes M. Larson, *History of the White Pine Industry in Minnesota* (Minneapolis: University of Minnesota Press, 1949), Chap. 6.

trade, now for the first time strictly a domestic one, assumed really large proportions. The total value of merchandise carried westward totaled $3,500,000 in 1860.

Following the Mormon settlement in Utah and accompanying the growing military and mining developments in the Rocky Mountain region during the fifties, a considerable trade grew up over a number of more northern routes. Thus by 1855, 304 wagons were engaged in hauling merchandise to Utah, and the traffic to this area increased tremendously with the so-called "Mormon War" of 1857. One of the most important of the wagon routes led from Nebraska City on the Missouri River up the Platte River Valley and on to Denver. A leading freighting concern at Nebraska City, that of Russell, Majors & Waddell, during the summer of 1860 employed 5,687 oxen, 515 wagons, and 602 men and transported nearly 3,000,000 pounds of goods. Though pony express lines carried small packages to the West coast and though postal service was developed, the great distance and the difficulties of mountain and desert travel prevented the development of an overland freight trade to the West coast. Even camels, introduced on the southern route by the United States Army during the latter part of the fifties, failed to solve the problem.[35]

As a result, the exchange of goods with the Pacific coast, which grew rapidly after 1848, was chiefly carried on by coastwise vessels sailing all the way around Cape Horn, perhaps the longest domestic trade route in the world. Westward, these vessels were heavily loaded with a vast array of merchandise from steam engines to pins and needles. Returning, they largely sailed in ballast, though they often carried gold, passengers, and sometimes wool, hides, skins, and wheat. The shorter route, involving transfer across Panama or Nicaragua, was important chiefly for passengers, for specie, and, after the completion of the Panama Railway in 1855, for light and valuable freight. This was the fastest and safest route to the Far West. Of the total emigrants to California from 1849 to 1859, about one fifth went via the Panama route.[36]

[35] Lewis Burt Lesley, Uncle Sam's Camels (Cambridge: Harvard University Press, 1929); Le Roy R. Hafen and Carl Coke Rister, Western America (New York: Prentice-Hall, Inc., 1941), Chaps. 14 and 26; R. L. Duffus, The Santa Fe Trail (New York: Longmans, Green and Co., 1930), pp. 85 ff.; Glenn Danford Bradley, The Story of the Santa Fe (Boston: Richard G. Badger, The Gorham Press, 1920), Chap. 1; Johnson and others, History of Domestic and Foreign Commerce in the United States, I, 248–250; Everett Dick, Vanguards of the Frontier (New York: D. Appleton–Century Company, 1941), pp. 342–343, 367; Josiah Gregg, The Commerce of the Prairies (Chicago: R. R. Donnelley and Sons Company, 1926); Winther, The Old Oregon Country, especially Chap. 11.
[36] John Haskell Kemble, The Panama Route, 1848–1869 (Vol. XXIX of University

THE VOLUME OF TRADE

Statistical treatment of the growth in the total volume or value of domestic commerce is most unsatisfactory. In the first place, detailed statistics such as are available for foreign trade do not exist; in the second place, the defining of domestic trade presents many pitfalls.[37] As a consequence, perhaps the best understanding of the growth of this commerce is to be obtained from the kind of description contained in the preceding pages. Nevertheless, it is worth while to note some comparisons of the total value of goods moved over particular routes; and to summarize the estimates of the total value of domestic trade which have been made for this period.

A number of rough statistical comparisons are possible between trade in the 1820's and 1850's. As the general level of prices for these two decades was roughly the same, value data are not appreciably influenced by price changes. The value of goods carried by wagon from Philadelphia to Pittsburgh in 1820 was estimated at $18,000,000. This appears high, but it may be compared with the total receipts by river at New Orleans, 1821–1822, and the annual value of traffic on the Erie Canal, 1825–1830, each of which totaled about $15,000,000.[38] The total value of downriver trade on the Susquehanna was estimated at $4,500,000 in 1826.[39] In contrast to these totals, it should be noted that the annual value of foreign trade varied from $109,000,000 to $181,000,000 during the twenties.

The estimates for the last decade of the period covered by this volume are of a different order of magnitude. Through traffic westward on the Erie Canal was valued at $94,000,000 when it reached its peak in 1853. Two years later the total value of all Erie Canal traffic was reported to be over $204,000,000. Receipts from the interior at New Orleans were valued at $185,000,000 in 1860.[40] Estimates of the value of trade on the Great Lakes for 1856 are $450,000,000 and $608,000,000. The latter sum is slightly larger than the total

of California Publications in History, Berkeley: University of California Press, 1943), pp. 205-209.

[37] See, for example, Chase Report on Foreign and Domestic Commerce, 1864, pp. 118–122.

[38] Johnson and others, History of Domestic and Foreign Commerce in the United States, I, 218 and 220.

[39] Ringwalt, Development of Transportation Systems in the United States, p. 13. But compare Niles' Weekly Register, XXXI (December 30, 1826), 283.

[40] Hunt's Merchants' Magazine, XXXV (1856), 358; Dixon, A Traffic History of the Mississippi River System, p. 165; Chase Report on Foreign and Domestic Commerce, 1864, p. 181.

value of American foreign commerce in that year.[41] Treasury computations for 1862, two years beyond the close of the period, evaluate the through freight passage westward over the Erie Canal and on four railroads, the New York Central, Erie, Pennsylvania, and Baltimore and Ohio, at $522,500,000.[42] The total value of American foreign trade was $687,000,000 in 1860.

One of the earliest estimates of the total value of domestic commerce was made by a writer in *Hunt's Merchants' Magazine* in 1843, who placed it at $900,000,000.[43] Secretary of the Treasury Robert J. Walker, making an estimate in 1846, reported that the value of American production exceeded $3,000,000,000, of which that part "interchanged among the several States of the Union" was worth at least $500,000,000.[44] A more elaborate estimate published in the *Andrews Report* of 1853 is reproduced in the following table:

TOTAL VALUE OF DOMESTIC COMMERCE

1851	Net		Gross	
	Tons	Value	Tons	Value
Lake commerce	1,985,563	$157,246,729	3,971,126	$314,473,458
River commerce	2,033,400	169,751,372	4,066,800	339,502,744
Aggregate	4,018,963	$326,988,101	8,037,926	$653,976,202
Estimate of 1852				
Coasting trade	20,397,490	$1,659,519,686	40,794,980	$3,319,039,372
Canal commerce	9,000,000	594,000,000	18,000,000	1,188,000,000
Railway commerce	5,407,500	540,750,000	10,815,000	1,081,500,000
Aggregate	34,804,990	$2,794,269,686	69,609,980	$5,588,539,372

The values shown in this report were secured by multiplying tonnage data (partly estimated) for important routes of trade by the estimated value a ton over each route. In order to avoid duplication and thus secure the "net" figures shown in the table, the "gross" figures were merely divided by 2. The resulting totals were, as Andrews was careful to point out, computed in "a very unsatisfactory way," but they are the best we have.[45] The table points to two important generalizations: by the fifties domestic trade had become much greater than

[41] *Hunt's Merchants' Magazine*, XXXVI (1857), 89. An official Canadian estimate of the value of the lake commerce for this same year placed it at $450,000,000. *Hunt's Merchants' Magazine*, XXXVII (1857), 223.

[42] *Chase Report on Foreign and Domestic Commerce*, 1864, p. 136.

[43] *Hunt's Merchants' Magazine*, VIII (1843), 322.

[44] *Report of the Secretary of the Treasury*, December 9, 1847, *House Executive Document* No. 6, 30 Cong., 1 Sess., p. 22.

[45] *Andrews Report* (*Senate Executive Document* No. 112, 32 Cong., 1 Sess., 1853), pp. 903–906.

foreign; and coastwise commerce was much more important than that over any other domestic route. Both of these conclusions fit well with what other knowledge we have and appear sound enough. On the other hand, the exact figures presented by Andrews will have to be very carefully restudied before they can be taken very seriously. It must be borne in mind, moreover, that Andrews' data are for the early fifties. In the decade 1851–1860 domestic commerce, at least on rivers, on the Great Lakes, and by railroad, experienced extremely rapid growth.

It must not be supposed that the domestic commerce grew at a constant rate from year to year, unaffected by the great cyclical disturbances of the period. Each of the major commercial crises put a damper on the growth of internal commerce, but in each period of prosperity, trade expanded rapidly to totals much higher than their previous levels. In major depressions such as that following 1839, tonnage totals might actually decline for a year or more. Thus New York State canal traffic declined slightly over the previous year in 1837, 1840, and 1842, but tonnage which had reached a prosperity peak in 1836 had more than doubled by 1847. Similarly, the value of Mississippi River trade, although declining slightly in 1839, 1841, 1842, and 1845, very nearly doubled between 1836 and 1847. Ton-miles of traffic on New York railroads increased by more than 100 per cent between 1853 and 1860, but suffered a slight decline from the 1856 level in 1857–1859. Nevertheless, the irregularities in the growth of domestic commerce should not be overemphasized, for at least before the fifties, fluctuations were repeatedly much less extreme than those experienced by foreign commerce.[46]

The tremendous growth of American internal trade during the forty-five years ending in 1860 was, of course, the result of many interacting factors. Fundamental was the adoption of the new instruments of transportation: canals, steamboats, and railroads. But many other influences played a part, especially the rapid settlement of the West, the growth of manufacturing, and the increase of foreign trade. Each was partly cause and partly effect; all were mutually interacting forces which taken together produced the transportation revolution and at least the beginnings in America of that whole series of rapid changes which has come to be termed the industrial revolution.

[46] Dixon, *A Traffic History of the Mississippi River System*, pp. 199, 215; Smith and Cole, *Fluctuations in American Business, 1790–1860*, pp. 72–73, 104–105; *Historical Statistics of the United States 1789–1945; A Supplement to the Statistical Abstract of the United States* (Bureau of the Census, Department of Commerce, Washington: Government Printing Office, 1949), p. 218; Albion, *The Rise of New York Port*, p. 411.

CHAPTER IX

Foreign Trade

THE very great increase which took place in the foreign commerce of the United States from 1815 to 1861 has been somewhat overshadowed by the even more rapid strides which were at the same time being taken by internal trade and industry. Probably foreign commerce was never again *relatively* so important a part of the whole American economy as in the period preceding the War of 1812. But this consideration should not be permitted to obscure the picture of remarkably rapid growth after 1815.

Examination of Chart 2 shows that although many year to year irregularities appear, the general trend of American foreign trade development was strongly upward to the Civil War. For the five years 1816–1820 the total foreign trade of the United States averaged $186,000,000 a year. This was the highest five-year average yet reached and may be compared with an average of $518,000,000 which was the annual value for the total foreign trade of the United Kingdom for the same period.[1] By the five-year period ending in 1860, American foreign trade had more than trebled, to average $616,000,-000 a year. This period from the close of the Napoleonic Wars to 1860 was one in which the United Kingdom, by virtue of its rapid industrialization, extensive foreign loans, and the dominant position of its merchant marine, was experiencing one of its great periods of foreign trade development. For the years 1856–1860 the annual value of its foreign commerce averaged $1,602,000,000. Yet it is significant that the United States, whose industrialization was still in its early stages and whose dependence on foreign loans was relatively small, nonetheless, in these forty-five years, increased its foreign

---

[1] For a summary of the foreign trade of the United Kingdom, 1816–1860, see Appendix A, Table 5.

trade at an even more rapid rate than did the United Kingdom. From 1816–1820 to 1856–1860 the total value of the foreign trade of the United States increased by 230 per cent; that of Great Britain by 205 per cent.

CHART 2

United States Merchandise Imports and Exports, 1815–1860

(See Appendix A, Table 4)

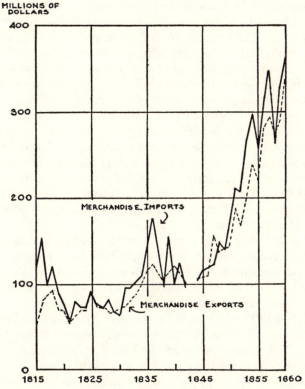

A statistical summary of the growth of the foreign commerce of the United States is shown in Appendix A, Table 4. Although this table gives a picture of major trends, it is inadequate, like most statistical summaries, in that it raises more questions than it answers: the reasons for the growth of foreign trade, the causes of its major fluctuations, and the relative significance of foreign commerce to American economy cannot be read directly from it. Such questions can be dealt with only by breaking down the totals into their significant components. Thus separation of exports from re-exports, examination of shifts in goods exchanged, exploration of the origin and destination of trade, and study of the balance of trade are fundamental to an interpretation of the statistics and to an understanding of the growth of American foreign commerce during this period.

THE RE-EXPORT TRADE

Some notion of the more important commodities involved and the chief countries of destination for re-exports may be gathered from Tables 6 and 7 in Appendix A. European ports from the Mediterranean to the Baltic absorbed large quantities of United States re-exports. These consisted of a great variety of tropical and semitropical products from the West Indies and Central and South America. Most important were sugar from Cuba, coffee from Cuba and Brazil, cocoa from Brazil, and dyewoods from Central America. Also, the products of the Far East, such as indigo, cotton textiles, tea, and spices, moved in appreciable quantities to European markets via American ports. Indigo and cotton cloth (chiefly nankeens) from the Far East were important only in the early years of the period. In the 1850's more than $1,000,000 worth of tea was sent annually from New York to both England and British North America, i.e., British possessions north of the United States.

After 1850 large quantities of Canadian wheat and flour were exported through American ports, chiefly New York. These re-exports were valued at over $4,000,000 at their peak in 1854 (wheat, $1,664,-067, and wheat flour, $2,643,902). Although most of these foodstuffs from Canada were re-exported to England, large shipments of flour (over $1,000,000 worth in 1854) went to the Maritime Provinces (New Brunswick, Nova Scotia, Newfoundland, and Prince Edward Island). This situation, in which the United States facilitated an important trade between two parts of British North America, was made possible by the opening up of cheap water and railroad transportation across the United States, the United States drawback law of 1846, and, finally, the action of three of the Maritime Provinces in removing all duties on Canadian wheat.

Europe was not only an important market for American re-exports but it also furnished many products which the United States re-exported to the rest of the world. These were largely manufactures consisting of cottons, woolens, linens, iron manufactures, and a host of miscellaneous items, some of the most important being wine and

Mediterranean fruits. In fact, the varied character of the re-exports makes any summary difficult. Among the many items are "botany specimens," "old junk and oakum," and "segars." In 1818 the Treasury report solemnly listed "Lions — No. of — 1." [2]

As would be expected, England was by far the most important source of the manufactured goods for United States re-export trade and, of these, cotton textiles were the most significant. This re-export trade in cotton textiles sharply reflects the changes which were resulting from the advance of the industrial revolution. Before the War of 1812 and for about a decade thereafter nankeens from the Far East, the product of handicraft industry, were important in the re-export trade. But re-exports of British cotton textiles grew very rapidly after 1815 and by the 1830's had almost entirely replaced those of India and China. The 1830's were the high point for re-export of British cotton. Thereafter American merchants exported increasingly large quantities of cheap cotton cloth from domestic mills, and the re-export trade in cotton manufactures declined in importance.

Only during the early years of the period were very large quantities of European goods reshipped to the Orient. The United States continued to have a large unfavorable balance with the Far East which was met, especially in the early part of the period, by annual shipments from the United States of millions of dollars of Mexican silver. Beginning about 1819, large quantities of English manufactures were exported directly from England to Canton by New York merchants. Timothy Pitkin reports that $893,836 worth of cotton and woolen cloth were thus shipped to China in 1827. But the sum remaining due to China was still very large and was covered by the increasing use of sterling bills. [3]

To the foreign markets of the Western Hemisphere, European products were re-exported in large amounts and, at least in the two decades preceding the Civil War, their value was often well over half that of total re-exports. Every American country from Chile to Canada received these re-exports, but Mexico in the early part of the period and Canada in the latter part were the most important. From 1820 through 1836 Mexico took more of American re-exports than any other country. The peak of this trade was reached in 1835 when this southern neighbor absorbed over $6,000,000 worth of American re-exports, an amount which was more than two fifths of

[2] *American State Papers: Commerce and Navigation*, II, 158.
[3] Timothy Pitkin, *Statistical View of the Commerce of the United States of America* (New Haven: Durrie & Peck, 1835), pp. 166, 251–254.

total re-exports for that year. The size of this trade reflects on the one hand the demand of New York merchants for silver to be sent to the Far East and on the other the Mexican need for European manufactured goods, especially cotton cloth. In 1835 the United States imported $8,265,855 worth of Mexican silver and re-exported to her $6,004,214 worth of foreign goods, $2,920,991 of which represented the value of re-exported cotton manufactures.

The re-export trade to British North America was negligible in the early part of this period. But re-exports to this region grew very rapidly during the forties and became of predominant importance in the decade of the fifties. The peak value of nearly $12,000,000 was reached in 1855. In that year re-exports to British North America were 46 per cent of total re-exports. The foreign commodities sent from New York to British North America included almost every possible item, both tropical staples and European manufactures. In 1855 the United States re-exported to British North America approximately $1,000,000 worth of each of the following commodities: tea, sugar, including molasses, woolen cloth, and cotton cloth. The tremendous development of this trade was due in part to the advantages which provincial merchants found in buying in a nearby market. The United States Consul for Canada and New Brunswick, Israel D. Andrews, writing in 1850, says of these merchants:

Instead of obtaining large stocks, by orders, from England, as they have formerly done, waiting several months for the completion of their orders, and being exposed at the same time to the risk of buying unsaleable stocks, they find it greatly to their advantage to go to the great American cities, where there are large assortments of goods. . . . They buy no larger stocks than they can readily dispose of, and in a few days after purchase have the goods upon their own shelves. Thus they have quick sales and certain profits.[4]

The re-export trade was carried on almost exclusively by five ports —New York, Boston, Philadelphia, New Orleans, and Baltimore. For the whole period 1821–1860, New York absorbed more than half of this trade, and Boston more than a fifth. Each of the five ports had a considerable share in the re-export trade at the beginning of the period, but New York gradually monopolized the trade to such an extent that by 1860 nearly three fourths of it was concentrated at that city.[5]

The United States, as the leading neutral maritime nation during the Napoleonic Wars, had developed a great indirect or re-export

4 *Senate Executive Document* No. 23, 31 Cong., 2 Sess., IV, 45.
5 See Appendix B.

trade. At times (1798–1800 and 1805–1807) re-exports were actually more valuable than exports of domestic production. They reached their highest point before the Civil War in 1806, when they were valued at $60,000,000 and amounted to nearly three fifths of the value of total exports. Although re-exports never again attained the relative importance they had held before 1815, they did continue as a significant though declining proportion of total trade down to 1860. Especially during the early decades of this period, a large re-export trade was a natural result of such factors as the unspecialized commercial organization of the time, the absence of common carriers running on regular schedule between any but a few major ports, and the slow and uncertain means which existed for the dissemination of market information. It will be seen from Table 4 in Appendix A that the annual value of re-exports increased from the low point of $6,500,000 in 1815 to approximately $24,000,000 in 1825.[6] An irregular decline followed which culminated in the low totals of the 1840's.

Late in the forties American re-export trade experienced marked revival, but its direction was significantly altered. Previously this indirect trade had been carried to almost every port of the world. China, the East Indies, South America, the West Indies, Russia, and Turkey had been important markets. After 1845 none of these regained its former significance. On the other hand, re-exports to Great Britain and British North America became of major importance. The combined re-exports to these two regions had constituted only 5 per cent of total merchandise re-exports in the decade 1821–1830. By the period 1851–1860 they had risen to 55 per cent of the total. Largely because of this increase, re-exports made a better showing in the fifties, and 1855 proved to be the best single year for the whole period, with re-exports valued at $26,000,000. But relative to total trade, re-exports had ceased to be of much significance. From 1821 through 1825 they had constituted about one fourth of the value of foreign exports, whereas during the last five years of the period they amounted to slightly more than one twentieth. Even this proportion was not maintained, and with the Civil War the re-export trade almost disappeared.

The United Kingdom was the chief rival of the United States for the re-export trade. The re-export trade of the two countries moved roughly parallel until about 1830, the annual value for United States re-exports being nearly one half that of the United Kingdom. But in

[6] See Appendix B.

the fourth decade, and even more clearly in the fifth, the value of the British re-export trade increased strongly, whereas the indirect trade of the United States lost ground. Finally, in the last decade of this period the United States re-exports turned definitely upward, but the average for the last five years was 12 per cent under that of the period 1816–1820. British re-export trade, on the other hand, advanced so rapidly that its value for 1856–1860 was 129 per cent greater than that for 1816–1820.[7]

Why did the United States lose to the United Kingdom in the struggle for this re-export trade? It is not without significance that in the period after 1830 the American merchant marine was not keeping pace in growth with total trade. A country whose shipping is carrying a decreasing percentage of its own exports and imports may not be expected greatly to increase its indirect trade. In this connection it may be noted that the increase in the American re-export business in the 1850's was in considerable part due to shipments to Canada, and these resulted in no small part from improved facilities for overland trade. Fundamentally, the decline in American re-exports is to be attributed not to the decreasing importance of the merchant marine but rather to the same basic causes which led to the relative decline in importance of the merchant marine itself. It may be merely noted here that capital to finance the indirect trade was abundant in England, whereas here it was limited in quantity and was, increasingly during the period, attracted to other investment fields such as canals, railroads, and manufacturing, all of which promised, or seemed to promise, higher returns.

IMPORTS FOR DOMESTIC CONSUMPTION

As an undeveloped yet rapidly growing country the United States had, during the period of this study, the greatest need for manufactured products of every description. Manufactured goods made up a large part of imports, varying from about one half to nearly three quarters of total merchandise imports. The demand for these products seemed insatiable, and whenever foreign credits expanded greatly, as they did in 1815–1818, 1836–1839, and in the 1850's, a tremendous influx of finished goods was easily absorbed.

Table 8 in Appendix A summarizes the record so far as the chief imports are concerned. Re-exports have been deducted so that the

[7] See Appendix A, Table 5.

figures given indicate "domestic" imports, i.e., imports for consumption, and not total imports. Cotton fabrics, woolens, and silk were, it will be seen, the chief manufactured imports, each one being at one time or another of first importance. Manufactures of flax were also substantial, averaging in value about one third those of cotton. If these four textile imports are taken together, their value was roughly one half that of all manufactures imported for domestic consumption and about one third the value of all commodities imported for domestic consumption.

Despite the tremendous growth in the United States of cotton textile manufacturing 1815–1860, cotton goods continued to be an import item of major importance and grew, at least in absolute value, to the end of the period. Previous to 1816, China and India had been the chief source for the coarser grades of cotton cloth.[8] But after the War of 1812, these cheaper grades were largely domestically produced, and imports were made up increasingly of the finer materials. These were almost exclusively of British manufacture. England was also the predominant source of supply for woolen and linen cloth. Small quantities of woolen manufactures came from the Continent, largely France and the Hanse towns. Considerable linen shipments came also from Scotland and Ireland, and, undoubtedly, much of the English exportation originated in Ireland. Silk was shipped to the United States chiefly from France and China, but imports of Chinese silk fell off rapidly in the later decades of the period. In some years large quantities of French silk reached America via English ports.

Iron and steel products constituted another major import. Pig and bar iron from Scandinavia were important in the early decades, but with the advent of the railroad era English rails became a leading import. In fact, most manufactured iron products, from tacks to ships' anchors, came from England, as did also a very great variety of other manufactured goods—books, buttons, clocks, hemp products, glass and earthenware of all kinds, jewelry, copper, lead products, and the like.

Of the nonmanufactured imports for home consumption, the leading items were the tropical or semitropical "foods"—sugar, coffee, and tea. America's appetite for sugar and coffee was increasing prodigiously. In 1821 the United States imported 37,500,000 pounds of brown sugar for domestic consumption; in 1860, over 660,000,000

[8] See Appendix B.

pounds, and this despite rapidly expanding domestic sugar production.[9] The increase is most strikingly shown by the fact that the annual per capita consumption of imported brown sugar rose from about four pounds at the beginning of the period to twenty-one pounds in 1860. Similarly, coffee consumption increased very rapidly during the same period. In the early 1820's Americans consumed each year less than two pounds per capita. In the decade before the Civil War, each person used, on the average, more than 5½ pounds per annum. Tea imports also increased, but not much more rapidly than the population, so that per capita consumption rose but slightly.[10]

The West Indies remained, as they had been in early American history, the chief source of sugar imports, although small amounts were brought from the Dutch East Indies and Brazil. Beginning with the fourth decade of the century, coffee came largely from Brazil. Previously Cuba and Haiti had been the most important sources of supply, but both declined in relative importance, and imports of Cuban coffee fell off greatly after 1844. China stood alone as the important source of tea.

Two other imports warrant brief comment. Alcoholic beverages were of considerable importance, though they declined in relative significance soon after the beginning of this period. Their total value was about equally divided between wine and spirits. Both were imported chiefly from France, but in the earlier part of the period wines from the Iberian Peninsula and the Wine Islands were imported in relatively large quantities. Changing tastes and the prosperity of well-to-do citizens are indicated by the fact that more than $1,300,000 worth of champagne was imported for consumption in 1860.

Hides and skins rose to some importance as imports before the end of the period, being valued at $10,500,000 in 1860. They came largely from South America and the East Indies and provided needed materials for the growing shoe and leather manufacturing industry of the United States.

Tables 9 and 10 of Appendix A show the distribution of American imports respectively by grand divisions and by leading countries. In view of the fact that finished manufactured goods typically made up about two thirds of the total value of American imports, it is not

[9] "Monthly Summary of Commerce and Finance of the United States," January, 1902, *House Document* No. 15, Pt. 7, 57 Cong., 1 Sess., XLIII, 2691, 2695, 2700.
[10] *Statement of Imports of Tea and Coffee into the U.S. Each Year from 1789 to 1882*, Quarterly Report No. 3, Series 1882–1883, of the Chief of the Bureau of Statistics, Treasury Department (Washington: 1883), pp. 427–428 and 446–447.

surprising to discover the dominant position of Europe in the import trade, nor to find that England, by far the most industrialized nation, furnished about two fifths of all American imports in value terms. Imports from France and Germany and other semi-industrialized areas of western Europe also rose rapidly during the period. On the other hand, imports from Russia, which was as yet quite unaltered by the industrial revolution, actually declined.

Southern North America and, to a lesser extent, South America were the chief sources of the tropical and semitropical products which, next to manufactures, were the largest imports. The West Indies were most important, though the percentage of total imports from this source showed some tendency to decline. But Cuban imports, always important, rose rapidly, so that by 1856–1860 more than three fourths of West Indian imports came from Cuba. Brazil, with its rapid rise to dominance in coffee production, was the chief source of imports from South America. Northern North America rose rapidly to importance in the last decade of the period. Asia was the only other import area from which America received appreciable imports. China and, to a much smaller extent, India were the chief countries in this trade which, although generally increasing throughout the period, did not quite share the rate of growth of total imports.

DOMESTIC EXPORTS

By far the major part of American purchasing power abroad arose from American commodity exports. But what commodities could America offer which would permit it to expand imports from $65,-000,000 in 1816 to $316,000,000 in 1860? The great tropical staples —tea, coffee, and spices—which found such profitable markets in Europe, could not be advantageously produced in the American climate. Domestic sugar production was, throughout the period, insufficient for home needs, and, until the discovery of gold in California, the export of mineral products was unimportant.

Fortunately, the United States did have one great staple, cotton. The rapid expansion of the demand for this product to feed the factories created by the industrial revolution is one of the most striking phenomena of the nineteenth century. The southern states could produce cotton at a relatively low cost and in seemingly unlimited quantities. In 1815 the United States exported 83,000,000 pounds of cotton valued at $17,500,000; by 1860 the quantity had risen to

1,768,000,000 pounds, worth nearly $192,000,000. For the period 1815–1860 as a whole this single product made up more than one half of the total value of domestic exports, and cotton alone paid for three fifths of total imports for consumption in 1860.[11]

No other product even approached the role played by cotton in the export trade. It is true that two commodities, wheat and tobacco, were strong contenders at the beginning of the period. For the years 1816–1820 wheat and wheat flour constituted 16 per cent of the value of domestic exports, unmanufactured tobacco 15 per cent, and cotton 39 per cent, but in terms of percentage of total exports this proved to be the high point for both wheat and tobacco.

The great staple of colonial times, tobacco, continued to be an important export, though of declining relative significance. Foreign demand was limited by competition from newly developed sources of supply as well as by highly restrictive taxes. In the United States, soil exhaustion in the old tobacco areas and the comparative advantage of cotton over tobacco contributed to its reduced importance. Exports of domestic tobacco were valued at $47,500,000 for the period 1816–1820, but this total was not reached again until 1851–1855. For the five years ending in 1860, tobacco exports were valued at $86,000,000, which was only 6 per cent of total domestic exports. As in the previous century, western Europe was the important market, and England the chief importer of unmanufactured tobacco.

Only intermittently did wheat play a major role in the exports of this period. In view of the fact that new farming lands in the West were being settled even more rapidly than the cotton areas of the new South, this may seem surprising. But the fact is that throughout the period, so far as the European market was concerned, the United States remained a marginal wheat-producing area. Only when European prices were unusually high, as for example in 1816–1818 and frequently after 1845, were large shipments of American wheat profitably disposed of in British markets. Not only did Great Britain remain largely self-sustaining, at least during the early part of the period, but flour from the Continent continued to have a competitive advantage over that from America. Even after the repeal of the British corn laws, when American flour exports greatly expanded, transportation costs (chiefly the cost of getting the wheat to the seaboard) were still so great that only in years of crop failures abroad or of special need when prices were unusually high did large quanti-

[11] See Appendix A, Table 11.

ties of American wheat or flour continue to reach the rapidly expanding British market.[12] Thus domestic exports of wheat and flour totaled $50,500,000 for 1816–1820 and constituted 16 per cent of total domestic exports. This percentage was not again equaled for any five-year period before the Civil War. The value of wheat exports was greatest for the five years ending in 1860 ($158,000,000) but even then amounted to but 11 per cent of total domestic exports.

Had it not been for the demand for American flour in the West Indies and South America, especially Brazil, flour exports would have approached the vanishing point in much of the period between 1820 and 1845. Here was an area in which the United States could compete on favorable terms with other sources of supply. On the other hand, this was at best a limited market, for, while under the impetus of the industrial revolution European (especially British) markets were expanding marvelously, those to the south increased but slowly and at times actually declined.

In addition to flour and wheat, the United States was, of course, in a position to produce tremendous quantities of other food products of the Temperate Zone, but none of these was exported in relatively large quantities. (See Appendix A, Table 11.) Only corn and rice were of appreciable importance among the grains, and the first of these, corn, amounted to more than 2 per cent of total domestic exports only in the five-year period which includes the Irish potato famine; and the second, rice, contributed 4 per cent to the value of domestic exports in 1816–1820 and only 1 per cent by the close of the period. Nor were meat and dairy products of great importance as exports. Pork and pork products, the most important of these, increased in value from $4,000,000 in 1816–1820 to nearly $54,000,000 in 1856–1860, when they represented about 4 per cent of the value of domestic exports. For all these food products the situation was similar to that for wheat and flour. Except for periods of exceptionally high prices, American provisions were still at a competitive disadvantage in western European markets, and the West Indian and South American markets failed to expand consistently. Finally, it may be noted that exports of fish, so important in colonial times, suffered both an absolute and a relative decline in this period.

By far the most significant of American nonagricultural exports were manufactured goods, which increased in value eightfold during

[12] Cf. Worthy P. Sterns, "The Foreign Trade of the United States from 1820 to 1840," *Journal of Political Economy*, VIII (December, 1899), 34–57, 452–497. See also Appendix B.

the period, thus eclipsing even raw cotton in rate of growth. Manufactured products, which were 7 per cent of total value exports in 1816–1820, equaled 12 per cent of the total in the last five years of the period, when they were valued at $167,000,000.[13] The nature of these manufactured exports is shown in the accompanying table, which lists in order of value the eight most important manufactured exports at five-year intervals, 1820–1860. The dominant position of cotton manufactures beginning in 1830 is noteworthy. Even in the previous decade cotton manufactures were, although not first, undoubtedly well up on the list, but they cannot be placed exactly at that time as they are not clearly separated in the original Treasury reports. In the early part of this period the chief foreign buyers of American cotton manufactures were Mexico and the West Indian Islands. In the 1840's Mexican imports of American manufactured goods declined in relative importance, and China, during much of the rest of the period, became the leading customer. Important shipments were made also to South America, to the West Indies, to Canada, and even to Africa and the East Indies.

Manufactures of cotton constitute the only important manufactured export which was to a large extent the product of relatively large-scale factory production. By the end of the period this was also beginning to be true of iron and steel products which, from eleventh place in 1820, moved steadily upward to second place in the final decade of the period. But before 1840, iron, and throughout the whole period practically all of the other manufactures, were largely the products of household or small-scale, neighborhood industries.

This is well illustrated by chemicals, which were the leading manufactured export in the 1820's and remained important throughout. About nine tenths of this category was made up of pot and pearl ashes, from which came potash, essential in the manufacture of such products as glass, soap, and explosives. The chief source of ashes was domestic fireplaces in the Middle and New England states. The process of leaching the ashes to produce pot and pearl ashes was always a neighborhood industry, carried on typically in a farmer's shed by not more than two or three workers.[14] Soap, spirits,

[13] The official classifications of products as "manufactured" or "unmanufactured" are necessarily arbitrary. Thus flour, butter, cheese, and naval stores are not included as manufactured products, whereas the following are so considered: soap, pot and pearl ashes, and refined sugar.

[14] Theodore J. Kreps, "Vicissitudes of the American Potash Industry," *Journal of Economic and Business History*, III (1930–1931), 640–653.

LEADING DOMESTIC EXPORTS OF MANUFACTURED PRODUCTS

(Values expressed in millions of dollars)

Rank	1820		1830		1840		1850		1860	
1	Chemicals, etc.	$1.0	Cotton, manuf.	$1.3	Cotton, manuf.	$3.5	Cotton, manuf.	$4.7	Cotton, manuf.	$10.9
2	Soap	0.8	Chemicals, etc.	1.2	Sugar, refined	1.2	Wood a	2.0	Iron and steel	5.9
3	Spirits, dist'l'd	0.5	Soap	0.6	Iron and steel	1.1	Iron and steel	2.0	Tobacco	3.4
4	Candles	0.3	Leather, manuf.	0.4	Tobacco, manuf.	0.8	Chemicals, etc.	0.9	Wood a	2.7
5	Leather, manuf.	0.2	Iron and steel	0.3	Chemicals, etc.	0.7	Soap	0.7	Chemicals, etc.	1.9
6	Wood a	0.2	Spirits dist'l'd	0.3	Wood a	0.6	Tobacco	0.6	Copper and brass	1.7
7	Wood b	0.2	Candles	0.2	Soap	0.5	Spirits, dist'l'd	0.3	Leather, manuf.	1.5
8	Tobacco, manuf.	0.1	Tobacco, manuf.	0.2	Spirits, dist'l'd	0.4	Sugar, refined	0.3	Spirits, dist'l'd	1.5

a Wood, not including household furnishings.
b Wood, household furnishings.

Source: Monthly Summary of Commerce and Finance, April, 1903, Bureau of Statistics, Treasury Department, *House Document* No. 15, Pt. 10, 57 Cong., 2 Sess., XLII, 3313–3315.

candles, leather, and "wood, other" (which included staves, shingles, boards, and so on) were largely the product of neighborhood or even household manufacture and were directly dependent upon cheap domestic materials. In fact, chemicals and soap, the two leading manufactured exports of the 1820's, might be looked upon as by-products of the agriculture of the period. Pot and pearl ashes, a product destined not for immediate consumption but for further use in manufacturing, were the only export of American manufacture which was sent chiefly to European markets. All the other important manufactured exports found their best markets in the West Indies (especially Cuba and Haiti), Mexico, South America, and, for the later decades, British North America.

Tables 12 and 13 in Appendix A show the destination of American exports. Table 12 gives percentages for total exports and, therefore, is not quite as significant for the purpose as Table 13, which is for domestic exports only. A study of these tables throws further light on the preceding analysis of exports. The leading position of Europe and especially the United Kingdom in American export trade serves again to illustrate the extent to which domestic exports were dominated by raw cotton. The place of southern North America and South America is a reflection of their demand for American foodstuffs and manufactured goods, a demand which was expanding throughout the period but not as rapidly as total exports. Taking the period as a whole, the absolute value of domestic exports increased to practically every part of the world. There was a tendency for the percentage of domestic exports sent to Europe and northern North America to increase moderately. Exports to Asia and South America declined slightly as a percentage of total domestic exports; for exports to the West Indies the percentage drop was very considerable, from 19 per cent in 1821–1825 to 7 per cent in 1856–1860.

THE GROWTH OF FOREIGN TRADE

The rapidly growing population of the United States offered an almost unlimited potential demand for the manufactured goods of Europe and for the tropical and semitropical foodstuffs of the South and the Far East. But the effective demand, the amount actually imported, was determined by American purchasing power, and this in turn was limited by the amount of American exports, by the services rendered to foreigners, and by loans from abroad. As exports were the predominant means of payment, attention will be centered primarily on analyzing the reasons for their development. Import changes, insofar as they do not parallel those in exports, are discussed in the last part of this chapter, which has to do with the balance of international indebtedness.

CHART 3

Domestic Exports and Imports for Consumption, 1815–1860

(See Appendix A, Table 4)

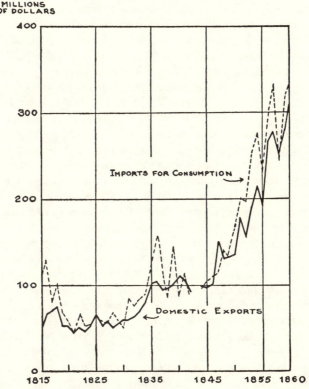

The annual growth of imports for consumption and domestic exports is shown in Chart 3. Two periods stand out in the growth of American domestic export trade: the rapid increase through 1818, followed by generally lower values throughout the twenties; and the growth in the value of domestic exports which began in the 1830's and, after a reaction in the following decade, reached tremendous proportions in the 1850's.

From the close of the War of 1812 through 1818 the value of

domestic exports was very high indeed. In fact, total values were higher than in any equal period before that time and were not exceeded until the fourth decade of the century. With the end of the war and the lifting of the British blockade, accumulated stocks of American goods, notably cotton and tobacco, were released for shipment abroad at prices that remained extremely high well into 1818. Moreover, until normal conditions of production could be restored in Britain and on the Continent, a tremendous market existed there for American wheat and flour at very high prices.

Despite the rapid growth in population and productivity during the decade of the twenties, the value of American domestic exports actually declined. Not until the five-year period ending in 1835 did domestic exports equal in value the totals attained in the five years ending in 1820. This unexpected development in the export trade has not been well understood. Certainly it cannot be held that foreign and American tariff legislation, the growth of a home market for American raw materials and foodstuffs, or increasing attention to internal trade caused a decline in American exports.[15] Doubtless renewed European tariff restrictions may have been a generally restraining influence, although it is impossible to locate important cases where this was true. As for the American tariff, it may be assumed on general principles that it also was a restricting factor. But as there was no very important legislation between 1816 and 1824 and as the value of domestic exports rose to their greatest heights (1818) and fell to their lowest point (1821) within this period, it may also be assumed that American tariff policy was not an important factor. As for the belief that the development of American manufacturing in the 1820's was taking so much raw material that more could not be exported, the notion seems absurd in view of the low prices then prevailing. Moreover, the question immediately arises as to why, in the 1850's, when American manufacturing industry was really developing at a tremendous pace, exports increased as never before. Finally, it is absurd to believe that a rapidly developing internal trade was a hindrance to foreign commerce in the twenties but a help in subsequent decades.

The fact of the matter is that the *volume* of domestic exports, far from declining, was actually *increasing* appreciably in this decade of supposed stagnation. Shipments of cotton, by far the most im-

---

[15] See Johnson and others, *History of Domestic and Foreign Commerce of the United States*, II, 37–40; and John H. Frederick, *The Development of American Commerce* (New York: D. Appleton–Century Company, 1932), pp. 86, 89.

portant export, averaged in the "depressed" twenties more than double (114 per cent increase) what they had during 1816–1820. Cotton exports, which were 128,000,000 pounds in 1820, had risen to 298,000,000 pounds in 1830. Most other commodities also showed substantial gains, although few increased as much as cotton. Thus comparing the physical volume of trade for 1816–1820 and 1821–1830, it is found that the average annual exports of tobacco increased 12 per cent; rice, 33 per cent; pork, 17 per cent; bacon and hams, 178 per cent; beef, 81 per cent; and pot and pearl ashes, 18 per cent. Against these must be set losses of 13 per cent for boards, planks, and scantling; 4 per cent for dried and smoked fish; and 14 per cent for wheat flour.[16] Lumber and fish were relatively unimportant in value exports, and the decline in flour exports was due, not to the fact that the home demand was taking the supply, but, as has been pointed out above, to the fact that prices were so low that European shipments were unprofitable.

Attempts to explain the great "decline" in American foreign trade in the twenties have gone astray largely because of failure to recognize the significance of the price revolution of 1819. No index of prices of American exports is available for this period, but Anne Bezanson's index for domestic commodities at Philadelphia probably gives a fair indication of the movement of prices for American exports. According to this study, the average monthly index of prices of domestic commodities as shown for January was 168.0 in 1816, 114.7 in 1820, and 85.2 in 1830.[17] In view of the importance of cotton in our foreign trade, the situation is probably best revealed by noting the effect of price changes on value exports of that commodity. Domestic exports of cotton rose from 92,000,000 pounds in 1818 to 298,000,000 pounds in 1830, but, as prices declined during the same period from an annual average of 33.9 cents a pound to 9.9 cents a pound, the value exports in the latter year were actually less than in the former.[18] It may be perfectly proper to call this situation a "decline" in trade but, if so, the correct explanation is in terms of prices and not of tariffs or the increasing importance of internal markets.

What explanation can be offered for the general upward sweep

[16] Computed from Charles H. Evans, "Exports, Domestic, from the United States to All Countries from 1789 to 1883, Inclusive," *House Miscellaneous Document* No. 49, Pt. 2, 48 Cong., 1 Sess. (1884), XXIV, 15 ff.
[17] Anne Bezanson and others, *Wholesale Prices in Philadelphia, 1784–1861* (Philadelphia: University of Pennsylvania Press, 1936), 352–353.
[18] *House Miscellaneous Document* No. 49, Pt. 2, 48 Cong., 1 Sess. (1884), XXIV, 28–29.

of exports which began in the early thirties, was checked temporarily after 1839, and culminated in the tremendous expansion of the fifties (see Chart 3)? The value of domestic exports for 1850–1859 was double that of the previous decade, and more than four times that of the decade of the twenties. Moreover, this tremendous increase is as impressive in terms of quantity as in terms of value. Thus in the 1840's the general level of prices was well under that for the 1820's. Yet, despite this fact, export values were much increased for the decade of the forties. Similarly, for the period 1850–1859, prices were roughly at the same level as they had been in the twenties, but the value of domestic exports had increased fourfold.

It has sometimes been held that favorable changes in commercial policy, both of the United States and of foreign nations, were an important factor in this great increase in foreign trade, especially in the tremendous growth after 1846. Undoubtedly the United States tariff reductions of 1846 and 1857 had a favorable influence on trade expansion. However, it should be noted that the high rates of the tariff of 1832 prevailed during the period of tremendous increase in foreign trade during the thirties,[19] and that despite the unprecedentedly high tariff following the Civil War, foreign commerce grew phenomenally. Nor can the Reciprocity Act of 1854 with Canada be regarded as a major factor in promoting the high trade values of the late fifties. Although that act did undoubtedly lend some stimulus to commerce, it must be noted in this connection that the great increase in trade between the United States and British North America came before, not after, the passage of the act; that the act was put into effect at a time when English markets for American foodstuffs were appreciably expanded because of the Crimean War; and that the impetus to the exchange of foodstuffs and raw material which resulted from the Reciprocity Agreement was offset, in part at least, by the higher duties on United States manufactured goods which were imposed by Canada soon after the passage of the act.[20] Finally, it should be emphasized that by 1860 American exports to British North America were less than 7 per cent of total exports.

Moreover, it is not clear that changes in their commercial policies by foreign countries were of great importance in affecting the total commerce during this period. Detailed consideration of these changes is impossible, but it may be noted that the period, especially after

[19] See Appendix B.
[20] Donald C. Masters, *The Reciprocity Treaty of 1854* (New York: Longmans, Green and Co., 1936), Chap. 4.

1845, was characterized by a general tendency toward freer trade, the outstanding example being the repeal of the British corn laws in 1846. Undoubtedly the reduction of trade restrictions was a favorable factor in trade growth, but it may be questioned whether that factor was of major significance. Even the repeal of the corn laws was not the chief explanation for the great increase in the grain trade after 1845. Much more important were the fundamental changes which had been brought about by the increased industrialization of England and the crop failures during the late forties in Britain and Ireland which raised prices and made imperative large food importations. In fact, the repeal was less the cause of the increased grain trade than the result of high corn prices and an actual scarcity of needed foodstuffs in Great Britain and Ireland.[21]

But, if it be concluded that changes in commercial policy were not of major importance, what were the chief factors which caused the great increase in American foreign commerce? In the first place, it is essential to note that practically all the countries of western Europe were greatly expanding their foreign commerce. The fundamental reason was the progress of the industrial revolution, and the fact that the rate of that progress was greatly stepped up in the 1850's as gold flowed from newly opened mines and rising prices afforded their usual stimulus to capitalistic production. There were special reasons why the United States should participate generously in these gains. Not only was population increasing in the United States at a rapid rate but the area of the country had been appreciably increased by the addition of Texas, the Southwest, and the West coast. Finally, and most important, cheap inland water transportation now supplemented by railroads which connected the rich Mississippi Valley with the Atlantic coast, put the United States into a position in which greatly expanded exports were possible—in fact, inevitable —whenever foreign demand would permit. Very briefly, then, these were the prime factors which caused the great expansion of American trade in the decades preceding the Civil War.

Before the War of 1812, no one port had dominated American foreign commerce. In early colonial times Boston held the leading position, which before the Revolution was yielded to Philadelphia. After about 1796 New York was generally in the lead. But none of these cities immediately achieved a commanding position. Such ports as Charleston, Baltimore, and New Orleans were important

[21] Frederick Merk, "The British Corn Crisis of 1845–46 and the Oregon Treaty," *Agricultural History*, VIII, No. 3 (July, 1934), 107 ff.

contenders at one time or another, and a host of smaller ports from Maine to Georgia carried on a considerable foreign trade. The tremendous increase in foreign trade between 1815 and 1860 brought drastic shifts in the relative position of American seaports. During this period New York achieved a dominant position, leaving its rivals on the Atlantic coast far behind, and two Gulf ports, New Orleans and Mobile, rose to major importance in the export trade.

New York seized the leadership at the very beginning of the period, and rapidly became the dominant port in American foreign trade. For the whole period 1821–1860 she had 60 per cent of total imports and 33 per cent of total exports. Of basic importance to this success was the unique excellence of New York Harbor and its advantageous location with respect both to the extensive coast line and to foreign ports. But other factors were also very important. Shortly after the war New York became the chief port for the receipt and distribution of English manufactures, especially textiles. The auction system adopted in New York City for the disposal of these wares helped greatly to make it the chief distribution center in the United States. The establishment of the transatlantic packet lines, with their fast and dependable service and rapid transmission of market information, gave New York traders another early advantage. The greatest handicap to all of the northern ports had always been a lack of exports. This obstacle New York overcame more successfully than any of its rivals. This was accomplished in two ways: through the Erie Canal and later the railroads she brought the produce of the rapidly developing West to her docks; and by aggressive action in the coastwise trade her merchants enslaved the cotton ports and brought their cotton, tobacco, and naval stores to the mouth of the Hudson in order to provide eastbound cargoes for her transatlantic ships.[22]

The foreign commerce of Boston increased greatly during the period, from a value of $17,000,000 in 1821 to $58,000,000 in 1860, but she trailed far behind New York, whose total foreign commerce was worth $383,000,000 in 1860. For a time in the forties Boston threatened to overcome the New York lead, for her trade advanced rapidly as she gained from her early railroad connections with the West and the superior transatlantic service provided by the Cunard Line. But the close of the decade saw the end of this threat, and much Boston business and even many Boston businessmen moved to New York. Throughout the period Boston retained her supremacy in the

[22] Albion, "New York Port and Its Disappointed Rivals, 1815–1860," pp. 602–629.

trade with Turkey, the Baltic, and the ports of the Far East. But on the main Atlantic routes Boston was decidedly secondary to New York, and the expanding cotton exports of New Orleans soon made the New England city a poor third in the total value of foreign commerce.

The foreign trade of Philadelphia showed almost no growth. Even at the end of the period her foreign commerce was less than it had been during the Napoleonic Wars. Relatively unsuccessful in her early attempts to open up advantageous connections with the West, she devoted her chief energies to developing manufactured products for the domestic market.

Baltimore's foreign trade, though considerably smaller than Philadelphia's at the beginning of the period, grew appreciably to equal it by the fifties. Baltimore absorbed much of the foreign trade of other Chesapeake ports and was an important factor in the West Indian and South American trade. The excellent keeping qualities of the Virginia and Maryland flour gave her an advantage in the important Brazilian market and she imported large quantities of coffee from Brazil and guano from the west coast of South America.[23]

Charleston, which had been a really important seaport before 1812, was rapidly outdistanced by its rivals following the war. The value of its imports was actually less in 1856–1860 than in 1821–1825. Foreign exports showed little change to the fifties but increased appreciably just before the Civil War. New York's development of the coastal trade was an important factor in the failure of Charleston's commerce to expand. In 1822–1824 coastwise shipments of cotton from Charleston had averaged about 16 per cent of foreign exports. By 1859 this percentage had risen to 45. For rice an even greater change resulted, with coastwise shipments appreciably exceeding foreign exports by the latter part of the fifties. For the whole period 1821–1860 the value of the imports of the South Carolina city was less than 1 per cent of the national total. Exports were under 7 per cent of the total for the whole country.[24]

The cotton ports on the Gulf grew tremendously. New Orleans, aided by the tremendous expansion of cotton growing and by the expanding receipts of food products from the Mississippi Valley, increased her exports from $5,000,000 in 1815 to $107,000,000 in 1860.

---

[23] See Frank R. Rutter, *South American Trade of Baltimore* (Johns Hopkins University *Studies in Historical and Political Science*, Vol. XV, No. 9, Baltimore: The Johns Hopkins Press, 1897), *passim*.

[24] Van Deusen, *Economic Bases of Disunion in South Carolina*, Chap. 5 and App. B and C; Albion, *The Rise of New York Port*, App. I.

For a number of years in the thirties and forties, New Orleans topped New York as an exporting center. Mobile also grew phenomenally, being the third largest exporting city in the last few years of the period. But none of the cotton ports except New Orleans developed an appreciable import trade, and even for that city imports continued throughout to be greatly overshadowed by exports. For the period 1821–1860 exports from New Orleans were nearly one fourth of the national total but imports were only one fifteenth.

THE BALANCE OF INTERNATIONAL INDEBTEDNESS

During most of the period 1815–1860 the United States had an unfavorable balance of trade (see Chart 2, p. 177). It might be assumed, therefore, that the United States was what has been termed an immature borrowing country, one whose balance of trade is unfavorable because large foreign imports are being paid for by loans from abroad. When the interest which must be paid on these foreign loans exceeds the amount of the new loans, exports exceed imports and the mature borrowing stage is said to have been reached. But no such interpretation of United States foreign trade development can be assumed before the balance sheet is examined in some detail. In order to do this the period has been divided as follows: 1815–1820, 1821–1837, 1838–1849, and 1850–1860.

The foreign trade of the United States, which had almost disappeared during the last year of the War of 1812, increased greatly during the years of peace immediately following. War-impoverished Europe was in no position to absorb an appreciable part of the great accumulated stock of British manufactures. So American markets were the one great outlet. In the peak year 1816, foreign imports into the United States were valued at almost $150,000,000, the largest total up to that time and one not surpassed for nineteen years. Exports also expanded rapidly, for in Europe disorganized production and poor harvests resulted in a great demand for American foodstuffs. Nevertheless, exports grew at a slower rate than imports, with the result that the United States had the unprecedentedly large import balance of $187,000,000 for the period 1815–1820.

How, it may be asked, was this large "unfavorable" balance met? To begin with, the reliability of the official export and import statistics must be examined. The records kept before 1821 are not as complete or as reliable as those since that time. Every ship's captain clearing from an American port was required to report the quantity and value of his cargo to the customs office before his ship could be cleared. As no duties were levied on exports, there was no monetary incentive to undervaluation. On the other hand, the ignorance or negligence of the master sometimes resulted in incorrect returns. The captain, when not himself the shipper, may have had a rather uncertain idea of the freight carried. Moreover, as there was no outward inspection of his cargo by port officials, he was in no danger of being found in error. So, although he had no reason to render false returns, neither had he an incentive to go to very much trouble to provide a full or correct one.[25]

There is no clear evidence that Treasury reports of exports were too high or too low. A Senate committee reporting in 1819 offers confusing comment. After demonstrating that the method of valuing certain re-exports was such as to undervalue them, the report concludes without further explanation that there are "sufficient reasons" to believe that the value of American exports have been overstated to an undetermined but probably not considerable extent.[26] On the other hand, as late as 1864, by which time considerable improvement had been made in the recording of export statistics, a special report from the Secretary of the Treasury held that the reports of exports were subject to large deficiencies.[27] Until clear proof is forthcoming of definite bias in the export statistics, the Treasury returns will have to be accepted as they stand as the best approximation available.

Before 1821 the customs records give the value of all imports subject to ad valorem duties, chiefly cotton and woolen textiles and iron manufactures. For goods paying specific duties, only quantity records were kept. And no record at all was made of goods entering free of duty. As a result there are no contemporary, official statistics of the annual value of total imports into the United States. But in 1835 the Treasury Department made a special study on the basis of which the annual value of total imports was computed for the years previous to 1821 and these figures have since that time been accepted as official.[28] By exactly what method these estimates were made is not known beyond this: that for 1815 they are based on Seybert's figures; that for the following years they are derived from manuscript notes, calculations, and comparisons with other years; and, finally,

[25] *American State Papers: Commerce and Navigation*, II, 391–393.
[26] *Ibid.*, pp. 392–393.
[27] Foreign Commerce of the United States, *Senate Executive Document* No. 55, 38 Cong., 1 Sess., p. 41.
[28] Report of the Secretary of the Treasury, App. C, *Senate Document* No. 2, 24 Cong., 1 Sess., pp. 32–33.

that goods entered free of duty were counted as worth $3,000,000 per annum.[29] For the purposes of this study the official statistics have been accepted as the most reliable for the years 1816–1820, but, for 1815, the official figure for total imports of $113,041,274 is open to such serious question that Pitkin's estimate of $83,080,073 has been taken instead.[30] By this procedure the total value of imports for the years 1815–1820 is found to be $612,758,073 and the excess of imports over exports $157,000,000.

To this large debit item must be added the net imports of specie during the period. Much silver had left the country just before and during the War of 1812, but following the close of the war the situation changed rapidly and, despite the very large drain to China and India, the supply of specie in the United States increased. Gallatin's estimates, the best available, show specie in American banks increasing from $17,000,000 at the beginning of 1815 to $19,820,240 by the end of 1819. At least $2,000,000 was added in 1820. It may be conservatively estimated, therefore, that at least $5,000,000 was due abroad to balance this net specie importation.[31] Adding this to the net merchandise import balance gives a total of $162,000,000 due abroad.

This debit was met chiefly from the earnings of the merchant marine and by foreign loans to this country. The earnings of American ships were an important credit item in the American balance of payments down to the Civil War. In the six years under consideration not only did American ships carry more than four fifths of the total American foreign commerce, but about one fifth of the tonnage was employed in the carrying trade between foreign ports. The net earnings of the American merchant marine may be estimated at about $143,000,000 for this period. If from this is deducted the earnings of American and foreign ships bringing merchandise imports to the United States, it is found that shipping as a net credit item in the balance sheet amounted to about $80,000,000 for the period.[32] And to this may be added about $4,000,000 received from the sale to foreigners of American-built ships.[33]

[29] *Ibid.*

[30] Pitkin, *A Statistical View of the Commerce of the United States of America*, p. 265. See also Appendix B.

[31] Albert Gallatin, "Considerations on the Currency and Banking System of the United States," in Henry Adams, ed., *The Writings of Albert Gallatin* (Philadelphia: J. B. Lippincott Co., 1879), III, 285–288, 291, 363; Sterns, "The Foreign Trade of the United States from 1820 to 1840," p. 37.

[32] See Appendix B.

[33] See Appendix B.

A final item on the balance of international payments, that arising from international loans, is difficult to estimate. So far as long-
term loans involving the transfer of securities is concerned, credits are
estimated to offset debits. The chief debit item was the interest on
that part of the national debt which was held abroad. This debt was
estimated at $30,000,000 in 1815. It probably remained at approximately this figure until 1820, when English investors again began
to buy American securities. During the War of 1812 considerable investments abroad had been made by American citizens, but most of
these were apparently liquidated in the years immediately after the
war. The interest on these American-owned foreign securities, their
redemption by the American owners, and, finally, the small new loans
from abroad in 1820 (all credit items) are believed to have been about
equal to the interest due on American securities owned abroad.[34]

But the situation was quite different for short-term credit on
merchandise. The tremendous flood of manufactured goods which
was sent to the United States right after the war was, to a very considerable extent, sold on credit. Niles estimated that mercantile
obligations due Europeans, amounting to not much less than $100,-
000,000, were canceled as the result of bankruptcies in America during this period.[35] Although Niles is one of the most reliable of contemporary observers, it must be noted that he cites this figure while
expounding his pet hobby—the curse of imported luxuries and the
need of protecting American industry. Allowing for this bias, his
estimate has been reduced to $70,000,000 to give what appears to be
the best approximation for mercantile loans as a net credit item during this period. Even with this reduction, credits from this source are
estimated at a sum nearly equal to the net earnings of American shipping for the years 1815–1820.[36]

On the basis of the foregoing analysis, a balance of payments has
been drawn up in the accompanying table. No attempt has been made
to estimate the value of certain minor items such as travelers' expenses and insurance payments. Moreover, no single item in the statement can be regarded as more than a fair guess by one who has
attempted to weigh the information available. But the general picture
should be substantially correct. Shipping earnings, commercial credit,
and receipts from sale of ships were not sufficient to offset the "un-

[34] Worthy P. Sterns, "The Foreign Trade of the United States from 1820 to 1840,"
p. 38, and "The Beginnings of American Financial Independence," *Journal of Political
Economy*, VI (March, 1898), 197–199.
[35] *Niles' Weekly Register*, XIX (September 16, 1820), 40.
[36] Appendix B.

favorable" balance of trade. And, as should be expected under these circumstances, sterling exchange, which had been at a heavy discount during the war, rose rapidly during 1815 and remained at a premium during most of the rest of the period.[37]

BALANCE OF INTERNATIONAL INDEBTEDNESS OF THE
UNITED STATES, 1815–1820

(*In millions of dollars*)

	Credits	Debits
Excess of merchandise imports [38]	$...	$157
Net specie imports	...	5
Net freights	80	...
Sale of ships	4	...
Defaulted mercantile loans	70	...
	$154	$162

For the decade 1821–1830 the net excess of merchandise imports was only $35,000,000. Five years showed a favorable and five an unfavorable trade balance. Beginning with 1831, however, imports predominated, reaching a peak in 1836 when they surpassed exports by $52,000,000. For the whole seventeen years the net surplus of imports was $185,000,000.

A summary statement of the balance of payments for this period is shown in the table below. This has been taken from the standard study of this subject by Charles J. Bullock and others.[39] It will be noted that the unfavorable merchandise balance is increased by $30,-000,000 to correct for the understatement of the pound sterling. When

BALANCE OF INTERNATIONAL INDEBTEDNESS, 1821–1837

1821–1837	Credit	Debit
Merchandise	$1,389,000,000	$1,574,000,000
Undervaluation of pound sterling		30,000,000
Specie	107,675,000	144,389,000
Freights	214,000,000	8,000,000
Capital and interest	125,000,000	60,000,000
Sale of ships	8,000,000	
Immigrants	11,000,000	
Tourists		11,000,000
Total	$1,854,675,000	$1,827,389,000

[37] Smith and Cole, *Fluctuations in American Business 1790–1860*, p. 25.
[38] See Appendix B.
[39] For this period as well as the following ones, chief dependence has been placed on Charles J. Bullock, John H. Williams, and Rufus S. Tucker, "The Balance of Trade of the United States," *Review of Economic Statistics*, Preliminary I (1919), 215–266, referred to hereafter as the *Bullock Study*.

an excess of specie imports of $37,000,000 is added to this there is a total excess of merchandise and specie exports of about $221,000,000. The debit balance was, as in the previous period, chiefly offset by freight earnings and loans. The American merchant marine prospered during this period and brought in net credits of $206,000,000. And this was further augmented by the sale of ships to the sum of $8,000,000.

The net credit arising from new foreign loans is, as always, difficult to estimate. To 1824 Europe took only small amounts of American securities. But, with the success of the Erie Canal and the faith which that successful undertaking inspired in securities issued by American states for the financing of internal improvements, there was an increased flow of British capital to this country which, in the flush times after 1834, became very large indeed. Bullock estimates that new foreign loans to the United States during this period amounted to $125,000,000, a figure which is probably an understatement.[40] Against this is set $60,000,000 of necessary interest payments. Specie brought in by immigrants is assumed to balance the expenditures of American travelers, but the figures given may be fairly wide of the mark.[41]

The balance for the years 1838–1849 is shown in the following table. The inclusion of the years 1838 and 1839 in this period, instead of in the preceding one, is clearly unfortunate.[42] Despite the temporary reaction of 1838, these two years are definitely like the preceding ones in that Europe was still rapidly extending credit to the United States and net imports for the two years taken together were very large indeed. Even including these two years, this period

BALANCE OF INTERNATIONAL INDEBTEDNESS, 1838–1849

1838–1849	Credit	Debit
Merchandise	$1,392,000,000	$1,358,000,000
Specie	78,300,000	114,400,000
Freights	236,000,000	22,000,000
Capital and interest	40,000,000	144,000,000
Sale of ships	6,150,000	. . . .
Immigrants	75,000,000	15,000,000
Tourists	. . . .	84,500,000
Mexican war and indemnity	. . . .	25,000,000
Total	$1,827,450,000	$1,762,900,000

[40] See Appendix B.
[41] See Leland Hamilton Jenks, *The Migration of British Capital to 1875* (New York: Alfred A. Knopf, Inc., 1927), p. 363, fn. 48.
[42] *Ibid.*

demonstrates sharply the changed situation which characterized the international balance of payments during the forties. Merchandise trade for the whole period shows a small credit balance ($34,000,-000); for the depression years 1840–1844 it amounted to $61,606,528. As Bullock points out, net specie imports ($36,000,000) almost exactly balanced the excess of merchandise exports during the twelve years of this period.

The merchant marine and the sale of ships together continued to contribute a large sum to the credit side of the balance—$220,-000,000 for the twelve years under consideration. And immigrants, entering in unprecedented numbers toward the close of the period, are estimated to have brought approximately $75,000,000 into the country, although from this must be deducted perhaps $15,000,000 to cover their remittances to the home countries. On the debit side tourists' expenses of $84,500,000 and the Mexican War Indemnity of $25,000,000 must be added.

International capital movements played a new role during this period. The failure of the second Bank of the United States in 1839 and the subsequent repudiation of their bonds by many of the states discouraged further foreign investment in the United States until near the close of the period. The result was that the $40,000,000 of new capital which was invested in the United States was short of covering interest on past and present debt by a little over $100,000,-000.[43] So for this period the balance of payments, showing as it does an excess of exports and interest payments exceeding new capital investments, takes on characteristics typical of the balance of payments of a mature debtor country. But the symptoms were premature, the result in large part of a temporary slump between two great periods of expansion, for not until well after the Civil War did the United States take its place clearly as a mature debtor nation.

In the last period, 1850–1860, imports predominated in every year except 1858; for the whole period 1850–1860 imports exceeded exports by $385,000,000. To this, as a further debit item, must be added travelers' expenses of about $165,000,000. This large unfavorable balance was more than met by the flow of gold abroad, now made possible by the rapid exploitation of the newly discovered California mines. This large credit item is augmented by $260,000,000 from foreign freights and the sale of ships, for the American merchant marine was experiencing a last spurt of prosperity before its great decline during and after the war. Finally, specie brought in by im-

[43] See Appendix B.

migrants, less their remittances abroad, may be estimated at $100,-000,000. Toward the end of the forties, European capital had again begun to seek American investments, and this movement assumed large proportions during the 1850's as railroad securities moved rapidly into favor with foreign investors. Large as these new investments were (approximately $190,000,000), they were not quite sufficient to equal the annual interest payments on the total foreign debt, which may be estimated at $203,000,000 for the period.

The balance sheet for this period is shown in the accompanying table. It is derived largely from Bullock's balance sheet for the period 1850–1873.[44] The general outline of the picture is believed to be reliable, although a fairly large error is indicated by the appreciable spread between total credits and debits. It would be a mistake, however, to conclude that this disparity necessarily arises chiefly from errors in estimating the invisible items. In this period merchandise trade is so large absolutely that a small percentage of error in the official figures of imports or exports greatly affects the balance sheet. Thus, if imports had been undervalued during this period by 10 per cent (a not impossible assumption), then more than $300,000,000 would be added to the debit side of the balance.

BALANCE OF INTERNATIONAL INDEBTEDNESS, 1850–1860

(*In millions of dollars*)

	Credits	Debits
Specie	$420	
New capital borrowed	190	
Immigrants [45]	100	
Freight	243	
Sale of ships	17	
Merchandise		$385
Interest		203
Tourists' expenses		241
Total	$970	$829

Except for the decade of the forties, when exports slightly exceeded imports, the United States had a generally unfavorable balance of trade during the sixty years before the Civil War. For the whole period 1815–1860 the excess of merchandise imports over merchandise exports amounted to $724,000,000. This, the most important debit item, along with specie imports up to 1846 and invisible items such as the amounts spent by American travelers abroad, was

[44] See Appendix B.
[45] See Appendix B.

consistently offset, as has been shown, by the earnings of the American merchant marine, sporadically by large loans from abroad, and after 1846 by tremendous exports of American gold.

Actually, of course, it was chiefly the growth of merchandise exports that made possible so great an expansion of imports. At no time during this period did any invisible item on the credit side of the balance of payments, or all of them together, approach exports as the principal offset to imports. Even in the period of their greatest relative importance as a payment for imports (1815–1820), the net earnings of the merchant marine were only 15 per cent of imports while for the same period exports were 76 per cent. In the last period, 1850–1860, merchant marine earnings were only 8½ per cent, whereas exports were 87 per cent of total imports.

Similarly, foreign loans were a very small item as compared with exports in making possible the great growth of merchandise imports. Even in 1816–1818 and 1835–1839, when foreign loans were relatively most important in this respect, they did not in their peak year come anywhere near equaling exports. In fact, foreign investments in the United States were relatively small before the Civil War. They were estimated by the Secretary of the Treasury to total $400,000,000 in 1860. This sum is only a little more than the value of American merchandise imports for that single year.

CHAPTER X

Manufacturing: Early Development

THE population of the United States increased less than four times between 1815 and 1860. During the same period the value of manufactured products grew about eightfold and their volume approximately twelvefold. Certain factors were fundamental: a rapidly growing population, rich natural resources, a stable and favorably disposed government, and the absence of social impediments to economic change and of restrictions on the free movement of goods over a wide area. To these conditions were added during the decades preceding the Civil War the great improvements in transportation which have already been discussed. By cheapening and facilitating the movement of goods this revolution in transportation made possible a great specialization, a rapidly developing division of labor between different sections of the nation, between town and country, and between manufacturing and agriculture. Accompanying this increased specialization came changes in the technique, organization, and scale of manufacturing which greatly enlarged output and paved the way for the tremendous industrial development which took place in the United States during the second half of the nineteenth century.

MANUFACTURES IN 1815

In 1815 the town of Mount Pleasant, Ohio, described as having a population of about 500 in addition to journeymen, laborers, and transient persons, possessed, according to *Niles' Register*, the following manufacturing interests: ". . . 3 saddler's, 3 hatter's, 4 blacksmith's, 4 weaver's, 6 boot and shoemaker's, 8 carpenter's, 3 tailor's, 3 cabinet maker's, 1 baker's, 1 apothecary's, and 2 wagon maker's shops—2 tanneries; 1 shop for making wool carding machines; 1 with a machine for spinning wool; 1 manufactory for spinning thread from *flax;* 1 nail factory; 2 wool carding machines." In addition, "Within the distance of six miles from the town were—9 merchant mills; 2 grist mills; 12 saw mills; 1 paper mill, with 2 vats; 1 woolen factory, with 4 looms, and 2 fulling mills." [1] If to these activities had been added the multifarious household manufactures of the time, including the making in the home of a wide variety of products from soap and candles to leather and maple sugar, a fair picture would be presented of the household-handicraft-mill complex which accounted for a large portion of the manufacturing in the United States in 1815. This organization of industry was dominant in most parts of the country until well into the forties and continued important in more remote areas until long after the Civil War.

Household manufacture, or usufacture,[2] was the chief form of industry at the beginning of the period of this study. The Embargo and Nonintercourse Acts and the War of 1812 had so restricted imports of manufactured goods, especially of textiles, that household production had greatly expanded. In the East and South, families that had come to depend upon British woolens, Irish linens, and Indian cottons now turned back again to the products of home spinning wheels and looms. According to the census of 1810 the value of all textiles made in American homes was about $38,000,000.[3] By 1816 Niles estimated their annual value at $120,000,000, stating: "Ten years ago, the hours lost in the country, by *waiting for bed time* in long winter evenings, were equal to the time necessary to make the essential articles to clothe the people." [4] Even allowing for Niles' soaring enthusiasm for manufactures, it seems clear that by the close of the war the household manufacture of textiles had been widely re-established in the more settled parts of the country.

Especially in the more populous East, and to some extent even in the smaller frontier communities, household manufacture was supplemented by the labors of a considerable number of craftsmen: cobblers, blacksmiths, curriers, coopers, hatters, tailors, weavers, and others. In sparsely settled areas many of these specialists were true journeymen traveling from house to house, living with the family, and typically utilizing the leather, yarn, cloth, or other materials

---

[1] *Niles' Weekly Register,* X (June 8, 1816), 334. (Duplicate page numbers will be found in this volume.)

[2] The term preferred by N. S. B. Gras. See his "Stages in Economic History," *Journal of Economic and Business History,* II, No. 3 (May, 1930), 406–408.

[3] *American State Papers: Finance,* II, 691.

[4] *Niles' Weekly Register,* X (July 13, 1816), 323.

produced by the family unit. In the larger communities where local markets were sufficient, craftsmen since early colonial times had set up little shops, often in their own homes. Here they made such items as hats, shoes, and clothing to order. Also, in or near leading seaports, shipbuilding and the production of ships' fittings, stores, and provisions provided an important industrial activity.

In the larger towns and cities the more successful and aggressive workers, on becoming master craftsmen, hired apprentices and journeymen, sometimes producing products for general sale in addition to those made solely in response to specific orders from customers. The workbench products of these artisans long continued to be of considerable importance. Charles Cist, writing of Cincinnati in 1841, said, "Our manufacturing establishments, with the exception of a few, . . . are, in the literal sense, manufactures,—*works of the hand.* These last embrace the principal share of the productive industry of our mechanics, and are carried on in the upper stories, or in the rear shops of the warerooms, in which they are exposed for sale. . . ."[5]

Again, only the newest and most isolated communities lacked the aid which came from gristmills and sawmills using the power derived from small streams or, more rarely, using animal or wind power. These neighborhood establishments performed tasks extremely burdensome if done without mechanical power and utilized processes too complicated or exacting for relatively unskilled management. The mills were typically small, involved but little capital outlay, and were often conducted by the local merchant. But, though small, they were thickly scattered over the countryside, for it must be remembered that on roads in the early nineteenth century few farmers could expect to take a load of grain to the mill and return home before nightfall if a round trip of more than ten or twelve miles was necessary.

Especially in the older, more settled communities, other small, neighborhood industries common in 1815 were iron works, paper mills, wool carding and fulling mills, potash plants, breweries, tanneries, and brickyards. Like the flour mills and sawmills, these were dependent upon local materials and their products were destined, in considerable part at least, for local use. Thus the typical iron works, whether in New Hampshire or Virginia, depended upon the iron from a nearby bog or mine and upon charcoal fuel provided by the

[5] Charles Cist, *Cincinnati in 1841: Its Early Annals and Future Prospects* (Cincinnati: The author, 1841), p. 238.

trees of the immediate countryside. The bar iron produced was shaped by craftsmen into nails, horseshoes, and agricultural tools, chiefly for nearby markets; indeed, often this work was done by the farmer-consumers themselves.

Of course, not all mill and furnace production was strictly for local or neighborhood use. So-called merchant flour mills had long existed, and they grew rapidly during 1815–1819 to meet the tremendous demand for flour in southern Europe and later to supply the expanding domestic market. By the year 1834 the output of one large Richmond producer, Columbian Mills, was 48,000 barrels of flour.[6] The greatest concentration of these mills was in the Chesapeake region, where cities like Richmond, Georgetown, Alexandria, and Baltimore enjoyed cheap water transportation for both raw materials and finished product. Merchant flour mills were not limited to this area but developed throughout the North wherever effective internal water transportation was available. Along the Susquehanna, the Brandywine, the Hudson, the Delaware, and a hundred smaller streams, neighborhood mills expanded to meet the needs of distant markets. And the same was true for some of the other mill and furnace industries, especially in the case of iron production. But for the most part, until the results of improved transportation began to be clearly felt, mills and furnaces produced largely for local or nearby consumption.

A few industries, though using local materials, produced largely for distant markets. Those flourishing in the South converted southern staples into suitable form for transportation to market, being small and widely scattered because of the necessity of being near the raw materials. Some of the most important of these were the plantation cotton gins, the sugar mills of Louisiana, and the tar kilns of the Carolinas. Distilleries produced rum in New England and whisky in Ohio and Kentucky in order to satisfy the demand of local as well as distant consumers. Similarly, the salt works of Virginia and New York catered to a wide domestic market.

But the growth of merchant mills and the production of goods for sale beyond the immediate vicinity, though significant portents, were of relatively small importance at the beginning of the period. For the most part American manufactures were located in the country, carried on in the household or small mill, and produced for home or neighborhood use. But these characteristics, typical of American manufacture in 1815, were radically altered in the following decades.

[6] Bruce, *Virginia Iron Manufacture in the Slave Era*, p. 127.

HOUSEHOLD MANUFACTURES

For the country as a whole the per capita value of household manufactures—goods made in the home chiefly for family use—was undoubtedly close to its peak in 1815. Though many manufacturing activities, and especially those in connection with the preparation of food, continued for many decades to be carried on in the home, the relative importance of household manufacture began to decline soon after the close of the War of 1812. According to estimates made in 1810 and 1820, about two thirds of the clothing worn in the United States was the product of household manufacture. The proportion for 1815 was surely no lower than this and it may well have been higher. In the more densely settled areas of New England and the Middle Atlantic states, household manufactures had declined after the close of the Revolution but experienced a considerable revival, especially in textiles, during the period of disturbed trade relations with Great Britain in 1808–1815.[7]

From their predominant position in 1815, household manufactures, outside the field of food preparation, had largely disappeared by 1860 in most parts of the country. This marked decline in the importance of household manufactures took place in two stages: from 1815 to 1830 decreases in the East were offset in part at least by considerable expansion in new frontier areas; and during 1830–1860 the decline in household industry was quite general, extending to practically every part of the country. In both periods this primitive form of production throve where transportation was most difficult and expensive; it was least able to hold its own wherever canals, steamboats, or railroads were introduced.

In New England the household manufacture of textiles, which had been greatly stimulated by the second war with England, does not appear to have flourished greatly after the close of that contest. An investigation made by Secretary of the Treasury Louis McLane indicates that between 1824 and 1832, except in a few areas remote from transportation, household manufactures in New England were being so rapidly abandoned that they declined between 50 and 90 per cent. Lowered prices and the greater efficiency of factory production were the chief reasons given. From Amesbury, Massachusetts, came the following statement: "Labor-saving machinery bringing the articles so much lower than can be made in houses, it is found most

[7] Victor S. Clark, *History of Manufactures in the United States* (3 vols., New York: McGraw-Hill Book Company, 1929), I, 438; *American State Papers: Finance*, II, 427.

profitable to purchase. The same time spent in a factory will produce at least ten times as much as it will in household manufacture." [8]

For the Middle Atlantic states the picture was somewhat mixed. Fragmentary data from the report referred to above indicate that before 1832 household manufactures were declining in New Jersey and eastern Pennsylvania, though increasing in Delaware and western Pennsylvania. For New York State, census data carefully examined by Arthur H. Cole point to increasing yardage from household looms until 1825, followed by a decline.[9] In the more accessible parts of the South, increasing specialization on a few profitable agricultural staples apparently led to a fairly rapid decline in household manufactures, though in the more remote mountain areas they remained important for decades. For the western frontier states, the peak of household production may have come about 1830; though still growing in the newer states, household manufacture was already declining in the older states of the West.[10]

Following 1830, household manufactures declined in importance in practically every part of the country. The reduction was most marked wherever the new transportation—canals, steamboats, or railroads—made easily available the products of domestic or foreign factories. Even the character of the frontier changed. The new states brought into the Union in the late forties and fifties were, in a sense, the product of improved transportation. Settlement clung largely to areas where transportation was available; consequently, even on the frontier, household manufacturing found but slight encouragement during the railroad age.

Federal census reports for this period, although notoriously inaccurate, probably correctly indicate the general trend. They show the average per capita value of household manufacture for the whole country as declining from $1.70 in 1840 to $1.18 in 1850 and $.78 in 1860. By 1860 the system had largely disappeared from the northern states. In the South, though declining, it lingered on, especially in areas most remote from transportation. Other available data rein-

[8] Secretary of the Treasury, *Documents Relative to the Manufactures in the United States House Document* No. 308, 22 Cong., 1 Sess. (Washington: 1833), I, 78, referred to hereafter as the *McLane Report on Manufactures*. See also pages 69, 87, 92, 912; Rolla Milton Tryon, *Household Manufactures in the United States 1640–1860* (Chicago: The University of Chicago Press, 1917), pp. 290–293; Arthur H. Cole, *The American Wool Manufacture* (2 vols., Cambridge: Harvard University Press, 1926), I, 182–184.

[9] Cole, *The American Wool Manufacture*, I, 184–185.

[10] *Ibid.*, I, 186–189; Tryon, *Household Manufactures in the United States, 1640–1860*, pp. 293–302.

force these conclusions. Thus Cole, noting the dependence of the household woolen industry on local carding and fulling establishments, finds the decline in the number of these establishments strongly supporting other census information. After a careful survey of woolen manufacture in the whole country, he concludes that household production exceeded factory output in 1830 by about 4 to 3, that rough equivalence had been reached by 1840, and that thereafter the factory product rapidly replaced that from the homes.[11] As long as textiles were produced in the home, linens were so important that nearly every farm had a small planting of flax. The decline in household manufactures is reflected in a sharply decreasing flax crop. Thus, acreage planted to flax in New York fell from 46,000 in 1844 to 13,000 in 1854. For the country as a whole, the number of pounds of flax produced declined from 7,700,000 in 1850 to 4,700,000 in 1860.[12]

HOUSEHOLD TEXTILE MANUFACTURES IN NEW YORK

Year	Total Yards in Millions	Per Capita Yards
1825	16.5	8.95
1835	8.8	4.03
1845	7.1	2.74
1855	.9	.27

Source: Rolla Milton Tryon, *Household Manufactures in the United States, 1640–1860* (Chicago: The University of Chicago Press, 1917), pp. 304–305, with permission of publisher.

Studies based on statistics available for the state of New York best illustrate what was happening to household manufactures. It will be seen from the accompanying table that household textile manufactures in that state were cut nearly in half from 1825 to 1835, declined slowly during the next decade, and had almost disappeared by 1855. Per capita yardage produced declined from 8.95 in 1825 to barely .27 in 1855. A careful study of the household manufacture of woolen cloth in New York State by Arthur H. Cole emphasizes graphically the relation between transportation developments and the decline of household manufactures. The figure on page 214, taken from Cole, indicates the location within the state of the counties showing the highest per capita household production of woolen fabrics at two different periods. It will be noted that in 1820 none of the counties where the household manufacture of woolen cloth was relatively important lay along the Hudson south of Albany, and that in 1845 not a single such county was traversed by the Erie Canal.

[11] Cole, *The American Wool Manufacture*, I, 190, 282–284.
[12] Jared Van Wagenen, "Flax and the Loom," *The Chronicle of Early American Industries*, III (March, 1947), 93; *Eighth Census of the United States: Agriculture*, p. lxxxix.

FIGURE 1

Household Manufacture of Woolen Cloths in New York State, 1820 and 1845

(Arthur Harrison Cole, *The American Wool Manufacture*. Cambridge: Harvard University Press, 1926, p. 280, with the permission of the publisher.)

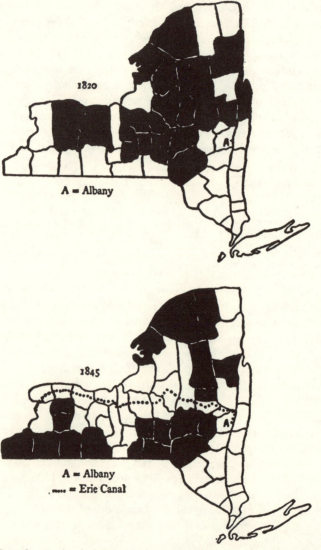

Note: In each case, the shaded area embraces that third of the counties in the state which showed the highest per capita household production of woolen fabrics, including those goods in which wool was mixed with cotton or linen.

PRODUCTION FOR THE MARKET

Accompanying the decline of household manufacture came a tremendous increase in production for the market. The shift from production for home use to production for sale frequently preceded, and was of at least equal importance with, the technological changes which will be described later in this chapter. Moreover, market-oriented production was a prime requisite of, though not to be confused with, the new factory system. This whole development of manufacturing for market sale, which took place between 1815 and 1860, was, like most important economic changes, neither orderly nor systematic. Rates of change varied from industry to industry, and no orderly progression appeared from one form of industrial organization to the next. The rapidly increasing demands of the market for manufactured products were met by three expedients: enlarged shop or handicraft production, the spread of the domestic or putting-out system, and the appearance of the factory system.

The last of these, the factory system, though of increasing importance during the whole period, did not become typical of American industry before the 1850's. It is dealt with in the following chapter. Here it is proposed to examine increased handicraft production and the domestic system. Both of these depended upon the capital and organizing genius of the merchant capitalist, the central organizing agent who assumed risks, provided capital, and became an expert in the technique of finding markets in which to sell at a profit those commodities which he had arranged to have produced at the lowest possible costs. Though workers in shop or home still provided their own tools, the raw materials were, often in the former and almost always under the latter system, owned by the merchant capitalist.

As custom or "bespoke" work declined in relative importance with the growing production of goods for impersonal market sale, the craftsman's shop tended to lose its function as a retail store and to become merely a small production unit. Here, often enough, the master craftsman became the "boss," directing the work indeed of an enlarged number of journeymen and apprentices, but selling the output to the wholesale merchant, i.e., the merchant capitalist, instead of dealing directly with the actual consumers. Moreover, instead of wide dispersion over the country certain crafts, such as shoemaking, tailoring, and hatmaking, came to be more concentrated in restricted areas. The effect of these changes on the workers is dealt with in a later chapter. The nature of these changes in craft production varied, of course, from trade to trade and from one section of the country to another. Thus, the impact of the increasing production of shoes for general market sale led to enlarged shop production in Philadelphia and New York, but in Massachusetts to the growth of the domestic or putting-out system.[13]

Despite this lack of uniformity, something of the general trend of shop development can be seen from looking briefly at the growth of hat manufacture at Danbury, Connecticut. In colonial days hats had been produced very largely to the order of the individual consumer, and in each local market either by resident craftsmen or by itinerant hatters. Later, especially after about 1800, production for general market sale through wholesale merchants became increasingly important and, from being widely dispersed over the whole country, hatmaking tended to be concentrated in a few areas where merchant capitalists found it advantageous to do their buying. Fairfield County, Connecticut, in which Danbury was the leading town, early became such an area. In 1802, merchants operating from this famous hatmaking center sold the handiwork of Danbury craftsmen as far away as Charleston. The increased output of hats in the Danbury area was at first achieved chiefly by multiplying the number of production units. Also, some of the shops grew rapidly in size, for one employing as many as fifty hands was reported in 1814. But though production was strictly for general market sale, primitive handicraft methods and relatively small shops remained typical until during the decade of the fifties, when something approximating the modern factory began to appear.

Then the use of coal and steam engines and the adoption of improved machines for hat production made rapid headway. A sharp decline in the number of establishments was accompanied by an increase in the size and aggregate output of those remaining. But it is important to note that this factory development came during the fifties, that in hatmaking, as in other lines of craft production such as cabinetmaking and tailoring, the first result of widening markets was to modify and enlarge shop production, not to bring about the immediate adoption of the factory system.[14]

In other lines of manufacture the enlarged market demand led to

[13] Described on pp. 217–220.

[14] W. H. Francis, *History of the Hatting Trade in Danbury, Conn.* (Danbury: H. and L. Osborne, 1860), *passim; Eighth Census of the United States: Manufactures,* pp. cliv–clxi.

the rise of the domestic or putting-out system. The merchant capitalist, seeking to meet the demands of the expanding market, furnished the raw materials to men and women who worked in their own homes to produce products which the merchant capitalist collected, assembled, finished if necessary in a central shop, and marketed, often at a very considerable distance. The system of production was, of course, far from universal, but is well worth some attention as one of the chief industrial forms which arose to meet the needs of the expanding market. This mode of production not only attained considerable importance in the manufacture of boots and shoes, where it had perhaps its most important development, but was significant also for the weaving of cotton and woolen cloth and for the making of such items as men's ready-to-wear clothing, buttons, carriage trimmings, horse whips, suspenders, and straw and palm-leaf hats.

During early colonial times, boots and shoes had been made for the most part in the home either by the farmer himself or with the help of an itinerant cobbler. Town dwellers typically secured their footwear on special order from the local cobbler's shop. But as early as 1760 the production of shoes for general market sale had become of some importance in eastern Massachusetts. The market for "store shoes," at first largely cheap brogans for southern slaves or for rough farm use in the North and West, expanded rapidly with the growing prosperity of the country and the improved quality of the shoes. To meet this demand the domestic system of production developed rapidly in the eastern states, especially in Massachusetts, New Jersey, and Pennsylvania.

Production was directed and organized by merchants or master craftsmen who supplied leather to men who worked each in his own home and with his own tools. Up to about 1810 a workman typically made the complete shoe. Thereafter the system underwent considerable change. As the volume of output was increased to meet the rapidly growing demand, central shops were developed. There most of the cutting was done in order to conserve materials and there, also, the finished products were assembled and inspected. As competition became stiffer, increasing emphasis was placed on securing a standardized product of good quality. Processes became constantly more specialized and the importance of careful supervision of production became so great that the work tended to be concentrated in the central shop. By the latter fifties this central shop took on more and more the characteristics of a modern factory, and the few processes still carried on by workers in their own homes represented merely the remnants of the domestic system.[15]

This pattern in the boot and shoe industry of orderly progression from the household and handicraft stage through the domestic to the factory system is not to be taken as typical of American industrial development. The domestic system was confined largely, though not exclusively, to the production of shoes, textiles, and various items of wearing apparel, and the conditions of its appearance differed greatly from one industry to another. In the production of both cotton and woolen cloth, the putting-out system at times played an important part in the weaving stage. The small cotton-spinning mills, which had such a considerable growth in New England before 1815, often marketed their yarn only after it had been put out for weaving on hand looms in nearby farm families. In Rhode Island the mill management at first made arrangements directly with each home weaver; later, contract weavers took over the negotiations but the mill retained ownership of the yarn. In Philadelphia, merchant weavers employed many full-time craftsmen to do home weaving of fine ginghams. But power looms and foreign competition were together too much for the home weaving of cottons. It disappeared in Rhode Island about 1827 and in Pennsylvania somewhat later. Similarly, the hand-loom weaving of woolen cloth was carried on under the domestic system after carding, finishing, and spinning of wool had become a mill or small factory process. In New England the introduction of power-loom weaving in the factories during the late 1820's doomed the putting-out system, but in Philadelphia the hand-loom weaving of woolen cloth, rugs, and hosiery persisted well into the middle of the century and retained an essentially domestic form of organization.[16]

A unique development came in the manufacture of straw and palm-leaf hats. Organized on the domestic system, this business expanded rapidly during the twenties, especially in New England, and continued this form of organization until well into the latter half of the century. The straw hats were a completely local product, being

[15] Blanche Evans Hazard, *The Organization of the Boot and Shoe Industry in Massachusetts before 1875* (Vol. XXIII of *Harvard Economic Studies*, Cambridge: Harvard University Press, 1921), *passim.*

[16] Caroline F. Ware, *The Early New England Cotton Manufacture* (Boston: Houghton Mifflin Company, 1931), pp. 50–52, 73–76, 93–94; Cole, *The American Wool Manufacture*, I, 220–226; Arthur H. Cole and Harold F. Williamson, *The American Carpet Manufacture* (Vol. LXX of *Harvard Economic Studies*, Cambridge: Harvard University Press, 1941), pp. 9–10; Edwin T. Freedley, *Philadelphia and Its Manufactures* (Philadelphia: Edward Young, 1858), pp. 232–256.

made from locally grown rye straw, which was bleached, split, and plaited into braids by New England farm women. Late in the twenties palm leaves began to be brought in from Cuba. They were distributed to farmhouses by wagon or were secured by the farm or village family from the local store. The hats were woven or braided in the homes "by women and children, the wives and daughters of farmers, in connection with the other household duties" and often in exchange for "store pay, principally calico, ribbons, etc. . . ." [17] Children as young as four years were sometimes employed. The merchant enterprisers who promoted this business collected the hats and often bleached, pressed, and trimmed them in central shops before sending them on to market. This home manufacture flourished on a small scale in many parts of the country, but only in Massachusetts did it assume considerable importance. There whole countrysides were given over to it as a part-time employment. Like most other hand industries, straw-hat making flourished in Philadelphia, where in the latter fifties it was still, in part at least, organized on a putting-out basis. [18]

At times the domestic system appeared as a special phase connected with early factory development. Thus, feet and legs of stockings were often knit in separate factories, the two parts being sewn together by homeworkers under the domestic system. Similarly, women and children working at home combined yarn spun in one factory with buttons and metal mountings produced in a second, and with elastic webbing woven in a third made the suspenders or galluses which formed an ornamental as well as useful feature of male attire. The domestic system also appeared in the ready-made clothing industry which arose to supply the necessary clothing for sailors and workers in seaport towns. The skilled tailor who had formerly worked in a central shop began to take his work home, where he received help, especially on the less skilled processes, from his wife and children. The invention of the sewing machine in 1846 promoted the

---

[17] McLane Report on Manufactures, I, 623, 805. See also C. O. Parmenter, History of Pelham, Mass. from 1738 to 1898 (Amherst, Mass.: Carpenter and Morehouse, 1898), pp. 255–256, 452–453.
[18] "Straw Bonnets," Harper's New Monthly Magazine, XXIX (October, 1864), 576–584; Eighth Census of the United States: Manufactures, pp. xc–xciv; McLane Report on Manufactures, I, 75, 82; Clark, History of Manufactures in the United States, I, 441; Carpenter and Morehouse, comp., The History of the Town of Amherst, Mass. (Amherst, Mass.: Carpenter and Morehouse, 1896), pp. 291–294; Freedley, Philadelphia and Its Manufactures, p. 281. Straw plaiting and straw-hat making became an important "cottage industry" in England at the time of its rapid growth in this country. See John G. Dony, A History of the Straw Hat Industry (Luton, England: Gibbs, Bamforth and Company, 1942), passim.

growth of the putting-out system in ready-made clothing, for it was found that routine sewing-machine work could be done effectively and inexpensively by women in their own homes. This industry, therefore, provides an interesting exception to the generalization that the mechanization of industry led to the development of the factory system, for in this case an important mechanical invention actually stimulated home rather than shop or factory production.[19]

The domestic system was essentially a modification of, or an outgrowth from, the shop craft system. It resulted from the demands for the production of standardized market goods. With the decline of production on the customer's order and specifications, no special advantage resulted from producing goods in a shop conveniently located for the consumer. Under conditions of acute labor scarcity, the domestic system, by placing manufacture in the home, tapped a tremendous pool of part-time labor, especially of women and children, which could be purchased at extremely low rates and would not otherwise have been utilized. In this predominantly agricultural country, most of these people lived in rural areas. Moreover, this system tended to thrive, especially in those more northern states where cold winters, by slowing down farm activities, often left members of rural families with a good deal of time on their hands. The effect of the growth of domestic production was to decentralize industry and disperse it over the countryside.

MACHINE TOOLS, INTERCHANGEABLE PARTS, AND POWER

At the same time that the household system of production was declining and the domestic system was reaching its fullest flowering in such industries as shoes and hats, far-reaching changes were taking place in the techniques of production in many industrial fields. The newly invented machines which so altered American manufacturing techniques during the nineteenth century were largely made of iron. Their construction required the use of machine tools. The advanced position of England in the ironworking industries and her early invention and use of machine-making machines account in part at least for the remarkable technical advances which marked British

[19] Clark, *History of Manufactures in the United States,* I, 441–442; Grace Pierpont Fuller, "An Introduction to the History of Connecticut as a Manufacturing State," *Smith College Studies in History,* I, No. 1 (October, 1915), 40–41, 47–48; Isaac A. Wile, *The Jews of Rochester* (Rochester: 1912), pp. 8–12; Cole, *The American Wool Manufacture,* I, 293; Jesse Eliphalet Pope, *The Clothing Industry in New York* (*University of Missouri Studies, Social Science Series,* Vol. I, Columbia: University of Missouri, 1905), pp. 12–17, 23.

manufacturing in the late eighteenth and early nineteenth centuries. In the art of constructing tool-making machinery, especially that of the heavier variety, England retained her predominance far into the nineteenth century. The heavy machine tools used in the United States were for the most part either imported from England or constructed here on the basis of British models. But in the designing and building of lighter machine tools, especially those used for the manufacture of small arms, clocks and watches, and textile and agricultural machinery, the United States played a major role.

Willingness to experiment and a general freedom from binding traditions gave American producers some advantage over their British rivals. But other factors also account for American leadership in the invention and use of light machine tools. The iron industry had been well established here since colonial times, and the making of hardware, pots and pans, and agricultural tools from the product of American furnaces was common from Massachusetts to Virginia. Considerable experience had also been gained in designing and building lathes and other machines for making wooden products and, in some cases at least, these methods were similar to ironworking techniques. And finally, British restrictions on the exportation of textile machinery forced the infant industry of the United States to make its own machines if it were to benefit from the new methods which were revolutionizing British production. British models were freely copied and often improved upon. But Americans also showed considerable originality. Thus, the slide and turret lathes, milling machines, and gear cutters were invented, or at least independently developed, in the United States.[20]

Along with machine tools came a unique American development: precision manufacture permitting the use of interchangeable parts. The idea appears to have been French in origin, but it was first put into successful practice in the United States by Eli Whitney and Simeon North in connection with the manufacture of small arms. By 1815 armories at Harpers Ferry, Virginia; Middletown, Connecticut; and Springfield, Massachusetts were seriously experimenting with this method, which embodied the fundamental principles of modern mass production. But prejudice against the new method of interchangeable parts, along with the persistence of technical difficulties which had not been completely overcome, continued so considerable that the technical superiority of the new method was not

[20] D. L. Burn, "The Genesis of American Engineering Competition," *Economic History*, II (January, 1931), 292–311.

generally recognized for small arms until about 1827. Nor could the
method be immediately extended to the manufacture of other products until much work was done on techniques and on standards of
interchangeability. But the rising standard of living in the United
States provided a rapidly expanding market for machine-made products, and American ingenuity presently proved especially effective
in developing methods permitting precision production of interchangeable parts. American machine shops made rapid progress in
the building and use of gigs, taps, and gauges. Using these and other
devices, American manufacturers were by the fifties utilizing interchangeable parts with great success in the production of such items
as clocks, watches, locks, agricultural implements, and sewing machines. And improvements of great significance were still being made.
The turret lathe, a machine tool essential to mass production technique was first built commercially by the firm of Robbins and Lawrence at Windsor, Vermont, in 1854; and the vernier caliper, a precision tool enabling ordinary workmen easily to make measurements
to a thousandth of an inch, became available in 1851 through the
efforts of J. R. Brown of Providence.[21]

The neighborhood mills of the early national period had been
driven by water power according to century-old methods and devices.
Especially for small mills, inefficient undershot wheels, which were
merely placed in the bed of small streams, were common. For the
larger installations, the breast or pitch-back type of water wheel
came to be preferred. Though clumsy, slow of operation, and costly
to install, these wheels, which depended on the weight of the water
and rotated in an upstream direction, sometimes developed as high
as 75 per cent of the energy potential. Because power was transmitted
to millstones and machines by wooden shafts and cogwheels, the
manufacturing processes were necessarily located near the water
wheel. Moreover, the amount of energy utilized was closely limited
by the strength of the wooden wheel and the transmission mechanism. Consequently, mills did not grow rapidly in size and small
streams were generally preferred to large ones.

[21] Joseph Wickham Roe, *English and American Tool Builders* (New Haven: Yale
University Press, 1916), *passim;* Clark, *History of Manufactures in the United States,*
I, 416–422; Frederick S. Blackall, Jr., *Invention and Industry—Cradled in New Eng-
land!* (New York: The Newcomen Society of England, American Branch, 1946), pp. 8–
21; Abbott Payson Usher, *A History of Mechanical Inventions* (New York: McGraw-
Hill Book Company, 1929), pp. 341–344; *Tenth Census of the United States: Manufac-
tures,* "Report on the Manufactures of Interchangeable Mechanism," by Charles H.
Fitch, II, 617–701; Felicia Johnson Deyrup, "Arms Makers of the Connecticut Valley,"
Smith College Studies in History, XXXIII (1948), 10–13, 87–99, 144–159.

Even before 1815, but especially in the two decades following, important though unspectacular changes added greatly to the effectiveness of water-power installations. Improved dams and canals increased the available power, and the gradual adoption of metal gears and leather belts for transmission purposes made possible the effective use of the added power. Larger rivers could now be used, and the Merrimack Manufacturing Company led the way in the twenties by a great water-power development at Lowell, Massachusetts. Installations there had developed about 2,500 horsepower by 1835. Other large-scale hydraulic developments followed at Lawrence and Holyoke, Massachusetts; at Saco, Maine; and at Philadelphia.

In the middle forties the cumbersome, slow-moving water wheels began to be replaced by hydraulic turbines. Invented in 1827 by the French engineer Benoit Fourneyron, these machines, as perfected and standardized in America during the late forties and fifties, proved more efficient, faster, less bulky, and more economical to install than water wheels. Though rapidly adopted during the fifties, the water turbine did not achieve a dominant position until after the Civil War, when it formed the basis of the modern hydraulic plant.[22]

The sensationally rapid adoption of steam power for river and railroad transportation was not duplicated in manufacturing production. Though successfully applied to manufacturing in the United States near the beginning of the century, the steam engine did not generally replace water power before the Civil War. As compared with water power, energy from the steam engine proved expensive. Its first cost was high, as was also its maintenance, for breakdowns were frequent and repairs costly. Even in Pennsylvania, where coal was available at minimum outlay, the annual cost per horsepower of steam was reported in 1839 to be four times that of water power.[23] The water flow in the Ohio River Valley fluctuated so greatly as to handicap appreciably mills dependent upon water wheels for power. As a result, steam mills were used in this region earlier than in the Atlantic states. Moreover, heat-using industries, such as glass- and ironmaking, tended to favor the early adoption of the steam engine. For the country as a whole, 46 per cent of the plants in the iron indus-

[22] Clark, History of Manufactures in the United States, I, 403–412; Jonathan Thayer Lincoln, "Material for a History of American Textile Machinery," Journal of Economic and Business History, IV (1931–1932), 267–276.

[23] Report of Lehigh Coal and Navigation Company, 1939, in Hazard's United States Register, II (March 4, 1840), 156. Cited by Clark, History of Manufactures in the United States, I, 410.

try were using steam power or water power and steam power in 1859. For the Ohio River Valley this percentage was 72.[24]

Although water remained the chief source of power for manufacturing as late as 1860, the use of steam power was spreading very rapidly in the two decades preceding the war. Additional water-power sites in the more densely settled parts of the East were no longer easily available for manufacturing expansion. Moreover, steam engines rapidly became less costly to buy, their operation was greatly improved, and, thanks to the revolution in transportation, cheap coal for fuel became available over wide areas. Even before 1850, six large steam textile mills had been erected in Massachusetts coastal towns north of Boston. The important manufacturing district in and around Fall River, Massachusetts, reached a critical point about 1850. Practically all of the available power from the Quequechan River had been developed, and an iron works, a print works, and a cotton mill were powered by steam. During the fifties two large steam cotton mills were added, so that by 1860 almost one fourth of the spindles operated in Fall River were steam-driven.[25]

IMPROVED TECHNIQUES OF MANUFACTURE

By 1815 the great series of inventions in the manufacture of cotton textiles had revolutionized that industry in Great Britain by mechanizing its chief processes and establishing the factory system of manufacture. Despite British attempts to retain a monopoly of these improved methods, they were, with brief lag, copied by American industry. By 1815 the Boston Manufacturing Company had installed power looms in its new factory at Waltham, Massachusetts, thus placing the American textile industry roughly abreast of the latest British technical developments. The years between 1815 and 1860 were marked both in England and in the United States by great improvements and refinements in practically every process of textile manufacture. Americans excelled especially in inventions increasing the speed of machine operation and making processes so automatic that they required less and less attention from the operatives. Especially notable in this connection was the development of the so-called "ring spinner," invented in 1828 by John Thorp of Providence

[24] Louis C. Hunter, "Studies in the Economic History of the Ohio Valley," *Smith College Studies in History*, XIX, Nos. 1–2 (October, 1933—January, 1934), 39–40.

[25] Clark, *History of Manufactures in the United States*, I, 408–411; Thomas Russell Smith, *The Cotton Textile Industry of Fall River, Massachusetts: A Study of Industrial Localization* (New York: King's Crown Press, 1944), pp. 43–47.

MANUFACTURING: EARLY DEVELOPMENT 225

and perfected soon after by William Mason of Taunton. It permitted spindle speeds three times those of the Arkwright spindles in general use at the time. Some indication of the technical progress is shown by the decline in the cost of producing cotton sheeting. In 1815 it had cost eighteen cents a yard; by 1860 it was two cents.

Improvements in woolen manufacture came more slowly than in cotton both in England and in the United States. But by 1830 technique in this industry had achieved the essentials of its modern form. Referring to conditions by that year Cole writes: "Within forty years, improvements, chiefly of American origin, had given a new significance to the power-driven carding machine borrowed from England; had made the spinning operation quasi-automatic by a development unknown abroad; had harnessed the loom to power, for the most part independently of foreign advance; and had largely removed hand processes from the cloth-finishing operations through the invention of machines so valuable that they were frequently copied by other nations in subsequent years." [26]

Following 1830, improvements permitted further mechanization, especially in the cleaning and carding of wool. Most of these inventions were of foreign origin but were promptly adopted in the United States because they economized labor. Though European producers made important advances in the technique of spinning wool, Americans were surprisingly slow to alter established practices in this part of the industry. But in weaving, a tremendous advance resulted in 1840 from the development of the Crompton loom at the Middlesex Mills in Lowell. Making feasible for the first time the weaving on power looms of fancy woolens, i.e., those involving figures or patterns, these machines came into rapid use both in the United States and abroad.

Roughly comparable progress was made in the development of machinery for the manufacture of products from hemp, flax, and silk and for the process of knitting. So, although many improvements remained for the future, by 1860 the whole textile industry was thoroughly mechanized. Brief mention should also be made of the remarkable changes inaugurated in carpet manufacture. Almost completely a hand industry before 1845, the making of carpets was well on the way to complete mechanization fifteen years later largely because of the power looms invented by Erastus B. Bigelow and developed by the Lowell Manufacturing Company. [27]

[26] Cole, *The American Wool Manufacture*, I, 86.
[27] *Ibid.*, 86–136, 307–312, 350–367; Cole and Williamson, *The American Carpet*

The small blast furnaces and forges scattered in almost every state of the Union were in 1815 little changed from colonial days. Fundamental technical changes which were already revolutionizing the British iron industry and were to be of such tremendous consequence in later industrial development in the United States came but slowly. In England the disappearance of forests as a source of charcoal was a major influence; in the United States the need to conserve labor was a controlling factor.

Two of the three major British innovations were introduced in America soon after 1815. The first was a rolling process by which the slabs or blooms from the furnaces were squeezed to expel the cinder and then rolled into bars. This machine, the rolling mill, greatly reduced the manpower required in the long-established practice of refining and shaping the iron by beating it with hammers. At about the same time the process of refining pig iron in open forges was improved by the introduction of the puddling process. In the older method the fuel came into direct contact with the pig iron as it was heated and worked; in the new process a reverberatory furnace heated the iron without bringing it into contact with the fuel. This method had the great advantage of permitting the substitution for charcoal of mineral coal, a fuel which could not be satisfactorily used with the traditional process because of the impurities it imparted to the iron when burnt in direct contact with it. By permitting large-scale operations and the use of coal, a decidedly cheaper fuel than charcoal, puddling gave a great impetus to the centralization of the whole iron industry.

The third major improvement, the use of coal in blast furnaces, was long delayed in the United States, becoming important only in the forties and not until the latter part of the fifties giving indication of its tremendous later development. Many reasons have been suggested for the failure to utilize this method, which had been successfully employed for many years in England. Certain it is that exhaustion of forests as a source of charcoal made necessary the British development. But, as Louis C. Hunter has shown, the abundance of wood in America is not a satisfactory explanation for the persistence of charcoal furnaces in the United States, for, even with the tremendous forests, charcoal was appreciably more expensive than coal. The explanation appears to lie in the peculiar characteristics of charcoal iron, its malleability and ease of welding, which suited the chief

---

Manufacture, pp. 22–34, 53–76; Ware, *The Early New England Cotton Manufacture,* pp. 82–85.

4

needs of the American market. For nails, hardware, and agricultural tools, the charcoal iron was better suited; moreover, it could be more satisfactorily worked by blacksmiths and farmers than that produced by coal or coke. On the other hand, iron made in blast furnaces using mineral fuel was highly suitable for railroad and other industrial purposes so that, especially after 1840, when this demand expanded so rapidly, the new technique rapidly gained a firm foothold.[28]

Brief mention can be made of only a few of the other new techniques and laborsaving devices which brought fundamental changes in almost every part of American industry. A new food-processing industry—the preservation of food by canning—developed from about 1820 as the processes of sterilization and enclosure in airtight receptacles became commercially feasible. Glass and tin cans were used. Though most important for sea foods, the process was, after about 1840, extended to include vegetables and fruits. During the fifties, following Gail Borden's development of the vacuum evaporation process, the canning of milk was begun. But mechanization had not advanced far and the techniques of the modern production line in the food industry were still a development of the future.[29]

The making of fur and woolen hats, previously a time-consuming hand industry, was largely mechanized by 1860. Fur-cutting machines, which greatly lightened the work of removing the fur from the pelt, and the shellac method of stiffening hat brims, which reduced the necessary labor by about 80 per cent, were both developed in the second quarter of the century. Finally, in 1846, a machine invented by Henry A. Wells for forming hat bodies increased labor productivity for this process about thirty times.[30]

The sewing machine, invented by Elias Howe in 1846 and improved by Allen B. Wilson and Isaac Singer, was rapidly introduced into the clothing and shoe trade during the fifties. These machines not only saved labor; they did work of an excellence impossible by

[28] Clark, History of Manufactures in the United States, I, 412–416; Louis C. Hunter, "Influence of the Market upon Technique in the Iron Industry in Western Pennsylvania up to 1860," Journal of Economic and Business History, I, No. 2 (February, 1929), 241–281; Louis C. Hunter, "Heavy Industries before 1860," in Harold F. Williamson, ed., The Growth of the American Economy (New York: Prentice-Hall, Inc., 1944), pp. 210–217; Bruce, Virginia Iron Manufacture in the Slave Era, pp. 136–139.
[29] Charles B. Kuhlmann, "The Processing of Agricultural Products in the Pre-Railway Age," in Williamson, ed., The Growth of the American Economy, pp. 201–203.
[30] H. H. Manchester, The Hat in America and the Ferry Hat Mfg. Company (New York: Ferry Hat Manufacturing Company, 1926), pp. 16–17; J. Leander Bishop, A History of American Manufacturers, from 1608 to 1860 (2 vols., Philadelphia: Edward Young and Company, 1864), II, 397, 412–413; Francis, History of the Hatting Trade in Danbury, Conn., pp. 10–16.

hand methods. Although crude pulping machines which reduced the rags to pulp had long been used in the United States, all paper was made by hand until 1817. In that year Thomas Gilpin, who operated a paper mill near Wilmington, Delaware, produced by a cylinder process the first machine-made paper in the United States. In this venture he undoubtedly benefited to some extent, at least, from developments abroad for the fundamental invention in the mechanization of paper-making, later called the Fourdrinier machine, had been patented in France by Nicholas-Louis Robert in 1799 and the first cylinder machine had been placed in operation in England by John Dickinson in 1809. In 1827 Henry Barclay of Saugerties, New York appears to have erected the first British-built Fourdrinier machine in America. The mechanization of this industry advanced very rapidly during the thirties and forties. By mid-century most of the paper manufactured in the United States was made by a single, progressive process which converted the pulp into great rolls of machine-made paper.[31]

Further examples might be cited of the rapid changes in industrial technique, but enough has been said to indicate their character and wide application. The marked acceleration of these changes may well be noted. Each succeeding decade brought forth a larger number of inventions and improvements, until in the fifties mechanization in nearly every industry moved forward at an unprecedented rate. Although the annual number of United States patents issued has many faults as a statistical series, it is of some interest in this connection. The total number of patents issued yearly from 1820 to 1830 averaged 535. Despite passage of a law in 1836 greatly tightening the conditions under which patents were granted, the number issued averaged 646 a year in 1841–1850 and 2,525 in the following decade.[32]

[31] Malcolm Keir, *Manufacturing* (New York: The Ronald Press Company, 1928), pp. 479–484; *Eighth Census of the United States: Manufactures*, pp. cxxvi–cxxvii; Lyman Horace Weeks, *A History of Paper-Manufacturing in the United States, 1690–1916* (New York: The Lockwood Trade Journal Company, 1916), pp. 172–181; Dard Hunter, *Papermaking: The History and Technique of an Ancient Craft* (New York: Alfred A. Knopf, 1947), pp. 341–368.

[32] Clark, *History of Manufactures in the United States*, I, 313.

CHAPTER XI

Manufacturing: The Factory System

THE FACTORY

THE period covered by this volume marks the significant beginnings of the factory system rather than its full flowering, years of important experimentation and uneven development from one industry to another and in different parts of the country. No rigorous definition of the terms "factory" or "factory stage" is here attempted; the actual process of industrial evolution does not tolerate clean-cut categories and precise definitions. But the terms are nevertheless useful as indicating a trend, the direction of change in the organization of industry in the course of which increasingly large aggregations of workers were assembled under the general supervision of an employer who, paying money wages and furnishing buildings, raw materials, and power-operated machines, organized the production of goods for general market sale. The trend was toward heavy capital investment, integration of industrial processes, and mass production. These and other characteristics noted in the following pages were symptoms of this new development, but all of them will not be found in every early *factory*, nor is it possible to draw a sharp distinction between the so-called mills and the early factories. Certainly the small neighborhood gristmill was a far cry from the modern factory; yet the larger merchant flour mills of the late eighteenth century evidenced many factory characteristics.

The early introduction of the factory system in the cotton textile industry and its development there along characteristic lines make it worthy of special attention. A beginning of sorts had been made before the War of 1812. After a number of others had failed to establish successful spinning mills using the British-invented Arkwright water frame, the Providence mercantile partnership of Almy and Brown had succeeded, with the help of Samuel Slater, in establishing a small mill or factory at Providence in 1791. By 1815 a number of these mills had sprung up, chiefly in southern New England, and were successfully spinning yarn. All were small, chiefly employed children from neighboring farms, and were dependent for weaving on the putting-out system. Following this successful beginning, many similar mills were erected on the small streams of Massachusetts, Connecticut, and Rhode Island. By 1845 these states were dotted from one end to the other with such mills, but concentration was greatest in the Blackstone Valley and in eastern Connecticut.[1]

This was doubtless a significant development, but the factory system in its most representative form did not arise directly from the gradual expansion of these small yarn mills but rather from a bold experiment organized at Waltham, Massachusetts, in 1813 under the name of the Boston Manufacturing Company and sponsored by Francis Cabot Lowell of Boston and a group of his fellow townsmen. None but wealthy men could have financed such a venture, and probably none but merchants used to the huge risks attendant upon foreign trade during the Napoleonic Wars would have had the initiative or courage necessary for a project involving such drastic innovations in the techniques of production and business organization. In fact, the spirit of this enterprise was prophetic of that willingness to risk huge private or public capitals on large and untried ventures which was presently exemplified by the organization of the Black Ball Line of packets, the digging of the Erie Canal, and the building of the railroads.

Lowell and the able group of Boston businessmen associated with him within six years put $600,000 into the Boston Manufacturing Company. They successfully introduced the power loom, an adaptation of the looms already in successful operation in England, and by integrating and standardizing the whole process of cotton cloth manufacture made mass production possible. The Waltham company, despite the difficult times following the war, was phenomenally successful. At Lowell (1822) and at Chicopee (1823), and before 1850 at numerous other places in Massachusetts and in New Hampshire and Maine, various members of this group of Boston businessmen, often called the Boston Associates, promoted the establishment of

---

[1] For interesting maps showing cotton mill location in these states in 1837 and 1845 see J. Herbert Burgy, *The New England Cotton Textile Industry* (Baltimore: J. Herbert Burgy, 1932), pp. 6–7.

other cotton factories on the Waltham plan. By 1850 these companies alone produced about one fifth of the total output of cotton cloth in the country, and their success with the factory form of organization had hastened its wide adoption not only in textiles but in many other fields.

What were the chief features of the Waltham plan of factory organization? (1) The principal processes of cotton cloth production —spinning, weaving, bleaching, dyeing, and in some cases, printing— were carried through in a single plant under unified management. (2) Total capital was large for the time, and ample funds were kept free for working capital. (3) Direction of the project was entrusted to persons selected for their general executive capacity rather than for their technical knowledge of the industrial processes. (4) A unique method was devised for supplying an adequate labor force. To permit manning their relatively large-scale operations, factories of the Waltham type recruited young women far and wide from New England farms and housed them in dormitories specially erected for the purpose. (5) Each factory produced a standardized cloth of relatively coarse weave which required little skill on the part of the operatives. The Waltham company specialized on sheetings and shirtings; the Hamilton Company at Lowell made, at least in its earliest years, such products as heavy drilling, jeans, and stripes; and the Merrimack Company, also of Lowell, concentrated on calicos. (6) Finally, factories of the Waltham type, instead of selling their product through a large number of jobbers and commission agents, disposed of their whole output through a single marketing agency.

Many factors contributed to the success of factories operated on the Waltham plan, but three are worthy of special emphasis: (1) substantial economies resulted from the maximum use of mechanical power and integration of processes; (2) mass production permitted specialization on low-cost, durable, coarse fabrics for which domestic demand was expanding with phenomenal rapidity; (3) strong financial backing provided ample working capital and the funds necessary for plant expansion.[2]

The striking success of the factory system in the production of cotton cloth inevitably led to attempts to introduce it elsewhere, especially in those industries where power-driven machinery was replacing hand processes. Until the twenties woolen factories were

[2] Ware, *The Early New England Cotton Manufacture*, Chaps. 4 and 5; Vera Shlakman, "Economic History of a Factory Town: A Study of Chicopee, Massachusetts," *Smith College Studies in History*, XX, Nos. 1–4 (October, 1934—July, 1935), 26–43.

small mills devoted to carding, finishing, and spinning. Weaving was still organized largely on a household or domestic basis. But the rapid installation of power looms during the twenties led to integrated operations and the appearance of huge factories. The Middlesex Company, organized at Lowell in 1830 with improved machinery and a capital of $100,000, was indicative of the trend of the following decades. Though many smaller mills widely scattered in the northern states continued to operate, the great factories developed in New England by 1860 exceeded in size even those devoted to cotton manufacture.[3]

The factory system of carpet manufacture, which grew rapidly beginning in the twenties, is worthy of comment in two respects: the factory stage, except in Philadelphia, where hand looms were important until after the Civil War, appeared without preliminary or intermediate stages except for some early household production of quite different material; and although small mills existed from the beginning, many factories were of relatively large size as compared with other textile industries.[4] The textile industry has been given special attention not only because it provided by the close of this period the example par excellence of the factory system but because since about the beginning of the century it had made a complete transition from the household to the factory system, a revolution in the organization of production not so fully accomplished in most other industries.

The small mill or neighborhood industries, which, as has been noted, were already widely prevalent in 1815, obviously possessed many characteristics of the factory. Thus, the merchant flour mills were fairly large-scale operations at least in terms of the size of physical plant and capital investment. Also, power-driven machinery was used and a more or less standardized product produced for a distant market. The changes which took place in these industries down to 1860 were largely matters of degree rather than of kind. Small neighborhood mills continued to exist in most parts of the country, while the merchant mills at such great centers as Baltimore and Rochester became larger and more mechanized and their marketing systems grew in complexity. The development of the other small factories or neighborhood mills of 1815—sawmills, glass manufactories, distilleries, tanneries, and salt works—was roughly similar,

[3] Clark, *History of Manufactures in the United States*, I, 453; Cole, *The American Wool Manufacture*, I, 219–226, 245–258.
[4] Cole and Williamson, *The American Carpet Manufacture*, pp. 16–23.

though a few had radically different histories. Except in frontier areas, carding and fulling mills had undergone a major metamorphosis; potash works grew in size for a period, then largely disappeared as potash ceased to be chiefly a by-product of farm fireplaces; cotton gins, tar works, and, in fact, many grist- and sawmills continued as small neighborhood projects little changed from colonial days.

The furnaces and forges of the beginning of the century already had certain factory characteristics—relatively large capital investment, use of power machinery, and production of a more or less standardized product, often for distant markets. Fully developed factory conditions in the iron industry came slowly, but by the later forties the anthracite furnaces and rolling mills of eastern Pennsylvania and western New Jersey were rapidly becoming major factory operations; indeed, just before the Civil War, when improved techniques of production and transportation permitted the merging of Michigan ore and Pennsylvania and Ohio bituminous coal in Pittsburgh furnaces, processes were so integrated as to bring the anthracite branch of the industry to a mature factory stage.

The translation of many of the shop or handicraft industries into the factory system was often gradual and unspectacular, and varied widely with the industry. As already noted, the boot and shoe industry reached the factory stage only on the eve of the Civil War. Even then, the workers were brought together into central shops or factories primarily in order to permit economies of operation and labor supervision. A usual characteristic of the mature factory system, the use of power-driven machinery, was still largely absent. Many of the shops of cabinet and coachmakers continued small throughout the period, but as early as the twenties some grew into factories making furniture, carriages, and wagons by the use of mass production methods and the use of power-driven woodworking machines.

The decline of household manufacturing after 1820 and the increase in the value of all manufactured products in the decades preceding 1860 give a rough indication of the general growth of the factory system. More significant, however, than any statistics of manufacturing are the census reports reflecting the growth of urbanization, for the factory system was a city development. Thus, the beginnings of the factory age are reflected in the census of 1830, which showed the first clear indication of a trend toward urbanization. And the rapid development of the factory system after 1840 is most clearly reflected in the tremendous increase in the rate of growth of American cities in the two decades before the Civil War. By 1860 the factory system was rapidly becoming important in practically every industrial field and the stage was set for its phenomenal development in postwar years.

PROFITS AND CAPITAL

The extraordinary growth of manufacturing from 1815 to 1860 merely reflected its relative profitability or comparative advantage. In competition with farming, trade, transportation, and land speculation, it was able to attract increasing supplies of labor and capital. The subject of industrial labor is dealt with in the following two chapters. It is the purpose here to note the general profitability of manufacturing and to explore the sources of the tremendous flow of capital into this field.

Data on profits in manufacturing are not abundant, and those which are available are often unsatisfactory: (1) The meaning of the rates of profit cited is typically not very clear because of lack of standard accounting practices. Thus, failure to deduct certain expenses such as depreciation sometimes inflates the rates of earnings reported. On the other hand, the practice sometimes adopted of reporting as profits only the amount earned in excess of the current rate of interest reduces the profit rate reported. (2) Profit information is chiefly available from hearings in connection with revisions of the tariff. Producers testifying before Congressional committees usually had a strong incentive to understate the profitability of their manufacturing enterprises.

Despite these limitations, contemporary reports of dividends and earnings are worth some attention. Of course, there were failures, a great many in depression years, and by no means all who tried their hands at manufacturing were able to succeed. Nevertheless, the profit record in manufacturing appears decidedly attractive. Rates of from 10 to 20 per cent seem to have been fairly common, and instances of much higher returns were not unusual.

In cotton manufacturing the records show generally high profits. During the period 1816–1826 the Boston Manufacturing Company averaged 18.75 per cent per annum, but returns of 6 per cent were reported during the highly competitive fifties. The Merrimack Company, organized in 1822, averaged annual dividends of 12 per cent until 1860, and the Appleton Company, which began operations in

1829, paid dividends averaging over 8 per cent for more than fifty years. These were large establishments, but many small ones also reported good earnings. Testimony in 1832 in connection with the *McLane Report on Manufactures*, though not altogether clear because of difficulties of definition, indicates that cotton manufacturers were earning about 6 per cent in New England, 7 per cent in New York State, 10 to 12 per cent in Delaware, 8 to 15 per cent in Pennsylvania, and from 12.5 to 25 per cent in Ohio. Leading New England cotton mills averaged dividends of about 10 per cent during the 1840's. A Congressional investigation before the enactment of the Walker Tariff of 1846 indicated that some cotton manufacturers were losing money and that others were clearing 20 to 25 per cent. A study published in 1845 showed the average annual dividends declared by the Lowell companies from the time of incorporation. Despite inclusion of the depression period 1837–1843, dividends averaged from 5.25 to 14 per cent. Textile mills of the South were paying 10 to 15 per cent and even higher in the forties. On the other hand, the record of many failures must not be overlooked, and certainly many of the smaller mills did not prove very profitable. Caroline Ware estimates, possibly somewhat too conservatively, that for the whole period 1816–1846 cotton textile profits in New England were only a little over 3 per cent on the capital investment.

The profits picture is none too clear for other industries, but the record often appears fairly favorable. Some of the large woolen mills did very well. Thus, the Middlesex Mills at Lowell average 16 per cent dividends for the whole period 1830–1860. Profits in iron manufacturing were subject to unusually wide fluctuations. Though failures were frequent in depression years, earnings of from 10 to 25 per cent appear to have been common in this industry. During boom times in the decade of the fifties, profit rates as high as 40 to 60 per cent were not unusual.

Finally, it may be noted that considerable fortunes for those days were made by men who entered manufacturing with practically no capital. Thus Samuel Slater, who started with little capital of his own but was aided by Almy and Brown, had begun cotton manufacturing in 1791 and left an estate valued at $690,000 in 1829, and Thomas Barrows earned about $500,000 between 1820 and 1850 in woolen manufacturing.[5]

[5] Fabien Linden, "Repercussions of Manufacturing in the Ante-Bellum South," *North Carolina Historical Review*, XVII, No. 4 (October, 1940), 314; Clark, *History of Manufacturing in the United States*, I, 372–378; Cole, *The American Wool Manufacture.*

Most American manufacturing began on a small scale, and the necessary capital was secured in relatively small amounts from exceedingly diverse sources. For the manufacture of such commodities as shoes, carriages, and furniture, the sum of a few hundred dollars was often sufficient to set up a business. The *McLane Report on Manufactures* gives data on literally hundreds of small manufactures whose total fixed and working capital was less than $1,000. As late as 1820 no Maine sawmill had been valued at more than $450. A woolen manufactory begun in North Adams, Massachusetts, is reported to have involved an initial expenditure totaling $1,100 for water-power site and building construction.[6] Probably very few manufactures started with quite such a small fixed investment. Of the Rhode Island factories reporting in 1832 to the Secretary of the Treasury, 68.4 per cent had a fixed capital investment of less than $50,000, and 18.4 per cent of less than $10,000. For the 119 cotton mills reporting, the average investment was about $43,000, and that for 22 woolen mills was close to $15,000.[7] The manufacture of iron has always required a relatively large fixed investment, but as late as 1857, rolling mills at Pittsburgh represented a capital investment averaging only a little over $150,000 for each plant.[8]

The initial capital invested in manufacturing came, as it had in Great Britain, in major part from mercantile profits. Repeatedly it is found that the gristmill, the potash works, or the fulling mill was owned and operated by the local storekeeper. Mercantile and manufacturing pursuits were typically closely tied together. The merchant manufacturer paid his help in store goods and obtained his store supplies as well as his raw materials in exchange for the products of his mill or factory. But though mercantile capital played a leading role, contributions came from almost every occupation: farming, land speculation, transportation, the professions, and handicraft production. Until about 1837 the last-named source of capital was especially important in expanding the production of boots and shoes under the domestic system.[9]

I, 226–231; Ware, *The Early New England Cotton Manufacture, passim;* Thomas G. Carey, *Profits on Manufactures at Lowell* (Boston: 1845), p. 8.

[6] Harvey A. Wooster, "Manufacturer and Artisan, 1790–1840," *Journal of Political Economy,* XXXIV, No. 1 (February, 1926), 72–76; Richard G. Wood, *A History of Lumbering in Maine 1820–1861* (*University of Maine Studies,* 2d series, No. 33, Orono: University Press, 1935), p. 159; Cole, *The American Wool Manufacture,* I, 229.

[7] Computed from *McLane Report on Manufactures,* I, 970–976.

[8] Louis C. Hunter, "Financial Problems of the Early Pittsburgh Iron Manufacturers," *Journal of Economic and Business History,* II, No. 3 (May, 1930), 531.

[9] See especially Clark, *History of Manufacturing in the United States,* I, 367–372; Ware, *The Early New England Cotton Manufacture,* pp. 127–128; Hazard, *The Or-*

The largest fortunes of the colonial and early national period had been made by merchants engaged in foreign trade. Though in the aggregate foreign commerce continued to grow after 1815, the high profits of the period of the Napoleonic Wars became much less common, and merchants, especially those engaged in the declining Far Eastern trade, tended to transfer their funds to domestic employment including manufacturing. Many of the small mills of southern New England were financed by such merchants. The funds which made possible the introduction of the large-scale factory system at Waltham, Lowell, and Chicopee came chiefly from representatives of great Massachusetts merchant families like the Lowells, Appletons, and Jacksons. Later, in the forties, many who had accumulated fortunes in whaling gradually transferred their capital to other employments including manufacturing. This process of withdrawal from foreign trade and reinvestment in manufacturing is well illustrated by John Perkins Cushing. One of Boston's famous China merchants, he began withdrawing his capital from foreign trade soon after 1828. In 1832 his investments in foreign trade were $454,500; at home they were $356,149. By 1839 his investments in foreign trade were less than $10,000; those at home over $1,000,000. Of Cushing's domestic investments, next to transportation, manufacturing was most important. His investments in the stock of manufacturing companies, which reached nearly $150,000 in 1835, had risen to nearly twice that sum by 1851.[10]

Firms in Boston, in Baltimore, and especially in New York that specialized in importing and distributing British cloth had accumulated a good deal of capital by the late twenties. Tariff hindrances to imports, especially after 1828, and prospects of attractive profits in domestic manufacture led many of these importers to withdraw funds from importing in order to finance textile mills and carpet factories.[11] Aaron Dennison, who pioneered in applying factory methods to watchmaking during the late forties and early fifties, secured capital

ganization of the Boot and Shoe Industry in Massachusetts before 1875, p. 68; Harvey A. Wooster, "A Forgotten Factor in American Industrial History," American Economic Review, XVI, No. 1 (March, 1926), 14–27 and, by the same author, "Manufacturer and Artisan, 1790–1840," Journal of Political Economy, XXXIV, No. 1 (February, 1926), 61–77.

10 Henrietta M. Larson, "A China Trader Turns Investor—A Biographical Chapter in American Business History," Harvard Business Review, XII, No. 3 (April, 1934), 351, 356. See also Evelyn H. Knowlton, Pepperell's Progress: History of a Cotton Textile Company, 1844–1945 (Vol. XIII of Harvard Studies in Business History, Cambridge: Harvard University Press, 1948), p. 17.

11 Cole and Williamson, The American Carpet Manufacture, pp. 13–15; Cole, The American Wool Manufacture, I, 228.

largely from small industrial capitalists, but when the Waltham Watch Company went bankrupt in 1857, necessary capital to salvage the venture came from Royal Elisha Robbins, a wealthy New York importer of watches.[12] Anson G. Phelps, who had made a fortune as an importer of tin, brass, and copper in New York City, utilized his large capital resources to become an important factor in developing the manufacture of copper sheets and wire in Connecticut during the thirties.[13] Leading merchants specializing in domestic commerce also made important capital contributions to manufacturing. Thus, Hartford and Springfield merchants were in 1815–1830 an important source of capital for the growing industries of the Connecticut River Valley. Caroline Ware points out that Philadelphia and Boston commission houses invested in New England cotton mills, and Louis Hunter shows that, when during the fifties railroads reduced the importance of Pittsburgh as a distributing center, local mercantile firms transferred their funds to iron manufacture.[14]

Once successfully established, manufacturing was often sufficiently profitable to be a major source of its own capital needs. Thus, Caroline Ware found that, for New England cotton textiles, expansion came largely through reinvestment of earnings.[15] A Waterbury, Connecticut, company, engaged in the manufacture of brass buttons, had a total investment of $6,500 in 1823. This had been increased to $20,000 by 1829, apparently from profits.[16] Many small firms like the Fall River Iron Works grew to very considerable size merely by plowing back profits. In 1821 this venture began with an original investment of $24,000. Although no new capital was added, and substantial dividends were paid out by subsidiary enterprises, this firm was worth $500,000 by 1845. Often profits from one field of manufacturing furnished capital for another. Thus, coal mining in western Pennsylvania provided capital for iron manufacture; profits from his glue and gelatin works permitted Peter Cooper to construct his great iron mills at Trenton, New Jersey; and earnings of the local iron works financed cotton mill development at Fall River.[17]

[12] Charles W. Moore, *Timing a Century: History of the Waltham Watch Company* (Vol. XI in *Harvard Studies in Business History*, Cambridge: Harvard University Press, 1945), pp. 26–27, 296.

[13] William G. Lathrop, *The Brass Industry in the United States* (Mount Carmel, Conn.: The author, 1926), pp. 58–59.

[14] Margaret E. Martin, "Merchants and Trade of the Connecticut River Valley, 1750–1820," pp. 203–210; Ware, *The Early New England Cotton Manufacture*, p. 142; Hunter, "Financial Problems of the Early Pittsburgh Iron Manufacturers," pp. 526–527.

[15] Ware, *The Early New England Cotton Manufacture*, p. 129.

[16] Lathrop, *The Brass Industry in the United States*, pp. 42–43.

[17] Hunter, "Financial Problems of the Early Pittsburgh Iron Manufacturers," p. 528;

(*Above*) An iron mill about 1850. A fast growing industry rapidly becoming mechanized. (*Bettmann Archive*) (*Below*) A cooper's shop, 1843. Small-scale production and handicraft methods long persisted in this industry. (*R. H. Gabriel, Pageant of America, V, 24*)

(*Above*) Felting hats. Hat making remained largely a hand-labor industry until the 1850's. (*R. H. Gabriel, Pageant of America, V, 21*) (*Below*) A bleachery at Waltham, 1853. Bleaching joined spinning and weaving as a large-scale factory occupation. (*Bettmann Archive*)

Moneylenders and banks helped to provide working capital for manufacturing concerns chiefly by note shaving, i.e., advancing cash on notes at a substantial discount. In a few industries where specialized marketing mechanisms had been developed, well-to-do distributors were able to provide needed capital. Commission merchants or selling agents often advanced cash on woolen cloth received on consignment from the woolen mills. Sometimes they provided loans secured by mortgages on buildings and machinery and thus enabled mills to pay cash for needed raw materials. Selling agencies also acted as bankers for some of the big cotton mills.[18]

But, far from providing capital for manufacturing, most distributors of manufactured products actually demanded financial help from producers in the form of long credits. In fact, with the exception of a few relatively large and prosperous firms, American manufacturers appear to have been chronically short of working capital. The same manufacturer who found himself faced with the necessity of paying cash for needed raw materials often discovered that he could dispose of his finished products only on long credits or in exchange for goods instead of money. The Britannia Company of Taunton, Massachusetts, was able to sell its wares in the early 1830's only by extending credit to buyers for one to nine months or even longer. Wherever in the North goods moved to market by canal or river, the winter season, by retarding delivery, increased capital needs. Pittsburgh iron manufacturers who were severely handicapped by lack of fluid capital had to meet not only this seasonal disadvantage but also faced the impossibility of sending their product to river markets whenever drought or floods interrupted navigation on the Ohio.[19]

Undeveloped marketing systems also added to the capital needs of the manufacturer. In many lines of industry it was customary to send goods to dealers to be sold on commission. Until disposed of, and this might be a matter of years, such goods tied up capital equal to their cost. Often much capital and energy had to be invested in buying supplies and selling the finished product. Clark notes that clockmakers in Connecticut had to interrupt production to go on long

---

Allan Nevins, *Abram S. Hewitt: with Some Account of Peter Cooper* (New York: Harper & Brothers, 1935), pp. 59 ff.; Smith, *The Cotton Textile Industry of Fall River, Massachusetts*, p. 31.

[18] Cole, *The American Wool Manufacture*, I, 212–213; Ware, *The Early New England Cotton Manufacture*, pp. 180–182.

[19] George Sweet Gibb, *The Whitesmiths of Taunton* (Vol. VIII of *Harvard Studies in Business History*, Cambridge: Harvard University Press, 1946), pp. 62–63; Hunter, "Financial Problems of the Early Pittsburgh Iron Manufacturers," pp. 531–535; Bruce, *Virginia Iron Manufacture in the Slave Era*, p. 126.

journeys for supplies or to peddle the finished clocks from horseback. As late as 1832 iron producers of western Pennsylvania distributed and sold iron from their own flatboats along the Ohio and Mississippi rivers.[20]

THE CORPORATION

Manufacturing, like domestic and foreign trade with which it was so closely allied, was usually organized as an individual proprietorship, a family enterprise, or a partnership. Before 1810 the corporate form of organization, though already common for banking, insurance, bridge and turnpike companies, was rare in manufacturing. With the growth of the factory system after 1815 and the appearance of large production units, especially in the manufacture of cotton and woolen cloth and carpets, the corporate form and also the unincorporated joint-stock associations became increasingly popular. The joint-stock associations were much like corporations but lacked formal state charters. Their legal status was not entirely clear, and of course they did not secure the special privileges sometimes granted by the states to the early incorporated companies. Both forms had a number of advantages. They facilitated the securing of capital from a larger group of persons than could ordinarily be brought together in a partnership, they provided continuity of operation, and they permitted the flexibility resulting from transferable shares. Limited liability, though often granted to corporation shareholders, was not always conferred by the state charters nor permitted by the courts in the early decades of the century. In 1830 a Massachusetts statute established the principle of limited liability for corporate shareholders. Thereafter other states gradually gave increasing recognition to this principle. New York, which had experimented with charters specifying double liability, unlimited liability, and limited liability, definitely adopted the last-named in 1848.[21]

Most corporation charters secured before 1860 were granted by special acts of state legislatures. But provision for incorporation under general laws became increasingly common after 1837, the year in which Connecticut passed a sweeping general act. Actually New York had provided for the incorporation, without special legislative action, of certain manufacturing concerns of limited capitalization

[20] Ware, *The Early New England Cotton Manufacture*, pp. 164–166; Clark, *History of Manufactures in the United States*, I, 356.

[21] Charles M. Hoar, "Legislative Regulations of New York Industrial Corporations, 1800–1850," *New York History*, XXII (April, 1941), 205–206.

as early as 1811. But popular distrust of corporations delayed the rapid spread of such legislation for more than twenty-five years. Following 1837, the movement for general laws grew so that before the decade of the fifties was over most of the important manufacturing states, including Maryland, New Jersey, New York, Pennsylvania, Indiana, Massachusetts, and Virginia, had passed permissive legislation. But all except Virginia still required special legislative action under certain conditions. Beginning with Louisiana in 1845, constitutional provisions necessitating incorporation under general laws were adopted by thirteen states before 1861.[22] But as late as 1860 incorporation under general acts remained the exception rather than the rule except where such procedure was mandatory, for more liberal charters were usually obtainable under special than under general laws.

The adoption of the corporate form by industry came most rapidly in the field of secondary manufacture. Thus, most of the larger textile mills and glass manufacturing plants were incorporated in the first quarter of the century. Firms engaged in primary manufacture, like saw- and gristmills and ironworks, were slow to adopt this new device. Though iron manufacturing was being rapidly incorporated during the 1850's, less than half the industry was so organized before the Civil War.

Incorporation of manufacturing establishments took place in three long waves. Beginning about 1805 the first rose to a peak in 1814 and subsided in 1820. The second wave grew until about 1836 or 1837 and then fell off in 1842. The third appears to have reached its highest point in the middle fifties and its trough in 1861. A study of special charters issued to Pennsylvania manufacturing corporations shows that 5 were issued before 1815, 81 during the years 1815–1850, and 93 in the single decade 1851–1860. Of the corporation charters granted to manufacturing and mining companies in the New England states, 591 were issued in the period 1800–1830, 803 from 1831 through 1843, and 1,853 in the years 1844–1862. The total number of incorporated manufacturing establishments in the United States probably doubled during the 1850's. This rapid increase clearly foretold the coming of the corporate age, but the fact must be emphasized that until well after 1860 most American manufacturing was still carried on by unincorporated units.[23]

[22] George Heberton Evans, Jr., *Business Incorporations in the United States, 1800–1943* (New York: National Bureau of Economic Research, 1948), p. 11.

[23] Thomas C. Cochran, "Business Organization and the Development of an Industrial Discipline," in Harold F. Williamson, ed., *The Growth of the American Economy*, pp.

The early corporations met with a great deal of suspicion, opposition, and criticism. As early as 1820 the American lawyer-economist Daniel Raymond wrote:

The very object . . . of the act of incorporation is to produce inequality, either in rights, or in the division of property. *Prima facie*, therefore all money corporations, are detrimental to national wealth. They are always created for the benefit of the rich, and never for the poor. The poor have no money to vest in them, and can, therefore, derive no advantage from such corporations. The rich have money, and not being satisfied with the power which money itself gives them, in their private individual capacities, they seek for an artificial combination, or amalgamation of their power, that its force may be augmented.[24]

This attitude was in part the reflection of a widespread hatred of special privilege and monopoly and to some extent at least the reaction of a predominantly agrarian population against new devices which seemed to give mysterious and imperfectly understood advantages to commercial and industrial interests.

But it was more than this, for small businessmen and conservative investors were often among those most critical of this new device. Curiously enough, corporations, many of which in the twentieth century spent liberally of their resources to point out the blessings of the free enterprise system, were attacked in this early period of corporate expansion as the arch enemies of individual enterprise, devices through which business was directed by groups of men who, not being the owners, could not possibly have the necessary degree of interest in the success of the enterprise. In fact, following the panic of 1857, there were many denunciations of corporate abuses, and the modern thesis, so emphasized by Berle and Means as well as by others, of the divergence in interest between ownership and management was explicitly developed. Thus an alarmed owner of stock in a number of New England manufacturing corporations wrote a pamphlet giving specific instances showing how management had

306–310; Shaw Livermore, "Unlimited Liability in Early American Corporations," *Journal of Political Economy*, XLIII, No. 5 (October, 1935), 674–687; Joseph G. Blandi, *Maryland Business Corporations, 1783–1852* (Johns Hopkins University *Studies in Historical and Political Science*, Vol. LII, No. 3, Baltimore: The Johns Hopkins Press, 1934), pp. 27–29; William Miller, "A Note on the History of Business Corporations in Pennsylvania, 1800–1860," *Quarterly Journal of Economics*, LV (November, 1940), 156–158; Oscar Handlin and Mary Flug Handlin, *Commonwealth: A Study of the Role of Government in the American Economy: Massachusetts, 1774–1861* (New York: New York University Press, 1947), pp. 173–174; W. C. Kessler, "Incorporation in New England: A Statistical Study, 1800–1875," *Journal of Economic History*, VIII (May, 1948), 43–62; Evans, *Business Incorporations in the United States, 1800–1943*, pp. 14–23.

[24] Daniel Raymond, *Thoughts on Political Economy* (Baltimore: Fielding Lucas, Jr., 1820), p. 427.

by proxies and other devices defied the owners and inquiring, "Can anybody doubt that . . . the officers in the possession of these great properties can continue to control them for their own purposes and in defiance of their owners?" [25]

MANUFACTURING IN 1860

The ten leading manufacturing industries in 1860 are listed in order of their importance in the accompanying table. The ranking shown is determined by the value added by manufacture, i.e., the

UNITED STATES MANUFACTURES, 1860

Item	Cost of Raw Material	Number of Employees	Value of Product	Value Added by Manufacture	Rank by Value Added
Cotton goods ...	$52,666,701	114,955	$107,337,783	$54,671,082	1
Lumber	51,358,400	75,595	104,928,342	53,569,942	2
Boots and shoes .	42,728,174	123,026	91,889,298	49,161,124	3
Flour and meal ..	208,497,309	27,682	248,580,365	40,083,056	4
Men's clothing ..	44,149,752	114,800	80,830,555	36,680,803	5
Iron (cast, forged, rolled, and wrought)	37,486,056	48,975	73,175,332	35,689,276	6
Machinery	19,444,533	41,223	52,010,376	32,565,843	7
Woolen goods ..	35,652,701	40,597	60,685,190	25,032,489	8
Carriages, wagons, and carts	11,898,282	37,102	35,552,842	23,654,560	9
Leather	44,520,737	22,679	67,306,452	22,785,715	10

Source: Computed from *Eighth Census of the United States: Manufactures*, pp. 733–742.

result obtained by subtracting the cost of raw materials from the value of the finished product. The census of 1860, the source of these data, though imperfect in many respects, was by far the most satisfactory census of manufacturing up to that time.

By 1840, and possibly even earlier, the making of cotton cloth had become the leading manufacturing industry in the United States. This rank was retained in subsequent decades as total cotton manufactures, which were valued at $46,000,000 in 1840, rose to $66,000,-000 in 1850 and $116,000,000 in 1860. It is not surprising, therefore, that the Census of Manufactures for 1860 opens with this statement: "The growth of the culture and manufacture of cotton in the United

[25] J. C. Ayer, *Some of the Usages and Abuses in the Management of Our Manufacturing Corporations* (Lowell, Mass.: C. M. Langley and Company, 1863), p. 18. See also Hartz, *Economic Policy and Democratic Thought: Pennsylvania, 1776–1860*, pp. 56–62.

States constitutes the most striking feature of the industrial history of the last fifty years." [26] From the first New England led in the cotton textile field. By 1860 nearly three fourths of the cotton manufacturing was carried on in this section, with Massachusetts responsible for the production of three times as much as either New Hampshire or Pennsylvania, the next most important producers.[27]

A major industry from colonial times, lumbering ranked second for the whole country in 1860 and was the leading manufacture in the western and southern states. This industry was dependent upon the location of the forests and the availability of transportation facilities. As older areas were cut over, the newer states tended to assume leadership. In 1860 about 38 per cent of the total value added by manufacture was contributed by the western states, 24 per cent by the Middle Atlantic, and 22 per cent by the southern states.

Aided by the sewing machine and the rapid introduction of the factory system, the boot and shoe industry had grown with great rapidity during the fifties, especially in New England. The value of boots and shoes produced in that region in 1860 exceeded by more than $850,000 the total production of footwear in the United States ten years earlier. The industry ranked third in 1860 and was even more highly concentrated in the East than the cotton textile industry, Massachusetts alone being responsible for more than one third of the total output. The four leading cities in boot and shoe manufacture— Philadelphia; Lynn and Haverhill, Massachusetts; and New York City —produced more than one fifth of the total for the country.

The manufacture of flour and meal, the fourth-ranking manufacture, was, like lumber production, as old as settlement in North America and widely scattered over the country. During the fifties the center of this industry, which had previously been located in the Middle Atlantic states, moved westward, so that by 1860 the western states were responsible for one half of the value added by manufacture in this industry.

The fifth-ranking item, men's clothing, like boots and shoes, gained

[26] *Eighth Census of the United States: Manufactures,* pp. ix, xix.

[27] Unless otherwise noted, manufacturing statistics are from the United States Census of Manufactures for 1860. The division of the states into sections follows the census of 1860: New England States (Maine, New Hampshire, Vermont, Massachusetts, Rhode Island, and Connecticut); Middle States (New York, New Jersey, Pennsylvania, Delaware, Maryland, and District of Columbia); Western States (Ohio, Indiana, Michigan, Illinois, Wisconsin, Iowa, Minnesota, Nebraska, Missouri, Kansas, and Kentucky); Southern States (Virginia, North Carolina, South Carolina, Georgia, Florida, Alabama, Mississippi, Louisiana, Texas, Arkansas, and Tennessee); Pacific States (California and Oregon); Territories (Utah, New Mexico, and Washington).

greatly from the sewing machine and expanded tremendously during the fifties. This important industry, which had not been in existence at the beginning of the period being discussed, developed rapidly during the forties as the declining cost of materials and cheaper production methods made ready-to-wear clothing available to a prosperous and rapidly growing middle class. In Cincinnati as early as 1840, nearly 4,000 women were employed in this industry and working in their own homes.[28] By 1860 New York State was responsible for more than one third of the total product, and the cities of New York, Philadelphia, Cincinnati, and Boston produced more than half of the output for the country.

Respectively sixth and seventh in rank were iron (cast, forged, rolled, and wrought) and machinery. Though production units were to be found in almost every part of the country, both industries centered chiefly in the Middle Atlantic states, with Pennsylvania the leading state. The iron industry expanded with great rapidity during the fifties; the value of bar, sheet, and railroad iron more than doubled, and the increase for machinery was apparently even greater. Problems of definition and classification are especially troublesome for statistics of iron and iron products. If the census designations had been broadened, the relative importance of both items would have been considerably increased. The importance of census definitions in determining rankings is well illustrated by the fact that if the two items, iron and machinery, had been combined in a single category called "Iron and Machinery," it would have become by a considerable margin the most important manufacturing industry in the country.

Some woolen cloth, the eighth-ranking manufacture, was made in almost every part of the country, but the big mills were located in New England, where about two thirds of this product was made. Only slightly less important were the products in ninth place—carriages, wagons, and carts; and in tenth place, leather.

The United States is such a large country and economic conditions vary so greatly from one section to another that generalization concerning conditions is often difficult and may be misleading. In a sense the country was still primarily a nation of farmers in 1860. Only one person out of five lived in places of more than 2,500 inhabitants, and of the total population only about 4 per cent were employed in manufacturing. On the other hand, if attention is focused on southern New England and on the Hudson and the Delaware

[28] Cist, *Cincinnati in 1841: Its Early Annals and Future Prospects*, p. 57, fn.

river valleys, an area of manufacturing development is discovered comparable to the most industrialized regions of Great Britain.

It will be seen from the accompanying table that whatever the measure used—capital invested, laborers employed, or value added by manufacture—the New England and Middle Atlantic states were the chief manufacturing regions. In both sections, capital, labor, and water power were relatively abundant, and transportation, which had developed more rapidly there than elsewhere in the country, provided easy access to raw materials and markets. The decline of agriculture in New England beginning early in the century helped to provide a labor force for manufacturing, and after 1815 the reduced profits in foreign trade and, still later, in whaling helped to make capital available. The Middle Atlantic states were in general closer to both raw materials and markets than New England, but the demands of manufacturing for labor and capital were met in the Middle Atlantic area by competition from within the region of a prosperous agriculture and from without by the trade and agriculture of the easily accessible West.

For the western states the great improvements in transportation tended on the one hand to discourage manufacturing development based primarily on regional isolation, and on the other to stimulate those which involved processing the products of agriculture and forestry. By 1860 the western states led the nation in the production of lumber, flour and meal, liquor, and packing-house products. This last was centered largely in Cincinnati, which became the pork-packing capital of the United States. Not identified as a separate industry there until 1818, it rapidly became by far the most important manufacture of that city. The census of 1840 not only shows it primary, but indicates that by-products such as candles and soap had become major products of the city. Though Cincinnati retained its position as the leading packing-house city of the country, in the two decades following, other western cities such as Chicago and St. Louis became increasingly important as the production of corn and hogs moved westward with the frontier.[29] The western states were first also in the production of agricultural machinery, a manufacture which found its greatest sale to the prairie farmers of the West.

The leading manufactures of the South in 1860, as well as for preceding decades, were lumber, tobacco, and flour and meal. Each involved the relatively simple processing of products of local ex-

[29] Isaac Lippincott, *A History of Manufactures in the Ohio River Valley to the Year 1860* (New York: The Knickerbocker Press, 1914), pp. 115–116, 177–182.

SECTIONAL EXHIBIT OF MANUFACTURING FOR 1860

Sections	Number of Establishments	Capital Invested	Cost of Raw Material	Number of Hands Employed		Annual Cost of Labor	Annual Value of Products	Value Added by Manufacture [a]
				Male	Female			
New England ...	20,671	$257,477,783	$245,523,107	262,834	129,002	$104,231,472	$468,599,287	$223,076,180
Middle	53,287	435,061,964	444,126,969	432,424	113,819	152,328,841	802,338,392	358,211,423
Western	36,785	194,212,543	225,618,813	194,081	15,828	63,573,307	384,606,530	158,987,717
Southern	20,631	95,975,185	86,543,152	98,583	12,138	28,681,195	155,531,281	68,988,129
Pacific	8,777	23,380,334	28,483,626	50,137	67	29,037,543	71,229,989	42,746,363
Territories	282	3,747,906	1,309,425	2,290	43	1,026,608	3,556,197	2,246,772
Aggregate	140,433	$1,009,855,715	$1,031,605,092	1,040,349	270,897	$378,878,966	$1,885,861,676	$854,256,584

[a] Computed.
Source: *Eighth Census of the United States: Manufactures,* p. 725.

tractive industries. A beginning had also been made before the Civil
War in the manufacture of cotton goods, machinery, iron, and other
industrial products. Numerous attempts to manufacture cotton cloth
with slave and with free labor were made in the South Atlantic states,
but except for those sponsored by William Gregg, an energetic
Charlestonian, few appear to have been profitable ventures. Iron
and iron products were produced by small establishments in almost
every southern state. But operations were typically on a small scale
and not very successful except in the vicinity of Richmond, Virginia,
where the industry gained a firm foothold. There four rolling mills,
fourteen foundries and machine shops, and other iron manufacturing
establishments, employed more than 1,600 mechanics in 1860 and
represented an investment of about $4,000,000. But as compared
with the total output of the nation, southern manufacturing production was still small. Of the many explanations offered for the industrial backwardness of this region, much of which had long been settled, the most convincing emphasize the effective competition for
both labor and capital of cotton growing and the slow development
of the southern transportation system.[30]

Appraisal of the general progress made in manufacturing before
1860 is peculiarly dependent upon the point of view, whether attention is limited to the years 1815–1860, or whether the perspective is
that of the whole century. The concluding table in this chapter per-
mits comparison of some of the more significant statistics for the
census dates 1810, 1860, and 1900. The period before 1860 was chiefly
one of significant beginnings. The fundamental changes in the techniques of production and the change-over to the factory system of
organization have been described earlier in this chapter. The rate
of manufacturing growth was extraordinarily rapid before 1860.
Value of product increased from about $200,000,000 to $2,000,000,-
000; thus, in fifty years it had increased ten times. Even more striking
in percentage terms are the increases in coal and iron production
shown in the table. Nevertheless, it must be emphasized—and the
table admirably brings this out—that in terms of absolute growth the
great period of manufacturing development came in the forty years
after 1860, when the annual value of manufactures rose from about
$2,000,000,000 to $13,000,000,000 and the capital invested increased
from about $1,000,000,000 to $10,000,000,000. Even more impressive,

[30] Seth Hammond, "Location Theory and the Cotton Industry," *Tasks of Economic History* (December, 1942), pp. 101–117; John G. Van Deusen, *Economic Bases of Dis-union in South Carolina* (New York: Columbia University Press, 1928), Chap. 7.

not only because of their basic importance in the new manufacturing economy but also because data are much more reliable than those for manufacturing, are the figures given in the accompanying table showing the increased production of coal and iron.

When by 1860 the eastern railway net had been substantially completed, the great revolution in transportation had taken place. Not so for manufacturing for, although a tremendously significant beginning had been made, the greatest period of development lay in the decades immediately ahead. Even more effectively than by the data contained in this table, this can be demonstrated by comparing the value of manufactures in the United States with that for the chief rivals abroad. In 1860 American manufactures were valued at a lower figure than those of the United Kingdom, France, or Germany. By 1894 the value of American manufactured products not only exceeded that of each of these countries but was not far from equaling all three combined.[31]

PROGRESS OF INDUSTRIALIZATION, 1810, 1859, AND 1899
(000's omitted)

	1810	1859	1899
Value of manufactures	$199,000 [a]	$1,886,000 [b]	$13,000,000 [b]
Capital invested in manufacture		1,010,000 [c]	9,817,000 [d]
Anthracite coal (short tons) [e]	(1829) 138	9,620	60,418
Bituminous coal (short tons) [e]	(1829) 102	6,013	193,323
Pig iron (long tons) [f]	54	821	13,621

a Source: Eighth Census of the United States: Manufactures, p. v.
b Biennial Census of Manufacturers, 1931, p. 19.
c Eighth Census of the United States: Manufactures, p. 729.
d Twelfth Census of the United States: Manufactures, Pt. 1, United States by Industries, VII, xcvii.
e Fourteenth Census of the United States: Mines and Quarries, XI, 258.
f Statistical Abstract of the United States, 1930, p. 755.

31 Twelfth Census of the United States: Manufactures, Pt. 1, United States by Industries, VII, lv.

CHAPTER XII

The Workers Under
Changing Conditions[1]

BACKGROUND AND BEGINNINGS

CERTAINLY not the least of the changes which make the first half of the nineteenth century of peculiar interest were those which affected the organization, the social status, and the well-being of labor. As transportation improved, as markets for standardized products developed, and as the domestic and factory systems arose, the whole manner of making a living underwent fundamental alteration. The story of this transition claims attention in this and the following chapter. They trace the path by which, between 1815 and 1860, most craftsmen, many men, women, and children from American farms, and, finally, increasing hordes of immigrants became a part of that great body of industrial wage earners now regarded as typical of capitalistic economy.

During the colonial and early national period skilled craftsmen in American towns—tailors, printers, coopers, cordwainers, and the like—had, as in England, formed their own craft organizations for fraternal and protective purposes and, often with the help of local legislation, had established an apprentice system for training labor. Apprenticeship requirements were often rather lax in America, where land was cheap and farming easily entered. Nevertheless, the craft system prevailing in American towns during colonial times continued on into the early national period. In this economy where labor was scarce, skilled craftsmen were relatively well paid. Workshops

---

[1] Throughout this chapter a great deal of use has been made of John R. Commons and associates, *History of Labour in the United States* (4 vols., New York: The Macmillan Company, 1918), Vol. I, often without specific footnote reference.

were small and typically operated by a master craftsman with an apprentice or two. In the larger shops might be found a few journeymen as well as apprentices. Most journeymen considered their status as temporary, an interlude to permit small savings before setting themselves up as master craftsmen.

As long as skilled workmen were engaged almost exclusively in supplying the local demand by filling orders for custom work, this system showed considerable stability. But it changed rapidly during the first half of the century as, in craft after craft, production for general market sale became more important than custom work, and the dominant role in marketing and production came to be played by that intermediary, the merchant capitalist, whose operations have been described in the preceding chapter. Village storekeepers, city merchants, and even a few of the more aggressive master craftsmen became merchant capitalists, buying the finished products or sometimes paying for having them made under the putting-out system, and selling them wherever markets could be found. In this pressure for market sale, price competition became the determining factor. The merchants marketing their goods in ever-widening areas put pressure on masters to produce as cheaply as possible. Under this compulsion those master craftsmen tended to survive who, organizing their shops for efficient and cheap production, reduced wages of their skilled workers and delegated the simple and less skilled processes to women and children. A few of the master craftsmen continued to do custom work of high quality for the well-to-do. But the great mass of them, coming gradually under the shadow of the merchant capitalist, produced a relatively cheap, standardized product for the rapidly expanding American market.

Caught in the midst of market changes which threatened them with declining wages, lowered status, and periods of ruinous unemployment, American workers were faced with extremely difficult problems of adjustment and even survival. Between the Revolution and 1815 journeymen shoemakers and printers in the larger American cities had organized craft societies and developed, at least to some extent, such fighting techniques as the strike and the closed shop. These early organizations were local in character, in part at least fraternal or social in purpose, and often ephemeral, lasting only for the duration of an industrial dispute. From the beginning such workers' organizations were opposed by militant employers who looked to the courts to curb the activities of workers' societies. Between 1805 and 1815, in at least six cases, unions were haled into court as being unlawful conspiracies. The decision in four of these went against the workers. In the most famous, the case of the Philadelphia Cordwainers in 1806, the jury found the workers "guilty of a combination to raise their wages." [2] Despite these difficulties, unions of such skilled craftsmen as printers, carpenters, shoemakers, and tailors were common immediately following the War of 1812 in the larger cities such as Philadelphia, Pittsburgh, Baltimore, New York, and Boston. But most of these trade societies were much too weak to survive a major industrial depression and practically all disappeared in the severe crisis of 1819–1820.

As economic conditions improved during the early twenties, workingmen's societies or unions again sprang up among the skilled workers in the larger cities. Printers, cordwainers, hatters, riggers, carpenters, and others formed trade unions, and as prices rose, especially during 1824 and 1825, many strikes were called. Most of these were designed to raise wages, though some sought a reduction of hours. A great deal of attention was attracted by the walkout of journeymen house carpenters of Boston in 1825. This strike for a ten-hour day was resolutely put down by the "gentlemen engaged in building," who in a public statement declared that the "spirit of discontent and insubordination" among the workers was a foreign importation and that a shorter workday would open "a wide door for idleness and vice." [3] But by 1827 unions were more active than ever before, and for the first time appeared the beginnings of a real American labor movement, not only in the sense that the trade unions grew in strength and combined on the local as well as on the national front, but also that workers in various occupations now united for reform, agitation, and political action.

THE EARLY LABOR MOVEMENT: WORKINGMEN'S SOCIETIES

The workingmen's societies continued their growth during the latter twenties and into the following decade. Many of the older organizations had been largely fraternal and protective, and master craftsmen as well as journeymen had been commonly eligible for membership. This situation showed signs of change after the mid-twenties. The fraternal and social aspects tended to disappear—or lingered on and new unions appeared in the trade to take over the

[2] John R. Commons and others, eds., A Documentary History of American Industrial Society (11 vols., Cleveland, Ohio: The Arthur H. Clark Company, 1910–1911), III, 236.

[3] Commons and associates, History of Labour in the United States, I, 161.

new functions—and fighting organizations intent on objectives connected with wages and hours began to take their place. This new emphasis drove a wedge between the journeymen and the masters and in most cases led to the exclusion of the masters from the unions which were now established.

Of course, it must be remembered that this early union movement did not include most workers. Common laborers, those employed in their own homes under the domestic system of industry, and the increasing band of factory workers played little or no part. These, the submerged majority too often simply lost sight of, will be given due consideration in the following chapter. But here attention is centered chiefly on the dramatic role of the craftsmen, the so-called artisans and mechanics, who in striving to carry on their ancient trades under the changing conditions of the transportation revolution brought the labor movement in this country to an early, though short-lived, maturity.

As will be pointed out presently, workers in the cities gave an unprecedented amount of attention to political activity from about 1827 to 1832. Nevertheless, unions also remained active and continued to grow during these years. In fact, the workers' political activity depended to no small extent on the workingmen's societies. The greatest wave of union growth came in the years of hectic price inflation, 1834–1836. From the summer of 1834 to the peak of prices in February, 1837, wholesale prices nearly doubled. Though wages were also advancing, their general rate of increase lagged so seriously behind the rising cost of living that wage workers, already concerned over their loss of status, became desperately alarmed over money earnings, which exchanged for less and less food and shelter.[4] Workers' societies flourished as never before. In the growing cities west of the Appalachians—Pittsburgh, Cleveland, Frankfort, and St. Louis—craftsmen organized societies and not infrequently sponsored spirited strikes. Unions flourished in New Orleans, and the typographical union was strong in many southern cities.[5] And in trades previously unorganized, such as whitesmiths, milliners, hand-loom weavers, and plasterers, unions now sprang up, formed more or less stable organizations, and, in at least some cases, secured wage increases or other advantages.

Societies for workmen in Philadelphia reached a total of 53 by

[4] Alvin H. Hansen, "Factors Affecting the Trend of Real Wages," *American Economic Review*, XV, No. 1 (March, 1925), 32.

[5] Richard B. Morris, "Labor Militancy in the Old South," *Labor and Nation*, IV, No. 3 (May–June, 1948), 35.

1836, a number more than twice that existing two or three years earlier. Between 1833 and 1837, 16 societies appeared in Newark, the same number was reported in Boston, 23 in Baltimore, and 52 in New York. In a few instances women and children formed temporary organizations and participated in walkouts. For short periods even seamstresses and shoebinders who worked in their own homes under the domestic system of manufacture had their own organizations. Though very few factory workers were organized in regular unions, joint action for strike purposes was not unusual. Thus about 2,000 persons, many of them women and children, walked out of the Paterson, New Jersey, textile mills in 1835 in protest against the 13½ hour day. This strike was broken when the employers made slight concessions in the working hours, and most of the workers returned to their machines. But the children of some of the leaders were denied re-employment. Nor were strikes unknown among the factory girls working in New England under the Waltham system, but there, as elsewhere, stable unions among factory operatives failed to develop at this time. The total number of trade unionists was estimated as at least 26,250 in 1834 and by 1836 at about 300,000 by a labor paper.[6] This latter figure must be a gross exaggeration, for the census of 1840 [7] gives the total employed in manufacturing and mechanical pursuits as under 800,000.

During the decade ending in 1837 the form of trade-union organization in the United States matured with striking rapidity. Both local federations and national unions made their first appearance. Late in 1827 fifteen Philadelphia workingmen's societies banded together to form the Mechanics' Union of Trade Associations, thus organizing the first city central or trades' union to be formed in the United States. Though weak and unable to hold its membership, this organization lasted until 1831 and proved a factor of considerable importance in the great upsurge of political activity by Philadelphia workers during 1828–1831. The next attempt at a city federation of unions came in 1833 in New York City. In that year the journeymen carpenters engaged in a bitterly fought strike to increase their wages. Other unions came to their aid, contributing about $1,200. With this help the carpenters were enabled to hold out for about a month and win their wage increase. Impressed with the obvious advantage of combined action, nine workingmen's societies federated soon after the settlement of the carpenters' strike, founding

[6] Commons and associates, *History of Labour in the United States*, I, 424.
[7] *Sixth Census of the United States*, p. 475.

the General Trades' Union of New York. The movement now spread rapidly to other parts of the country. By the end of 1833 trades' unions had been organized in Baltimore, Washington, and Philadelphia, and by 1836 such organizations were to be found in at least 13 American cities including three—Pittsburgh, Cincinnati, and Louisville—to the west of the Appalachians. The trades' unions formed in 1833 and the years immediately following largely avoided politics and laid chief stress on mutual aid in disputes with employers.

A few of these city trades' unions were brought together in 1834 to form the National Trades' Union. Its first convention was held at New York in August, 1834, with delegates present from Boston, Brooklyn, Poughkeepsie, Newark, and Philadelphia. This group, the first national labor organization in the United States bringing together workers from different crafts, held conventions again in 1835 and 1836. The national conventions apparently accomplished little, but they passed resolutions and served as a sounding board for labor opinions. The convention of 1836 was held in Philadelphia, with 35 delegates in attendance representing New York, New Jersey, Maryland, Ohio, and Pennsylvania. Many of the proposals put forward at this convention for improving the bargaining power of labor, including the suggestion of a "general strike," have a very modern ring.

As markets widened with improved transportation, skilled craftsmen in a number of trades gradually came to feel the desirability of extending their membership beyond the limits of a single city. In an attempt to meet this need, five national unions were formed in 1835 and 1836. The two strongest were established by the cordwainers and by the printers. But for a brief period organizations extending beyond a single local market existed also among the combmakers, carpenters, and hand-loom weavers. Each of these unions held at least one so-called national convention. Although chief attention appears to have been given to an attempt to standardize wages, other problems common to the particular trades were considered. Thus, the printers sought to deal with the breakdown of the apprenticeship system and the hand-loom weavers to investigate the threat of competition both from imports and from the power loom. But these national organizations, like the trades' unions, were much too new and weak to survive the economic cataclysm of 1837. They disappeared completely and not until 1852 did a national union again appear on the American scene.[8]

[8] Commons and associates, *History of Labour in the United States*, pp. 335–453; Harry A. Millis and Royal E. Montgomery. *Organized Labor* (New York: McGraw-Hill Book Company, 1945), pp. 30–33.

The hostile attitude of the courts toward labor organizations did not end with the early conspiracy trials already mentioned, but continued into the twenties and thirties. But the specific contention that a combination to raise wages was illegal tended to disappear, giving way, as in the New York Hatters' case of 1823, to the charge that the workers were conspiring to injure others. From 1829 to 1842 most of the labor cases involved the closed-shop issue, i.e., the right of the workers to determine with whom they would or would not work. One of the most important of these was the case of the Geneva, New York, shoemakers who were found guilty by the supreme court of the state in 1835. The shoemakers had forced an employer to discharge a worker who was willing to work for less than the union wage. The court declared: "In the present case, an industrious man was driven out of employment by the unlawful measures pursued by the defendants, and an injury done to the community, by diminishing the quantity of productive labour, and of internal trade." [9]

This decision served as a precedent by which in the following year the New York tailors were also found guilty of conspiracy because of strike efforts to enforce a closed shop. In this case the judge fined the union leaders, pointed out that in the United States honest journeymen of true moral worth would by skill and industry become master mechanics, and remarked that combinations, largely the work of foreigners, were not advantageous for the journeymen themselves. Though welcomed in some conservative quarters, this decision led to a great outcry from labor and its friends. A labor paper, *The National Laborer*, June 4, 1836, declared: "If an American judge will tell an American jury that these barriers which the poor have thrown up to protect themselves from the gnawing avarice of the rich, are unlawful, then are the mechanics justified the same as our Fathers were justified in the days of the revolution in 'Arming for Self Defence'!" [10] And a protest meeting held in New York City attracted, so it was reported, a large crowd of 27,000 persons.[11]

A revulsion of feeling seems to have followed this decision. In two similar court cases which followed later in 1836—the Hudson shoemakers and the Philadelphia plasterers—juries returned verdicts of not guilty. And then in 1842 Chief Justice Shaw of the Supreme Judicial Court of Massachusetts rendered his precedent-making decision in the famous case of Commonwealth v. Hunt. Here for the

[9] Quoted in Commons and associates, *History of Labour in the United States*, I, 407.
[10] *Ibid.*, 410.
[11] *Ibid.*, 410–411.

first time it was clearly and forcefully affirmed that workers might lawfully organize trade unions and that such organizations were not per se unlawful. Judge Shaw indeed went even further, holding that strikes for the purpose of securing the closed shop were legal.[12]

THE EARLY LABOR MOVEMENT: POLITICS

It will be remembered that property qualification upon suffrage had been retained by most states following the American Revolution and that not until the early twenties did such important states as New York and Massachusetts abandon property requirements on voting. Perhaps the very newness of their voting privileges gave the workers a naïve confidence in their ability to improve their condition through organized political action. At any rate, they believed that in forming their own political groups lay one method by which they might improve their lot. Around them they saw a tremendous, expanding economy—cities rapidly increasing in population, vast new agricultural lands attracting settlers, canals and steamboats revolutionizing commerce, trade thriving, and merchants and bankers prospering. Yet amidst all this growth and promise of better things to come, they felt passed by, for their position in society and their working conditions deteriorated as their status as wage workers rather than independent craftsmen became confirmed, and their level of living remained dishearteningly low. So it was that between 1828 and 1833 local workingmen's parties appeared in about fifteen states and in a few won some local victories. They were "workingmen's parties" in the sense that they directed their appeal for votes chiefly to poorer persons who worked with their hands. At times they included farmers. In the cities their chief membership appears to have come from craftsmen, whether independent operators or wage earners, but they often included professional men and small businessmen. The latter, indeed, were often indistinguishable from independent craftsmen.[13]

The first and perhaps the most successful early venture into politics, at least as measured by its effectiveness in electing candidates, came in Philadelphia and its vicinity. This area, at the end of the twenties the most industrialized in America, was the scene of acute

[12] *Ibid.*, 162–165, 404–412.
[13] Sidney L. Jackson, *America's Struggle for Free Schools* (Washington: American Council on Public Affairs, 1941), pp. 154–158; Arthur B. Darling, "The Workingmen's Party in Massachusetts, 1833–1834," *American Historical Review*, XXIX, No. 1 (October, 1923), 81–86.

labor discontent. Living conditions in the Philadelphia slums were almost incredibly bad. Resentment against the increasing contrasts of urban wealth and poverty, excessively long hours of labor, low wages, lack of provision for free public education, imprisonment for small debts—these and other causes of discontent brought about in 1827 what was apparently the first labor party in America.[14] At a meeting of the Mechanics' Union of Trade Associations of that city held in May, 1828, the question was raised of taking political action to help toward securing the ten-hour day as well as other important objectives. The constituent unions approved political action and candidates were nominated for the fall elections. Failure of the workers' candidates to be elected led to more careful planning and organization the following year.

The Republican Political Association of the Working Men of the City of Philadelphia was formed in May, 1829; the vigorous campaigns waged in that year and the next, despite bitter opposition, achieved considerable success. Thus in 1829 the Working Men's party elected twenty of its candidates in Philadelphia, enough to hold the balance of power, and in 1830, although it lost in the city and county elections, it made a very good showing in some of the suburbs, especially in Northern Liberties, where the workingmen elected all eight of their candidates for commissioner. This was the last year in which the Working Men's party succeeded in electing candidates. After 1831 the party disappeared, and its members were largely absorbed into the Jacksonian wing of the "Republican" party. The national election of 1832 aroused so much interest as to overshadow local political groups. But this was merely the final blow. The politically inexperienced Working Men's party had been easily victimized by professional politicians, who had rather quickly used it for their own ends. Lacking a state-wide organization, the whole movement, at least as an independent party, rapidly disappeared.

In another large city, New York, the workingmen made a temporarily successful bid for political power. There in 1829 a hurriedly organized Working Men's party elected a number of candidates in the fall elections, including Ebenezer Ford, the president of the carpenters' union, who thus became the first labor member of the New York State Assembly. Moreover, the movement spread to other cities of the state, and in the spring elections of 1830 farmers and workers

[14] William A. Sullivan, "Philadelphia Labor during the Jackson Era," *Pennsylvania History, Quarterly Journal of the Pennsylvania Historical Association*, XV, No. 4 (October, 1948), 305–320.

united to win sweeping victories in such towns as Troy, Albany, and Salina.[15]

But the labor vote in New York had already reached its crest. It fell off sharply in later elections, and by 1832 practically all of the workers had returned to the old parties. In fact, the short time elapsing between the organization of the Working Men's party and the New York election in the fall of 1829 was a chief factor in the initial victories, for within a year the Working Men's party was torn by schismatic struggles from which it never recovered. It had attracted leaders of unusual ability but of messianic fervor. The machinist Thomas Skidmore was most active in establishing the party, but his great interest lay in egalitarian reforms, chiefly those involving the redistribution of property in land. The new party was hardly three months old when, his leadership challenged, he withdrew with a small group of his disciples to form the Poor Man's party. More serious was the split in the ranks over the extreme educational teachings of Frances Wright and Robert Dale Owen. Both had joined enthusiastically in helping the party in the election of 1829 but, the election over, they moved determinedly to win it over to support their panacea for the ills of society—the care and education of all children under the guardianship of the state. That this proposal, which involved removing children from parental influence at a tender age and placing them in state-operated boarding schools, was actually endorsed by some strong labor groups is probably less an indication of the radical thinking of the time than a tribute to the remarkable ability and attractiveness of Frances Wright. But the Owenites were little more successful than Skidmore. Workers became alarmed when the followers of Owen were denounced as infidels bent on destroying the family, and the New York State convention of the party held August 25, 1830, came under the influence of more conservative and realistic, though less high-minded, political leaders. State guardianship was repudiated and, though a local labor ticket was nominated, this group, now known as the Cook-Guyon faction, endorsed Tammany candidates for state office. The Owenites, of course, nominated their own candidates. Hopelessly split by these dissensions, the labor groups lost their following and were reabsorbed into the older political parties by 1832.[16]

The movement for workingmen's parties extended to most other

[15] Philip S. Foner, *History of the Labor Movement in the United States* (New York: International Publishers, 1947), pp. 133–134.

[16] *Ibid.*, pp. 136–137, 158.

northern states and though such parties were generally weak and short-lived, they created a good deal of interest. Over fifty newspapers in states from Maine to Missouri presented the workingmen's point of view. In Delaware the movement reached its crest in 1830 when its candidates won in a number of districts, thirteen out of eighteen charter officers elected in the borough of Wilmington being nominees of the Working Men's Association. Here as elsewhere the leaders themselves were often not actually workingmen in the twentieth-century meaning of the term. In this period, as indeed in later ones in American history, reformers, small businessmen with their own axes to grind, and ambitious politicians often became prominent as leaders of workingmen's movements.[17]

In the New England states workingmen's groups appeared in many localities in 1830, public meetings were held, and in a few places their candidates ran successfully. As elsewhere, this political movement seems to have faded out as interest turned more and more to the national election in 1832. But local political activity was revived again in 1833 and 1834 under the aegis of the New England Association of Farmers, Mechanics, and Other Working Men. This organization became a political factor in 1833 and 1834 when workingmen's candidates were nominated for state offices in Massachusetts. The movement received some support from skilled mechanics, but common laborers or factory operatives do not appear to have participated in the conventions or to have voted for labor candidates. Its chief strength came from farmers and intellectuals of western Massachusetts, including men like Samuel Clesson Allen of Northfield and the historian George Bancroft of Northampton, who believed they saw in the rising tide of urbanization and industrialization a threat to those who labored, in contrast to those who consumed.[18]

Though workingmen's parties as distinct organizations had largely disappeared before 1832, it should not be supposed that workers withdrew from the political arena. Jackson's sweeping victory in the election of 1832 was due in part at least to the workers in eastern cities who rallied to his support following his July 10, 1832, veto of the bill to recharter the Bank of the United States. Daniel Webster rose in the Senate to condemn in resounding and horrified periods the statement in the veto message "that the rich and powerful too often bend

[17] Joseph Dorfman, *The Economic Mind in American Civilization, 1606–1918* (3 vols., New York: The Viking Press, 1946–1949), Vol. II, Chap. 24, and "The Jackson Wage-Earner Thesis," *American Historical Review*, LIV, No. 2 (January, 1949), 296–306.

[18] Darling, "The Workingmen's Party in Massachusetts, 1833–1834," pp. 81–86.

the acts of government to their selfish purposes," but many workers cast their ballots for Old Hickory.[19]

Following the election of 1832, workers continued to participate in politics, though ordinarily not as a separate party. Sometimes they ruled from within the Democratic fold as in Massachusetts, where in 1836 they united with the radical wing to gain control of the Democratic party. At other times they fought the conservative wing of the Democratic party and in state or local elections organized revolts led by workingmen. Such, in part at least, were the Loco Focos and Equal Rights parties in New York and Pennsylvania. Not infrequently the workingmen held the balance of power and succeeded in securing the election of their own representatives. Thus in 1834 they first forced Tammany to nominate for representative in Congress Ely Moore, president of the General Trades' Union of New York, and then secured his election as the first representative of organized labor to sit in the Congress of the United States.

THE EARLY LABOR MOVEMENT: OBJECTIVES AND DECLINE

The objectives which workers sought directly through their trade societies and those which they strove for through political action were generally different. Chiefly by use of the strike the unions sought to raise or maintain wages, protect or establish the closed shop, maintain apprenticeship regulations, and shorten the length of the working day. The aims sought through political activity now call for brief examination. The objectives sought by the workers through political action, so far as they can be apprehended through the pronouncements of workers' organizations and especially of the so-called workingmen's parties, show considerable agreement from one part of the country to another. Two reforms were almost everywhere given greatest emphasis: the extension of free education and the abolition of imprisonment for debt.

The agitation for free public schools and an improved educational system did not originate with so-called workingmen's groups, and certainly others, including employers, were often active in this cause. To some extent the more well-to-do part of the population favored extending popular education as the best protection available against the ignorant masses and their tendency to "abuse" the use of the ballot. But once aroused, the workers appear to have made popular

[19] Andrew Jackson, *Veto Message, July 10, 1832*, in *Miscellaneous Documents of the House of Representatives*, 53 Cong., 2 Sess. (1893–1894), II, 590.

education one of their most cherished objectives. With the possession of the ballot they began to realize the necessity of proper schooling so that they could use their new privilege intelligently.[20] "The right of suffrage which we all enjoy," declared workingmen at a meeting in New York City in 1830, "cannot be understandingly exercised by those whose want of education deprives them of the means of acquiring such information as is necessary for a proper and correct discharge of this duty." [21] Workers especially resented the implication of pauperism reflected upon their children who attended the public schools, for outside New England free public education was provided for the poor only.

Certainly the conditions patently called for reform. One million children between the ages of five and fifteen were estimated to be attending no school in 1833, and a few years later over half the children in Pennsylvania were said to be in the same situation.[22] Even in New England, where conditions were presumably best, many towns failed to provide the schooling required by law, women teachers were paid at rates comparable with the lowest factory wages, and "the little red schoolhouse" was in incredibly bad repair and frequently had no toilet facilities of any kind. In Connecticut some women teachers, although boarding themselves, received as little as $1.00 a week, and in Vermont as late as 1860 men teachers averaged about $1.05 a day as compared with $1.25 a day for mechanics, $1.50 to $2.00 for peddlers, and $2.00 or more for horse doctors.[23]

Workmen were hardly less unanimous in their condemnation of the almost universal practice of imprisonment for debt. At a public meeting held in New York City in 1829 it was declared to be "a remnant of the feudal system, calculated only for barbarians, disgraceful

[20] Merle Curti, The Social Ideas of American Educators (New York: Charles Scribner's Sons, 1935), pp. 79–80; Jackson, America's Struggle for Free Schools, passim; Philip R. V. Curoe, Educational Attitudes and Policies of Organized Labor in the United States (New York: Teachers College, Columbia University, 1926), pp. 8–47.

[21] Craftsman, September 4, 1830. Quoted by Commons and associates, History of Labour in the United States, I, 283. On the general faith in education see Arthur Alphonse Ekirch, Jr., The Idea of Progress in America, 1815–1860 (No. 511 of Studies in History, Economics and Public Law, New York: Columbia University Press, 1944), Chap. 7.

[22] F. T. Carlton, Economic Influences upon Educational Progress in the United States, 1820–1850 (University of Wisconsin, Bulletin No. 221, Economics and Political Science Series, Vol. IV, No. 1, Madison: 1908), p. 103; Commons and associates, History of Labour in the United States, I, 182.

[23] Newton Edwards and Herman G. Richey, The School in the American Social Order (Boston: Houghton Mifflin Company, 1947), p. 324; Vermont Board of Education, Fourth Annual Report (Burlington: 1860), p. 101; James Truslow Adams, New England in the Republic, 1776–1850 (Boston: Little, Brown & Company, 1926), pp. 363–367.

to the age and country in which we live, depriving individuals of the only means of being serviceable to themselves, their families, or the public." [24] Nor do their charges seem greatly exaggerated. Incarceration for debt was so common that in 1829 the Boston Prison Discipline Society found that 75,000 persons were annually jailed for debt in the United States and that more than half of these owed less than $20. In notorious cases widows with dependent children, the old, and the infirm were thrown into prison for unpaid obligations of less than a dollar.[25]

Other political objectives commonly sought by the workingmen at this time must be summarized more briefly: (1) They advocated mechanics' lien laws to give the workers protection against defaulting employers, a remedy much needed at a time when wages were often paid at intervals of six months or even longer. (2) They urged abolition of the militia system by which the wealthy got off with small fines which were easily paid, but workers, finding it difficult or inconvenient to serve, were faced with terms in jail. (3) They favored the abolition of licensed monopolies, especially banks. To them banks and bankers represented the "money power," the very center of political reaction. But they also had specific objections, for laborers suffered from being paid their wages in depreciated bank paper. In addition they feared the monopoly of credit wielded by banks in many communities. (4) Lotteries were opposed as a form of gambling which impoverished and demoralized the poor. (5) Finally, they sponsored measures designed to restrict competition from prison labor, to obtain simplification of court procedure, and to reform the tax system.

None of these reforms were originated by the workers' parties, nor were workingmen the only ones who supported them. The liberal traditions of Jeffersonianism lingered on in many communities, on the frontier and in rural areas of the East. Even from among the professional groups and from businessmen in the growing urban centers the reform movements often secured considerable support and leadership. Nevertheless in most of the eastern states the workers played an important role in achieving these goals.

The workingmen were especially active in Rhode Island. There a small group of wealthy persons, by limiting the suffrage, held ab-

[24] As quoted by Commons and associates, *History of Labour in the United States*, I, 281.

[25] *Ibid.*, pp. 178–180; Arthur M. Schlesinger, Jr., *The Age of Jackson* (Boston: Little, Brown & Company, 1945), pp. 134–136; Sullivan, "Philadelphia Labor during the Jackson Era," pp. 309–310.

solute political power and vetoed practically all democratic or reform measures. By threatening armed rebellion under Thomas W. Dorr, the poor and disenfranchised masses finally forced radical changes, including the adoption in 1843 of manhood suffrage, with property qualifications largely, though not completely, eliminated. Having finally secured the vote, the workers in this little state, which was one of the earliest to be industrialized, rapidly forced the introduction of most of the labor-championed reforms, including relatively generous provisions for free public instruction.

An examination of the philosophy of this early American labor movement shows a marked preoccupation with what was believed to be a growing gulf between the rich and the poor. Langdon Byllesby, a Philadelphia printer and publisher, declared: ". . . the profits of . . . improvements in the arts, instead, as would seem just, of *tending to benefit and relieve the whole of its members in the burdens of their toil,* go only to the enrichment of *a few,* and depression of a great majority." [26] Substantially this sentiment was repeated by every labor party of the time. Workingmen in New York City asserted in 1830 that they had "seen with surprise and alarm, the neglect which these interests [the producing classes] have received, and the greater consideration which has been bestowed upon the moneyed and aristocratical interests of this State." [27] A statement drawn up by two trade-union leaders seeking to establish the ten-hour day in Boston, 1835, read: "The work in which we are now engaged is neither more nor less than a contest between *Money* and LABOR: *Capital* which can only be made productive by *labor* is endeavoring to crush *labor* the only source of all wealth." [28]

These and other statements might be cited to illustrate the trend of thought of the workers and even of many small businessmen and others who at times identified themselves with the workingmen. Middle-class leaders attuned to the temper of the times forcefully enunciated these popular sentiments: Andrew Jackson in his veto message of 1832; John Greenleaf Whittier through editorials in the *American Manufacturer* and *Essex Gazette;* William Cullen Bryant and William Leggett in their writings in the New York *Evening Post;* and finally George Bancroft in his public statements. Of these we can quote only from a communication of Bancroft's which, though

[26] Langdon Byllesby, *Observations on the Sources and Effects of Unequal Wealth* (New York: Lewis J. Nichols, 1826), p. 77.

[27] Proceedings of Workingmen of Auburn in *Mechanics' Press,* July 17, 1830, quoted by Commons and associates, *History of Labour in the United States,* I, 233.

[28] As quoted from the *Boston Post* by Schlesinger, *The Age of Jackson,* p. 167, fn. 22.

made public in 1834, fourteen years before the issuance of the Communist Manifesto, has certain similarities to it in spirit and language, if not in doctrine. Bancroft wrote of "The feud between the capitalist and the laborer, the house of Have and the house of Want . . ." declaring:

Political influence is steadily tending to the summit level of property; and this political influence of wealth must be balanced by the political power of numbers. Even then this political influence often controls elections, and often with a giant's tread, stalks into the halls of legislation.

When the merchant demands that his interests should prevail over those of liberty, it is the clamor of capital. . . .

When a life and trust company ask for privileges, which enable capital to consume the moderate profits of the farmer by tempting him to incur the hazards of debt, it is the clamor of capital, deafening the voice of benevolence and legislative wisdom.

When the creditor demands that the debtor may once more be allowed to pledge his body and his personal freedom, it is the clamor of capital.

When "vested rights" claim a veto on legislation, and assert themselves as the law paramount in defiance of the constitution which makes the common good the supreme rule, it is the clamor of capital, desiring to renew one of the abuses of feudal institutions.

When the usurer invokes the aid of society to enforce the contracts, which he has wrung without mercy from the feverish hopes of pressing necessity, it is the clamor of capital, which like the grave, never says, It is enough.

When employers combine to reduce the wages of labor, and at the same time threaten an indictment for conspiracy against the combinations of workmen, it is the clamor of capital.[29]

For a few brief years in the thirties an identity of political and economic interests seemed about to be recognized as workingmen through trade unions and political action struggled for what they believed their rights. But it was a false dawn in labor history. The crises of 1837 and 1839 and the deep depression which followed broke the spell. Trade unions melted away and the workers ceased to be a distinct factor in national or, for the most part, even in local politics. Though many of the reforms, such as free public education and the abolition of imprisonment for debt, were achieved, labor did not for a long time regain either political strength or unity of thought.

The panic of 1837 marked the demise of the early labor movement in the United States, but it was by no means the sole cause of its disappearance. It cannot be too often emphasized that the workers involved in this early movement were not in appreciable num-

[29] George Bancroft in a letter to Messrs. S. Judd, J. H. Flint, S. Parsons, C. Clark, C. P. Huntington, J. Wright, October 1, 1834, *Boston Courier,* October 23, 1834.

bers either common laborers or factory workers; instead, they were chiefly skilled craftsmen whose status, because of the rapid extension of markets, was being swiftly changed, chiefly for the worse. For a brief period these hard-pressed craftsmen held an important place on the stage of history. Their forward-looking program coincided with the great humanitarian movements of the first part of the nineteenth century. Their philosophy was in part an inheritance from the American and French revolutions and in part an adaptation of Jeffersonian principles to urban conditions. In part, also, it was the natural result of granting suffrage to the poor workers who had previously been denied this privilege. They naïvely assumed that equal political rights would be easily and quickly translated into equality in economic bargaining power.

Utopianism on the one side and the slavery controversy on the other absorbed the great reform impetus of the early century, and fundamental changes in marketing and production left the skilled craftsmen a stranded and not very important minority on the national scene. The new patterns of production—the domestic system and the factory system—with their utilization of women and children and their emphasis on cheapness rather than skill, were alone probably enough to have wrecked the early American labor movement. But add the fact that the great era of foreign immigration now set in and it is not difficult to understand why the development of a firmly based labor movement was delayed for many years.

INDUSTRIAL WORKERS IN COUNTRY HOMES

The emphasis which has been given in the preceding pages to the role played in the labor movement before about 1840 by craftsmen in the few good-sized cities must not be permitted to divert attention from other important labor developments in the decades following the War of 1812. During this period thousands of men and women were finding manufacturing employment in their own homes under the domestic system, while others, rapidly growing in numbers and closely resembling the modern industrial proletariat, were becoming familiar with the discipline of the factory.

In New England, and especially in Massachusetts, Connecticut, and Rhode Island, before about 1850, conditions were most favorable for building up an industrial labor force. There, increasingly after 1820, farmers on the poorer soils found themselves unable to compete successfully with western producers. Under these conditions the hill town farmer was faced with three alternatives: (1) He could stick it out on his stony soil, grasping whatever expedients presented themselves in order to supplement his meager income from agriculture. If he followed this course one answer lay in the domestic system—manufacture in the home for market sale. Another was that the farmers' daughters might leave the farm at least for a few years to work in a distant factory. (2) The farmer might move his whole family to some nearby town, where all could be employed as factory operatives. (3) Finally, he could migrate westward, taking his family with him. Those farm families that did not follow this last alternative during the period before 1850 provided most of the labor force which made possible the growth in the United States of both the domestic and the factory system of manufacture.[30]

Workers under the domestic system have been given surprisingly little attention by labor historians. Though numerous only in the North Atlantic states, especially New England, and though largely part-time workers, the men, women, and children employed under this system were in the decades before the Civil War a very appreciable part of the industrial labor force of the nation. If those in Massachusetts who were devoting at least a part of their time to producing shoes, straw and palm-leaf hats, or similar goods are counted, then as late as 1845 and possibly well into the 1850's, probably more Massachusetts workers were manufacturing goods under the domestic system than under any other.[31]

Though the domestic system later became primarily an urban phenomenon identified largely with the sweated trades, it remained in New England before the fifties almost exclusively a village and rural development. Working in their own homes and free to determine the hours and conditions of labor which suited them best, these workers were subjected to less industrial discipline than the craft workers of the cities and stand in striking contrast to the almost completely regimented cotton-mill operatives in such centers as Waltham and Chicopee. In shoemaking, the occupation under the domestic system most dependent upon male labor, the workers had unusual freedom. Not only could they do their work when and where they wished, but the men often had alternative forms of income and em-

[30] See Margaret R. Pabst, "Agricultural Trends in the Connecticut Valley Region of Massachusetts, 1800–1900," *Smith College Studies in History*, XXVI, Nos. 1–4 (October, 1940—July, 1941), *passim*.
[31] *Statistical Tables: Exhibiting the Condition and Products of Certain Branches of Industry in Massachusetts for the Year Ending April 1, 1837* (Boston: 1838), pp. 201–204; *Statistics of the Condition and Products of Certain Branches of Industry in Massachusetts for the Year Ending April 1, 1845* (Boston: 1846), pp. 373–377.

ployment close at hand. The shoemakers of eastern Massachusetts often kept a cow or two and raised much of their own food. They went hunting when they wished, and for many the sea was so close at hand that they could easily turn to fishing for an alternative source of income. At Marblehead many of those who made shoes in the winter followed the sea in the summer. On the other hand, wages relative to those paid other skilled craftsmen were very low, often averaging only $4 a week or a little more. Pay for the shoes made was typically received in store goods; so in actual purchasing power, earnings in this, the most important sector of the domestic system, must often have been under $150 a year.[32]

Most other manufacturing occupations organized under the domestic system chiefly involved the labor of women and children, usually on a part-time basis. The braiding of straw and the making of straw and palm-leaf hats were typical of this employment. New England farm women and children thus found spare-time employment, especially during the winter, when the usual farm tasks were least pressing. The Puritan dislike of idleness, combined with the promise of a small supplementary income, led whole countrysides to engage in this type of work. Such home labor was socially approved, for even the doctors' and ministers' wives participated, and entire communities took it up. The census taker at Greenwich, Massachusetts, reported in 1855 that almost all the women of the town made hats "when occupied with nothing of more importance." [33] And employment in home industry must have been about as general in the adjoining town of Prescott, which, with a population of less than 800, reported that 50,000 palm-leaf hats valued at $10,000 were produced in the year ending April 1, 1837.[34]

Not a great deal is known as to the pay which these domestic workers received, though the *McLane Report on Manufactures* indicates that women and girls working on shoes often averaged 25 cents a day or less. In fact, wages as low as 8 and 9 cents a day are reported, but these must have been paid to young girls or for less than full-

[32] Norman Ware, *The Industrial Worker 1840–1860* (Boston: Houghton Mifflin Company, 1924), pp. 38–44; Clark, *History of Manufactures in the United States,* I, 394–395; Percy Wells Bidwell and John I. Falconer, *History of Agriculture in the Northern United States, 1620–1860* (Washington: Carnegie Institution of Washington, 1925), pp. 253–254; *McLane Report on Manufactures, passim,* but see especially I, 238.

[33] *Statistical Information Relating to Certain Branches of Industry in Massachusetts for the Year Ending June 1, 1855* (Boston: 1856), p. 648.

[34] *Statistical Tables: Exhibiting the Condition and Products of Certain Branches of Industry in Massachusetts for the Year Ending April 1, 1837* (Boston: 1838), p. 81.

time employment of women.[35] By dint of long hours on the part of women and children, the total family income must in some cases have been substantially increased. Thus computations based chiefly on the Massachusetts Census of 1837 indicate that in the town of Prescott, where nearly every family apparently gave at least some attention to making palm-leaf hats, the annual family income from this source, assuming all families to have been so employed, averaged more than $50. This was a very appreciable sum in a day when the annual net income from a farm was often between $200 and $300, and might be even less, and when a Lynn fisherman was doing better than average if he cleared more than $100 in five months.[36]

A careful observer reported in 1827 that although the power loom had greatly reduced the remuneration of hand weavers, whole families willing to combine farming and weaving could "make a very comfortable livelihood" in the vicinity of Philadelphia.[37] But wherever the domestic system persisted, rates of remuneration became distressingly low. In the thirties the needle trades were being rapidly developed on the domestic system in New York and Philadelphia; by the fifties most tailoring of ready-made garments was conducted on this basis, and the worst aspects of the sweating system were beginning to appear.

[35] See McLane Report on Manufactures, I, 237–239.

[36] McLane Report on Manufactures, I, 275, 805; Statistical Tables: Exhibiting the Condition and Products of Certain Branches of Industry in Massachusetts for the Year Ending April 1, 1837 (Boston: 1838), p. 81; Hazard, The Organization of the Boot and Shoe Industry in Massachusetts before 1875, passim; Thomas Mooney, "General View by an Irish 'Perpetual Traveller,' " in Vol. VII of Commons and others, eds., A Documentary History of American Industrial Society, p. 72.

[37] A Letter, on the Present State of the Labouring Classes in America, by an intelligent Emigrant at Philadelphia, pamphlet (Bury: John Kay, 1827), pp. 6, 7.

CHAPTER XIII

The Emergence of the Wage Earner

WORKERS UNDER THE RHODE ISLAND SYSTEM

AS the result of a number of factors, including the enclosure movement, a large surplus population had appeared in eighteenth-century
England. There the unemployed agricultural laborers, with their
wives and children, provided a cheap supply of workers to operate
the machines of the rapidly expanding cotton mills of Lancashire.
No such surplus was to be found in the United States. Even in New
England, where some labor power was available for manufacturing,
to bring it to the factory was a serious problem. In the days before
the streetcar and the automobile, the worker was not available for
factory employment unless he lived within easy walking distance of
the factory. In attempting to solve this problem of providing a sufficient number of operatives to tend the machines, employers developed two distinct types of factory organization. In southern Massachusetts, Rhode Island, Connecticut, and the states to the south and
west, the Rhode Island or family system evolved. In most of Massachusetts and the states to the northward, the Waltham or boardinghouse system predominated, though many small mills used the Rhode
Island system.

As the name implies, the family system often involved the hiring
of whole families, and depended largely upon the labor of women,
boys, and girls. Often small textile mills depended upon farmers'
daughters from the immediate neighborhood.[1] Cotton mills utilizing
the family system were ordinarily equipped with the spinning mule,
which required men for the heavy work but also provided much light
labor which could be done by women and even small children.

[1] A Letter, on the Present State of the Labouring Classes in America, p. 7.

The stocking weaver, 1839. Handicrafts-men in this industry found increasing competition from the power looms after the early thirties. (*Bettmann Archive*)

Making straw hats under the domestic system. The whole family found employment in the home. (*Harper's Magazine, XXIX [1864], 580*)

A shoe factory, Lynn, Massachusetts, about 1850. Mechanization was only just beginning before 1860. (*Bettmann Archive*)

Logging, 1858. In the north, work in the woods gave winter employment for farmers. (*R. H. Gabriel, Pageant of America, V, 217*)

(*Below*) Rivermen. They floated a thousand miles down the Ohio-Mississippi Rivers and before the steamboat era walked back. (*Old Print Shop*) (*Right*) Coal miner. His job was hard, dirty, and completely unmechanized. (*J. T. Adams, Album of American History, III, 393*)

(*Below*) Dock workers, New York Harbor. (*Brown Brothers*)

Most contemporary opinion regarded the employment of women and children as doubly beneficial: it provided them with productive occupation, and it also helped to keep them from falling into habits of idleness and vice. By 1820 about 45 per cent of the cotton-mill workers in Massachusetts were children; the comparable figure in Rhode Island was 55 per cent. Later this proportion declined somewhat, data for 1832 indicating that in cotton mills the percentage of children was about 21 per cent in Massachusetts and 41 per cent in Rhode Island.[2] The term "children" is loosely used in most early records. The upper age limit appears to have been at least sixteen and, in some cases, fourteen or fifteen. The woolen industry also employed women and children, but heavy work required the employment of a considerable number of men. The tariff investigation of 1828 indicated that, for the firms reporting, women constituted about 41 per cent of the workers, and children about 17 per cent; and the *McLane Report on Manufactures* shows the number of women had risen to about 49 per cent but of children had been reduced to about 8 per cent.[3]

Only very small mills could secure an adequate labor force from nearby farm or village families. The early factories were ordinarily dependent upon water power and hence were not usually erected in the centers of population. So to build up a labor supply employers frequently were forced to erect tenements, not a few of which, with their identical entrances, factorylike construction, absence of sufficient windows for adequate light, and generally run-down appearance, to this day add a rather grim note to the otherwise attractive appearance of many a New England village. Millowners favored large families because of the desire to utilize the cheap labor of children. The whole system tended to be paternalistic, with employers requiring sobriety and good behavior of their tenants. Some of the more enlightened employers did something toward providing for schooling of the children on Sundays. The contemporary British practice of recruiting orphaned and destitute children was indeed tried in a few instances but was never of appreciable importance, if for no other reason than that large numbers of such children were not available.[4]

A considerable effort was made by employers to secure operatives from Europe for factory work. But except for a few foremen and

---

[2] Ware, *The Early New England Cotton Manufacture*, pp. 210–211.

[3] Cole, *The American Wool Manufacture*, I, 239–240; *McLane Report on Manufactures*, I, 66–577; *American State Papers: Finance*, V, 778–845.

[4] Cole, *American Wool Manufacture*, I, 235–237; Ware, *The Early New England Cotton Manufacture*, pp. 210–212, 225–226.

skilled mechanics, largely English and Scottish, relatively few came over to work in American mills before the 1840's.[5] In the South, Negro slaves as well as white persons were used for factory labor. Sometimes they even worked together in the same factory, as in Virginia at the Tredegar Iron Company.[6] But wherever the Rhode Island system prevailed, the main source of factory operatives was native white families.

As might be expected in a predominantly agricultural country, wages and working conditions approximated those on the farm. Family wages appear to have compared favorably with what many, at least in New England, could secure from farming. But incomes were certainly very low in money terms. The investigations of 1828 and 1832 give numerous instances of male factory operatives receiving about 90 cents per day, women about 40 cents, and children 25 cents.[7] Illustrative of one of the factories paying very low wages was the Phoenix Manufacturing Company of Paterson, New Jersey, which manufactured sail duck. The company reported in 1828 that it employed 265 hands, who did not receive board and were paid as follows: [8]

109 men	$ .65 a day
42 boys, 8 to 14 years of age	1.375 a week
61 women	2.375 a week
53 girls, 8 to 12 years of age	1.375 a week

Factory operatives under the Rhode Island system probably received lower wages than did similar workers under the Waltham system or unskilled laborers in some of the larger cities. But clear-cut comparisons are impossible, for under the Rhode Island system wages were usually paid in large part in trade at a company-owned store. Thus, as late as 1831, Samuel Slater required workers to sign an agreement to patronize his store.[9] Even where wages were paid in money, payment was often made only at three- to six-month intervals. On the other hand, workers under the family system may have gained something from the fact that factories were often located in small and remote

[5] Theodore F. Marburg, "Aspects of Labor Administration in the Early Nineteenth Century," *Bulletin of the Business Historical Society*, XV, No. 1 (February, 1941), 2–6; Commons and others, *A Documentary History of American Industrial Society*, IV, Supplement, 29; Cole, *American Wool Manufacture*, I, 234–235.

[6] Bruce, *Virginia Iron Manufacture in the Slave Era*, p. 309.

[7] *American State Papers: Finance*, V, 783–857; *McLane Report on Manufactures*, *passim*.

[8] Cole, *The American Wool Manufacture*, I, 242. See also *History of Wages in the United States from Colonial Times to 1928*, Bulletin No. 499 of the United States Bureau of Labor Statistics (Washington: 1929), pp. 90–93.

villages, where food costs were low and some supplementary income was available from gardening or part-time farming.[10]

As on the farms, hours of labor were extremely long—in summer from sunrise to sunset, and in winter the machines were often kept going until eight or nine o'clock in the evening by the help of candle-light. Thus the year-round factory workers averaged about 68 to 72 hours a week. The intensity of application, especially for the children, whose work often involved intermittent rather than continuous activity, was surely less than in the modern factory. Nevertheless, such long hours must have been burdensome, even where work was light, for barely enough time remained on weekdays for eating, sleeping, and going to and from work. Children put in the same long hours as adults, and the records show that in some instances, at least, they were kept awake by having water thrown in their faces or disciplined by use of the whip. Conditions were surely detrimental to health and made proper schooling impossible. Although a few of the states passed laws before 1860 restricting the hours of labor for children and requiring school attendance, none of this legislation seems to have been well enforced. The tender age at which many boys and girls began work and the responsibilities which they assumed at an age when most children today are still in school amaze the mid-twentieth century reader. Thus Caroline Ware tells of a boy who, at the ripe age of thirteen, was entrusted to repair and set in operation the machinery of a cotton mill in Tiverton, Rhode Island. He had at that time been a cotton-mill operative for seven years. Another lad, nineteen years of age, became superintendent of the Pawtucket Thread Mill in 1826. He qualified for this responsible position by no less than eleven years' experience in the business.[11]

Early factory workers in the United States nowhere formed strong or enduring unions. But temporary organizations often sprang up at times of serious disputes with employers. A number of bitterly fought strikes by workers in factories of the Rhode Island type occurred in 1828–1829 and again in 1833–1836. One of the first strikes by factory workers took place at Paterson, New Jersey, in 1828. Operatives, in large part children, opposed a change of the dinner hour. The militia was called out and the strike broken. In the fall of 1828 an extensive though unsuccessful strike lasting for more than three months

10 Marburg, "Aspects of Labor Administration in the Early Nineteenth Century," pp. 6–8; Ware, The Early New England Cotton Manufacture, p. 226.

11 Ware, The Early New England Cotton Manufacture, p. 211; Edith Abbott, Women in Industry (New York: D. Appleton and Company, 1910), pp. 338–349; Report of Massachusetts Bureau of Statistics of Labor (Boston: 1870), p. 107.

was conducted by the spinners of Philadelphia and vicinity and a group of weavers conducted a walkout in Baltimore the following year.[12]

One of the most bitterly contested strikes in New England was that of the weavers in the plant of the Thompsonville Manufacturing Company at Thompsonville, Connecticut. In 1833 when these workmen struck for higher wages their leaders were thrown into jail on the charge of conspiring to ruin the business of the employer. Three separate trials were held, but the last (1836) resulted in a verdict favoring the workmen. The strike itself had been broken off after five or six weeks, and the workers forced to accept lower wages.[13] During 1834–1836 at least four strikes of factory operatives took place in Pennsylvania and one each in Delaware and New Jersey. This last, that at Paterson, in 1835, was one of the most extensive of the period, involving 20 mills and 2,000 workers.[14]

WORKERS UNDER THE WALTHAM SYSTEM

In contrast to the Rhode Island system stood the Waltham or boardinghouse plan, which was inaugurated by the Boston Manufacturing Company in 1814 and came to prevail throughout northern New England wherever mills were erected by the Boston Associates. This system was designed to provide an ample and satisfactory labor force for large-scale factories located on water-power sites in rural areas, where practically no factory labor was available. The core of the plan involved recruiting young women from New England farms and housing them in dormitories or boardinghouses erected near the factories.[15]

This boardinghouse system was designed not only to provide

[12] Commons and associates, *History of Labour in the United States*, I, 418–419.
[13] Commons and others, *A Documentary History of American Industrial Society*, Vol. IV, *Supplement, passim*.
[14] Commons and associates, *History of Labour in the United States*, I, 313–314, 418–422.
[15] The discussion of the Waltham system is based largely on Massachusetts, House Document, No. 50, *Special Report on The Hours of Labor*, March 12, 1845 and No. 153, *Report on Limitation on Hours of Labor*, April 10, 1850; Hannah Josephson, *The Golden Threads* (New York: Duell, Sloan and Pearce, 1949); Harriet H. Robinson, *Loom and Spindle* (New York: Thomas Y. Crowell Company, 1898); *Mind amongst the Spindles, A Miscellany, Wholly Composed by the Factory Girls*, Selected from the *Lowell Offering*, with an introduction by the English editor, and a letter from Harriet Martineau (Boston: Jordan, Swift and Wiley, 1845); Ware, *The Early New England Cotton Manufacture*, Chap. 8; Shlakman, "Economic History of a Factory Town: A Study of Chicopee, Massachusetts," Chap. 3; Louis Taylor Merrill, "Mill Town on the Merrimack," *New England Quarterly*, XIX, No. 1 (March, 1946), 19–31.

economical food and shelter for the girls, but to ensure an environment which would be sufficiently respectable to overcome the prejudice of conservative, rural New England against industrial employment. Widows of the highest respectability were placed in charge of the dormitories, and the rules for the operatives' behavior remind one of those enforced today in the most exclusive eastern preparatory schools for girls. The factory girls were typically required to be in their rooms by 10 P.M., to attend church services regularly, and in general to be modest and industrious. Although such regulations would surely be looked upon by present-day workers as paternalistic and an intolerable interference in their private lives, they were not generally so regarded at the time. Instead, during the heyday of this system and before its decadence in the late forties and in the fifties, both the girls and their parents welcomed this surveillance as concrete evidence that the mills were run by godly men who sought to protect the reputation of the operatives.

Francis C. Lowell, who had much to do with first developing this system at Waltham, showed a shrewd understanding of rural New England, for he was remarkably effective in attracting large numbers of farm girls into the textile mills. The decline of household manufacture had somewhat lightened the tasks of women in the home, and occupations, such as schoolteaching, were not yet open on a very extensive scale to the ambitious country girl. So, as soon as it developed that factory employment was respectable and did not hurt their chances of marriage, young women from New England and New York State eagerly sought employment in such rapidly developing mill towns as Lowell, Chicopee, and Manchester. Few, if any, were forced into the factories by grinding poverty. Rather, they were attracted by the opportunity of earning money which might be used to help support their parents, educate a brother, add to a marriage dowry, finance a term at Mount Holyoke Seminary, or merely provide themselves with better clothing. In addition, for many it was adventure, a chance for a few years to exchange the irksome routine of accustomed home duties for the excitement of working in a factory and living in a dormitory.

What was the life of these girls, the "female operatives," in this industrial experiment? As on the farm and in the mill of the family type, the hours seem inhumanly long by modern standards—from sunrise to sunset in summer and on into the evening by candlelight during the winter. It does not seem possible they could have worked a twelve-hour day and even longer at the tension of most modern factory work. Contemporary records do not present a clear picture. Evidence of an easy work pace, permitting even an occasional opportunity for the operative to read or knit, contrasts with other testimony of mounting pressure for production and harsh discipline. Undoubtedly conditions varied from time to time and from place to place, with apparently a general tendency for working conditions to worsen after the thirties. Wages for female operatives at Lowell appear to have averaged about $2.50 to $3.00 a week before 1850. The cost of board and room which was deducted from this came to about $1.25. At the Pepperell Mills in Biddeford, Maine, during the fifties, earnings of female warp spinners averaged from $2.52 to $3.48 a week and for female weavers from $2.14 to $3.84. Weekly earnings of men employees were somewhat higher, annual averages for carding room pickers varying from $3.75 to $4.77 and for weavers from $5.52 to $6.78. Low as these wages now seem, they appear to have been higher than those paid women textile workers under the Rhode Island system and compare very favorably with the earnings of women schoolteachers.[16]

The living conditions of the mill girls would hardly be judged attractive by modern standards. The dormitories were typically compact structures providing barely enough room for eating and sleeping. As many as six or eight girls shared a room. Sometimes, to the horror of the British visitor Harriet Martineau, who in other respects viewed Lowell through rosy glasses, the girls slept three in a bed.[17] Sanitary arrangements left much to be desired, for behind the dormitories were rows of outdoor toilets and pigpens interspersed with wells from which came the drinking water. Yet, on the whole, living conditions were certainly better than those common in the poorer areas of the large cities at the time, and probably no worse than in many a crowded home in the country.

Factory conditions under the boardinghouse system were hardly idyllic during the twenties and thirties, although they were generally better than in the following decades or even under the family system. Hours were long and many operatives must have had little time or energy for social life. The occasional walkouts of the workers, chiefly to oppose reductions in their wages, give evidence of at least some discontent. The first of these strikes was conducted in 1828 by the factory girls in Dover, New Hampshire, but the one involving the largest numbers and causing the most comment at the time was

[16] Robinson, *Loom and Spindle*, pp. 30–32; Knowlton, *Pepperell's Progress*, App. 23.
[17] Harriet Martineau, *Society in America* (2 vols., New York: Saunders and Otley, 1837), II, 140.

the strike at Lowell in February, 1834. These sporadic and generally unsuccessful protests found some echo in the labor press of the time, where the long hours and the wages of less than two cents an hour were bitterly condemned.[18] On the other hand, at least before the forties, most operatives expected to return to the farm after a few years of factory work and so tended to regard their factory work as an exciting and stimulating experience. Surely they were a remarkable group of women, these New England farm girl operatives of the early nineteenth century. While their brothers sailed before the mast seeking adventure on the seven seas or studied for the ministry at country colleges like Dartmouth, Williams, and Amherst, or sought their fortunes in Boston, New York, or the West, they created a unique chapter in American labor history. Despite long hours they formed improvement circles which met evenings, often at a local church, where they studied French or wrote articles for their own literary magazines. Though working a seventy-hour week, they attended the lyceum of an evening to hear a series of lectures by Ralph Waldo Emerson on historical biography or a religious discourse by Professor A. P. Peabody of Harvard University.[19]

LABOR MOVEMENT 1840–1860: REFORMS

The great reform movements which characterized the 1840's provided in part a natural refuge for those who had seen their hopes of great things from the political action of labor or from labor unions disappear in the acute depression of the late thirties. But the ebullient spirit of the "fabulous forties" was a manifestation of other more general influences: the great humanitarian movement which agitated Europe as well as the United States; a spirit of adolescent enthusiasm which seemed to possess Americans as they came to realize their great growth and magnificent future prospects; and, finally and somewhat paradoxically, a shrinking from reality, an attempt to flee from the immediate and less attractive results of the revolution in transportation and industry.

These influences, whether the result of youthful idealism or a retreat from reality, led to a mass impulse to embrace magic nostrums for social ills, to a pathetic eagerness to adopt even the most bizarre

18 See Bertha Monica Stearns, "Early Factory Magazines in New England," *Journal of Economic and Business History*, II, No. 4 (August, 1930), 685–705; Allan MacDonald, "Lowell: A Commercial Utopia," *New England Quarterly*, X, No. 1 (March, 1937), 37–62.

19 *Mind amongst the Spindles*, p. xv; Robinson, *Loom and Spindle*, pp. 74–75.

short cuts to Utopia. So New England intellectuals found refuge in the mists of transcendentalism and contemplation of the soul and the oversoul. The new woman sought emancipation by appearing in bloomers, and faddists in every city took up with mesmerism, phrenology, or phrenomagnetism. Perhaps most logical of all were the Millerites, who having set the hour and day for their escape from the problems of this world, disposed of their worldly possessions, and, garbed in ascension robes, assembled ready for the Second Coming and the triumphant flight to a heavenly Utopia.

Most affected by these enthusiasms of the forties was the middle class. The rising industrialists had for the most part become so enamored with the game of money-making that they wished neither to change the game nor to permit a modification of the rules. And the workers themselves, absorbed with the immediate problem of providing needed food and clothing, often had little time for utopian dreaming. Nevertheless, workingmen were appreciably affected by four of the great movements of the decade. Two of them, associationism and land reform, were clearly utopian. Two others, cooperation and especially the ten-hour movement, were closer to reality.

Associationism was based chiefly on the teachings of the Frenchman Charles Fourier, who envisaged an organization of production which would preserve the cherished harmonies of the past and at the same time avoid the alarming problems of the new industrialism. Robert Owen had established his communistic colony at New Harmony, Indiana, in the twenties, but it had lasted for only a year. Owenite as well as religious communities of one kind or another continued to be established in the United States from time to time and had considerable growth in the forties. But they had even less following among the workers than had Fourierism. In phalansteries, each containing 1,500 to 2,000 members, production was to be so organized that each person would best realize the fulfillment of his own passions or instincts and avoid monotony by flitting easily from job to job, thus, according to Fourier, gratifying the butterfly instinct. Remuneration was to go to capital, labor, and management according to a predetermined mathematical pattern.

Associationism might have caused little stir in this country had it not been for that remarkable pair of propagandists, Albert Brisbane and Horace Greeley. Brisbane, a wealthy young American, while studying in Europe during the thirties, came under the influence of Fourier's teachings and discovered what was to him a revolutionary idea—that manual labor, instead of being a curse inflicted on man since Adam's fall, was honorable and, under proper conditions, could be made delightful and attractive. After returning to the United States, Brisbane converted the publisher of the New York *Tribune*, Horace Greeley, to associationism, and in 1842 he began contributing a column on Fourierism to Greeley's paper. Other writers soon joined the movement, and several journals were published solely to spread the Fourierist doctrine. Almost at once a group of enthusiasts established the first Fourierist community, the Sylvania Phalanx, in western Pennsylvania, and before the decade was over at least thirty-four phalansteries had been set up at different places across the country from Massachusetts to Wisconsin. Most of them lasted less than two years, and all had disappeared by 1860. Agriculture was the chief occupation in most Fourierist settlements, but in one, that at Northampton, Massachusetts, silk manufacture became the central activity. Though but few workingmen actually became members of Fourierist communities, the associationist leaders were for a time able to secure much favorable attention from labor groups, with the result that to some extent the attention of workers was diverted from other and generally more feasible programs.[20]

The prophets of land reform, the chief of whom was George Henry Evans, competed with the associationists for the attention of the workers during the forties. Evans's Utopia stressed the need for equal distribution of property in land and envisaged the establishment of more or less self-sufficient communities, "rural republican townships," where farmer-craftsmen would produce and exchange their products in simple harmony. Both Fourierism and land reform therefore represent attempts to discard the whole transportation revolution by setting up self-sufficing communities not dependent on canals or railroads. In fact, the two utopias are so essentially similar that one is tempted to assert that their chief difference was one of vocabulary. But there were some important contrasts. Whereas the Fourierists expected private persons to furnish the capital and the phalansteries to flourish as commercial ventures needing only a charter of incorporation from the state, the land reformers placed their hope on political action, recognizing that private capital would

[20] See, for example, Ware, *The Industrial Worker, 1804–1860*, Chap. 11; Foner, *History of the Labor Movement in the United States*, pp. 170–178; Horace Greeley, *Recollections of a Busy Life* (New York: J. B. Ford and Company, 1868), Chaps. 19 and 20; Alice Eaton McBee, "From Utopia to Florence: The Story of a Transcendentalist Community in Northampton, Mass., 1830–1852," *Smith College Studies in History*, XXXII (1947), Chap. 2; Arthur Eugene Bestor, Jr., *Backwoods Utopias* (Philadelphia: University Press, 1950).

probably be antagonized by some of their more egalitarian proposals.

With their slogan of "Vote yourself a farm" and under the able leadership of Evans, who had been active in labor politics in the Jacksonian era, the land reform group managed to attract much attention during the mid-forties and at times to capture control of the groping workingmen's organizations. Evans's dogmatic insistence that land reform should be the first aim of labor rather than cooperatives, the ten-hour movements, or trade-union activity tended further to becloud the already confused thinking of labor groups. Though it achieved a few local political triumphs, the movement largely disappeared in the early fifties or in watered-down form became merely an agitation for free public lands for actual settlers.[21]

A third movement of the time, the formation of cooperative societies—both producers' and consumers'—was much more an actual working-class movement than the two just considered. A number of producers' cooperative ventures had sprung up during the thirties, particularly in Philadelphia and vicinity, but had disappeared in the hard times beginning in 1837. In the forties a new and much more vigorous movement for self-employment arose. Lynn shoemakers and New York City seamstresses organized cooperative ventures as early as 1845, but the movement for producers' cooperation really began to take hold in 1848, when the iron molders of Cincinnati organized a successful shop. During the following three or four years, producers' cooperatives sprang up in many parts of the country, often as the aftermath of unsuccessful strikes. Molders at Wheeling, Virginia, and Steubenville, Ohio, and at Pittsburgh and Sharon, Pennsylvania, imitated the Cincinnati workmen, and the tailors in Boston organized a cooperative workshop which employed thirty or forty men and showed a net profit at the end of the first year. The movement seems to have spread most rapidly in New York City, where by 1851 producers' cooperatives had been formed among tailors, shirt sewers, bakers, shoemakers, carpenters, and others.

Involving many more people than producers' cooperation was the movement for consumers' cooperation, which, getting started in 1845, reached its peak in 1852–1853 and, at least in New England, must be regarded as a major reform movement. In the fifteen years before the Civil War more than eight hundred consumers' cooperative societies, or protective unions as they were called, were organized.

[21] Ware, *The Industrial Worker, 1840–1860*, Chap. 12; Helene Sara Zahler, *Eastern Workingmen and National Land Policy, 1829–1862* (No. 7 of Columbia University *Studies in the History of American Agriculture*, New York: Columbia University Press, 1941), *passim*.

THE EMERGENCE OF THE WAGE EARNER

Most of the cooperative retail stores were members of the New England Protective Union, which through its Central Agency did much of the buying. Some notion of the magnitude of the business done by 1852 can be gained from the fact that in that year the value of purchases made by the Central Agency exceeded one million dollars, the total trade of the retail stores being estimated at four million dollars. At least thirty to forty thousand persons were members of protective societies, and many more were familiar with the movement and purchased goods at the cooperative stores.

The rapid growth of consumers' cooperatives was aided by the associationists, who gave this movement their blessing in the belief that it might be an important first step which would lead to the establishment of genuine phalansteries. To the workmen the protective societies made a twofold appeal: the philosophy of cooperation seemed to many to offer a possible escape from the growing threat of industrialism; and the possibility of buying goods at low prices was of immediate and practical interest to workers, many of whom found their wages rising less rapidly than prices.

The enthusiasm for cooperation reached its peak in the early fifties and then declined rather rapidly, relatively few cooperative ventures surviving beyond 1860. Many reasons have been suggested for the failure of cooperatives to strike deep roots at this time. The tendency of Americans to be on the move from place to place and the nonhomogeneous character of the urban population, especially as immigration increased after 1846, created conditions fundamentally unfavorable for the growth of local societies. Consumers' and producers' societies shared two serious weaknesses: they were practically always seriously starved for capital; and they found great difficulty in securing able and responsible managerial talent. In addition, consumers' cooperatives in New England got into serious trouble by permitting credit accounts, and their coordinating agency, the New England Protective Union, was torn by internal dissension which apparently arose from personal rivalries for power.[22]

Finally, there was the movement for the shorter working day. In 1830 workingmen commonly worked about 12½ hours a day. Thirty years later most skilled mechanics and common laborers had achieved the 10-hour day, and even factory workers averaged 11 hours or perhaps a little less. This great reduction of hours was brought about by

[22] Edwin C. Rozwenc, *Cooperatives Come to America: The History of the Protective Union Store Movement, 1845–1867* (Mount Vernon, Ia.: Hawkeye-Record Press, 1941), *passim;* Ware, *The Industrial Worker, 1840–1860,* Chap. 13.

agitation which had been begun in the Jacksonian years, became a strong working-class movement during the forties, and received considerable help from middle-class leaders and politicians during the fifties.

Against bitter opposition from conservative groups, President Van Buren had decreed the general 10-hour day for federal employees in 1840. By that time many skilled workmen had already achieved this goal, though for the most part their efforts had been unsuccessful in New England. In the forties the 10-hour movement spread throughout the country and especially among the factory workers, many of whom worked from 12 to 14 hours a day. The workers demanded this reduction not only because the excessively long hours led to too great physical exhaustion, but also because they believed time for study and public affairs was necessary in order that they might become better citizens. Workingmen believed that they should suffer no reduction of pay with the shorter hours, but employers generally contended not only that wages must be reduced if hours were shortened but also that the shorter hours were undesirable per se because they would expose the workers to unaccustomed temptations and lead inevitably to drunkenness and vice.

The 10-hour movement grew rapidly in New England and especially in Massachusetts during the early forties. The factory girls of Lowell and the mechanics of Fall River were leaders in the agitation, which up to 1844 was confined largely to protests in workers' publications and the circulation of petitions requesting legislative relief. But in October of that year was held at Boston the first New England Convention. This meeting, representing workers from many parts of New England, strongly urged 10-hour legislation. Meetings were held in following years to 1848. Though this association ordinarily spoke out for a reduction of working hours, its effectiveness was lessened by the utopian leaders who seized control of the annual conventions to promote their schemes.

Elsewhere also the 10-hour agitation was a favorite cause with the workers. In the Pittsburgh cotton mills the female workers struck in an unsuccessful attempt to control their hours in 1843 and again in 1845. In 1848 the women operatives of western Pennsylvania succeeded, after a bitter strike involving some violence, in forcing a 10-hour day, but they had to agree to a 16 per cent wage reduction. Female operatives in New England mills also attempted walkouts to force shorter hours but were not successful.

The agitation, especially the petitions and political pressures brought upon the legislatures, was not entirely without result, and a number of states passed 10-hour legislation: New Hampshire in 1847, and Pennsylvania, Maine, New Jersey, Ohio, and Rhode Island by 1853. These laws were generally regarded as a fraud by the workers. They certainly did not force the 10-hour working day, for each law had an escape clause which made it possible for the employer and employee to "agree" on longer working hours. In Massachusetts the workers refused to accept such empty legislation. All they were able to secure were repeated legislative investigations which, though actually bringing some of the facts to light through the testimony of workers, resulted in weak reports and no action. Laws were passed by a number of states regulating child labor and requiring school attendance, but they appear to have meant little, for almost no effort was made to enforce them.

The struggle for the 10-hour day petered out in the latter forties and when revived in 1852 was, at least in New England where so many of the factory workers were now foreigners, less a movement of the workers themselves than of middle-class reformers and politicians. Conventions were again held, petitions were circulated, and some political support was recruited, but little progress was made toward effective state legislation limiting hours for adults. However, in actual fact some progress was made toward reducing hours. Skilled mechanics throughout the country and now even in Massachusetts were able to force the 10-hour day largely through strikes or union action. And, finally yielding to popular pressure, many of the great mills in such places as Lowell and Salem reduced the hours of their operatives to 11 a day, but the 10-hour day for these workers was not realized until after 1860.[23]

LABOR MOVEMENT 1840–1860: TRADE UNIONS [24]

The trade-union movement took on new life in the early fifties, but it should not be supposed that unions were unimportant throughout the previous decade. Though they had largely died out in the disturbed period following the panic of 1837, they began to reappear

[23] Abbott, Women in Industry, pp. 343–344; Alba M. Edwards, "The Labor Legislation of Connecticut," Publications of the American Economic Association, 3d series, VIII (1907), 2–13; Foner, History of the Labor Movement in the United States, Chap. 11; Ware, The Industrial Worker, 1840–1860, Chaps. 8, 9; Burdine, "Governmental Regulation of Industry in Massachusetts, 1776–1860," pp. 144–151.
[24] Commons and associates, History of Labour in the United States, Vol. 1, Chap. 7; Ware, The Industrial Worker, 1840–1860, Chaps. 14, 15; Foner, History of the Labor Movement, Chap. 12.

in the early forties. Even at the depths of the depression in 1840, small and often weak associations of craftsmen were formed in the larger seaboard cities. Among those organizing were the bookbinders, blacksmiths, tailors, stonecutters, and house carpenters. The widespread union movement of the thirties did not immediately return, although as the decade advanced the union movement did grow generally stronger. It gained most when business conditions were improving but tended to slump badly during periods of unemployment. The emphasis which writers have placed on the utopian theories prevalent during the forties, the attention almost inevitably given to such leaders as Greeley and Evans and to such experiments as Brook Farm and the North American Phalanx, and finally the natural tendency to notice such much advertised gatherings as the World Conventions and Industrial Conferences, have not infrequently obscured the basic importance of the craft unions during this era.

In 1843–1844 and again in 1846–1847 strikes were common in nearly every American city and the number of local craft unions greatly increased. In the spring of 1850 a major revival of trade unionism got under way and by 1853–1854 had reached full tide, with skilled workers in all the eastern cities organized and conducting an unprecedented number of strikes. A single issue of a New York newspaper might note as many as twenty-five or thirty strikes, and in other eastern cities the number of strikes was almost as great. But though many of the unions had strengthened their treasuries and developed stronger fighting organizations than ever before, they were for the most part still too weak to survive periods of serious unemployment. The business recession of late 1854 caused the disappearance of many unions, as did also that of 1857. But some survived and others reappeared after each depression, so that in 1860 unions were to be found among the skilled craftsmen in most American cities.

The period of this study closes with the greatest strike in American history before the Civil War. On February 22, 1860, the shoemakers in Lynn and Natick, Massachusetts, struck for higher wages, and sent representatives to the other shoe towns of eastern Massachusetts, New Hampshire, and Maine, calling upon the men and women workers in the industry not only to walk out for higher wages but to form mechanics' associations and to insist upon union recognition. The strike spread to practically the whole shoemaking area of New England and involved possibly as many as twenty-five towns and twenty thousand workers. Women shocked conservatives by parading in a great demonstration in Lynn, the workers pledged themselves to abstain from intoxicating beverages and to conduct themselves resolutely but in orderly fashion, and preachers and even some businessmen sympathized with the strikers in Lynn when Boston police were brought in on the plea of keeping order. Within a few weeks most of the employers granted the wage demands, and in a few places they also agreed to recognize the union.

Superficially the union history of the period 1840–1860 may not seem to differ from that of the previous twenty-year period. The unions were still for the most part local, weak, and with an undisciplined membership. They flourished during years of prosperity and melted away during depressions. Political action and the strike were used as circumstances dictated. Attempts were made, as in the earlier period, to form city centrals or city industrial congresses, as they were called in the latter forties and early fifties. But for the most part these attempts at federation were even less effective than the similar ventures of the thirties, for almost without exception they fell promptly under the dominance of one reform group or another.

Somewhat more successful were the attempts to re-establish national trade unions in order to match national unions with nation-wide markets. First to be organized on a national scale were the printers, who held their first annual convention in 1852 with delegates present from twelve cities. Eight or nine other important national unions were formed by 1857, but the panic of that year wiped out all but three—the National Typographical Union founded in 1852, the Hat Finishers' National Association founded in 1854, and the Journeymen Stone Cutters Association founded in 1855. A few others, including the National Union of Iron Molders with William H. Sylvis as the outstanding leader, appeared between 1857 and the Civil War.[25] But none were very strong and most did little more than hold national conventions and pass resolutions.

Despite these surface similarities, the labor movement was in these years undergoing fundamental changes of enduring importance. In the first place, two influences, hardly more than hinted at before 1840, became increasingly important—the factory system and increased immigration. Both of these tended to retard the develop-

---

[25] The early struggles to form the molders' union are dealt with in Jonathan Grossman, *William Sylvis, Pioneer of American Labor* (New York: Columbia University Press, 1945), pp. 22–44.

ment of American trade unions and a self-conscious labor movement. The new factory workers were without traditions of organization and consisted to a large extent of women and children and recent immigrants, groups especially difficult to organize into strong unions even under the most favorable conditions. As the factory system of textile manufacture expanded in the late forties and during the fifties, the operatives were increasingly provided from a greatly augmented flow of European immigrants. Complaints of competition from foreign workers had been voiced in Fall River as early as 1842 and in Rhode Island a few years later. By 1860 Irish immigrants supplied more than half the operatives in this part of New England. Industrial workers had been so scarce in Boston previous to 1845 as definitely to discourage manufacturing development. The large numbers of Irish who crowded into that city in the following fifteen years created such a surplus of cheap labor that manufacturing was tremendously stimulated.[26]

In Lowell and other textile cities the Waltham or boardinghouse system crumbled under the impact of increasing numbers of foreign-born operatives. In order to find farm girl recruits for the expanding factories at Lowell, Dover, and Chicopee, the agents, who secured them on a commission basis and brought them back to the mills in long black wagons, were required to range farther and farther. By the late forties they were seeking them as far away as upstate New York and Canada. At first the Irish had been used only as common laborers and roustabouts in these New England mill towns, but beginning in the early forties these newcomers, both the men and the women, increasingly took their places as operatives of the textile machines. With this change many of the distinctive features of the Waltham system rapidly disappeared.

During this decade competition grew in the industry, wages were lowered, and the girls were forced to tend more machines. The "young ladies of the loom" now began to surrender their dream of culture. They either returned to their New England farm homes or, resigning themselves to a continuing status as wage earners, remained to labor alongside the Irish and, toward the very end of the period, the French Canadians, both of whom worked willingly for extremely low wages and demanded few cultural advantages. The change was not unacceptable to the employers, who were apparently satisfied to be able

[26] Smith, *The Cotton-Textile Industry of Fall River, Massachusetts*, p. 36; Oscar Handlin, *Boston's Immigrants, 1790–1865* (Vol. L of *Harvard Historical Studies*, Cambridge: Harvard University Press, 1941), pp. 80–89; Clark, *History of Manufactures in the United States*, I, 398–399.

to substitute tractable foreigners for the increasingly independent and militant daughters of New England.[27]

Actually the effect of the great increase of foreign born after 1846 was mixed. Insofar as this tremendous immigration added to the shifting character of the labor population, and especially as these new workers were Irish whose background was almost completely rural and untouched by trade unions, these newcomers definitely retarded the development of strong unions in the United States. On the other hand, the skilled workers coming in, especially from England and Germany, brought with them a relatively mature tradition of labor organization. Thus what beginnings there were of a labor movement among the textile mill workers were largely due to English operatives who had been union members before they emigrated. Even more important were the Germans, many of whom brought with them not only craft skills but strong traditions of craft loyalty and some experience of union organization. In cities with large numbers of German immigrants like New York and St. Louis, the Germans formed their own unions. At times this served to split and hence weaken the workers in their negotiations with their employers. But though language and custom were a barrier, native and immigrant groups were usually forced into cooperation by the very identity of their interests and the impossibility of one succeeding without the other.

Many of the Germans coming over, following the failure of the 1848 revolutions, brought with them an interest in the liberal and radical doctrines then current in Europe. They furnished many able reform and trade-union leaders, most of whom had been considerably influenced by the doctrines of Marx and Engels. The most vigorous and orthodox of these leaders was Joseph Weydemeyer, who acted as a sort of press agent for Marx in the United States during the fifties and attempted to spread Marxian socialism by writing and speaking. He appears to have met with but slight success even among his fellow immigrants.[28]

Certain trends in union development which had appeared much earlier became intensified in the fifties. The benevolent and fraternal aspects now tended completely to disappear. More and more workers

[27] Shlakman, "Economic History of a Factory Town: A Study of Chicopee, Massachusetts," pp. 138–150; Ware, *The Industrial Worker, 1840–1860*, pp. 81–82; Ware, *The Early New England Cotton Manufacture*, Chap. 8; Merrill, "Mill Town on the Merrimack," pp. 29–31.
[28] Karl Obermann, *Joseph Weydemeyer, Pioneer of American Socialism* (New York: International Publishers, 1947), *passim*.

lost their old attitude of independent craftsmen on their way to becoming masters and recognized their status as that of wage earners
who would probably remain such. With this change in outlook, the
skilled workers tended to take their union membership with a new
seriousness and to establish stronger and more permanent organizations. Thus a new emphasis was placed upon building up war chests
for strike purposes; more important, the notion of union recognition
and collective bargaining agreements began to be emphasized. By
about 1854, many unions in the leading cities had abandoned the old
custom of agreements with individual employers for general agreements with employers as a group. Though still weak and with many
battles still to fight, the American trade-union movement was already
showing signs of development which were to become typical in the
latter decades of the century.

COMMON LABORERS AND SLAVES

The transportation revolution greatly increased the number of
persons engaged in constructing and operating transportation facilities. During the Napoleonic Wars, the number of sailors employed
had rapidly expanded, and this growth continued into subsequent
decades as packets, clippers, and steamships transformed ocean
transportation. In 1836 the number of seamen employed in foreign
and domestic shipping was estimated to be 63,000. Though a sprink-
ling of foreign-born sailors had always formed a part of the crew
of most United States ships, the chief source of recruits for the sailing
fleet, at least until some time in the thirties, had been native sons,
mostly from New England. For about two decades following 1815,
ambitious Yankee lads, many from Cape Cod and Maine, sought adventure as well as a fair living by going to sea where, like their sisters who entered the factories at Waltham and Lowell, they displayed
a zeal for knowledge quite without precedent in their calling.

Beginning in the thirties, the character of the crews began to
change as the number of foreigners increased rapidly, despite the
law of 1817 requiring that at least two thirds of the crews on American vessels be American citizens. Wages were low and conditions of
living grew so hard that fewer and fewer New England farm boys
were attracted to the sea. Perhaps no class of workers was treated
worse or had fewer rights, not excepting Negro slaves. In fact, like
the slaves they were subject to involuntary servitude, for if seamen
left their ship they could be, and often were, arrested and imprisoned.

Finally, masters of vessels resorted increasingly to crimping and shanghaiing, so that by the fifties the finest ships in the world, the American clippers, carried a motley crew in which a few experienced sailors, mostly foreign, worked with drunks and waterside loafers who were "recruited" just as the ship was about to sail.[29]

The construction of the turnpikes, canals, and railroads created an unprecedented demand for unskilled workers. Some of this labor, especially that for turnpike construction, was supplied by nearby farmers, but to a very large extent the canals and railroads were built by immigrants. As early as 1818, more than 3,000 persons were employed in building the Erie Canal. Nearly 2,000 workers were employed in the northern section of the Ohio Canal in 1825. In 1828, 5,000 men were employed in constructing the Pennsylvania canals, and in the following year over 3,100 were working for the Chesapeake and Ohio Canal Company, which advertised abroad that it needed 10,000 workers. Over 3,000 men were employed in constructing the James River and Kanawha Canal in 1837. Wages were often low, working and living conditions almost incredibly bad, and fevers and sickness of all kinds prevalent. Wages were reported to average $10 to $12 a month in 1831, though they often fell to $5 in the winter or even less. Mathew Carey shows in detail how most canal laborers could not earn enough to provide a wife and two children with a minimum of subsistence even though the wife were fortunate enough to earn fifty cents a week. He estimates that of the canal workers "five per cent return to their families in the winter, with broken constitutions, by fevers and agues, one half of whom are carried off to an untimely grave." [30] When the Erie Canal was being dug through the Montezuma marshes near Syracuse in the summer of 1819, a thousand men were reported ill with fevers and many died. An outbreak of cholera disrupted work on the Chesapeake and Ohio Canal in 1832. This project, as well as most others, was slowed up for at least part of nearly every summer because of sickness among the laborers.[31]

[29] Daniel Drake, *Hospitals in the Valley of the Mississippi, House Document* No. 195, 24 Cong., 1 Sess. (1836), p. 3; Albion, *Square-Riggers on Schedule*, pp. 140–173; Morison, *The Maritime History of Massachusetts, 1783–1860*, pp. 256–260, 352–357; Clark, *The Clipper Ship Era*, pp. 119–133; Richard B. Morris, "Labor Controls in Maryland in the Nineteenth Century," *Journal of Southern History*, XIV, No. 3 (August, 1948), 393–394.

[30] Mathew Carey, *Address to the Wealthy of the Land* (Philadelphia: W. F. Geddes, 1831), p. 6, fn.

[31] *Ibid.*, pp. 4–10; Ernest Ludlow Bogart, *Internal Improvements and State Debt in Ohio* (New York: Longmans, Green and Co., 1924), pp. 25, 38; Gates, *The Illinois Central Rail-road and Its Colonization Work*, pp. 89, 94–98; Sanderlin, *The Great*

Outbreaks of violence were not uncommon among the men who, before the days of the steam shovel and the bulldozer, dug the canals and made the cuts and fills for the railroads. On the Chesapeake and Ohio Canal project, after weeks of grueling labor and of living in "miserable and filthy shanties," Irishmen from Cork turned on their countrymen, the "far-downs," and relieved the strain and tedium of their lives by a bloody battle fought with helves, clubs, and guns.[32] More often, however, their resentment turned against their employers as they sought to remedy some special injustice or to secure better wages or working conditions. In the summer of 1831 several hundred construction laborers on the Baltimore and Ohio Railroad, being deprived of their wages by an absconding contractor, rioted and destroyed property.[33] Sometimes little or no violence occurred, the men merely refusing to work until wage or other concessions were made. In any case, they seem to have gained little from their sporadic revolts, for police or troops moved in wherever difficulties arose. Federal troops were called out in 1834 to quell rioting by the Chesapeake and Ohio workers.[34] In another instance, in 1855, leaders of construction workers who struck against the North Eastern Railroad in South Carolina were sentenced to prison for two months and fined $5 each because they "inspired terror," though no actual violence seems to have been done. They were seeking by group action to secure an increase of wages from $1.00 to $1.25 a day.[35]

In addition to the men employed in constructing internal improvements, even more were engaged in operating the rapidly expanding facilities for internal commerce. Occupational statistics before the Civil War are seriously defective. Certainly many men were engaged in road transportation; more than a thousand wagoners must have been employed between Philadelphia and Pittsburgh at the beginning of this period. Of course, canals and railroads decreased the need for long-distance road transportation, but at the same time this short haul business greatly increased, especially at

National Project, pp. 71–79; William Forbes Adams, Ireland and Irish Emigration to the New World from 1815 to the Famine (New Haven: Yale University Press, 1932), pp. 151, 187; Harlow, Old Towpaths, pp. 53–54, 73; Benjamin W. McCready, On the Influence of Trades, Professions, and Occupations in the United States, in the Production of Disease (Baltimore: The Johns Hopkins Press, 1943), pp. 38–40.

[32] Niles' Weekly Register, XLV (February 1, 1834), 382, XLVII (December 6, 1834), 218.

[33] Ibid., XL (July 16, 1831), 338–339.

[34] Ibid., XLV (February 1, 1834), 282–283.

[35] Morris, "Labor Militancy in the Old South," pp. 33–34. Also see Sanderlin, The Great National Project, pp. 116–122.

important river, canal, and railroad centers. Thus, an analysis of the occupational statistics for Boston in 1850 shows more than 1,300 persons classified as drivers, teamsters, truckmen, and cabmen.[36] Thousands of men operated boats on rivers, lakes, and canals, the total number so employed being estimated at 43,000 in 1836. On the Ohio-Mississippi River system a hardy race of rivermen developed who took the flatboats through to New Orleans, despite the fact that, because of accidents and sickness, on the average only three out of a boat crew of five returned. They also manned the keelboats on the long and backbreaking upriver trip, and later they made up the crews of the river steamers. By 1851 the number of men employed on steamboats on the Ohio-Mississippi River system was reported to be nearly 15,000. Other thousands worked on the canals where drivers had to be satisfied with $8 to $12, although steersmen might receive as high as $20 a month. Harlow estimates the working population on the Erie Canal in the early forties as about 25,000, and he notes a missionary source to the effect that there were possibly about 10,000 boys employed on New York canals in 1848.[37] The United States Census reported the number of men employed by the railroads as 4,831 in 1850 and 36,567 in 1860.[38] These totals are undoubtedly too small, for records supplied by Massachusetts railroads in 1860 show 6,268 railroad employees in that state alone.[39]

Of other early laborers—those in fishing, logging, and mining—there is little to be said; indeed, not a great deal is known. Almost the same is true for the large number of women—native women, but also, especially after 1830, many Irish and German girls, who were the domestic and personal servants of the period. By 1860 they numbered over 1,000,000 persons.[40] Finally, brief note may be taken of the casual laborers in the cities, those whom Mathew Carey refers to as "hod men, wood pilers, scavengers, and various other classes." These men, who probably did not average much more than 200 days' employment a year and whose wages, one builder reported, fell as

[36] Drake, *Hospitals in the Valley of the Mississippi*, p. 2; Baldwin, *The Keelboat Age on Western Waters*, p. 184; Handlin, *Boston's Immigrants, 1790–1865*, p. 238.

[37] Hunter, *Steamboats on the Western Rivers*, p. 443; Baldwin, *The Keelboat Age on Western Waters*, pp. 85–91; Harlow, *Old Towpaths*, pp. 328–329.

[38] J. D. B. De Bow, *Statistical View of the United States: A Compendium of the Seventh Census* (Washington: Beverley Tucker, 1854), p. 127; *Eighth Census of the United States: Population*, pp. 672–673.

[39] Computed from *Returns of the Railroad Corporations in Massachusetts, 1860, Public Document* No. 46 (Boston: 1861).

[40] P. K. Whelpton, "Occupational Groups in the United States, 1820–1920," *Journal of the American Statistical Association*, XXI, No. 155 (September, 1926), 339.

low as 25 cents a day in the winter and 62.5 cents in the summer, were probably least well off of all workingmen in the period.[41]

The Negroes of the North lived largely in the cities, where, for the most part, they constituted but a small part of the population. In Philadelphia they were more numerous than elsewhere and in 1820 possibly included in their number a majority of the artisans of that city. Changing economic conditions and the bitter opposition of white workers had greatly reduced the number of skilled colored workers by the middle thirties. In northern cities generally, few Negroes became skilled workers. Natives as well as foreigners typically refused to work with them or to permit them to join their unions. Though a small number of the more fortunate were caterers, coachmen, or waiters, most were common laborers competing for the lowest-paid jobs. They were seldom able to secure employment in such occupations as stevedoring, except when brought in by employers to break a strike of white workers.[42]

In the slave states, much of the nonagricultural work was done by slaves. Practically everywhere they were the chief source of common labor: as construction hands on roads, canals, and railroads; as roustabouts, longshoremen, and scavengers in the towns and cities; and as workers in mines and forests and on fishing boats. But some white laborers and a few free Negroes were to be found in all of these fields, though in most regions they were a small minority. Some white laborers were used in the mines, and gangs of Irishmen were frequently hired for construction work in Maryland and Virginia. In fact, they were sometimes preferred where work was dangerous or a great deal of sickness prevailed because, not involving a capital investment, the Irishmen were more expendable than the slaves. Most of the domestic servants in the towns were female slaves, although a small number of white females also were so employed.[43]

Both slave labor and free labor were in common use in southern factories. Often a factory employed both black and white laborers. In Richmond, the slaves working chiefly in tobacco, cotton, iron, and

[41] Carey, *Address to the Wealthy of the Land*, p. 7.

[42] Charles Lionel Franklin, *The Negro Labor Unionist of New York* (No. 420 of *Studies in History, Economics and Public Law,* New York: Columbia University Press, 1936), pp. 22–23, 28–29, 60–61; Joseph G. Rayback, "The American Workingman and the Antislavery Crusade," *Journal of Economic History,* III, No. 2 (November, 1943), 156–157.

[43] Ulrich Bonnell Phillips, *American Negro Slavery* (New York: D. Appleton and Company, 1918), pp. 402–404; Luther Porter Jackson, *Free Negro Labor and Property Holding in Virginia, 1830–1860* (New York: D. Appleton–Century Company, 1942), pp. 54–64.

flour factories and mills numbered 5,667 in 1846 and 6,326 in 1856. During the fifties tobacco factories in Richmond and Petersburg increased their slave labor force but also now added free blacks and, in 1858, white women. They were influenced, no doubt, by the rapidly increasing price of slaves. At least where the employer owned his own slaves, the workers became an overhead cost instead of a variable one, as under the wage system. This consideration, as well as others, has led one student to conclude that the use of slave labor on an extensive scale in factories was proving an unprofitable venture by the middle fifties.[44]

As artisans and in the skilled trades generally, slaves were used throughout the South, although in most areas and for most trades the whites were apparently the more numerous. The larger plantations often had their own slave craftsmen—carpenters, blacksmiths, wheelwrights, and the like. In the towns, slaves were to be found in nearly every trade. At Charleston in 1848, coopers, carpenters, and masons and bricklayers were the most numerous of the craftsmen.[45]

Factory owners, building contractors, and master craftsmen in some cases owned their own workers; but in most cases they hired at least part of their slave help. Even domestic servants appear frequently to have been secured by hire rather than owned. Rates of hire on an annual basis for prime Negro men in Georgia were reported at a peak of $150 in 1818 and ranged from $100 to $125 in the twenties. Prices were higher in the following decade, but down again in the depressed forties, with the Georgia Railroad paying only $75 or less for section hands. In the fifties rates advanced sharply, reaching their highest point in 1860. In that year first-rate hands employed in Petersburg tobacco factories brought $225, and a blacksmith in Louisiana cost $430 for the year.[46]

The practice became common in the cities of permitting slaves who were skilled workers or especially able or dependable to hire themselves out or even to conduct a small business such as huckstering. In such cases, the master required a regular share of the man's

[44] Phillips, *American Negro Slavery*, p. 410; Jackson, *Free Negro Labor and Property Holding in Virginia, 1830–1860*, pp. 52–64; Foner, *History of the Labor Movement in the United States*, pp. 259–261; Linden, "Repercussions of Manufacturing in the Ante-Bellum South," pp. 326–327.

[45] Phillips, *American Negro Slavery*, pp. 402–414; *A Statistical View of the United States: A Compendium of the Seventh Census*, pp. 80–81; John Hope Franklin, *The Free Negro in North Carolina, 1790–1860* (Chapel Hill: The University of North Carolina Press, 1943), Chap. 4, *passim*.

[46] Phillips, *American Negro Slavery*, pp. 405–410; Sterling D. Spero and Abram L. Harris, *The Black Worker: The Negro and the Labor Movement* (New York: Columbia University Press, 1931), pp. 5–6.

earnings. Sometimes a slave who was on his own hired other slaves to work for him. Such arrangements constituted a curious combination of the slave and the wage systems. White labor resented this competition and sought, ineffectively, to have it curtailed.[47] Sometimes a slave working in this way was able to get enough money ahead to buy his own freedom. But the black's new status might, economically at least, be worse than it was as a slave, for free Negroes were subjected to many special restrictions not only as to the occupations in which they could engage but also as to place of residence and freedom of movement. Both white laborers and slaveowners resented the competition of the free blacks. Nevertheless, a few, especially in Louisiana, where there was relatively less prejudice against them, rose to some prominence in business and even in the professions.[48]

THE LEVEL OF LIVING

An important statistical study bearing on the level of living was made by Alvin Hansen in 1925. Utilizing chiefly data from the *Aldrich Report,* he computed an annual index of real wage rates, daily and weekly, which fluctuated greatly with price changes from year to year but averaged by decades showed the following movement 1820–1860: [49]

Years	Index (1913 = 100)
1820–1829	46
1830–1839	48
1840–1849	56
1850–1859	52

According to this study the rate of real wages advanced from the twenties through the thirties and forties, declined in the fifties, and registered a net increase of 13 per cent from the first to the last decade. It must be emphasized that these indices are for *rates* of wages, and that they are based on generally unsatisfactory data. A more recent study based on elaborate price investigations not avail-

[47] Spero and Harris, *The Black Worker,* pp. 5–9; Phillips, *American Negro Slavery,* pp. 411–415; Commons and others, *A Documentary History of American Industrial Society,* II, 360–368.
[48] Phillips, *American Negro Slavery,* Chap. 21; *A Statistical View of the United States: A Compendium of the Seventh Census,* pp. 80–81; Jackson, *Free Negro Labor and Property Holding in Virginia, 1830–1860, passim;* Franklin, *The Free Negro in North Carolina, 1790–1860, passim.*
[49] Hansen, "Factors Affecting the Trend of Real Wages," pp. 32–33. The *Aldrich Report* referred to here and elsewhere in this chapter is an elaborate historical study entitled *Wholesale Prices, Wages, and Transportation.* It is published as *Senate Report* 1394, Pts. 1–4, 52 Cong., 2 Sess. (1893)

able to Hansen indicates a similar trend. An index (1900 = 100) of real wage rates for fully employed workers, constructed by Jürgen Kuczynski, shows the index to be 69 for 1821–1826, 72 for the two periods 1827–1834 and 1835–1842, 83 for 1843–1848, and 79 for 1849–1858. Bearing in mind the increased employment in industry of women and children over this period, it may be doubted if average rates of real wages for all workers advanced as much as the index shows.[50] Moreover, lacking employment information, no generalization can be made as to the average annual real earnings of workers. Moreover, the data upon which this index is erected are none too satisfactory. The whole subject needs further study.

The chief advances in wage rates went to the skilled workmen, especially those in the building trades in the larger cities. Scattered information for common labor shows no clear trend for the three decades before 1860. Rates of more than a dollar a day were certainly unusual before the fifties, but at least in New York they rose above that figure during some of the more prosperous years of that decade. Using the *Aldrich Report,* Edith Abbott computed an average annual wage for unskilled labor from 1840, which fluctuates from 79 to 95 cents a day from 1840 through 1853 and from $1.00 to $1.03 during the next seven years. Applying Hansen's index of the cost of living to these data brings out no clear trend in real wages for this group of workers but does show the purchasing power of a day's work to have been slightly higher in 1860 than in 1840. Sharing least in the improvements of the times were the factory workers. In fact, many of them must have been worse off in the fifties than in the previous decade. Spinners who averaged about $2.73 a week in 1842 received $2.85 in 1860. This was an increase of 5 per cent in money wages but a decrease in purchasing power because prices were nearly 10 per cent higher in 1860. Factory weavers were in general even worse off, for their money wages actually declined substantially over the same period.[51]

As these figures suggest, the level of living varied greatly among different groups of workers. Certainly many received incomes too small to permit decent living conditions. In 1851 Greeley's New York

[50] Jürgen Kuczynski, *A Short History of Labor Conditions under Industrial Capitalism* (3 vols., London: Frederick Muller, Ltd., 1943), II, 20–24, 40–44.

[51] Sixteenth Annual Report of the Bureau of Statistics of Labor, Commonwealth of Massachusetts (1885), pp. 238–312; Ware, *The Industrial Worker, 1840–1860,* Chaps. 4 and 7; Edith Abbott, "The Wages of Unskilled Labor in the United States, 1850–1900," *Journal of Political Economy,* XIII, No. 3 (1905), 321–367, and *Women in Industry,* App. C, pp. 365–373; *History of Wages in the United States and Colonial Times to 1928, Bulletin* No. 499, United States Bureau of Labor Statistics (Washington: 1929), pp. 253–254, 363–415. See also the *Aldrich Report, passim.*

Tribune published the following minimum budget for a worker's family of five: [52]

BUDGET FOR FAMILY OF FIVE FOR ONE WEEK

Barrel of flour, $5.00, will last eight weeks $0.62½
Sugar, 4 lbs. at 8 cents a pound .... .32
Butter, 2 lbs. at 31½ cents a pound .... .62½
Milk, 2 cents a day .... .14
Butcher's meat, 2 lbs. beef a day at 10¢ a lb. 1.40
Potatoes, ½ bushel .... .50
Coffee and tea .... .25
Candle light .... .14
Fuel, 3 tons of coal per annum, $15.00; charcoal, chips, matches, etc., $5.00
    per annum .... .40
Salt, pepper, vinegar, starch, soap, soda, yeast, cheese, eggs .... .40
Household articles, wear and tear .... .25
Rent 3.00
Bed Clothes .... .20
Clothing 2.00
Newspapers .... .12
    Total $10.37

Concerning this budget, which was submitted by John Campbell of Philadelphia, the contributor wrote: ". . . have I made the working-man's comforts too high? Where is the money to pay for amusements, for ice-creams, his puddings, his trips on Sunday up or down the river in order to get some fresh air, to pay the doctor or apothecary, to pay for pew rent in the church, to purchase books, musical instruments?" [53] That the *Tribune* budget figures were not unreasonably low seems to be indicated by the fact that two years later the conservative New York *Times* published a workingman's budget which assumed fifty weeks' employment a year at $12 a week. Prices had advanced appreciably since 1851 and the *Times* budget was for a family of four, whereas the *Tribune* provided for a family of five.[54]

Very few workmen received incomes equal to the figure assumed by the *Tribune*. Foremen and a few of the highly skilled, especially those in the relatively well paid building trades, apparently had a comfortable living if their employment were continuous. Thus some blacksmiths, engineers, machinists, masons, and carpenters received $12.00 a week or even more in 1851, although others received as much as two or three dollars less. But many highly skilled workers received less than this minimum budget. Top wages for German smiths

[52] *Daily Tribune*, New York, May 27, 1851, p. 7.
[53] *Ibid.*; Ware, *The Industrial Worker, 1840–1860*, p. 33.
[54] New York *Times*, November 8, 1853.

and wheelwrights in New York City were $7.50 a week in 1850.[55] In 1851, according to the *Aldrich Report,* some house painters received $10.25 a week, but others as low as $9.00 or even less. The wages of common labor and factory workers fell far below the budget figure. Few common laborers made more than a few cents over $1.00 a day, or about $6.00 a week, when steadily employed. Some received appreciably less. Weekly wages for factory workers were also extremely low. For men, wages of $5.00 to $6.00 were common, and for women $3.00 to $4.00.[56] By 1860 few workmen even in such skilled trades as watchmaking and printing were earning as much as $12.00 a week.[57]

Among the most poorly paid were the women needle workers. Toiling 14 to 18 hours a day in their own squalid homes under cheerless and unsanitary conditions, they were often fortunate to earn 14 to 25 cents a day or $.84 to $1.50 a week. Even these small earnings were not always actually paid, for employers, taking advantage of the weak bargaining position of the women, would sometimes withhold all or part of the wages due. In 1830, when the cost of living was only slightly higher than later in 1851, Mathew Carey estimated that in Boston, New York, Philadelphia, and Baltimore eighteen to twenty thousand women, many of them widows with small children, earned their living at such occupations as seamstresses, shoebinders, and so on, and that, generously estimated, their annual income was $55.00. Of this, $26.00 went for lodging and at least $6.50 for fuel, leaving $22.50 a year for all other expenses, including food and clothing.[58]

With wages of many workers falling so seriously below what was regarded as a minimum level, it is not surprising that pauperism and conditions of extreme urban poverty became a serious problem during this entire period. The situation was appreciably aggravated by the increasing flow of immigrants, some of whom, despite legislation designed to prevent it, were dumped on American shores directly from poorhouses abroad, and others arrived so ill or infirm that, unable to care for themselves, they had to be moved almost directly from shipboard to poorhouse. As early as 1819 New York City had a

[55] Commons and associates, *History of Labour in the United States,* I, 583.

[56] Based chiefly on quotations in the *Aldrich Report;* wages cited are from Ware, *The Industrial Worker, 1840–1860,* Chaps. 4 and 7; Commons and associates, *History of Labour in the United States,* I, 581–586, 610–611.

[57] *Hunt's Merchants' Magazine,* XLII (June, 1860), 750.

[58] Mathew Carey, *To the Editor of the New York Daily Sentinel,* pamphlet, March 22, 1830, pp. 1–4. See also by the same author, *Address to the Wealthy of the Land,* pp. 10–16.

Society for the Prevention of Pauperism, which was deploring the increasing number of indigent in that city.[59] Even in the supposedly prosperous early thirties, Mathew Carey, writing of conditions among the poor in Philadelphia, reported wages extremely low and living conditions revoltingly bad. In one part of the city he found 55 families, including 253 persons, living in 30 tenements without toilet facilities of any kind.[60]

Boston, New York, Philadelphia, and Baltimore struggled with the problems of an increasing number of paupers and living conditions in crowded tenements which were almost unbelievably squalid. In 1846, the number of paupers in New York City was declared to be over 50,000, or one person in every seven.[61] The state of New York, which showed a population of 3,831,590 according to the federal census of 1860, relieved or supported over 228,000 town and country paupers in 1859. Living conditions among the very poor almost beggar description. Thousands in New York and Boston lived crowded into dark unsanitary basements and subbasements. Handlin writes of these underground dwellings of the very poor Irish immigrants in Boston: [62]

. . . Built entirely beneath the street level, they enjoyed no light or air save that which dribbled in through the door leading down, by rickety steps, from the sidewalk above. Innocent of the most rudimentary plumbing, some normally held two or three feet of water, and all were subject to periodic floods and frequent inundations by the backwater of drains at high tide. Above all, there was little space. Some windowless vaults no more than eighteen feet square and five feet high held fourteen humans.

The New York City cellar population had been reduced from about 29,000 in 1850 to 20,000 in 1859, but more than half the city's population was reported living under extremely bad slum conditions.[63]

Finally, even the level of living described above was never secure from the threat of unemployment. This insecurity of the worker in his new status as a wage earner arose not only from the seasonal and

[59] Marcus Lee Hansen, The Atlantic Migration, 1607–1860 (Cambridge: Harvard University Press, 1940), p. 108.
[60] Mathew Carey, Letters on the Living Condition of the Poor (2nd edition), pp. 16–17.
[61] Evans in The Working Man's Advocate, July 6, 1844, cited by Ware, The Industrial Worker, 1840–1860, p. 27.
[62] Handlin, Boston's Immigrants, 1790–1865, p. 113. Reproduced by permission of Harvard University Press.
[63] Martin, The Standard of Living in 1860, pp. 170–173, 287–290; Handlin, Boston's Immigrants, 1790–1865, pp. 93–124; McMaster, A History of the People of the United States, VI, 82–85.

intermittent character of much employment and the technological unemployment inevitable in a period of phenomenally rapid change in industry, but also from the repeated crises and depressions which temporarily paralyzed commerce and closed down many industrial plants. Thanks to the transportation revolution, the great cities housed increasing thousands of workers who were completely divorced from the land. Unlike those who toiled under the rural domestic system or in the small shops and factories common in small towns and semirural communities, the city worker could seldom resort to part-time subsistence farming or turn his hand temporarily to fishing or woodcutting. Moreover, low wages left practically no margin for savings, and welfare agencies, even where they had appeared, were unprepared to provide adequate unemployment relief.[64]

Though repeated minor business fluctuations often caused much distress, the workers' difficulties are best illustrated by the major crises.[65] In 1837 a New York mob, following a meeting called to protest unemployment and the high cost of living, broke open warehouses in the "flour riots" of that year. Horace Greeley declared in January, 1838, that of the 200,000 wage earners in New York City, about one third were wholly or in large part unemployed, and that not less than 10,000 persons were in "utter and hopeless distress." Soup kitchens were established. Proposals for work relief projects did not materialize, but some help was furnished from public soup kitchens, which provided to many of those worst off some bread and a pint of soup a day.[66]

Similar conditions prevailed in the great crisis of 1857. Unemployment was widespread but, as for all the early crises, accurate statistics are not available. Estimates of those unemployed in New York City vary from 25,000 to 100,000. Approximately 20,000 were said to be out of work in Chicago and 3,000 in Louisville, Kentucky.[67] Expenditures for poor relief were increased, though they remained inadequate. According to poor law statistics for the state of New York, more than 260,000 persons, about 7.4 per cent of the total

[64] Leah Hannah Feder, *Unemployment Relief in Periods of Depression* (New York: Russell Sage Foundation, 1936), Chap. 2; David M. Schneider, *The History of Public Welfare in New York State, 1609–1866* (Chicago: The University of Chicago Press, 1938), pp. 179 ff.

[65] For a discussion of business fluctuations, see Chapter XV.

[66] Schneider, *The History of Public Welfare in New York State, 1609–1866*, pp. 272–278; Reginald Charles McGrane, *The Panic of 1837* (Chicago: The University of Chicago Press, 1924), pp. 130–136.

[67] Feder, *Unemployment Relief in Periods of Depression*, p. 19; George W. Van Vleck, *The Panic of 1857* (New York: Columbia University Press, 1943), pp. 75–76; Schneider, *The History of Public Welfare in New York State, 1609–1866*, p. 273.

population, were granted some relief in 1858. About half of these were in New York City.[68] Protest meetings, the largest of which attracted as many as 10,000 men and women, were reported in New York City and Philadelphia; 40,000 unemployed workers were reported as having paraded in New York City, mobs did some damage, and on one occasion there, federal troops were called out to protect the Subtreasury Building in Wall Street.[69] Of course, many of those on relief were not employable persons, and at least some who participated in protest meetings were employed workers. Yet the numbers involved give some indication of the insecurity of the worker's position and his dissatisfaction with the level of living he was able to secure.

On balance, were workers "better off" generally in 1860 than they had been in 1815? Had the immediate results of the transportation revolution and the beginnings of the industrial revolution raised the level of living for most laboring men? No clear answer can be given. Cost of living indices indicate some improvement, perhaps, in the quantity of food and clothing available, but they are too imperfect statistically to warrant much confidence. But even though the statistics were above reproach, the query would remain unanswered, for in addition to the *quantitative* changes taking place between 1815 and 1860, there were accompanying alterations in modes of living and making a living, changes in the social, intellectual, religious, technological, political, and economic environment—in short, *qualitative* changes of the most fundamental kind, involving every aspect of man's life.

[68] Schneider, *The History of Public Welfare in New York State, 1609–1866*, p. 278.
[69] *Ibid.*, pp. 272–278; Van Vleck, *The Panic of 1857*, pp. 75–76; McMaster, *A History of the People of the United States, 1883–1913*, VIII, 287–288, 296–301.

CHAPTER XIV

Financial Institutions

ESTABLISHMENT OF THE SECOND BANK OF THE UNITED STATES

EARLY in January, 1817, the second Bank of the United States opened for business in Carpenter's Hall, Philadelphia. The first Bank of the United States had occupied this building when it had ceased functioning as a national bank six years before. It was appropriate that the second Bank should begin at the old stand for, although the new Bank was considerably larger, its organization was substantially similar to that of its predecessor. And it was an augury of the Bank's future financial power that in 1821 it should move from the modest quarters where the old Bank had quietly performed its functions to a sumptuous temple built for its occupancy and designed by William Strickland on the lines of the Parthenon in Athens.

Why should the same political party and even the same persons who had refused to recharter the Bank of the United States in 1811 have voted to establish an even larger institution in 1816? The chief reason was the war, a war which had been fought on the military front with an inefficiency and ineptness rivaled only by the administration of the government's finances. Congress failed to pass adequate tax laws until the war was nearly over, and the administration of the Treasury under William Jones and George W. Campbell proved almost incredibly bad. By the beginning of 1815 the credit of the United States had fallen to its lowest ebb since the founding of the federal government. The War Department was pressed to find enough money to pay a bill for $30, and the Treasury could not secure funds to meet the interest on that part of the public debt held in New England. Banks had multiplied during the war and greatly extended their note issues. By the autumn of 1814 most banks outside New

England had been forced to suspend specie payments. The currency consisted of a flood of bank notes circulating at varying discounts and of increasing quantities of United States treasury notes, also of fluctuating value. Prices had risen to the highest point for the whole nineteenth century.

As one means of bringing some order out of this chaos and assisting the government in financing the war, sentiment grew for the re-establishment of a national bank. Leaders in promoting this movement were John Jacob Astor, David Parish, Stephen Girard, and other wealthy merchants whose patriotic sentiments were in happy accord with their personal financial interests. They believed the establishment of a national bank would aid the government to finance the war and would also raise the price of government stock, in which they were heavy investors. With their approval President James Madison appointed and the Senate confirmed in October, 1814, Alexander Dallas as Secretary of the Treasury. An able Philadelphia lawyer known to favor the establishment of a national bank, he and Senator John C. Calhoun were most active in drawing up plans for the new bank charter. After a great deal of debate and compromise, a bill satisfactory to the administration was prepared. President Madison overcame his constitutional scruples and, despite the efforts of Daniel Webster and John Randolph, who led two opposition groups, the act was passed and approved by the President April 10, 1816.[1]

The charter provided that the capital of the second Bank of the United States should be $35,000,000,[2] of which one fifth was to be subscribed by the federal government. The shareholders were to elect twenty directors of the Bank, and the President of the United States was to appoint five. The new institution could issue notes in denominations of not less than $5, which would be accepted by the government in payment for taxes; the total value of notes issued was not to exceed $35,000,000. Notes must be redeemed in specie or the Bank was to forfeit 12 per cent per annum on any part of its circulation not so redeemed. The federal government was to receive $1,500,000 from the Bank in return for the charter privilege.

[1] Raymond Walters, Jr., *Alexander James Dallas* (Philadelphia: University of Pennsylvania, 1943), pp. 186–217, and "The Origins of the Second Bank of the United States," *Journal of Political Economy*, LIII, No. 2 (June, 1945), 115–131; Burton Alva Konkle, *Thomas Willing* (Philadelphia: University of Pennsylvania Press, 1937), pp. 207–209; Kenneth L. Brown, "Stephen Girard, Promoter of the Second Bank of the United States," *Journal of Economic History*, II, No. 2 (November, 1942), 125–148.

[2] For a detailed comparison of the charters of the two banks see Davis R. Dewey, *The Second Bank of the United States* (National Monetary Commission, Vol. IV, No. 2, Senate Document No. 571, 61 Cong., 2 Sess., Washington: Government Printing Office, 1910), pp. 163–175.

Although earlier proponents had looked upon it mainly as a means of aiding the Treasury in financing the war, the chief objects sought by the Bank's sponsors in 1816 were to force the state banks to resume specie payments and to establish a satisfactory national currency. In view of later controversies as to the Bank's function, it is worth noting that Secretary Dallas regarded it as much more than merely a giant commercial bank. He wrote to Calhoun on December 24, 1815: ". . . it is not an institution created for the purposes of commerce and profit alone, but more for the purposes of national policy, as an auxiliary in the exercise of some of the highest powers of the Government." [3] Nevertheless many, including some government officials and officers of the bank, did not hold this broad view but appear to have regarded the Bank as merely a great financial institution chiefly obligated to make profits for its stockholders.

Unfortunately the Bank got off to a bad start and soon headed into serious trouble. President Madison and Secretary Dallas had agreed that the Bank should be under strong Republican influence and succeeded in having William Jones, an ardent Republican politician of Philadelphia, elected as the first president. That this man who during the war had shown notorious incompetence as the Secretary of the Navy and the Acting Secretary of the Treasury should have been chosen for this key position is difficult to understand. Apparently his contemporaries regarded him as a loyal political follower and a trustworthy individual. At any rate, he at once adopted a loose, expansionist policy for the Bank, seemingly with the purpose of maximizing profits for stockholders. Branches were promptly opened up in the more important commercial cities of the country, and loans and discounts were rapidly expanded, especially in these branch offices.

Trouble first developed in the branches, which were subjected to little or no control by the parent institution. The Baltimore branch from the beginning fell into the hands of a ring of unscrupulous operators who easily robbed it of more than a million dollars before they were exposed and the branch was forced into the hands of a receiver. Most of the members of the board of directors of the parent bank speculated in the bank's own stock, and Jones himself accepted a present of $18,000 which his officers "earned" for him by this kind of speculation. Whether in the branches or in the main office in Philadelphia, wherever one might look, there was malfeasance, misfea-

[3] Ralph C. H. Catterall, *The Second Bank of the United States* (Chicago: The University of Chicago Press, 1903), p. 19, fn. 5.

sance, or merely administrative incompetence. In January, 1819, President Jones was permitted to resign. In less than two years he had built up the greatest financial institution in the country and brought it perilously close to bankruptcy.[4]

The Bank was saved by Langdon Cheves, a respected South Carolina lawyer, who became president in 1819 and remained in that position until 1823. Brought in to restore the financial soundness of the institution, he promptly and decisively tightened the administration, for the first time brought the branches under control, sharply reduced the loans outstanding, and began action to collect on the defaulted debts of both state banks and individuals. By 1820 the notes of the Bank in circulation had been reduced to about $3,500,000 from over $8,000,000 in 1818, and loans to $31,401,000 from $41,181,-000. Cheves's methods promptly returned the Bank to financial soundness, but his conservative policies resulted in reduced dividends to stockholders. As a result, the stockholders became restive and within a few years felt that the Bank needed more creative leadership. Cheves resigned in the fall of 1823, to be succeeded by Nicholas Biddle, a brilliant, strong-willed man, thirty-seven years old, who had already made a favorable reputation for himself as a writer, as a member of the Pennsylvania senate, and as one of the government directors of the Bank.

Long before Biddle took over, the Bank had aroused the bitter hostility of the state banks. In fact, the Bank of the United States could do little which did not evoke the jealousy of these local institutions. When Jones, following a policy of expansion, had established branches in western and southern cities, the local banks protested against such competition and secured state legislation designed to curtail the operations of the branches. Two states, Indiana (1816) and Illinois (1818), prohibited by provisions in their state constitutions the establishment within their borders of any but state banks. Other states, including Maryland, Tennessee, Georgia, North Carolina, Kentucky, and Ohio, levied taxes upon the branches of the Bank of the United States which would have driven the Bank from the states imposing them had it not been for favorable action by the United States Supreme Court. In one of his most famous decisions, McCulloch v. Maryland,[5] Chief Justice John Marshall in 1819 declared that the second Bank of the United States was a necessary

[4] William M. Gouge, *A Short History of Paper-Money and Banking in the United States* (New York: B. & S. Collins, 1835), pp. 31–32; Catterall, *The Second Bank of the United States,* Chap. 2.

[5] 4 Wheaton 316 (1819).

and proper instrument of the United States government for carrying out its fiscal operations and was therefore constitutional. Moreover, he found the attempt of the state of Maryland to tax the Bank unconstitutional because, said he, if this were permitted then a state might ". . . tax all the means employed by the government, to an excess which would defeat all the ends of government." [6]

When, under Cheves, the Bank reversed its expansionist policy and called in its loans, the hostility of state banks was even greater than when its operations were being extended. The drastic contraction was accompanied by a wave of failures which meant bankruptcy for many business firms and financial institutions, especially in the West and South. With many of the state banks which survived this debacle the second Bank of the United States was often on bad terms chiefly because it reasonably enough insisted that the state banks should not remain for long periods indebted to it for huge sums. Under Jones the branch of the Bank of the United States in Savannah, Georgia, had extended credits of about $200,000 to the state banks of that city. The Bank of the United States under Cheves tried to reduce this debt and made an extremely liberal offer permitting the state banks to use $100,000 without interest if they paid all in excess of that amount. The state banks, in repelling this offer, attacked the Bank of the United States as a "mammoth" come to destroy them. Not until the dispute had gone to the Supreme Court was the Bank of the United States able to enforce its claims against the Savannah banks.[7]

THE BANK UNDER BIDDLE

Under Biddle the Bank soon began cautiously to expand its operations and to assume a position of strength and prosperity. Growth, relatively moderate through 1828, accelerated thereafter. Bank notes issued averaged $4,500,000 in 1823, $11,000,000 in 1828, and $19,-000,000 in 1831. Emphasis was placed on commercial loans of short maturity and transactions in domestic bills of exchange greatly increased. These latter totaled nearly $9,000,000 in 1823, rose to $21,-400,000 in 1828, and reached $49,500,000 by 1831. At the same time, earnings increased greatly. By 1828 a surplus of $1,500,000 had been accumulated, and in the latter half of that year the Bank began pay-

[6] 4 Wheaton 432 (1819). For his almost equally well known decision declaring the Ohio tax unconstitutional, see Osborn v. Bank of the United States, 9 Wheaton 738 (1824).

[7] Osborn v. Bank of the United States, 9 Wheaton 738 (1824) and United States Bank v. Planters' Bank, 9 Wheaton 904 (1824).

ing dividends at the rate of 7 per cent per annum, a rate which was continued as long as the Bank retained its federal charter.[8]

The operations of the Bank had at last reached a scale sufficient to permit it to perform the dominant role for which it had been originally cast. From the beginning it had proved an efficient fiscal agent for the federal government, not only acting as a safe depository for Treasury funds but also successfully transferring these funds from one part of the country to another and meeting government drafts for disbursement at each of its branches. For the years 1816–1827, the Bank transferred funds for the United States Treasury, averaging about $28,000,000 a year at a saving estimated at more than $1,000,000. Moreover, the government secured necessary funds quickly and economically from the Bank of the United States whenever borrowing was necessary.[9]

In the second place, the Bank of the United States helped to create a sound national currency both by maintaining specie payments on its own notes and by bringing pressure on the state banks to do the same. During the presidency of Jones the Bank had attempted to accept the notes of all of its branches at face value whenever they were presented at any of its offices. This practice could not be continued, for western branches expanded their note issues to meet the need for exchange on the East, with the result that the eastern branches accepting these notes were stripped of their specie. The policy was changed, therefore, to one which honored bank notes at face value in specie only at Philadelphia and at the branch of issue; at a distance from the place of issue notes circulated at a small discount, usually less than 1 per cent. This discount was much less than ordinarily existed before the Bank was established, but it did give critics of the Bank an opportunity to accuse it of not maintaining a uniform currency.[10]

On February 20, 1817, after the Bank of the United States had been in actual operation for only a little over a month, it was able to get the state banks to resume specie payments, and from that time on, assisted by the United States Treasury, it did much to force state banks to remain on a specie-paying basis. However, it must be noted that during much of the period 1818–1822 many of these local institutions were only nominally on a specie basis. Many could not

[8] Catterall, *The Second Bank of the United States*, pp. 504–512.

[9] *Ibid.*, Chap. 19.

[10] Albert Gallatin, "Considerations on the Currency and Banking System of the United States" (1831) reprinted in Adams, ed., *The Writings of Albert Gallatin*, 3 vols., III, 340–346; Catterall, *The Second Bank of the United States*, Chap. 17.

possibly have paid out specie if the Bank of the United States had insisted on their meeting their outstanding obligations to it. As times improved in the late twenties and early thirties, most state banks were better able to meet specie demands, but even under favorable circumstances their issues typically provided a satisfactory currency for local purposes only. At any distance from the place of issue their notes usually circulated at a considerable discount.[11]

In the third place, the Bank of the United States helped to make credit and currency more abundant in the West and the South. To a very considerable extent the Bank of the United States built up its business outside the eastern states on the basis of capital raised in those states. In doing this it aided the frontier areas by helping to provide both the capital and the currency needed for their development.[12]

In modern practice the chief function of a central bank is to act as a bankers' bank, guiding its activities not for the purpose of making a profit but so as to forward the public good by discouraging tendencies to overexpansion in the economy, and giving prompt relief to banks and business in times of crisis. This central banking function, insofar as it was carried out between 1815 and 1824, was chiefly performed not by the Bank of the United States but by the United States Treasury. Before 1819 it was the Treasury which was most vigorous in attempting to restore specie payments and restrict credit expansion. And in the period of severe liquidation which followed, it was again the United States Treasury, not the Bank of the United States, which through specie deposits went to the aid of hard-pressed state banks and helped them to weather the storm.[13]

After 1823, under the direction of Biddle, the Bank of the United States for a time began to assume real leadership as a central bank. In the sharp crisis of 1825, Biddle, seeing trouble coming, placed a restraining influence on credit expansion by the banking community, and, after the bubble burst, during the period of severe liquidation he wisely expanded loans, thus easing the impact of the crisis on the financial and business community. Again in 1828 he took somewhat similar action to protect the public interest. But in 1832, when he finally acted to check the overexpansion of business at that time, his position was basically changed, for he was then putting a check on an inflationary movement to which the Bank itself had unwisely

[11] Catterall, *The Second Bank of the United States*, Chap. 18.
[12] *Ibid.*, Chap. 17; Dewey, *The Second Bank of the United States*, pp. 234–241.
[13] Esther Rogoff Taus, *Central Banking Functions of the United States Treasury, 1789–1941* (New York: Columbia University Press, 1943), pp. 27–32.

lent assistance. Later, in 1833–1834, Biddle used the tremendous power of the Bank against the general good to force a disastrous contraction on the business community in his effort to win his personal war with President Jackson.[14]

Unwisely, as later events proved, Biddle applied for recharter of the second Bank of the United States in January, 1832, four years before the existing charter expired. He thus threw down the gauge of battle to Andrew Jackson in an election year. Congress passed a bill to continue the Bank with little change, and President Jackson vetoed it, July 10, 1832. The veto message declared the Bank unconstitutional and condemned it as a device for giving financial advantage and power to a small and irresponsible group of wealthy persons living in eastern cities and even in foreign countries. Biddle threw the whole influence of the Bank against the election of Jackson, who was re-elected by an overwhelming vote.

But this did not end the feud over the Bank. Suspicious of it and vindictive as well, Jackson believed that the government should promptly begin to remove its deposits from the Bank and force it to prepare to wind up its affairs. William J. Duane had been made Secretary of the Treasury early in 1833, soon after Louis McLane left that position to head the State Department. When Duane, a puppet of McLane, who was very close to the bank group, refused to accept the removal policy, Jackson forced his resignation and appointed his Attorney General, Roger B. Taney, Secretary of the Treasury. Taney definitely opposed the Bank and had been one of the chief drafters of the President's veto message on the bill to recharter. Actually no appreciable shift of existing deposits took place but, as new government receipts came in, they were simply placed on deposit in state banks.

Nicholas Biddle, no less headstrong than Jackson and still hoping to force the recharter of his bank, fought back. Believing that only a drastic credit contraction would convince the administration and the country of the folly of permitting the Bank to go out of existence, Biddle began in August, 1833, to curtail credit and, despite growing protests even from favorably disposed business and banking leaders, continued the curtailment to September, 1834. To William Appleton, president of the branch of the Bank of the United States

---

[14] *Ibid.*, pp. 32–34; Fritz Redlich, *The Molding of American Banking, Men and Ideas* (New York: Hafner Publishing Company, 1947), pp. 135–145; Catterall, *The Second Bank of the United States*, pp. 106–107, 142.

at Boston, he wrote in January, 1834: "Nothing but the evidence of suffering abroad will produce any effect in Congress." [15] And early in the next month he wrote to another correspondent: ". . . all the other Banks and all the merchants may break, but the Bank of the United States shall not break." [16] Biddle succeeded in precipitating a crisis which in 1834 forced discount rates as high as 18 to 36 per cent and brought great distress to the business community. But by this display of power he ruined whatever chances the Bank may have had for recharter. Many business leaders, even those of conservative tendencies, now turned against that institution. Biddle had demonstrated what his enemies had charged: the ability of the Bank to affect the whole course of business of the country and his willingness to use that power to the public detriment and his own personal advantage.[17]

The subsequent history of the Bank is quickly told. Having failed in 1834 to frighten the government into giving it a new charter, the Bank reversed its policy and greatly expanded its operations. On the expiration of its United States charter in 1836 it secured a new one from the state of Pennsylvania and continued in business until October, 1839, when, caught with greatly overextended loans, it found itself in serious financial straits and forced to suspend specie payments. It never really recovered and was forced into liquidation in 1841.[18]

It is worth noting that this controversy over the Bank still goes on, with students disagreeing in their evaluation of the relative positions of Biddle and Jackson on the recharter of the bank, their conclusions apparently being affected chiefly by their general economic philosophy. Those who are most conscious of the direct disadvantages to business of a chaotic system of state banking, who emphasize the need for a rational over-all banking control, who believe that a prime concern of government should be to aid business in order that it may prosper and thereby, presumably, benefit everyone—in short, all those who in general hold to a Hamiltonian philosophy tend to side

[15] Reginald C. McGrane, ed., *The Correspondence of Nicholas Biddle* (Boston: Houghton Mifflin Company, 1919), p. 219.

[16] *Ibid.*, p. 221.

[17] Catterall, *The Second Bank of the United States*, pp. 326–331, 338–345; Schlesinger, *The Age of Jackson*, Chap. 9.

[18] See McGrane, *The Panic of 1837*, Chaps. 3 and 6; Bray Hammond, "Jackson, Biddle, and the Bank of the United States," *Journal of Economic History*, VII, No. 1 (May, 1947), 11–23; and by the same author, "The Chestnut Street Raid on Wall Street, 1839," *Quarterly Journal of Economics*, LXI (August, 1947), 605–618.

with Biddle and the Bank. Staunchly defending the personal integrity of Biddle, they tend to agree with Catterall's statement in his classic work on *The Second Bank of the United States* that

Jackson and his supporters committed an offense against the nation when they destroyed the bank. The magnitude and enormity of that offense can only be faintly realized, but one is certainly justified in saying that few greater enormities are chargeable to politicians than the destruction of the Bank of the United States.[19]

In the other camp are those who, following a Jeffersonian approach, condemn the Bank and believe Jackson's instincts essentially sound in opposing it. Passing over the disputes as to the character of the chief protagonists, they emphasize the fact that the charter gave tremendous economic privileges and irresponsible power to a small group of wealthy men. They conclude that, lacking a truly national bank, it was better to suffer the disadvantages of unsatisfactory state banking than to risk a system which placed almost unlimited power in the hands of individuals not directly responsible to the people. This attitude is well summarized by George Bancroft, who wrote in 1834:

the great objection in my mind to the continuance of the present United States Bank, lies in its tendency to promote extreme inequalities in point of fortune. It forms a part of a system of deadly hostility to the policy which the country should pursue. The Bank is possessed of immense resources and commanding influence; its sympathies, its prejudices, are all on the side of wealth; and its existence has a steady and evident tendency to conciliate for capital a controlling influence on legislation.[20]

It is surely important to remember that the modern theory of central banking has taken a long time to develop; neither Biddle nor Jackson should be condemned for possessing only a hazy understanding of central banking principles more than one hundred years ago. Because the abuses of uncontrolled state banking became notorious or because the second Bank of the United States operated at times *somewhat like* a modern central bank, it does not follow that Biddle's bank should have been rechartered. Though often assumed to be, the second Bank of the United States was not an acceptable central bank from the standpoint of either the state banks or the public.

In the first place, it must not be supposed that the antagonism of the state banks to the Bank of the United States arose merely because of its pressure on them to observe sound practices and maintain specie payments. Actually the Bank of the United States was a great

---

[19] Catterall, *The Second Bank of the United States*, p. 476.
[20] Letter addressed to Messrs. S. Judd, J. H. Flint, S. Parsons, C. Clark, C. P. Huntington, and J. Wright, printed in the Boston *Courier*, October 23, 1834.

commercial bank which sought profits from commercial loans just as did other banks. In the competition for business, the federal charter gave the Bank of the United States an overwhelming advantage which it might use, if it wished, against a competitor institution.

In the second place, and again contrary to what is often assumed, the charter of the second Bank of the United States did not create a responsible central bank. Neither by law, as in the case of the Federal Reserve, nor by tradition, as was formerly the case for the Bank of England, was the Bank of the United States an agent with clearly recognizable public responsibilities. In fact, Biddle made considerable point of his independence. It is true, as shown above, that especially in 1825 and 1828 he did conduct the operations of the Bank for the benefit of the entire economy. Later, however, he did not hesitate to use the whole weight of the Bank, both economic and political, for his own personal advantage. No nation today would long tolerate such a situation, nor did the government or the people deem it endurable in Jackson's day.

Finally, expressions of fear of the note-issuing powers of the national bank cannot be dismissed cavalierly as mere demagoguery or as the result of ignorant objections by hard-money fanatics. Similar objections to the operations of the Bank of England had been recently voiced by such respectable English authorities as David Ricardo and his followers.[21]

EXPERIMENTS IN STATE BANKING

"It has come to be a proverb," wrote Amasa Walker in 1857, "that banks never originate with those who have money to lend, but with those who wish to borrow." [22] This should be remembered, along with the additional fact that, once in operation, privately owned banks were conducted primarily to gain profits for their officers and owners and not directly for any public purpose, such as providing a safe and uniform currency or stabilizing business. When these considerations are borne in mind and when it is remembered that state legislatures and the public were generally very ill-informed on the

[21] For recent statements favorable to the Bank, see Hammond, "Jackson, Biddle, and the Bank of the United States," pp. 1–23, and a review of Schlesinger's *Age of Jackson* in *Journal of Economic History*, VI (May, 1946), 79–84. For a viewpoint favorable to Jackson, see Claude G. Bowers, *The Party Battles of the Jackson Period* (Boston: Houghton Mifflin Company, 1922), Chaps. 8, 9, 11, and 12; Schlesinger, *The Age of Jackson*, Chaps. 7–9; Carl Brent Swisher, *Roger B. Taney* (New York: The Macmillan Company, 1935), Chaps. 9–13.

[22] Amasa Walker, *The Nature and Uses of Money and Mixed Currency, with a History of the Wickaboag Bank* (Boston: Crosby, Nichols & Company, 1857), p. 53.

whole subject, it is not surprising to find during the period before the Civil War much bad banking as well as unwise and ineffective legislation on banks. A great deal of experimentation was carried on in the various states, and gradually a number of systems evolved which, proving useful, were widely copied by other states. Following brief mention of some of the chief weaknesses of the state banking systems, a few of the more significant state experiments are described below.

The state banks were designed primarily to make money for their owners, who ordinarily paid in but little specie on their stock purchases. Indeed, it was common practice for the stockholder to pay for at least a considerable part of his bank stock by his personal note, against which he pledged the bank stock as security. Moreover, the owners and officers expected to be favored borrowers of the bank. Of course, bank profits depended upon the bank's extending its loans and discounts, and the tendency was therefore for it to seek every means possible to achieve this end and to avoid having to pay out specie on its outstanding notes or deposit liabilities. As long as credit was expanding and no unusual demand for specie appeared, difficulties might not develop. But serious trouble almost certainly began the moment any unusual demand for specie arose. In times of general suspension the banks which could not redeem their notes in specie might not immediately go bankrupt, but their notes would circulate at a discount. A few might manage to put their affairs in shape and resume specie payments; many, unable to meet their obligations, would eventually be forced into liquidation.[23]

The so-called wildcat banks were those which went to extremes in attempting to avoid having their notes returned and exchanged for specie. Located in the deep woods where wildcats might more easily find their way than bank note holders, these banks sought to delay or prevent the return flow of their notes. But it was ordinarily not necessary to secure such great inaccessibility in order to obtain considerable advantage. As long as transportation and communication were relatively slow and no effective clearing system had developed, mere distance from the centers of commerce was a valuable asset to a bank. Thus country banks had an advantage over those in the city, and banks in the frontier area could more easily delay the return of their notes than could those in the more settled parts of the country. Some banks even hired agents to place their notes in circulation at distant points, and sometimes banks in one part of the

[23] For fluctuations in the number of banks and in bank circulation, see page 325.

country agreed to pay out the notes of those in remote areas. During the fifties, Illinois banks made a practice of placing in circulation such large quantities of the notes of Georgia banks that the Middle West became flooded with the bank paper of that southern state.[24]

One of the earliest improvements in banking appeared in New England, where the Suffolk system came into operation in the mid-twenties. Though Boston banks had been unusually successful in maintaining specie payments both during and following the War of 1812, the notes of country banks circulated in that city at discounts varying, in part at least, with their distance from Boston. The Boston banks continually found it necessary to return these notes to the banks of issue. Their messengers laden with country bank notes would present them for redemption at the bank issue, receive specie in exchange, and, having packed it in kegs, would return to Boston. But this process had to be continually repeated, for the country bank notes soon reappeared in Boston, where they tended to make up a large portion of the circulating medium. On the other hand, the notes of the Boston banks, being easily convertible into specie, quickly returned to the bank of issue.

As it was greatly to the advantage of the Boston banks to keep their own notes in circulation, they cooperated with the Suffolk Bank of Boston to establish a system, in full operation by 1825, which was primarily designed to curtail the circulation of country banks and so permit an expansion by the city banks. Under this system the Suffolk Bank made arrangements to receive country bank notes and to present them promptly at the bank of issue for specie redemption unless the country bank arranged for redemption in Boston. Under this pressure most country banks in the New England states agreed to keep deposits with the Suffolk Bank and thus ensure the prompt honoring of their notes. As a result, the discount on the notes of these country banks disappeared, and Boston merchants were largely freed of the troublesome necessity of receiving payment for goods in depreciated bank paper. The Suffolk Bank thus successfully performed one of the functions of a central bank by furnishing an effective clearing system for bank notes and holding such notes at par with specie.

The original hope of the city banks that the circulation of outside banks would be reduced was not realized. But the Suffolk Bank soon discovered that the profits arising from the deposits of the country banks more than offset the expense of operating the clearing system and so kept the plan in operation. Until the latter fifties the Suffolk

24 Pierce, *A History of Chicago*, II, 124–128.

Bank operated the system without competition. Then, beginning in 1858, a rival institution, the Bank of Mutual Redemption, which had been promoted by some of the country banks, took over part of the business. The two institutions came to terms and the system of par clearance continued to work smoothly.

Despite numerous attempts to imitate Boston's system, neither New York nor Philadelphia was able to put a very effective bank note clearing scheme into successful operation. Not until the adoption of the National Banking System in 1862 did the notes of country banks cease to circulate at a discount in those cities. A similar situation prevailed over most of the rest of the country except for Illinois and Indiana, whose state-owned banks were able to force par collection; for Louisiana, where banking outside New Orleans was done largely by branches of the New Orleans institutions; and for Cincinnati, where in 1858 a successful system similar to that of the Suffolk Bank went into operation.[25]

The safety-fund system of banking created by New York State in 1829 was designed to give greater protection to bank creditors and especially to holders of bank notes. It contained two important innovations: (1) A board of three commissioners was established, and charged with the responsibility of making quarterly inspections of the operations of each bank. This provision was much more sweeping than any previously tried in the United States. Even the charter of the second Bank of the United States, though of course permitting examination by an agent of the United States Secretary of the Treasury, made no provision for periodic examination by experts. This requirement of the New York act was very soon copied by other states and came to be regarded as an essential feature of a sound banking system. (2) As the name implies, a safety fund was built up out of which creditors of the banks could be paid if the banks failed to satisfy the holders of their notes or deposits. Each bank in the system had to contribute annually .5 per cent of its capital until the fund reached 3 per cent of the total capital of all the banks in the system. As these deposits were used to meet the liabilities of defaulting banks, the remaining members had to continue contributions until the fund was again built up to 3 per cent. On the surface the

[25] Wilfred S. Lake, "The End of the Suffolk System," *Journal of Economic History*, VII, No. 2 (November, 1947), 183–207; Davis R. Whitney, *The Suffolk Bank* (Cambridge: 1878), *passim*; Leonard C. Helderman, *National and State Banks* (Boston: Houghton Mifflin Company, 1931), pp. 29–34; Davis R. Dewey, *State Banking before the Civil War*, National Monetary Commission, IV, No. 2, *Senate Document* No. 581, 61 Cong., 2 Sess., 82–104; Redlich, *The Molding of American Banking, Men and Ideas*, pp. 71–78.

system appeared to be working well enough until 1840, when a wave of bank failures began. By 1843 the fund was in real difficulties, and in 1845 the legislature provided for a state loan to make up current deficits in the fund. No new banks were added to the safety-fund system after 1838.

The chief weakness lay in assessing contributions to the fund on the basis of bank capital instead of on note circulation. The effect was to penalize the New York City banks, whose capitals were large but whose note issues were seldom excessive. On the other hand, the country banks, whose capitals were small and who were most likely to overextend their note issue and get into trouble, made relatively small contributions to the fund and so felt little pressure to contract their note issue. In fact, the very existence of this safety fund made it dangerously easy for country banks to increase their circulation. The safety-fund provision of the New York law of 1829 was not generally copied at the time, though Vermont set up a very similar system in 1831 which continued in one form or another until after the Civil War. Michigan also adopted a safety-fund provision in 1836, but it was never of any real importance.[26]

Of the state banking laws adopted before the Civil War, the New York Free Banking Act of 1838 most influenced subsequent legislation. The National Banking System established in 1862 was largely patterned on it, and many states copied its two important features: the granting of bank charters without special legislation, and the protection of note issue by requiring the deposit of securities with a public agency. Before 1838 the state governments granted charters to banks only by special legislative acts. The privileges conferred under these charters were recognized as being semimonopolistic and of such value to the grantees that they were practically always required to make special grants or payments to the state. Moreover, high returns were often anticipated from state investments in the bank stock. Not infrequently members of the state legislature also expected to be rewarded for their favorable votes. The popular opposition to banks, including the feeling against the second Bank of the United States, was due in part at least to this special privilege aspect of banking. The attitude was well reflected in an upstate New

[26] The most detailed study is Robert E. Chaddock, *The Safety-Fund Banking System in New York, 1829–1866*, National Monetary Commission, Vol. IV, No. 2, Senate Document No. 581, 61 Cong., 2 Sess., *passim*. See also Redlich, *The Molding of American Banking, Men and Ideas*, pp. 88–95; Helderman, *National and State Banks*, pp. 11–14; Bray Hammond, "Free Banks and Corporations," *Journal of Political Economy*, XLIV, No. 2 (April, 1936), 184–209.

York petition of 1837 which stated that " 'moneyed corporations with special and exclusive privileges' were as unrepublican as titles of nobility." [27]

In adopting the Free Banking Act of 1838 the New York legislature attempted to introduce competition into the banking field, to increase the banking facilities available to the public, and at the same time to ensure the safety of note issue. The act provided that any group of citizens, upon complying with certain general conditions, should be granted a charter and permitted to carry on a banking business. Special legislation was not necessary to secure a charter, and payments no longer needed to be made either to the state or to the lawmakers. But along with this increased freedom, the act provided a new device for ensuring the safety of bank note issue. Notes were to be issued to banks by the state comptroller, but only after that official had received a deposit of approved bonds equal to the amount of the notes, or there had been deposited with him New York State real-estate mortgages to twice the value of the notes issued. It was also provided that banks not redeeming their notes in specie must pay an annual interest charge of 14 per cent to holders of such notes.

On the whole, the scheme was fairly successful in protecting bank note holders, though the original specifications as to the securities which might be deposited had to be appreciably tightened. In a period when the bonds of many states depreciated greatly in value, accepting them at par value as security for note issue did not provide adequate protection. Amendments to the law gradually limited the securities acceptable for deposit against note issue to specified bonds of the state of New York and the federal government. But the supply of bonds against which notes were authorized became so limited as to introduce an inelasticity into the note issue which was later regarded as a considerable disadvantage. Nevertheless, the system, especially as improved during the forties, gave a very high degree of protection to holders of notes of New York state banks.[28]

The success of the free banking system in New York and the widespread belief that the evils of banks could be overcome by encouraging competition among them [29] led to the wide adoption of free-

[27] Helderman, *National and State Banks*, p. 18, quoted from *Senate Documents*, 1837, Vol. I, No. 10 (January 18, 1837).

[28] See especially Redlich, *The Molding of American Banking, Men and Ideas*, Chap. 7; Helderman, *National State Banks*, pp. 14–24.

[29] On this banking theory as well as others of the time see Lloyd W. Mints, *A History of Banking Theory in Great Britain and the United States* (Chicago: The University

banking statutes in other states, not infrequently with very little or no advantage. Influenced by New York's experience, Michigan adopted a free banking law even before such legislation was passed by the Empire State. The results were disastrous, "a caricature of the New York system," says Sumner, "[which] . . . produced a swarm of small, swindling concerns." [30] In Indiana and Wisconsin free banking acts were passed in 1852 and 1853, respectively, which led to some of the worst wildcat banking of the period.

As originally passed, the New York Free Banking Act required banks to keep a specie reserve of 12.5 per cent against note issues. But this provision was repealed in 1840, and the credit for inaugurating a sound reserve requirement goes to Louisiana, which in its celebrated law of 1842 required all note and deposit liabilities to be covered—one third in specie and the remainder by short-term paper. The excellent performance of New Orleans banks during the crisis of 1857 testified to the soundness of this arrangement. In 1858 Massachusetts passed an act requiring a 15 per cent reserve against notes and deposits, and when the National Banking System was established four years later, a similar deposit requirement became a basic feature of that law.[31]

Finally, at the very time when the decentralized free banking system was becoming increasingly popular, state banks or banking systems, in large part owned and controlled by the state governments, flourished in some of the southern and western states. These centralized state banks produced no more uniform results than did other systems. One of the oldest of the state-owned and -operated institutions was the Bank of the State of South Carolina. From its organization in 1812 through the Civil War it acted as a safe and efficient fiscal agent for the state and, though dealing largely in agricultural loans, managed to remain solvent and on a specie basis even in such crisis years as 1837 and 1839. Its success appears to have been due not to any unique charter provisions but simply to an enviable record of sound and honest management.

Unlike the Bank of the State of South Carolina, which had to meet

of Chicago Press, 1945), Chaps. 8 and 9, and Harry E. Miller, *Banking Theories in the United States before 1860* (Vol. XXX of *Harvard Economic Studies,* Cambridge: Harvard University Press, 1927), *passim.*

[30] William Graham Sumner, *A History of Banking in the United States* (Vol. I in William Dodsworth, ed., *A History of Banking in All the Leading Nations,* 4 vols., New York: The Journal of Commerce and Commercial Bulletin, 1896), p. 329.

[31] Dewey, *State Banking before the Civil War,* pp. 217–224; Stephen A. Caldwell, *A Banking History of Louisiana* (No. 19 of *Louisiana State University Studies,* Baton Rouge: Louisiana State University Press, 1935), pp. 77–78.

competition from other state-chartered institutions, the second State Bank of Indiana, 1834–1857, enjoyed until 1852 a complete monopoly of banking in that state. As originally organized, it consisted of ten branches which were under the close control and supervision of a central control board. The state, in addition to owning half the stock, elected the president and kept considerable control over the institution. The charter contained a number of sound provisions. For example, it provided that each branch was liable for the debts of all the others. On the other hand, it was completely lacking in such safeguards as required specie reserves and loan limitations. Nevertheless, it was phenomenally successful at a time when political corruption was rife in the state and when most western states were operating with extremely weak and unsatisfactory banking systems. Favored by able management, it flourished from the beginning, serving as an efficient fiscal agent for the state government and giving tremendous help to farmers and merchants. When the State Bank of Indiana wound up its business following January 1, 1857, it was able to retire its circulation, meet all its obligations, and show a surplus of more than $1,000,000. In addition it had paid out annual dividends of from 11 to 22.5 per cent.[32]

On the other hand, some of the state ventures in banking brought financial ruin both to the state bank and to the state. The Bank of the State of Alabama created December 20, 1823, was one of these. Entirely owned and controlled by the state government, it became a part of a political machine. It proved very useful in securing votes for candidates, for members of the state legislature freely promised bank loans for those who gave them their votes. By 1843 more than $16,000,000 was owed to the bank, nearly half of which was found to consist of bad or doubtful debts. By 1844 this bank and all its branches had been placed in liquidation. The state debt had been increased about $11,000,000 by this banking venture, a very considerable amount, for the annual interest charge on this sum came to several times the usual cost of running the state government. Banks owned and operated by the states were also seriously unsatisfactory in Illinois, Kentucky, and Mississippi.[33]

[32] Earl Sylvester Sparks, *History and Theory of Agricultural Credit in the United States* (New York: Thomas Y. Crowell Company, 1932), pp. 98–99, 258–260; Helderman, *National and State Banks*, pp. 34–38, 46–55; Logan Esarey, *State Banking in Indiana, 1814–1873* (*Indiana University Studies*, Vol. X, No. 2, Bloomington: Indiana University, 1912), pp. 247–277. State banking monopolies were also successful in Missouri and Iowa.

[33] Helderman, *National and State Banks*, pp. 84–87; Sparks, *History and Theory of Agricultural Credit in the United States*, pp. 101–103; William O. Scroggs, "Pioneer

OTHER FINANCIAL INSTITUTIONS

The banks of issue, predominantly commercial banks, to which major attention has been given in this chapter, performed two functions of great importance: they supplied a large part of the circulating medium of the country; and they made available to business needed capital funds. Though state and local governments and sometimes even private and unauthorized corporations occasionally issued paper which was used as money, the chief institutions issuing paper money were the commercial banks. But in the performance of the second function—the provision of needed capital—the banks of issue were greatly aided by other institutions. Stocks and bonds, along with the organized agencies for dealing in them: systems of note brokerage, lotteries, savings banks, and insurance companies—all these played a part in making available the savings and credit which were essential for the great transportation and industrial development of the age. As sources of capital, credit institutions were generally much less specialized than in the twentieth century. It is true that the note-issuing banks were largely what might be designated as commercial banks, and that they specialized largely, though not exclusively, in short-term commercial loans. On the other hand, many banks of issue, especially in the West and the South, made a large share of their loans for long periods often with real estate as security. Again, although the savings banks in the decade or two before the Civil War had come to specialize in long-term obligations, especially mortgages, it may be pointed out that savings institutions often invested in the capital stock of commercial banks, and that it was not at all unusual for them to deposit funds in commercial banks and to receive interest on such deposits.

The securities issued by governmental units or the rapidly multiplying private corporations provided an increasingly important method through which savings were collected and made available for investment. And, gradually, financial institutions arose to facilitate the flotation and marketing of these securities. Even before 1815 commercial banks as well as unincorporated banks and brokerage houses aided in the marketing of securities, both public and private. This practice continued, becoming of increased importance during the early thirties, when security issues expanded greatly. Leading private banks or brokerage houses engaged in this service were Astor

Banking in Alabama," in Edwin Francis Gay, ed., *Facts and Factors in Economic History* (Cambridge: Harvard University Press, 1932), pp. 402–423.

& Sons, Brown Brothers & Co., E. W. Clark & Co., and Nevins, Townsend & Co.[34]

Paralleling this development of investment banking came the early stock exchanges, which facilitated trading in securities and provided investors with publicly announced price quotations. The first of these exchanges appeared at Philadelphia near the beginning of the century. The New York Stock Exchange was established in 1817 and soon became the chief center in the country for security transactions, although thousand-share days did not arrive until the early thirties. The Boston Stock Exchange was the only one on which industrial securities were important in the years before the Civil War.[35]

At the time when organized markets were appearing for bonds and stocks, note brokers developed a growing business in short-term commercial paper.[36] For a commission these brokers found buyers for the notes or bills of exchange of businessmen who for one reason or another did not receive sufficient direct accommodation from the banks. Though expanding, the note brokerage business remained small scale and limited to a local market in the leading commercial cities until about 1840. Thereafter markets dealt in local bonds, and the commercial paper offered for sale in one city might actually be disposed of to banks in distant sections. New York early established its primacy in this business. By 1860 Boston was second, and the business of note brokerage had become common in practically every large commercial city in this country.[37]

Lotteries, though of rapidly decreasing importance after about 1830, were decidedly significant institutions for the collection of capital from those who had only the smallest sums to invest. Tickets were often divided up into fractional parts selling for as little as 12.5 cents, thus permitting the poorest laborers to participate. But persons of considerable economic standing, including bankers and businessmen, must be included among the substantial purchasers of lottery tickets. This business appears to have expanded greatly following

[34] Myers, *The New York Money Market*, I, 23–24; Henrietta M. Larson, "E. W. Clark & Co., 1837–1857," *Journal of Economic and Business History*, IV, Pt. 2, No. 3 (May, 1932), 430–460.

[35] Myers, *The New York Money Market*, I, 16–18.

[36] The "note broker" referred to here should not be confused with the dealer in bank notes. Actually most brokerage houses dealt both in commercial paper or promissory notes and in bank notes.

[37] Albert O. Greef, *The Commercial Paper House in the United States* (Vol. LX of *Harvard Economic Studies*, Cambridge: Harvard University Press, 1938), Chap. 1.

the War of 1812. New York State had used lotteries to raise money as early as 1800 but had never collected more than about $25,000 in any one year until 1816, when receipts rose to $257,000. A special investigating committee for that state reported in 1819 that $585,000 had been raised by lotteries, and that over $500,000 was still to be collected on those which had been authorized. Of the money already raised, the three largest sums were for the following: Roads, $109,000; Hudson River Improvement, $108,000; Union College, $111,000. In Philadelphia there were only three lottery offices in 1819, but they grew to 60 in 1827 and to 200 in 1833. In the city of Boston the business done by lotteries in 1832 was estimated at $1,000,000. In 1832 the value of lottery tickets authorized in nine eastern states is reported to have exceeded $53,000,000.

But this method of raising capital did not long continue of much importance. To some extent its decline may have resulted from the moral crusade against gambling which was part of the great reform movement of the period. New York prohibited the authorization of new lotteries as early as 1821, and by 1833 leading states such as New York, Pennsylvania, and Massachusetts had all passed prohibitive legislation. But the decline of lotteries was also due to the rise of new financial institutions which tended to take their place. The increasing opportunities to invest in stocks and bonds provided a rival opportunity for speculation and investment. In fact, the same brokers who dealt in lottery tickets also sold the securities of corporations.[38]

Though they later became important sources of capital in the United States, savings banks were not originated for this purpose but were founded by public-spirited citizens who sought, by encouraging habits of thrift in the very poor, to accomplish two ends: to aid these unfortunate persons to escape the evils of extreme destitution; and to relieve the community of at least some of the burden of poor relief. The first incorporated savings bank in the United States was established in Philadelphia in December, 1816. By 1819 similar institutions had been founded in Boston and New York. All were mutual institutions and influenced by British experiments along similar lines. Once started, the movement grew slowly through the

[38] A. R. Spofford, "Lotteries in American History," *Annual Report of American Historical Association for the Year 1892* (Washington: Government Printing Office, 1893), pp. 177–190; McMaster, *A History of the People of the United States*, VII, 154–157; Larson, "S. & M. Allen—Lottery, Exchange, and Stock Brokerage," pp. 424–445; Don C. Sowers, *The Financial History of New York State from 1789 to 1912* (*Studies in History, Economics and Public Law*, Vol. LVII, No. 2, New York: Columbia University Press, 1914), pp. 135–138; Handlin and Handlin, *Commonwealth*, pp. 251–252.

thirties and then with considerable acceleration during the two following decades. Total savings bank deposits reached $7,000,000 in
1835, $43,000,000 in 1850, and $150,000,000 in 1860. Most of this development came in the mutual organizations in New York State and
Massachusetts. The philanthropic character of the early banks soon
gave way to business management as the institutions proved amply
self-supporting. The depositors were not typically the very poor
but chiefly persons of moderate and even substantial income.[39]

The growth of business and the need of the individual to protect his dependents under the new conditions of industrialization
and urbanization led to the rapid development of new forms of insurance. Marine insurance had, of course, been long in existence.
Early in this period formal companies completed the taking over of
this business from the associations of individuals which had been so
important before 1800. American marine insurance companies also
began to compete without serious disadvantage with British firms.
Up to the great New York conflagration of 1835, fire insurance had
been written on a small scale in the United States, largely, though
not exclusively, on a local basis, and often by marine insurance companies. This tremendous fire emphasized not only the need for insurance protection but also, because many New York companies
failed, the desirability of companies spreading their risks by doing
business over an area much wider than a single city. Both stock and
mutual companies grew rapidly during the forties and fifties, so
that by 1860 fire and marine insurance in force in the United States
totaled nearly $3,000,000,000.

Life insurance developed much less rapidly. Some life policies
and annuities had been written by the early marine and fire insurance companies, but in 1812 the first company specializing in life
insurance was incorporated in Philadelphia. This was the Pennsylvania Company for Insurances on Lives and Granting Annuities.
Thereafter other companies gradually appeared in the field, many
doing a trust business which often overshadowed their insurance
activity. After 1843 came rapid development. Most of the companies were now mutual in form. Substantial progress had been made
in developing mortality tables, and the demand for life insurance
was stimulated on the one hand by the growing industrialization of
the country and on the other by the increasing use of agencies with

[39] Redlich, *The Molding of American Banking, Men and Ideas*, Chap. 9; John P.
Townsend, "A History of Savings Banks in the United States," in Dodsworth, ed., *A History of Banking in All the Leading Nations*, II, 439–444.

modern selling methods. The total amount of insurance in force in the United States was apparently less than $10,000,000 in 1840 and possibly not equal to even half that figure. But in 1860 it totaled more than $160,000,000.[40]

[40] Shepard B. Clough, *A Century of American Life Insurance: A History of the Mutual Life Insurance Company of New York 1843–1943* (New York: Columbia University Press, 1946), pp. 22–122; Marquis James, *The Metropolitan Life: A Study in Business Growth* (New York: The Viking Press, 1947), pp. 13–18; Solomon Huebner, "History of Marine Insurance" and F. C. Oviatt, "History of Fire Insurance in the United States" in Lester W. Zartman, ed., *Property Insurance* (New Haven: Yale University Press, 1914), pp. 18–22 and 70–98, respectively; J. Owen Stalson, *Marketing Life Insurance: Its History in America* (Vol. VI of *Harvard Studies in Business History*, Cambridge, Mass.: Harvard University Press, 1942), pp. 31–378. Also see Marquis James, *Biography of a Business, 1792–1942* (Indianapolis: The Bobbs-Merrill Company, 1942), pp. 95–147.

CHAPTER XV

Money, Prices, and
Economic Fluctuations

NOTES, DEPOSITS, AND COINS

THE number of incorporated commercial banks in the United States grew from 88 in 1815 to 1,562 in 1860, and their aggregate note issue from $45,500,000 to $207,000,000 over the same period. This very appreciable expansion is shown in the accompanying table; from 1834 statistics for bank deposits are added. Beginning with 1834 the statistics, while far from perfect, are more reliable than those indicated for earlier years, which are merely Gallatin's estimates.

The table gives some indication of the extreme fluctuations which took place in banking facilities. Thus the rise in bank note circulation from $61,000,000 in 1830 to $149,000,000 in 1837 and then its decline to $59,000,000 in 1843 were of revolutionary proportions, reflecting the change from great prosperity to severe depression. But to a considerable extent the over-all figures summarized in the table tend to iron out the precipitous changes which not infrequently took place in particular states. Virginia, with four banks in 1815, had three times that number in 1816 but was reduced to four again in the twenties, whereas little Rhode Island, which had fourteen in 1815, increased this number to thirty in 1820 and to forty-seven in 1830. Notes in circulation totaled over $10,000,000 in Pennsylvania in 1815 but had fallen to about $3,000,000 by 1819.[1] At least in some areas

[1] Gouge, A Short History of Paper-Money and Banking, pp. 47, 60–61; Members of the Staff, Board of Governors of the Federal Reserve System, Banking Studies (Washington: Board of Governors, 1941), pp. 417–418; Albert Gallatin, "Considerations on the Currency and Banking System of the United States," in Adams, ed., The Writings of Albert Gallatin, III, 352–363.

BANKING STATISTICS, 1815–1860

Year	Number of State Banks	Bank Notes (*in millions of dollars*)	Deposits (*in millions of dollars*)
1815	208	45	...
1816	246	68	...
1820	307	45	...
1830	330	61	...
1834	506	95	76
1835	704	104	83
1836	713	140	115
1837	788	149	127
1838	829	116	85
1839	840	135	90
1840	901	107	76
1841	784	107	65
1842	692	84	62
1843	691	59	56
1844	696	75	85
1845	707	90	88
1846	707	106	97
1847	715	106	92
1848	751	129	103
1849	782	115	91
1850	824	131	110
1851	879	155	129
1852	815	161	137
1853	750	146	146
1854	1,208	205	188
1855	1,307	187	190
1856	1,398	196	213
1857	1,416	215	230
1858	1,422	155	186
1859	1,476	193	260
1860	1,562	207	254

Source: William M. Gouge, *A Short History of Paper-Money and Banking* (New York: B. & S. Collins, 1835), p. 61; and Members of the Staff, Board of Governors of the Federal Reserve System, *Banking Studies* (Washington: Board of Governors, 1941), pp. 417–418.

even more violent fluctuations in note circulation marked the business decline following 1837. Bank circulation fell in Louisiana by 85 per cent from 1837 to 1843, and in Ohio 88 per cent from 1836 to 1843.[2]

[2] Walker, *The Nature and Uses of Money and Mixed Currency, with a History of the Wickaboag Bank*, pp. 29–30; Caldwell, *A Banking History of Louisiana*, p. 127.

For the period of this study the money of the country can be divided into three categories: notes, bank deposits, and specie. Each of these merits brief examination. During the existence of the second Bank of the United States its notes were of considerable importance, usually constituting from around one tenth to almost one third of the total bank notes in circulation.[3] But of course the chief source of paper money was the state banks. As has already been pointed out, their notes circulated at varying degrees of discount, depending upon the distance from the place of issue and the reputation of the bank itself. In order to inform merchants and others who dealt in money, so-called bank note detectors were printed in the leading commercial centers. These guides not only indicated the discount at which valid notes circulated in a given market, but also gave information as to spurious and counterfeit notes. This latter service was essential because, with notes being issued by hundreds of independent institutions and often on very poor paper with crudely engraved designs, the temptation to fraud and counterfeiting became more than many people could resist. Condy Raguet reports:

> Bicknell's Counterfeit Detector and Bank Note List, of 1st Jan. 1839, contains the names of 54 banks that had *failed* at different times; of 20 *fictitious* banks, the pretended notes of which are in circulation; of 43 banks besides, for the notes of which there is *no sale;* of 254 banks, the notes of which have been counterfeited or altered; and 1395 descriptions of counterfeited and altered notes then supposed to be in circulation, from one dollar to five hundred.[4]

But, as though this were not enough, the paper money situation was further complicated in two respects. In the first place, the banks did not always confine their paper issues to what were, strictly speaking, bank notes—that is, to promissory notes payable to bearer on demand. Most important were the post notes, which were payable not to the bearer but to order and at a future specified date, sometimes, though not always, with interest. Their use appears to have been common in the North in 1815–1830, in the South in the 1830's and 1840's, and to have disappeared during the 1850's. Another kind of circulating bank paper consisted of notes issued at one place but payable at another. Finally, there were the branch drafts of the

---

[3] Gallatin, "Considerations on the Currency and Banking System of the United States," pp. 291, 296; Catterall, *The Second Bank of the United States,* p. 503; Federal Reserve, *Banking Studies,* 1941, p. 417.

[4] Condy Raguet, *A Treatise on Currency and Banking* (Philadelphia: Grigg & Elliot, 2d ed., 1840), p. 164, fn. See also William H. Dillistin, *Bank Note Reporters and Counterfeit Detectors, 1826–1866* (*Numismatic Notes and Monographs* No. 114, New York: The American Numismatic Society, 1949), *passim.*

second Bank of the United States, drafts drawn by branches on the cashier of the Bank of the United States at Philadelphia. Circulating like regular bank notes, they were an expedient designed to avoid a restriction in the charter of the second Bank. A provision in this charter effectively limited the issue of genuine bank notes through the burdensome requirement that the president and cashier of the Bank must both sign all notes issued, whether of the mother bank or its branches.[5]

In the second place, in addition to the issues of chartered banks, there circulated considerable quantities of paper money or scrip, often of doubtful legality, issued by public or private agencies. Private banks, unincorporated agencies operating under the common law, insurance companies, and even railroads issued their promises to pay which often circulated as money. Though prohibited by its charter from issuing bank notes, George Smith's Wisconsin Marine and Fire Insurance Company issued certificates of deposit. These certificates circulated widely in the Middle West and, because of Smith's record of meeting promptly all demands on him, were often preferred over bank notes. By 1851 nearly $1,500,000 of these certificates of deposit were outstanding.[6] Chartered in 1835, the Ohio Railroad was forbidden to use any part of its capital for banking purposes. Yet it managed to put a large quantity of notes into circulation, several hundred thousand dollars of which became worthless in 1842.[7] Ernest L. Bogart reports that in Ohio, 1838–1839, even libraries and orphan asylums were doing a banking business and issuing their own notes.[8] Finally, despite the clearly illegal character of the notes, a number of states circulated their own treasury notes, and in time of stress municipalities followed suit, issuing their promises to pay, often in small denominations and in such form that they readily became part of the circulating medium of the country.[9]

Of bank deposits little need be said except to point out that, despite the relatively small attention they received from contemporary writers, they were of major importance in the great mer-

[5] Fritz Redlich, "Bank Money in the United States during the First Half of the Nineteenth Century," *Southern Economic Journal*, X, No. 3 (January, 1944), 212–221.
[6] James, *The Growth of Chicago Banks*, I, 203. See also Larson, "E. W. Clark & Co., 1837–1857," p. 447; and Dewey, *State Banking before the Civil War*, pp. 180–181.
[7] C. P. Leland, "The Ohio Railroad," *Magazine of Western History*, XIII, No. 6 (April, 1891), 742–756.
[8] Ernest L. Bogart, *Financial History of Ohio* (University of Illinois *Studies in the Social Sciences*, Vol. I, Nos. 1–2, Urbana: University of Illinois, 1912), p. 274.
[9] Sparks, *History and Theory of Agricultural Credit in the United States*, p. 253; John Bach McMaster has a good description of the paper money system at the close of the War of 1812. See his *History of the People of the United States*, IV, 295–309.

cantile centers of the East. This neglect has undoubtedly resulted because they were not as subject to abuse as bank notes were and their use was confined to the relatively well-to-do who dealt primarily with the large banks in eastern seaports. It is surely a mistake to suppose that the use of bank checks was unimportant until just before the Civil War. A shrewd observer, Mathew Carey pointed out as early as 1816 that deposits rather than bank notes or specie furnished the chief medium of payment in the great commercial cities.[10] The data presented in the table on page 325 show that annually from 1834 to 1855 notes and deposits were of almost equal value. Since 1855 the value of deposits has always exceeded that of the bank note issue in the United States.[11]

The third kind of money in circulation—the gold and silver coins —formed, along with bullion, the basis upon which both bank notes and deposits rested. Under the leadership of Hamilton, the nation had adopted a bimetallic system at a ratio of 15 to 1 in 1792, and a mint had been established which began operations late in that year. For decades the United States mint operated on a very small scale. Even those few coins which it did turn out were largely exported. So the coins in circulation remained until about 1837, as they had been during the colonial period, a heterogeneous collection. Many were light in weight and nearly all were from foreign mints. At least until the middle of the century Spanish silver dollars and United States silver half dollars were the chief large coins in circulation. Below these circulated Spanish, English, French, and Dutch fractional silver and the United States copper coins. Not until after 1853 was there a sufficiency of fractional money.[12] In his report of 1820, Secretary of the Treasury William H. Crawford complained that, because of the scarcity of small silver coins, tickets in denomination of 6.25, 10, 12.5, 25, and 50 cents were "issued by mayors and corporation officers" to meet the acute need for small change.[13]

The mint ratio of 15 to 1 established by the act of 1792 had favored silver over gold, and this situation persisted until 1834, when the law was changed. Gold was relatively more valuable in the market; hence very little came to the mint. Despite the favorable mint ratio for silver, the mint output of silver coins was small. This small mint out-

[10] Mathew Carey, *Essays on Banking* (Philadelphia: M. Carey, 1816), pp. 182–183.
[11] Federal Reserve, *Banking Studies,* 1941, p. 417. See also Myers, *The New York Money Market,* I, 87–93.
[12] Neil Carothers, *Fractional Money* (New York: John Wiley & Sons, 1930), pp. 76–79.
[13] *American State Papers: Finance,* III, 500.

put of United States silver coins was due to a number of causes, among which technical backwardness at the small, horse-powered mint in Philadelphia and poor management there were of considerable importance. When the law fixing the mint ratio was changed in 1834 and 1837 so as to establish a ratio of about 16 to 1, the previous situation was reversed. As the market value of gold was less than 16 to 1, gold was now overvalued at the mint and silver undervalued. This new situation, combined with improvements at the mint and in the administration of the law, now led to a great increase in mint output, mostly, of course, in gold coins. But, curiously enough, the amount of silver in circulation also greatly increased. The market premium on silver was so small as hardly to compensate for the cost of its shipment abroad, and there were actually heavy imports of silver from Mexico from 1834 to 1843. Furthermore, the newly minted gold coins flowing into bank reserves released into general circulation many silver dollars and half dollars.

The situation remained fairly stable, with bimetallism really working surprisingly well, until toward the end of the forties. From 1837 to about 1850 the silver in a dollar had possessed a market value of close to $1.01 in gold, but with the rapid increase of California gold after 1849 the relative value of silver advanced rapidly in world markets. Early in 1851 a silver dollar brought $1.035 in gold and the advantage in exporting the white metal became decisive. As fractional silver coins contained the same proportions of silver as did the dollar, they also could be profitably melted down or shipped abroad; hence an acute shortage of small change rapidly developed. In order to remedy the situation so far as fractional coinage was concerned, Congress passed the Subsidiary Coinage Act of 1853. By lowering the silver content of the half dollar, quarter, dime, and half dime, this law made these coins more valuable as money than as bullion and within a short time fractional currency became more abundant than ever before in the nation's history.[14]

There can be no question that the disordered condition of the country's money, and especially of that part of it consisting of paper, must have caused a great deal of trouble and annoyance to those who were continually involved in monetary transactions. Merchants and manufacturers at times suffered serious loss because of having to accept depreciated or doubtful paper. Undoubtedly, also, the inconvenience of a nonuniform currency added to their cost of doing business. However, business was customarily able to pass on these

[14] Carothers, *Fractional Money*, Chaps. 7–11.

losses to employees or customers and, at least in some cases, actually to enlarge its earnings by currency manipulation. Workmen repeatedly complained that their wages were seriously reduced because employers forced them to accept depreciated paper at its face value. Merchants, constantly making money transactions and therefore much better informed than their customers as to the market value of bank notes, often picked up an additional profit because of such knowledge. Neil Carothers reports that storekeepers in the South and Southwest managed to make a substantial additional profit by giving in change dimes and half dimes when Spanish reals (12.5 cents) and medios (6.25 cents) should have been returned.[15]

Rapidly rising prices often force those on relatively fixed money incomes, including wage earners whose wages do not increase as rapidly as prices, to curtail consumption, thus permitting society as a whole to increase its savings. This phenomenon undoubtedly characterized the great price rise during the thirties, but the mistake must not be made of ascribing that inflationary movement, common also to western Europe, as peculiarly due to state banking and the disorganized currency in the United States. Yet the monetary and banking conditions existing in the nation at that time, in addition to their inflationary effect, did have a peculiar influence on capital formation. To the extent that bank issues were used to finance internal improvements or other capital expenditures, they often led to a forced saving somewhat different from that caused by increases in the general level of prices. Thus, in those cases in which the bank paper lost all or part of its value, the holder did the saving not because of rising prices but because the money he held declined in value relative to specie or some other standard. In the same way, those who purchased the stock issued by state banks continued their abstinence longer than they had planned when the bank failed and the stock became worthless. But actually, as has been noted above, the stockholders of these early banks often contributed very little capital. The chief sacrifice, therefore, seems to have been made by those who, receiving money for goods or services, held the money while it depreciated in value either in terms of prices or in terms of the standard money of the time.

PRICES

As New York was the leading commercial center in the United States, the index of wholesale prices for that city may be selected

[15] *Ibid.*, pp. 103–104.

as best representing price movements in the country as a whole. The index for New York prices shown in Chart 4 pictures the main movements for the years 1815–1860. The period opens, it will be noted, with prices at a very high level. In fact, if the chart showed price movements for the whole nineteenth century it would indicate no price level higher than that reached in January, 1815. The downward movement from that peak flattened out while still at a very high level during 1817 and 1818, and then took an abrupt plunge to a low point in March, 1821. This decline, one of the most drastic in all United States history, represents a reduction in the wholesale price level of close to 50 per cent.

CHART 4

All-Commodity Index of Wholesale Prices with Variable Group-Weights at New York, Annually, 1815–1860

(Base: 1824–1842

(Computed from data appearing in Arthur Harrison Cole, *Wholesale Commodity Prices in the United States, 1700–1861*. Cambridge: Harvard University Press, 1938, p. 137.)

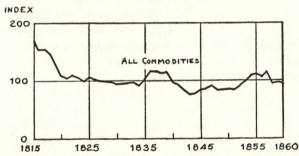

With brief recoveries in 1822 and 1825, prices drifted downward to the end of the decade. Then in 1830 there began a reverse swing which, though briefly interrupted in 1834, brought the index to twin peaks in 1837 and 1839. The ensuing decline was unusually severe and prolonged. By March, 1843, prices had fallen about two fifths from their peak in February, 1837, and more than three fifths from the high point in January, 1815. This marked the lowest point reached by wholesale prices during the century. From this bottom level, prices moved irregularly higher, with brief peaks in 1845 and 1847, until in 1852 another strong upward movement began which carried wholesale prices to a level almost as high as that reached in 1839. From August, 1857, to July of the next year, prices declined about 20 per cent, a loss only partially recovered in the next two years.

Taking the whole period 1815–1860, the trend of prices appears to have been definitely downward, a condition which follows largely from the extremely high level before 1819. More helpful for analyzing long-run price movements than the concept of the secular trend is that of long waves as developed by Kondratieff and applied by various students to American data. According to this view, one great wave of prices reached its lowest point about 1789, and a new one starting then reached its crest around 1815 and its lowest ebb in 1843. The upward swing from this later year was the beginning of a new long wave which rose to its highest point during or soon after the Civil War and subsided to its trough near the close of the century.[16]

The peculiar monetary and banking developments in the United States, 1815–1860, the political battles which were fought around them, and the special attention devoted to them by contemporaries must not lead to the assumption that American price trends and business conditions were determined solely by local conditions and but little affected by world trends. Such an inference, it must be emphasized, is quite unjustified, as any careful study of the general history of price behavior and business fluctuations quickly demonstrates. The long-run trend of prices in the United States during the nineteenth century shows no important deviations from that in western Europe. Even the short-run price movements show a close, though by no means identical, pattern in England and America, a fact readily evident from an examination of Norman J. Silberling's index for British commodity prices.[17]

Unfortunately, index numbers of the general price level have the fault that, like any average, they may conceal quite as much as they reveal, but it is not possible here to attempt a detailed examination of the price behavior of individual commodities or commodity groups. Nevertheless it is worth while to draw attention to the movement of price indexes for agricultural products as compared to those for industrial products. Careful analysis of the movement of wholesale prices at Philadelphia shows that most of the upward pressure which raised the general level of prices in the thirties and again in the fifties came from agricultural products. The unmistakable downward trend of the index for industrial prices may well have been the result of the

[16] Arthur Harrison Cole, *Wholesale Commodity Prices in the United States, 1700–1861* (Cambridge: Harvard University Press, 1938), p. 107; Joseph A. Schumpeter, *Business Cycles* (2 vols., New York: McGraw-Hill Book Company, 1939), I, 252–311; II, 461–471.

[17] Norman J. Silberling, "British Prices and Business Cycles, 1779–1850," *Review of Economic Statistics*, Prelim. Vol. V, Supp. 2 (October, 1923), pp. 230–231.

technological improvements of the age. At least this conclusion is strengthened by an examination of the behavior of the prices of subgroups and even of individual items. For example, a study of the price changes for the commodities included in the industrial commodities index shows that, of these, the prices of goods ready for immediate consumption declined most persistently.[18]

The extensive studies which have been completed under the sponsorship of the International Committee on Price History made it possible for the first time to observe the simultaneous movement of prices in different market areas of the United States. Studies for New York, Philadelphia, Charleston, New Orleans, and Cincinnati indicate, despite technical differences in compiling the indexes, that price movements in all markets were closely tied together. It might be expected that as a result of the transportation revolution the general price level in the different American markets would show a growing tendency to move more closely in unison over the period 1815–1860. To some extent this seems to have been the case, though the picture is blurred by the presence of other factors.[19]

Much more easily demonstrable is the effect of improved transportation on prices for identical commodities in different markets. Thomas Berry's comparisons of Cincinnati prices with those at New York and New Orleans are particularly illuminating in this respect. He shows that lard prices averaged 5.1 cents a pound lower in Cincinnati in 1816–1820 than in New Orleans and 4.8 cents less a pound than in New York City. By 1856–1860 these differentials stood at only .7 cents and .4 cents a pound, respectively. For other important Ohio Valley exports the trend was similar, though not typically so drastic in percentage terms. Thus flour, which was worth $2.16 less a barrel in Cincinnati than in New Orleans in 1816–1820, averaged only 63 cents less a barrel in 1856–1860, and the shrinkage in the differential on this item between Cincinnati and New York City was even greater. For typical Ohio Valley imports, the decline in price differences during the years of the transportation revolution is equally impressive. In the period just preceding the Civil War, coffee cost 1.5 cents more a pound in Cincinnati than in New York or New Orleans. In the five years following 1815 this difference had averaged at least 16 cents a pound.[20]

Interest rates during the years 1815–1860 tended to be high in

[18] Bezanson and others, Wholesale Prices in Philadelphia, 1784–1861, pp. 392–393.
[19] Cole, Wholesale Commodity Prices, Chap. 8; Berry, Western Prices before 1861, pp. 97–102.
[20] Berry, Western Prices before 1861, pp. 102–119.

the United States, though they varied greatly with such factors as place, time, and business conditions. Most states prescribed legal rates, usually 6 or 7 per cent, but such legislation was not effective. Usually, rates were much higher outside the centers of commerce than in them, and in the West as compared with the East. Interest rates on conservative mortgage loans in the West in the twenties ranged from 8 to 10 per cent and even higher. At the same time, rates on commercial loans in Ohio varied from 20 to 36 per cent, the smaller loans bringing the higher rates of interest.

On the other hand, the Massachusetts Bank of Boston regularly discounted commercial loans in the early twenties at rates of 5 to 6 per cent. By the fifties, rates on "good" commercial paper in Cincinnati usually ranged between 8 and 12 per cent, though for brief periods it rose much higher. During the same decade, rates on comparable short-term paper in New York City, while more volatile than those in the West, were usually appreciably lower. Commercial-paper rates in New York showed a definite tendency toward a seasonal rise in the autumn. Extremely high rates on money were characteristic of the financial crises of the period. Thus, in October, 1857, the rate of discount touched a high of 60 in Cincinnati and 36 in New York, but by the next summer had fallen to a rate of 8 to 12 per cent in the western city and to 4.5 per cent in the eastern city.[21]

THE POSTWAR BOOM AND THE CRISIS OF 1819

In its aftermath the War of 1812 brought to America, and especially to its agricultural population, a period of unusual prosperity lasting nearly to the end of 1818. It is true that the optimism which marked the end of the war was followed by a short period of falling prices and business uncertainty. But by the end of 1815 a strong upward movement was under way. With the wartime restrictions on trade removed, Americans demanded the foreign goods of which they had been deprived by the blockade. These were readily available, for foreign manufacturers, especially the British, had accumulated large stocks ready for shipment. Nor was the purchasing power lacking which would permit a major trade revival. On the one hand, American agricultural income expanded greatly as foreign buyers,

[21] Berry, *Western Prices before 1861*, pp. 486–498, 513; N. S. B. Gras, *The Massachusetts First National Bank of Boston, 1784–1934* (Vol. IV of *Harvard Studies in Business History*, Cambridge: Harvard University Press, 1937), p. 108; Smith and Cole, *Fluctuations in American Business, 1790–1860*, pp. 76–78, 83, 125–127; *Hunt's Merchants' Magazine*, XXXII (March, 1855), 355.

especially the British, took tremendous quantities of American wheat and flour, tobacco, and cotton at top prices. On the other hand, and supplementing this, large quantities of British goods were shipped over on credit to American importers, who in turn sold them to domestic distributors with liberal arrangements as to future payment. Under this stimulus, agriculture, commerce, and the carrying trade enjoyed unusual prosperity.

Other factors also contributed to the general expansion. The chaotic banking and currency system which had been inherited from the war undoubtedly presented difficulties for business. But, aided by the continued suspension of specie payments after the war, the state banks grew in number, their note issue rising by more than 50 per cent from 1815 to 1816. Neither pressure from the Bank of the United States, which began operations early in 1817, nor the general resumption of specie payments at about the same time had much effect in restraining the general business and credit expansion. By the end of 1818 the Bank of the United States had itself increased the inflationary pressures by placing more than $8,000,000 of notes in circulation and making loans of over $41,000,000. Moreover, the resumption of specie payments by state banks had been more nominal than real, and very little, if any, contraction had taken place in their circulation.[22]

Commerce and industry in towns and cities, though benefiting from the agricultural prosperity and the tremendous foreign trade expansion, faced certain problems of adjustment in the midst of the general prosperity. Falling prices for manufactured goods required careful management from merchants and raised especially difficult problems for manufacturers. Many small manufacturing companies which had sprung up during the war and in the period of trade restrictions preceding it faced grueling competition from cheap foreign imports following 1814. In some cases, as for example in the manufacture of cotton goods, they had to deal with declining prices for their finished products at the same time that costs of raw materials were rising. Some firms were forced out of business; others continued operation but at sharply reduced profits. But merely because some firms failed and those which survived complained bitterly of foreign competition in their campaign for higher tariff protection, it should not be concluded that times were generally bad or that all manu-

[22] See p. 325 above and Gouge, *A Short History of Paper-Money and Banking*, p. 34; Catterall, *The Second Bank of the United States*, pp. 23–39; Berry, *Western Prices before 1861*, p. 380.

facturing was being rapidly wiped out. Actually, through innovations and technical improvements of one kind or another, many manufacturing firms survived, new mills and factories were established each year, and at least some of the manufacturing ventures registered very satisfactory profits.[23]

Finally, in view of the importance of capital commitments for construction purposes in later business fluctuations in the United States, it is interesting to note that at least some of the impetus to expansion during the postwar boom appears to have originated from that source. The volume of shipbuilding, which had fallen to less than 30,000 tons in 1814, rose to nearly 156,000 tons in 1815, and, though declining, held to more than 86,000 tons through 1819.[24] While this considerable investment was being made in shipping, substantial sums, although much less than are to be met with later, were being spent on internal improvements, especially in the Middle Atlantic states, where Pennsylvania, New York, and Maryland were in the midst of a turnpike-building boom. In Pennsylvania alone more than $10,000,000 was spent on turnpikes, canals, and bridges from 1811 through 1821.[25] And it will of course be remembered that in 1817 New York State had vigorously launched her $10,000,000 Erie and Champlain canal-building projects.

The panic of 1819 reflects the colonial character of the American economy. With the return of good crops abroad in the autumn of 1818, British markets for American foodstuffs collapsed and grain prices fell sharply. At the same time England moved into a major financial and industrial crisis, and the prices paid for American cotton and tobacco broke sharply. With this change in conditions English creditors ceased to expand loans and demanded payment on those due. As a result, specie tended to move out of the United States and the greatly overextended credit system was badly strained. There followed the most severe panic since the beginning of commercial banking in America near the end of the eighteenth century. Many of the state banks failed, and the Bank of the United States

[23] Samuel Batchelder, *Introduction and Early Progress of the Cotton Manufacture in the United States* (Boston: Little, Brown & Company, 1863), p. 71; "Cultivation, Manufacture and Foreign Trade of Cotton," *House Executive Document* No. 146, 24 Cong., 1 Sess. (1836), p. 51; Clark, *History of Manufactures in the United States*, I, 379; Ware, *The Early New England Cotton Manufacture*, pp. 66–75; Cole, *The American Wool Manufacture*, I, 230.

[24] *Annual Report of the Commissioner of Navigation, 1901, House Document* No. 14, 57 Cong., 1 Sess., p. 585.

[25] Evans, *Business Incorporations in the United States, 1800–1943*, pp. 13–22; Durrenberger, *Turnpikes*, p. 50 ff.

avoided bankruptcy only by sharply contracting its loans, an action which, of course, made matters even worse for the business community.

Perhaps no crisis in United States history so suddenly prostrated the agricultural part of the economy. With the collapse of prices, farm purchasing power nearly ceased to exist, and large rural areas were left with almost no circulating medium. Bank paper became greatly depreciated or, in some cases, actually worthless, as the weaker institutions were forced into bankruptcy. Conditions were so bad in Ohio that the Bank of the United States was compelled to close its branch in Cincinnati as creditors defaulted on their loans and land values all but disappeared. Stay laws designed to protect insolvent debtors were passed by many state legislatures in the South and West. States resorted to desperate expedients to retain or create an adequate circulating medium. Ohio adopted legislation prohibiting the acceptance of bank notes at a discount, and Kentucky created the Bank of the Commonwealth, designed to issue paper money without pretense of specie backing, in order to assist hard-pressed debtors. But though generally bankrupt and without an adequate circulating medium, the farming areas did have plenty of necessary food, household industry supplied the most pressing needs for finished goods, and, by a general resort to barter, at least some trade and exchange continued.[26]

Writing at Philadelphia, one of the cities most affected by the crisis, Mathew Carey declared: ". . . that the enlivening sound of the spindle, the loom, and the hammer has in many places almost ceased to be heard—that our merchants and traders are daily swept away by bankruptcy one after another—that our banks are drained of their specie—that our cities exhibit an unvarying scene of gloom and despair—that confidence between man and man is almost extinct—that debts cannot in general be collected—that property cannot be sold but at enormous sacrifices—that capitalists have thus an opportunity of aggrandizing themselves at the expense of the middle class to an incalculable extent—that money cannot be borrowed but at extravagant interest—in a word, that with advantages equal to any that Heaven has ever bestowed on any nation, we exhibit a state

[26] Gouge, *A Short History of Paper-Money and Banking*, pp. 35 ff.; Berry, *Western Prices before 1861*, pp. 380–405; Samuel Rezneck, "The Depression of 1819–1822: A Social History," *American Historical Review*, XXXIX, No. 1 (October, 1933), 44–47; Thomas H. Greer, "Economic and Social Effects of the Depression of 1819 in the Old Northwest," *Indiana Magazine of History*, XLIV, No. 3 (September, 1948), 227–243.

of things at which our enemies must rejoice—and our friends put on sackcloth and ashes!" [27]

How many "artificers and manufacturers" were actually unemployed throughout the country is not known. Bishop says 40,000 to 60,000; Carey thought the number reached 100,000. James Flint, naming 500,000 as without employment, made an absurdly high estimate.[28] In the agrarian-handicraft economy of 1820, *unemployment* was not a very precise term. Probably the clearest view of the situation is reflected by statements such as the following by Niles: "Hatters, shoe-makers, and taylors, and even blacksmiths, whose work seemed to be indispensable, have lost, in general, much of their former businesses—from a fourth to one half." [29]

THE CRISES OF 1837 AND 1839

A surge of sustained economic growth characterized the years from 1820 to 1839. Expansion, innovation, and technological change proceeded with but slight interruption from the minor recessions which came at irregular intervals during the period. Much of this story of economic development has been told elsewhere in this volume. Here it must suffice to note the nature of the twin crises, 1837 and 1839, and some of the more important developments leading up to them.

The depression of 1819–1821 appears to have had a generally adverse effect on manufacturing. But it would be a mistake to accept the opinion of the protectionist Friends of National Industry that industry was prostrated; in fact, it should be noted that the most rapidly growing manufacturing industry, cotton textiles, expanded vigorously right through much of the depression. Caroline Ware reports that by the autumn of 1820 cotton factories were busily installing power looms, and employers were already resorting to newspaper advertisements to secure needed labor. Niles, reviewing the situation in 1821, showed that cotton textile manufacturing was expanding rapidly in Pawtucket, Philadelphia, and Paterson. Rapid growth characterized cotton textile manufacture during the twenty

[27] Mathew Carey, *Addresses of the Philadelphia Society for the Promotion of National Industry* (Philadelphia: M. Carey and Son, 1819), p. v.

[28] Bishop, *A History of American Manufactures from 1608 to 1860*, II, 250 [Mathew Carey], *The New Olive Branch*, Letter 5, Philadelphia, August 16, 1830 (2nd ed., no place or date of publication), p. 2; James Flint, *Letters from America* (Edinburgh: 1822), letter of August 15, 1820, p. 248; Malcolm Rogers Eiselen, *The Rise of Pennsylvania Protectionism* (Philadelphia: The author, 1932), pp. 43–45.

[29] *Niles' Weekly Register*, XVIII (April 15, 1820), 115.

years ending in 1839. In that period the capital invested in the mills of one city—Lowell, Massachusetts—exceeded the original cost of the Erie Canal. The best available measure of the growth of this industry is the total number of spindles employed. These numbered 220,000 in 1820, rose to 800,000 by 1825, and reached 1,750,000 in 1835. Much less spectacular than the growth in cotton textiles, but still substantial, was the marked expansion of other industries such as woolens, iron and machinery, and shoes and leather products.[30]

Construction activity was, of course, by no means confined to manufacturing. The reader need merely be reminded that between 1816 and 1840 the huge sum of $125,000,000 was invested in canal construction; that steamboat building rose from about 1,400 tons in 1821 to successive peaks of 15,400 in 1832 and 33,500 tons in 1837; that tonnage of sailing vessels constructed remained relatively high throughout the period and exceeded 100,000 tons during six of the years from 1820 through 1839; that substantial turnpike and bridge construction continued in most areas; that from 1830 to 1840 more than 3,000 miles of railroad were completed; and, finally, that the rapid settlement of the West and the growth of urban centers entailed expanding outlays for residences, barns, stores, churches, schools, and courthouses. This investment activity during the twenties and thirties greatly added to the productivity of the economy and contributed to a full use of capital and labor; fortunately, it did not, until well into the thirties, lead to seriously speculative excesses or to an appreciable inflation of prices. For the most part the new investments promptly proved their worth, and many were sufficiently successful to provide ample funds for further expansion out of profits. Thus at Lowell and elsewhere in New England new mills were financed in considerable part from current business earnings. Or, to take another example, income from tolls on the Erie Canal was great enough to contribute substantially toward its enlargement.

Despite the fact that labor and resources were to an increasing extent being diverted to construction projects and away from the production of goods for immediate consumption, the prices for consumption goods did not tend to rise during the twenties. In fact, the general price level moved gradually downward, with prices for manufactured goods receding more rapidly than those for agricultural

[30] Niles' Weekly Register, XXI (September 15, 1821), 39; Bishop, History of American Manufactures, II, 250, 268–269; Clark, History of Manufactures in the United States, I, 378–380; Ware, The Early New England Cotton Manufacture, pp. 66–78; Hunt's Merchants' Magazine, I (1840), 89; House Executive Document No. 146, 24 Cong., 1 Sess. (1836), p. 51.

products. The productivity of the newly opened western lands, the improvements in manufacturing techniques, and the lowered costs of transportation all helped to increase the goods and services that were made immediately available at the very time when a growing proportion of the economy was being devoted to building capital equipment.

This highly desirable condition of healthy growth gradually deteriorated, as in the middle thirties it gave way to feverish activity, to an emphasis on speculative ventures, and to increasingly unwise commitments. Although some solid growth continued, danger signals presently began to appear in nearly every major field. Land speculation became almost universal. The annual income from sales of public land rose from only $2,300,000 in 1830 to $14,800,000 in 1835, and to the all-time high of nearly $25,000,000 in 1836. Despite rising costs for labor and material, manufacturing expansion also accelerated, and elements of weakness began to appear. An ill-starred boom in silk manufacturing was well under way by 1835, and in the following year the number of manufacturing companies granted state charters experienced a mushroomlike growth.[31]

Especially significant was the disappointing nature of many of the newly constructed public works, particularly canals. The canal-building boom, which followed the completion of the Erie in 1825, persisted for fifteen years despite mounting discouragements, increasing costs for labor and materials, costly prolongations of expected construction periods, and, finally, as began to be abundantly evident in the late thirties, returns from tolls so disappointing as to bankrupt private companies and saddle state governments with unprecedented debts. Here was a serious point of weakness, offset only in part by the appreciable success of many of the early railroad ventures. Much of the manpower and resources devoted to constructing great public projects like the Pennsylvania Public Works or the privately owned ones such as the New Haven and Northampton Canal was not only irretrievably lost, but the purchasing power paid out for the construction of such projects and flowing into the market through the hands of laborers and suppliers of materials became merely inflationary. It added to the demand for consumption goods and services while, unlike the earlier and more successful ventures, making but slight contributions toward increasing their supply. But

[31] Clark, *History of Manufactures in the United States*, I, 575; Bishop, *A History of American Manufactures from 1608 to 1860*, II, 391–394; Evans, *Business Incorporations in the United States, 1800–1943*, pp. 15–17.

the promoters and investors of that time, like those in other "new eras" of expansion, were carried away with a spirit of optimism which finally led to foolish investments and extravagant ventures.

The banking system had recovered slowly after the failures of 1819–1820 but, except in parts of the West and South, where disturbed conditions were somewhat prolonged, the needs of expanding business for currency and credit appear to have been adequately met by a conservative enlargement of banking facilities. From 1820 to 1830 the number of banks grew from 307 to 330, and bank notes issued expanded from $44,900,000 to $61,300,000. In the thirties the tempo of credit expansion rapidly rose. The number of banks grew to 506 by 1834 and to 788 by 1837, and bank note circulation soared to $95,000,000 in 1834 and $149,000,000 in 1837.[32] Four major factors made this extreme expansion possible: (1) the generally lax control under which most state banks operated; (2) the stimulus to state bank expansion resulting from the refusal to recharter the Bank of the United States and the shifting of government deposits to the state banks; (3) the expansionist policy adopted by the Bank of the United States after 1834; and (4) the large loans which flowed in from London as state bonds, issued largely to finance banks and internal improvements, found a rapidly expanding market abroad. This credit expansion helped, of course, to make possible the great increase in capital goods and at the same time doubtless also facilitated the general rise of prices which, beginning in 1830, had assumed alarming proportions by 1836.

The crash of 1837 did not come entirely without warning. Alarmed by banking excesses in the western states and the tremendous speculation in land, the Treasury Department had as early as April 6, 1835, refused to receive bank notes in denominations of less than $5. Other precautionary actions followed, and finally the Specie Circular was issued July 16, 1836. It required that all payments for public lands made to federal agents must, with certain minor exceptions, be made in gold or silver. This requirement led banks in the West and Southwest to bolster their specie supply by drawing on eastern financial centers. The specie drain on eastern banks came at a time when foreign influences were becoming unfavorable. During the years 1835–1836 England experienced a considerable boom. Banks increased greatly in number and in the volume of their loans. A drain on the gold reserve of the Bank of England began in the spring of 1836 and led to increases in the Bank's rate of discount in

[32] See p. 325.

July and again in September. By autumn the Bank of England took even more energetic measures to avoid a serious crisis, going to the aid of the Agricultural and Commercial Bank of Ireland, which had got into serious difficulty, and issuing regulations designed to curtail the operations of the English Joint Stock Banks, some of which had been making large purchases of American bills.[33]

A veritable flood of American securities, mostly state bonds to finance public improvements, had come onto the American market in 1836. At the same time, the balance of foreign trade turned sharply against the United States. American imports from abroad expanded tremendously, with the result that imports exceeded exports in the year ending September 30, 1836, by the unprecedented total of $52,-000,000. This tremendous purchase of foreign goods was, of course, chiefly the result of the wave of prosperity in the United States. Another factor possibly worthy of mention was the poor grain crop in the United States, which had actually led to the importation of British wheat in 1836. At any rate the large adverse trade balance of 1836 might have brought no serious, immediate difficulties had credit continued easy and had British banks been willing to accept payment in American bills or securities. But with the credit situation grown very tight in both countries, a major banking crisis was precipitated in the United States in the spring of 1837.

The New York and Philadelphia banks had managed to get through the autumn of 1836 without undue strain on their specie reserves, but at the beginning of the following year they were faced with a new difficulty, the distribution of the surplus revenue under the act of July, 1836. About $37,000,000 had to be transferred to the states during 1837 in quarterly payments of more than $9,000,000, which were due on the first day of January, April, July, and September. The requirements for the distribution were such that its payment involved moving large government deposits from the eastern financial centers to banks in rural areas. The eastern banks successfully accomplished the January 1 transfer and then with great effort that of April 1. But before this second payment had been made, a crisis arose in the cotton export trade, which had been heavily financed by British firms. These British firms, finding themselves unable to rediscount the bills drawn by southern cotton brokers and commission men against shipments of the cotton crop of 1836, returned the bills protested. Cotton prices fell precipitously. About the

[33] W. Marston Acres, *The Bank of England from Within 1694–1900* (2 vols., London: Oxford University Press, 1931), II, 463–464.

middle of March, leading cotton houses failed in New Orleans, and before the end of the month their New York correspondents had been brought down with them. On May 10, New York banks suspended specie payments, and were promptly followed by those in Boston and Philadelphia.[34]

The spring and summer of 1837 brought a spate of commercial failures and a general stagnation of business in which New York City and New Orleans appear to have been the hardest hit. Unemployment was widespread, and in New York City labor discontent manifested itself in huge protest meetings and rioting.[35] Manufacturing suffered from loss of markets, though the assertion in *Niles' Weekly Register* under a New York dateline of September 5, 1837, that nine tenths of the factories in the eastern states had closed their doors is the type of contemporary "evidence" which needs to be viewed with great skepticism.[36] The shoe industry, still organized in the domestic stage, was badly depressed, but there is little to indicate that manufacturing in general suffered prolonged shutdowns.[37] Perhaps the experience of Leonard, Reed & Barton, manufacturers of britannia ware in Taunton, Massachusetts, was not untypical of many small mills or factories. In 1837 this plant operated with a reduced staff during the month of July, was closed during August, in part probably because of "seasonal dullness," and by December was in full operation. During 1838 the plant operated at capacity.[38]

Agriculture, though adversely affected by falling prices, was far from prostrated. Prices of imported products fell more than those of domestic goods, and prices of foodstuffs held up better than those of most other domestic items. Western farmers continued to be fairly prosperous during 1837 and 1838. Unlike foreign trade, which experienced extreme fluctuations, domestic commerce, as measured by Arthur Cole's index, experienced only a moderate decrease. This measure stood at 107 in 1836, declined to 100 in 1837 and 96 in 1838, and rose to 103 in 1839.[39]

[34] John Crosby Brown, *A Hundred Years of Merchant Banking* (New York: Privately printed, 1909), pp. 78–79; Myers, *The New York Money Market*, I, 64–67; McGrane, *The Panic of 1837*, pp. 91–98.

[35] McMaster, *A History of the People of the United States*, VI, 391–393; Schneider, *The History of Public Welfare in New York State, 1609–1866*, pp. 258–265.

[36] *Niles' Weekly Register*, LIII (September 16, 1837), 34.

[37] Clark, *History of Manufactures in the United States*, I, 380–381; Ware, *The Early New England Cotton Manufacture*, pp. 99–103; McGrane, *The Panic of 1837*, pp. 130–132; Hazard, *The Organization of the Boot and Shoe Industry in Massachusetts before 1875*, pp. 63–65.

[38] Gibb, *The Whitesmiths of Taunton*, p. 96.

[39] Smith and Cole, *Fluctuations in American Business, 1790–1860*, p. 73. See also Berry, *Western Prices before 1861*, p. 434.

The crisis of 1837 must be regarded as primarily a banking and commercial phenomenon not immediately changing the underlying expansionist trend of American industry. The chief centers of trade suffered severely from banking difficulties and the collapse of commercial credit as, for about a year, prices traced an uneven decline. But specie payments were resumed in the spring of 1838, and by summer of that year business turned sharply upward. The great trading ports quickly took on new life as prices, especially those for American farm products, rose sharply. In the winter of 1838–1839 the general price level reached a new peak only slightly lower than that of 1836–1837. Imports, which had fallen off in 1837 and 1838, expanded rapidly to a figure only a little less than that for 1836, and bank note circulation, which had been sharply off in 1838, rose rapidly in 1839.

Strong underlying factors were working toward continued growth. The British credit had expanded again in 1837–1838. Despite the panic of 1837, confidence in American securities had persisted, and foreign investors continued to stand ready to absorb an increasing flood of state bonds. The years 1836 right through 1838 mark the high tide of state bond issues for expenditures on internal improvements. B. U. Ratchford points out that American states issued more bonds during these three years than in the whole previous half century.[40] Pennsylvania was still expending enormous sums on her state works through the thirties. Maryland, pushing the construction of both the Chesapeake and Ohio Canal and the Baltimore and Ohio Railroad, was raising additional millions for the purpose. In 1838 New York authorized a loan of $4,000,000 for the enlargement of the Erie Canal, and in the West expenditures for internal improvements were beginning to accumulate in a really big way. In 1836 Illinois projected a whole series of railroads, canals, and river improvements; in the following year Michigan voted to borrow $5,000,000 for internal improvements; in 1837–1839 Indiana added $7,000,000 to her public debt for canal, railroad, and turnpike construction; and as late as 1839 Ohio made large appropriations for canal building.[41]

The revival of 1838–1839 could not be maintained. In the summer of 1839 credit again tightened in England and specie began to move from New York to London. The Bank of the United States, deeply involved in disastrous cotton speculation, was forced to suspend specie payments October 9, 1939. Other banks followed, and a panic gripped

[40] Ratchford, *American State Debts,* p. 80.

[41] McGrane, *The Panic of 1837,* pp. 104–144; Benton, "The Wabash Trade Route in the Development of the Old Northwest," p. 61; *Niles' Weekly Register,* LVII (October 26, 1839), 142–143; *North American Review,* LVIII (1844), 109–157.

the economy which, at least on the surface, seemed similar to that of 1837. But this time no help came from a revival of foreign trade, expanding investments in internal improvements, or renewed purchases by the British of American state bonds. With only minor and temporary recoveries, the American economy moved into an ever-deepening depression in the three years following 1839.

Continuously from the early twenties until late in 1839 new investments in the cities and on the farms, in manufacturing, and especially in transportation had buoyed up the economy, sustained internal trade at a high level, and produced a stimulating flow of purchasing power. But by the end of 1839 the game was up. Many of the more recent state projects like those of Illinois, Michigan, and Indiana were ill-conceived and mismanaged. Even those in the older states, like the State Works of Pennsylvania and the Chesapeake and Ohio Canal, were proving of limited worth, their completion was long delayed, and they gave no prospect of immediate returns such as would justify the tremendous investment. The credit of the states was exhausted, and British investors had become thoroughly frightened. One after another, most construction projects were stopped. The prosperity so long sustained by expanding investments in new homes, factories, and means of transportation was over for the time being.

RENEWED EXPANSION AND THE CRISIS OF 1857

The depression of 1839–1843 proved to be one of the most severe in United States history. Prices did not fall as sharply as in 1819–1820, but they continued their downward course for nearly four years. From their highest monthly average in 1839 to their lowest in 1843, the wholesale prices fell by about one fourth at Philadelphia, two fifths at New York, and more than one half at Cincinnati and New Orleans.[42] The acreage of public lands sold in 1842 measured less than 6 per cent of the 1836 peak. Real-estate values shrank, especially in the West.[43] Land in the city of Chicago by 1842 retained only 14 per cent of its market value six years earlier.[44] From February, 1839, to the same month in 1843, prices of railroad stocks declined a little more than 50 per cent.[45]

[42] Computed from Cole, *Wholesale Commodity Prices in the United States, 1700–1861*, pp. 135, 144, 179, and 181.

[43] Smith and Cole, *Fluctuations in American Business*, p. 185.

[44] Homer Hoyt, *One Hundred Years of Land Values in Chicago* (Chicago: The University of Chicago Press, 1933), pp. 41–42.

[45] Smith and Cole, *Fluctuations in American Business, 1790–1860*, p. 179.

The depression fell with especial force upon farmers, as agricultural prices fell even more drastically than those for manufactured products.[46] Nevertheless, farming communities were more or less self-sustaining, and in bad times farmers worked as hard as or harder than they had worked in prosperous ones. Partly at least for this reason and partly also because large new areas in the West were just coming into production, the volume of internal trade did not fall off as drastically as might have been expected. Thus at its low point in 1842 Cole's index for internal trade was only 12 per cent below 1839 and by 1844 had returned to the 1839 level. In this connection it may be noted that the tonnage of freight received by river at New Orleans registered substantial annual increases from 1839 to 1843 and almost doubled over that four-year period.[47] Also, despite the general depression, steamboat building on western rivers expanded rapidly in 1841 and 1842, and by 1844 the tonnage constructed exceeded that of any previous year.[48]

The depression had pretty well run its course by 1843. During that year the United States began a fourteen-year period of phenomenal growth. With temporary setbacks, the chief of which came in 1847–1848 and 1854, the economy rode forward on a tremendous wave of expansion. The growth of population and immigration, the rapid filling up of the Mississippi Valley and the beginnings of settlement in the Far West, the discovery of gold in California (1848) and Australia (1851), the increase of the merchant marine and the expansion of foreign trade, the rise of factory production—these and other influences played a part. But here it must suffice to focus attention on two strategic factors: railroad building and other construction, and the behavior of the credit system.

New capital investment in productive equipment—factories, ships, telegraph lines, and railroads—underlay the growth and stimulated this expansion of the economy, as had similar expenditures on capital goods in the preceding decades. But the dominant role now played by railroad investment was something new. Only a little over 3,000 miles of railroad had been completed in 1840. This rose to about 8,500 miles by 1850 and to nearly 24,000 miles by 1857. Railroad construction had involved an outlay of about $372,000,000 by 1850. In the next seven years this amount rose by $600,000,000 to make the total investment in American railroads approximately

[46] Bezanson and others, *Wholesale Prices in Philadelphia, 1784–1861*, p. 392.
[47] Switzler, *Report on the Internal Commerce of the United States*, pp. 199, 221.
[48] Berry, *Western Prices before 1861*, p. 557.

$1,000,000,000.[49] The magnitude of these totals is apparent when it is realized that nearly five times as much capital was invested in railroads during 1850–1857 as in canals during the whole period 1816–1840.

Furthermore, the building of railroads gave much greater indirect encouragement to investment in capital equipment than did canals. Outlays for canal construction and operating equipment led primarily to a demand for consumption goods by laborers and by suppliers of horses, mules, stone, sand, and lumber. About the same might be said for railroads insofar as the preparation of the right of way was concerned. But the rails, the locomotives, and to some extent the freight and passenger cars, altogether an appreciable part of the total cost of a new railroad, necessitated additional large investments in capital equipment which took the form of furnaces, rolling and rail mills, foundries, and locomotive works. For example, according to an estimate of 1854, the total capital invested at that time merely in locomotive building came to $3,000,000.[50]

As in the earlier expansion, British investments were again important in the years preceding 1857. In the expansion before 1839 such investments had largely taken the form of the purchase of the state bonds issued to finance banks and internal improvements. In the later expansion it was primarily bonds of privately owned American railways that were marketed abroad. By 1857 foreign holdings of American securities probably totaled between $250,000,000 and $350,000,000, the net increase of foreign investments in the United States for the years 1850–1860 being estimated at $190,000,000.[51]

Most of those who have written on American financial history before 1860 have been advocates of a more centralized banking system and strong believers in "sound money." Almost to a man they have condemned the banking of the time and described its weaknesses in great detail. Certainly during the forties and fifties there was much irresponsible banking as well as an inconvenient lack of uniformity and stability of value in the bank notes which made up most of the circulating medium. Possibly, also, the failure of business to recover more rapidly from the depression in the early forties was in part chargeable to the imperfect banking system. But at the same time

---

[49] Bezanson and others, *Wholesale Prices in Philadelphia, 1784–1861*, p. 392; Ringwalt, *Development of Transportation Systems in the United States*, pp. 115–146.

[50] Freedley, *Philadelphia and Its Manufactures*, p. 304. See also Norman J. Silberling, *The Dynamics of Business* (New York: McGraw-Hill Book Company, 1943), pp. 213–216; Berry, *Western Prices before 1861*, p. 511.

[51] See p. 205; also Van Vleck, *The Panic of 1857*, p. 36.

it is well to remember that the much-maligned banking and currency arrangements of that day proved adequate to facilitate, or at least did not prevent, one of the greatest periods of expansion and prosperity the country has ever experienced.

Currency and credit, which had suffered a serious contraction during the 1840's, expanded moderately as business revived during the middle and later years of the decade, much as they had during the 1820's. Not until 1851 did either the volume of bank notes or that of bank deposits exceed the previous high points which had been reached in 1837. But following 1851 the volume of notes and deposits rose much more rapidly.[52] An increasing flow of gold from California mines, a tremendous expansion of commerce and industry, and a growing spirit of optimism and speculation accompanied this expansion, which, with a brief shock in 1854, continued down to the autumn of 1857.

The background for the crisis of 1857 presents certain familiar parallels with that of 1839. A long-continued wave of new investment came to an end as sources of capital abroad dried up and new domestic investments were discouraged by increasing evidence that profits on new projects were not living up to expectations. A general credit expansion prevailing in France and England after 1855 found the Bank of France in a weakened position and repeatedly forced to draw specie from the Bank of England. This pressure as well as others brought a consistently high bank rate in London which on the one hand discouraged British investment in American railroad bonds and on the other tended to attract specie from New York.

With the revival of business after the depression of the early forties, New York had become more than ever the financial capital of the country. Banks in New York had a tremendous business in foreign and domestic exchange, and country banks throughout the United States and Canada found it advantageous to keep deposits in the institutions of that city against which drafts could be drawn at any time. As a result, country banks fell into the habit not only of keeping such deposits in New York but of using them as a sort of reserve to be drawn on in emergencies. Moreover, banks outside New York City were encouraged in this practice by a number of New York City banks which paid interest on such bankers' deposits. This the New York banks were able to do by lending on the call loan market the funds so deposited.

This whole situation had obvious advantages in that it facili-

[52] See p. 325.

tated exchange transactions, economized reserves by pyramiding them, made excess funds easily available to investors, and increased the earnings of country banks. On the other hand, it had the great disadvantage of leaving the banking and credit system of the country extremely vulnerable in case of a serious crisis. Thus if, when credit was tight, the outside banks should make large withdrawals of their deposits in New York City banks, then the New York banks would have to call their loans in order to secure the necessary funds. These call loans on which the banks would seek to realize were made on the security of stocks and bonds on the theory that such holdings could be easily and quickly liquidated should need arise. But, at least under panic conditions such as developed in 1857, call loans proved far from liquid. Security prices fell so rapidly and so many wished to sell that sales which returned the full value of the call loans often could not be made. Moreover, this weakness was all the more serious because the banks had not yet learned to work together closely in meeting crisis conditions, nor was there any adequate provision, except through the cessation of specie payments, by which credit could be temporarily increased and unnecessary failures avoided at the outset of a panic.[53]

The end of the Crimean War in 1856 brought lowered prices for American cereals and also a reduced demand for American shipping. Nevertheless, the year was one of general prosperity and tremendous foreign trade. The level of prices moved up strongly to a new peak in the middle of 1857 amidst general confidence in continued prosperity. But at least as early as July some adverse signs began to appear. In that month a number of important New England textile mills closed down because of lack of demand for their product. As was usual in August, demand for funds increased and credit became tight in New York, but not alarmingly so.

Then, rather suddenly, panic began to grip the country. On August 24, 1857, the New York branch of the leading Ohio bank, known as the Ohio Life Insurance and Trust Company, closed its doors, and the parent institution failed soon afterward as news leaked out of a staggering embezzlement by its cashier. This shock to confidence was followed by mounting failures of banks, railroads, and commercial firms. As country banks sought to withdraw their funds from New York City, city banks tried to strengthen their position by calling their loans on securities and reducing their commercial loans, and brokers and businessmen threw securities and property onto the

[53] Myers, *The New York Money Market*, Vol. I, Chaps. 6 and 7.

market in a desperate attempt to meet maturing obligations. Runs developed on New York banks, each of which, without joining the others in any plan of concerted action, tried to bolster its own position. The stronger New York banks were able to hold out through October 13, when, with one exception, they collapsed. By October 14, most banks throughout the nation had suspended specie payments, and commerce and industry seemed to be seized with almost complete paralysis.

The crisis of 1857 has sometimes been viewed as a brief but severe financial panic which did not deeply affect the economy as a whole and from which a prompt recovery was made. It is true that the banking crisis, although severe, was not prolonged. Gold flowed in promptly from California and from abroad. Specie payments were resumed in New York by December 14 and in much of the rest of the country early in 1858. Despite this rapid banking recovery, the crisis of 1857 must be regarded as marking a major business and commercial recession. One authority reports that it was followed by over 5,100 failures involving liabilities of nearly $300,000,000.[54] Widespread unemployment appeared in eastern cities and, reaching serious proportions in 1858, placed unprecedented burdens on relief agencies and, as in 1837, led to public demonstration of labor unrest.[55] For a time new investment largely ceased as the building of factories, railroads, and ships sharply declined. New railroad mileage, which had reached a peak in 1854, had by 1857 shrunk by more than one third and by 1858 by about one half.[56] The gross tonnage of all vessels built in the United States had fallen by 1859 to only one third of the 1856 total.[57] Studies of the volume of trade by both Cole and Berry clearly indicate that the recession following 1857 was the sharpest since that following the crisis of 1839.[58] As late as August, 1859, a writer in *Hunt's Merchants' Magazine* asserted: "The United States can boast of having more idle men and vessels of *all classes*, than any other country in the world of the same population." [59]

[54] A. Barton Hepburn, *History of Coinage and Currency in the United States and the Perennial Contest for Sound Money* (New York: The Macmillan Company, 1903), p. 166.
[55] Feder, *Unemployment Relief in Periods of Depression*, pp. 19–36; Schneider, *The History of Public Welfare in New York State, 1609–1866*, pp. 272–280.
[56] Ringwalt, *Development of Transportation Systems in the United States*, p. 145.
[57] *Historical Statistics of the United States 1789–1945: A Supplement to the Statistical Abstract of the United States* (Bureau of the Census, Department of Commerce, Washington: Government Printing Office, 1949), p. 211.
[58] Smith and Cole, *Fluctuations in American Business, 1790–1860*, p. 104; Berry, *Western Prices before 1861*, pp. 270–271.
[59] *Hunt's Merchants' Magazine*, XLI (August, 1859), 185.

By 1859–1860 conditions were considerably improved, and a general recovery seemed to be emerging. But political uncertainties and the increasing tension between the North and the South now began to overshadow all developments and to become the dominant factor affecting the trend of business.

CHAPTER XVI

The Role of Government

". . . it is the duty of the legislator to find employment for all the people, and if he cannot find them employment in agriculture and commerce, he must set them to manufacturing." [1] This statement made in 1820 by Daniel Raymond, author of the first general text in economics to be written in the United States, well characterizes American thought during a period when the responsibility of the state for economic conditions was generally taken for granted. A committee of the Senate of the Commonwealth of Massachusetts demonstrated a similar point of view when making a report in 1825 on child labor in factories. Apparently without expectation of any contrary viewpoint, this committee observed: ". . . this is a subject always deserving the parental care of a vigilant government." [2] Daniel Webster apparently held no consistent philosophy as to the role of the state, but as one of the ablest debaters in the United States Senate he developed great shrewdness in selecting for attack the weakest arguments of his opponents. In an important debate on the subtreasury in 1838 he held up to scorn a noninterventionist viewpoint, declaring: "Let the Government attend to its own business, and let the people attend to theirs. . . . These ominous sentences Mr. President, have been ringing in my ears ever since they were uttered yesterday, by the member from New York." [3]

During the decades covered by this study, Americans, though much given to debates concerning the interpretation of the constitution, were not much interested in elaborate theories as to the proper role of government in economic affairs. They believed that economic

[1] Raymond, *Thoughts on Political Economy*, p. 367.
[2] Quoted in Abbott, *Women in Industry*, p. 342. Cf. Hartz, *Economic Policy and Democratic Thought: Pennsylvania, 1776–1860*, pp. 200–201.
[3] Daniel Webster, Senate speech, January 31, 1838, *The Writings and Speeches of Daniel Webster* (8 vols., Boston: Little, Brown & Company, 1903), VIII, 140.

conditions should constantly improve and that the government had a simple and direct obligation to take any practicable measure to forward such progress. Why should they fear the power of the state? Was it not their own creation in which the people themselves were sovereign? So issues tended to be considered on the basis of simple expediency. Or if theoretical questions were raised, nine times out of ten they dealt with constitutional interpretations having to do with whether a particular activity fell within the powers of the federal or the state government and not whether *any* action by government was theoretically defensible or desirable.

Most Southerners, it is true, objected bitterly to the protective tariff but insofar as their arguments were not of a constitutional nature they rested their case for the most part not on general laissez-faire principles but on the concrete charge that the tariff was a tax on the South for the benefit of the North. In the North, especially in New England, a school of academic economists who preached laissez-faire doctrine did develop, but it appears to have had but little influence before the Civil War either on popular thinking or on state policy. These New England professors, the orthodox followers of the British classical school of economists, combined the teachings of Adam Smith with liberal quotations from the Bible to develop a laissez-faire defense for business—a philosophy which was to be used by corporations to prevent unwelcome regulation by the state and to justify employers in objecting to legislation affecting the hours and conditions of labor.[4]

But this was a development which reached appreciable importance only after the Civil War. Far more typical of the early decades of the nineteenth century was a New York pamphleteer who, in arguing for a protective tariff to aid manufacturing and labor, declared: "Those who rely upon mere individual enterprise for the promotion of *national industry*, pursue a false light. The motives and projects which lead to national or civic prosperity or greatness, are too extensive and responsible, and are too dependent upon *aggregate ability* to be assumed by solitary individuals, or to be within the scope of their operations. The efforts of unaided genius may *exhibit*, but cannot realize the resources of a nation." [5]

Present-day writers, and especially those who fear the growing

[4] Michael J. L. O'Connor, *Origins of Academic Economics in the United States* (New York: Columbia University Press, 1944), *passim;* Dorfman, *The Economic Mind in American Civilization, 1606–1918*, II, 713–771.

[5] [John Woodward], *Plain Sense on National Industry* (New York: G. L. Berch and Company, 1820), pp. 48–49.

power of the government and increased economic activities of the state, not infrequently make nostalgic reference to an earlier period in American history when a policy of laissez faire had general acceptance and government did not interfere in any appreciable degree with the activities of business. The exact time when this idyllic condition is supposed to have prevailed is seldom made more definite than are most references to the "good old days." But the following pages which describe the actual practice of governmental intervention lend no support to those who would place the heyday of laissez faire in the United States during the period of this study.

FISCAL OPERATIONS OF THE FEDERAL GOVERNMENT

No major nation in modern history has experienced less difficulty in meeting its financial needs than did the United States in the years between the second war with England and the Civil War. Conditions were so favorable to the Treasury from 1816 through 1836 that there was a deficit in only three years; in all the others there was a surplus running at times to many millions. Congress was repeatedly perplexed as to how to dispose of so-called redundant revenues, and in 1826 a Senate committee actually complained "of the serious inconvenience of an overflowing Treasury." [6]

Before the War of 1812 the ordinary annual expenditures of the federal government had never quite reached $11,000,000. But as a result of the war they rose to $35,000,000 in 1814. For many years thereafter annual disbursements remained typically under $20,000,-000 until they rose rapidly to a total of $37,000,000 in 1837. In the following nine years they averaged below $30,000,000 until another record sum, $57,000,000, was expended in 1847. From that time on, annual expenditures averaged well over $40,000,000 until, increasing rapidly in the middle fifties, they were $74,000,000 in 1858.

Except for the short Mexican War, the whole period was an extraordinarily peaceful one. The increased sums expended were used chiefly for the civil administration and for the Army and Navy. But disbursements for these purposes seem to have risen not so much because of pressing need as because surplus funds were so often available. When temporary deficits followed the more flush periods, public expenditures declined, but never to their previous levels. Also, of course, large sums were expended for debt reduction.

[6] *American State Papers: Finance*, V, 502. This passage is quoted by James A. Maxwell, *The Fiscal Impact of Federalism in the United States* (Vol. LXXIX of *Harvard Economic Studies*, Cambridge: Harvard University Press, 1946), p. 12.

The federal debt, which reached a peak at a little over $86,000,-
000 in 1803, fell to about $45,000,000 shortly before the War of 1812
and rose to $128,000,000 in 1815 just after the war's close. This debt,
the largest before the Civil War, amounted to about $15 per capita.
By January, 1835, it had been entirely paid off. Although deficits accumulated during depression years and Mexican War expenditures
caused a new debt to arise, it never became large. By 1860 it amounted
to only $65,000,000, or about $2.06 per capita. This unparalleled
achievement by which a great modern nation completely retired
its public debt, and thereafter for many years held its indebtedness
to a very low per capita figure, was made possible by two fundamental
conditions: the tremendous growth and prosperity of the United
States; and freedom from major war. But it was also the result of
mounting public revenues which in part fortuitously and without
intention poured into the Treasury from the customs and from the
sale of public lands.

After almost criminal delay in providing adequate funds with
which to prosecute the War of 1812, Congress finally passed a substantial tax measure in 1814 which increased duties on imports,
doubled the direct taxes which had been imposed in 1813 on land,
dwelling houses, and slaves, and assessed internal revenue duties on
a long list of items. These new taxes, which went into effect shortly
before the war ended, combined with a tremendous surge of imports,
so multiplied Treasury receipts that the deficit was converted into
an unprecedented surplus. By 1817 Congress, with a decisiveness
characteristic of its behavior only when reducing taxes, had removed
practically all of the war levies.

The federal government was left with two significant sources
of revenue: public land sales, and the duties on imports. Together
these were more than adequate to meet all revenue needs. Nevertheless, they presented a serious problem: (1) if the law were left
unchanged, that is if the price of public lands and the duties on imports were unaltered, the revenue collected annually showed a general tendency to increase greatly and also to fluctuate violently from
year to year depending upon general business conditions; and (2) if
an attempt were made to change the law and reduce revenues, a
host of new problems arose because both the price of public land
and the tariff rates presented many-sided political issues which often
enough much more vitally concerned Congress than did their pro-
spective yield to the Treasury.

Viewing the whole period 1815–1860, we may regard the redundant receipts of the federal Treasury as partly merely fortuitous and as partly the result of legislation adopted largely because of non-fiscal considerations. Despite a reduction of the price of land in 1820 and the lower level of tariff rates after 1832, total revenues, with only occasional temporary declines, surged strongly upward in each successive decade. It will be seen from Chart 5 that revenue from the sale of public lands increased gradually until the 1830's, when boom

CHART 5

Receipts of the Federal Government, 1815–1860

Annual Report of the Secretary of the Treasury, 1932, pp. 362–363.

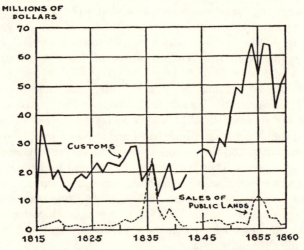

times in the West carried receipts from this source to nearly $25,000,-000 in 1836. In that year, the only one in American history before the First World War, revenue from imports took second place as a source of Treasury receipts. In the mid-fifties public land sales rose to a substantial figure—$10,000,000 in 1856—but they never again equaled or even approximated customs revenues as a source of Treasury income. Revenue from customs duties varied with the volume of imports. Even the substantial reduction of rates in 1846 was much more than offset by increased trade, which at its peak in the fifties resulted in receipts from customs duties exceeding $60,000,000 a year.

Treasury operations exerted an almost continuous influence on banking and business conditions. The Secretary of the Treasury promoted the idea of establishing the second Bank of the United States and took a leading part putting it into operation. During its first years, when the Bank was so badly mismanaged, it was the United States Treasury rather than the Bank whose influence helped to keep the state banks on a specie basis and to secure some stability and uniformity in the currency. And when crisis conditions appeared beginning in 1818, it was the Treasury which, by making special deposits in weakened state banks, helped to avoid runs and specie suspensions. Again in 1824 the Treasury, making use of surplus funds, paid the maturing portion of the federal debt before it was due in order to relieve a monetary stringency which seriously threatened the business community.[7]

From 1825 to 1832, when the second Bank of the United States was at its strongest, the direct influence of the Treasury declined. But this situation changed quickly with Jackson's veto of the bill to recharter the Bank in 1832. Beginning in the fall of 1833 federal funds were deposited in state banks. At first federal depository banks, the so-called "pet banks," were carefully chosen. But standards were soon relaxed and the availability of federal funds helped to encourage a great deal of unsound banking. The surplus in the federal Treasury grew to unprecedented proportions in 1835 and 1836, and by depositing these huge sums in state banks the federal government did much to promote an unhealthy credit expansion.

After having contributed in this way to the inflationary trend, the government presently became alarmed and took two important steps which helped to precipitate the sharp crisis of 1837. The first of these was the Specie Circular issued by the Treasury on July 11, 1836. Designed to discourage speculation in western lands and to reduce the growing obligations of western banks to the federal Treasury, it required, with certain exceptions, that payments to the government for public lands must be made in specie. Government officials hoped that one of the effects of this measure would be to cause Easterners to send specie to the West in order to buy land. In this way it hoped that the specie position of western banks would be improved. The chief effect was rather to increase the difficulties of the western banks by raising doubts as to the soundness of their note issues.

The act providing for a distribution to the states of the surplus accumulated in the federal Treasury also contributed to the developing crisis. No longer was there a national debt to which surplus funds

[7] Taus, *Central Banking Functions of the United States Treasury, 1789–1941*, pp. 27–31.

could be applied, and as revenues from both public land sales and customs duties poured into the Treasury, a large surplus was built up. By June 1, 1836, this surplus exceeded $41,000,000, and the movement for distribution among the states became irresistible. A law was passed in June, 1836, which provided for doling out to the states most of the Treasury surplus in quarterly installments during 1837. In order to avoid constitutional objections, the grants to the states were made in the form of loans and, indeed, have long remained on the books of the federal government as "unevaluable funds." But it was well understood at the time that no repayment would ever be required.

The states received a little over $28,000,000 in three quarterly payments during 1837. The fourth installment was never paid, for by the fall of that year the country was in the grip of a severe crisis, banks had suspended specie payments, and the federal government was forced to issue treasury notes in order to obtain funds with which to meet current obligations. The distribution of the surplus funds to the states contributed to the severity of the crisis by forcing a shift of federal deposits among the many depository banks. The chief difficulty arose in those states where public land sales had been concentrated. The banks in those states had received tremendous sums on deposit from the federal government and had promptly expanded their loans. The allocation of the surplus funds to the states was made on the basis of their electoral vote, i.e., their representation in Congress according to the census of 1830. This meant that some of the least populous of the western states which had huge deposits because of public land sales were to receive only a small share of the surplus funds. Michigan was one of the states most unfavorably affected. Its banks had received Treasury deposits of $2,267,000, but its share in the surplus came to only $382,000.[8]

The causes of the crisis of 1837 were no less complicated than the causes of all major crises. In part the expansion and the financial crash were world-wide phenomena. But this fact does not warrant our excusing the government of the United States for its financial measures which, on the one hand, encouraged an unhealthy inflation through improperly safeguarded deposits in "pet" banks, and on the other helped to precipitate the crisis by the Specie Circular and the distribution of the surplus revenue.

Once the crisis had become the panic of 1837, the Treasury could

[8] Edward G. Bourne, The History of the Surplus Revenue of 1837 (New York: G. P. Putnam's Sons, 1885), passim.

give little or no aid to the business or banking community, for its funds were largely tied up in suspended banks. Mortality among business and banking firms was perhaps the worst in United States history. Though conditions improved in 1838, a new wave of failures accompanied the drop in cotton prices in the second half of 1839, and bankruptcies and liquidations became a recurring story to 1843.

From 1837 to 1840 Treasury receipts were for the most part kept in the possession of the Treasury officials who collected them. Then, briefly, with the passage of the Independent Treasury Act of 1840, funds were deposited at subtreasury offices established in leading cities. But with the repeal of this law in the following year, the practice was revived of depositing Treasury funds in specie-paying state banks. Finally, in 1846, after the Democrats had returned to power, they passed an act providing for an independent or subtreasury system similar to that of 1840–1841. This law was designed to separate completely the operations of the United States Treasury from all connection with or dependence upon banks. To this end subtreasuries were established in six leading cities and charged with the responsibility of receiving, acting as custodians of, and paying out public funds. Moreover, all the receipts and disbursements of these offices had to be made in gold and silver coins or treasury notes.

The new system succeeded in removing the Treasury from dependence on the state banks and, by placing it on a specie basis, protected it from the losses formerly suffered when banks failed to redeem their notes at par or to meet their deposit obligations. But though the Treasury was now independent of the banks, the banks and the business community were still very much affected by the operations of the Treasury. The Mexican War was fought without either a serious inflation or a banking crisis, in part, at least, as a result of the restraining effect of the independent Treasury on the commercial banks. Without anyone willing it, Treasury operations continued to be a vital factor in business conditions. When government revenues exceeded disbursements, specie accumulated in the Treasury, banks found their reserves dwindling, credit became tight, and a crisis was likely to ensue. On the other hand, when government disbursements exceeded collections, specie flowed into the channel of trade to become, perhaps, a decisive stimulant to business.

Problems arising from such situations repeatedly forced extremely difficult decisions upon the Secretary of the Treasury during the fifties. In 1853 surplus funds accumulating in the Treasury threatened to cause a serious crisis, and Secretary James Guthrie quickly threw money into circulation by buying silver bullion and paying off part of the debt before it was due. In 1857, when credit again became tight, the Secretary of the Treasury attempted to relieve the situation by bond purchases. This time, at least according to some students, he entered the market too soon and actually helped to exaggerate the speculative movement, which ended in the serious crisis following the failure of the Ohio Life Insurance and Trust Company in August, 1857. Whatever the policy of the Secretary of the Treasury should have been at this time, the point of emphasis here is the major role unavoidably played by the government because of the magnitude of its specie operation.[9]

THE PROTECTIVE TARIFF

The height and nature of the duties imposed on imports by the federal government were determined by two objectives: revenue, and protection to home industries. Though not always mutually exclusive, these two purposes were at least so ill-mated as to lead to almost constant difficulties in drawing up tariff measures and to cause a great deal of confused thinking. One aspect of this problem can hardly be treated without some attention to the other, but the interest here is in the tariff as an interventionist device, a method by which the state attempted to extend its help or "protection" to selected parts of the economy.

A protective element had been present in the very first tariff act, that of 1789, but Hamilton's ambitious protective system had not been adopted by Congress. Until the War of 1812 rates remained relatively low, less than 20 per cent on the value of dutiable products, and revenue consideration clearly overshadowed the protective features. In July, 1812, as a war revenue measure, Congress doubled the duties on imports for the duration of the war and for one year thereafter. By 1816 the federal treasury was overflowing with revenue, and duties might well have been returned to the prewar level. But protectionist sentiment intervened, proving sufficiently strong to make the act of 1816 mildly protectionist. The new rates, though generally less than those prevailing during the war, were higher than the previous peacetime levels. But they were still very low as compared to some later

[9] For good general treatments of the material covered in this section see William J. Shultz and M. R. Caine, *Financial Development of the United States* (New York: Prentice-Hall, Inc., 1937), Chaps. 8–11; Davis R. Dewey, *Financial History of the United States* (New York: Longmans, Green and Co., 1934), Chaps. 7, 9–11; and Taus, *Central Banking Functions of the United States Treasury, 1789–1941*, pp. 27–64.

acts. The act provided for a general level of rates on dutiable goods of about 20 per cent. Cotton and woolen cloth were to pay a duty of 25 per cent, which was to be reduced after three years to 20 per cent. Moreover, all cotton cloth was to be valued at no less than 25 cents a square yard for purposes of assessing the duty. This last provision was designed to keep out the cheap cottons of the Far East, but in actual practice it also proved extremely effective against English cottons when prices fell drastically in 1819. A special tariff act in 1818 repealed the provision in the earlier law that the rate on cotton and woolen textiles should be reduced to 20 per cent after three years, and substantially increased the duty on pig and bar iron and iron manufactures.

Less a party measure than later tariffs, the mildly protective act of 1816 aroused no strong opposition and actually found considerable support in the South. Even John C. Calhoun was among those voting for it. But such general agreement on tariff legislation soon disappeared. The continued flood of manufactured imports in 1817 and 1818 and then the severe depression of 1819–1820 brought an aggressive and persistent demand for greatly increased duties on manufactured goods. Centered in Pennsylvania, this sentiment was also strong in all the Middle Atlantic states, southern New England, Ohio, and Kentucky. In this area great numbers of small manufacturing businesses had sprung up during the years of trade restrictions, 1808–1809 and 1812–1814. The European importations and the sharp price declines of 1819–1820 bankrupted many of these ventures and seemed to many manufacturers to present difficulties which could be overcome only if the federal government promptly adopted protective legislation.

If this depression-born enthusiasm for protection had been confined merely to the owners of manufacturing ventures, the political pressures for high import duties might not have been very effective. But, fortunately for the protectionists, they now easily recruited enthusiastic support from farmers, workers, and printers. American farmers were bitterly resentful of declining prices. In March, 1817, farm crops in Pennsylvania reached their highest monthly levels between the Revolution and the Civil War; by 1821 they had fallen by more than 50 per cent. Grain farmers were especially affected. For the whole period 1784 through 1861 the index of grain prices reached its highest annual average in 1816, its lowest in 1821. Wheat and wheat flour, the most important cash crop in such states as Pennsylvania and Maryland, suffered especially. Thus Philadelphia superfine flour, which brought more than $14 a barrel in the spring of 1817, had fallen to $4 and even less four years later in 1821.[10] The high prices were in large part the result of short crops in Europe which led to tremendous exports; the price decline coincided with the almost complete cessation of such exports after 1818. With prices so low that it hardly paid farmers to haul wheat to the mill, and with little prospect of a revival of the European demand, the wheat growers of Pennsylvania, Maryland, Connecticut, and Ohio were easily convinced that their only hope lay in enlarging the home market by protection to domestic manufacturing. In addition, other farmers, like the hemp growers of Kentucky and the sheep raisers of Ohio, Pennsylvania, and Vermont, found it easy to ascribe their depression hardships to imports of hemp and wool and to see a remedy in higher duties.

From an entirely new group, the workers in manufacturing, or mechanics as they were called, also came strong support for the protectionists. The depression of 1819–1820 produced for the first time the phenomenon in America of industrial unemployment, of workers discharged from manufacturing employment and dependent upon charity for subsistence. The number of unemployed in Philadelphia in 1819 was estimated at from 7,288 to 20,000 out of a total population of about 110,000. Similarly, in the western manufacturing center of Pittsburgh, employment in 1819 had fallen to one third the total for 1815. Some of these were workers in textile mills and iron works; others were unemployed mechanics working in small shops where their interest was closely identified with that of the master workman or manufacturer.[11] In their distress the workmen, like their masters, blamed their condition on foreign competition and demanded increased duties. The Philadelphia shoemakers became so converted to the protectionist viewpoint that they naïvely carried it to its logical conclusion, declared New Englanders "a species of foreigners," and requested the governor and legislature of Pennsylvania to prohibit the sale of New England shoes in Pennsylvania.[12]

Finally, the protectionist cause now received invaluable support from able writers and publicists. The free trade teachings of Adam Smith and J. B. Say, which had greatly influenced the leaders of

[10] Bezanson and others, *Wholesale Prices in Philadelphia, 1784–1861*, p. 354; Cole, *Wholesale Commodity Prices in the United States, 1700–1861, Statistical Supplement*, pp. 178–195.
[11] Eiselen, *The Rise of Pennsylvania Protectionism*, pp. 44–45.
[12] *United States Gazette*, April 25, 1818, cited in Eiselen, *The Rise of Pennsylvania Protectionism*, p. 53.

American thought, were for the first time effectively challenged by writers of systematic texts on political economy. Most important of these was Raymond, whose *Thoughts on Political Economy* attacked the whole Smithian system and defended protective duties as a cure for unemployment. Greatly influenced by his observation of conditions during the depression of 1819–1820, he presented a strong protectionist and nationalist viewpoint which was soon adopted by other able writers, men such as Willard Phillips, Friedrich List, and, somewhat later, Henry C. Carey. Even more influential were two publicists, those indefatigable workers in the protectionist vineyard, Hezekiah Niles and Mathew Carey. *Niles' Weekly Register,* issued from Baltimore, reached a national audience with the gospel of protection to native industries. Few publications circulated more widely, were more often quoted by other papers, or were more generally respected. Also, the successful Philadelphia printer and pamphleteer, Mathew Carey, worked and wrote tirelessly for the cause. Neither was a great thinker or system builder, but both lost no opportunity to reiterate the doctrine that prosperity, employment, and national strength depended upon prosperous native manufactures, which in turn could not succeed without proper protective duties.[13]

Massachusetts was not at first one of the states clamoring for an upward revision of the tariff of 1816. The usual explanation for this emphasizes the fact that commercial interests partial to free trade continued relatively strong in the state until after 1824, when manufacturing became relatively more important and the majority of Massachusetts votes in Congress shifted over to the protectionist side. Although this was part of the picture it should not be permitted to obscure the fact that the representatives of cotton textile factories of Massachusetts were not especially active in urging higher tariffs in 1820 and 1824 because the Boston Associates, who were busily developing the Waltham system, were doing very well. In the first place, their influence had secured relatively high protection in the tariff act of 1816 under the minimum valuation clause for imported textiles; and in the second place, their improved methods and general efficiency permitted them to continue profitable production right through the depression of 1819–1821.[14]

[13] Norval Neil Luxon, *Niles' Weekly Register, News Magazine of the Nineteenth Century* (Baton Rouge: Louisiana State University Press, 1947); Kenneth Wyer Rowe, *Mathew Carey: A Study in American Economic Development* (Johns Hopkins University *Studies in Historical and Political Science,* LI, No. 4, Baltimore: The Johns Hopkins Press, 1933); Dorfman, *The Economic Mind in American Civilization, 1606–1918,* Vol. II, Chap. 22.

[14] Ware, *The Early New England Cotton Manufactures,* Chap. 4; F. W. Taussig,

The position of the South was overwhelmingly antitariff after 1816. Dependence of that area on foreign markets for disposal of its cotton and tobacco and failure of the South to develop manufacturing on a considerable scale convinced southern leaders that the protective system hurt their foreign markets and increased the prices they had to pay for manufactured goods.

The rising tide of protectionist sentiment led to an attempt to pass an act appreciably increasing the tariff in 1820. This bill passed the House and failed by only one vote in the Senate, but a similar measure won easily in 1824. Rates on important manufactures as well as on the products of the farm, mines, and quarries were solidly increased by this act and then given a further boost in 1828 when, with the passage of the so-called Tariff of Abominations, rates reached their highest general level before the Civil War. This latter measure, the result of political maneuvering, was especially distasteful to New England representatives. At the same time that they voted for high duties on textiles, they were forced also to approve rates which penalized wool manufacturers by high duties on raw wool, shipbuilders by high duties on hemp and ship iron, and rum manufacturers by a high tariff on molasses. Special tariff acts in 1830 and a general revision in 1832 modified the provisions of the act of 1828 most objectionable to New England manufacturers by reducing rates on needed imported materials. They also helped temporarily to reduce redundant Treasury receipts by placing such commodities as sugar, tea, and coffee on the free list.

Though the tariff act of 1832 had reduced rates to a level about equal to that of the tariff of 1824, it was definitely and systematically protective in intent. The act was bitterly resisted by the Southerners because it seemed definitely to fasten the protective system upon the country. Leading the opposition, South Carolina called a state convention which declared the tariff acts of 1828 and 1832 nullified after February 1, 1833. President Jackson replied with his famous toast, "The Federal Union—it must be preserved." The crisis passed with the adoption of the Compromise Tariff of 1833. This measure provided that by July 1, 1842, duties should be lowered to 20 per cent, a level close to the average duties imposed under the tariff of 1816. This reduction was to be made in steps, one tenth in each of the years 1834, 1836, 1838, and 1840, and six tenths in 1842, of which one half was to come on January 1 and the rest on July 1.

The Tariff History of the United States (New York: G. P. Putnam's Sons, 1892), pp. 29–36.

Though these reductions were made as planned, the low level finally reached by the middle of 1842 was not permitted to prevail for more than a few weeks. The strongly protectionist Whig party had gained control of the government, the deep depression beginning in 1839 had led to a popular demand for remedial legislation, and temporary Treasury deficits seemed to indicate a need for higher duties. On August 30, 1842, a new tariff act went into effect which substantially raised duties. But in 1844 the Democrats returned to power, business improved, and Treasury surpluses reappeared. Over strong opposition from New England and the Middle Atlantic states, the so-called Walker Tariff was adopted in 1846. Though still mildly protective, this act brought a general lowering of rates. It also greatly simplified the form of tariff legislation by classifying all dutiable commodities in a small number of groups or schedules and provided for single ad valorem rates on each schedule.

There followed a decade during which protective sentiment was at low ebb. Times were good and Treasury receipts more than ample. In line with growing free-trade sentiment and in order to reduce redundant funds in the Treasury, the tariff act of 1857 was passed to lower duties still further. The free list was enlarged in this tariff, and rates now averaged less than 20 per cent. In harmony with European trends, the United States appeared to be moving toward a policy of genuine free trade.

The panic of 1857 broke in August. The Treasury ran sizable deficits and had to resort to borrowing to meet current obligations. Manufacturing interests in New England and New York (especially the manufacturers of woolens, who benefited from lowered rates on imports of raw wool) seem to have been fairly well satisfied with the tariff of 1857. But not so the iron and steel interests of Pennsylvania or the sheep raisers of Ohio and Vermont. The rising Republican party, making a high protective tariff one of the chief planks in its platform, won the election of 1860. In 1861, after some of the southern members had withdrawn, Congress passed the Morrill Tariff for the twin purposes of increased revenue and higher protection.[15]

The foregoing paragraphs give but the briefest outline of tariff legislation and hardly do justice to a subject which was a leading political issue of the period. But the economic significance of the tariff seems to have been not unlike that of the medicinal importance to the Chinese of the chief American export to them, the ginseng

[15] Richard Hofstadter, "The Tariff Issue on the Eve of the Civil War," *American Historical Review*, XLIV, No. 1 (October, 1938), 50–55.

root. The inert ingredients of this plant were believed by the Chinese to have marvelous curative properties, just as the tariff was thought, often by both its friends and its enemies, to have an almost magic effect upon business conditions, raising or lowering the general level of wages, precipitating business panics, or promoting eras of prosperity. Thus protectionists regarded the lowered tariff of 1833 as the cause of the panic of 1837 and advocates of free trade believed the Walker Tariff of 1846 to be the fundamental reason for the prosperity of the early fifties. Of course, a change in the duties on imports may sometimes be a factor affecting the course of business, but that any of the tariff acts passed before 1860 played a very important role in causing either good or bad times has yet to be demonstrated.

The tariff was one of many factors influencing the development of manufacturing in the United States, 1815–1860, but its exact role is not easily determined because of two major difficulties: frequent changes took place in the level, form, and administration of import duties; and other important and often-changing influences were present. In addition, questions such as the following repeatedly arise: Did the duty on the finished manufactured products compensate, and if so, to what extent, for the tariff on necessary raw materials? Did protection to one industry stimulate or possibly retard the growth of some others? Did duties which reduced foreign competition stimulate or discourage technological change in the protected American industry? In view of these as well as other difficulties, it is perhaps hardly surprising that careful students are extremely cautious in drawing conclusions as to the influence of the tariff. One of the ablest of American economic historians, writing in the first decade of the twentieth century, said of American tariff history before 1860: "It is not going too far to say that no important feature in our economic development during that period can be attributed unmistakably to tariff legislation. No important industries can be said to have been created or prevented from growth by that legislation. Other influences determined the main features of development, and the tariff policy did nothing more than modify them a little, where it had any effect at all." [16] Studies made in subsequent decades have tended to confirm the soundness of the foregoing statement,[17] though some theoretical

[16] Guy Stevens Callender, *Selections from the Economic History of the United States, 1765–1860* (Boston: Ginn and Company, 1909), p. 488.

[17] Taussig, *The Tariff History of the United States*, pp. 1–154; Clark, *History of Manufactures in the United States*, I, 274–312; Chester Whitney Wright, *Wool-Growing and the Tariff* (Vol. V of *Harvard Economic Studies*, Boston: Houghton Mifflin Company, 1910), Chaps. 3–5; Cole and Williamson, *The American Carpet Manufacture*, Chaps. 3 and 6; Cole, *The American Wool Manufacture*, Vol. I, Chaps. 7 and 17.

analysis indicates the possibility that protection may have helped somewhat toward raising the real wages of labor.[18]

OTHER ECONOMIC ACTIVITIES OF THE FEDERAL GOVERNMENT

Special attention has now been given to the fiscal operations of the federal government, to the protective tariff, and, in earlier chapters, to the ambitious federal ventures into the various fields of transportation. Aside from its fiscal operations, the economic activities of the federal government may be roughly classified into those involving government ownership or operation, those supplying special help or protection to industry, and, finally, those chiefly of a regulatory character. In considering each of these fields of activity, only the more important governmental activities which have not already been described will be given attention.

Though the national government did not own and operate many economic projects, some of its ventures were of considerable importance. The United States Post Office is, of course, the most obvious example of this type of activity. As shown in Chapter VII, the government rapidly improved and extended its postal services during the forties and fifties. By 1860, when its annual expenditures equaled more than $19,000,000,[19] the Post Office was among the very largest business enterprises in the country. It will also be remembered that the longest and most expensive of all the turnpikes, the National Road, as well as a number of frontier military roads, was built by the federal government. But none of these roads remained long in federal hands, for they were soon turned over to the states through which they passed. Other federal projects of some importance include the lighthouse service, the mint, river and harbor improvements, armories, Indian factories, hospitals for seamen, and the first telegraph line. Of these the last three may be singled out for brief attention.

The government Indian trading posts, or "factories" as they were usually called, were established by act of Congress in 1796 in the hope that they would be of real help to the Indians by rescuing the trade from its debased character through the yardstick of fair competition and would assist the United States in winning over the friendship of the Indians. The factories were located on the frontier and manned by federal employees who sold supplies to the Indians at cost and took in exchange skins and furs. Though faced with aggressive com-

---

[18] Wolfgang F. Stolper and Paul A. Samuelson, "Protection and Real Wages," *Review of Economic Statistics*, IX (November, 1941), 58–73.
[19] *Annual Report of the Postmaster General*, 1948, p. 152.

petition from private companies which extended liberal credit and often provided the Indians with alcoholic beverages, the government factories were able to give some benefits to the Indians and to retain so substantial a part of the fur trading business that John Jacob Astor's American Fur Company found it worth while to bring pressure to bear on Congress to repeal the act establishing the government factories. This repeal was accomplished apparently without serious difficulty in May, 1822. Leading officials of the American Fur Company lobbied in Washington as Senator Thomas H. Benton, the company's attorney, saw the bill through Congress. It was promptly signed by President Monroe, who raised no objection to the bill and was doubtless glad to be able to do a favor for his personal friend John Jacob Astor.[20]

The relatively small extent to which the federal government actually went into business was due in part, at least, to the widespread belief that the federal constitution limited federal projects to those having to do with defense, the mails, Indian affairs, and interstate and foreign commerce—that all projects not clearly permitted by the Constitution were closed to the federal government and open only to the states or their subdivisions. With the exception of transportation, not many new fields existed where the federal government might easily have entered during this period. But where a real need for federal ownership of facilities appeared, practically no opposition to it seems to have developed.

In the one field where, at the beginning of United States history, federal social insurance seemed to be needed—that is, for sick and disabled seamen—compulsory sick insurance by the federal government was adopted without serious objection on either constitutional or other grounds. In the first decades of United States history, sailors were the one class of workmen who traveled far from their own homes and who might find themselves ill and stranded in a distant part of the country. They were essentially the responsibility of the nation rather than of the jurisdiction in which they fell ill. Following British and state precedents, the United States government enacted legislation in 1798 which provided that masters of vessels must withhold

[20] For the debate in Congress on the bill see *Annals of Congress*, 17 Cong., 1 Sess. (1821–1822), pp. 317–424. See also *American State Papers: Indian Affairs*, II, 326–364; Hiram Martin Chittenden, *The American Fur Trade of the Far West* (2 vols., New York: The Press of the Pioneers, 1935), I, 14–17; Kenneth Wiggins Porter, *John Jacob Astor, Business Man* (Vol. I in *Harvard Studies in Business History*, 2 vols., Cambridge: Harvard University Press, 1931), II, 709–714; Edgar B. Wesley, "The Government Factory System among the Indians, 1795–1822," *Journal of Economic and Business History*, IV, Pt. 2, No. 3 (May, 1932), 503–510.

20 cents monthly from the wages of each seaman and that out of the funds thus collected the federal government should provide temporary relief for sick and disabled seamen. Amended in minor details and extended to cover those engaged in navigation on the lakes, canals, and rivers, this law remained in force throughout the years covered by this study. The law was not always efficiently administered, but to 1861, twenty-seven federal hospitals were erected by the government for this purpose, and over $7,000,000 was spent, of which about $4,600,000 came from seamen's contributions and the remainder from the federal treasury.[21]

In order to build an experimental line to test out the magnetic telegraph, toward the development of which he had made significant contributions, Samuel F. B. Morse was desperately in need of capital. When this was not forthcoming from private sources, Morse finally, in 1843, persuaded Congress to appropriate enough money to permit a line to be built from Washington to Baltimore under his supervision. When placed in operation the following year, this government-owned utility demonstrated the practical effectiveness of the new instrument of communication. The United States government not only owned this, the first magnetic telegraph line in the United States, but proceeded to operate it with the Postmaster General, Cave Johnson, in charge. Morse now tried his best to sell his patent to the government. And the Postmaster General, who had earlier been skeptical, urged that the telegraph should be taken over and operated, like the mails, as a government monopoly. But Congress, becoming engrossed with other matters, refused to act. Finally, the money-making possibilities of the telegraph began to be sensed and private capital rapidly took over.[22]

The principal methods by which the federal government gave special assistance to state or private economic ventures have already been described elsewhere in this volume and so need only be mentioned here. They include tremendous aid to internal improvements, tariff protection to native industries, as well as ship subsidies and legislation designed to protect the merchant marine, including the exclusion of foreign ships from the coastwise trade. To these positive attempts of the national government to help special groups should

---

[21] Henry W. Farnam, *Chapters in the History of Social Legislation in the United States to 1860* (Washington: Carnegie Institution of Washington, 1938), pp. 231–242. See also Hunter, *Steamboats on the Western Rivers*, pp. 462–463.

[22] Robert Luther Thompson, *Wiring a Continent: The History of the Telegraph Industry in the United States, 1832–1866* (Princeton: Princeton University Press, 1947), pp. 16–34.

be added two others not previously described: the large annual grants made to the cod fishing industry, and the procurement activities of government departments.

Bounties to the cod fishing industry, which had been provided as early as Washington's first term, found their justification in the tariff duty on salt and the advantage to national defense of having a large training school for sailors. An act of Congress passed in 1819 somewhat increased the earlier bounty and provided that government payments, varying with the tonnage of the fishing vessels, should be divided between the owners and crew of such boats as had spent four months during the year at sea. Congress laid down conditions for payment of the bounty, which went a long way toward federal control of the organization of the industry. Three fourths of the crew and the master must be United States citizens, and before the boat put out to sea, a United States examiner must check on the crew, the equipment, and the seaworthiness of the vessel. The crew could not be paid wages based on hourly or daily rates but must share in the catch. And the federal bounty itself had to be divided, three eighths to the owner and five eighths to the crew. Despite the fact that the duty on salt was several times reduced, the bounty remained unchanged from 1819 to 1866, and in the aggregate amounted to a very substantial sum totaling nearly $11,000,000 for 1819–1859 and averaging $265,655 per annum. The peak year was 1857, when the bounty to the codfisheries reached nearly $500,000.[23]

Finally, among the promotional activities of the federal government must be noted the stimulus afforded industrial development by government procurement policies. Most effective in this respect were the efforts to encourage the establishment of small-arms manufacturing. Beginning in 1798, it became the practice of the government to make liberal advances to small-arms makers in order to provide them with the capital necessary to make arms needed by the Army and the state militia. Interest was not charged on these advances, which were often so liberal as to leave only small sums due the manufacturer when the arms were finally delivered to the government. Though largely abandoned between 1830 and 1840, this contract system was markedly successful, not only in bringing the industry into existence, but in promoting a spirit of mutual cooperation which greatly stimulated technological advance; moreover, it led to the adoption of the

[23] Raymond McFarland, *A History of the New England Fisheries* (Philadelphia: University of Pennsylvania, 1911), pp. 162–170; and Johnson and others, *History of Domestic and Foreign Commerce of the United States*, II, 163–164.

system of utilizing interchangeable parts. No doubt the American economy would have evolved a system of production based upon the use of interchangeable parts in the course of time, but its early growth appears to have been in no small part the fruit of governmental subsidy and initiative.[24]

The regulatory activities of the federal government, so important today, had important beginnings before 1860, but the field of recognized need was much narrower in the economy of that time. In the field of foreign commerce the responsibility of the federal government was admitted, and, as has been shown in an earlier chapter, detailed legislation not only for regulating foreign commerce but for controlling the merchant marine had become customary by this period. Thus legislation protecting seamen and requiring that a certain percentage of the crew of ships flying the American flag should be citizens of the United States had long been on the statute books. In 1819, 1847, 1848, and 1855, Congress passed laws designed to protect immigrants from overcrowding and unsanitary conditions on their passage across the Atlantic. Unfortunately most of this legislation was so loosely worded or so poorly enforced as to be quite ineffective.[25]

In the realm of internal commerce the need for action by the federal government had not yet become widely evident nor had the courts more than begun that long series of interpretations which later gave such a broad meaning to the term "interstate commerce." Nevertheless in one field—interstate steamboat operation—where the public demanded protection from careless and irresponsible operators, Congress established in 1838 and improved in 1852 a fairly elaborate system of inspection and regulation, and the courts validated such regulation even though it applied to steamboats operating on a river lying entirely within the limits of one state.[26] Of course relations with the Indians were a responsibility of the federal government, and this fact gave rise to legislation as, for example, the prohibition of the sale of alcoholic beverages to the Indians and the requirement that traders with the Indians should be licensed by the federal government. Finally, it may be noted that federal legislation regulating bankruptcies was passed in 1841 but was actually in effect for less than two years, for the law was repealed in 1843.[27]

[24] Deyrup, "Arms Makers of the Connecticut Valley," Chap. 2 and pp. 117–120.
[25] Henry Pratt Fairchild, *Immigration* (New York: The Macmillan Company, 1913), pp. 61–62, 81–87; Farnam, *Chapters in the History of Social Legislation in the United States to 1860*, pp. 242–252.
[26] Hunter, *Steamboats on the Western Rivers*, Chap. 13.
[27] Charles Warren, *Bankruptcy in United States History* (Cambridge: Harvard University Press, 1935), pp. 68–87.

STATE FINANCE AND BORROWING [28]

The fluctuations in state debts provide a rough index of state activity in promoting ventures in banking and internal improvements. The accompanying table presents the statistical picture of these debts, and the pages which immediately follow provide a summary of the following four periods in state financial history from the standpoint of debt development:

1) 1815–1829: Gradual growth of state debts
2) 1830–1840: First great debt expansion
3) 1841–1852: Collapse and slow revival of state credit
4) 1853–1860: Second great debt expansion

From about 1815 to 1829 the states were in a remarkably strong financial position. Largely freed from debt by the act of 1793, under

BOND ISSUES OF STATES, 1820–1838

(in thousands of dollars)

State	1820 to 1825	1825 to 1830	1830 to 1835	1835 to 1838	Total
Alabama	$ 100	....	$ 2,200	$ 8,500	$ 10,800
Arkansas	....	....	....	3,000	3,000
Illinois	....	....	600	11,000	11,600
Indiana	....	....	1,890	10,000	11,890
Kentucky	....	....	....	7,369	7,369
Louisiana	1,800	....	7,335	14,000	23,135
Maine	....	....	555	....	555
Maryland	58	$ 577	4,210	6,648	11,493
Massachusetts ..	....	....	....	4,290	4,290
Michigan	....	....	....	5,340	5,340
Mississippi	....	....	2,000	5,000	7,000
Missouri	....	....	....	2,500	2,500
New York	6,873	1,624	2,205	12,229	22,931
Ohio	....	4,400	1,701	....	6,101
Pennsylvania ...	1,680	6,300	16,130	3,167	27,277
South Carolina ..	1,250	310	....	4,000	5,560
Tennessee	....	....	500	6,648	7,148
Virginia	1,030	469	686	4,133	6,318
Total	$12,791	$13,680	$40,012	$107,824	$174,307

Source: Tenth Census of the United States; Valuation, Taxation, and Public Indebtedness, VII, 523.

which the federal government took over their past obligations, and having no need to expend appreciable sums, most of the states easily

[28] In addition to the works specifically referred to below, the following standard works have been drawn upon in preparing this section: Ratchford, *American State Debts,* Chaps. 4 and 5, and Reginald C. McGrane, *Foreign Bondholders and American State Debts* (New York: The Macmillan Company, 1935), *passim.*

met current needs out of current revenues. To some the War of 1812 brought unexpected defense expenditures, but the states had been largely reimbursed for these outlays by 1820. New York, with outstanding obligations of about $3,000,000, was the only state having a sizable public debt in 1815.

To the end of the twenties state disbursements continued to be relatively small, for neither schools nor public roads, to say nothing of the other services furnished by modern state governments, had yet become a heavy charge against state revenues. Thus in 1825 Massachusetts was almost free of debt. Its annual expenditures were $198,500, of which the three leading items were $93,600 for salaries, $51,400 for charitable outlays, and $17,600 for penal purposes. In that year the per capita state tax was only 35 cents, apparently the lowest it has ever been.[29] Detailed expenditures for Ohio, first published in 1822, show a total of $77,000 spent in that year, largely for the machinery of government, though $10,000 went for the penitentiary and smaller sums for printing expenses, the militia, and so on.[30] Finally, it may be noted that for the whole period 1796–1825, $13,301,000 was spent on common schools in the state of New York. But of this total the state treasury contributed less than $1,000,000 and local taxation produced about $3,000,000; more than two thirds came from the gifts of individuals.[31]

Even with their rather rudimentary systems of taxation, the states found little difficulty in securing the funds necessary for disbursements as limited as those just indicated. And the task was further lightened because most of the states secured more or less revenue from the sale of public lands, and many had an appreciable income from investments. A considerable number of the states received substantial returns on bank stock, much of which had been received in exchange for charter privileges. But these were by no means the only securities held. Thus in 1822 five states owned United States bonds worth more than $700,000. Pennsylvania, whose holdings of securities were especially large, earned $127,000 on its investments in 1820, a sum larger than that received from all other sources. So taxes were generally light. In a number of the older states in the East, property and poll taxes were avoided for considerable periods. Thus Pennsylvania in 1820 raised ample revenues largely from license fees and taxes

[29] Charles J. Bullock, "Historical Sketch of the Finances and Financial Policy of Massachusetts from 1780 to 1905," *Publications of the American Economic Association*, 3d series, VIII, No. 2 (1907), 23–24.

[30] Bogart, *Financial History of Ohio*, pp. 76–77.

[31] Sowers, *The Financial History of New York State from 1789 to 1912*, p. 193.

on bank dividends. New York had a general property tax from 1815 through 1826 but had none from the latter year until 1843. Appreciable sums were raised from the tax on lotteries during the years 1816–1820. Approximately $750,000 came from this source in this five-year period.[32] In the early twenties Massachusetts revenues were derived about half from property and poll taxes and half from a tax on banks.[33] The southern and western states, on the other hand, were chiefly dependent on general property taxes, but the rates were generally low. From 1819 through 1825 in Ohio, where, for purposes of taxation, land was placed in three categories according to quality, the amount of tax on 100 acres was in no year higher than $1.50 for land of the first rate, $1.125 for second rate, and $.75 for third rate.[34]

The growth of state debts for the purpose of financing internal improvements, largely canals, was gradual until about 1830. The total amount borrowed by the states 1820–1830 was only a little over $26,000,000, and two states, New York and Pennsylvania, were responsible for more than half of this sum. Then in the 1830's the first real boom in state-financed internal improvements took place. During 1830–1838 states borrowed nearly $150,000,000, and by 1838 the total of their outstanding debt amounted to $170,806,187. According to the Tenth Census of the United States,[35] this debt was contracted for the following purposes:

Banking	$52,640,000
Canals	60,201,551
Railroads	42,871,084
Turnpikes	6,618,868
Miscellaneous	8,474,684
Total	$170,806,187

Borrowing for banking purposes was largely confined to western and southern states; in fact, two thirds of it arose from borrowing by Louisiana, Mississippi, and Alabama. But the greater part of the debt increase for internal improvements was incurred by eastern, chiefly Middle Atlantic, states, with Pennsylvania and New York together responsible for over one third of the total.

As long as the boom lasted, the states had little trouble in borrowing by selling their bonds either at home or abroad. The past record of the states in meeting their financial obligations without difficulty

[32] Ibid., p. 649.
[33] Bullock, "Historical Sketch of the Finances and Financial Policy of Massachusetts from 1780 to 1905," pp. 28–30.
[34] Bogart, Financial History of Ohio, p. 182.
[35] Tenth Census of the United States: Valuation, Taxation, and Public Indebtedness, VII, 526.

bred optimism, and the rapid retirement of the federal debt not only freed funds for reinvestment but greatly impressed foreign lenders, who did not always distinguish clearly between federal and state obligations. Even the panic of 1837 was not a decisive blow. A number of the states were caught with important works under way which were largely useless unless completed, and the improvement of conditions in 1838 made many believe the business reaction to be a temporary one.

But the era came definitely to an end with the second crisis, which broke in 1839. By that time the states had definitely exhausted their credit, and it had become apparent that the expected returns on their investments in banks and internal improvements would not materialize. Instead of receiving the major part of their income, as had been expected, from their investments in banks or internal improvements, the states were suddenly faced with the necessity of taxing their citizens in order to meet the interest on debts incurred in order to promote banking or public works projects. The shock was more than most of the heavily indebted states were prepared to meet. By December, 1842, Florida, Mississippi, Arkansas, Indiana, Illinois, Maryland, Michigan, Pennsylvania, and Louisiana had defaulted on at least some of their obligations, and Ohio and New York were saved from similar humiliation only by taking extraordinary measures.

Efforts at further borrowing were now hopeless, and for nearly a decade the states struggled to recover financial solvency. One effort directed to this end was the agitation for legislation requiring the national government to assume the states' debts. This was strongly favored by Pennsylvania and Maryland, two heavily indebted states, and naturally also by foreign investors holding the bonds of American states. But though strenuous efforts were made to get favorable legislation during 1840–1843, Congress refused to come to the aid of the states.

Three states and the Territory of Florida actually repudiated bonds having principal values approximately as follows:

Arkansas	$ 500,000
Florida	4,000,000
Michigan	2,270,000
Mississippi	7,000,000

Arkansas and Michigan could claim some legal justification for their action, but no sound case can be made out for the other two. The bondholders and their descendants, many of them residents of foreign countries, have never ceased protesting this action, and from time to time still attempt to collect what they believe due them. The immediate result of this debt repudiation was, of course, to make investors wary of buying state obligations of any kind. This feeling was still so strong in the fifties as to hurt the foreign market for the bonds of American states.

The other states, those which had fallen into grave financial difficulties but did not repudiate their obligations, were forced to take strenuous measures to meet interest payments on their swollen debts. Most states now sold the securities and the public works they owned for what these would bring. Thus Louisiana, which had gone into debt to the extent of about $23,000,000 to subsidize banking, recovered something over $3,000,000 by selling bank stock, and Pennsylvania sold her system of public works, which had originally cost about $30,000,000, for approximately $11,000,000. In addition, though some put it off as long as possible, practically all of the states in financial difficulties now had seriously to begin to tax. In an attempt to avoid levying substantial general property taxes, a number of states imposed taxes on banks and other corporations while others attempted to raise money by licenses on occupations. Attempts to impose state income and inheritance taxes brought in but little revenue. Finally, most states were forced to lean heavily on general property taxes and, as a consequence, to give some attention to improving the administration of this tax. The older system of collecting a fixed sum an acre or a unit had been gradually abandoned as higher rates led to insistent demands for more refined methods of valuation. Also, as the tax rates became heavier, complaints grew of inequalities arising from appraisal standards, which varied from one locality to another, and led to the establishment of state equalization boards.

The need for greatly increased revenues to service the swollen state debts led to some attempts to economize, but before long, and especially as prosperity returned in the fifties, most states rapidly increased their expenditures. These increases are, of course, partly explained by the almost universal tendency of governmental bodies to enlarge their disbursements when times are good and prices rising. Nevertheless, one aspect of the mounting disbursements warrants brief attention.

In the northern and western states there was a strong tendency after about 1840 to increase expenditures for charitable, correctional, and penal institutions. In part, of course, this resulted from the rapid increase in population. In addition, the humanitarian movement of the forties stressed the need for prison reform and emphasized the responsibility of the state for the care of paupers and the physically or mentally handicapped. In Massachusetts in 1825 state expenditures for charitable and penal purposes were $69,000. By 1850 they had risen to nearly $200,000, and were $654,000 in 1855 and $523,000 in 1860.[36] A similar trend in Ohio shows annual expenditures for charitable, correctional, and penal institutions averaging less than $10,000 for 1822–1829, moving irregularly higher during the next two decades to $73,000 in 1850, and then expanding greatly with annual disbursements averaging nearly $300,000 for 1856–1860.[37]

During the years 1841–1853 some states were able to reduce their indebtedness while others increased it, but for the period as a whole the total debt of the states changed very little. Reported as standing at $190,000,000 in 1841, the aggregate debt of the states had increased twelve years later by only $3,000,000. But then, from 1853 to the Civil War, state debts experienced a second though less hectic period of rapid expansion, rising from $192,500,000 to $257,500,000.

A few states, notably Alabama, Illinois, and Louisiana, actually reduced their indebtedness during these years. But during the same time others incurred new debts amounting to about $90,000,000. New York was the only state now involved which had been a heavy borrower in the early boom. Traffic on the Erie Canal had so expanded as to make necessary a very expensive enlargement, and capital was now borrowed by the state for that purpose. The other important borrowers during this period—Missouri, North Carolina, Tennessee, and Virginia—increased their debts chiefly to finance railroad construction.

This was a decade, it will be remembered, of such tremendous enthusiasm for railroads that undoubtedly the increase in state debts for this purpose would have been much larger had it not been for a number of important restraining influences: (1) some of the states had not yet recovered their credit and were burdened with heavy debts incurred during the thirties; (2) nineteen states had been so affected by the severe crises following the boom of the thirties that they had amended their constitutions so as to impose debt limitations upon themselves; (3) foreign investors were still reluctant to invest in the

[36] Bullock, "Historical Sketch of the Finances and Financial Policy of Massachusetts from 1780 to 1905," pp. 44–46.
[37] Bogart, *Financial History of Ohio*, pp. 134, 136.

obligations of American states; and (4) the federal government was beginning to assume an important part of the financial burden of railroad building through grants of public lands for this purpose.

ECONOMIC ACTIVITIES OF THE STATES

The political changes brought about by the American Revolution had little effect upon either the theory or the practice of the relation of government to economic life. The wide area of economic regulation typical of the colonial days continued with little change in the newly formed states during the early national period and into the decades covered by this study. In fact, the tremendous economic changes following 1815, for the most part, actually led to expanded governmental action. And, as the Constitution seemed to place close limits on the functions of the federal government, the chief responsibility for taking over new activities fell upon the states. Most of these economic activities of the states, especially those having to do with transportation and banking, have already been described. In any case the economic interests of the state governments were of so many different kinds and varied so much from state to state that only a summary treatment is possible here. For this purpose the economic functions of the states may be classified under three heads: (1) those of a regulatory character; (2) those whose purpose was primarily to protect or subsidize some economic interest; and (3) those which involved state participation in industry either through mixed enterprise or through full-fledged state ownership and control.

Typical of the long-established regulatory activities is the assize of bread. Detailed specification as to the size and price of loaves of bread which might be sold in American cities was not uncommon even after 1815. In 1818, five hundred underweight loaves of bread were seized in Charleston and, as required by law, were advertised to be given to the poor.[38] As late as 1851 the legislature of the state of Iowa, in granting a charter to the city of Davenport, provided among numerous taxing and regulatory powers the right "to regulate the weight, quality and price of bread to be sold and used in the city." [39] But as markets outgrew local limits, state regulation became of increased importance, and legislatures concerned themselves with establishing

[38] *Niles' Weekly Register,* XIV (August 8, 1818), 407.
[39] Ivan L. Pollock, *History of Economic Legislation in Iowa* (Iowa City: Clio Press, 1918), pp. 280, 357. See also Bayrd Still, "Patterns of Mid-Nineteenth Century Urbanization in the Middle West," *Mississippi Valley Historical Review,* XXVIII, No. 2 (September, 1941), 192–193.

state-wide standards for weights and measures. Especially common were official inspections designed primarily to ensure honest quality and measurement of articles destined for export. Thus, the state of Pennsylvania provided inspection programs for such products as "flour, fish, beef, pork, hogslard, flaxseed, butter, biscuits, harness and leather, tobacco, shingles, potash and pearlash, staves, heading and lumber, ground black-oak bark, pickled fish, spirituous liquors, and gunpowder." [40] With the transportation revolution came the gradual disappearance of the family cow, and this fact led to the necessity of protecting the common milk supply. In 1856 Massachusetts adopted legislation designed to prohibit the adulteration of milk, and two years later made illegal the feeding of distillery waste.[41]

Municipal regulation of markets, of hackney rates, and of transportation of goods by wagon or dray was common in 1815. The growth of canals and railroads had led by 1860 to an increasing amount of regulation, largely but not exclusively through provisions in corporation charters, which included not only rates and fares but also such matters as speed, prevention of accidents, and standards of service. Gas, water, and even ice companies came in for similar attention from the states.[42]

The appearance of the factory system and the growing numbers of industrial wage workers raised new problems for the state legislatures and marked the beginning of modern labor legislation. Acts were passed by some eastern states providing for compulsory school attendance by children employed in factories, prohibiting child labor before a specified minimum age, and, in a few states, setting limits on the maximum number of hours of labor a day or week for factory workers. But as has already been noted in Chapter XIII, the state labor legislation adopted in the forties and fifties was ineffectively drafted and poorly enforced.[43] Nonetheless, these state labor laws are of interest as indicating the reopening of a large field of state control which had been of wide importance during the colonial period and was destined to be the center of much attention again in the twentieth century.

Other regulatory actions by the states can merely be mentioned,

[40] Hartz, *Economic Policy and Democratic Thought: Pennsylvania, 1776–1860*, p. 205.

[41] Edmund E. Vial, "Milk Supply," *Encyclopaedia of the Social Sciences*, X (New York: The Macmillan Company, 1933), 475.

[42] Hartz, *Economic Policy and Democratic Thought: Pennsylvania, 1776–1860*, pp. 251–261; Handlin, *Commonwealth*, pp. 240–241, 220–221; Martin, *The Standard of Living in 1860*, p. 264, fn.

[43] See pages 282–283.

although some, like those controlling the chartering of corporations, were of the greatest significance. Licenses, like those on peddlers and brokers, and taxes, like those on sales at auctions, for example, were commonly utilized for regulatory purposes.[44] The great reform and humanitarian movement of the time was reflected in legislation regulating or prohibiting the sale of lottery tickets and alcoholic beverages. Periods of depression, as well as the new humanitarianism, led to legislation protecting debtors, providing for mechanics' liens, and modifying the earlier legislation on imprisonment for debt.

Much state activity in the economic field arose from the effort to subsidize or give special assistance to particular economic groups or interests, i.e., for states within their own limits to favor certain interests just as did the federal government on a national scale through the tariff. Thus New York lent state funds directly to farmers on mortgage security, and the state of Maine made a brief and costly excursion into the field of farm relief in the late thirties when it offered bounties on the production of wheat and corn, which took more than $150,000 out of the state treasury in 1839.[45] Agricultural fairs and societies were often state-subsidized, especially in the northern states. At least nine states offered bounties on silk culture during the thirties and forties, and one of these, Massachusetts, paid to have a manual written on this subject for general distribution.[46]

Between 1812 and 1830 Vermont made generous provision for exemption from taxation for local manufacturing establishments, and the state of New York, by a law adopted in 1817, freed textile mills from taxation and their employees from jury duty and militia service.[47] Industrial fairs, sometimes with premiums for winning entries paid out of state funds, were also tried.[48] The General Assembly of

[44] Many state laws regulated peddlers and auctions. See Fred Mitchell Jones, *Middlemen in the Domestic Trade of the United States, 1800–1860* (University of Illinois *Studies in the Social Sciences*, Vol. XXI, No. 3, Urbana: University of Illinois, 1937), pp. 40–43, 62–63; Burdine, "Governmental Regulation of Industry in Pennsylvania, 1776–1860," pp. 133–139.

[45] Sowers, *The Financial History of New York State from 1789 to 1912*, pp. 261, 268–272; Fred Eugene Jewett, *A Financial History of Maine* (No. 432 of *Studies in History, Economics and Public Law*, New York: Columbia University Press, 1937), p. 37.

[46] *Tenth Census of the United States: Manufactures*, II, 919; Hartz, *Economic Policy and Democratic Thought*, App. V, p. 333.

[47] Frederick A. Wood, *History of Taxation in Vermont* (*Studies in History, Economics and Public Law*, Vol. IV, No. 3, New York: Columbia College, 1894), pp. 80–81; Dixon Ryan Fox, *The Decline of Aristocracy in the Politics of New York* (Vol. LXXXVI of Columbia University *Studies in History, Economics and Public Law*, New York: Longmans, Green and Co., 1919), p. 324.

[48] Samuel Rezneck, "The Rise and Early Development of Industrial Consciousness in the United States, 1760–1830," *Journal of Economic and Business History*, IV, Pt. 2, No. 4 (August, 1932), 801–805.

Ohio passed an act in 1823 which exempted from taxation ironworks, glassworks, and textile mills.[49] A number of southern states added grants of land to exemption from taxes in order to encourage iron manufacture.[50] Bounties on ship building are reported to have been offered by both Louisiana and Alabama in 1852.[51] The state of California attempted to hasten the completion of transcontinental telegraph lines by offering generous subsidies to the first two projects making connection with eastern lines.[52]

Interesting because they involved attempts to stimulate local production as against both foreign and out-of-state competitors were the measures taken by the state of New York to protect salt manufacture. In the early forties the canal board permitted a drawback on Erie Canal tolls of 3 cents a pound on all locally produced salt shipped outside the state, and later, when this device was found illegal, the legislature paid a bounty on local salt shipped outside the state, with the result that the New York product sold more cheaply in Massachusetts than at home. In addition, very high canal charges were imposed on foreign salt in an attempt to exclude the imported product from interior markets.[53] Though most of these measures appear to have been rather ineffective in achieving their objects, they do illustrate the general attitude toward state help for economic interests.

But the period of this study was especially remarkable for the degree to which the state governments actually participated in economic enterprises, both through mixed corporations and by complete ownership and control. These activities have already been described elsewhere in this volume, so that only certain aspects need be commented upon here. Of course it should not pass unnoticed that two fields involving large investment, i.e., through roads or turnpikes, and public education, were rapidly taken over by the state and local governments following 1830, although a considerable beginning had already been made even earlier.

Particularly significant is the fact that when the great public works of the period were projected it was usually taken for granted that they should be state enterprises. This was true for a number of

[49] Thomas H. Greer, "Economic and Social Effects of the Depression in 1819 in the Old Northwest," *Indiana Magazine of History*, XLIV, No. 3 (September, 1948), 234.

[50] Lester J. Cappon, "Trend of the Southern Iron Industry under the Plantation System," *Journal of Economic and Business History*, II, No. 2 (February, 1930), 358.

[51] Clark, *History of Manufactures in the United States, 1607–1860*, I, 470.

[52] Thompson, *Wiring a Continent*, p. 349.

[53] Sowers, *The Financial History of New York State from 1789 to 1912*, pp. 138–140; Israel D. Andrews, "Communication from the Secretary of the Treasury," 1852, *Senate Executive Document* No. 112, 32 Cong., 1 Sess., pp. 441–442.

reasons: (1) The semimonopolistic character of the projects made private control seem dangerous to the public interest. (2) Their purpose was typically to help some important interest within the state or to defeat some powerful out-of-state threat. Thus Mississippi set up and financed a state bank in order to make credit easily available to agriculturists, and Pennsylvania built her great State Works under the spur of competition from New York and Baltimore projects. (3) The large amounts of capital needed were not yet generally available from private sources. (4) If large profits were expected, then it was believed desirable that the whole state should benefit from such profitable investments; and, if losses might follow, then it seemed just that the burden should be borne by the whole people through taxation. (5) Little or no prejudice existed against state enterprise.

Most of the great canals were largely state projects, but the railroads, though largely financed with government help, were for the most part built and operated by private corporations. Yet in the beginning it was generally believed that the railroads should be state enterprises, as indeed they were in part, at least, in such states as Pennsylvania, Georgia, Michigan, and Indiana. In Maryland, the Baltimore and Ohio Railroad, though a private corporation, was largely financed by the city and the state. The huge investment in the Erie Canal caused the citizens of the state of New York to hesitate to create a competitive transportation system. But many felt that railroads should be owned by the state. This view was expressed by the New York businessman, Samuel B. Ruggles, when he wrote in 1838 that "the very idea of employing a private company to construct and manage a public work involves a political absurdity and a paradox in terms." [54]

After the crisis of 1839 the amount of state participation in economic activity tended to decline. This was especially true in states such as Pennsylvania, Ohio, and Indiana, where large investments in internal improvements, especially canals, proved productive of little revenue and burdened the state with such a large debt that bankruptcy was narrowly avoided. In an effort to regain solvency and to avoid heavy taxes, Pennsylvania sold a large part of its investments in private corporations during the forties and disposed of its public works in the following decade. With depleted treasuries and badly

[54] D. G. Brinton Thompson, *Ruggles of New York: A Life of Samuel B. Ruggles* (No. 524 of *Studies in History, Economics and Public Law,* New York: Columbia University Press, 1946), p. 103.

shaken credit, most of the states were not in a position to assume the same role in railroad building which they had played in canal construction. Moreover, it must be emphasized that, by the forties and during the fifties, private capital was much more abundant and available than it had been earlier.

For the first time there now appeared the beginnings of that critical attitude toward state enterprise which later came to be regarded as typical in the United States. This was especially true in Pennsylvania, where administration of the state's works had been inefficient and generally corrupt, although probably no more so than in the case of many private ventures. Moreover, this sentiment was now reinforced by popular propaganda put forth by those interests, chiefly the Pennsylvania Railroad, which in seeking to reduce competition from state projects and to take them over, began to press the viewpoint that state enterprise was unnatural and unwise. No doubt this propaganda would have been less effective if conditions had not been favorable. Yet, at least in its beginnings, the sentiment against state enterprise in Pennsylvania appears to have owed much to agitation by corporations which were seeking to take over state projects.[55]

Taking the period of this study as a whole, it must be concluded that the government, far from playing a neutral part, was an active and extremely important economic factor in the industrial development of the time. The fiscal operations of both federal and state governments, especially because of their close connection with banking and currency, crucially affected conditions in the whole country. The regulatory activities of the federal government made a small beginning even though limited by constitutional provisions, but the states, suffering from no comparable restrictions, did not hesitate to extend economic regulation into many fields. Promotional activities—tariffs by the national government and premiums and bounties by state governments—were widely used with the hope, often illusory, of benefiting home industries. Finally, in no other period of American history has the government been so active in financing and actually promoting, owning, and controlling banks and public works including turnpikes, bridges, canals, and railroads.

[55] Hartz, *Economic Policy and Democratic Thought: Pennsylvania, 1776–1860,* *passim.*

CHAPTER XVII

The National Economy in 1860

RESOURCES AND EXTRACTIVE INDUSTRIES

BETWEEN 1815 and 1860 Florida, Texas, and the Far West were added to the territorial possessions of the United States, with a resulting increase in area of 1,307,000 square miles or about 76 per cent. Though significant for the future, the addition of this vast area had a relatively small influence on American industrial development before 1860. Some trade and agricultural activity appeared, and the discovery of gold in California in 1848 led to the rapid settlement of that region. But for the most part this newer territory remained but sparsely populated and largely unexploited until later in the century.

According to the census of 1860, the total population of the United States had reached 31,443,321, with 19,690,000 accredited to the North; 11,133,361 to the South; and only 619,000 to the West.[1] Of every seven persons, one was a Negro and one was of foreign birth. Immigration, which had been small in the generation ending with the War of 1812, grew rapidly thereafter. More than 5,000,000 entered between 1819 and 1860, and of these more than half arrived during the fifties. Over one half of the immigrants came from Great Britain and Ireland, and about one third from Germany.

Resources in one extractive industry, fur trading and trapping, had been so fully exploited that the product had actually begun to decline. Though fur traders and trappers still operated widely in the West and Far West, their business had been generally dwindling since the thirties. Expanding settlement and destructive methods tended to reduce the supply, and, at the same time, there appeared seriously unfavorable demand developments. During the thirties

[1] As in 1940 Census: North includes New England, Middle Atlantic, East and West North Central; South includes South Atlantic, East and West South Central; West, Mountain and Pacific states.

the market fell off sharply as silk came to be preferred for hats. Also nutria, chiefly South American, became more fashionable than muskrat fur.

On the Great Plains the vast herds of bison afforded an increasing source of hides. Only small amounts of meat were salvaged. By the 1840's hundreds of thousands were being slain annually; 800,000 was the contemporary estimate for the 1859–1860 season.[2] They were so numerous—the total number was estimated at 15,000,000—that this tremendous slaughter continued for two decades after 1860 before the herds were largely killed off.

Fishing, an activity even older than the fur trade, experienced a vigorous growth in the decades following the War of 1812. Expanding domestic markets took an increasing portion of the enlarged catch, and foreign markets, especially those of the West Indies, absorbed surpluses at advantageous prices. As in earlier years, the cod-fisheries remained most important. But productive new fisheries—mackerel, herring, halibut, and lobster—were added. The catch was taken chiefly off the coast of New England and the Maritime Provinces by Americans from fishing towns and villages scattered along the coast from Long Island Sound to Maine. Oysters became one of the most favored American delicacies during this period, the earliest canals and railroads being used to transport barrels of fresh oysters westward in order to give variety to the diet of frontier America. The most productive natural oyster beds were found in Chesapeake Bay and northward along the New Jersey coast. Before the close of this period the business of transplanting oysters to more northern waters had been so considerably developed that Connecticut became a leading producer.

Whaling grew phenomenally after 1812, and in some years its value product may have been about equal to that for the rest of the fishing industry. The demand for the products of this sea mammal, especially for illuminating oil, seemed insatiable. Whalers from the ports of New York and New England pursued their quarry to the remotest seas, with the result that the United States became the main producer of whale bone and oil. Whaling gave employment to more than 12,000 men in 1860. Over one half of these workers had their homes in New Bedford, the chief center of the industry.

The total value of the product of American fisheries cannot be determined with any close degree of accuracy. The 1860 census figure of $14,000,000 was admittedly based on seriously incomplete informa-

[2] *De Bow's Review*, XXIX (December, 1860), 783.

tion. On the other hand, Kettell's estimate of $48,000,000 seems too high.[3] At any rate, the contribution of this industry to the national product appears to have been small, amounting to appreciably less than half that from either mining or lumbering.

Mineral production, which, just before the Civil War, stood on the threshold of its period of phenomenal growth, had made only a very small beginning in 1815. From early colonial times iron had been produced in small quantities in many places along the eastern seaboard. By 1860 this was still true, but more than half of the output now came from Pennsylvania, and production in the Ohio and Cumberland valleys was becoming especially important. Development of the rich ores of the Lake Superior region benefited from the opening of the St. Marys Canal in 1855. By 1860 ore from the lake region accounted for almost one tenth of total pig iron production in the United States.

Like iron, copper production had remained relatively small-scale and came from widely scattered deposits. But during the fifties output was considerably increased, both from the Ducktown district on the border where Tennessee joins Georgia and also from the fabulously rich mines of the Upper Peninsula of Michigan. Exploitation of this latter field began in the early 1840's but did not at first become profitable despite the uncovering of rich deposits. During the next decade, however, with the aid of Boston and Pittsburgh investors, Michigan mines showed handsome profits and by 1860 accounted for three fourths of the total national product.[4]

Small quantities of lead had long been produced in the Missouri and the Wisconsin tristate areas. Following 1815 the output from the latter, often referred to as the Galena district, expanded considerably, reaching its maximum in the period 1845–1850. Thereafter output declined as the deposit of easily available ore became exhausted. The output from these two areas was valued at around $1,500,000 annually for the years 1845–1847.[5] Small quantities of gold had been mined in the southern Appalachians before the discovery of the metal in

[3] For statistics on fishing see *Eighth Census of the United States: Manufactures*, *passim*; *Eighth Census of the United States: Mortality and Miscellaneous Statistics*, pp. 527–551; *Eighty Years Progress of the United States* (2 vols., New York: L. Stebbins, 1861), I, 386 (article by Thomas P. Kettell).

[4] Murdoch, *"Boom Copper": The Story of the First U.S. Mining Boom*, Chaps. 3–12, *passim*.

[5] *Hunt's Merchants' Magazine*, XVIII (March, 1948), 292, and XLI (July, 1859), 126; William J. Tenney, ed., *The Mining Magazine*, I (November, 1853), 523; *Niles' Weekly Register*, XXXVIII (May 8, 1830), 204; Joseph Schafer, *The Wisconsin Lead Region* (Madison: State Historical Society of Wisconsin, 1932), *passim*.

California in 1848. Following that year, the California output grew so rapidly that during the fifties gold became the most valuable mineral product of the United States. In 1857 the output of the California mines was valued at nearly $50,000,000.[6]

The existence of vast coal beds in the United States was known in the early national period and even before, but their exploitation awaited the development of cheap transportation and improvements in the technique of their use. Both of these difficulties were sufficiently overcome by the second quarter of the century as to permit a rapid extension of coal mining. For bituminous the chief development came in the mines of the Pittsburgh area, which greatly increased their output to meet the growing needs of the Ohio River Valley. As soon as canals and railroads brought the anthracite of northeastern Pennsylvania to tidewater, this fuel came rapidly into extensive use in the chief coastal cities, both for heating homes and for industrial use. By 1860 the coal production of the United States was valued at $20,000,000, and the great era of coal production had begun. In only twenty years after that date it had increased by about 400 per cent.[7]

In 1859 at Oil Creek, Pennsylvania, the first drilled oil well came into production. The product had long been known, and real progress in the refining process had been made during the fifties. Now, at the very end of this period, a beginning was made toward effective exploitation of one of the most valuable natural resources of the United States.

Lumber production was more than fourteen times greater in 1859 than it had been in 1819.[8] Despite generations of exploitation, during which millions of acres of forest had been burned merely to clear the land for farming, much lumber was still being produced in 1860 in such older states as Connecticut, New York, and Pennsylvania. The census for that year shows the two last states as responsible for about one fourth of the total lumber output. Though regarded as an old lumbering area, the vast forests of Maine were far from exhaustion in 1860, and the industry was just entering upon its great period of rapid growth in Michigan, Wisconsin, and Minnesota. Bangor was the leading lumber market in Maine, and Albany in New York. By 1860 the output of Wisconsin forests had become so great that Chicago had become the greatest lumber center in the world. From as

[6] *Hunt's Merchants' Magazine*, XLI (July, 1859), 80.

[7] *Eighth Census of the United States: Manufactures*, p. 735; Eavenson, *The First Century and a Quarter of American Coal Industry*, p. 420.

[8] *United States Yearbook of Agriculture*, 1933, p. 748.

far north as the St. Croix River tremendous rafts of lumber and logs were being floated down the Mississippi to St. Louis. From southern forests hard pine and cypress shingles moved in growing quantities to northern markets, but the great period of southern exploitation was still to come. By the census referred to above, the gross value of lumber produced in the United States exceeded $100,000,000.[9] In terms of hands employed, as well as value of product, it was, although much less important than agriculture, next to it the leading extractive industry of the United States.[10]

URBANIZATION

It has often been noted that the rapidity of western settlement and the development of western agriculture reflected the revolutionary improvements in transportation, upon which so much emphasis has been placed in preceding chapters. But with attention firmly focused on the western movement, students have tended to overlook the fact that this was the period in American history of the most rapid urbanization. Basic to this city growth was the increasing production of the expanding West and the growing specialization and exchange made possible by improved methods of transportation and communication.

As noted in the first chapter, the proportion of the population living in cities (that is, places of 2,500 or more) was only 6.1 per cent in 1820, and there had been little change since the census of 1810. But from this time on until the Civil War, the cities grew at a more rapid rate than ever before or since in United States history. By 1860 close to 20 per cent of the population were city dwellers. In the forty years between 1820 and 1860 the total population of the United States rose by 226 per cent, but the proportion living in cities increased by 797 per cent. The most rapid urbanization took place in the two decades preceding the Civil War. Total population increased 35.9 per cent during the forties and 35.6 per cent in the fifties; during the same decades urban population grew 92.1 per cent and 75.4 per cent, respectively. In 1820, only 12 cities had a population exceeding 10,000 and only 2 were greater than 100,000. Forty years later, in 1860, 101 cities exceeded 10,000, 8 exceeded 100,000, and New York had passed 1,000,000.

[9] *Eighth Census of the United States: Manufactures*, p. 738.
[10] James Elliott Defebaugh, *History of the Lumber Industry of America* (2 vols., Chicago: The American Lumberman, 1906–1907), *passim;* Agnes M. Larson, *History of the White Pine Industry in Minnesota* (Minneapolis: University of Minnesota Press, 1949), Chaps. 1–6.

The fifteen cities exceeding 50,000 in population, according to the census of 1860, are shown in the accompanying table. These cities, like those in 1820, owed their pre-eminence chiefly to the demands of commerce. The five largest cities in order of size were, as in 1820, the great seaports of New York, Philadelphia, Baltimore, Boston, and New Orleans. Each had benefited not only from the increase of foreign trade, but especially from the greatly increased domestic flow of goods which now moved coastwise and by river, canal, and railroad. Of the next seven cities in order of rank, only Newark was chiefly important as a seaport; all the others owed their growth in large part to the development of commerce by river, canal, or lake, although for each the railroad rapidly began to play a major role.

By 1860 the great era of the industrial city had not yet arrived. However, manufacturing had already become a factor in urban growth and cannot be entirely ignored. New Orleans stands out as the one very large city which was almost completely commercial. Only 3 per cent of its total population was engaged in manufactures in 1860. In New York and Boston 10 and 11 per cent, respectively, of the population were so engaged. Two of the greatest commercial cities—Philadelphia with 17 per cent employed in manufactures, and Cincinnati with 18 per cent—owed their importance almost as much to industry as to commerce. Finally, predominantly manufacturing cities were already appearing with the comparable percentages running 26 for Newark, 36 for Lowell, and 45 for Lynn.[11] Lynn was

THE LEADING CITIES IN 1860

Rank in Order of Population	Name of City	Population	Percentage Engaged in Manufacture
1	New York	1,080,330	9.5
2	Philadelphia	565,529	17.5
3	Baltimore	212,418	8.0
4	Boston	177,840	10.8
5	New Orleans	168,675	3.0
6	Cincinnati	161,044	18.3
7	St. Louis	160,773	5.8
8	Chicago	109,260	4.9
9	Buffalo	81,129	6.9
10	Newark	71,941	26.2
11	Louisville	68,033	9.8
12	Albany	62,367	9.3
13	Washington	61,122	3.9
14	San Francisco	56,802	2.6
15	Providence	50,666	22.0

Source: Eighth Census of the United States: Mortality and Miscellaneous Statistics, p. xviii.

[11] Computed from *Eighth Census of the United States: Mortality and Miscellaneous Statistics,* p. xviii.

the smallest of these, with a population of 19,083. These were the fore-runners of the industrial cities of a later period.

This urban growth, as well as that of large suburban areas, was greatly facilitated by developments in city transportation almost as revolutionary as were the contemporary advances in long-distance transportation. The first marked improvements came with the intro-duction of steam ferries and omnibuses. The former appeared on the Hudson in 1811 and came into general use after 1815. Replacing the unreliable sail-driven craft, they greatly facilitated transportation of persons in the seaport cities. Steam ferries were especially welcome to insular New York. Sailing vessels, which might require several hours to tack their way across the Hudson River, rapidly gave way to steam-driven vessels, which could be depended upon to make the crossing in a matter of minutes.

On city streets omnibuses began to be introduced before 1830. These horse-drawn vehicles carrying twelve to twenty passengers, or even more, helped appreciably toward meeting the problem of rapid transit in the growing urban areas. Early fares were high—10 to 12.5 cents in Philadelphia and 9 cents in Boston. But rates declined, being ultimately only 5 or 6 cents, and omnibus lines operating over the more important streets became an accepted aspect of urban life in America.[12]

Much superior to the omnibuses and of growing importance in the last two decades of the period were the newly built railroads, which promptly developed a heavy local traffic where their lines went through urban or suburban areas. Thus the Boston and Worces-ter Railroad sold its first annual ticket to a commuter in 1838 and by 1843 had put on a special commuters' train, which ran between Bos-ton and West Newton. In 1857 this railroad reported carrying nearly half a million passengers between Boston and stations no farther from the city (ten miles) than Auburndale.[13] In this same year, a local observer wrote: "If by horse one can go eight miles per hour, the diameter becomes sixteen miles, and area two hundred and one square miles; and, if by railroad he moves thirty miles per hour, the diameter becomes sixty miles, and the area 2,827 miles. The effect

[12] Frederic W. Speirs, *The Street Railway System of Philadelphia: Its History and Present Condition* (Johns Hopkins University *Studies in Historical and Political Science*, Vol. XV, No. 3, Baltimore: The Johns Hopkins Press, 1897), 10; Ringwalt, *Develop-ment of Transportation Systems in the United States*, p. 64; Handlin, *Boston's Immi-grants, 1790–1865*, p. 99.

[13] *Twenty-eighth Annual Report of the Directors of the Boston and Worcester Rail-road Corporation for the Year Ending November 30, 1857* (Boston: David Clapp, 1858), pp. 7, 8; and *1858*, p. 4.

of such diffusion is plainly seen about Boston, (Massachusetts). People who in 1830 were mostly confined to the city, now live in Dorchester, Milton, Dedham, Roxbury, Brookline, Brighton, Cambridge, Charlestown, Somerville, Chelsea, Lynn, and Salem; places distant from two to thirteen miles." [14]

But the greatest change in short-distance passenger transportation came in the fifties when street railways with horse-drawn cars became the chief agency for the mass movement of persons in all of the major cities. In New York the five principal street railways were reported to have carried nearly 35,000,000 passengers in 1858. The longest horse-drawn railroad in Boston, the Metropolitan Railroad Corporation, transported nearly 6,500,000 persons in 1860 at an average rate of speed of six and one half miles an hour. Philadelphia was relatively slow in turning to street railways, completing its first one in 1857. But by 1858 it had five lines in operation which were estimated to be carrying 46,000 passengers daily; two years later it had 148 miles of street railway tracks, a greater mileage than any other city. Rates were low, only 5 cents in Boston and New York, and 7 cents in Philadelphia, and service was frequent, with the result that whole new urban areas were opened up as possible living sites for workmen, who had previously been forced to dwell under excessively crowded conditions very close to their work. Thus, Handlin points out that the rapid spread of horsecar lines in Boston in the fifties led to major population shifts, with large numbers of Irish workmen invading residential areas previously closed to them because of transportation difficulties.[15]

General sanitary and health conditions in the fast-growing American cities left much to be desired. In fact, growth of the cities took place despite bad conditions of urban living, not because of appreciable improvements. Streets and alleys, even of the largest cities, were typically not only rutted and full of mud holes, but frequently ankle-deep in garbage, ashes, and filth. Everywhere hogs, dogs, geese, and hordes of rats—and in the South, vultures—acted as scavengers. Most large cities had some rudimentary systems for the disposal of sewage and storm water, but none were extensive or at all

[14] Vose, *Handbook of Railroad Construction*, p. 4.

[15] Handlin, *Boston's Immigrants, 1790–1865*, pp. 99–100; Martin, *The Standard of Living in 1860*, pp. 261–262; Speirs, *The Street Railway System of Philadelphia: Its History and Present Condition*, pp. 16–17; *Return of the Railroad Corporations in Massachusetts, 1860* (Boston: 1861); *The Fifth Return of the Metropolitan Railroad Corporation for the Year Ending November 30, 1860*, p. 3; Vose, *Handbook of Railroad Construction*, p. 4; *Eighth Census of the United States: Mortality and Miscellaneous Statistics*, p. 332; *Hunt's Merchants' Magazine*, XLIV (1861), 375.

adequate to the growing needs. Even in the largest centers of population, water closets were a luxury of the rich, and brimming outdoor toilets, especially in the slum areas, presented with every rain an offense to the senses and a threat to health which seem incredible to city dwellers of the mid-twentieth century.

Most large cities had made some provision for an unfiltered public water supply from nearby rivers or lakes. Progress during the fifties was especially rapid, and the 83 systems operating in 1850 had been increased to 148 in 1860. Nevertheless, a few cities like Milwaukee, Portland, and Providence had no public water systems, and even in those cities which had such works, most people still depended upon wells for drinking water.

Little wonder, therefore, that conditions in American cities were notoriously unhealthy and mortality rates were shockingly high. The statistics, though not fully trustworthy, indicate that death rates were much higher for the cities than for the country as a whole and that New York City's death rate was nearly twice that for London. Down to the Civil War and beyond, epidemics of such diseases as cholera, yellow fever, typhus, and smallpox swept devastatingly through the crowded and unsanitary urban areas. Physicians were generally ill-trained and not often available to care for the poorer people. But this lack of physicians was not always a disadvantage, for medical knowledge was still compounded, in considerable part, of fads and ignorance. Not until 1863 was the first disease microbe identified and the way opened for intelligent control of communicable diseases. The surprising fact is that urban growth was unchecked despite the high mortality rates.[16]

THE GROWTH OF WEALTH AND INCOME

Every record of the years from 1815 to 1860 testifies to the tremendous increase in national wealth, not only in terms of the annual volume of consumption goods and services produced, but also in the unprecedented additions to capital equipment—in roads, canals, ships and steamboats, railroads, factories, and machines. Unfortunately, accurate measurement of this growth in wealth and income is rendered impossible by the lack of adequate statistical records. Yet on the basis of the data available, estimates have been made

[16] Arthur Charles Cole, *The Irrepressible Conflict, 1850–1865* (Vol. VII in *A History of American Life*, Arthur M. Schlesinger and Dixon Ryan Fox, eds., New York: The Macmillan Company, 1934), pp. 179–187; Handlin, *Boston's Immigrants 1790–1865*, Chap. 4; Martin, *The Standard of Living in 1860*, Chap. 8.

which, although subject to substantial error, are worthy of brief notice.

A study which includes only the taxable value of property—and hence probably involves considerable understatement—indicates that national wealth, as so measured, rose from $3,273,000 in 1825 to $16,-160,000 in 1860, or nearly 400 per cent.[17] Estimates for total realized national income show about the same percentage advance. Adjusted for changes in the general price level, they indicate that the average per capita income rose from $168 in 1819 to $300 in 1860.[18] As 1819 was a year of deep depression, it may perhaps be roughly estimated that per capita real income in dollars of constant purchasing power rose by about 50 per cent from 1815 to 1860. About all that can be said as to the reliability of this figure is that, on the basis of what is generally known about the period, the estimate appears fairly plausible.

It would be interesting to know how the increased average per capita income was divided among different occupations and economic groups. According to Alvin Hansen's study, real wages increased nearly 40 per cent from 1820 to 1860.[19] If this is compared with the 50 per cent rise in average per capita income, the implication is that wage earners shared somewhat less than proportionally in the increased income. But the statistical series is not sufficiently reliable to warrant confidence on this point, nor is general descriptive material available such as to justify confident generalization in this respect.

Certainly within the wage earning class marked variations appeared in the extent of the benefit received by different groups. The very poor, the paupers, and the handicapped appear to have been as badly off at the end of the period as they were at the beginning, and there were more of them—possibly even proportionally more— in part, at least, because of the heavy influx of immigrants during the fifties. At least the conditions of urban poverty described in the preceding section of this chapter indicate that many on the lowest rungs of the economic ladder did not benefit from the increased productivity of the period. Some skilled craftsmen, like the hand-loom weavers, actually experienced a degradation of their living conditions as they found themselves forced to compete with the machine or to accept factory employment. On the other hand, workers who pos-

[17] *Historical Statistics of the United States, 1789–1945,* p. 9.
[18] Robert F. Martin, *National Income in the United States, 1799–1938* (New York: National Industrial Conference Board, 1939), p. 6.
[19] Hansen, "Factors Affecting the Trend of Real Wages," p. 32.

sessed mechanical skills—skilled metalworkers, tool makers, and those in the building trades—the demand for whose services expanded rapidly, appear to have gained more than other workmen.[20]

Without attempting to deal with the extremely difficult problem of the extent to which agriculture shared in the gains of the transportation revolution, the question remains as to how the businessmen, the urban owners and managers of enterprises, fared. Two mutually reinforcing circumstances led to the rapid development of the role of the entrepreneur. In the first place, the transportation revolution and the beginnings of the industrial revolution in the relatively undeveloped economy opened up unique opportunities for risk taking and profit. And in the second place, Americans of that age, especially those in the northern states, met the rapidly developing opportunities for material gain with unusual energy and enthusiam. The spirit of adventure, aggressiveness, and willingness to make sacrifices in the hope of economic advantage, which characterized American merchants in the foreign trade and drove settlers to develop the West so rapidly despite all obstacles and uncertainties, also dominated the businessmen who played so active a part in planning, organizing, financing, and managing new ventures in transporting and manufacturing goods.

The indications seem clear that this entrepreneurial group at least retained its proportionate share, and probably more, of the increase in wealth and income. It must not be forgotten, however, that risks were great and that there were many failures, especially during the recurrent financial crises. How far such business losses offset the gains is impossible to say, but certain it is, at least, that the number of wealthy men increased greatly between 1815 and 1860. By the close of the War of 1812 two men, Stephen Girard and John Jacob Astor, had already accumulated great wealth. Possibly there were three or four others like William Gray of Boston who could be regarded as millionaires in that they owned property valued at $1,000,000 or more. Girard's estate was valued in 1831 at about $8,000,000, Astor's in 1848 at more than $20,000,000.

According to a contemporary estimate, New York had 14 millionaires in 1846, 19 persons with property worth $500,000, and 137 whose wealth was estimated to reach at least $250,000.[21] By 1855

[20] History of Wages in the United States from Colonial Times to 1928 (Bulletin No. 499 of the Bureau of Labor Statistics, Washington: Government Printing Office, 1929), passim.

[21] M. Y. Beach, Wealth and Wealthy Citizens of New York, reproduced in Henry

the number of millionaires in New York had risen to 20. Three years later, 25 were claimed for Philadelphia. For Boston, 18 had been reported in 1850. Foreign trade and land speculation appear to have supplied the foundation for most of this wealth, but banking and manufacturing were increasingly important.[22]

The well-to-do businessmen of the northern cities, like the great planters in the slave states, constituted the most powerful class in the community. And business success, never lightly regarded in the commercial centers of the North, became more than ever the prize sought by the able and ambitious. The leading merchants of the colonial period had often been men of broad culture and superior education. Many took an interest in politics and held important governmental positions. This became less true in the early national period after about 1810, as position and success came to be measured more and more by a purely monetary standard. Fewer of the business elite than ever before had more than an elementary education, and among some, at least, the feeling developed that it was hardly necessary for success. And the direct participation of businessmen in politics declined sharply.[23]

Between 1815 and 1860 it was apparently somewhat easier than in earlier decades for farmers and laborers to rise in business to positions of wealth. Apprentices, those with little or no schooling, and those with only an elementary education, stood a better chance of business success than at any time before or since in American history. Yet, although this was true in a relative sense, the majority of successful businessmen continued to come from families ranking in the upper- and upper middle-income groups and from the sons of fathers who were business or professional men or government servants.[24] It was still true, as C. Wright Mills has observed, that "the best statistical chance of becoming a member of the business elite . . . [was] to be born into it." [25]

Wysham Lanier, *A Century of Banking in New York* (New York: George H. Doran, 1922), pp. 151–184.

[22] E. T. Freedley, *Opportunities for Industry and the Safe Investment of Capital* (Philadelphia: J. B. Lippincott Company, 1859), pp. 51–52; Freedley, *Philadelphia and Its Manufactures*, p. 128, fn.; Martin, *The Standard of Living in 1860*, pp. 291–292.

[23] C. Wright Mills, "The American Business Elite: A Collective Portrait," *Tasks of Economic History* (December, 1945), pp. 28–39; Harvey J. Wexler, "How to Succeed in Business, 1840–1860," *Explorations in Entrepreneurial History*, I, No. 1 (January, 1949), 28.

[24] Mills, "The American Business Elite: A Collective Portrait," pp. 28–39.

[25] *Ibid.*, p. 29.

A NATIONAL ECONOMY

1860 the colonial orientation of the American economy as described in the first chapter of this volume had disappeared, and a national economy had taken its place. No longer were more than nine tenths of American agriculture and industry concentrated within a narrow strip extending no farther inland than a hundred miles from the Atlantic coast, nor was dependence upon foreign trade and European markets the almost universal characteristic of the economy. The changes described in the previous chapters, especially those of the transportation revolution, had resulted in the creation of a new and really national economic orientation.

It is true that London was still the financial capital of the world and that America still looked to Great Britain for large extensions of credit. Nevertheless, domestic sources of capital had expanded rapidly, and eastern merchants, although often still dependent on foreign capital, were increasingly able to assume the burden of granting the long credits still customary in domestic commerce. Even in foreign trade, American importers and exporters were beginning to compete on more nearly equal terms with British merchants.

Although foreign commerce had grown tremendously, as has been shown in Chapter IX, it had become largely overshadowed by the domestic trade. The great export staples, cotton and tobacco, were still sent abroad in tremendous quantities, and wheat exports, which had declined after the years immediately following the War of 1812, were again rising to renewed importance in the fifties. But the extreme dependence on foreign markets for disposing of American wheat and tobacco had been greatly reduced. This followed not only from the increasing diversification of American agriculture and industry but also from the tremendously expanded home market for domestic products. Early in the period, home consumption had absorbed a very large part of the wheat production and, despite the greatly expanded tobacco output during the fifties, more than half of that crop was consumed in the United States.

Even for cotton, the exports of which grew so tremendously that this one product may be said to have dominated foreign trade, two developments must be noted. First, though just before the Civil War Great Britain was still absorbing more than half of the United States cotton crop and only about one fourth of the total production was being taken by American factories, American consumption, which had been annually under 100,000 bales until 1823, had risen to about 1,000,000 bales by the end of the fifties. Second, the financing and marketing of this staple had been taken over more and more by New York businessmen. So, although the South with its continued dependence upon cotton monoculture retained an economy of the colonial type, it did so increasingly as a part of the larger national economy of the United States.

The growth of domestic commerce had contributed to the decline of merchant capitalism, possibly already past its zenith in 1815, and by 1860 the organization of both foreign and domestic trade had reached a degree of specialization and a country-wide integration typical of modern national economies. Banking and finance had become a separate calling which was further differentiated with the rise of commercial banks, savings banks, insurance companies, note brokers, clearinghouses, and stock exchanges. With the rise of factories, manufacturing had become separated from marketing, and with the transportation revolution the actual moving of goods in foreign and domestic trade had become largely the responsibility of common carriers. Those who actually traded in goods, whether foreign or domestic, had also become highly specialized operators. Among those were the wholesale merchants who bought and sold goods in large quantities for their own account, and whose business had benefited from the decline of the auctions after the 1820's; commission merchants or factors often specializing in a particular product and buying and selling goods for others; brokers who did not actually receive the goods at all but brought buyer and seller together; and retailers, both those who had specialty shops in the large cities and those much more typical the country over who sold to consumers almost every conceivable product and service.

New York had firmly established itself as the great distributing center of the nation for both domestic and foreign goods. Here, centered in Pearl Street, were the jobbers and wholesalers to whose establishments came by coastwise vessel and railroad train country retailers from the South and West. Traveling salesmen, though increasing rapidly, were as yet relatively few in number. Retailers and wholesalers flocking to the metropolis on the Hudson divided their time between visiting the countinghouses to buy supplies for the coming season and enjoying a holiday in the big city. But not all storekeepers could afford an annual trip to New York. So regional jobbing centers grew rapidly, especially in the decade preceding 1860, with places like Augusta, Memphis, and Louisville in the

innati, St. Louis, and Chicago in the West, becom-
g importance.[26] Certain cities became trading centers
ommodities and developed highly specialized market-
s. Thus, by 1860 cotton was sold by sample in New
Orleans, and tremendous quantities of grain changed
han.. icago and Buffalo merely on the basis of recognized
grades. Boston had become the leading wool market of the country,
St. Louis led in the marketing of furs, while Chicago and Albany
were the leading marts for lumber.

This emerging national economy of 1860 had a new orientation.
The great cities of the East no longer faced the sea and gave their
chief attention to shipping and foreign trade. Their commerce centered increasingly now at the railroad stations rather than at the
docks, and the commercial news from Mobile, Memphis, Louisville,
Cleveland, and Chicago was awaited with greater interest than that
from Liverpool, Marseilles, or Antwerp. But though the American
economy now faced the rapidly developing West, the leadership and
the organizing genius remained concentrated in the great eastern
cities. There, on Wall Street, State Street, and Broad Street, the leaders of the emerging era of finance capitalism were beginning to appear. By means of well-placed investments, by speculation and manipulation on the stock and produce exchanges, and by membership
on the boards of directors of banks, insurance companies, cotton mills,
and railroads, these rising entrepreneurs, the successors of the older
sedentary merchants, were soon to play the directing role in the emerging national economy of stocks and bonds and debentures.

[26] Fred Mitchell Jones, *Middlemen in the Domestic Trade of the United States,
1800–1860* (University of Illinois *Studies in the Social Sciences,* Vol. XXI, No. 3, Urbana: University of Illinois, 1937), *passim;* Lewis E. Atherton, *The Pioneer Merchant
in Mid-America* (*University of Missouri Studies,* Vol. XIV, No. 2, Columbia: The
University of Missouri, 1939), *passim;* Theodore F. Marburg, "Manufacturer's Drum-
mer, 1832," *Bulletin of the Business Historical Society,* XXII, No. 2 (April, 1948), 40–56.

Bibliography

GENERAL

MOST comprehensive historical works on the period 1815–1860 do not emphasize the economic side of American historical development. However, John Bach McMaster, *A History of the People of the United States* (8 vols., New York: D. Appleton and Company, 1883–1913), Vols. 4–8, gives much detailed material on economic conditions, culled largely from newspaper sources. Edward Channing, *A History of the United States* (6 vols., New York: The Macmillan Company, 1905–1925), Vols. 4–6, though generally slighting economic aspects, is occasionally excellent on particular topics. For the more limited period covered, Allan Nevins, *Ordeal of the Union* (New York: Charles Scribner's Sons, 1947), includes much on economic conditions. Though they emphasize social history, much material on economic conditions and industrial development may be found in three volumes in Arthur Meier Schlesinger and Dixon Ryan Fox, eds., *A History of American Life* (12 vols., New York: The Macmillan Company, 1927–1944): John Allen Krout and Dixon Ryan Fox, *The Completion of Independence, 1790–1830;* Carl Russell Fish, *The Rise of the Common Man, 1830–1850;* and Arthur Charles Cole, *The Irrepressible Conflict, 1850–1865.*

Charles A. Beard and Mary R. Beard, *The Rise of American Civilization* (2 vols., New York: The Macmillan Company, 1927), emphasizes economic factors, and Louis M. Hacker, *The Triumph of American Capitalism* (New York: Simon and Schuster, 1940), stresses the rise of capitalism in the period covered by this volume. Arthur M. Schlesinger, Jr., *The Age of Jackson* (Boston: Little, Brown & Company, 1945), is a recent interpretive study in which unusual attention is devoted to the economic background. For the relations of economic developments to intellectual history, see Merle Curti, *The Growth of American Thought* (New York: Harper & Brothers, 2d ed., 1943). For the contemporary development of economic

399

thought, consult Joseph Dorfman, *The Economic Mind in American Civilization, 1606–1918* (3 vols., New York: The Viking Press, 1946–1949), Vol. II.

By far the most useful contemporary periodical, both for descriptive articles and statistical data, is *Hunt's Merchants' Magazine and Commercial Review*, New York, Vols. 1–63, 1839–1870. More sectional in their coverage but still invaluable are *De Bow's Commercial Review of the South and West*, New Orleans, Vols. 1–39, 1846–1870, and *Hazard's Register of Pennsylvania*, Philadelphia, Vols. 1–16, 1828–1835. Important, especially for the earlier years, when it stood alone, is *Niles' Weekly Register*, Baltimore, Vols. 1–75, 1811–1849. Much material similar to that available in the foregoing periodicals but occasionally providing valuable supplementary information will be found in J. D. B. De Bow, *Industrial Resources and Statistics of Southern and Western States*, New Orleans, Vols. 1–3, 1852–1853, and *Eighty Years Progress of the United States* (2 vols., New York: L. Stebbins, 1861). In addition, the newspapers, especially those of the leading ports, frequently provide information not available elsewhere.

The many travel accounts available for this period are chiefly valuable for social history, but they also provide many passages dealing briefly and often superficially with economic aspects. They are especially enlightening on the standard of living and the conditions of travel. References to the most useful of these may be found in the bibliographical sections of the three volumes in *A History of American Life* series referred to above.

Good historical maps on industrial and transportation aspects are to be found in Charles O. Paullin, comp., *Atlas of the Historical Geography of the United States* (Washington: Carnegie Institution of Washington, 1932); and Clifford L. Lord and Elizabeth L. Lord, comps., *Historical Atlas of the United States* (New York: Henry Holt and Company, 1944). *Historical Statistics of the United States, 1789–1945, A Supplement to the Statistical Abstract of the United States* (Bureau of the Census, Department of Commerce, Washington: Government Printing Office, 1949), is the best compilation in the field indicated.

POPULATION AND IMMIGRATION

On population the decennial reports of the United States Census are, of course, indispensable, with that for 1860 by far the most sat-

isfactory up to that time. The data provided on urbanization and occupations are of great interest, but unfortunately those for the latter
are largely unreliable. Not to be overlooked is the useful summary of
statistics for the 102 largest cities in 1860 which appears in the
*Eighth Census of the United States: Mortality and Miscellaneous
Statistics,* 1860. *A Century of Population Growth in the United States,
1790–1900* (Washington: Government Printing Office, 1909), provides a convenient statistical summary. A useful analytical presentation is provided by Warren S. Thompson and P. K. Whelpton, *Population Trends in the United States* (New York: McGraw-Hill Book Company, 1933). Old but still the standard work on urban growth is Adna
Ferrin Weber, *The Growth of Cities in the Nineteenth Century* (Vol.
XI of Columbia University *Studies in History, Economics and Public
Law,* New York: The Macmillan Company, 1899).

An excellent critical bibliography on immigration may be consulted in David F. Bowers, ed., *Foreign Influences in American Life*
(Princeton: Princeton University Press, 1944), pp. 195–206. Standard historical studies of immigration which give appreciable attention to the period 1815–1860 are Henry Pratt Fairchild, *Immigration,
a World Movement and Its American Significance* (New York: The
Macmillan Company, 1913); and George M. Stephenson, *A History
of American Immigration, 1820–1924* (Boston: Ginn and Company,
1926). The latter provides a good bibliography. Marcus Lee Hansen,
The Atlantic Migration, 1607–1860 (Cambridge: Harvard University
Press, 1940), emphasizes European influences and is the most complete general treatment of the period before 1860. Though useful,
Carl Wittke, *We Who Built America* (New York: Prentice-Hall, Inc.,
1939), is chiefly devoted to the period after the Civil War. Generally
excellent and especially valuable because of their economic emphasis
are Oscar Handlin, *Boston's Immigrants, 1790–1865* (Vol. L of *Harvard Historical Studies,* Cambridge: Harvard University Press, 1941)
and Robert Ernst, *Immigrant Life in New York City, 1825–1863* (New
York: King's Crown Press, 1949). More studies of this kind are badly
needed. Studies of the contributions of special racial groups are, from
the standpoint of industrial history, disappointing. References to
these works will be found in the bibliographies mentioned above.

INTERNAL TRANSPORTATION: GENERAL

The standard work covering the history of internal transportation
during the period of this study is Caroline E. MacGill and others,

History of Transportation in the United States before 1860 (Balthasar Henry Meyer, ed., Washington: Carnegie Institution of Washington, 1917). The earlier J. L. Ringwalt, *Development of Transportation Systems in the United States* (Philadelphia: J. L. Ringwalt, 1888), is still useful. Both are mines of information, generally though not always reliable, and disappointing because of poor organization and spotty coverage. The former contains an extensive bibliography. Useful general accounts by contemporaries are Henry V. Poor, *History of the Railroads and Canals of the United States of America* (New York: 1860), and Henry S. Tanner, *A Description of the Railroads and Canals of the United States Comprehending Notices of All the Works of Internal Improvement Throughout the Several States* (New York: T. R. Tanner & J. Disturnell, 1840). "Report on the Physical Characteristics of the Railroads . . ." *Tenth Census of the United States: Transportation*, IV, 299–387, and *Hunt's Merchants' Magazine and Commercial Review* (referred to above) provide much detailed statistical information. Archer Butler Hulbert, *Historic Highways of America* (16 vols., Cleveland: The Arthur H. Clark Company, 1902–1905), is an ambitious project chiefly on highways but includes two volumes on canals and one on waterways. Seymour Dunbar, *A History of Travel in America* (4 vols., Indianapolis: The Bobbs-Merrill Company, 1915), is popular and discursive. Though emphasizing travel, it devotes some attention to general transportation development. Both of the foregoing have but limited interest for the economic historian. On early development in the Far West see: Oscar Osburn Winter, *The Old Oregon Country, A History of Frontier Trade, Transportation, and Travel* (Indiana University Publications, Social Sciences Series No. 7, Bloomington: Indiana University, 1950).

Many of the general texts on transportation or railroads have introductory chapters containing useful summaries. Among these are William Z. Ripley, *Railroads: Rates and Regulation* (New York: Longmans, Green and Co., 1912); Stuart Daggett, *Principles of Inland Transportation* (New York: Harper & Brothers, 1928); D. Philip Locklin, *Economics of Transportation* (Chicago: Business Publications, Inc., 1935); and Sidney L. Miller, *Inland Transportation: Principles and Policies* (New York: McGraw-Hill Book Company, 1933). For excellent pictorial material see Malcolm Keir, *The March of Commerce* (Vol. IV of *Pageant of America*, New Haven: Yale University Press, 1927).

Of the regional and state studies of transportation, Ulrich Bonnell Phillips, *A History of Transportation in the Eastern Cotton Belt to 1860* (New York: Columbia University Press, 1908); Wheaton J. Lane, *From Indian Trail to Iron Horse: Travel and Transportation in New Jersey, 1620–1860* (Princeton: Princeton University Press, 1939); and Edward Chase Kirkland, *Men, Cities and Transportation, A Study in New England History, 1820–1900* (2 vols., Cambridge: Harvard University Press, 1948), are so outstanding that they are essential reading for an understanding of the period. Also useful are William F. Gephart, *Transportation and Industrial Development in the Middle West* (Columbia University *Studies in History, Economics and Public Law*, Vol. XXXIV, No. 1, New York: Columbia University Press, 1909); John Henry Krenkel, *Internal Improvements in Illinois, 1818–1848* (Urbana: University of Illinois, 1937); Charles Clinton Weaver, *Internal Improvements in North Carolina Previous to 1860* (Johns Hopkins University *Studies in Historical and Political Science*, XXI, Nos. 3 and 4, Baltimore: The Johns Hopkins Press, 1903), pp. 121–206; and Isaac Figley Boughter, "Internal Improvements in Northwestern Virginia: A Study of State Policy Prior to the Civil War," *University of Pittsburgh Bulletin*, Vol. XXVIII, No. 4 (December, 1931). A popular account well worth consulting is Charles Henry Ambler, *A History of Transportation in the Ohio Valley* (Glendale, Cal.: The Arthur H. Clark Company, 1932). Three studies by Carter Goodrich make a major contribution to our understanding of the movement for internal improvements: "National Planning of Internal Improvements," *Political Science Quarterly*, LXIII (March, 1948), 16–44; "The Virginia System of Mixed Enterprise: A Study of State Planning of Internal Improvements," *Political Science Quarterly*, LXIV (September, 1949), 355–387; and "The Revulsion Against Internal Improvements," *Journal of Economic History*, X (November, 1950), 145–169.

HIGHWAYS

Two valuable studies with an economic emphasis have been made of the turnpikes: Joseph Austin Durrenberger, *Turnpikes: A Study of the Toll Road Movement in the Middle Atlantic States and Maryland* (Valdosta, Ga.: Southern Stationery and Printing Company, 1931); and Philip Elbert Taylor, "The Turnpike Era in New England" (unpublished thesis, Yale University, 1934). Worth consulting for descriptive detail is Frederic J. Wood, *The Turnpikes of New England and Evolution of the Same through England, Virginia and Maryland* (Boston: Marshall Jones Company, 1919). For the development in New York State see Oliver W. Holmes, "The Turnpike Era," *Conquering the Wilderness* (Vol. V of *History of the State of New York,* A. C. Flick, ed., New York: Columbia University Press, 1934), pp. 257–291. The detailed story of one company is told in J. Orin Oliphant and Merrill W. Linn, "The Lewisburg and Mifflinburg Turnpike Company," *Pennsylvania History*, XV, No. 2 (April, 1948), 86–119. Three works have appeared in Jay Monaghan, ed., *The American Trails* series (Indianapolis: The Bobbs-Merrill Company, 1947–1948): Robert Lee Kincaid, *The Wilderness Road;* Jay Monaghan, *The Overland Trail;* and Philip D. Jordan, *The National Road.* Apparently designed for hammock rather than desk reading, they chiefly provide anecdotes and atmosphere, but each has a useful bibliography. Jordan's volume on the National Road, though definitely for the "general reader," provides the best study yet available on that important highway.

On road construction see Nathan C. Rockwood, *One Hundred Fifty Years of Road Building in America* (New York: Engineering News, 1914). William Kingsford, *History, Structure, and Statistics of Plank Roads, in the United States and Canada* (Philadelphia: A. Hart, 1851), and W. M. Gillespie, *A Manual of the Principles and Practice of Road-making* (New York: A. S. Barnes and Company, 1852), provide interesting contemporary accounts by plank-road enthusiasts. On bridges the most useful are Henry Grattan Tyrrell, *History of Bridge Engineering* (Chicago: The author, 1911); Wilbur J. Watson, *Bridge Architecture* (Cleveland: J. H. Jansen, 1927); Wilbur J. Watson and Sara Ruth Watson, *Bridges in History and Legend* (Cleveland: J. H. Jansen, 1937); Adelbert M. Jakeman, *Old Covered Bridges* (Brattleboro, Vt.: Stephen Daye Press, 1935); and D. B. Steinman, *The Builders of the Bridge: The Story of John Roebling and His Son* (New York: Harcourt, Brace and Company, 1945).

Much has been written on stagecoaches and taverns, mostly emphasizing the colorful and the quaint. See Alice Morse Earle, *Stage-Coach and Tavern Days* (New York: The Macmillan Company, 1935); Elise Lathrop, *Early American Inns and Taverns* (New York: Tudor Publishing Company, 1935); and Oliver W. Holmes, "The Stage-Coach Business in the Hudson Valley," New York State Historical Association, *Quarterly Journal*, XII (July, 1931), 231–256.

CANALS

On canals, though undocumented and popular in style, Alvin F. Harlow, *Old Towpaths* (New York: D. Appleton and Company, 1926), provides the best general treatment. Much statistical and descriptive material relative to canals may be found in Inland Waterways Commission, *Preliminary Report, Senate Document* No. 325, 60 Cong., 1 Sess., 1908; and *Tenth Census of the United States: Transportation*, IV, 731–764. A detailed history of the New York canals is Noble E. Whitford, *History of the Canal System of the State of New York, Supplement to the Annual Report of the State Engineer and Surveyor of the State of New York, 1905* (2 vols., Albany: 1906). A general study of Pennsylvania canals, T. B. Klein, *The Canals of Pennsylvania and the System of Internal Improvements* (Harrisburg: 1901), is still useful. For state-owned canals in Pennsylvania consult Avard Longley Bishop, "The State Works of Pennsylvania," *Transactions of the Connecticut Academy of Arts and Sciences* (New Haven: The Tuttle, Morehouse and Taylor Press, 1908), XIII, 149–297, and his "Corrupt Practices Connected with the Building and Operation of the State Works of Pennsylvania," *Yale Review*, XV (February, 1907), 391–411.

Chester Lloyd Jones, *The Economic History of the Anthracite-Tidewater Canals* (No. 22 of University of Pennsylvania *Publications in Political Economy and Public Law*, Philadelphia: The John C. Winston Company, 1908), provides a sound study of the waterways indicated. Wayland Fuller Dunaway, *History of the James River and Kanawha Company* (Columbia University *Studies in History, Economics and Public Law*, Vol. CIV, No. 2, New York: Columbia University Press, 1922), pp. 249–480, is an exhaustive and useful work. Christopher Roberts, *The Middlesex Canal, 1793–1860* (Vol. LXI of *Harvard Economic Studies*, Cambridge: Harvard University Press, 1938), provides a careful study of a relatively unimportant waterway. The Dismal Swamp Canal is described in Clifford Reginald Hinshaw, Jr., "North Carolina Canals before 1860," *North Carolina Historical Review*, XXV, No. 1 (January, 1948), 1–56. On Ohio canals, valuable studies are provided in Charles N. Morris, "Internal Improvements in Ohio, 1825–1850," *Papers of the American Historical Association*, III, No. 2 (1889), 107–136; and C. P. McClelland and C. C. Huntington, *History of the Ohio Canals, Their Construction, Cost, Use and Partial Abandonment* (Columbus: Ohio State Archaeological and

Historical Society, 1905). James William Putnam, *The Illinois and Michigan Canal: A Study in Economic History* (Vol. X of *Chicago Historical Society's Collection,* Chicago: The University of Chicago Press, 1918), provides a careful study of the canal indicated, but the student will also wish to consult Bessie Louise Pierce, *A History of Chicago* (2 vols., New York: Alfred A. Knopf, Inc., 1937–1940). Though inadequate, Elbert Jay Benton, *The Wabash Trade Route in the Development of the Old Northwest* (Johns Hopkins University *Studies in Historical and Political Science,* Vol. XXI, Nos. 1–2, Baltimore: The Johns Hopkins Press, 1903), remains the standard work on Indiana canals. The most recent, and certainly one of the very best of the canal studies, is Walter S. Sanderlin, *The Great National Project: A History of the Chesapeake and Ohio Canal* (Johns Hopkins University *Studies in Historical and Political Science,* Vol. LXIV, No. 1, Baltimore: The Johns Hopkins Press, 1946).

STEAMBOATS

Most of the general works on transportation, including those of MacGill and Ringwalt, referred to above, devote surprisingly little attention to steamboat development. The report by T. C. Purdy on "Steam Navigation in the United States," in the *Tenth Census of the United States: Transportation,* IV, 653–720; and John H. Morrison, *History of American Steam Navigation* (New York: W. F. Sametz and Company, 1903), though inadequate in many respects, continue to be the best available general treatments of the subject. Carl D. Lane, *American Paddle Steamboats* (New York: Coward–McCann, Inc., 1943), combines a brief, well-balanced historical sketch with many fine reproductions of old steamboat prints. Statistical tables indicative of steamboat development frequently appeared in *Hunt's Merchants' Magazine.*

Excellent on the eastern steamboats are Robert Greenhalgh Albion, *The Rise of New York Port [1815–1860]* (New York: Charles Scribner's Sons, 1939); and two books by Wheaton J. Lane, that referred to above and *Commodore Vanderbilt: An Epic of the Steam Age* (New York: Alfred A. Knopf, Inc., 1942). On the lake steamship reliable information attractively presented is available in two books by Harlan Hatcher: *Lake Erie* (New York: The Bobbs-Merrill Company, 1945), and *The Great Lakes* (New York: Oxford University Press, 1944). Older but still worth consulting is James Cooke Mills,

Our Inland Seas, Their Shipping and Commerce for Three Centuries
(Chicago: A. C. McClurg and Company, 1910).

On the western steamboat, the new book by Louis C. Hunter,
Steamboats on the Western Rivers (Cambridge: Harvard University
Press, 1949), makes a major contribution. This truly excellent study
combines sound historical scholarship with careful economic analysis to provide by far the best work on American steamboat history
which has yet appeared. Two good studies are available on the steamboats of the upper Mississippi: Mildred L. Hartsough, *From Canoe
to Steel Barge on the Upper Mississippi* (Minneapolis: The University
of Minnesota Press, 1934); and William J. Petersen, *Steamboating on
the Upper Mississippi* (Iowa City: State Historical Society, 1937).
Ambler, *A History of Transportation in the Ohio Valley*, referred to
above, tells the story for the indicated area, but more reliable for the
origin and development of the western steamship is Louis C. Hunter,
"The Invention of the Western Steamboat," *Journal of Economic History*, III, No. 2 (November, 1943), 202–220. For conditions on the
great western branches of the lower Mississippi River a useful account is Grant Foreman, "River Navigation in the Early Southwest,"
Mississippi Valley Historical Review, XV, No. 1 (June, 1928), 34–55.
Most older books on the western steamboat were written in romantic
or popular vein. Of these may be cited Hiram Martin Chittenden,
History of Early Steamboat Navigation on the Missouri River (2 vols.,
New York: Francis P. Harper, 1903); and E. W. Gould, *Fifty Years
on the Mississippi; or Gould's History of River Navigation* (St.
Louis: Nixon-Jones Printing Co., 1899).

Forty-two volumes are now available in the *Rivers of America
Series* (New York: Rinehart & Company). They excel in local color,
sprightly style, and folksy anecdote, but make only slight contributions to transportation history.

RAILROADS

In addition to the transportation histories listed above, a number
of general railroad histories are worth consulting. The best are two
older ones: Charles Francis Adams, *Railroads: Their Origin and
Problems* (New York: G. P. Putnam & Co., 1878); and Henry M.
Flint, *The Railroads of the United States: Their History and Statistics* (Philadelphia: John E. Potter and Company, 1868). Of more
recent date are two popular works: Slason Thompson, *A Short His-*

tory of American Railways, Covering Ten Decades (New York: D. Appleton and Company, 1925); and John W. Starr, Jr., *One Hundred Years of American Railroading* (New York: Dodd, Mead & Company, 1928).

William H. Brown, *The History of the First Locomotives in America* (New York: D. Appleton and Company, rev. ed., 1874); E. P. Alexander, *Iron Horses; American Locomotives, 1829–1900* (New York: W. W. Norton & Company, 1941); and Robert H. Thurston, *A History of the Growth of the Steam-Engine* (New York: D. Appleton and Company, 4th rev. ed., 1907), provide information on early technical developments, but often more satisfactory on this subject are the histories of individual railroad lines, such as those listed below. Frederick A. Cleveland and Fred Wilbur Powell, *Railroad Promotion and Capitalization in the United States* (New York: Longmans, Green and Co., 1909), continues to be the best summary of early railroad financing. Henry V. Poor, *Manual of the Railroads of the United States for 1868–69* (New York: H. V. and H. W. Poor, 1868), pp. 9–32, provides a sketch of American railway development including useful statistical summaries.

Some of the most interesting and at the same time most valuable work on railroad history appears in regional transportation studies such as those by Phillips, Lane, and Kirkland listed above, to which should be added Jules I. Bogen, *The Anthracite Railroads* (New York: The Ronald Press Company, 1927); Robert E. Riegel, "Trans-Mississippi Railroads during the Fifties," *Mississippi Valley Historical Review*, X, No. 2 (September, 1923), 153–172; Thelma M. Kistler, "The Rise of Railroads in the Connecticut River Valley," *Smith College Studies in History*, Vol. XXIII, Nos. 1–4 (October, 1937—July, 1938); and Cecil Kenneth Brown, *A State Movement in Railroad Development* (Chapel Hill: The University of North Carolina Press, 1928). Also useful is the series of articles on the South by Robert S. Cotterill in the *Mississippi Valley Historical Review*: "The Beginnings of Railroads in the Southwest," VIII, No. 4 (March, 1922), 318–326; "Southern Railroads and Western Trade, 1840–1850," III, No. 4 (March, 1917), 427–441; and "Southern Railroads, 1850–1860," X, No. 4 (March, 1924), 396–405. A good summary of railroad conditions at the end of the period covered by this volume is Carl Russell Fish, "The Northern Railroads, April, 1861," *American Historical Review*, XXII, No. 4 (July, 1917), 778–793.

Histories of particular railroad companies are legion, varying greatly in quality, but the better ones provide indispensable material.

Especially distinguished for their scholarly qualities and as rich mines of valuable information are Paul Wallace Gates, *The Illinois Central Rail-road and Its Colonization Work* (Vol. XLII of *Harvard Economic Studies,* Cambridge: Harvard University Press, 1934); and Richard C. Overton, *Burlington West: A Colonization History of the Burlington Railroad* (Cambridge: Harvard University Press, 1941). Of the many others, among the most useful for the period before 1860 are Edward Hungerford, *The Story of the Baltimore & Ohio Railroad, 1827–1927* (2 vols., New York: G. P. Putnam's Sons, 1928); Samuel Melanchthon Derrick, *Centennial History of the South Carolina Railroad* (Columbia: The State Company, 1930); Frank Walker Stevens, *The Beginnings of the New York Central Railroad: A History* (New York: G. P. Putnam's Sons, 1926); Edward Harold Mott, *Between the Ocean and the Lakes: The Story of the Erie* (New York: J. S. Collins, 1902); William Bender Wilson, *History of the Pennsylvania Railroad Company* (2 vols., Philadelphia: H. T. Coates and Co., 1899); George H. Burgess and Miles C. Kennedy, *Centennial History of the Pennsylvania Railroad Company, 1846–1946* (Philadelphia: The Pennsylvania Railroad Company, 1949); and *A Century of Progress, History of the Delaware and Hudson Company, 1823–1923* (Albany: The Delaware and Hudson Company, 1925).

Three biographical studies shed light on early railroad leadership: Henry Greenleaf Pearson, *An American Railroad Builder, John Murray Forbes* (Boston: Houghton Mifflin Company, 1911); Archibald Douglas Turnbull, *John Stevens, an American Record* (New York: The Century Company, 1928); and Allan Nevins, *Abram S. Hewitt: With Some Account of Peter Cooper* (New York: Harper & Brothers, 1935).

The standard works on federal aid have been Lewis Henry Haney, *A Congressional History of Railways in the United States to 1850* (University of Wisconsin, *Bulletin* No. 211, *Economics and Political Science Series,* Vol. III, Madison: 1903); John Bell Sanborn, *Congressional Grants of Land in Aid of Railways* (University of Wisconsin, *Bulletin* No. 3, *Economics, Political Science, and History Series,* Vol. II, Madison: 1899); and Thomas Donaldson, *The Public Domain; Its History, with Statistics* (Washington: Government Printing Office, 1884). But much valuable work has been done more recently on this subject. See Federal Coordinator of Transportation, *Public Aids to Transportation* (4 vols., Washington: Government Printing Office, 1938–1940), and the studies by Gates and Overton referred to above.

Best on the early express companies is the popularly written Alvin

F. Harlow, *Old Waybills; The Romance of the Express Companies* (New York: D. Appleton–Century Company, 1934). This may be supplemented by A. L. Stimson, *History of the Express Companies: And the Origin of American Railroads* (New York, 1858); and Henry Wells, *Sketch of the Rise, Progress, and Present Condition of the Express System* (Albany: Van Benthuysen's Printing House, 1864). This whole subject badly needs further investigation.

COMMUNICATIONS

Good on the early history of the Post Office is Wesley Everett Rich, *The History of the United States Post Office to the Year 1829* (Vol. XXVII of *Harvard Economic Studies*, Cambridge: Harvard University Press, 1924), but a detailed scholarly study is lacking for later years. However, Daniel C. Roper, *The United States Post Office* (New York: Funk & Wagnalls Company, 1917), and Alvin F. Harlow, *Old Post Bags* (New York: D. Appleton and Company, 1928), provide useful, popular histories.

Although emphasizing aspects not strictly economic in nature, two valuable studies of American newspaper development are William A. Dill, *Growth of Newspapers in the United States* (Lawrence: University of Kansas, 1928), and Frank Luther Mott, *American Journalism* (New York: The Macmillan Company, 1947). For a more specialized study, consult Harold A. Innis, "The Newspaper in Economic Development," *The Tasks of Economic History* (December, 1942), pp. 1–33. On magazines, most useful is Frank Luther Mott, *A History of American Magazines* (3 vols., New York: D. Appleton and Company, 1930), Vols. I and II.

Outstanding on the history of the telegraph is Robert Luther Thompson, *Wiring a Continent* (Princeton: Princeton University Press, 1947). Also of considerable interest is Alvin F. Harlow's sprightly *Old Wires and New Waves: The History of the Telegraph, Telephone, and Wireless* (New York: D. Appleton–Century Company, 1936). Two useful older studies are Charles Frederick Briggs and August Maverick, *The Story of the Telegraph* (New York: Rudd & Carleton, 1858), and George B. Prescott, *History, Theory, and Practice of the Electric Telegraph* (Boston: Ticknor & Fields, 1860). A detailed account of the first Atlantic cable is given in Henry M. Field, *History of the Atlantic Telegraph* (New York: Charles Scribner & Co., 1866).

MERCHANT MARINE

Although much has been written on the history of the American merchant marine, no satisfactory general history has been available until very recently. The publication of John G. B. Hutchins, *The American Maritime Industries and Public Policy, 1789–1914* (Vol. LXXI of *Harvard Economic Studies,* Cambridge: Harvard University Press, 1941), has admirably filled this gap. Able historical writing and sound economic analysis combine to make this by far the most useful general treatise. An excellent bibliography is included. Of the earlier works, one of the best is Hans Keiler, *American Shipping: Its History and Economic Conditions* (Jena: Fischer, 1913). Winthrop L. Marvin, *The American Merchant Marine: Its History and Romance from 1620 to 1902* (New York: Charles Scribner's Sons, 1910), and John R. Spears, *The Story of the American Merchant Marine* (New York: The Macmillan Company, 1910), are popular accounts. William W. Bates, *American Marine: The Shipping Question in History and Politics* (Boston: Houghton Mifflin Company, 1893), provides a strongly protectionist survey. The chapter entitled "The Maritime Industries of America," by J. R. Soley in Nathaniel Southgate Shaler, ed., *The United States of America* (2 vols., New York: D. Appleton and Company, 1894), is an old but still useful summary. Adam W. Kirkaldy, *British Shipping: Its History, Organization and Importance* (New York: E. P. Dutton & Co., 1914), is a standard English work useful to the student of American development. But for a convenient summary of British growth, see Abbot Payson Usher, "The Growth of English Shipping, 1572–1922," *Quarterly Journal of Economics,* XLII (May, 1928), 465–478.

Two recent works by Robert Greenhalgh Albion make major contributions to the maritime history of the period. His *Square-Riggers on Schedule* (Princeton: Princeton University Press, 1938) is indispensable to a study of the packets, and his *The Rise of New York Port [1815–1860]* (New York: Charles Scribner's Sons, 1939) gives invaluable material not only on the development of shipping from that port but also on the general maritime history of the period. Samuel Eliot Morison, *The Maritime History of Massachusetts, 1783–1860* (Boston: Houghton Mifflin Company, 1921), a classic in its field, has valuable and interesting chapters on this period. Each of these books has a comprehensive bibliography. Worth consulting but of limited usefulness is William Hutchinson Rowe, *The Maritime History of*

Maine: Three Centuries of Shipbuilding & Seafaring (New York: W. W. Norton & Company, 1948). Frank C. Bowen, *A Century of Atlantic Travel, 1830–1930* (Boston: Little, Brown & Company, 1930), is a potpourri of incidents and information.

Somewhat popular and discursive reading on the sailing ships is available in E. Keble Chatterton, *Sailing Ships and Their Story* (Boston: Lauriat, 1935); and in R. A. Fletcher, *In the Days of the Tall Ships* (London: Brentano's Ltd., 1928). Arthur H. Clark. *The Clipper Ship Era* (New York: G. P. Putnam's Sons, 1910), is a standard work in this field but should be supplemented, as should practically all older books on ships and shipping, by careful reading of the works by Hutchins and Albion referred to above. Reliable, attractively presented, and a mine of detailed material on the clippers is Carl C. Cutler, *Greyhounds of the Sea: The Story of the American Clipper Ship* (New York: G. P. Putnam's Sons, 1930). Octavius T. Howe and Frederick C. Matthews, *American Clipper Ships, 1833–1858* (2 vols., Salem, Mass.: Marine Research Society, 1926–1927), goes into great detail on the history of individual ships. For an excellent summary of clippers in their most important trade, see Raymond A. Rydell, "The California Clippers," *Pacific Historical Review*, XVIII, No. 1 (February, 1949), 70–83.

David Budlong Tyler, *Steam Conquers the Atlantic* (New York: D. Appleton-Century Company, 1939), provides the most useful summary of the development of steam in ocean transportation. Also of special value are G. Gibbard Jackson, *The Ship under Steam* (New York: Charles Scribner's Sons, 1928); Arthur J. Maginnis, *The Atlantic Ferry, Its Ships, Men, and Working* (New York: The Macmillan Company, 1893); Robert H. Thurston, *A History of the Growth of the Steam-Engine* (New York: D. Appleton and Company, 1907); W. Mack Angas, *Rivalry on the Atlantic* (New York: Lee Furman, Inc., 1939); and T. C. Purdy, "Report on Steam Navigation in the United States," *Tenth Census of the United States: Transportation*, IV, 653–720.

On commercial policy relating to the merchant marine, the best general treatment is that by Hutchins, referred to above. Vernon G. Setser, *The Commercial Reciprocity Policy of the United States, 1774–1829* (Philadelphia: University of Pennsylvania Press, 1937), is the best general source for the limited period it covers. F. Lee Benns, *The American Struggle for the British West India Carrying-Trade, 1815–1830* (Vol. X of *Indiana University Studies*, Bloomington: University of Indiana Press, 1923), treats in detail the aspect indicated by the title. Lloyd W. Maxwell, *Discriminating Duties and the American Merchant Marine* (New York: The H. W. Wilson Company, 1926), covers the period of this volume with a political emphasis. Other surveys will be found in Emory R. Johnson, T. W. Van Metre, G. G. Huebner, and D. S. Hanchett, *History of Domestic and Foreign Commerce of the United States* (2 vols., Washington: Carnegie Institution of Washington, 1915); and in Paul Maxwell Zeis, *American Shipping Policy* (Princeton: Princeton University Press, 1938). W. W. Bates, in his work cited above, attacks the abandonment of discriminating duties during this period. His position is vigorously assailed by E. S. Gregg, "A Case against Discriminating Duties," *Journal of Political Economy*, XXX, No. 3 (June, 1922), 404–411. Of numerous governmental reports, most useful are two by Joseph Nimmo, Jr., Chief of Division of Tonnage in the Treasury Department, in 1870 and 1871, respectively. See *House Executive Document* No. 111, 41 Cong., 2 Sess., and *House Executive Document* No. 76, 41 Cong., 3 Sess.

Two special studies are available on subsidies to shipping: Marguerite M. McKee, "The Ship Subsidy Question in United States Politics," *Smith College Studies in History*, Vol. VIII, No. 1 (October, 1922); and Royal Meeker, "History of Shipping Subsidies," *Publications of the American Economic Association*, VI, No. 3 (August, 1905), 1–171. An excellent factual synopsis appears in Jesse E. Saugstad, *Shipping and Shipbuilding Subsidies*, United States Department of Commerce, *Trade Promotion Series* No. 129, 1932.

Detailed statistics on the merchant marine are to be found in the annual reports of the Secretary of the Treasury. For the earlier years of the period see *American State Papers, Commerce and Navigation*. Many useful summaries are scattered through government reports. A convenient compilation appears in the Annual Report of the Commissioner of Navigation to the Secretary of Commerce, June 30, 1914. More complete summaries, especially for the later periods, and graphical representations accompany the Nimmo reports referred to above. For the first three years of the period covered by this volume Adam Seybert, *Statistical Annals* (Philadelphia: Thomas Dobson and Son, 1818), is useful, as is also Timothy Pitkin, *Statistical View of the Commerce of the United States of America* (New Haven: Durrie & Peck, 1835), for a longer period. J. S. Homans, Jr., *An Historical and Statistical Account of the Foreign Commerce of the United States* (New York: G. P Putnam & Co., 1857), also provides detailed statistical summaries. British shipping statistics for this period are conveniently brought together in William Page, *Commerce and Industry* (2 vols., London: Constable and Company, Ltd., 1919), Vol. II.

The only attempt to deal in some detail and yet comprehensively with the domestic commerce of the United States for the period covered by this volume is to be found in Parts II and III of Volume I of Emory R. Johnson, T. W. Van Metre, G. G. Huebner, and D. S. Hanchett, *History of Domestic and Foreign Commerce of the United States* (2 vols., Washington: Carnegie Institution of Washington, 1915), Both of these parts are the work of T. W. Van Metre. Though decidedly useful, they provide only a start on the work which needs to be done on this subject. An excellent special study is Louis Bernard Schmidt, "The Internal Grain Trade of the United States, 1850–1860," *Iowa Journal of History and Politics*, XVIII, No. 1 (January, 1920), 94–124. *The Philadelphia-Baltimore Trade Rivalry, 1780–1860* (Harrisburg: The Pennsylvania Historical and Museum Commission, 1947), by James Weston Livingood, though worthy of attention, gives more emphasis to agencies of transportation and less to internal commerce than might be anticipated from the title. For a study of internal trade in Ohio see Ernest L. Bogart, "Early Canal Traffic and Railroad Competition in Ohio," *Journal of Political Economy*, XXI (January, 1913), 56–70. Many of the studies of transportation referred to in preceding sections of this chapter are useful on internal commerce. See also the two books by Albion cited under the previous heading.

No general collection of the statistics of domestic trade has ever been made and is badly needed. *Historical Statistics of the United States, 1789–1945, A Supplement to the Statistical Abstract of the United States* (Bureau of the Census, Department of Commerce, Washington: Government Printing Office, 1949), is particularly disappointing in this respect. Data must be found chiefly in the annual reports of canals and railroad companies, reports of chambers of commerce, scattered through such contemporary periodicals as *Hunt's Merchants' Magazine* and *De Bow's Review*, and in various government documents. Of the last the most useful are Israel D. Andrews, *Report on the Trade and Commerce of the British North American Colonies* (the so-called *Andrews Report*), Senate Document No. 112, 32 Cong., 1 Sess. (1853); Joseph Nimmo, Jr., *Report on the Internal Commerce of the United States, House Document* No. 46, Pt. 2, 44 Cong., 2 Sess. (1877), and *House Document* No. 32, Pt.

3, 45 Cong., 3 Sess. (1879); *Preliminary Report of the Inland Waterways Commission, Senate Document* No. 325, 60 Cong., 1 Sess.
(1908);*Eighth Census of the United States: Agriculture;* and *Tenth
Census of the United States: Transportation*, IV, *House Miscellaneous
Document* No. 42, Pt. 4, 47 Cong., 2 Sess.; William F. Switzler, *Report on the Internal Commerce of the United States*, Part II of Commerce and Navigation, Special Report on the Commerce of the Mississippi, Ohio, and Other Rivers, and of the Bridges Which Cross
Them (Treasury Department *Document* No. 1,039b, Bureau of Statistics, Washington: Government Printing Office, 1888); and Frank
Haigh Dixon, *A Traffic History of the Mississippi River System* (National Waterways Commission *Document* No. 11, Washington: Government Printing Office, 1917).

For internal trade organization a standard general treatment is
Fred Mitchell Jones, *Middlemen in the Domestic Trade of the United
States, 1800–1860* (University of Illinois *Studies in the Social Sci-
ences*, Vol. XXI, No. 3, Urbana: University of Illinois, 1937). *The
Southern Country Store, 1800–1860* (Baton Rouge: Louisiana State
University Press, 1949), by Lewis E. Atherton, emphasizes the in-
tegrating function of the country merchant. On the role of the ped-
dler, the same author's "Itinerant Merchandising in the Ante-Bellum
South," *Bulletin of the Business Historical Society*, XIX, No. 2
(April, 1945), 35–59, is an excellent brief account. One of the best
studies on a special aspect of commercial organization is Ray Bert
Westerfield, "Early History of American Auctions—A Chapter in
Commercial History," *Transactions of the Connecticut Academy of
Arts and Sciences*, XXIII (May, 1920), 159–210. Richardson Wright,
Hawkers & Walkers in Early America (Philadelphia: J. B. Lippincott
Company, 1927), is lively and popular. Useful for early frontier mer-
chandising is Sister Marietta Jennings, *A Pioneer Merchant of St.
Louis, 1810–1820* (No. 462 of *Studies in History, Economics and Pub-
lic Law*, New York: Columbia University Press, 1939). See also the
references in the following section which have to do chiefly, though
by no means exclusively, with the organization of foreign trade.

Biographies of merchants often give an intimate view of the commercial organization of the period. Some of the most useful of these
are Kenneth Wiggins Porter, *John Jacob Astor, Business Man* (2 vols.,
Cambridge: Harvard University Press, 1931); William Hurd Hillyer,
James Talcott, Merchant and His Times (New York: Charles Scribner's Sons, 1937); Walter Barrett (pseudonym used by J. Scoville),
The Old Merchants of New York City (New York: Carleton, 3d ed.,

1865); Freeman Hunt, *Lives of American Merchants* (2 vols., New York: Derby & Jackson, 1858); Frank R. Kent, *The Story of Alexander Brown & Sons* (Baltimore: Privately printed, 1925); Robert T. Thompson, *Colonel James Neilson* (New Brunswick, N. J. Rutgers University Press, 1940); and Sarah Forbes Hughes, ed., *Letters and Recollections of John Murray Forbes* (2 vols., Boston: Houghton Mifflin Company, 1899), Vol. I.

FOREIGN TRADE

Surprisingly little careful analytical work has been done on the general history of foreign trade during this period. Emory R. Johnson and others, *History of Domestic and Foreign Commerce of the United States,* remains the standard reference work; and Worthy P. Sterns, "The Foreign Trade of the United States from 1820 to 1840," *Journal of Political Economy,* VIII (1900), 34–57 and 452–490, which, despite its title, covers only the years 1820–1830, is the most useful detailed study.

The general surveys of American commerce available give only slight attention to the period 1815–1860. Brief, conventional treatments will be found in Clive Day, *History of Commerce in the United States* (New York: Longmans, Green and Co., 1925); and John H. Frederick, *The Development of American Commerce* (New York: D. Appleton–Century Company, 1932).

With reference to the commerce of particular ports or areas, the following are especially valuable: Robert Greenhalgh Albion, *Square-Riggers on Schedule* (Princeton: Princeton University Press, 1938), and *The Rise of New York Port [1815–1860]* (New York: Charles Scribner's Sons, 1939); Samuel Eliot Morison, *The Maritime History of Massachusetts, 1783–1860* (Boston: Houghton Mifflin Company, 1921); and Frank R. Rutter, *South American Trade of Baltimore* (Johns Hopkins University *Studies in Historical and Political Science,* Vol. XV, No. 9, Baltimore: The Johns Hopkins Press, 1897). A detailed study of United States trade with the Far East is Tyler Dennett, *Americans in Eastern Asia* (New York: Barnes & Noble, Inc., 1941).

Two special studies shed light on the effects of commercial policy: C. R. Fay, *The Corn Laws and Social England* (Cambridge: The University Press, 1932), which deals with America's grain trade with the United Kingdom; and Donald C. Masters, *The Reciprocity Treaty of 1854* (New York: Longmans, Green and Co., 1936), which has an excellent chapter dealing with the effect of the reciprocity treaty on the trade between British North America and the United States. Also useful are the two so-called *Andrews Reports,* which were written to promote reciprocity between Canada and the United States: Israel D. Andrews, "Report on the Trade, Commerce, and Resources of the British North American Colonies," *Senate Executive Document* No. 23, 31 Cong., 2 Sess. (1851), and "On the Trade and Commerce of the British North American Colonies, and upon the Trade of the Great Lakes and Rivers," *Senate Executive Document* No. 112, 32 Cong., 1 Sess. (1853).

On the international balance of indebtedness see Charles J. Bullock, John H. Williams, and Rufus S. Tucker, "The Balance of Trade of the United States," *Review of Economic Statistics,* Preliminary I (1919), 215–266; and Leland Hamilton Jenks, *The Migration of British Capital to 1875* (New York: Alfred A. Knopf, Inc., 1927).

Many of the books cited above under other headings provide much material on the organization of foreign trade. Of these the chapters on the commercial organization in New York in Robert Greenhalgh Albion, *The Rise of New York Port [1815–1860],* are especially useful. Detailed analyses of the organization of American merchant and industrial capitalism are yet to be made, but excellent brief statements by N. S. B. Gras are available in a number of places, including *Business and Capitalism* (New York: F. S. Crofts & Co., 1939), and as an introduction to Kenneth Wiggins Porter, *The Jacksons and the Lees* (2 vols., Cambridge: Harvard University Press, 1937). The latter work is unusually valuable, not only for the introduction by Gras but also for the documentary material and Porter's illuminating introduction. On the subject indicated by its title, Norman Sydney Buck, *The Development of the Organisation of Anglo-American Trade, 1800–1850* (New Haven: Yale University Press, 1925), is indispensable. Chief attention is given to the organization of the trade in imported British manufactures and cotton exports. On the merchant bankers, Ralph W. Hidy, "The Organization and Functions of Anglo-American Merchant Bankers, 1815–1860," *Tasks of Economic History* (December, 1941), pp. 53–66 and *The House of Baring in American Trade and Finance* (Vol. XIV of *Harvard Studies in Business History,* Cambridge: Harvard University Press, 1949) should not be overlooked. An excellent localized study which throws much light on the organization of both foreign and domestic trade is Margaret E. Martin, "Merchants and Trade of the Connecticut River Valley, 1750–1820," *Smith College Studies in History,* XXIV, Nos. 1–4 (October, 1938—July, 1939).

The statistical material on American foreign commerce is exceedingly voluminous, widely scattered, often confusing and, at least before 1821, not always reliable. Care must be exercised at all times to distinguish between data which do and those which do not include gold and silver. The most detailed statistics will be found, of course, in the annual reports of the Secretary of the Treasury on Commerce and Navigation. Before 1822 these will be found in *American State Papers: Commerce and Navigation,* and for subsequent years they are often printed as special Congressional documents. Annual statistics for the more usual series have now been brought together in *Historical Statistics of the United States, 1789–1945, A Supplement to the Statistical Abstract of the United States* (Bureau of the Census, Department of Commerce, Washington: Government Printing Office, 1949). Many special summaries are to be found in various government publications. Consult for detailed annual tables especially useful for studying the balance of trade, *Historical Tables of Commerce, Finance, Tonnage and Immigration of the United States* (United States Treasury Department, Washington: n.d.); for domestic exports by countries, Charles H. Evans, "Exports, Domestic, from the United States to All Countries from 1789 to 1883, Inclusive," *House Miscellaneous Document* No. 49, Pt. 2, 48 Cong., 1 Sess. (1884), pp. 1–266; for a detailed breakdown of commerce with European countries, "Statistical Tables Exhibiting the Commerce of the United States with European Countries from 1790 to 1890," *House Miscellaneous Document* No. 117, 52 Cong., 2 Sess. (1893); for similar studies of American commerce with the countries of the Western Hemisphere, "Monthly Summary of Commerce and Finance of the United States," *House Document* No. 573, Pt. 12, 55 Cong., 2 Sess. (June, 1899), pp. 3274–3428; and for exports of domestic manufacturers, "Monthly Summary of Commerce and Finance of the United States," *House Document* No. 15, Pt. 10, 57 Cong., 2 Sess. (April, 1903), pp. 3241–3339.

MANUFACTURING

The most complete and useful general history of manufacturing is Victor S. Clark, *History of Manufactures in the United States* (3 vols., New York: McGraw-Hill Book Company, 1929). About half of Volume I is devoted to the period between the Revolution and the Civil War. An extensive bibliography will be found in Volume III. An older general treatment, J. Leander Bishop, *A History of American*

Manufactures, from 1608 to 1860 (2 vols., Philadelphia: Edward Young & Company, 1864), Vol. II, which covers the years 1789–1860, provides a useful compilation of descriptive material. Much briefer in their attention to the period of this study and generally popular in presentation are Malcolm Keir, *Manufacturing* (New York: The Ronald Press Company, 1928); Frederic William Wile, *A Century of Industrial Progress* (New York: Doubleday, Doran & Company, 1928); Albert S. Bolles, *Industrial History of the United States* (Norwich, Conn.: The Henry Bill Publishing Company, 1879); and John George Glover and William Bouck Cornell, *The Development of American Industries* (New York: Prentice-Hall, Inc., 1933). Harold F. Williamson, ed., *The Growth of the American Economy* (New York: Prentice-Hall, Inc., 1944), gives more attention to manufacturing development before the Civil War than do most general economic histories. Excellent summaries appear in Chapter 10, "The Processing of Agricultural Products in the Pre-Railway Age," by Charles B. Kuhlmann; in Chapter 11, "Heavy Industries before 1860," by Louis C. Hunter; and in Chapter 12, "Light Manufactures and the Beginnings of Precision Manufacture before 1861," by Constance M. Green.

For contemporary materials chiefly of a statistical nature, the various United States Census Reports, though faulty in many respects, are indispensable. By far the most reliable and complete before the Civil War is the volume on Manufactures in the *Eighth Census of the United States,* 1860. The *Tenth Census of the United States: Manufactures,* II (1880), contains useful historical essays, of which that by Carroll D. Wright, "Report on the Factory System of the United States," pp. 527–606, is outstanding. Valuable state censuses of manufacturing were taken by New York, Massachusetts, and Connecticut. For New York see *Censuses of the State of New York for the Years 1821 and 1825,* in *Journal of the Assembly of New York,* 45 Sess. (Albany: 1822), Appendix A; and *New York Senate Journal,* 49 Sess. (Albany: 1826), Appendix A; and *Censuses of the State of New York for the Years 1835, 1845, 1855.* For Massachusetts see *Statistical Tables: Exhibiting the Condition and Products of Certain Branches of Industry in Massachusetts, for the Year Ending April 1, 1837* (Boston: Dutton and Wentworth, 1838); *Statistics of the Condition and Products of Certain Branches of Industry in Massachusetts, for the Year Ending April 1, 1845* (Boston: Dutton and Wentworth, 1846); and *Statistical Information Relating to Certain Branches of Industry in Massachusetts, for the Year Ending June*

1, 1855 (Boston: William White, 1856). For Connecticut see *Report of the Secretary of State Relative to Certain Branches of Industry* (Connecticut House of Representatives *Document* No. 26, May Sess., 1839, Hartford: 1839), and Daniel P. Tyler, ed., *Statistics of the Condition and Products of Certain Branches of Industry in Connecticut, for the Year Ending October 1, 1845* (Hartford: 1846). Material largely from United States census reports is summarized in Timothy Pitkin, *A Statistical View of the Commerce of the United States of America* (New Haven: Durrie & Peck, 1835), Chapter 11. Of the federal investigations of manufacturing growing out of the disputes over the tariff, by far the most valuable is the so-called *Mc-Lane Report on Manufactures, Documents Relative to Manufactures in the United States, House Document* No. 308, 22d Cong., 1 Sess. (2 vols., Washington: 1833). Though defective as a statistical study, it provides a mine of detailed information.

On particular industries, chief attention has been given to textile manufacturing. For contemporary accounts see Nathan Appleton, *The Introduction of the Power Loom* (Lowell: B. H. Penhallow, 1858); R. H. Baird, *The American Cotton Spinner* (Philadelphia: A. Hart, 1851); and Samuel Batchelder, *Introduction and Early Progress of the Cotton Manufacture in the United States* (Boston: Little, Brown & Company, 1863). Two studies, Arthur H. Cole, *The American Wool Manufacture* (2 vols., Cambridge: Harvard University Press, 1926), and Arthur H. Cole and Harold F. Williamson, *The American Carpet Manufacture* (Vol. LXX of *Harvard Economic Studies*, Cambridge: Harvard University Press, 1941), are models of scholarship and come close to being definitive works. Melvin Thomas Copeland, *The Cotton Manufacturing Industry of the United States* (Vol. VIII of *Harvard Economic Studies*, Cambridge: Harvard University Press, 1912), the standard general work on the cotton textile industry, has only one brief chapter on the period before 1860, but Caroline F. Ware, *The Early New England Cotton Manufacture* (Boston: Houghton Mifflin Company, 1931), is excellent for New England and gives some incidental information on the Middle Atlantic states. Broadus Mitchell, *The Rise of Cotton Mills in the South* (Johns Hopkins University *Studies in Historical and Political Science*, Vol. XXXIX, No. 2, Baltimore: The Johns Hopkins Press, 1921), has an introductory section covering the beginnings of this industry in the South. *William Gregg, Factory Master of the Old South* (*University of North Carolina Social Study Series*, Chapel Hill: The University of North Carolina Press, 1928), by the same author, tells the story of the leading advocate of cotton textile manufacturing in the South and sheds much light on the early vicissitudes of this industry. A much-used account by an early writer is the work by Samuel Batchelder referred to above. An excellent picture of the operations of an important cotton mill will be found in the opening chapters of Evelyn H. Knowlton, *Pepperell's Progress: History of a Cotton Textile Company, 1844–1945* (Vol. XIII of *Harvard Studies in Business History*, Cambridge: Harvard University Press, 1948). Studies of firms making textile machinery will be found in George Sweet Gibb, *The Saco-Lowell Shops* (Vol. XVI of *Harvard Studies in Business History*, Cambridge: Harvard University Press, 1950), and Thomas R. Navin, *The Whitin Machine Works Since 1831* (Vol. XV of the same series, 1950).

James M. Swank, *History of the Manufacture of Iron in All Ages* (Philadelphia: The American Iron and Steel Association, 2d ed., 1892), though quite inadequate, is the best available general study of the subject indicated by the title. J. P. Lesley, *The Iron Manufacturer's Guide to the Furnaces, Forges and Rolling Mills of the United States* (New York: John Wiley, 1859), is a detailed contemporary description of the industry. Essential to an understanding of the development of iron manufacturing are such special studies as Louis C. Hunter, "Influence of the Market upon Technique in the Iron Industry in Western Pennsylvania Up to 1860," *Journal of Economic and Business History*, I, No. 2 (February, 1929), 241–281, and "Financial Problems of the Early Pittsburgh Iron Manufacturers," *Journal of Economic and Business History*, II, No. 3 (May, 1930), 520–544; Lester J. Cappon, "Trend of the Southern Iron Industry under the Plantation System," *Journal of Economic and Business History*, II, No. 2 (February, 1930), 353–394; Kathleen Bruce, *Virginia Iron Manufacture in the Slave Era* (New York: The Century Company, 1931); and Arthur Cecil Bining, "The Rise of Iron Manufacturing in Pennsylvania," *Western Pennsylvania Historical Magazine*, XVI, No. 4 (November, 1933), 235–256.

Available for the growth of shipbuilding is the excellent John G. B. Hutchins, *The American Maritime Industries and Public Policy, 1789–1914* (Vol. LXXI of *Harvard Economic Studies*, Cambridge: Harvard University Press, 1941). Though the volume is largely devoted to a later period, the introductory chapters should be consulted in Charles W. Moore, *Timing a Century: History of the Waltham Watch Company* (Vol. XI in *Harvard Studies in Business History*, Cambridge: Harvard University Press, 1945). Blanche Evans Hazard,

The Organization of the Boot and Shoe Industry in Massachusetts before 1875 (Vol. XXIII of *Harvard Economic Studies*, Cambridge: Harvard University Press, 1921), though limited to one state, has some general applicability and is a highly useful study. An outstanding study of a small manufacturing firm is George Sweet Gibb, *The Whitesmiths of Taunton* (Vol. VIII of *Harvard Studies in Business History*, Cambridge: Harvard University Press, 1946).

Of the regional or local studies of manufacturing, the following are among the most useful: Vera Shlakman, "Economic History of a Factory Town: A Study of Chicopee, Massachusetts," *Smith College Studies in History*, XX, Nos. 1–4 (October, 1934—July, 1935); Louis C. Hunter, "Studies in the Economic History of the Ohio Valley," *Smith College Studies in History*, XIX, Nos. 1–2 (October, 1933—January, 1934); Grace Pierpont Fuller, "An Introduction to the History of Connecticut as a Manufacturing State," *Smith College Studies in History*, Vol. I, No. 1 (October, 1915); Thomas Russell Smith, *The Cotton Textile Industry of Fall River, Massachusetts: A Study of Industrial Localization* (New York: King's Crown Press, 1944); Constance McLaughlin Green, *Holyoke, Massachusetts* (New Haven: Yale University Press, 1939), and *History of Naugatuck, Connecticut* (New Haven: Yale University Press, 1948); Harry J. Carman, "The Rise of the Factory System," *The Age of Reform* (Vol. VI in Alexander C. Flick, ed., *History of the State of New York*, 10 vols., New York: Columbia University Press, 1934); Clive Day, "The Rise of Manufacturing in Connecticut, 1820–1850," *Tercentenary Commission of the State of Connecticut* (1935); Isaac Lippincott, *A History of Manufactures in the Ohio River Valley to the Year 1860* (New York: The Knickerbocker Press, 1914); and Felicia Johnson Deyrup, "Arms Makers of the Connecticut Valley," *Smith College Studies in History*, Vol. XXXIII (1948). For southern industrial developments, a fair summary will be found in Emory Q. Hawk, *Economic History of the South* (New York: Prentice-Hall, Inc., 1934), Chapter X. On the factory system in the South see Fabian Linden, "Repercussions of Manufacturing in the Ante-Bellum South," *North Carolina Historical Review*, XVII (October, 1940), pp. 313–331.

Adequate studies of the organization of manufacturing before 1860 do not exist. Rolla Milton Tryon, *Household Manufactures in the United States, 1640–1860* (Chicago: The University of Chicago Press, 1917), is the only general study of this subject available and provides hardly more than a good beginning. No general study of the domestic system as it appeared in the United States has been made.

For the domestic system, as well as for the rise of the factory system, the best treatments are to be found in the special industry studies cited above. But N. S. B. Gras, "Stages in Economic History," *Journal of Economic and Business History*, II, No. 3 (May, 1930), 395–418, and Louis M. Hacker, *The Triumph of American Capitalism* (New York: Simon and Schuster, 1940), provide interpretive treatments well worth examination.

No comprehensive history primarily concerned with the early technological developments in American manufacturing has yet appeared. The small popular presentation, Roy T. Bramson, *Highlights in the History of American Mass Production* (Detroit: The Bramson Publishing Company, 1945), comes closest to meeting this need. Helpful for that part of the subject indicated by its title is Edward Cressy, *A Hundred Years of Mechanical Engineering* (New York: The Macmillan Company, 1937). A number of valuable works covering a broader field are available, the best of which are Abbott Payson Usher, *A History of Mechanical Inventions* (New York: McGraw-Hill Book Company, 1929); Joseph Wickham Roe, *English and American Tool Builders* (New Haven: Yale University Press, 1916); and Dirk J. Struik, *Yankee Science in the Making* (Boston: Little, Brown & Company, 1948). Especially helpful on this subject are some of the special studies referred to above, particularly Felicia Johnson Deyrup, "Arms Makers of the Connecticut Valley."

Long a neglected subject, the use of the corporate form of organization has recently been receiving attention, but two older studies are still worth consulting: Victor S. Clark, *History of Manufactures in the United States*, referred to above, and G. S. Callender, "The Early Transportation and Banking Enterprises of the States in Relation to the Growth of Corporations," *Quarterly Journal of Economics*, XVII (1903), 111–162. Of the more recent studies, the following are especially useful: Shaw Livermore, "Unlimited Liability in Early American Corporations," *Journal of Political Economy*, XLIII, No. 5 (October, 1935), 674–687; Joseph G. Blandi, *Maryland Business Corporations, 1783–1852* (Johns Hopkins University *Studies in Historical and Political Science*, Vol. LII, No. 3, Baltimore: The Johns Hopkins Press, 1934); William Miller, "A Note on the History of Business Corporations in Pennsylvania, 1800–1860," *Quarterly Journal of Economics*, LV (1940), 150–169; Oscar Handlin and Mary F. Handlin, "Origins of the American Business Corporation," *Journal of Economic History*, V, No. 1 (May, 1945), 1–23; W. C. Kessler, "A Statistical Study of the New York General Incorporation Act of 1811,"

Journal of Political Economy, XLVIII, No. 6 (December, 1940), 877–882, and "Incorporation in New England: A Statistical Study, 1800–1875," *Journal of Economic History,* VIII (May, 1948), 43–62; and John W. Cadman, *The Corporation in New Jersey* (Cambridge: Harvard University Press, 1949). Louis Hartz, *Economic Policy and Democratic Thought: Pennsylvania, 1776–1860* (Cambridge: Harvard University Press, 1948), and Handlin and Handlin, *Commonwealth,* deal with the corporative development. Each provides an excellent discussion of the role of the corporation before 1860. The most comprehensive statistical study is George Heberton Evans, Jr., *Business Incorporations in the United States, 1800–1943* (New York: National Bureau of Economic Research, 1948).

LABOR

Basic to any study of labor history for 1815–1860 are the publications of John R. Commons and his associates. Volumes 1–8 of John R. Commons and others, eds., *A Documentary History of American Industrial Society* (11 vols., Cleveland: The Arthur H. Clark Company, 1910–1911), provide a rich mine of source materials, and the first volume of John R. Commons and associates, *History of Labour in the United States* (4 vols., New York: The Macmillan Company, 1918), is still one of the best and most reliable of general labor histories, though some of its interpretations are now seriously questioned. Philip S. Foner, *History of the Labor Movement in the United States* (New York: International Publishers, 1947), one of the more recent of labor histories, provides, on the basis of a great deal of research in contemporary materials, an interesting synthesis with strong left-wing emphasis. Jürgen Kuczynski, *A Short History of Labour Conditions under Industrial Capitalism* (3 vols., London: Frederick Muller, Ltd., 1943), Vol. II, offers the best statistical analysis of wages for the period 1815–1860. The text is shorter than Foner's but the viewpoint is similar.

Most of the general labor histories do not emphasize the period before 1860, but useful summaries will be found in Mary Beard, *A Short History of the American Labor Movement* (New York: Harcourt, Brace and Howe, 1920); Harold U. Faulkner and Mark Starr, *Labor in America* (New York: Harper & Brothers, 1944); Herbert Harris, *American Labor* (New Haven: Yale University Press, 1939); and Foster Rhea Dulles, *Labor in America* (New York: Thomas Y. Crowell Company, 1949). One of the best short treatments of union history may be found in Chapter II of Volume III of Harry A. Millis and Royal E. Montgomery, *Organized Labor* (New York: McGraw-Hill Book Company, 1945). Also available is the older Selig Perlman, *A History of Trade Unionism in the United States* (New York: The Macmillan Company, 1922).

Norman Ware, *The Industrial Worker, 1840–1860* (Boston: Houghton Mifflin Company, 1924), stands out among the special studies as an unusually fine piece of historical writing. Two studies by Edith Abbott, *Women in Industry* (New York: D. Appleton and Company, 1910), and "The Wages of Unskilled Labor in the United States, 1850–1900," *Journal of Political Economy*, XIII, No. 3 (June, 1905), 321–367, are still most useful. Most of the industry studies referred to in the manufacturing section provide information on labor history, Caroline F. Ware, *The Early New England Cotton Manufacture* (Boston: Houghton Mifflin Company, 1931), and Vera Shlakman, "Economic History of a Factory Town; A Study of Chicopee, Massachusetts," *Smith College Studies in History*, Vol. XX, Nos. 1–4 (October, 1934—July, 1935), being especially helpful in this respect. Source materials on the Waltham system are listed in footnote references in the text. The student should not overlook two valuable committee reports: *Massachusetts House Document* No. 50, March 12, 1845, and No. 153, April 10, 1850. For an interesting and reliable account of working conditions under the Waltham system see Hannah Josephson, *The Golden Threads, New England Mill Girls and Magnates* (New York: Duell, Sloan and Pearce, 1949). Unfortunately this study is largely undocumented but it does include a good bibliography. Among the books available on special aspects of the labor movement, the student should not overlook two excellent specialized studies: Edwin C. Rozwenc, *Cooperatives Come to America* (Mount Vernon, Ia.: Hawkeye-Record Press, 1941), and Helen Sara Zahler, *Eastern Workingmen and National Land Policy, 1829–1862* (No. VII of Columbia University *Studies in the History of American Agriculture*, New York: Columbia University Press, 1941). Good summaries of many of the general reform movements of the time will be found in Alice Felt Tyler, *Freedom's Ferment: Phases of American Social History to 1860* (Minneapolis: The University of Minnesota Press, 1944. A voluminous literature exists on the early communistic communities. Worthy of special attention is Arthur Eugene Bestor, Jr., *Backwoods Utopias, The Sectarian and Owenite Phases of Communitarian Socialism in America: 1663–1829* (Philadelphia: University of Pennsylvania Press, 1950), which besides being an excellent study of

Owenism is valuable for its bibliography and its checklist of American communist communities.

Two biographies of labor leaders may be cited. Chapter 2 of Jonathan Grossman, *William Sylvis, Pioneer of American Labor* (No. 516 of *Studies in History, Economics and Public Law,* New York: Columbia University Press, 1945), throws light on the activities of the molders' union in the fifties; and Karl Obermann, *Joseph Weydemeyer, Pioneer of American Socialism* (New York: International Publishers, 1947), tells of the beginnings of Marxian socialism in the United States with some tendency to overemphasize its influence. Material on early labor legislation is disappointing, but Henry W. Farnam, *Chapters in the History of Social Legislation in the United States to 1860* (Washington: Carnegie Institution of Washington, 1938), and Charles E. Persons, "The Early History of Factory Legislation in Massachusetts," in Susan M. Kingsbury, ed., *Labor Laws and Their Enforcement* (New York: Longmans, Green and Co., 1911), provide at least a beginning.

Brief descriptions of Negro labor before 1860 appear in Charles H. Wesley, *Negro Labor in the United States, 1850–1925* (New York: Vanguard Press, 1927), and in W. E. Burghardt Du Bois and Augustus Granville Dill, *The Negro American Artisan* (Atlanta: The Atlanta University Press, 1912). Among the useful special studies of the northern Negro, which give at least some attention to the period of this volume, are Edward Raymond Turner, *The Negro in Pennsylvania* (Washington: The American Historical Association, 1912), and W. E. Burghardt Du Bois, *The Philadelphia Negro* (No. 14 in *Political Economy and Public Law Series,* Philadelphia: University of Pennsylvania, 1899).

Southern nonagricultural Negro labor has received little attention in the general labor histories. Ulrich Bonnell Phillips's contributions are of unusual value in this field. See especially his *American Negro Slavery* (New York: D. Appleton and Company, 1918), Chaps. 21 and 22, and *Life and Labor in the Old South* (Boston: Little, Brown, and Company, 1939). Also see the introductory chapter of Sterling D. Spero and Abram L. Harris, *The Black Worker: The Negro and the Labor Movement* (New York: Columbia University Press, 1931).

Extensive studies on the position of the free Negro have appeared recently for two states: John Hope Franklin, *The Free Negro in North Carolina, 1790–1860* (Chapel Hill: The University of North Carolina Press, 1943); and Luther Porter Jackson, *Free Negro Labor and Property Holding in Virginia, 1830–1860* (New York: D. Appleton–Century Company, 1942). The latter book is an unusually valuable economic study and gives a much wider coverage of labor history than is indicated by its title.

Statistical materials on prices are commented on in the following section. For wages the great collection of source material is *Senate Report* No. 1,394, Pt. 1, 52 Cong., 2 Sess. (1893), the so-called *Aldrich Report*, which provides much detailed data back to 1840. Information on rates in Massachusetts for the whole period of this study will be found in *Sixteenth Annual Report of the Massachusetts Bureau of Statistics of Labor, Public Document* No. 15 (August, 1885). These statistical materials have been used by Abbott in the works mentioned above and more recently by Alvin H. Hansen in "Factors Affecting the Trend of Real Wages," *American Economic Review*, XV, No. 1 (March, 1925), 27–42. A little-used but a detailed and decidedly useful compilation of wage data is the *History of Wages in the United States from Colonial Times to 1928* (Washington: United States Bureau of Labor Statistics, 1929). Census data by occupational groupings are brought together in P. K. Whelpton, "Occupational Groups in the United States, 1820–1920," *Journal of the American Statistical Association*, XXI, No. 155 (September, 1926), 335–343. But all such material from early census reports must be used with great care because of the inadequacy of the original data.

For nonstatistical material on the level of living of the working class, both Edgar W. Martin, *The Standard of Living in 1860* (Chicago: The University of Chicago Press, 1942), and Oscar Handlin, *Boston's Immigrants, 1790–1865* (Vol. L of *Harvard Historical Studies*, Cambridge: Harvard University Press, 1941), are excellent. A careful description of the condition of the very poor and the handicapped, and the measures taken for their relief, is available for one state in David M. Schneider, *The History of Public Welfare in New York State, 1609–1866* (Chicago: The University of Chicago Press, 1938). Unemployment in the fifties is treated in Leah Hannah Feder, *Unemployment Relief in Periods of Depression* (New York: Russell Sage Foundation, 1936), Chap. 2. The following prize essay written by a New York physician in 1837, now reprinted, provides a valuable contemporary comment on living conditions: Benjamin W. McCready, *On the Influence of Trades, Professions, and Occupations in the United States, in the Production of Disease* (Baltimore: The Johns Hopkins Press, 1943).

FINANCIAL INSTITUTIONS, PRICES, AND ECONOMIC FLUCTUATIONS

Among the more valuable contemporary writings on banking history are two papers by Albert Gallatin, "Considerations of the Currency and Banking System of the United States," III, 231–364, and "Suggestions on the Banks and Currency of the Several United States, in Reference Principally to the Suspension of Specie Payments," in Henry Adams, ed., *The Writings of Albert Gallatin* (3 vols., Philadelphia: J. B. Lippincott Company, 1879), III, 365–488. Useful statistics appear in an appendix to both studies. Later banking statistics are conveniently summarized in *Banking Studies* by members of the Staff Board of Governors of the Federal Reserve System (Washington: Board of Governors, 1941), pp. 417–418. Another contemporary work, William M. Gouge, *A Short History of Paper-Money and Banking in the United States* (New York: B. & S. Collins, 1835), contains excellent historical chapters. *The Journal of Banking from July 1841 to July 1842* (Philadelphia: J. Van Court, 1842), edited by Gouge, provides a wealth of interesting detail for the time period indicated. Condy Raguet, *A Treatise on Currency and Banking* (Philadelphia: Grigg & Elliot, 2d ed., 1840), is another indispensable contemporary study, more theoretical and less descriptive than Gouge's treatise. A later work, also a classic of the period, is Amasa Walker, *The Nature and Uses of Money and Mixed Currency, with a History of the Wickaboag Bank* (Boston: Crosby, Nichols & Company, 1857).

The two standard financial histories are William J. Shultz and M. R. Caine, *Financial Development of the United States* (New York: Prentice-Hall, Inc., 1937); and Davis Rich Dewey, *Financial History of the United States* (New York: Longmans, Green and Co., 12th ed., 1934). Both give a good deal of attention to the period of this volume and contain excellent bibliographies, but their chief emphasis is on public finance, a topic dealt with in the following section of this chapter. A host of older studies deal with money and banking history in more or less detail for the years 1815–1860. Among these are Charles F. Dunbar, *Chapters on the Theory and History of Banking* (New York: G. P. Putnam's Sons, rev. ed., 1907); A. Barton Hepburn, *A History of Currency in the United States* (New York: The Macmillan Company, rev. ed., 1924); William Graham, *A History of Banking in the United States* (New York: The Journal of Commerce and Commercial Bulletin, 1896); and Horace White, *Money and Banking, Illustrated by American History* (Boston: Ginn and Company, 2d ed., 1902). On currency history, J. Laurence Laughlin, *The History of Bimetallism in the United States* (New York: D. Appleton–Century Company, 4th ed., 1892), should be consulted, along with the indispensable and more recent Neil Carothers, *Fractional Money* (New York: John Wiley & Sons, 1930).

Among the more useful specialized studies are the following published by the National Monetary Commission: Davis R. Dewey, *State Banking before the Civil War,* National Monetary Commission, *Senate Document* No. 581, 61 Cong., 2 Sess., Vol. IV, No. 2; Robert E. Chaddock, *The Safety Fund Banking System in New York, 1829–1866,* National Monetary Commission, *Senate Document* No. 581, 61 Cong., 2 Sess., Vol. IV, No. 2; David Kinley, *The Independent Treasury of the United States and Its Relations to the Banks of the Country* (Washington: Government Printing Office, 1910; also published as *Senate Document* No. 587, 61 Cong., 2 Sess.); and John Thom Holdsworth and Davis R. Dewey, *The First and Second Banks of the United States* (National Monetary Commission, Vol. IV, No. 1, Washington: Government Printing Office, 1910; also published as *Senate Document* No. 571, 61 Cong., 2 Sess.). On the state banks Leonard C. Helderman, *National and State Banks* (Boston: Houghton Mifflin Company, 1931), and Earl Sylvester Sparks, *History and Theory of Agricultural Credit in the United States* (New York: Thomas Y. Crowell Company, 1932), provide helpful summaries.

A uniquely valuable interpretive study of western state banking is Bray Hammond, "Banking in the Early West: Monopoly, Prohibition, and Laissez Faire," *Journal of Economic History,* VIII, No. 1 (May, 1948), 1–25. Interesting especially because of its emphasis on the role of individual leaders and because it traces, and possibly magnifies, European influences, is Fritz Redlich, *The Molding of American Banking, Men and Ideas* (Vol. II of *History of American Business Leaders,* New York: Hafner Publishing Company, 1940–1947), Pt. 1. A good short history of banking in one state is Stephen A. Caldwell, *A Banking History of Louisiana* (No. 19 of *Louisiana State University Studies,* Baton Rouge: Louisiana State University Press, 1935). Outstanding among local banking studies is F. Cyril James, *The Growth of Chicago Banks* (2 vols., New York: Harper & Brothers, 1938).

The work by Redlich referred to above is especially valuable for its treatment of the second Bank of the United States. Ralph C. H. Catterall, *The Second Bank of the United States* (Chicago: The University of Chicago Press, 1903), has long been accepted as the standard work on this subject. The judicious tone of this study has tended to conceal its partisan approach and limited perspective. For important new light on the movement to charter the second Bank, see Raymond Walters, Jr., "The Origins of the Second Bank of the United States," *Journal of Political Economy,* LIII, No. 2 (June, 1945), 115–131; and Kenneth L. Brown, "Stephen Girard, Promoter of the Second Bank of the United States," *Journal of Economic History,* II, No. 2 (November, 1942), 125–148. The controversy over the rechartering of the Bank has resulted recently in fresh attempts at interpretation. For the pro-Biddle analysis, see Bray Hammond, "Jackson, Biddle, and the Bank of the United States," *Journal of Economic History,* VII, No. 1 (May, 1947), 1–23, and his "Public Policy and National Banks" (a review of Arthur M. Schlesinger, Jr., *The Age of Jackson*), *Journal of Economic History,* VI (May, 1946), 79–84; and for the pro-Jackson view, see Arthur M. Schlesinger, Jr., *The Age of Jackson* (Boston: Little, Brown & Company, 1945); and Carl Brent Swisher, *Roger B. Taney* (New York: The Macmillan Company, 1935).

A fairly recent book by Esther Rogoff Taus, *Central Banking Functions of the United States Treasury, 1789–1941* (New York: Columbia University Press, 1943), makes an appreciable contribution to our understanding of banking before 1860 along lines indicated by its title. Available on banking theory during this period are Lloyd W. Mints, *A History of Banking Theory in Great Britain and the United States* (Chicago: The University of Chicago Press, 1945); and Harry E. Miller, *Banking Theories in the United States Before 1860* (Vol. XXX of *Harvard Economic Studies,* Cambridge: Harvard University Press, 1927).

A number of excellent studies are available on finance and financial institutions in addition to those indicated above. Margaret G. Myers, *Origins and Development* (Vol. I of *The New York Money Market,* 4 vols., New York: Columbia University Press, 1931); Albert O. Greef, *The Commercial Paper House in the United States* (Vol. LX of *Harvard Economic Studies,* Cambridge: Harvard University Press, 1938), and Joseph Edward Hedges, *Commercial Banking and the Stock Market before 1863* (Johns Hopkins University *Studies in Historical and Political Science,* Vol. LVI, No. 1, Baltimore: The Johns Hopkins Press, 1938), are best in their respective fields. Good brief surveys of fire and marine insurance history will be found in Solomon Heubner, "History of Marine Insurance," in Lester W. Zartman, ed., *Property Insurance* (New Haven: Yale University Press, 1914), pp. 1–38, and in F. C. Oviatt, "History of Fire Insurance in the United States," pp. 70–98, in the same volume. Three studies of particular insurance companies, Shepard B. Clough, *A Century of American Life Insurance: A History of the Mutual Life Insurance Company of New York, 1843–1943* (New York: Columbia University Press, 1946); Marquis James, *The Metropolitan Life: A Study in*

Business Growth (New York: The Viking Press, 1947), and his *Bi-ography of a Business, 1792–1942* (Indianapolis: The Bobbs-Merrill Company, 1942), provide an excellent picture of the early history of life insurance in the United States. Old and inadequate, but still the best on the history of lotteries, is A. R. Spofford, "Lotteries in American History," *Annual Report of American Historical Association for the Year 1892* (Washington: 1893), pp. 171–195.

Earlier studies in price history have been largely superseded by those sponsored by the International Committee on Price History. These have been excellently summarized in Arthur Harrison Cole, *Wholesale Commodity Prices in the United States, 1700–1861* (Cambridge: Harvard University Press, 1938), and detailed statistics made available in the *Statistical Supplement* to that study. Of the detailed works resulting from this effort and covering the period of this volume, Anne Bezanson, Robert D. Gray, and Miriam Hussey, *Wholesale Prices in Philadelphia, 1784–1861* (Philadelphia: University of Pennsylvania Press, 1936), and Thomas Senior Berry, *Western Prices before 1861: A Study of the Cincinnati Market* (Vol. LXXIV of *Harvard Economic Studies*, Cambridge: Harvard University Press, 1943), merit special attention.

The most useful single work on business fluctuations and financial crises is Walter Buckingham Smith and Arthur Harrison Cole, *Fluctuations in American Business, 1790–1860* (Vol. L of *Harvard Economic Studies*, Cambridge: Harvard University Press, 1935). Older studies of business fluctuations, devoted in part at least to the period covered in this volume, such as Otto C. Lightner, *The History of Business Depressions* (New York: The Northeastern Press, 1922), and Ira Ryner, "On the Crises of 1837, 1847, and 1857, in England, France, and the United States: An Analysis and Comparison," *University Studies of the University of Nebraska*, V, No. 2 (April, 1905), 143–189, are no longer worth much attention, but Willard Long Thorp, *Business Annals* (New York: National Bureau of Economic Research, 1926), is still useful, especially as it facilitates international comparisons. For pertinent price series and their analyses, Smith and Cole, *Fluctuations in American Business, 1790–1860;* Cole, *Wholesale Commodity Prices in the United States, 1700–1861;* and the price studies by Berry and by Bezanson, Gray, and Hussey, referred to above, are indispensable. All of these, and especially Berry's study, go beyond a mere presentation of price data. For a theoretical approach to the American business cycle before 1860, see Norman J. Silberling, *The Dynamics of Business* (New York: McGraw-Hill

Book Company, 1943); and Joseph A. Schumpeter, *Business Cycles* (2 vols., New York: McGraw-Hill Book Company, 1939).

No detailed analysis of the crisis of 1819 is available, but the following article tells part of the story: Thomas H. Greer, "Economic and Social Effects of the Depression of 1819 in the Old Northwest," *Indiana Magazine of History*, XLIV, No. 3 (September, 1948), 227–243. For the situation in the thirties and covering more than the title indicates, see Reginald Charles McGrane, *The Panic of 1837* (Chicago: The University of Chicago Press, 1924). For a later crisis, George W. Van Vleck, *The Panic of 1857: An Analytical Study* (New York: Columbia University Press, 1943), provides a parallel study. Descriptive and emphasizing social aspects are three articles by Samuel Reznek: "The Depression of 1819–1822: A Social History," *American Historical Review*, XXXIX, No. 1 (October, 1933), 28–47; "The Social History of an American Depression, 1837–1843," *American Historical Review*, XL, No. 4 (July, 1935), 662–687; and "The Influence of Depression upon American Opinion, 1857–1859," *Journal of Economic History*, II, No. 1 (May, 1942), 1–23.

THE ROLE OF GOVERNMENT

The two standard general texts on the history of public finance are Davis Rich Dewey, *Financial History of the United States* (New York: Longmans, Green and Co., 12th ed., 1934), and William J. Shultz and M. R. Caine, *Financial Development of the United States* (New York: Prentice-Hall, Inc., 1937), referred to above. The first is notable for wide coverage of material and an extensive bibliography; the second is more interesting, is better balanced, and gives more attention to interpretation. Older and much more detailed for the period of this study is Albert Sidney Bolles, *The Financial History of the United States, from 1789 to 1860* (3 vols., New York: D. Appleton and Company, 1883), Vol. II. Of the special studies of federal finance, Esther Rogoff Taus, *Central Banking Functions of the United States Treasury, 1789–1941* (New York: Columbia University Press, 1943), is an excellent recent book emphasizing an important aspect insufficiently stressed in earlier works; and Edward Gaylord Bourne, *The History of the Surplus Revenue of 1837* (New York. G. P. Putnam's Sons, 1885), is an old and reliable study of the subject indicated. A detailed and authoritative study of federal loans is Rafael A. Bayley, *The National Loans of the United States, from July 4, 1776, to June 30, 1880* (Washington: Government Printing Office, 1881), also published in the *Tenth Census of the United States Valuation, Taxation and Public Indebtedness*, VII, 350–370, 425–444. On the independent treasury, David Kinley, *The History, Organization and Influence of the Independent Treasury of the United States* (New York: Thomas Y. Crowell Company, 1893), and David Kinley, *The Independent Treasury of the United States and Its Relations to the Banks of the Country* (Washington: Government Printing Office, 1910; also published as *Senate Document* No. 587, 61 Cong., 2 Sess.), are detailed and reliable studies. Reginald Charles McGrane, *The Panic of 1837*, referred to above, offers a brief but interesting chapter on the preliminaries for the passage of the bill establishing the independent treasury in 1840. For contemporary materials and documents, most useful are the annual reports of the Secretary of the Treasury and especially Jonathan Elliot, *The Funding System of the United States and of Great Britain* (Washington: Blair and Rives, 1845; also published as *House Executive Document*, 28 Cong., 1 Sess. [1843–1844], Vol. II).

No satisfactory general history of state or local financing is available for the period of this study. Richard T. Ely, *Taxation in American States and Cities* (New York: Thomas Y. Crowell Company, 1888), though of some value, is out-of-date and poorly organized. Of the detailed accounts available for many of the states, the following are among the most useful: Fred Eugene Jewett, *A Financial History of Maine* (No. 432 of *Studies in History, Economics and Public Law*, New York: Columbia University Press, 1937); Ernest Ludlow Bogart, *Financial History of Ohio* (University of Illinois *Studies in the Social Sciences*, Vol. I, Nos. 1–2, Urbana: University of Illinois, 1912); Charles J. Bullock, *Historical Sketch of the Finances and Financial Policy of Massachusetts from 1780 to 1905* (American Economic Association, *Publications*, 3d series, Vol. VIII, No. 2, 1907); Don C. Sowers, *The Financial History of New York State from 1789 to 1912* (*Studies in History, Economics and Public Law*, Vol. LVII, No. 2, New York: Columbia University Press, 1914); and Frederick A. Wood, *History of Taxation in Vermont* (*Studies in History, Economics and Public Law*, Vol. IV, No. 3, New York: Columbia College, 1894). Especially useful for its statistical materials is a "History of State Debts" presented in the *Tenth Census of the United States: Valuation, Taxation, and Public Indebtedness*, VII, 521–645. Two excellent studies on the state debts are Reginald C. McGrane, *Foreign Bondholders and American State Debts* (New York: The Macmillan Company, 1935); and B. U. Ratchford, *Ameri-*

can State Debts (Durham, N.C.: Duke University Press, 1941).

Despite the tremendous amount of writing which has been done on the tariff, the number of items offering much help to the economic historian remains small. F. W. Taussig, *The Tariff History of the United States* (New York: G. P. Putnam's Sons, 1892), provides by far the best general study of the period. Its bias is definitely a free-trade one. From the protectionist viewpoint, Edward Stanwood, *American Tariff Controversies in the Nineteenth Century* (2 vols., Boston: Houghton Mifflin Company, 1904), is perhaps the best. The emphasis is on political aspects, and it is so largely merely a digest of Congressional speeches on the subject as to make dull and repetitious reading. Orrin Leslie Elliott, *The Tariff Controversy in the United States, 1789–1833* (Palo Alto, Cal.: Ieland Stanford Junior University, 1892), also has a political emphasis but is useful for the limited period covered. Of the special studies, Malcolm Rogers Eiselen, *The Rise of Pennsylvania Protectionism* (Philadelphia: The author, 1932), and Chester Whitney Wright, *Wool-Growing and the Tariff* (Vol. V of *Harvard Economic Studies*, Boston: Houghton Mifflin Company, 1910), are excellent. The former has not received the attention from students which it deserves. Chapter 3 of John Dean Goss, *The History of Tariff Administration in the United States* (*Studies in History, Economics and Public Law*, Vol. I, No. 2, New York: Columbia University Press, 1891), is still useful for the aspect of the subject indicated in the title. The contemporary material is hopelessly voluminous and partisan. The speeches of Senator Henry Clay, for protection, and of Senator George McDuffie, against, tell a large part of the story. Orations by Daniel Webster on both sides of the question are available. Through 1824 his pronouncements state the free-trade position; thereafter they reflect the popular protectionist arguments. A useful collection of such materials is Frank W. Taussig, *State Papers and Speeches on the Tariff* (Cambridge: Harvard University Press, 1893).

On the general attitude toward the role of the state in economic affairs, Joseph Dorfman, *The Economic Mind in American Civilization, 1606–1918* (3 vols., New York: The Viking Press, 1946–1949), Michael J. L. O'Connor, *Origins of Academic Economics in the United States* (New York: Columbia University Press, 1944), and Merle Curti, *The Growth of American Thought* (New York: Harper & Brothers, 2d ed., 1943), are most useful. For the actual participation of the state and federal governments in economic affairs, specialized studies such as those cited above under other topics must be consulted. But worth special notice in this respect are Charles Warren, *Bankruptcy in United States History* (Cambridge: Harvard University Press, 1935); Arthur P. Miles, *An Introduction to Public Welfare* (Boston: D. C. Heath and Company, 1949); William Clinton Heffner, *History of Poor Relief Legislation in Pennsylvania, 1682–1913* (Cleona, Pa.: Holzopfel, 1913); and David M. Schneider, *The History of Public Welfare in New York State, 1609–1866* (Chicago: The University of Chicago Press, 1938).

Recently, long overdue attention has been given to the economic activities of the state governments. The following essays appearing in the *Tasks of Economic History*, December, 1943, are statements preliminary to more detailed studies which have been promised: Oscar Handlin, "Laissez-Faire Thought in Massachusetts, 1790–1880"; Louis Hartz, "Laissez-Faire Thought in Pennsylvania, 1776–1860"; and Milton S. Heath, "Laissez Faire in Georgia, 1732–1860." Two of the promised studies have already appeared: Oscar Handlin and Mary Flug Handlin, *Commonwealth: A Study of the Role of Government in the American Economy: Massachusetts, 1774–1861* (New York: New York University Press, 1947); and Louis Hartz, *Economic Policy and Democratic Thought: Pennsylvania, 1776–1860* (Cambridge: Harvard University Press, 1948).

EXTRACTIVE INDUSTRIES OTHER THAN AGRICULTURE

Scholarly studies, or even competent analytical surveys, in the extractive industries other than agriculture are almost nonexistent. On fur trading and trapping, the standard work is the rambling, anecdotal, and poorly organized Hiram Martin Chittenden, *The American Fur Trade of the Far West* (2 vols., New York: The Press of the Pioneers, Inc., 1935). One of the best brief, popular accounts is Everett Dick, *Vanguards of the Frontier* (New York: D. Appleton–Century Company, 1941), Chaps. 1 and 2. A competent Canadian study, Harold A. Innis, *The Fur Trade in Canada* (New Haven: Yale University Press, 1930), gives some incidental information for the United States. The story of the Rocky Mountain fur trade is delightfully told in the recently published Bernard De Voto, *Across the Wide Missouri* (Boston: Houghton Mifflin Company, 1947). The illustrations are superb and the bibliography is extensive. Best on the economic aspects and especially on the American Fur Company are Grace Lee Nute, "The Papers of the American Fur Company: A Brief Estimate of Their Significance," *American Historical Re-*

view, XXXII, No. 3 (April, 1927), 519–538; and Kenneth Wiggins Porter, *John Jacob Astor, Business Man* (2 vols., Cambridge: Harvard University Press, 1931). Valuable chapters on the early fur trade in Oregon are now available in Winther, *The Old Oregon Country*, referred to above. A good popular account of the bison is E. Douglas Branch, *The Hunting of the Buffalo* (New York: D. Appleton and Company, 1929).

For statistical materials as well as for a brief historical description of fishing, the *Eighth Census of the United States: Mortality and Miscellaneous Statistics*, pp. 527–551, should be consulted. A useful brief account of the fisheries of New England will be found in T. W. Van Metre, "American Fisheries," in Emory R. Johnson and others, eds., *History of Domestic and Foreign Commerce of the United States* (2 vols., Washington: Carnegie Institution of Washington, 1915), II, 157–168; and a much longer one in Raymond McFarland, *A History of the New England Fisheries* (New York: D. Appleton and Company, 1911). An older account is George Brown Goode and associates, *The Fisheries and Fishery Industries of the United States* (Washington: Government Printing Office, 1884–1887). Among the best special studies are Harold A. Innis, *The Cod Fisheries* (New Haven: Yale University Press, 1940); and Elmo Paul Hohman, *The American Whaleman* (New York: Longmans, Green and Co., 1928). The former stresses political aspects and the latter working conditions. Still useful also is Walter S. Tower, *A History of the American Whale Fishery* (No. 20 of University of Pennsylvania *Series in Political Economy and Public Law*, Philadelphia: The John C. Winston Company, 1907).

A good brief, general treatment of American mining history is that of Louis Hunter, "Heavy Industries before 1860," in Harold F. Williamson, ed., *The Growth of the American Economy* (New York: Prentice-Hall, Inc., 1944). Very few historical studies of mining give much attention to the period before 1860, but some useful material will be found in the following: Howard N. Eavenson, *The First Century and a Quarter of American Coal Industry* (Baltimore: Waverly Press, 1942); Angus Murdoch, *"Boom Copper": The Story of the First U.S. Mining Boom* (New York: The Macmillan Company, 1943); Walter Renton Ingalls, *Lead and Zinc in the United States* (New York: Hill Publishing Company, 1908); Thomas A. Rickard, *A History of American Mining* (New York: McGraw-Hill Book Company, 1932); Glenn Chesney Quiett, *Pay Dirt: A Panorama of American Gold-Rushes* (New York: D. Appleton–Century Company, 1936);

and Joseph Schafer, *The Wisconsin Lead Region* (Madison: State Historical Society of Wisconsin, 1932). *Hunt's Merchants' Magazine* has many articles on mining, but by far the best contemporary source is the *Mining Magazine*, Vols. I–XIII (July, 1853–April, 1861).

On lumbering, much can be learned from such firsthand accounts as Isaac Stephenson, *Recollections of a Long Life, 1829–1915* (Chicago: Privately printed, 1915); and John S. Springer, *Forest Life and Forest Trees* (New York: Harper & Brothers, 1851). The story of eastern lumbering is told in James Elliott Defebaugh, *History of the Lumber Industry of America* (2 vols., Chicago: The American Lumberman, 1906–1907). More detailed are such state studies as Richard G. Wood, *A History of Lumbering in Maine, 1820–1861* (*University of Maine Studies*, 2d series, No. 33, Orono: University Press, 1935); and W. F. Fox, *A History of the Lumber Industry in the State of New York*, Department of Agriculture, Bureau of Forestry, *Bulletin* No. 34, 1902. On western lumbering before 1860, interesting material will be found in such older studies as Captain Edward W. Durant, "Lumbering and Steamboating on the St. Croix River," *Collections of the Minnesota Historical Society*, X, Pt. 2 (St. Paul: The Society, 1905), 645–675; William H. C. Folsom, "History of Lumbering in the St. Croix Valley, with Biographic Sketches," *Collections of the Minnesota Historical Society*, IX (St. Paul: The Society, 1901), 291–324; and Daniel Stanchfield, "History of Pioneer Lumbering on the Upper Mississippi and Its Tributaries, with Biographic Sketches," *Collections of the Minnesota Historical Society*, IX (St. Paul: The Society, 1901), 325–362. An excellent recent study is Agnes M. Larson, *History of the White Pine Industry in Minnesota* (Minneapolis: University of Minnesota Press, 1949). Finally, worth notice is the popularly written Richard G. Lillard, *The Great Forest* (New York: Alfred A. Knopf, Inc., 1947).

WEALTH AND INCOME

Estimates on national wealth and income before 1860 are based on the early decennial censuses and other data often even less reliable. Faulty as it undoubtedly is, the best estimate of national wealth is to be found in Horatio C. Burchard, *Annual Report of the Director of the Mint*, 1881, *House Executive Document* No. 2, 47 Cong., 1 Sess. The study begins with 1825. These figures are conveniently summarized in *Historical Statistics of the United States, 1789–1945*, p. 9. The best study of income is to be found in Robert F. Martin, *National In-*

come in the United States, 1799–1938 (New York: National Industrial Conference Board, 1939). Most of the same data are also available in *Conference Board Studies in Enterprise and Social Progress* (New York: National Industrial Conference Board, 1939). A detailed breakdown of income data by industries is presented, but because of the inadequacy of the underlying statistics, it is of doubtful value for the years covered by this volume.

On the share of the national product going to the wage earner, see references under the topic "Labor" above. The share as well as the role of the entrepreneur is dealt with incidentally in many of the books referred to above. *Hunt's Merchants' Magazine* carries many articles on the merchant, including biographical sketches of leading merchants and essays dealing with the training and capacities needed for success in business. The biographies, with some additions, are printed in Freeman Hunt, *Lives of American Merchants* (2 vols., New York: Derby & Jackson, 1858). But few of these are very satisfactory, and the student will do well to turn to the *Dictionary of American Biography* and to utilize the biographical references indicated there.

An interesting contemporary source on great fortunes is M. Y. Beach, *Wealth and Wealthy Citizens of New York*. This was published annually from 1842 to 1855 with some variations in title. The issue for 1845 is reproduced in Henry Wysham Lanier, *A Century of Banking in New York* (New York: George H. Doran, 1922). Most of the individuals treated in Gustavus Myers, *History of the Great American Fortunes* (3 vols., Chicago: Charles H. Kerr & Company, 1911), lived at least part of their lives during the period covered by this volume.

The role of the entrepreneur, a subject which has been given increasing attention, is emphasized in N. S. B. Gras, *Business and Capitalism* (New York: F. S. Crofts & Co., 1939), but with little special attention to conditions in America in the decades preceding 1860. The same may be said for the articles appearing in the publication *Explorations in Entrepreneurial History*, which was issued in 1949 for private distribution in connection with a special study of entrepreneurship at the Harvard School of Business Administration, but special attention may be called to Harvey J. Wexler, "How to Succeed in Business, 1840–1860," I, No. 1 (January, 1949), 26–29. The two best discussions dealing specifically with the period covered by this volume are Robert Greenhalgh Albion, *The Rise of New York Port* [*1815–1860*], Chap. 13; and C. Wright Mills, "The American Business Elite: A Collective Portrait," *Tasks of Economic History* (December, 1945), pp. 20–44. .

Appendices

Appendix A

TABLE 1

UNITED STATES MERCHANT MARINE STATISTICS BY YEARS, 1815–1861

Year Ended [f]	I [a] Registered Tonnage of the United States	II [b] American Tonnage Entered and Cleared in United States Foreign Trade	III [c] Percentages of Value of American Foreign Trade Carried in U.S. Vessels	IV [d] American Proportion of Total Tonnage of All Vessels Cleared in Foreign Trade (%)
1815	824,295	1,389,508		
1816	800,760	1,754,922		
1817	804,851	1,560,272		
1818 [e]	589,944	1,510,202		
1819	581,230	1,567,158		
1820	583,657	1,602,506		
1821	593,825	1,570,045	88.7	90
1822	582,701	1,501,709	88.4	88
1823	600,003	1,586,032	89.9	86
1824	636,807	1,769,311	91.2	90
1825	665,409	1,841,120	92.3	91
1826	696,221	1,895,218	92.5	89
1827	701,517	1,898,903	90.9	88
1828	757,998	1,765,785	88.9	85
1829 [e]	592,859	1,817,748	89.5	87
1830	537,563	1,938,987	89.9	88
1831	538,136	1,895,456	86.5	77
1832	614,121	1,924,487	83.1	71
1833	648,869	2,253,601	83.8	68
1834	749,378	2,208,690	83.0	66
1835	788,173 [g]	2,753,270	84.5	68
1836	753,094	2,570,907	84.3	65
1837	683,205	2,566,342	82.6	63
1838	702,962	2,711,735	84.2	69
1839	702,400	2,969,207	84.3	71
1840	762,838	3,223,955	82.9	69
1841	788,398	3,266,065	83.3	69
1842	832,746	3,046,562	82.3	68
1843	856,930 [g]	2,411,606	77.1	70
1844	900,471	3,988,362	78.6	69

TABLE 1 (*Cont.*)

UNITED STATES MERCHANT MARINE STATISTICS BY YEARS, 1815–1861

Year Ended [f]	I [a] Registered Tonnage of the United States	II [b] American Tonnage Entered and Cleared in United States Foreign Trade	III [c] Percentages of Value of American Foreign Trade Carried in U.S. Vessels	IV [d] American Proportion of Total Tonnage of All Vessels Cleared in Foreign Trade (%)
1845	904,476	4,089,463	81.7	69
1846	943,307	4,372,142	81.7	70
1847	1,047,454	4,303,752	70.9	65
1848	1,168,707	4,854,762	77.4	64
1849	1,258,756	5,412,045	75.2	62
1850	1,439,694	5,205,804	72.5	60
1851	1,544,663	6,254,868	72.7	62
1852	1,705,650	6,466,112	70.5	62
1853	1,910,471	7,770,802	69.5	63
1854	2,151,918	7,663,507	70.5	65
1855	2,348,358	7,930,373	75.6	65
1856	2,302,190	8,923,848	75.2	65
1857	2,268,196	9,302,021	70.5	66
1858	2,301,148	8,885,675	73.7	67
1859	2,321,674	10,563,015	66.9	68
1860	2,379,396	12,087,209	66.5	71

a *Annual Report of the Commissioner of Navigation*, 1914, pp. 186–188.

b The figures for 1815–1820 are computed from tables for tonnage entered presented by the Commissioner of Navigation, Eugene Tyler Chamberlain, in *Report of the Merchant Marine Commission* (1905), *Senate Report* No. 2,755, 58 Cong., 3 Sess., III, 1765. The figures for tonnage "entered" were doubled to secure a total for "entered and cleared." If the ratio between tonnage entered and tonnage cleared existing in the 1820's was the same for 1815–1820 as in the following years, then the totals secured by this method are somewhat higher than they should be. For 1821–1861 data are from *Annual Report of the Commissioner of Navigation*, 1914, p. 150.

c *Annual Report of the Commissioner of Navigation*, 1914, pp. 148–149.

d *Annual Report of the Commissioner of Navigation*, 1914, p. 150.

e The official records were corrected in this year.

f For Column I, 1815–1834 year ending December 31, 1835; 1842 year ending September 30; and 1843–1861 year ending June 30. For Column II, fiscal year.

g Less than full year.

TABLE 2

AVERAGE FREIGHT RATES A TON-MILE
FOR 1816, 1853, AND 1860

Means of Transportation	1816	1853 [d]	1860
	cents a ton-mile		
Turnpikes	30.00 up [a]	15.00	15.00 [a]
Mississippi-Ohio River, downstream	1.30 [b]		.37 [c]
Mississippi-Ohio River, upstream	5.80 [b]		.37 [c]
Ohio River		0.80	
Hudson River	6.20 [e]	0.70	
Illinois River		1.20	
Erie Canal		1.10	.99 [f]
Ohio Canal		1.00	
Wabash-Erie Canal		1.90	
Illinois Canal		1.40	
Pennsylvania Main Line Canal		2.40	
Chesapeake and Ohio Canal (coal)		0.25	.25 [d]
New York Central Railroad		3.40	2.06 [f]
Erie Railroad		2.40	1.84 [f]
Western Railroad—Buffalo to Chicago		2.50	
Western Railroad—Boston to Albany		2.30	
Pennsylvania Railroad		3.50	1.96 [g]
Western lakes, short voyage		0.10	
Western lakes, long voyage		0.05	

a See above pp. 133–134.

b For 1815. See Berry, *Western Prices before 1861*, pp. 45, 53.

c Average for first 6 months of year, the season during which most goods were shipped. Upstream rates are taken to be the same as downstream although they were often lower. Thomas Senior Berry, *Western Prices before 1861: A Study of the Cincinnati Market* (Vol. LXXIV of *Harvard Economic Studies*, Cambridge: Harvard University Press, 1943), pp. 56–57, 559.

d *Hunt's Merchants' Magazine*, XXXI (July, 1854), 123, except for the Chesapeake and Ohio Canal, for which see Walter S. Sanderlin, *The Great National Project: A History of the Chesapeake and Ohio Canal*, Johns Hopkins University *Studies in Historical and Political Science*, LXIV (1946), 313.

e *Niles' Weekly Register*, VI (May 14, 1814), 169.

f *Nimmo Report*, 1879, p. 110.

g *Aldrich Report, Senate Report* No. 1,394, Pt. 1 (1893), 52 Cong., 2 Sess., III, 19. This source gives rates in 1860 for the New York Central and the Erie Railroad slightly lower than those appearing in the table.

TABLE 3

TIME REQUIRED FOR FREIGHT SHIPMENTS FROM CINCINNATI TO
NEW YORK CITY, 1815–1860 BY VARIOUS ROUTES AND METHODS

Date	Route	Average Time Elapsed
1817	Ohio River keelboat to Pittsburgh, wagon to Philadelphia, wagon or wagon and river to New York	52 days [a]
1843 and 1851	Ohio River steamboat to Pittsburgh, canal to Philadelphia, railroad to New York	18–20 days [b]
1852	Canal across Ohio, Lake Erie, Erie Canal, and Hudson River	18 days [c]
1850's	Steamboat to New Orleans and packet to New York	28 days [d]
1852	All rail via Erie Railroad and connecting lines	6–8 days [c]

a Partly estimated by the author and may well be on the low side. See Berry, *Western Prices before 1861*, p. 27; *Niles' Weekly Register*, X (June 1, 1816), 231; Wheaton J. Lane, *From Indian Trail to Iron Horse* (Princeton: Princeton University Press, 1939), p. 157.

b Berry, *Western Prices before 1861*, pp. 88, 92.

c Robert Greenhalgh Albion, *The Rise of New York Port* [*1815–1860*] (New York: Charles Scribner's Sons, 1939), p. 119.

d Louis Hunter, *Steamboats on Western Rivers* (Cambridge: Harvard University Press, 1949); Robert Greenhalgh Albion, *Square-Riggers on Schedule* (Princeton: Princeton University Press, 1938), p. 317. Partly estimated by the author.

TABLE 4

UNITED STATES MERCHANDISE EXPORTS AND IMPORTS, 1815–1860

Year [a]	Total Exports	Domestic Exports	Re-exports	Total Imports
1815	$ 52,557,753	$ 45,974,403	$ 6,583,350	$113,041,274 [b]
1816	81,920,052	64,781,896	17,138,156	147,103,000
1817	87,671,569	68,313,500	19,358,069	99,250,000
1818	93,281,133	73,854,437	19,426,696	121,750,000
1819	70,142,521	50,976,838	19,165,683	87,125,000
1820	69,691,669	51,683,640	18,008,029	74,450,000
1821	54,596,323	43,671,894	10,924,429	54,520,834
1822	61,350,101	49,874,079	11,476,022	79,871,695
1823	68,326,043	47,155,408	21,170,635	72,481,371
1824	68,972,105	50,649,500	18,322,605	72,169,172
1825	90,738,333	66,944,745	23,793,588	90,189,310
1826	72,890,789	52,449,855	20,440,934	78,093,511
1827	74,309,947	57,878,117	16,431,830	71,332,938
1828	64,021,210	49,976,632	14,044,578	81,020,083
1829	67,434,651	55,087,307	12,347,344	67,088,915
1830	71,670,735	58,524,878	13,145,857	62,720,956
1831	72,295,652	59,218,583	13,077,069	95,885,179
1832	81,520,603	61,726,529	19,794,074	95,121,762
1833	87,528,732	69,950,856	17,577,876	101,047,943
1834	102,260,215	80,623,662	21,636,553	108,609,700
1835	115,215,802	100,459,481	14,756,321	136,764,295
1836	124,338,704	106,570,942	17,767,762	176,579,154
1837	111,443,127	94,280,895	17,162,232	130,472,803
1838	104,978,570	95,560,880	9,417,690	95,970,288
1839	112,251,673	101,625,533	10,626,140	156,496,956
1840	123,668,932	111,660,561	12,008,371	98,258,706
1841	111,817,471	103,636,236	8,181,235	122,957,544
1842	99,877,995	91,799,242	8,078,753	96,075,071
1843	82,825,689	77,686,354	5,139,335	42,433,464
1844	105,745,832	99,531,774	6,214,058	102,604,606
1845	106,040,111	98,455,330	7,584,781	113,184,322
1846	109,583,248	101,718,042	7,865,206	117,914,065
1847	156,741,598	150,574,844	6,166,754	122,424,349
1848	138,190,515	130,203,709	7,986,806	148,638,644
1849	140,351,172	131,710,081	8,641,091	141,206,199
1850	144,375,726	134,900,233	9,475,493	173,509,526
1851	188,915,259	178,620,138	10,295,121	210,771,429
1852	166,984,231	154,931,147	12,053,084	207,440,398
1853	203,489,282	189,869,162	13,620,120	263,777,265
1854	237,043,764	215,328,300	21,715,464	297,803,794
1855	218,909,503	192,751,135	26,158,368	257,808,708
1856	281,219,423	266,438,051	14,781,372	310,432,310
1857	293,823,760	278,906,713	14,917,047	348,428,342
1858	272,011,274	251,351,033	20,660,241	263,338,654
1859	292,902,051	278,392,080	14,509,971	331,333,341
1860	333,576,057	316,242,423	17,333,634	353,616,119

a Year ending September 30 for 1815–1842 and year ending June 30 for 1844–1860. The totals for 1843 are for the nine months beginning November 1, 1842 and ending June 30, 1843.
b This is the accepted official figure but is probably too high.

TABLE 4 (*Cont.*)

UNITED STATES MERCHANDISE EXPORTS AND IMPORTS, 1815–1860

Imports for Consumption	Total Foreign Trade	Excess of Exports + Imports −	Year [a]
$106,457,924	$165,599,027	$60,483,521 −	1815
129,964,844	229,023,052	65,182,948 −	1816
79,891,931	186,921,569	11,578,431 −	1817
102,323,304	215,031,133	28,468,867 −	1818
67,959,317	157,267,521	16,982,479 −	1819
56,441,971	144,141,669	4,758,331 −	1820
43,596,405	109,117,157	75,489 +	1821
68,395,673	141,221,796	18,521,594 −	1822
51,310,736	140,807,414	4,155,328 −	1823
53,846,567	141,141,277	3,197,067 −	1824
66,395,722	180,927,643	549,023 +	1825
57,652,577	150,984,300	5,202,722 −	1826
54,901,108	145,642,885	2,977,009 +	1827
66,975,505	145,041,293	16,998,873 −	1828
54,741,571	134,523,566	345,736 +	1829
49,575,099	134,391,691	8,949,779 +	1830
82,808,110	168,180,831	23,589,527 −	1831
75,327,688	176,642,365	13,601,159 −	1832
83,470,067	188,576,675	13,519,211 −	1833
86,973,147	210,869,915	6,349,485 −	1834
122,007,974	251,980,097	21,548,493 −	1835
158,811,392	300,917,858	52,240,450 −	1836
113,310,571	241,915,930	19,029,676 −	1837
86,552,598	200,948,858	9,008,282 +	1838
145,870,816	268,748,629	44,245,283 −	1839
86,250,335	221,927,638	25,410,226 +	1840
114,776,309	234,775,015	11,140,073 −	1841
87,996,318	195,953,066	3,802,924 +	1842
37,294,129	125,259,153	40,392,225 +	1843
96,390,548	208,350,438	3,141,226 +	1844
105,599,541	219,224,433	7,144,211 −	1845
110,048,859	227,497,313	8,330,817 −	1846
116,257,595	279,165,947	34,317,249 +	1847
140,651,838	286,829,159	10,448,129 −	1848
132,565,108	281,557,371	855,027 −	1849
164,034,033	317,885,252	29,133,800 −	1850
200,476,308	399,686,688	21,856,170 −	1851
195,387,314	374,424,629	40,456,167 −	1852
250,157,145	467,266,547	60,287,983 −	1853
276,088,330	534,847,558	60,760,030 −	1854
231,650,340	476,718,211	38,899,205 −	1855
295,650,938	591,651,733	29,212,887 −	1856
333,511,295	642,252,102	54,604,582 −	1857
242,678,413	535,349,928	8,672,620 +	1858
316,823,370	624,235,392	38,431,290 −	1859
336,282,485	687,192,176	20,040,062 −	1860

Source: Historical Tables of Commerce, Finance, Tonnage and Immigration of the United States, Treasury Department, Bureau of Statistics (Washington: 1894?).

TABLE 5

FOREIGN TRADE OF THE UNITED KINGDOM, 1815–1860

(*Real value in millions of dollars*) [a]

Year	Exports [b]	Re-exports [b]	Imports [c]	Total Foreign Commerce
1815	$281.3	$75.6	$315.8	$597.1
1816	236.2	64.7	198.7	434.9
1817	241.9	49.4	257.8	499.7
1818	257.3	52.1	414.2	671.5
1819	208.3	47.5	276.0	484.3
1820	235.2	50.7	265.0	500.2
1821	247.2	51.0	218.9	466.1
1822	256.8	44.3	217.9	474.7
1823	251.5	41.3	254.9	506.4
1824	282.7	49.0	262.6	545.3
1825	270.2	44.0	389.3	659.5
1826	244.8	48.4	271.7	516.5
1827	298.1	47.2	329.3	627.4
1828	301.0	47.8	298.1	599.0
1829	320.6	51.0	280.8	601.4
1830	334.6	41.0	303.8	638.4
1831	342.7	51.6	330.7	673.4
1832	365.3	53.0	272.2	637.4
1833	383.0	47.2	270.7	653.8
1834	409.9	55.5	312.0	721.9
1835	443.8	62.3	305.6	749.4
1836	475.0	60.3	389.8	864.8
1837	417.6	64.4	365.5	783.0
1838	512.0	61.9	403.0	914.9
1839	536.3	62.3	463.8	1,000.1
1840	567.0	67.0	462.3	1,029.3
1841	568.9	71.7	440.4	1,009.3
1842	553.8	66.1	371.3	925.1
1843	641.4	67.9	382.0	1,023.4
1844	710.5	70.1	403.9	1,114.4
1845	734.4	79.2	481.8	1,216.1
1846	723.2	79.3	445.8	1,168.9
1847	711.5	97.5	537.3	1,248.7
1848	734.8	89.4	494.4	1,229.3
1849	925.1	124.4	517.8	1,442.9
1850	960.2	106.5	492.0	1,452.2
1851	1,043.4	115.5	549.4	1,592.8
1852	1,068.2	113.5	533.9	1,602.1
1853	1,178.2	135.0	710.0	1,888.2
1854	563.5	90.7	796.7	1,360.2
1855	567.9	102.2	707.6	1,275.5
1856	677.4	113.8	842.9	1,520.3
1857	711.5	117.3	895.4	1,606.9
1858	680.3	112.8	773.3	1,453.6
1859	757.7	123.0	852.1	1,609.8
1860	800.5	139.3	1,020.0	1,820.6

TABLE 6

VALUE OF IMPORTANT RE-EXPORTS EVERY FIFTH YEAR, 1821–1860

Year	Cotton Manu- factures	Wheat and Wheat Flour	Sugar and Molasses	Tea	Coffee	Woolens
1821	$1,581,143	Not listed	$1,560,417	$242,372	$2,087,479	$379,252
1825						
1830	1,989,464	Not listed	691,166	892,807	1,046,542	229,767
1835	3,697,837	Not listed	575,202	927,525	1,333,777	368,732
1840	1,103,489	Not listed	1,406,901	1,359,866	930,398	360,177
1845	502,553	Not listed	867,013	927,187	842,475	156,646
1850	425,630	$1,074,690	709,498	737,178	1,316,363	174,934
1855	2,012,554	1,892,040	1,712,138	2,036,389	1,453,977	2,327,701
1860	1,059,533	670	2,433,684	1,985,203	2,268,691	201,276

Year	Flax Manu- factures	Dyewood and Barilla	Cocoa	Indigo	Iron and Steel	Alcoholic Beverages[a]
1821	$245,848	$112,855	$228,219	$416,968	$256,628	$410,704
1825						
1830	923,546	331,701	148,294	440,863	265,743	613,506
1835	354,690	459,907	370,535	96,619	348,323	398,325
1840	425,466	631,314	146,901	179,210	190,076	318,067
1845	159,626	349,067	152,630	94,686	112,018	160,820
1850	129,878	598,334	124,578	14,565	140,939	283,390
1855	278,850	780,401	66,638	53,790	1,628,591	461,722
1860	180,611	317,162	271,987	48,175	280,185	464,820

a Includes value of bottles.

Sources: American State Papers: Commerce and Navigation, II, 602, for 1821. For other years see annual reports of the Secretary of the Treasury.

NOTES FOR TABLE 5

a English pounds were converted into United States dollars at the following ratios: 1815–1834, £1 = $4.80, and 1835–1860, £1 = $4.8665. The result for the years 1815–1834 is only approximate, but is more accurate than the result obtained from using the "official" par of £1 = $4.44⅘. Cf. Arthur H. Cole, "Evolution of the Foreign-Exchange Market of the United States," *Journal of Economic and Business History,* I (May, 1929), 406–407, fn. 1.

b William Page, *Commerce and Industry* (2 vols., London: Constable and Company, Ltd., 1919), II, 70–71.

c Werner Schlote, *Entwicklung und Strukturwandlungen des Englischen Aussenhandels von 1700 bis zur Gegenwart* (Jena: G. Fischer, 1938), pp. 124–125. Cf. Albert H. Imlah, "Real Values in British Foreign Trade, 1798–1853," *Journal of Economic History,* VIII (November, 1948), 133–152. This valuable study was not available at the time Chapter IX was written. Though small differences appear between the data here used and those computed by Imlah, they are not such as to affect significantly the conclusions drawn.

TABLE 7

VALUE OF MERCHANDISE RE-EXPORTS FROM THE UNITED STATES TO PRINCIPAL COUNTRIES
BY FIVE-YEAR PERIODS, 1816–1860

Five-Year Period	Belgium	France	Germany	Italy	Netherlands
1816–1820 b	Included in Netherlands	$12,128,872 a	$5,985,226 a	$5,721,555 a	$11,522,769 a
1821–1825		8,886,808	5,980,529	3,696,791	7,595,825
1826–1830		6,601,245	5,653,069	2,592,439	4,698,799
1831–1835		9,483,351	6,046,968	1,642,219	5,219,755
1836–1840	$1,917,850	8,076,138	4,704,721	1,686,386	3,209,709
1841–1845	1,129,836	2,072,443	2,963,980	1,679,379	1,351,896
1846–1850	1,936,844	2,389,112	2,494,643	1,710,611	1,230,214
1851–1855	4,754,387	2,887,666	3,258,690	1,497,392	1,056,079
1856–1860	7,550,395	2,978,516	7,486,278	730,961	970,275

Five-Year Period	United Kingdom	South America	Mexico	West Indies	Canada and the Maritime Provinces	China
1816–1820	$4,310,792 a	$13,564,332		$14,283,139		
1821–1825	3,849,792	8,796,197		11,509,993		
1826–1830	4,270,532	8,551,932	$16,583,022	9,643,092		
1831–1835	7,940,824	5,643,550	21,516,671	7,764,720	$206,393	$2,274,568
1836–1840	10,771,929	3,887,505	12,094,070	2,986,305	780,848	907,459
1841–1845	6,930,328	2,923,961	3,117,710	3,048,749	2,079,467	387,738
1846–1850	6,283,823	4,402,046	4,297,760	4,106,747	8,663,669	397,543
1851–1855	17,600,730	5,583,673	4,186,556	4,437,275	32,537,370	529,438
1856–1860	15,912,384		5,047,550		25,069,235	962,826

a Including gold and silver.
b See Appendix A, Table 4, footnote (a).
Source: Computed from annual reports of the Secretary of the Treasury.

TABLE 8

LEADING IMPORTS INTO THE UNITED STATES FOR DOMESTIC CONSUMPTION, 1821–1860

(Values expressed in millions of dollars)

Year [a]	Cotton Manufacture		Woolen Manufacture		Silk Manufacture		Flax Manufacture		Iron and Steel (arms included)	
	Value	% of total	Value	% of total	Value	% of total	Value	% of total	Value	% of total
1821	$5.8	13	$6.9	16	$3.4	8	$2.3	5.0	$3.0	7
1825										
1830	5.9	12	5.6	11	4.8	10	2.1	4.0	5.7	11
1835	11.7	10	10.7	9	15.8	13	5.1	4.0	8.6	7
1840	5.4	6	6.2	7	8.5	10	3.5	4.0	7.1	8
1845	13.4	13	8.6	8	9.5	9	2.6	2.0	8.9	8
1850	19.7	12	12.0	7	17.3	11	5.3	3.0	17.5	11
1855	15.7	7	22.1	10	23.5	10	5.9	3.0	23.9	10
1860	31.5	9	37.7	11	32.7	10	11.1	3.0	21.2	6

Year [a]	Tea		Coffee		Sugar		Hides and Skins		Alcoholic Beverages	
	Value	% of total	Value	% of total	Value	% of total	Value	% of total	Value	% of total
1821	$1.1	2	$2.4	6	$2.0	5	$0.8	2.0	$3.3	8
1825	2.2	3	2.0	3	2.6	4				
1830	1.5	3	3.2	6	3.9	8	2.1	4.0	1.6	3
1835	3.6	3	9.4	8	6.2	5	3.3	3.0	5.1	4
1840	4.1	5	7.6	9	4.2	5	2.3	3.0	3.6	4
1845	4.8	5	5.4	5	4.0	4	0.1	0.1	2.6	2
1850	4.0	2	9.9	6	6.9	4	4.7	3.0	5.1	3
1855	4.9	2	15.5	7	13.3	6	7.7	3.0	5.7	2
1860	6.9	2	19.6	6	28.9	9	8.9	3.0	10.8	3

a See Appendix A, Table 4, footnote (a).
Source: Computed from annual reports of the Secretary of the Treasury.

TABLE 9

PERCENTAGE DISTRIBUTION OF IMPORTS INTO THE UNITED STATES BY CONTINENTS

Year	North America		South America	Europe	Asia	Oceania	Africa
	Northern	Southern					
1821	0.7	21.7	2.9	64.2	9.8	0.1	0.7
1830	0.6	17.2	7.8	64.0	10.0	a	0.4
1840	1.2	15.7	8.8	62.8	10.9	0.2	0.5
1850	3.0	9.3	9.2	71.0	7.2	a	0.4
1860	6.7	12.5	9.9	61.3	8.3	0.3	1.0

a Less than one tenth of 1 per cent.
Source: Statistical Abstract of the United States, 1938, p. 458.

TABLE 10

VALUE OF MERCHANDISE IMPORTED INTO THE UNITED STATES BY
COUNTRIES AND AREAS BY FIVE-YEAR PERIODS, 1821–1860

(*Values expressed in millions of dollars*)

Five-Year Period a	United Kingdom b		France b		Russia b, c		Germany b		British N.Am. Colonies	
	Value	% of total	Value	% of total	Value	% of total	Value	% of total	Value	% of total
1821–1825	$151.3	41	$33.7	9	$11.7	3.0	$9.5	3	$1.8	0.5
1826–1830	138.7	38	42.6	12	11.3	3.0	11.5	3	1.7	0.5
1831–1835	220.0	41	77.4	14	12.6	2.0	16.0	3	4.4	1.0
1836–1840	254.4	39	117.2	18	12.5	2.0	21.5	3	7.8	1.0
1841–1845	178.4	37	83.7	18	7.5	2.0	10.5	2	5.1	1.0
1846–1850	285.7	41	126.7	18	6.2	1.0	29.7	4	8.1	1.0
1851–1855	564.7	46	157.1	13	6.1	0.5	62.1	5	41.2	3.0
1856–1860	601.6	37	212.5	13	6.1	0.4	80.2	5	102.0	6.0

Five-Year Period a	Cuba d		Total West Indies d		Argentina d		Brazil d		China e	
	Value	% of total	Value	% of total	Value	% of total	Value	% of total	Value	% of total
1821–1825	$32.6	9	$69.9	19			$7.0	2		
1826–1830	29.3	8	60.1	17	2.9	1	11.7	3		
1831–1835	44.4	8	78.4	15	6.1	1	21.5	4	$29.8	6
1836–1840	56.3	9	90.9	14	3.9	1	25.4	4	31.4	5
1841–1845	39.2	8	63.2	13	7.4	2	29.0	6	25.5	5
1846–1850	52.0	7	76.4	11	6.4	1	40.3	6	32.4	5
1851–1855	88.3	7	121.3	10	12.2	1	67.8	5	49.5	4
1856–1860	156.9	10	205.9	13	15.8	1	101.3	6	53.7	3

a See Appendix A, Table 4, footnote (a).
b *House Miscellaneous Document,* Vol. XVI, 52 Cong., 2 Sess.
c 1854–1860 inclusive, "Russia in Europe."
d *House Document* No. 573, Pt. 12, 55 Cong., 2 Sess.
e Annual reports of the Secretary of the Treasury.

TABLE 11

VALUE OF LEADING DOMESTIC EXPORTS OF THE UNITED STATES, 1815–1860

(*Values expressed in millions of dollars*)

Year c	Cotton a Unmanuf.		Tobacco a Unmanuf.		Wheat a and Flour		Corn and a Corn Meal		Rice a	
	Value	% of total	Value	% of total	Value	% of total	Value	% of total	Value	% of total
1816–1820	$121.5	39	$47.5	15	$50.6	16	$7.6	2	$13.1	4
1821–1825	123.4	48	28.1	11	25.4	10	4.1	2	8.7	3
1826–1830	133.1	49	27.8	10	25.6	9	4.4	2	11.4	4
1831–1835	207.6	56	31.5	8	30.1	8	4.5	1	11.2	3
1836–1840	321.2	63	43.0	8	29.0	6	4.3	1	11.0	2
1841–1845	256.8	55	42.6	9	33.9	7	4.8	1	9.9	2
1846–1850	296.6	46	39.0	6	82.2	13	40.3	6	13.7	2
1851–1855	491.5	53	55.3	6	97.5	10	21.9	2	10.7	1
1856–1860	744.6	54	86.5	6	157.7	11	24.7	2	11.3	1

Year c	Beef,a Tallow, Hides, and Horned Cattle		Pork (pick-a led), Bacon, Lard, and Live Hogs		Dried a Smoked or Pickled Fish		Staves, Shin-a gles, Boards, and Hewn Timber		Domestic b Manu- factures	
	Value	% of total	Value	% of total	Value	% of total	Value	% of total	Value	% of total
1816–1820	$3.7	1	$4.2	1	$6.8	2.0	$15.5	5	$21.1	7
1821–1825	3.9	2	7.3	3	5.1	2.0	7.6	3	27.9	11
1826–1830	3.6	1	7.8	3	4.7	2.0	8.7	3	32.3	12
1831–1835	4.0	1	9.2	2	4.8	1.0	9.5	3	36.2	10
1836–1840	2.8	1	7.7	2	4.1	1.0	10.7	2	46.4	9
1841–1845	6.9	1	13.6	3	3.9	1.0	9.4	2	50.9	11
1846–1850	10.5	2	36.3	6	3.4	1.0	10.8	2	70.1	11
1851–1855	12.6	1	37.1	4	2.4	0.3	17.6	2	126.4	14
1856–1860	21.8	2	53.9	4	3.9	0.3	29.3	2	167.3	12

a *House Miscellaneous Document* No. 49, Pt. 2, 48 Cong., 1 Sess., Vol. XXIV.
b *House Document* No. 15, Pt. 10, 57 Cong., 2 Sess., XLII, 3242.
c See Appendix A, Table 4, footnote (a).

TABLE 12

PERCENTAGE DISTRIBUTION OF EXPORTS FROM THE UNITED STATES
BY CONTINENTS

Year	North America		South America	Europe	Asia	Oceania	Africa
	Northern	Southern					
1821	4.4	22.0	4.1	65.3	3.6	0.1	0.6
1830	3.9	20.5	6.4	66.1	2.7	a	0.3
1840	4.9	13.9	4.6	74.4	1.3	0.3	0.6
1850	6.6	9.9	5.4	75.2	2.1	0.1	0.7
1860	6.9	8.8	4.7	74.8	2.4	1.5	1.0

a Less than one tenth of 1 per cent.
Source: Statistical Abstract of the United States, 1935, p. 431.

TABLE 13

VALUE OF DOMESTIC EXPORTS OF THE UNITED STATES BY COUNTRIES
AND AREAS OF DESTINATION BY FIVE-YEAR PERIODS, 1821–1860 [a]

(*Values expressed in millions of dollars*)

Five-Year Period [c]	United [a] Kingdom		Total [b] West Indies		France [a]		Total South [b] America		Cuba [b]	
	Value	% of total	Value	% of total	Value	% of total	Value	% of total	Value	% of total
1821–1825	$118.3	46	$49.5	19	$30.3	12	$15.2	6	$15.4	6
1826–1830	113.3	41	47.8	17	44.9	16	18.0	7	19.0	7
1831–1835	180.3	48	49.4	13	56.5	15	17.7	5	18.9	5
1836–1840	263.1	52	54.2	11	85.3	17	19.8	4	23.9	5
1841–1845	214.2	45	56.2	12	70.3	15	24.4	5	22.7	5
1846–1850	343.2	53	63.9	10	75.9	12	32.5	5	26.3	4
1851–1855	476.0	51	73.1	8	113.0	12	49.0	5	32.6	4
1856–1860	678.8	49	100.5	7	160.3	12	67.0	5	49.4	4

Five-Year Period	British [b] North America		Netherlands [a]		Germany [a]		British [b] West Indies	
	Value	% of total	Value	% of total	Value	% of total	Value	% of total
1821–1825	$10.0	4	$10.8	4	$6.8	3	$5.7	2
1826–1830	10.3	4	12.6	5	8.1	3	2.8	1
1831–1835	16.9	5	10.4	3	11.9	3	8.1	2
1836–1840	16.5	3	12.1	2	14.1	3	11.2	2
1841–1845	24.7	5	12.4	3	19.3	4	16.9	4
1846–1850	24.3	4	9.9	2	19.6	3	20.6	3
1851–1855	53.7	6	10.4	1	32.3	3	20.1	2
1856–1860	102.5	7	18.8	1	62.0	4	25.0	2

a Computed from *House Miscellaneous Document* No. 117, 52 Cong., 2 Sess., Vol. XXVI, *passim*.
b *House Document* No. 573, Pt. 7, 55 Cong., 2 Sess., pp. 3274 ff.
c See Appendix A, Table 4, footnote (a).

Appendix B

Footnote   *Comment*

5   These percentages include shipments of gold and silver which tend to magnify the importance of New York.

6   Totals for re-exports were at all times somewhat understated. Goods on the free list, especially if not obviously the products of tropical countries, often appear as domestic exports. This was true, for example, of Canadian wheat and flour after these products were placed on the free list under the Reciprocity Treaty of 1854. Only where drawback payments were actually claimed can we be sure that the record is reasonably complete.

8   By the 1840's, the course of trade had been completely reversed. Boston merchants who had imported Calcutta nankeens for the American market were in this later period selling in India coarse cottons woven on Massachusetts looms.

12   Sterns emphasizes the importance of the high cost of internal transportation as a deterrent to the exportation of American foodstuffs, 1820–1830 (see especially pp. 40–42). But he fails to show clearly that it was not *absolute* transportation costs but their height *relative* to commodity prices which was the crucial factor.

19   The reductions of the act of 1833, it will be remembered, were not appreciably in effect until after 1839.

30   For an explanation of the reason for rejecting the official figure for 1815 see Worthy P. Sterns, "The Beginnings of American Financial Independence," *Journal of Political Economy*, VI (1897–1898), 191. But Stern's contention that the official figures for imports are generally too high by about 20 per cent cannot be accepted for the years 1816–1820. He believes that American prices rather than foreign prices were used to determine the value of imports subject to specific duties. Although this may have been true for certain earlier years, it cannot be clearly demonstrated for 1816–1820. Pitkin, whose totals are substantially the same as the official figures for 1816 and 1817, does seem to imply that he used domestic prices in his computations for 1815–1817 (p. 176), but a comparison of the prices which he actually used with those reported for that period in contemporary price lists indicates that the prices he used were generally below the New York or Philadelphia quotations, sometimes very much lower. Moreover, it must be remembered that this was a period especially notorious for the undervaluation of imports to avoid the payment of duties. See *American State Papers: Finance*, III, 234–240 and *Hunt's Merchants' Magazine*, XXXVII (1857), 664.

32   On the basis of *Treasury Reports* the tonnage for this period may be reckoned as 4,302,845 for one year. Earnings are figured at $33.33 a ton. This

figure, which is used by Sterns for the following period, is lower than the $40 a ton used by him for the years 1790–1820. The smaller figure is preferred because (1) it compensates somewhat for the overstatement of registered tonnage (see *American State Papers: Commerce and Navigation,* II, 398 and 406), and (2) Sterns estimated $40 a ton earnings on the assumption that ships made three trips to France each year. The average was probably under three at this time, for the Senate Committee on Commerce and Navigation reported in 1819 that tonnage engaged in trade with Europe arrived "generally twice, and sometimes thrice, in the year." (*American State Papers: Commerce and Navigation,* II, 398.) Total carrying charges for imports are figured at 10 per cent of the value of merchandise imports, or $64,271,927. This subtracted from total earnings of American shipping (i.e., $143,428,023) equals $79,156,096, the net amount due the United States from abroad for shipping services. See Worthy P. Sterns, "The Beginnings of American Financial Independence," *Journal of Political Economy,* VI (1897–1898), 194–195, and "The Foreign Trade of the United States from 1820 to 1840," *Journal of Political Economy,* VIII (1900), 53.

33   American shipping totaling 79,725 tons sold for an estimated price of $50 a ton. For tonnage sold to foreigners see the annual reports on *Tonnage* made by the Secretary of the Treasury, *American State Papers: Commerce and Navigation,* II. Cf. Worthy P. Sterns, "The Beginnings of American Financial Independence," *Journal of Political Economy,* VI (1897–1898), 193–194.

36   Sterns accepts the $100,000,000 estimate without reduction. "The Beginnings of American Financial Independence," *Journal of Political Economy,* VI (1897–1898), 200.

38   Using Pitkin's rather than the official estimate for 1815. If the official figure is used, the debit item for imports is $187.

40   Cf. Leland Hamilton Jenks, *The Migration of British Capital to 1875* (New York: Alfred A. Knopf, Inc., 1927), pp. 48–49. See especially the footnotes. Certainly Bullock's figure of $125,000,000 for new capital investments is appreciably too small if it is meant to include mercantile credit, which increased very rapidly after 1834. If mercantile credit extended by foreigners to United States citizens is not included, we should expect to find total debits for the period exceeding total credits. Yet the reverse is true for the balance sheet offered. Furthermore, it is very confusing in the light of the credit balance of $27,000,000, which his balance sheet shows, to find Bullock stating: "At the end of period there was an unsettled balance against us . . . ." (p. 219), and to discover that Jenks, following Bullock, refers to "an unsettled balance of payments against us of about $27,000,000" (p. 363, fn. 49).

43   Forty million dollars of new capital seems a considerable underestimate, for very large sums were still being lent to the United States in 1838 and 1839. See Reginald C. McGrane, *Foreign Bondholders and American State Debts* (New York: The Macmillan Company, 1935), pp. 17–20; and Leland Hamilton Jenks, *The Migration of British Capital to 1875* (New York: Alfred A. Knopf, Inc., 1927), pp. 88 ff.

44   Bullock's methods and data have been taken over except as noted in footnotes to the accompanying table.

45   Following Bullock's method, 2,968,194 immigrants at $50 equals $148,-409,700. But he takes no account of immigrant remittances, which by this period must have been appreciable. If such remittances are estimated at $48,000,000, the net credit due to immigrants is $100,000,000.

Index

Street railroads, 391

Streets, city, 391

Strickland, William, architect, 76, 301

Strikes, 251–257, 273–274, 284–285, 288
  and cooperatives, 280
  for ten-hour day, 282–283
  under Waltham system, 276–277

Subsidiary Coinage Act of 1853, 329

Subsidies, federal, to cod fishing, 369–370
   to merchant marine, 117, 129–131
   of newspaper transportation, 150
   to ocean steamship lines, 120–121
   state, 380–383

Subtreasury system (*see* Independent
  Treasury)

Suburban areas, growth of, 390

Suffolk Bank, 313–314

Suffolk system, 313–314

Suffrage, and free education, 262
  in Rhode Island, 263–264
  property qualifications, 257

Sugar, 13, 166, 185, 364
  carried by packets, 107
  in domestic trade, 158
  imports, 183–184
  market for, 169
  marketed through New Orleans, 9
  movement by Mississippi, 164
  prices, 160
  re-exported, 178, 180
  upriver shipment of, 159

Sugar mills, 210

Sumner, William Graham, on banking,
  317

Sunday schools, for factory workers, 271

Supercargoes, 12, 104

Superior district, iron, 6

Surplus revenue, distribution of, 342
  distribution to states, 357, 358

Surveys, railroad, 94–95

Suspenders, production by domestic system, 217, 219

Suspension bridge, 28–29

Susquehanna River, flatboats, 136
  lumber trade on, 171
  use for power, 5

Susquehanna and Tidewater Canal, 41–
  42, 44, 54
  cost of construction, 53
  state aid, 51

Swivel truck, 83

Sylvania Phalanx, 279

Sylvis, William H., union leader, 285

T

T rail, 81

Tailoring, 215–216
  shop production in, 216

Tailors, cooperatives, 280
  and domestic system, 219–220
  industrial dispute, 256
  unions, 252, 284

Tammany and labor, 261

Taney, Roger B., Attorney General, 308

Tanneries, 209

Taps, 222

Tar kilns, 210

Tariff, 194, 201, 237, 335, 360–367,
  370
  Act of 1816, 360–361, 363
  Act of 1818, 361
  Act of 1824, 364
  Act of 1828, 364
  Act of 1832, 364
  Act of 1833, 364, 366
  Act of 1842, 365
  Act of 1846, 365–366
  Act of 1857, 365
  Act of 1861, 365
  attitude toward, 353
  Bill of 1820, 364
  on Canadian wheat, 178
  duties on railroad iron, 95
  effect of exports, 192
  as source of revenue, 355–356

Tariff of Abominations, 364

Taunton, Mass., britannia ware manufacture, 343

Taxation, railroads, 89

Taxes, 380
  exemption from, 380–381
  federal, 355
  state, 373–376
   on branches of second Bank of the
    United States, 304–307

Tea, 178, 180, 185, 364
  clipper trade, 111
  imports, 183–184
  overland export to Ohio Valley, 159

Teachers, 12
  wages, 262

Teamsters, effect of railroads on, 156

Telegraph, 369
  development of, 151–152
  for dispatching trains, 84

Tenements for workers, 271

Ten-hour movement, 252, 258, 264, 278, 282–283
Tennessee, debt, 377
Texas, railroad aid, 94
Textile machinery, use of machine tools in manufacture of, 221
Textile manufacturing, capital invested in, 236
  corporations in, 241
  factory system in, 229–234
  failures in, 235
  improvements in, 224–225
  state aid, 380–381
  at Waltham, 230–231
Textile mills, in 1857, 349
  dependent on local labor, 270–271
  financing of, 237
  foreign workers in, 285
  unemployment in, 362
  use of steam engine in, 224
  Waltham system, 274–277
Textiles, carried by packets, 107
  domestic trade routes for, 168
  household manufacture of, 208, 211, 213
  overland export to Ohio Valley, 159
  sales at auction, 11–12
  statistics of imports, 199
  tariff, 364
  transportation from Lowell, 154
Thompsonville Manufacturing Company, 274
Thorp, John, inventor, 224–225
Thoughts on Political Economy, by Daniel Raymond, 363
Timber, movement by western steamboats, 64
Times, New York, 296
Tobacco, 192
  carried by packets, 107
  coastwise trade in, 157, 168
  eastward shipment of, 161–162
  exported via New York, 126–127
  exports of, 186, 193, 335, 396–397
  manufacturing in South, 246
    slave labor, 292–293
  market for, 169
  receipts at New Orleans, 164
  and tariff, 364
  trade, 8
    of New York, 196
  transportation in Ohio Valley, 158
Toilets, 392

Toll charges, as expense of turnpike transportation, 134
Toll roads (*see* Turnpikes)
Towboats (*see* Barges)
Trade, coastwise, closed to foreign shipping, 129
  domestic, 153–175, 396–397
    as affecting foreign commerce, 192
    disadvantage of high cost, 132–133
    effect of crisis of 1837, 343
    lead, 154
    with Pacific Coast, 172
    volume and value of, 173–175, 346
  foreign, 176–206, 396–397
    advantage of low cost, 132–133
    carried in American vessels, 123–124
    federal regulation of, 371
    growth of, 190–198
    indirect, 129
    and merchant marine, 126
    source of manufacturing capital, 246
  organization of, 10–14
    (*See also* Foreign trade)
Trade routes, on Atlantic, 105
  coastwise trade, 117
  domestic, 153–175, 169–172
Trading posts, federal, for Indians, 367–368
Tramps, ocean, 104–105
Tramways, 76–77, 81
Transatlantic cable, 152
Transcendentalism, 278
Transcontinental Railroad, 86
Transients (*see* Tramps)
Transportation, workers, 290–291
Travel, cost and speed of, 141–148
Travelers' expenses, as affecting the balance of international indebtedness, 201–206
Treasury Department, administration of, 301
  and banks, 356–360
  records of foreign commerce, 199
  and second Bank of the United States, 306–307
Treasury notes, 302, 358
  issued by states, 327
Tredegar Iron Company, workers in, 272
Trenton, N.J., 9
  iron manufacture at, 238
Tribune, New York, 279, 295–296
Troy, N.Y., railroad ownership, 91–92
  workingmen's parties in, 258–259

Whaling, 385
  as source of manufacturing capital, 237,
    246
Wheat, 178
  cost of railroad transportation, 135
  cost of wagoning, 133
  eastward shipment of, 167
  exports of, 186–187, 335, 396–397
  freight rates, Chicago to New York,
    135
  imports from England, 342
  in Pacific Coast trade, 172
  prices, 192, 361
  rail shipments at Chicago, 165–166
  receipts at New Orleans, 164
  shipments by water, 167
  shipped from West, 151
  subsidy, 380
Wheeling, Virginia, 19, 22
Wheelwrights, slave, 293
  wages, 297
Whig Party and tariff, 365
Whipple, Squire, bridgebuilder, 28
Whiskey, manufacture of, 210
White, Josiah, 39
White Star Line, 119
White Water Canal, 47, 54
Whitesmiths' union, 253
Whitney, Eli, inventor, 221
Whittier, John Greenleaf, as editorial
    writer, 264
Wildcat banking, 312–313, 317
Willamette River, steamboats on, 65
Williams College, 277
Wilmington, Del., 9, 260
Wilson, Allen B., inventor, 227
Winchester, Va., 23
Wine, 178–179
  cost of, in Atlantic travel, 146
  exports, 184
Wine Islands, imports from, 184
Wing dams on Lehigh River, 39
Wisconsin, 98
  downriver shipments from, 163
  free banking, 317
  lead mining, 6, 386
  lumber production in, 387
  plank roads in, 31
Wisconsin Marine and Fire Insurance
    Company, 327
Women, in cotton textiles, 231
  as domestic servants, 291
  emancipation of, 278

Women (Cont.)
  employment under Rhode Island sys-
    tem, 270–271
  hours of labor under Rhode Island sys-
    tem, 273
  needle workers, wages, 297
  straw and palm-leaf hat making, 268–
    269
  strikes, 285
  teachers, 262
  unions, 254
  wages, 272
  under Waltham system, 274–277
  workers, ten-hour movement, 282–283
Wood, export of, 190
  as locomotive fuel, 84
  for ship construction, 127
  as steamboat fuel, 60
  for steamship construction, 119
  as western steamboat fuel, 66
Wooden rails, 80–81
Wool, carding mills, 209
  market, 398
  in Pacific Coast trade, 172
  raw, tariff, 364, 365
Woolen cloth, 180
  domestic system weaving, 217
  duty on, 361
  hand-loom weaving, 218
  manufacturing, 245
Woolen goods, factory production of, 231–
    232
  imports, 183
  manufacture, 225
  tariff, 365
Woolen manufacturing, capital for, 236
  employment of women and children,
    271
  growth of, 339
  profits in, 235
  tariff, 364
Woolens, 178–179
  British, 208
  household manufacture of, 213
  statistics of imports, 199
Worcester, Mass., and canal transportation,
    37
Workers, in domestic system, 266–269
  and free public education, 261–262
  income, 393–394
  opportunities, 395
  under Rhode Island system, 270–274
  in seaports, 12–13